The English Setter, Adonis

No. 1 of the American Kennel Club Stud Book,
published in Volume 1, 1878, of the National American Kennel Club.

THE COMPLETE DOG BOOK

The Complete
DOG BOOK

B 43

The History and Standard of Breeds
Admitted to AKC Registration,
and the Training, Feeding, Care
and Handling of Pure-Bred Dogs

NEW REVISED
EDITION

An official publication of The American Kennel Club

GARDEN CITY BOOKS, Garden City, N.Y.

Breed Standards Corrected
to June 1, 1964

New and revised standards are published when adopted in the American Kennel Club's official magazine, Pure-Bred Dogs—American Kennel Gazette.

PREFACE

IN THE history of the dog lies the history of all peoples; in his development, the development of all races, and in his faithfulness, a reflection of the finer instincts of humankind. The years have brought a better appreciation of the dog and his importance to man, yet the bond of companionship linking the two extends back into the dim beginnings of civilization.

The dog is mentioned in some of the earliest parts of the Old Testament. In the course of the Bible's references to him, we learn of the great diversity of breeds and types, the most definite of these having been bequeathed to us by the Egyptians and Assyrians.

What is presumed to be the oldest picture showing dogs is found on the tomb of Amten, in Egypt, which dates to the fourth dynasty, or between 2900 and 2751 B.C., when hunting scenes depicted dogs of the sighthound type. From later Egyptian dynasties comes evidence of three other types of dog, while monuments in Assyria before the Christian Era give additional views of ancient-dog kinds.

Like man and with man, the dog has migrated ever westward, making his home wherever and however his master has wanted. The partnership has endured through happiness and sorrow; it has persisted even when disasters shook the earth; and it has been so selfless as to attract the attention of our great philosophers.

Each year enlarges the horizon of knowledge in the field of dogs, as scientist and researcher, veterinarian and fancier—in fact, all who are interested in the welfare of the dog—work together to perfect him mentally and physically for the part he now plays as intelligent helpmeet of man. To further this end, The American Kennel Club has compiled this volume which includes present-day methods of dog feeding, care, and handling, exhaustive researches into the history of his past, and breed standards of perfection which attempt to delineate each ideal pure-bred specimen of the future.

The breed standards and the information incorporated in the historical articles have been furnished in the main by the parent club sponsoring each breed. The photographs, too, have been secured from the same source, except in a few instances where none could be obtained. It should not be thought that these pictures portray the most typical specimen of their respective breeds. To be exact, there is no one best specimen of any breed, but rather several, and any one of them might be held worthy of the honor of representing its breed were a photograph, suitable for reproduction, available at the moment required.

The American Kennel Club acknowledges with gratitude the assistance of those who co-operated in the preparation of this volume: The New York State Veterinary College of Cornell University, various club officers, and other breed authorities for their valuable advice; also the New Bedford *Standard Times* for permission to reproduce the unique, historical photograph of the English Setter, Adonis, as our frontispiece. The chapters on diseases, care and management were written by R. W. Kirk, D.V.M., the anatomical sketches were drawn by S. Edwin Megargee, and the book was edited by Josephine Z. Rine.

CONTENTS

PART I: TRAINING, BREEDING, CARE, AND MANAGEMENT

FIRST STEPS IN TRAINING

THERE ARE a certain number of basic things a civilized dog should do when you tell him to, to make your life and his easier. They are: walking at your side in the streets, called "heeling" in the jargon of training, sitting, and lying down on command, staying where you tell him to, coming when you call him, and standing and holding his position at your command. The fact that these "exercises" are exactly those included in the requirements for the Companion Dog degree awarded in obedience competition by the AKC is by no means a coincidence. We feel that they are the minimum requirements of a civilized dog—sufficient to make him easy to live with and a pleasure to own, a true companion as the title implies.

A fair amount of precision in their performance is required in obedience competition. While we recommend that you train your dog to do properly whatever he is doing, there is of course no necessity for the perfection in home training that is striven for in the competition ring. There is, however, one absolute requirement identical in ring and home —your dog must learn to obey you instantly, with one and only one command or order. The truest sign of the poorly trained dog is the repeated command or commands, quite generally given in a rising voice, and only reluctantly complied with by the dog.

Background to Training

Dogs are not unlike young children. They are curious and investigative, and with no ill will in the world they will try various modes of behavior and ways of doing things. It is up to you to channel these natural attempts at coping with their world into the paths you desire— those acceptable to you, and later those actually useful and helpful. A dog, like a child, has certain wants and needs. He will experiment with different methods of attracting your attention to them (once he has learned you are the fount and source of most of his requirements in this world) until he finds one or several which work. Dogs are basically pragmatists. Having little or no moral sense, they use the methods which result in the maximum results combined with the minimum discomfort to them.

Thus if your dog learns that he gets what he wants by constant whining (the child analogy holds remarkably well here), he will whine. If he learns that he gets attention through refusal to eat, he will refuse to eat. If he learns that relieving himself on your Aubusson carpet (a considerable convenience as compared to waiting until he is let outside) brings less discomfort by way of discipline than the discomfort of waiting, he will happily shower the carpet. But if he learns from his first contact with you that your ways of doing things result in praise and comfortable relations, while other ways result in firm, unvarying correction, he is simply going to take the easier way out. Making the right way (your way) the easier way is a fair definition of training.

The foundation stone of training is confidence. It is a two-way thing, meaning your dog's confidence in you, and yours in him. First, he must have confidence that you are fair and trustworthy, which may come as a surprise to you, but although dogs most assuredly don't think in such terms, they operate using the principles. He must have confidence that a certain action is always greeted with the same reaction. In training this means that certain actions are always prohibited, and certain others always encouraged. That way he can live in a secure world, without worrying about how you will react to what he does. Vacillation is the deadly enemy of good training, undercutting security completely. And security is of the utmost importance to any puppy or dog.

Praise and Correction

Under confidence comes the subheading, a vitally important one, of praise and correction. Praise means what it implies, obvious approval when your dog has done something right, which is easy enough. But it also means praise after you have corrected or disciplined your dog. This is not so obvious, but it is important. It is because of the desirability of maintaining smooth and happy relations with your dog. One of the basic mistakes made by many home trainers is that of continued anger at a dog that has misbehaved, or has been seemingly unable to absorb a training lesson. This has no effect on a dog except a harmful one. He cannot remember, after only a few minutes, what it was he did, or didn't do, and he only knows you are displeased with him. All of which teaches him nothing except that you're not as easy to get along with as might be.

Of course you should never have been angry with him in the first place, but humans are human, and the best trainers lose their tempers once in a while. The reason they are the best trainers is that they show it as little as possible, and have learned to control it.

Therefore, rule: when you have corrected your dog for either omission or commission, praise him at once. Let him know that the point has been made, but nonetheless you are still friends. Do this no matter how many times you've had to make the identical correction. It takes a few times for any correction to sink in. Your praise afterwards won't lessen the impact of the correction, but it will reassure him that all is well between you, and the training can progress without hard feelings on either side.

As to corrections themselves, they are with one exception mild and non-violent. We recommend as strongly as possible that you do not strike your dog, ever, or at least hardly ever. The exception is that in which your dog actually threatens to bite, which does happen, although rarely. In this circumstance you will have to judge, from your knowledge of your own dog, how to handle it. You may have to hit him. But even then, once it is over, remember to praise and comfort him afterward, for he wants to get along.

In any other situation, don't hit him. And this includes with your hand, with a rolled-up newspaper, with a stick; in short, with anything at all. And don't threaten to hit him, which is almost worse than actually hitting him. That is what makes dogs "hand shy," cringing at an upraised hand or even a hand near them. If when he sees a hand raised near him he has good reason to expect that someone is going to swing at him, he has every reason in the world to try to skitter away.

In the lines of hitting, it should be obvious why you shouldn't hit him with a stick, but the rolled-newspaper myth is widespread enough to deserve a paragraph of discussion. The idea, generally, is that it doesn't hurt a dog—it is simply the loud whack that scares him and punishes him. This is faulty thinking from several angles. First, if you're thinking along lines of scaring him into doing what you want him to, or desisting from what you don't want, you're on the wrong track already. And second, deliberately teaching a dog to be frightened of sudden loud noises comes close to criminal behavior. Third and perhaps most important, it is unlikely that you will have a rolled newspaper in your hand at all times, or even close to hand. This is the really fatal flaw in the fabric, for a correction, to be effective at all, must be administered immediately, not in ten seconds' time.

The main point of good and positive corrections is that they must be immediate and somehow connected with the act. If they are constructive corrections, they must show the dog instantly what he ought to be doing. For example, if you are teaching your dog to sit, and he does not, you must instantly show him what he ought to be doing by guiding him to a sitting position with your hands. And if it is a disciplinary correction, it must be as fast as humanly possible, and as closely as possible connected with the misdeed. As an example—when you are teaching your dog not to jump up on people, the knee which throws him off balance at the moment of his jump is an excellent disciplinary correction. Note that neither of these involves any unpleasantness from you to him, no shouting, no hitting or beating, no recriminations. And note also that there is no mention anywhere here of "punishment." A dog is never punished; he is corrected. This may seem to you a fine point, but it is in such fine points that lies the difference between good and bad training.

One further point before we go on to the actual details of training and housebreaking. Never, under any imaginable circumstances, correct or discipline your dog when you have called him to you, or when he has come to you of his own accord. The dog has a mind which makes direct and short-term connection. If he comes to you and you correct or discipline him, he will not connect it with whatever he was doing before, but with the fact that he came—the most recent thing he did before the roof fell in. After a few times, he'll be a little reluctant about coming, and perhaps soon he won't come at all. You have only to put yourself in his position (a very good idea when considering any aspect of training, incidentally), imagining a friend asking you to come to him, then shouting at you or hitting you when you arrive. Very soon you'd get very cautious about approaching him. Your dog feels much the same way. Don't ever do it. If he has done something wrong at a distance, either get to where he is for your correction, or forget about it until you have the opportunity to do it right.

Housebreaking

There are two basic housebreaking situations: one in which housebreaking can be accomplished directly, and another in which paperbreaking is an intermediate stage. Direct housebreaking is by far the more preferable, but your ability to do this will be dictated by your living accommodations. If you have a yard of any sort directly outside your door, then it is not only possible but best to housebreak directly. If you live in a city apartment, as many dog owners do, the intermediate paperbreaking may be called for.

Direct housebreaking is simple. Basically, it means taking the puppy outside frequently, allowing him to relieve himself, and then returning him to the house. When he is in the house, confine him either in a large sleeping-living box or crate or, if you are able to keep a close watch on him, keep him tied on a short leash or rope (six feet or so) in the kitchen. In either case, the puppy will be restricted to a small area in which he must play and sleep, and he will be very reluctant to soil that area. If he does inadvertently soil it—and these accidents will happen—

chastise him mildly and take him outside immediately to the area he has used before, to remind him that the only permissible place is there. But be fair to him. A young puppy has to eliminate quite often, so in the early days before he has had a chance to build up any sort of control, take him out often. Do definitely take him out about an hour after each feeding. As he grows older, he will be able to contain himself for longer periods and the necessary outings will be reduced to around four a day, but let him work up slowly to that.

Don't worry about the close confinement inside. The novice dog owner tends to think that it is unfair to the new pup to keep him in close quarters, but experienced owners and trainers know that it is, if anything, a kindness to the puppy because it allows him to get the house-breaking done with efficiently and over with. Most of the housebreaking trouble you may have heard of results from "kind" owners who let an unhousebroken pup have the run of the house. The pup gets into the habit of soiling the floors, and for years after he may have to be corrected constantly. As between two weeks or so of close confinement and ef-ficient housebreaking, and possibly years of dissatisfaction and continual corrections, there seems an obvious choice. If you make a point of play-ing with your pup in his confinement area, and when you are outside with him, your future relations won't suffer either. Do what needs to be done, with firmness, kindness, and love.

The housebreaking problem in an apartment is somewhat more diffi-cult. Your vet may advise you not to take the puppy out into city streets until his shots protect him against diseases he might pick up there. And it may simply be physically inconvenient to make many trips from a high-floor apartment to the busy street. In this case, set up a paper-breaking room, preferably the kitchen, in which the pup is to be con-fined. Cover the entire floor with several thicknesses of newspaper, and wait for the pup to use them. Pick up the soiled papers and replace them, and continue in this fashion for a day or two. Then leave a small corner of the room bare, and hope he doesn't use it. If he does, chastise him mildly and put him on the papers, letting him know that it is there and only there he is to go.

As the days go by and he seems to come to understand the paper idea, widen the bare area until you have a papered area equivalent to about two full newspaper sheets. Until he is old enough to go to the street, keep him using that area, replacing the soiled papers as they are used. Then begin street walks with him until he learns that the street is the place to go, and remove the papers. At that point, watch carefully for any indication of need for relief—he may search frantically for the papers—and take him out promptly.

As with direct housebreaking, keep him absolutely confined, in this case to the paper-breaking room, until he has completely learned his lesson. It won't hurt him.

At nighttime in either city or country, make it easier for him by exercising a bit of caution on the water intake—it will help him control the outgo. Don't give him water for at least two hours before his bedtime, and make sure he is taken out, or allowed access to the papers, just before the household retires. You'll be surprised how long even quite a young puppy can hold it if he has relieved the immediate pressures of eating and drinking.

The Collar and Leash

When it comes to the serious training of your dog, we recommend that you wait until he is about six to eight months old before beginning. Until then he will have little power of concentration, and concentrated lessons will only confuse him. In any case, he deserves to enjoy his brief puppyhood before going on to serious life, so don't push him too hard at first. On the other hand, if you read this with an older dog in mind, don't hesitate to start a dog of any age in training. Despite the old adage, a dog can be trained if he can still move around.

While heeling is not the most important of the exercises, it is the first that should be taught, for it forms the foundation on which the others are built. In preparation for this training, you should have a training collar and leash. The collar to use is the metal chain-link variety, with metal rings at each end. Get the right size for your dog (about one inch longer than the measurement around the largest part of his head) and learn to put it on properly for training. Slip the chain through one of the rings so the collar forms a sort of loop, sliding through one ring, with the other ring left for attachment to the leash. This training collar has been found to be the most effective one for its purpose, which is to control the dog during training—to exert as much control as you need, or as little. When you use it, bear in mind that in the wrong hands it can be harmful to the dog; in really thoughtless hands it can be an instrument of torture. You must never, repeat *never*, use the training collar to exert a constant pull on your dog's neck, for that will only choke and damage him. Like nearly every other useful device, the training collar can be misused, but when properly used it is of great help in training.

The proper method of use is: when you want to get your dog's attention, or urge him into a desired position or in some direction, give a light, quick snap or tug on the leash, which *momentarily* tightens the collar about his neck. Then release the pressure instantly, and the correction will have been made. Use it this way and you will have no problems; misuse it and the harm can be great. We can only leave it to your good judgment and sense to use it properly.

The proper way of putting the collar on your dog is with the loose ring at the right of the dog's neck, the chain attached to it having come over the neck and through the holding ring, rather than under the neck. It seems a small point, but as the dog is at your left during most of training, this arrangement is what makes the collar effective, as it allows the collar to loosen instantly when you have finished the quick snap on the leash. With the proper training leash (leather or webbing, six feet long and half to full inch wide), you are ready to begin.

Introduce him gently to the apparatus. Put the collar on and let him wear it for a day before trying anything else. Then snap the leash onto the collar and let him drag that around for a while to get used to it, being careful that he doesn't get it tangled with something and get panicky. Then when he is used to the leash being on, take up your end of it and walk around with him, putting little or no pressure on. Gradually, over a short period, increase your control until he learns that, while it restrains him, it is nothing to be afraid of. When you have reached the point where you can persuade him to come along in the general direction you want to go by gentle snaps of the leash, you are ready to begin with heeling proper.

Heeling

From this point on, you should establish regular training periods, of about fifteen minutes to half an hour in length, once or twice a day. Any longer will be fatiguing for him, and you too, and training will suffer unless his mind is fresh and alert. Nothing is worse for training than boredom, either on his part or yours, from overlong sessions. During each training session, keep everything quite businesslike, but don't, of course, leave out the praise and friendliness. Then after each session, take a little time to play and romp with him, just to ease off the pressure and make sure your relations are friendly and good.

To begin heeling, get him more or less at your left side, then start off walking, giving him the command, "Mike, heel!", using his name, followed immediately by the command word. Give the command just as you take the first step, and simultaneously give him a light snap with the leash to persuade him to come along. Use only as much force as is necessary to get him moving with you. As you are walking along, continue to urge him to walk just at your left side, with his head about opposite your left leg and level with it, by snapping the leash as you go to urge him forward or back, right or left, into position. Each time give the command "Heel!" as you snap. And each time you snap and command, follow it with praise. It need only be a brief word or two, as "That's it, good boy!" It will take a good deal of work before he understands what is going on, for this is the first time he has had to perform at command, but if you are kind and patient and skillful, he will soon learn, and without rancor.

The entire secret of successful heel training is learning the art of the snap of the leash. The training collar is not meant for choking a dog, although you will hear it called "choke collar." And it will indeed choke him if you use it to tow him along with a steady pull. The proper method is the quick snap and equally quick release of pressure, the snap being nothing more than a quick tug which tightens the chain collar momentarily around his neck to get his attention, and at the same time urges him in the proper direction. If you will remember *always* to use the collar and leash for quick snaps and releases, never hard enough really to hurt him, and especially never maintaining continual pressure, you will be well along in training skills.

Equally important is the praise you give him after each snap correction. However mild your corrections, each is a discomfort to him, and if you praise him immediately, it will take the sting out without removing the lesson.

Work on the heeling until you are able to give him only one command, "Mike, heel!", as you start walking, and do not have to use the leash for correction at all. From walking largely in a straight line, begin to make circles and corners, turnabouts and other maneuvers, keeping him at your side with continual snaps and praise, until you are confident that he is walking with you of his own accord. Then you are ready to begin teaching the sit.

Sit

The sit is taught first by having your dog sit when you stop walking while he is heeling. It can be begun quite early. When you stop, give the command, "Sit!", and while your left hand guides his rear down to a sitting position, your right hand holds his head up and in position with the leash. With your hands and the leash, make him stay in the sitting position a moment, then give the heel command and start up. Again stop, give the sit command, guide him into position, and have him stay seated a little longer.

Gradually, as he gets the idea, you will be able to abandon first the command, and finally the leash and hand correction. He will sit automatically when you come to a stop, waiting either for you to start up again or for his release through an established release command, such as "Okay!"

Finally, when he has learned quite fully the meaning of sit, and learned to do it when you stop walking, you are ready to teach the sit from any position. Put the collar and leash on and give him the "Sit!" command, guiding him into position just as you did before. Concentrate on this phase, continuing the pure sit training until he will sit on command with no corrections, and then begin to introduce the "Stay."

Stay

In the stay, your dog is simply required to stay in his sitting position until released by you. To teach it, sit him, on leash, and immediately tell him "Stay!", repeating the command in a coaxing but firm voice, keeping your hands on him if necessary to reinforce the command. The first few times, don't try to make him stay more than ten or twenty seconds, then release him. But slowly increase the time, cutting down on the continued commands, until he will stay on one command for at least three minutes. You'll find it's a handy bit of training.

At this point it might be well to reinforce our earlier statements on "one command and one only." The truly trained dog will do what he is told the first time he is told. Otherwise he cannot be called trained. This should not be taken to mean that you should not use second and third and however many commands you may need during the initial training, but you must arrive at the point where you need only say "heel" once to get him started, or "sit" just once to get him sat. Once he has the idea of what you want him to do, give the command only once, in a firm but pleasant tone, and then use the leash and collar to be sure he does what he is told. There is never any need to be rough; simply be firm and unequivocal. The command means the action, and nothing else. It is absolutely fatal to training to have to give a command a second time, whether pleading or shouting furiously, once your dog knows what the command is about. Don't do it.

Stand-Stay

Once he has mastered heeling and sitting, and sitting and staying, he is ready to learn the stand-stay. The usefulness of this may escape you at first, but you will find it indeed a very valuable thing. As only one example, you will find brushing and grooming far and away easier if your dog will stand firmly in position when told to.

This, too, is taught from the heel. As you are heeling along with him, and as you slow down to come to a halt, give him the command, "Stand!" As you do so, stop his forward motion with the leash, and before he has a chance to sit as he has learned to, block the forward and downward motion of his rear with your left hand, fingers extended, just in front of the top of his right hind leg. Don't grab him, just block him. If he still attempts to sit, don't chastise him, for he's only trying to do what you've first taught him. Simply start up again with the "Heel!" command and after a few steps, stop again, using your left hand more firmly to prevent his sitting. He will probably be a little confused at this point, but your praise will reassure him. As he is standing, give him the "Stand!" command repeatedly, to let him know you want him to stay in that position, and also give him the "Stay!" command. This command he will know from the sit-stay training, and he will soon get the idea of what you want him to do.

Continue this training until he will stand firmly at your side until you start up heeling again. If he tries to sit, simply start up heeling again with the command, then stop after a step or two and again give the stand-stay command. Mix this training in with normal sits when you stop walking. He may at first be quite confused, and you may have to reinforce the sit with commands again for a short while. Soon it will become clear to him that he is to sit unless there is a command to the contrary, and to stand when he hears the word.

Now you can begin to leave him a little while he is either sitting or standing at the stay. Whichever position he is in, give him a firm command, "Stay!" At the same time, bring your right hand around, fingers extended, and hold it just in front of his nose, palm to him, for a second, as a "stay" signal. With the leash still in your hand, take a step away from him. If he attempts to move or follow you, give him a firm "No!" and then repeat the "Stay!", if necessary guiding him back into position with your hands and leash. Here again be prepared for natural confusion, for up to now you have wanted him to go with you when you started walking. Keep at it until he learns that he is now to stay unless given a countercommand to heel, or is released. Step away again and move slowly until you are at the distance of the leash. Stay there only a few seconds before coming back to praise him and release him. As the training sessions go on, slowly increase the time you are away from him until you can stay away for at least a minute while he holds the stand position, and three minutes while he holds the sit. Then you can begin to move around him while he is sitting or standing. Still holding the leash, walk away from him and circle around him, being careful that the leash neither tugs on him nor drags across his face. Continue this until he will stay quietly and confidently for the times listed above, during which you can walk away from him to the front or back or sides and circle him several times. Don't try to stop him from turning his head to watch you, but deal with any breaks from position gently and firmly, giving the correction and then praise when he has resumed his position, then reinforcing it with the command again, and leaving once more.

Here again we will remind you of the necessity of praise for your dog after every correction, and whenever he does something right by himself. It is to gain your praise that he works and learns. We haven't said "praise him" after every sentence, for it would be boring and repetitious for you as you read this. But praise is never boring to your dog. So read each of these paragraphs as though after every sentence we wrote: "Praise him."

Down

Teaching the down comes naturally at this point, for he has learned the meaning of commands—that there is something he must do either actively or passively, at your commands—and another item is simply further accomplishment along the same lines. Sit him at your side, then kneel beside him and reach over his back with your left arm, taking hold of his left front leg near his body with your left hand, and his right front leg similarly with your right hand. Tell him "Down!" and as you do so, lift him gently into the down position by lifting his front feet off the floor or ground and easing his body down until he is indeed lying down.

We recommend this method because it involves no struggle between you and your dog. He is comforted by the fact that you are there with your arm around him, and there is no pressure of leash or hand for him to fight by bracing his front legs, and his rear is already on the ground.

When he is down, release your grasp on him slowly, sliding your left hand around and leaving it on his back, continually telling him "Down, stay!" and keep him in position for a few seconds. Then release him and get him into sitting position, by command, for another try. Continue this until he goes down at command without your having to lift him, and will stay quietly until released, without any pressure of your left hand on his back. Then give the command without putting your hands into the ready position. Soon, by gentle and steady progress over a period of days, you will be able to stand erect and give only the one command, "Down!" to have him flop at your side. From this you can improvise until he goes down when several feet away from you, still on leash.

When he has learned the down, leave him at the stay, as before with the sit and stand, first walking away only briefly and then for longer periods and then circling him. You will find it will be easier this time, for he knows now what "Stay!" means.

Come

Once your dog has mastered all these, it is time to teach him to come to you on command. While this is perhaps the most important thing your dog should learn, it is placed here in the training schedule for several very good reasons. Among them are: he has learned to work at command, just as in the down, and more important, he has acquired the abilities to heel and sit, both of which are used in the preliminary "come" training.

This is how it is done: after all the preceding training, when you are heeling one day, suddenly take a step backward and tell him, "Mike, come!" As you give the command, give a snap on the leash to turn him around to his right as he is walking, and get him headed back toward you. When he is turned around, keep walking backward, urging him to come toward you with continued gentle snaps of the leash and repetitions of the "Come!" command. And remember to praise him, for this is a confusing turn of events for him. Then, when he is in full stride toward you, stop, and as he reaches you, give the command, "Sit!" It may be necessary to guide him into a sitting position directly in front of you, but there is a very good chance you won't have to. Get him into a sitting position directly in front of you and facing you, and the first "recall" is completed. Tell him "Stay!" and walk around into position, then start up at heel again for another try.

Continue working in this vein until you have only to step backward and give the command with no leash urging, and he turns and walks to you, sitting in front without further command. From this, the progression to the recall from a sitting position at a distance is simple. Get him sat, and step away from him to the end of the leash, then give the "Come!" command. If he hesitates, give him a slight snap on the leash to let him know what you want, and he will get up, come to you, and sit again in front.

The entire idea behind this method is that there is never a brute strength contest between you and him. He is already in motion when you first give him the "Come!" while heeling, and there is no tugging on him with the leash to get him up from a sit or down when he hasn't the slightest idea what "Come!" means. By the time you do introduce the ordinary recall, he does know what it means, and will respond to the command, so there is only a reminder snap to get him in motion.

These, the heel, sit, stand, stay, down, and recall, are the basic lessons, and once these are firmly learned on leash, you are ready for the final step, which is obedience without a controlling leash in your hand. In preparation for this, you must be absolutely, totally sure that he obeys your commands without hesitation on leash. Work on them for a while until there is no slightest doubt in your mind. This is a crucial point in training, and the one at which training often breaks down. Many home trainers give the on-leash work a lick and promise, barely getting their dogs to do what they tell them, and then trying it without leash control. It is invariably fatal to the training, and we cannot recommend more strongly that you have the on-leash work down firmly and confidently before taking the leash off and giving a command.

But once you are sure of yourself and your dog, go ahead. Get him seated at your side as you have been doing. Take off the leash and start up with the heel command. You will probably be greatly surprised to find that he heels with you, but it is no surprise at all if the previous training has been good. Go through the whole routine, the stands, downs, stays and recalls, just as if he still had the leash on. In most cases, if all has gone well before, all will go well now. If not, put the leash back on for correction of whatever parts he is unsure about. Work on that part until you both have it properly, and then take the leash off and try it again. It will work, and you will have a trained dog, which is what this is all about. One point of caution though: when trying the recall off leash, don't do it from a great distance at first. Do it from only six feet or so, and work up to a distance slowly. It is like everything else in training: slow, gradual progress is the way.

To close this section, we will repeat that the moving force of training is confidence. Your confidence in yourself as a trainer, and in your dog as an intelligent being. And your dog's confidence in you as a kind, fair, and firm master and owner. Through patience and the application of the methods we have outlined here, you can and will have a well-trained dog. It isn't done in a day or a week or a month, but doing it can be fun and not work if you go about it right. And the result will be a trained dog, a joy to own and a true companion.

ROUTINE CARE

The AVERAGE pet owner buys a dog which he expects will become a companion and a friend. As such, the dog becomes part of the family and his welfare is usually carefully supervised. The dog must be kept healthy and clean and appear well groomed. He will then be an acceptable household companion and an individual to which you can refer with pride. Maintaining a dog in this condition is not difficult, but requires attention to certain details at regular times. This regularity of attention is most important.

Feeding

Feeding is one place where regularity is paramount. Regular times, regular amounts, and relatively stable, uniform diet will be most satisfactory. When you bring your new puppy home at six to eight weeks of age, he will already have been started on a diet schedule. Be sure to obtain specific directions for feeding from the previous owner and do not change the pup's schedule when you first take him home. Sudden changes often produce intestinal upsets, and any changes made should be gradual. At this point it is well to stop and decide what type of food will be economically possible and most convenient for you to give your dog for the rest of his life. It is well to start the pup on this diet (be it canned food, meal, meat, biscuits, or table scraps) at an early date and let him know that it is *his* food. Too many of us spoil our dogs by catering to their whims in the food line. Of course we will stick up our nose at hot dogs if we feel that by doing so we can get steak—and dogs use the same psychology!

Puppies are fed on basic principles similar to those used for babies. It is better (and necessary) to feed small amounts of food at frequent intervals than it is to feed large amounts once or twice daily. By feeding frequently, the total amount of food ingested may be increased, and still the pup's stomach is not overloaded. Young puppies should be fed four times daily. Once at each household mealtime, and once at bedtime. At three or four months of age this can be reduced to three times daily; at six months of age to twice daily and after one year, once daily may be adequate. However, most dogs are more content if fed twice daily. The heavier meal should be at night if you want the dog to sleep or if he is a field dog, and the heavier meal in the morning if you want your dog to be alert at night as a watchdog.

Correct feeding is especially important in the larger breeds, particularly during their growing period. Some of these dogs weigh only a pound or two at birth and in ten to twelve months grow to 100 pounds or more. It takes a human being ten to twelve years to attain the same growth. Because these large breeds grow so fast, attention should be given to see that their diets are particularly well fortified with calcium and phosphorus, vitamin D and good quality proteins. If you must try to cut corners on feeding a large dog, wait until he reaches maturity, or better yet, get a smaller breed that you can maintain correctly.

Another particularly critical time in a dog's growth period is the age around three to four months when he is getting his immunization injections. An animal at this time is being asked to meet the challenge of his "shots," and to build up an immunity within his body. The building blocks for this immunity are derived from protein. If your dog is not given a rich protein diet he may not have the necessary material to build himself a good immunity and you, accordingly, are not getting the protection for your dog that you are paying for. This factor may be an important point in cases where vaccinated dogs do contract disease at a later date.

Young dogs usually are given vitamin and mineral supplements during their first year of life. It is best to check with your veterinarian for specific products and doses to use for your dog during this period.

Feeding one or two dogs is most easily done by making use of commercial dog foods. Most well known and reputable feed concerns have spent much time and research money in formulating rations which are fairly complete and well balanced. These rations are sometimes modified by selling or packaging requirements, however. Fat is a point in question. Because an adequate fat level may decrease the shelf life of the food, the fat is often curtailed. For this reason if feeding exclusively processed food (especially meals and biscuits) it is desirable to add animal fat to the ration daily. This can be added in the form of lard, meat trimmings, butter, cream, etc. A dog can utilize up to 25 per cent of his food as fat *if* other requirements are met too, so be generous with the fat supplemented.

The amount to feed a dog is often in question. It is difficult to make a general statement here because each individual varies tremendously in his basic requirements. Such things as basal metabolism, nervous temperament, amount of exercise or work done, growth or pregnancy requirements, etc. will change the quantity of food needed, so that two individuals of the same weight may need vastly different quantities of food. You should judge the amount to give the dog by the response and condition of that individual. If your dog is ravenously hungry and still doesn't gain weight in spite of increased feeding, it may be advisable to check with your veterinarian.

Here are some rules of thumb which may help you to get a foundation for feeding quantities. You will notice that they vary greatly, too.

Wet meal or canned food—one ounce per pound of body weight of the dog per day. (This is usually enough for young, growing dogs.) One-half to three-quarter ounce per pound of body weight for the dog per day. (This is usually enough for maintenance of older animals.)

Dry meal—One to two pounds of dry meal per thirty-five pounds of dog. (This measure is oftentimes useful in estimating quantities of meal to mix when feeding several dogs.)

There are often people who prefer to feed table scraps or especially prepared menus for their pets. These suggestions may be helpful as guides and to help squash some old superstitions.

Spaghetti, macaroni and other high-starch foods are not desirable feeds, especially if highly seasoned.

Raw meat, milk, and candy do not cause worms.

Starch has not been proven to be the cause of eczema, and can be digested by dogs if well cooked.

Grass is not a tonic and, in fact, may cause intestinal and stomach upsets. Garlic is not a good worm remedy.

Bones are not necessary for dogs to chew on. They can cause much trouble if small, brittle bones are fed. If you must give bones, give large, solid knuckles, etc., never steak, chop, or chicken bones.

Remember, the dog is basically a carnivore, and meat should form a large part of his diet. Raw meat is to be preferred to cooked, as there is considerable vitamin loss from cooking. Partial cooking is a good compromise.

Vegetables are beneficial and should be included. Cooked, green and leafy vegetables are especially good.

Toast, cooked cereals, breakfast foods, etc. are well utilized by dogs.

The quantity of these miscellaneous foods to be given, again, will vary with the individual. If meat forms a large percentage of the quantity, feed the same amounts as previously given for canned foods.

Feeding sick dogs is a special problem. Keeping a dog eating and taking fluids is fundamental to most nursing care, as this helps the animal to maintain his strength. Often special food that is normally relished by the dog can be presented with a little coaxing and finesse that will obtain success in making the animal eat. Warming food to increase aromas may help, and rubbing some of the food on his lips and gums may stimulate his interest. Oftentimes great patience and perseverance are necessary to obtain results. Those foods which are highly nourishing and easily digested are especially beneficial. Such foods as strained baby meats, chopped liver, soft-boiled eggs, bouillon, toast, boiled milk, cooked cereals, etc., are desirable for feeding sick dogs. Sick dogs are usually best fed small amounts of nutritious food at frequent intervals.

The Coat

Care of the dog's coat is a factor which will greatly influence his general appearance. The skin is an organ of the body which quickly reflects the dog's general health. In order to have a good looking coat it is essential that the dog be basically well fed and in robust good health. If your dog has this fundamental good health, the grooming his coat receives is next in importance. A dog should be bathed as little as possible and usually only when excessively dirty or contaminated with something of offensive odor or appearance. Excessive washing removes natural oils and causes the coat to become dry and harsh. When necessary, bathing should be done with a mild castile soap or coconut-oil shampoo. Stand the dog in a tub or basin, plug his ears with cotton and place a bland ophthalmic ointment, or a few drops of mineral oil, in his eyes. Wet the dog with the water, apply the soap and work up a good lather. Be sure to rinse well when finished. It is a good precaution to keep the dog inside until thoroughly dry. This process may be hastened by vigorously rubbing the dog with rough towels. Once he is clean, the dog can best be kept that way by regular brushing and combing.

Each breed varies somewhat as regards hair coat and the best method of caring for it. Shorthaired dogs are best brushed, terrier type dogs require periodic plucking to remove dead hair and to "trim up" their appearance. In-between times, careful brushing and combing are needed. The longer-coated dogs usually are first carefully combed and may be brushed only to give an added sheen or luster to the hair. When grooming your dog, be sure to get the brush down to the dog's skin, as the massaging action stimulates blood circulation which is beneficial in promoting skin health. This massaging also helps to loosen and remove any flakes or dandruff which may be present. If you can comb and brush your dog daily, it is best to do so. However, brushing several times a week will keep the average dog looking neat and clean. Vigorous and frequent grooming is particularly important when the dog is shedding, as it helps to remove the dead hair. Some dogs shed once or twice yearly, and at these times it is desirable to help the process to early completion by plucking or removing dead hair tufts. Some dogs, especially the smooth, short-coated breeds that are kept indoors much of the time, shed almost constantly. Continual brushing and grooming may be helpful in reducing the quantities of hair which are left about the house.

Mats in the hair are often difficult to remove. They can sometimes be teased apart using only one or two teeth of the comb. Occasionally they must be cut out. You must be careful here, as it is easy to cut the skin, too. Cutting also leaves a bare, gouged area in the animal's coat. If the mat must be removed by cutting, try to work the comb all the way through the mat but close to and parallel to the skin, then cut the mat off outside the comb. Mats are most often found as solid masses of hair behind the ears, under the legs, etc., and are caused by inadequate grooming.

The Nails

Part of the grooming routine includes care of the nails, eyes, and ears. A dog's nails should be cut periodically so that they just clear the floor. If they are allowed to grow long, they may cause the foot to splay or spread, and they may even grow around in a circle and back into the dog's skin. This is most apt to happen to the dewclaws, which are not in wear, and which are often covered by long hair so they may not be observed readily. Cutting nails is easy with the special dog nail trimmer. The cut should be made just outside the pink blood line seen on white nails. In pigmented nails the cut must be judged by noting the curvature of the underside of the nail. The hooklike projection is removed. Frequency of cutting depends upon the type and amount of exercise the dog receives. Usually once every two months is adequate. It is very difficult to cut nails with an ordinary scissors and we recommend that you do not attempt it. The special nail trimmers can be purchased at most pet stores.

The Eyes

The dog's eyes need regular care, too. Breeds which have large, protruding eyes are especially predisposed to injuries, foreign bodies, and other accidental scratches and bruises. This constant irritation of the eyes eventually produces a chronic infection, and the dog may appear red-eyed and have a slight discharge from the corner of the eyes. Such individuals are benefited by washing the eyes with a warm boric-acid solution or a salt solution composed of one teaspoonful of table salt per pint of water. After the eyes are thoroughly cleaned, some cotton or cloth patches can be soaked in good warm water and held in place over the eyes for five to ten minutes. This stimulates blood flow to the part. Yellow mercuric oxide ophthalmic ointment can now be squeezed directly onto the eyeball. This line of treatment is beneficial for mild irritations and should be instituted twice daily for five to seven days. If your dog has only an accumulation of mucus in the corners of his eyes on waking mornings, all that is necessary is to wipe out the discharge using the salt and water solution described above.

The Ears

Ears often cause a dog much pain and suffering. They are delicate areas and easily infected. Most ear trouble starts from irritation of the lining inside the ear. Soap, water, strong medicines, ear mites, foreign objects, excessive wax secretion, etc., will all cause irritation and eventually lead to trouble. Some dog owners call this kind of irritation canker, or otorrhea. The affected animal will shake his head, scratch, hold the bad ear down, show evidence of pain, and usually present an ear which smells offensively and has a pasty, dark-colored discharge. Treatment of a well-established case is difficult, and response is slow. However, if the dog is just beginning to show symptoms of irritation, fill the ear with warm mineral oil, massage the base of the ear to allow the oil to loosen dirt and wax particles and then wipe out as much of the oil as you can with cotton held in your fingers. Treatment can be continued daily. It will kill mites, is soothing and perfectly safe to use. Never wash the ears with water, alcohol, or peroxide. Unless used for a specific purpose by your veterinarian, they may cause a further increase in irritation. Dogs with lop ears or hair-filled ear canals are predisposed to more ear trouble than individuals with erect ears. This is basically a condition of air circulation, as the open ears dry out better and do not produce the good media for infections to grow in that covered ears do. In very severe or chronic ear infections, your veterinarian may suggest a surgical procedure which opens up the ear canal and lets it drain and dry out. Some cases heal spectacularly following this surgery. However, if you take proper care of the ear to keep it clean and dry and seek professional advice before infection becomes deep seated, most ear troubles can be easily remedied.

External Parasites

Fleas: External parasites often infest the dog's coat. The most commonly encountered ectoparasites are fleas, lice, and ticks. Fleas are very small brown bugs which are flattened laterally (like a coin standing on edge). They move about rapidly through the dog's hair and are difficult to catch, but they can catch *you* easily enough. Fleas can jump, too. They are difficult to eradicate because they do not spend all of their time on the dog's body. Eggs are found in bedding, in cracks in the floor, in sand or dirt spots, etc.; the eggs hatch, and a new flea starts looking for something to feed on. If animals are around they prefer them, but if not, humans are readily accepted. Sometimes a family gets rid of the dog and immediately becomes severely "flea bitten." Dogs can pick up fleas from grass and brushy lawn or woods areas. Fleas deposit a black excreta, and in a heavily infested dog the coat may be covered with these dark, cinderlike deposits.

Defleaing the dog is worthless unless an attempt is made to clean up the premises and other possible sources of reinfestation. Thorough vacuuming of rugs and spraying of floors, sand piles, dog beds, and houses with 5 per cent DDT solutions are usually effective. It is impossible, of course, to treat entire grass areas, so that regular use of flea powders or the new flea collars may be desirable during the summer months. Flea powders which contain rotenone and/or 5 per cent DDT are quite safe and effective for fleas on *dogs*. The animal can be dusted daily during severe infestations; the powder should be dusted on and worked down into the coat by rubbing against the grain of the hair. Apply most of the powder around the head, neck, and ears and down the top of the back. The new flea collars are fine, but their effectiveness tends to wear off. Various sprays and dips are available for treating flea infestations, but some of them are very toxic if not used properly or if the dog licks too much of the material from his coat. Certain flea soaps are very efficient flea killers, but too frequent use may remove excessive amounts of oil from the hair coat. Ingestion of infected fleas is the method of spreading one type of dog tapeworm (*Dipylidium caninum*), so flea control is paramount to tapeworm control, too.

Lice: Lice are much easier to eradicate because they spend all of their life cycle on the dog. Lice are small, blue-black (rice size) parasites which are attached to the skin and adjacent hair. They are especially thick on the ears and neck of affected dogs. Lice do not move about rapidly and spread from dog to dog usually by direct body contact. Lice lay small eggs or "nits" which are light colored, waxy bodies that are tightly fixed to the hair shaft. Heavy louse infestations are very annoying to the dog, and in addition to the itching and scratching produced, the animal may be severely run down and anemic from supporting his "little friends." Most of the flea remedies previously mentioned will control lice, but treatment must be repeated at seven-day intervals to catch the new generations of lice hatching out of their protected wax-covered shells. Nits can be killed by washing the dog in a 5 per cent vinegar solution, but several treatments at weekly intervals are still to be recommended.

Ticks: Ticks are similar to fleas in that much of their life cycle is spent off the animal. In appearance they vary in size from brownish-red, flattened parasites one-quarter inch or so in diameter up to large, fat gray bodies that look like coffee beans. Ticks are the means of spread of Rocky Mountain spotted fever and other diseases communicable to man. They are very prevalent in wooded lands of the interior and are also abundant along the sandy beaches of many of our ocean resorts. Immature ticks rest on the branches of trees and shrubs of these areas, and when an animal passes by, they drop off on that animal and obtain the blood meal which is needed for the completion of their life cycle. Ticks also infest houses and buildings, and it is common to find them crawling up the walls of such infested places.

In our experience, ticks are not well controlled by DDT or most of the older insecticides. Chlordane and Lindane in proper dilution do a creditable job of killing ticks and they possess a residual action which lasts from two to four weeks if the animal does not become wet. However, they are very toxic, so should only be applied by experienced people. Much stronger solutions of Chlordane may be applied to buildings and infested areas, and very satisfactory control results can be obtained. Occasionally a dog will have one or two ticks and the owner wants to pick them off. If this is summarily done, the mouth parts of the tick (which are attached to the animal's skin) may be broken off and left behind to start an infection. Easy, safe removal is accomplished by soaking the tick with alcohol and then pulling it off with very gentle traction as it loosens its hold.

Internal Parasites

Worms: Worming is a subject open to much controversial opinion. It is undoubtedly true that at least as much damage is done to dogs from worming and overworming as is done by the worms themselves. If worms are not the trouble (and there is a good chance that they are not), indiscriminate worming is the worst possible treatment that could be administered to the dog; furthermore, if the dog is sick or run down, what might be a reasonable dose of worm medicine for a healthy dog becomes a lethal dose for the sick dog.

Dogs may be infested with at least four common types of intestinal parasites, and remedies effective against one type of worm may be ineffective against the others. If you guess wrong on the medication, you may not even be removing the worms you think you are. However, there is no need to guess. Today, any veterinarian can microscopically examine a specimen of the dog's stool and tell you exactly what types of worms are present. He can also dispense the correct worm medicine if any is needed, and tell you how to use it.

Roundworms, or ascarids, are most commonly encountered in pups or young dogs. They may be passed to the puppy *before* birth, or they may ingest the worm eggs from contamination early in their lives. Ascarids may be passed periodically in the stool. They look like strips of thin spaghetti about one to three inches long and are often curled or coiled like springs. They are white, firm, and round. Affected pups may eat excessively, be pot-bellied, have diarrhea and hiccup occasionally. Treatment as to fasting, administration of laxatives, etc. depends on the medication used, and this may be varied depending on the condition of the dog. As dogs grow older, they may become tolerant or immune to the ascarids so that they are not so deleterious to the animal's health.

Hookworms are also commonly encountered in puppies, but dogs of any age can be seriously infested. This worm, too, may be passed to the puppies before birth or at an early age. Debilitated animals are easy prey, and a heavy infestation may cause death. These worms are tiny, white, hairlike parasites which have hooklike mouth parts for chewing and attaching themselves to the intestinal lining. A heavily parasitized dog may be weak and anemic from loss of blood. He may have thin, mucoid bowel movements that are always diarrhealike and often contain blood. Worming such animals is a delicate procedure. They often need blood transfusions to build them up for the worming. Mild infestations may produce unthriftiness, loss of weight, poor coat, chronic diarrhea, and other symptoms.

Whipworms are more commonly seen in older dogs. They are usually very difficult to remove because they inhabit the colon and the cecum, a blind outpouching of the intestinal tract that may be by-passed by the worm medicine. Whipworms are small, round, sharply tapered white worms. Symptoms may be vague and include intermittent diarrhea, generally poor condition, dry harsh coat, etc. Treatment is often effective with medicine given by mouth, but usually some medicine must be deposited right in the blind pouch. This is accomplished by introducing it through the rectum. If this treatment fails, it may be necessary to remove the cecum surgically. Diagnosis of all the above worm infestations can be made easily by microscopic fecal examinations.

Tapeworms more often involve older or mature dogs. There are two more or less common tapeworms which claim the dog for their host for part of their life cycles. They are: *Dipylidium*, which spends part of its cycle in the flea (ingestion of an infected flea is necessary before the dog can become infected), and *Taenia* which spends part of its cycle in the rabbit or mouse so that ingestion of viscera is necessary before the dog can become infected. The head end, or scolex, of these worms attaches to the intestinal linings and the rest of the parasite streams out into the lumen of the intestine like a rope floating in a river. As the parasite is flat and segmented, and the segments are all produced at the scolex, or head end, the whole worm becomes longer and longer. Eventually some of the segments break off and appear in the stool. Unless the scolex is removed, the parasite will soon grow again.

Often the segments from the stool will become attached to the hair around the anus of the dog. These segments may dry and fall off. They are commonly found in the dog's bed and look like pieces of dried rice. Finding these dried up segments, or seeing the fresh segments in the stool, plus voracious appetite, loss of weight, and generally poor condition are usually indicative of tapeworm infestation. Treatment with severe purgatives will remove many of the segments but may not remove the heads. Special tapeworm remedies given orally will usually accomplish this, but reinfestation often occurs.

Dogs are occasionally infested with *Coccidia*, small microscopic bodies which invade the tissues lining the intestinal walls. They are rarely encountered and general good sanitation helps in limiting the disease. Dogs are also parasitized with heartworms, or *Dirofilaria*. These parasites are transmitted from dog to dog by mosquitoes and other biting insects. The larvae develop in the mosquito that has drawn blood from an infected dog. Upon injection into a normal dog during the stinging process, they move to the dog's heart, where they develop into adult worms. These parasites are three to five inches long and actually interfere with the action of the heart. Dogs so affected tire easily, may have a chronic cough, and also may lose weight. Diagnosis is made by microscopic analysis of a blood sample drawn from the dog in question. These parasites are very prevalent in the south and are becoming no rarity as far north as New Jersey and New York. Treatment is by intravenous injection of arsenic and antimony compounds, and results are not always completely satisfactory, although many cures are safely and thoroughly accomplished.

FIRST AID

FIRST AID is important, not only to alleviate pain, but to prevent further complications of those injuries already sustained. Most injured animals are not only in pain, but frightened and apprehensive of anyone who approaches them (even the owner) for fear of being hurt again. They must be handled very carefully and gently and it is always a wise precaution to muzzle the dog first. A muzzle can be fashioned from bandage, cord, strips of cloth, or even heavy string. The cord is looped around the dog's mouth and tied firmly under his chin. The long ends are then extended from the chin around behind the head and tied again to prevent the muzzle from slipping forward over the nose. Small injured dogs are best lifted by grasping the nape of the neck with one hand and the loose skin over the hips with the other. This method prevents further twisting and injury to the legs, as they hang straight down when the animal is picked up. Larger animals are best moved onto a board, rug, or blanket and picked up on the makeshift stretcher.

Bleeding

The very first thing to look for after the dog is muzzled is bleeding. Small cuts and abrasions can be treated by clipping the hair away and cleaning the area with mild soap and water. An antiseptic such as tincture of metaphen should be applied. Deeper wounds can be treated the same way except that they should be covered with sterile gauze and a pressure bandage applied. Wounds that bleed excessively will probably need professional care. Until this can be obtained, a tourniquet may be applied near the wound but between the wound and the heart. Tourniquets which must remain in place a long time should be loosened every ten minutes to allow the blood to flow again.

Shock

If an animal loses a great deal of blood or suffers severe crushing injuries and acute pain, he may go into shock. This is a serious state which often leads to death. The animal seems numbed and dazed, may be cool to touch and may have pale-colored lips and tongue. While rushing him to the hospital, keep him warm and wrapped in blankets and, if he can be kept lying down, have his head lower than the rest of his body. Never try to force liquids into a dazed or shocked animal—fluids may run into his lungs.

Fractures

Broken bones are the usual result of automobile accidents, or falls from windows, fire escapes, etc. The first-aid problem is to keep the broken limb straight and immobilized while taking your pet to the hospital. Handle the animal as little as possible, and lift him gently as described previously. When you want to set him down again, keep the affected side uppermost.

The veterinary profession has made marvelous progress in orthopedic therapy and, in fact, one splint designed by a veterinarian is now used in the repair of fractures in humans. The type of splint applied depends upon the fracture. It may be made of plaster of Paris or adhesive tape, or the leg may have been surgically opened and the broken bones screwed or pinned together. In any case, the splint will probably have to remain in place for about a month. If your dog is allowed to go home with the splint still on, be sure and follow directions for the care and handling of the dog and note when he should be returned to the veterinarian for checkups. Splints occasionally slip out of adjustment, so if there is any question about your pet's condition or progress, contact your veterinarian for specific advice.

Burns

Simple burns such as occur from hot water, grease, or touching hot irons, etc. can usually be handled by applying a sterile ointment which is soothing, protects the burned surface and serves to keep air away from it. A bland ointment is quite satisfactory, but vaseline or even butter, lard, or cold cream can be used in a pinch. Larger burns should also have a light bandage for additional protection. Burns are not only painful, slow-healing, and prone to infection, but they may also leave ugly scars which as hairless areas will detract from your dog's appearance. Burns from acids or alkalies should first be flushed with dilute baking soda or dilute lemon juice solutions respectively, and then treated as regular burns.

Owners often try to apply turpentine or kerosene to remove paint or grease spots from their dogs. These oils produce painful burns. Treatment by the application of vegetable cooking oil, followed by gentle washing with mild soap and water and further application of oil is often soothing and healing. You can remove the paint by clipping the hair in the involved areas. Small spots are best just allowed to wear off.

Dogs that are very seriously burned may also go into shock, and, of course, they require hospital treatment.

Foreign Bodies

Foreign bodies are common in the mouth, ears, and eyes of dogs. Hunting dogs are especially susceptible to these accidents. Objects in the eyes are very painful and unless removed promptly, may seriously injure the eye. Removing seed or weed particles, or pieces of stone or dirt is fairly simple. A piece of cotton can be wrapped around a match stick and the tip of the cotton moistened with water. The dog's eyelids can be spread open and the moistened cotton swab used to wipe out the offending object. Following such removal a few drops of mineral oil or a little mercuric oxide ophthalmic ointment can be applied to protect the eye from further irritation and to promote healing.

Bones are often accidentally wedged in a dog's mouth between the teeth. The animal will salivate, hold his jaw open and paw at his mouth. It is often difficult to remove the bone unless the animal is first anesthetized. In any case, careful manipulation is needed, as rough twisting and turning may result in fracture of the jaw, or teeth, and laceration of the gums. Unless you can see the object in question, it is best not to fool with the animal too much—better take him to your veterinarian.

Fish hooks are commonly caught in a dog's lips and mouth. Treatment here is simple but painful. The hook must be pushed on through so that the barb end protrudes. This is cut off with a pair of pliers or wire nippers and the rest of the fish hook backed out. The hooks are usually rusty or badly contaminated, so clean and apply tincture of metaphen to the injured area.

Country dogs that run at large in the northern regions often encounter porcupines. Fighting or biting at the porcupine results in a dog being pierced with the barblike quills of the animal. We have seen some dogs following such a fight with literally thousands of quills piercing the skin. Such cases are best treated by your veterinarian as the animal must be anesthetized for the painful process of removal. With a large number of quills, many will be broken off under the skin and may produce severe infections. If the dog has only a few quills, they may be removed at home. A small pointed-nosed pair of pliers will work satisfactorily. There is a trick to removing quills cleanly, too—do not jerk or snap them out, just keep a steady pull, and all at once they give way and slide out. They are not so apt to break off this way, but it is more painful for the dog.

Electric shock is occasionally encountered, as puppies often play with electric outlet cords. The pup usually chews into the cord, suddenly stiffens out and falls over in a rigid manner. Always pull the plug from the wall before touching the dog. If you can feel the dog's heart beating, but he is not breathing, initiate artificial respiration at once and have someone call your veterinarian for further instructions. Artificial respiration is given by laying the dog on his side and alternately depressing and releasing the chest by pressing on the rib cage at its most posterior margin. Aromatic inhalants are beneficial in some cases, too.

Poisoning

Poisoning is not quite as common as some people believe, but we are still encountering too many poisoning cases. The majority of these are accidental or caused by carelessness. We rarely see poisoning which we look upon as being deliberate acts, but they undoubtedly do exist. Poisons may act by a local caustic or burning action, or they may act by being absorbed into the dog's system and thereby producing a general effect. Those which produce a generalized action are by far the more common. Because of this, speed in getting treatment for the dog is essential. If the poison can be removed before it has an opportunity to be absorbed, the problem is much less serious than if one must attempt to treat a "late" case of poisoning. Poisons do not always have to be ingested either. Many of the new insecticides are extremely toxic to dogs if applied incorrectly. (It is usually best to ask your veterinarian for his recommendation of a safe, effective powder or medicine to use for the particular parasite you are trying to kill.)

If you should find your dog just licking his chops after having finished the last morsel of something you know to be poisonous—find the container the ant or rat poison or the medicine came in. Call your veterinarian and read him the label of contents so he will know exactly what the problem is. He can then advise you to not worry, if such is the case, or prescribe correct first-aid treatment if needed. If you cannot locate your veterinarian, the following principles will usually be of some help, although not always the most specific treatment.

First cause the dog to vomit. This can be accomplished by giving two teaspoonfuls of hydrogen peroxide orally every five minutes until vomiting occurs. Usually, one or two doses produce the desired effect. After the vomiting stops, give the dog a dose of equal parts of mineral oil and milk of magnesia. The total dose (half of each) will vary from one tablespoonful for small terriers up to four tablespoonfuls for the larger breeds. This combination will directly counteract some poisons, and will help evacuate the intestinal tract while at the same time the oil coats and protects the delicate intestinal lining. Even after this treatment has been given, it is still best to contact your veterinarian for specific advice on your special problem.

Administration of Medicine

Medicine is not difficult to administer to most dogs, but occasionally an animal is encountered that is extremely obstreperous. Here are a few hints which often make the job easier. Some medicines are tasty, or at least tasteless, and can be conveniently included in the dog's food or milk. Cod-liver oil, mineral oil, and milk of magnesia can often be given this way. Many pills can often be administered in this manner, too. However, if a dog bites down on a piece of meat and encounters a hard object (such as the pill) he will immediately spit it out. Accordingly, it is better to crush the pill into a powder (by rolling it under the bowl of a spoon) and mixing it with the food.

A much more positive and effective method of giving medications orally is to force the dog to take them. Capsules, pills, and other solid forms can be given by standing along the dog's right side, grasping his muzzle over the top of his nose so that the fingers of the left hand press in on the lips and squeeze them against the teeth. This will usually cause the dog to start to open his mouth. As he does so the lips are curled inward around the points of the teeth. If the dog attempts to close his mouth, he will bite his own lips. The capsule is held in the fingers of the right hand and pushed deeply into the dog's throat. The hand is quickly withdrawn, the mouth closed, and the animal's head elevated while the throat is stroked. Usually the dog will lick his nose when he has swallowed the capsule. If he should spit it out, merely repeat the process of giving it again.

Liquid medicines are more difficult to administer, as the dog may move his head and cause the medicine to be spilled. Liquids are best administered from a vial or small bottle—a spoon is an awkward, clumsy implement to use. It is essential to have someone hold the dog's head steady and just slightly elevated. Insert two fingers inside the corner of the lips and pull the lips outward away from the teeth. This forms a funnel-like pouch into which the medicine may be poured. It will trickle between the teeth and as the animal tastes it, he will usually swallow. Some dogs clench the teeth and do not allow the medicine to enter between them; to overcome this, insert the handle of a spoon between the teeth. Once the dog starts to swallow, he usually takes the medicine satisfactorily.

BREEDING AND WHELPING

THE average male dog in good health is capable of mating at any time of year and during the major portion of his life. Puberty usually occurs at six to eight months of age, and senility arrives at such varied times as to be hard to state. Usually disease processes will influence the time when a male dog can no longer be used as a stud. If a dog is used often for breeding (once or twice weekly) he should be especially well fed, with emphasis on a high-protein diet. It is also important that he receive adequate exercise, for a dog in lean, hard condition will prove to be a more active sire than will an overfed, soft individual. The first time a male is used for breeding he will undoubtedly be more successful if he is used with a proven matron. Conversely, a maiden bitch is best bred the first time to an accomplished stud.

The average female dog in good health is capable of mating and producing young twice yearly. However, this is often not possible and usually not advisable. A young pup should not be bred her first season. She should be given time to grow and develop fully, receive all her vaccinations, and have her puppy "high jinks" before she settles down to the business of parenthood.

The Reproductive Cycle

The bitch, like most other animals, has a rhythmic reproductive cycle. This cycle varies somewhat with breeds and, of course, with individuals. The average bitch may show her first "season" at six to eight months of age, although some breeds do not show estrus until twelve months of age. The reproductive cycle is divided into four sections:

A. Proestrum lasts for approximately nine days and it is at that time during the cycle when the external genitalia are enlarged and swollen and a bloody discharge occurs.
B. Estrum or true "heat" also lasts approximately nine days and is the time during which sexual desire is strongest and during which ovulation occurs. Ovulation is the casting off of the eggs from the ovary, and it usually happens on the first or second day of *estrus*. However, the ovum is not ready for fertilization until one or two days after ovulation. Because of this it is best to breed a bitch on the twelfth day after she first shows signs of being in season (swollen genitalia and bloody discharge). This

is best for the average dog. Not *all* animals are the same, so if difficulty is encountered determining the day to breed, your veterinarian can make vaginal smears of the bitch during the estral period to help determine the best day for breeding.

C. & D. Following estrum, there are two periods called anestrum and metestrum which are rest periods of two and three months respectively during which the bitch acts normal and is "out of season."

If you do not want to breed your dog, be sure to keep her *confined*, not just tied up. There is an old saying that to keep a dog unbred, put her in your house, bar all the doors, shutter the windows, put a board over the chimney, and even then sometimes the inevitable happens. Keep her confined at least twenty-one days. If *mésalliance* does occur, your veterinarian can give hormone injections which *may* prevent conception.

Gestation

The gestation period in the bitch is sixty-three days (date from day conceived until day whelped). The fertilized ovum floats free in the uterus for about twenty days, during which time it is nourished by a fluid called uterine milk. After this time it becomes stuck or implanted in the uterus and a cuff-like band of tissue attaches the embryonic pup to its mother. This cuff is called the placenta, and there is one for each pup. Diagnosis of pregnancy can be made around the thirty-fifth day by having your veterinarian palpate the abdomen of the bitch. X-rays show the fetal skeleton about the forty-fifth day. In a primipara the nipples may be enlarged and pink by the thirtieth day; the breasts may be enlarging by the fiftieth day, and milk may be present the last day or two before whelping. A few hours before giving birth the vulva enlarges, the animal's body temperature falls slightly, food may be refused, and the animal may act restless and want to keep off by herself. During the pregnancy it is advisable to have provided the bitch with a low-sided, roomy box which she can call her own, and to which she can become accustomed. Newspapers make good bedding, and just before whelping the bitch will tear them up and make herself a nest. It is a good idea to place the box in an out-of-the-way warm place. If it can be located so that you can "peek" into it without the bitch seeing the observer, so much the better.

SIXTY-THREE DAY WHELPING TABLE

Service January	1	2	3	4	5	6	7	8	9	10	11	12	13	14	15	16	17	18	19	20	21	22	23	24	25	26	27	28	29	30	31
Whelping March	5	6	7	8	9	10	11	12	13	14	15	16	17	18	19	20	21	22	23	24	25	26	27	28	29	30	31	Apr. 1	2	3	4
Service February	1	2	3	4	5	6	7	8	9	10	11	12	13	14	15	16	17	18	19	20	21	22	23	24	25	26	27	28			
Whelping April	5	6	7	8	9	10	11	12	13	14	15	16	17	18	19	20	21	22	23	24	25	26	27	28	29	30	May 1	2			
Service March	1	2	3	4	5	6	7	8	9	10	11	12	13	14	15	16	17	18	19	20	21	22	23	24	25	26	27	28	29	30	31
Whelping May	3	4	5	6	7	8	9	10	11	12	13	14	15	16	17	18	19	20	21	22	23	24	25	26	27	28	29	30	31	June 1	2
Service April	1	2	3	4	5	6	7	8	9	10	11	12	13	14	15	16	17	18	19	20	21	22	23	24	25	26	27	28	29	30	
Whelping June	3	4	5	6	7	8	9	10	11	12	13	14	15	16	17	18	19	20	21	22	23	24	25	26	27	28	29	30	July 1	2	
Service May	1	2	3	4	5	6	7	8	9	10	11	12	13	14	15	16	17	18	19	20	21	22	23	24	25	26	27	28	29	30	31
Whelping July	3	4	5	6	7	8	9	10	11	12	13	14	15	16	17	18	19	20	21	22	23	24	25	26	27	28	29	30	31	Aug. 1	2
Service June	1	2	3	4	5	6	7	8	9	10	11	12	13	14	15	16	17	18	19	20	21	22	23	24	25	26	27	28	29	30	
Whelping August	3	4	5	6	7	8	9	10	11	12	13	14	15	16	17	18	19	20	21	22	23	24	25	26	27	28	29	30	31	Sept. 1	
Service July	1	2	3	4	5	6	7	8	9	10	11	12	13	14	15	16	17	18	19	20	21	22	23	24	25	26	27	28	29	30	31
Whelping September	2	3	4	5	6	7	8	9	10	11	12	13	14	15	16	17	18	19	20	21	22	23	24	25	26	27	28	29	30	Oct. 1	2
Service August	1	2	3	4	5	6	7	8	9	10	11	12	13	14	15	16	17	18	19	20	21	22	23	24	25	26	27	28	29	30	31
Whelping October	3	4	5	6	7	8	9	10	11	12	13	14	15	16	17	18	19	20	21	22	23	24	25	26	27	28	29	30	31	Nov. 1	2
Service September	1	2	3	4	5	6	7	8	9	10	11	12	13	14	15	16	17	18	19	20	21	22	23	24	25	26	27	28	29	30	
Whelping November	3	4	5	6	7	8	9	10	11	12	13	14	15	16	17	18	19	20	21	22	23	24	25	26	27	28	29	30	Dec. 1	2	
Service October	1	2	3	4	5	6	7	8	9	10	11	12	13	14	15	16	17	18	19	20	21	22	23	24	25	26	27	28	29	30	31
Whelping December	3	4	5	6	7	8	9	10	11	12	13	14	15	16	17	18	19	20	21	22	23	24	25	26	27	28	29	30	31	Jan. 1	2
Service November	1	2	3	4	5	6	7	8	9	10	11	12	13	14	15	16	17	18	19	20	21	22	23	24	25	26	27	28	29	30	
Whelping January	3	4	5	6	7	8	9	10	11	12	13	14	15	16	17	18	19	20	21	22	23	24	25	26	27	28	29	30	31	Feb. 1	
Service December	1	2	3	4	5	6	7	8	9	10	11	12	13	14	15	16	17	18	19	20	21	22	23	24	25	26	27	28	29	30	31
Whelping February	2	3	4	5	6	7	8	9	10	11	12	13	14	15	16	17	18	19	20	21	22	23	24	25	26	27	28	March 1	2	3	4

Whelping

Labor is initiated by interaction of hormones within the individual, and may last from four to five hours up to thirty-six hours and still be normal. Some pups may be born head first and some hind end first. Both are normal presentations. The average bitch will have her puppies easily and take care of them, and the *less we interfere, the better!* There are some things we must do, however, if the bitch fails to accomplish them. If the bitch does not clean the membranes off the pup, this should be done so that the head is exposed and breathing can begin. The umbilical cord may have to be cut about two inches from the pup's abdomen, and tincture of iodine applied to the cord. If the mother will not cuddle the pups to her and clean and warm them, it is desirable to rub them vigorously with a rough towel to dry them and stimulate circulation. Place them in a small box with a towel-covered hot-water bottle in the bottom until the bitch has completed whelping.

Newborn pups need two things; warmth and fluids. Keep them very warm, especially if the bitch is a slow whelper and disinclined to care for her new offspring. It may be necessary to feed the pups a few dropperfuls of formula or of a solution of one teaspoonful of Karo in one cup of water heated to body temperature. This can be repeated every two hours until the bitch will nurse the puppies properly.

If the bitch seems to be slow in producing a pup which is partially protruding, you can grasp its limbs with a piece of sterile gauze and apply gentle, steady traction. Never insert your fingers or anything else into the vagina. If you are worried about any phase, contact your veterinarian for advice immediately.

Signs of trouble during whelping:

In labor too long without giving birth to a pup, (over six hours).
Excessive pain.
Excessive straining.
Trembling, shivering, cold extremities.
Collapse and exhaustion.
Vomiting.

You can usually tell when the whelping is complete because the bitch will act content and at rest, will mother and feed the pups, and will have gone several hours without any straining. However, it is always advisable to have a veterinarian examine her to be sure. Sometimes X-rays are made and injections of hormones administered. The injection is beneficial in two ways; it causes the uterus to contract and expel any fluid or placental shreds left behind, and it stimulates the let-down of milk in the breasts.

It is *most* important that the pups receive the colostrum or the first milk of their dam, as this milk is high in vitamins A and D which the pups lack; and it is high in globulin, the protein factor which helps give them immunity to those diseases to which their dam is immune. This milk is also somewhat laxative. In order for the pups to receive the greatest benefits from the colostrum, however, it must be ingested during the first twenty-four hours of their lives. Exclusive formula feeding should not be used during this time unless absolutely necessary.

As each pup is born, it is cleaned and licked off and the placenta, or afterbirth, is eaten by the mother. This material is best moved along out of her stomach, so a laxative such as milk of magnesia is often indicated the day following whelping. Dosage varies from one to two teaspoonfuls for the smaller terriers up to two to four tablespoonfuls for the very large breeds. If the bitch should have inadequate milk, or if you should be called upon to raise an orphaned litter, so that you have to "hand feed" the puppies, you are in for a difficult job.

Orphan Puppies

Raising orphaned pups entails attention to details in three general categories. Proper *thermostatically controlled* heat is probably the most important item, and the one most apt to be inadequate. During the first week of life the temperature should be maintained at 85°–90°F.; during the second week 80°–85°F.; and during the third week 75°–80°F.

The formula employed in feeding the pups is also important to their successful survival during the first ten days. Actually, commercial powdered milk which is compounded to simulate bitch's milk is convenient, economical, and most satisfactory. This product can be procured from any veterinarian and from certain large pet supply shops. An emergency (but quite good) formula can be compounded at home by using the top one half of a bottle of unshaken, unhomogenized whole cow's milk (you want the cream in the formula). To this is added one raw egg yolk. The formula is well mixed and stored in several small bottles (each containing the quantity for one feeding) in the refrigerator. The pups should be fed every eight hours. The formula should be warmed to about 100°F. and fed with an ordinary baby bottle. Usually the holes in the rubber nipple should be enlarged so the milk will drip out slowly when the bottle is turned over. Very small or weak pups can be easily fed from an eye dropper. The amount to feed depends upon the breed and size of the pup. Day-old Beagles require slightly more than a quarter of an ounce of formula every eight hours. The quantity is increased as they grow, of course.

Sanitary requirements of the pups during the first week are often misunderstood. After each feeding the pup should be "burped" by massaging the abdomen gently or by bouncing the pup in the palm of the hand. The massage often stimulates defecation and urination. If these acts do not occur, a small pledget of cotton soaked in warm water should be used to massage the pup's abdomen and the region under the tail. This usually stimulates elimination. After several days, urination and defecation occur more spontaneously, but cleanliness is still important. The pup should be wiped over with a damp cloth or even given a *light* application of baby oil. Orphaned pups should be kept in separate compartments (such as shoe boxes) as they tend to suckle each other's tails and genitalia.

It may be possible by two weeks (when the pups' eyes open) to get them started eating from a dish. To initiate this, get them good and hungry and then push their noses into a saucer of formula. When they are eating well from a dish, they may be fed four times daily. However, it is better to feed more often than may be necessary than to feed them too few times daily.

Weaning

With a normal nursing litter, the pups should be fed supplementally from a dish as early as they can walk around and learn to eat from a dish. This is usually around three weeks of age. First food should be plain milk, followed later by the addition of Pablum or some cereal mush. Cooked eggs, cottage cheese, scraped raw beef muscle, corn oil, and raw liver are other food items which can be fed to young pups at the time of weaning. Gradually bits of dog meal or dog meat chopped fine and partially cooked can be added. By the time the pups are from five to six weeks of age they will be eating more and more from their dish and less and less from their dam. The bitch will be getting sick of their mauling by this time, too, and the combination of these factors usually makes weaning a simple and automatic procedure.

When it is decided to wean the litter, separate the dam from them for several days and drastically curtail her food and water intake. This helps to reduce her milk production. Even so, some individuals develop swollen and caked breasts. Gentle massage, two or three times daily, with camphorated oil is usually beneficial in overcoming this congestion.

Eclampsia

There is a serious condition called eclampsia which is seen in lactating canines. It is almost never seen with a first litter and usually occurs from fourteen to thirty days after whelping. It is more common in individuals that have large litters and whose pups are very fat and healthy looking. Eclampsia is caused by overproduction of milk, so that excessive calcium is taken from the dam to form the milk. It is usually successfully treated *if seen in time* by the veterinarian. Call him immediately if the symptoms develop. The bitch may stagger, walk drunkenly (*i.e.* with poor co-ordination) she may pant and drool excessively, pace the floor nervously, look alert and even wild-eyed, be jumpy to noise, and finally go into spasms of convulsions (fits). Fortunately, it is not a common condition, and if the owner seeks veterinary service promptly the treatment with calcium injections is usually successful.

Feeding

Feeding a bitch correctly during pregnancy and lactation is most essential to safeguarding her future health and to optimum development of the pups. It is during the last three or four weeks of pregnancy that the pups do most of their growing within the uterus, so until this time the dam can be fed her normal diet. This should be well balanced, vitamin rich, and not too fattening. During this time abundant exercise is most desirable. The last three weeks of pregnancy the dam will show a great enlargement of her abdomen and her appetite will increase considerably. The diet may have to be increased as much as 50 per cent. Most of this increase should be good-quality meat. Liver or dairy proteins are especially desirable. During this later period of pregnancy, an abundant supply of calcium, phosphorus, iron and vitamins D and A are most important. They can be supplied as bone meal, iron pills, calcium powders, etc. The human prenatal capsules, while somewhat expensive, are a made to order item for canines in that condition, too.

After whelping, the dam should be fed lightly the next day, and then gradually put on a full diet again. As the puppies grow their demands for milk increase and the mother's food should be increased accordingly. *Some* females require twice as much food while nursing pups as they do normally. Foods which seem to help stimulate formation of milk are liver, raw meat, and milk or milk products. At weaning time the bitch's food should be sharply restricted, as previously mentioned.

MAJOR INFECTIOUS DISEASES AND
INDICATIONS OF OTHER SERIOUS ILLNESS

THIS section is presented with the intention of furthering the average dog owner's basic understanding of diseases which might commonly affect his pet. It is not intended as a doctor book but as a presentation of facts which may help you to better understand your dog's illness.

Your responsibility is early recognition of abnormal symptoms and accurate reporting of these symptoms to the veterinarian. You must speak for your pet. You must also be able to follow directions exactly in order to carry out home medications effectively.

Diseases will be discussed individually with indications of cause, method of spread, general symptoms, and the principles of treatment. Specific remedies are not given because each case must be treated individually, and dosage of medicines for different breeds, ages, and sizes of dogs are not the same. Information about prophylactic treatment is given elsewhere.

Distemper

Distemper is the most common of the infectious diseases which plague our nation's dogs. It is caused by a virus and it is a very highly contagious disease. The infection is air-borne (like a cold), and can be spread on contaminated dishes, bedding, shoes, and clothing because the virus is present in urine, saliva, and eye and nasal discharges of infected dogs. Once contaminated, articles or premises remain dangerous for a considerable time unless thoroughly cleaned and disinfected. While much work has been done recently in research laboratories to study this disease (mostly on prophylactic measures), there is still a great deal to be investigated before veterinarians will feel that it has been conquered. Despite the rapid strides in therapy, distemper is still the number one killer of dogs. The virus is so omnipresent that very few dogs are not exposed to the disease many times during their lifetime. Because it is so prevalent, it is usually a disease of young animals, although an old animal never before exposed could contract the disease just as easily. A dog that has suffered the disease and recovered possesses a lifelong immunity.

The incubation period may run from several days to fourteen days, although it may vary. Symptoms are extremely varied because the disease may attack any system in the body and because the viral infection is usually complicated by so-called secondary bacterial infections (due to weakness of the patient). Some outbreaks of distemper are more virulent than others, so the mortality per cent may vary greatly from year to year.

Generally, a distemper-sick pup acts sleepy and dopey, and acts as if he has a "cold." He will not eat well, has runny nose and eyes and often a slight cough. He will have a fever. He may also have diarrhea and vomit occasionally. Some animals apparently recover from this stage, but fourteen to thirty days afterwards develop convulsions, or fits; they lie on their sides and thrash their legs, champ their jaws, and salivate profusely. These fits last from a minute or two to fifteen or twenty minutes. They are a most serious development and indicate that the virus has invaded the nervous system. Prognosis then is apt to be poor because, while many of the animals survive, they may be left mentally retarded, or paralyzed, or they may have a permanent muscle twitch (called chorea). Some dogs make a perfect recovery, however. Curiously, most dogs that have the nervous type of infection eat ravenously. This is no cause for optimism, however.

During a convulsion it is best to leave the animal alone. He is not "mad" and will not attack you, but if you get a finger between those champing jaws, of course you will be bitten.

In treating a dog, it is generally true that excellent nursing care is a fundamental necessity. Keeping the animal warm, dry, and clean is most important. Keeping the eye and nasal discharges wiped away and applying ophthalmic ointment to the eyes and nasal drops in the nose are beneficial. Use of vitamin tonics together with the feeding of adequate fluids such as water, milk, and broths are also important aids. Because the disease is caused by a virus, the new "wonder drugs" are ineffective in combating the virus itself. However, they are often used to obviate the possibility of the weakened animal coming down with a secondary bacterial infection (such as pneumonia). Veterinarians sometimes use immune serums and blood transfusions to combat the virus itself. Many cases of distemper are hospitalized and many are treated at home. Either way, it is essential that the treatment be under the close direction of a veterinarian. The course of the disease is long and recovery is slow. Convalescence may take six to eight weeks. Just as the physician can give us no *sure* cure for the cold, the veterinarian can give us no *sure* cure for distemper. However, because of extensive research, distemper can now be prevented and satisfactory recovery from infection with the disease is becoming more commonplace. The future looks bright.

Infectious Hepatitis

Hepatitis is the "new disease" you have heard so much about. Like distemper, it is caused by a virus and is highly contagious. Unlike distemper, it is not air-borne. It is easily transmitted by direct contact though, especially when articles are contaminated with urine or saliva from infected dogs. Recovered animals may shed the virus in their urine for long periods of time even though the "carrier" appears normal and healthy. The disease is very prevalent in some localities and usually affects very young puppies. (If a pup gets distemper and hepatitis together, he will not usually survive.)

Hepatitis is a very acute disease characterized by sudden onset, high fever, and very marked depression. Affected pups may vomit, have sore throats, and grunt with pain when picked up under the chest. This disease is often difficult to differentiate from distemper.

Hepatitis in dogs affects primarily the liver and blood vessels. Because it is such an acute condition, dogs may appear normal in the morning and be dead by nightfall. Prompt treatment is necessary. Nursing care is important, but your veterinarian may also use antibiotics and injections of immune serum. Blood sugar and fluids may also be given intravenously. Occasionally an animal that has recovered will develop a milky cloudiness of both eyes. This condition is usually temporary if properly treated. Recovery from hepatitis confers permanent immunity upon an individual.

Leptospirosis

This disease in dogs is caused by spirochetelike organisms that are also present in other animals (rats) and can be transmitted to man. These spirochetelike organisms are called *Leptospira canicola,* and *Leptospira icterohaemorrhagia,* and they attack primarily the dog's kidneys. The organisms may be spread in the urine of infected animals and one form of the disease is spread by contamination with rat urine. There is a larger percentage of males affected than of females. This is probably due to the male's inquisitive sniffing habits, which cause him to be exposed to infected urine. Unless the dog is properly treated, the urine of the recovered animal spreads the *Leptospira* for many months. Damage done to the kidney by this disease may again trouble the animal during old age, when kidney function becomes less efficient. The disease may be acute or subacute.

Symptoms may include fever, depression and dopeyness, vomiting, soreness to pressure over the loin, stiff-legged gait, red eyes and gums, and sometimes jaundice. As this disease is transmittable to man, it is important to thoroughly wash after handling or cleaning the dog. Veterinarians treat the disease with blood transfusions and injections of penicillin and streptomycin. Recovery *may* take place in two weeks, but treatment must be done by your veterinarian.

Rabies (Hydrophobia)

Rabies is one of the most feared of infectious diseases, as any animal contracting it dies. It may be transmitted to man. There is no treatment, although there is a preventative. Rabies is a specific encephalitis caused by a virus which attacks the nervous system of the animal and is present also in the salivary glands. When an infected animal bites another, the saliva transfers the virus to the new victim. If bleeding is immediately encouraged, the wound thoroughly scrubbed with soap and water, and a series of injections given the bitten animal (or if he has previously been vaccinated), his chances of escaping the disease are good. However, once symptoms develop, the animal is sure to die. The incubation period is usually three to six weeks, but may be as long as six months.

There are two main syndromes of the disease, the dumb and the furious forms. In dumb rabies the animal becomes lethargic and wants to be left alone. He soon becomes paralyzed, slips into a coma, and dies. If an animal has rabies, he will usually die within seven days of the onset of the disease. In furious rabies, the animal has a change in disposition—either he becomes more friendly or more aloof. He may seem nervous and easily disturbed, get a wild-eyed expression and a peculiar bark. His jaw may become paralyzed, and he may run aimlessly over the countryside. Anyone or anything that gets in his way may be snapped at. The animal will chew furiously at sticks, stones, pieces of metal, etc. Rabid dogs are said to fear water (hence the name *hydrophobia*) and in fact cannot drink or swallow. Because they salivate profusely, some people feel they have a "bone in the throat" and attempt to remove it. Needless to say, this is a foolhardy exposure to infection.

If *you* are bitten by a dog, or cat, contact your physician for the professional treatment he may deem necessary and keep track of the dog, or cat, that did the biting. Sometimes neighborhood dogs are involved, so that this problem is not too difficult. If the dog lives more than seven days, he probably did not have rabies when he bit you. Bite wounds of the face and neck are the most dangerous. If *your dog* is bitten by another animal, contact your veterinarian for further professional advice. Never destroy a dog that has been biting people or that is suspected of being rabid. Lock him up in a room or a garage and call the public-health authorities. If you live in an area where rabies is endemic, it pays you to keep your dog vaccinated.

Skin Diseases

To the average dog owner, a dog with skin trouble has "mange." While many dogs do have mange, at least an equal number have eczema and dermatitis. Mange itself can be somewhat complicated and there are three main forms:

a) Otodectic, or ear mange, caused by relatively large mites which inhabit the ear canal, especially of dogs with hair-filled ears. These mites set up a severe irritation which causes much itching and head shaking. Filling the ear with plain mineral oil daily will eventually kill these mites. Incidentally, never probe or poke into the ear with swabs or sticks. That is a job for your veterinarian. The mineral oil can be removed by swabbing out the ear with cotton held around the index finger.

b) Sarcoptic mange is usually seen as patchy, crusty areas of the body, legs, abdomen, etc. It also itches, especially in warm weather, and has a peculiar mouselike odor. This form of mange is transmittable to man. It is usually treated with medicated baths and may respond in four to six weeks.

c) Demodectic mange is more common in short-coated dogs and appears as thin-haired, dark skinned areas of the face, head, and legs. It is also called red mange. This form of mange is very refractory to treatment and may take eight to ten weeks to clear up. Some cases are incurable. Bitches that have once had the trouble may pass the condition on to their pups. This is true even though the dam's skin looks perfectly healthy. Diagnosis of mange is made by scraping the skin and examining the collected debris under the microscope for the mites.

Chronic eczema is a noncontagious skin affliction which may be caused by a myriad of factors. Some cases are caused by hormonal upsets, dietary inadequacies, infected anal sacs (the pouches on each side of the dog's anus), allergies and chronic irritations (such as too much bathing). Cases of eczema are most difficult to clear up as each case is a separate individual problem with a complicated solution. Accordingly, treatment varies, too. General principles to follow which may be of benefit in treatment include the administering of a laxative, removal of fleas or other parasites, vigorous brushing to stimulate skin blood circulation and addition of lard to the diet. Other treatment is often used, but should be directed by the veterinarian.

Fungus infections such as ringworm are quite commonly encountered in dogs. They may be seen as round, patchy, crusty areas within which the hair is brittle and sometimes stubby and broken off. This condition is important to man because it is easily transmitted to him and may become a serious infection. In dogs the infection can be successfully treated, but the entire animal must be treated at least once to catch the newly affected areas which are not yet apparent to the eye. Therefore professional treatment is necessary for diagnosis and initial medication.

Vitamin deficiencies, tumors of the skin, and tumors of glands within the body may also cause skin abnormalities, and correction of these basic lesions may involve X-ray, ultraviolet therapy, or even surgery.

Constipation

Impaction of the bowel may be dietary in nature, or it may be due to rheumatism, or to an inflamed prostate or anal sacs (all of which produce pain if the animal strains, so he puts it off). Correct treatment must attempt to remove the causative factor. Administration of plain mineral oil for two days followed by a laxative dose of milk of magnesia often relieves the situation, but a soap and warm water enema is usually more prompt and efficacious in removing the impacted material. Liver (which is laxative) included in the diet for several days is often beneficial in preventing recurrence. One word of caution here. Never administer human laxative tablets to dogs. The ingredients of some of them are poisonous to dogs and may actually cause the animal's death.

Diarrhea

Dysentery, or diarrhea, is usually caused by indigestion from overeating or eating unwholesome food. However, worms, intestinal infections, and certain systemic diseases may also cause diarrhea. It is the body's reaction to an irritating substance and its attempt to get rid of it. By the time a case of diarrhea is really noticeable, the animal's intestinal tract is sore and inflamed. Treatment should be aimed at soothing and protecting these inflamed surfaces giving them an opportunity to rest and, most important, doing nothing to further the irritation. It is felt that withholding food for six to eight hours will help rest the intestinal tract, and administering one to four teaspoonfuls of milk of bismuth every three to four hours will help to soothe and protect the inflamed membranes. Liquids may be somewhat curtailed temporarily. After the short initial rest period, it is desirable to begin feeding the animal soft, easily digested foods that will not cause irritation, but which will be nourishing and strengthening. Desirable foods include soft-boiled eggs, toast, boiled milk, or soft cereals such as cream of wheat, etc. Mild diarrhea caused by dietary upset will respond in two to three days to this line of treatment. More serious diarrheas need professional help.

Vomiting

This symptom is very commonly encountered in dogs because they can retch voluntarily, and at the first indication of stomach upset or discomfort, they promptly empty the organ. Vomiting is such a common symptom in so many different illnesses that a complete list would be prohibitively long. However, a few causes are car sickness, overeating, eating unwholesome food or objects, foreign bodies in the stomach, so-called nervous stomachs in high strung dogs, foreign bodies or twists in the bowel, kidney disease, infectious diseases, and many toxic conditions in addition to poisonings.

Obviously, no treatment can apply to all cases of vomiting unless determination and removal of the cause is accomplished first. There are some general principles that one should adhere to until correct diagnosis has been made and treatment prescribed. First, give no food or drink. Allow the stomach complete rest. Keep the animal warm and quiet, and if he seems excessively thirsty, let him lick ice cubes (but not drink the fluid). This can be accomplished by placing the cubes in a strainer which in turn is fitted into a bowl or pan. Occasionally administration of milk of bismuth, as outlined under diarrheas, will be of benefit in cases of simple stomach upset. Large amounts of liquid usually aggravate the condition and are definitely to be avoided.

Abnormalities of the Urinary System

As animals age, the wear and tear of twenty-four-hour functions begins to tell on some of their vital organs. In dogs, the kidneys may be especially affected, and as a result of this "wearing out" process, they function less efficiently. The kidneys perform much like a filter, and as kidney function fails, it takes more fluid passing through the filter to do the work required. This, then, is the reason older dogs often drink large quantities of water and urinate excessive amounts. These symptoms are signs of urinary abnormality.

Some dogs will have an inflammation of the bladder, and some may even have stones formed in their urinary passages. Of course, these are serious occurrences which may require surgical treatment. Blood clots or red color in the urine, especially when associated with straining, are indications of serious trouble. There is very little in the way of treatment that dog owners can do for most urinary disease. If an old dog wants to drink a lot, be sure to allow him all he wants. Sometimes dietary changes may be helpful in relieving the work load of the kidney. Other treatments should be prescribed by the veterinarian.

Convulsions

This symptom is very startling and rather awesome. Our first reaction is sympathy for the poor dog having the convulsion. However, if the animal has already fallen down and is not apt to become tangled in furniture, fall down the stairs, or otherwise injure himself, the best course is to leave him alone. The convulsion will soon pass and the dog can easily be handled then. If the animal is in a situation where he may injure himself, it may be advisable to hold him down. If this is done, be careful to keep the fingers away from his mouth, as severe bite wounds may result. During convulsions the dog will not be vicious or attempt to attack you. He is too busy with troubles of his own and usually oblivious to what is going on about him.

Convulsions are most commonly caused by a virus infection of the brain, especially distemper. However, other irritating factors may be influencing the condition. Ear infections, parasite infestations, epilepsy, etc. may also be involved. Do not worm dogs that have convulsions. This may be exactly the wrong thing to do and may even cause the animal's death.

PROPHYLACTIC IMMUNIZATION

THE SUBJECT of prophylactic immunization is a very important one, which will be discussed by following the pup from birth to maturity. Distemper, infectious hepatitis, leptospirosis, and rabies are the diseases for which vaccines are usually administered. When a puppy is born and nurses the mother for the first time, he receives colostrum or her "first milk," which is very high in the protein globulin. This protein is a substance which contains antibodies against those diseases to which the mother is immune. (If the mother is not immune to a disease, there will be no antibodies in her milk against that disease.)

If the pup ingests this globulin during the first twenty-four hours of life, he becomes immediately and passively protected against those diseases for which antibodies are present. (Passive immunity is that produced from an outside source, such as another dog, without any effort by the individual's body; active immunity is that produced by the animal's own body.) Dr. James Gillespie at the laboratory for the diseases of dogs at Cornell University has developed a test to measure the amount of immunity a specific dog has to distemper and to hepatitis. This test can be performed on a dog of any age. It is available to the public and can be arranged through your local veterinarian. The test is important for two reasons:

(1) It can tell you whether a specific animal is immune or susceptible to distemper and to hepatitis.

(2) By a procedure called nomographing, the results of the refined test can be used to tell the titer or amount of immunity possessed by the individual dog. Some animals carry very high titers of immunity; others carry very low or marginal titers of immunity; and others carry no titer at all, and so are susceptible.

It has been found that bitches pass protection against distemper to their puppies in the colostrum, which is ingested during the first twenty-four hours of life. The degree of protection, and hence the duration of the protection of the puppy and directly related, or can be graphed as a straight line. This line is called the nomograph. It can be used by the veterinarian to determine (even before their birth) how long a puppy will be immune to distemper after birth and when he can be safely and accurately vaccinated in order to produce his own active immunity. The test is best run on bitches during gestation, and is made on a sample of blood which can be taken from the animal by the local veterinarian. If the normograph information is not available on specific puppies, it is desirable that they receive passive immunity against distemper and hepatitis in the form of serum which is produced from the blood of other dogs immuned to the diseases in question. Injections of such serum (temporary or puppy shots as they are often called) must be given every ten days until the puppy is at least twelve weeks old. The reason for this is that after each serum injection the pup has a reasonable degree of protection, but the protection rapidly decreases until it is dissipated, between nine and eighteen days after the injection.

Most serum injections available commercially are polyvalent, which means that they will protect the puppy against several different diseases.

Relatively permanent protection against infectious hepatitis can be conferred by a single injection of a killed tissue vaccine. This vaccine can be given at ten to twelve weeks of age. The active immunity produced by this vaccine is solid and lasts for a long time. The vaccine cannot produce disease itself nor can it produce any carrier state. It would be wise to vaccinate dogs with this product early in life, especially if the animal is to travel to shows, field trials, or other gatherings of dogs. A live type of hepatitis vaccine is also available, and a single injection of this produces a solid, long-lasting immunity.

Permanent active immunization against distemper can be accomplished in several ways. Dog people usually refer to them as "one-, two-, or three-shot" methods. The single injection is vaccination with a modified virus of distemper. The live virus has been altered in its characteristics so that it can no longer produce the disease in a dog. This altering is accomplished by growing the virus in fertile chick eggs or by passing it through laboratory animals until the virus has been modified or attenuated. It is then frozen and dried so it can be preserved in the live state. Vaccination by this method should give a very solid, lasting immunity but does embody some degree of risk, as occasionally an animal will develop a mild reaction. These reactions are seldom of a serious nature, however. For optimum results the dog to be vaccinated should be in robust good health, parasite-free, and be free from the effects of any passive immunizations (either serum injections or colostrum). The monetary cost of this injection is usually equal to the total of two or three injections in the other methods, as the product is more expensive to produce.

The "two-shot" method of vaccination is not as universally popular as the other systems; it consists of an injection of serum to confer passive immunity, followed by an injection of the live active virus itself. This method can conceivably produce the disease, so there is some risk involved. However, it does develop a very solid immunity.

The permanent immunity engendered by the system of three vaccinations is the most common method in use today. Each of these injections is a killed-tissue vaccine. The repeated stimulation of the dog's own immune processes is said to produce antibody formation. However, unless the dog is challenged by contact with the disease, the immunity produced may not be as long-lived as with other methods of vaccination. Distemper is so universally prevalent, though, that some contact is almost inevitable. Veterinarians have had very successful results with this vaccine, and as it cannot produce the disease, reactions are almost unheard-of. It is important that the dog be in good health, well fed, and free of parasites before receiving these vaccinations too. The time interval between injections (fourteen to twenty-one days) must be adhered to rigidly, and following completion of the course, contact with other dogs (not necessarily sick ones) is desirable. Booster vaccinations at three- to six-month intervals are especially desirable during the first year following the initial course of vaccination with the killed-tissue product.

Keeping the dog population of an area vaccinated is one good method of controlling severe epidemics of rabies in the area. By all means co-operate with your health authorities in these matters. They are not only helping to protect your animals, they are protecting human lives too.

Rabies vaccinations are required for shipment of dogs interstate, into Canada, for entrance at some shows, etc. Vaccination can be accomplished by two methods. The older method is one injection of a killed-tissue vaccine produced by the Semple method. This vaccine produces a good immunity for one year. It is probably the best method to use when immunizing cats. By giving two or three injections of this vaccine to dogs at weekly intervals, stronger immunity is produced. The second method of vaccination is the one being advocated at the present time for the use in vaccinating dogs routinely. It is a single injection of an altered live virus vaccine. This vaccine produces immunity which lasts at least three years, and it may last even longer.

Leptospirosis is an acute disease which is quite prevalent in some areas of the country. About 10 per cent of many dog populations have been exposed to the disease and have developed an immunity to it. During an outbreak in a particular area, it may be wise to have your dog immunized against leptospirosis. This can be done by one injection of a killed-tissue vaccine administered by your veterinarian. The protection, however, is probably not good for the life of the dog.

After completing any vaccination series, always remember that no protection is perfect, once in a while the immunity is not complete or solid and a so-called "break" may result. This is indeed a rare occurrence, and as laboratory research progresses, we trust it will soon be eliminated.

TERMINOLOGY

American Kennel Club: The American Kennel Club is a non-profit organization devoted to the advancement of pure-bred dogs. Its members are clubs which conduct dog shows, field trials, and obedience trials under its rules. It adopts, through its board of directors and the delegates of its member clubs, rules applying to these events and participation in them. It maintains a stud book and publishes the *Stud Book Register* as well as an official monthly magazine, *Pure-Bred Dogs—American Kennel Gazette.* Its reference library contains one of the most extensive collections of dog books in the world. And it conducts a breeder information service equipped to answer all manner of questions about dogs.

Almond eyes: The eye set in surrounding tissue of almond shape.

Angulation: The angles formed by a meeting of the bones; mainly, the shoulder, upper arm, stifle, and hock.

Apple head: An irregular roundedness of topskull, in greater or less degree humped toward its center.

Apron: Longer hair below the neck on the chest. Frill.

Babbler: The hound that barks when not on the trail.

Balanced: A consistent whole; symmetrical, typically proportioned as a whole or as regards its separate parts; i.e., balance of head, balance of body, or balance of head and body.

Bandog: A dog tied by day, released at night. Tiedog.

Barrel: Rounded rib section.

Bat ear: An erect ear, rather broad at the base, rounded in outline at the top, and with orifice directly to the front. (French Bulldog.)

Bay: The prolonged bark or voice of the hunting hound.

Beard: Thick, long hair growth on the underjaw.

Beauty spot: A distinct spot, usually round, of colored hair, surrounded by the white of the blaze, on the topskull between the ears. (Blenheim Spaniel, Boston Terrier.)

Beefy: Overheavy development of the hindquarters.

Belton: A color designation. An intermingling of colored and white hairs, as blue belton, lemon, orange, or liver belton. (English Setter.)

Bench show: A dog show at which the dogs competing for prizes are "benched" or leashed on benches.

Best in show: A dog-show award to the dog adjudged best of all breeds.

Bevy: A flock of birds.

Bilateral cryptorchid: See Cryptorchid.

Bird dog: A sporting dog trained to hunt birds.

Bitch: A female dog.

Bite: The relative position of the upper and lower teeth as they meet when the mouth is closed. *See* Level bite, Scissors bite, Undershot, Overshot.

Blaze: A white stripe running up the center of the face usually between the eyes.

Blinker: A dog that points a bird and then leaves it, or, upon finding a bird, avoids making a definite point.

Blocky: Square or cubelike formation of the head.

Blooded: A dog of good breeding; pedigreed.

Bloom: The sheen of a coat in prime condition.

Blue merle: Blue and gray mixed with black. Marbled.

Board: To feed, house, and care for a dog for a fee.

Bobtail: A tail docked very short. Also, a name frequently given to the Old English Sheepdog.

Bolt: To drive or "start" an animal out of its earth or burrow.

Bone: The relative size (girth) of a dog's leg bones. Substance.

Bossy: Overdevelopment of the shoulder muscles.

Brace: Two dogs of a kind. A couple.

Breeching: Tan-colored hair on the inside of the thighs. (Manchester Terrier.)

Breed: Pure-bred dogs more or less uniform in size and structure, as produced and maintained by man.

Breeding particulars: Sire, dam, date of birth, sex, color, etc.

Brindle: A fine even mixture of black hairs with hairs of a lighter color, usually tan, brown, or gray.

Brisket: The forepart of the body below the chest, between the forelegs, closest to the ribs.

Brock: A badger.

Broken color: Self color broken by white or another color.

Broken-haired: Rough, wire coat.

Broken-up face: A receding nose, together with a deep stop, wrinkle, and undershot jaw. (Bulldog, Pekingese.)

Brood bitch: A female used for breeding. Brood matron.

Brush: A bushy tail; a tail heavy with hair.

Bullbaiting: An ancient sport in which the dog baited or tormented the bull.

Burr: The inside of the ear; i.e., the irregular formation visible within the cup.

Butterfly nose: A particolored nose; i.e., dark, spotted with flesh color.

Buttocks: The rump or hips.

Button ear: The ear flap folding forward, the tip lying close to the skull so as to cover the orifice, and pointing toward the eye.

Bye: A field-trial term. In the drawing of braces, the odd dog left, which runs alone.

Canine: A group of animals—dogs, foxes, wolves, jackals.

Canines: The two upper and two lower sharp-pointed teeth next to the incisors. Fangs.

Castrate: To remove the testicles of the male dog.

Cat-foot: The short, round, compact foot like that of a cat. The foot with short third digits.

Catch dog: A dog used to catch and hold a hunted animal, so the huntsman can take it alive.

Challenge certificate: An award of the Kennel Club, England, corresponding to the AKC best of breed award.

Champion: A dog that has demonstrated superiority at duly authorized competitions such as dog shows or field trials.

Character: Expression, individuality, and general appearance and deportment as considered typical of a breed.

Cheeky: Cheeks prominently rounded; thick, protruding.

Chest: Forepart of the body between the shoulder blades and above the brisket.

China eye: A clear blue eye.

Chiseled: Clean-cut in head, particularly beneath the eyes.

Choke collar: A leather or chain collar fitted to the dog's neck in such a manner that the degree of tension exerted by the hand tightens or loosens it.

Chops: Jowls or pendulous flesh of the lips and jaw. (Bulldog.)

Chorea: A nervous jerking caused by involuntary contraction of the muscles, usually affecting the face or legs.

Clip: The method of trimming the coat in some breeds, notably the Poodle.

Cloddy: Low, thickset, comparatively heavy.

Close-coupled: Comparatively short from withers to hipbones.

Coat: The dog's hairy covering.

Cobby: Short-bodied, compact.

Collar: The marking around the neck, usually white. Also a leather or chain for restraining or leading the dog, when the leash is attached.

Companion Dog (CD); *Companion Dog Excellent* (CDX): Obedience-test titles.

Condition: Health as shown by the coat, state of flesh, general appearance and deportment.

Conformation: The form and structure, make and shape; arrangement of the parts in conformance with breed-standard demands.

Corky: Active, lively, alert.

Couple: Two hounds.

Coupling: A leash or collar ring for controlling two dogs together.

Couplings: The body between the withers and the hipbones; used to express comparative length, as "long or short in the couplings," or "long- or short-coupled."

Coursing: The sport of chasing the hare by Greyhounds.

Cow-hocked: When the hocks turn toward each other.

Crank tail: A tail carried down and resembling a crank in shape.

Crest: The upper, arched portion of the neck.

Cropping: The cutting or trimming of the ear leather for the purpose of inducing the ears to stand erect.

Crossbred: A dog whose sire and dam are representatives of two different breeds.

Croup: The back part of the back, above the hind legs.

Crown: The highest part of the head; the topskull.

Cry: The baying or "music" of the hounds.

Cryptorchid: The adult whose testicles are abnormally retained in the abdominal cavity. Bilateral cryptorchidism involves both sides; that is, neither testicle has descended into the scrotum. Unilateral cryptorchidism involves one side only; that is, one testicle is retained or hidden, and one descended.

Culotte: The longer hair on the back of the thighs.

Cur: A mongrel.

Cushion: Fullness or thickness of the upper lips. (Pekingese.)

Dam: The female parent.

Dappled: Mottled marking of different colors, no one predominating.

Deadgrass: Tan or dull straw color.

Derby: Field-trial competition for young, novice sporting dogs usually between one and two years of age.

Dewclaw: An extra claw or functionless digit on the inside of the leg; a rudimentary fifth toe.

Dewlap: Loose, pendulous skin under the throat.

Diehard: Nickname of the Scottish Terrier.

Dish-faced: When the nasal bone is so formed that the nose is higher at the tip than at the stop; or, a slight concaveness of line from the stop to the nose tip.

Disqualification: A fault that, when so specified by a breed standard, renders the dog ineligible to compete or ineligible to win a prize in organized competition.

Distemper teeth: Teeth discolored or pitted as a result of distemper or other enervating disease or deficiency.

Dock: To shorten the tail by cutting.

Dog: A male dog; also used collectively to designate both male and female.

Dog show: An exhibition for dogs that are judged each in accordance with its breed standard.

Domed: Evenly rounded in topskull; convex instead of flat. Domy.

Double coat: A top coat of more or less weather-resisting hair, and an under-coat of softer hair for warmth.

Down-faced: When the nasal bone inclines toward the tip of the nose.

Down in pastern: When weak or faulty pastern joints, tendons, or muscles cause pronounced angulation at the pastern and let the foot down.

Drag: A trail prepared by dragging along the ground a bag impregnated usually with animal scent.

Drahthaar: Wirehair (German)

Drawing: Selection by lot of dogs to be run, and in which pairs, in a field-trial stake.

Drop ear: The leather long and hanging straight down.

Dropper: A bird-dog cross.

Dry neck: The skin taut; neither loose nor wrinkled.

Dual champion: A dog that has won both a bench-show and a field-trial championship.

Dudley nose: Flesh-colored.

Elbow: The joint between the upper arm and the forearm.

Elbows out: Turning out or off from the body; not held close.

Ewe neck: Concave curvature of the top neckline.

Expression: Color, size, and placement of the eyes, which together are responsible for the countenance as distinctive of the breed.

Eyeteeth: The upper canines.

Faking: To change the appearance of a dog by artificial means with the object of deceiving the onlooker as to its real merit.

Fall: Hair overhanging the face.

Fancier: A person especially interested and usually active in some phase of the sport of pure-bred dogs.

Fangs: See Canines.

Feathering: Longer fringe of hair on ears, legs, tail, or body.

Feet east and west: The toes turned out.

Fetch: The retrieve of game by the dog; also the command to do so.

Fiddle front: Forelegs out at elbows, pasterns close, and feet turned out. French front.

Flag: A long-haired, fringed tail; said usually of Setters.

Field trial: A competition for hunting dogs which are judged on ability to find game, also on range, speed, and style of working.

Flank: The side of the body between the last rib and the hip.

Flare: A blaze that widens as it approaches the topskull.

Flat bone: The leg bone whose girth is elliptical rather than round.

Flat-sided: Ribs insufficiently rounded as they approach the sternum or breastbone.

Flews: Upper lips pendulous particularly at their inner corners.

Flush: To drive birds from cover, to force them to take flight. To spring.

Flying ears: Any characteristic drop ears or semi-prick ears that stand or "fly."

Forearm: The bone of the foreleg between the elbow and the pastern.

Foreface: The front part of the head, before the eyes. Muzzle.

Foster mother: A bitch or other animal, such as a cat, used to nurse whelps not her own.

Foul color: A color or marking not characteristic.

Frill: See Apron.

Fringes: See Feathering.

Frogface: Extending nose accompanied by a receding jaw, usually overshot.

Front: The forepart of the body as viewed head on; i.e., forelegs, chest, brisket, and shoulder line.

Furrow: A slight indentation or median line down the center of the skull to the stop.

Futurity stake: A class at dog shows or field trials for young dogs which have been nominated at or before birth.

Gait: The manner in which the dog walks or runs.

Game: Hunted wild birds or animals.

Gay tail: The tail carried up.

Gazehound: Greyhound or other sight-hunting hound.

Geld: See Castrate.

Genealogy: Recorded family descent.

Goose rump: Too steep or sloping a croup.

Grizzle: Bluish-gray color.

Groom: To brush, comb, trim, or otherwise make neat the coat.

Groups: The breeds as grouped in six divisions to facilitate judging.

Gun dog: The dog trained to assist the huntsman.

Guns: Sportsmen who do the shooting at field trials.

Gun-shy: When the dog fears the sight or sound of a gun.

Hackles: Hair on neck and back raised involuntarily in fright or anger.

Ham: Muscular development of the hind leg just above the stifle.

Handler: A person who exhibits a dog in the show ring or field trial.

Hard-mouthed: The dog that bites or marks with his teeth the game he retrieves.

Harefoot: A foot whose third digits are longer; hence, an elongated foot.

Harlequin: Patched or pied coloration, usually black on white. (Great Danes.)

Harness: A leather strap shaped around the shoulders and chest, with a ring at its top over the withers.

Haw: A third eyelid or membrane in the inside corner of the eye.

Heat: Seasonal period of the female. Estrum.

Heel: See Hock; also a command to the dog to keep close beside its handler.

Height: Vertical measurement from the withers to the ground; referred to usually as shoulder height. *See* Withers.

Hie on: A command to urge the dog on; used in hunting or in field trials.

Hock: The tarsus or collection of bones of the hind leg forming the joint between the second thigh and the metatarsals; the dog's true heel.

Holt: The lair of the fox or other animal in tree roots, bank, drains or similar hideouts. Lodge.

Honorable scars: Scars from injuries suffered as a result of work.

Hound: A dog commonly used for hunting by scent or sight.

Hound-marked: A coloration composed of white, tan, and black. The ground color, usually white, may be marked with tan and/or black patches on the head, back, legs, and tail. The extent and the exact location of such markings, however, differ in breeds and individuals.

Hound jog: The usual pace of the hound.

Hucklebones: The top of the hipbones.

Inbreeding: The mating of closely related dogs of the same standard breed.

Incisors: The upper and lower front teeth between the canines.

Interbreeding: The breeding together of dogs of different varieties.

Isabella: Fawn or light bay color.

Judge: The arbiter in the dog-show ring, obedience trial, or field trial.

Kennel: Building or enclosure where dogs are kept.

Kink tail: The tail sharply bent.

Kiss marks: Tan spots on the cheeks and over the eyes.

Knuckling over: Faulty structure of carpus (wrist) joint allowing it to double forward under the weight of the standing dog; double-jointed wrist, often with slight swelling of the bones.

Layback: Receding nose accompanied by an undershot jaw.

Lead: A strap, cord, or chain attached to the collar or harness for the purpose of restraining or leading the dog. Leash.

Leather: The flap of the ear.

Level bite: When the front teeth (incisors) of the upper and lower jaws meet exactly edge to edge. Pincer bite.

Liam: Leash.

License: Formal permission granted by the AKC to a person to judge or handle dogs at shows under its jurisdiction; or formal permission to a non-member club to hold a show or a trial.

Line breeding: The mating of related dogs of the same standard breed, within the line or family, to a common ancestor, as, for example, a dog to his granddam or a bitch to her grandsire.

Lippy: Pendulous lips or lips that do not fit tightly.

Litter: The puppies of one whelping.

Liver: A color; i.e., deep, reddish brown.

Loaded shoulders: When the shoulder blades are shoved out from the body by overdevelopment of the muscles.

Loin: Region of the body on either side of the vertebral column between the last ribs and the hindquarters.

Lower thigh: *See* Second thigh.

Lumber: Superfluous flesh.

Lumbering: An awkward gait.

Lurcher: A crossbred hound.

Lymer: A hound of ancient times led by a liam.

Mad dog: A rabid dog.

Mane: Long and profuse hair on top and sides of the neck.

Mantle: Dark-shaded portion of the coat on shoulders, back, and sides. (St. Bernard.)

Mask: Dark shading on the foreface. (Mastiff, Boxer, Pekingese.)

Match show: Usually an informal dog show at which no championship points are awarded.

Mate: To breed a dog and bitch.

Median line: *See* Furrow.

Merle: A coloration, usually blue-gray with flecks of black.

Miscellaneous class: A competitive class at dog shows for certain breeds not recognized by the AKC.

Molera: Incomplete, imperfect or abnormal ossification of the skull.

Mongrel: A dog whose parents are of mixed-breed origin.

Monorchid: A unilateral cryptorchid. *See* Cryptorchid.

Music: The baying of the hounds.

Mute: To run mute, to be silent on the trail; i.e., to trail without baying or barking.

Muzzle: The head in front of the eyes—nasal bone, nostrils, and jaws. Foreface. Also, a strap or wire cage attached to the foreface to prevent the dog from biting or from picking up food.

Muzzle band: White marking around the muzzle. (Boston Terrier.)

Non-slip Retriever: The dog that walks at heel, marks the fall, and retrieves game on command; not expected to find or flush.

Nose: Organ of smell; also, the ability to detect by means of scent.

Occiput: Upper, back point of the skull.

Occipital protuberance: A prominently raised occiput characteristic of some gun-dog breeds.

Open bitch: A bitch that can be bred.

Open class: A class at dog shows in which all dogs of a breed, champions and imported dogs included, may compete.

Orange belton: See Belton.

Organized competition: Competition governed by the rules of a club or society, such as the AKC, organized to promote the interests of pure-bred dogs.

Otter tail: Thick at the root, round, and tapering, with the hair parted or divided on the underside.

Out at elbows: Elbows turning out from the body as opposed to being held close.

Out at walk: To lease or lend a puppy to someone for raising.

Outcrossing: The mating of unrelated individuals of the same breed.

Overhang: A heavy or pronounced brow. (Pekingese.)

Overshot: The front teeth (incisors) of the upper jaw overlapping the front teeth of the lower jaw when the mouth is closed.

Pace: A gait which tends to promote a rolling motion of the body. The left foreleg and left hind leg advance in unison, then the right foreleg and right hind leg.

Pack: Several hounds kept together in one kennel. Mixed pack is composed of dogs and bitches.

Paddling: Moving with forefeet wide, inducing a body swing.

Pads: Tough, shock-absorbing projections on the underside of the feet. Soles.

Paper foot: The foot with thin soles or pads.

Parti-color: Variegated in patches of two or more colors.

Pastern: Commonly recognized as the region of the foreleg between the carpus or wrist and the digits.

Peak: *See* Occiput.

Pedigree: The written record of a dog's descent for three generations or more.

Penciling: Black lines dividing the tan on the toes. (Manchester.)

Pied: Comparatively large patches of two or more colors. Piebald, parti-colored.

Pigeon breast: A narrow chest with protruding breastbone.

Pig jaw: *See* Overshot.

Pile: Dense undercoat of soft hair.

Pincer bite: *See* Level bite.

Plume: A feathered tail carried over the back.

Poach: When hunting, to trespass on private property.

Point: The immovable stance of the hunting dog taken to indicate the presence and position of game.

Points: Color on face, ears, legs, and tail when correlated—usually white, black or tan.

Police dog: Any dog trained for police work.

Pompon: A rounded tuft of hair left on the end of the tail when the coat is clipped. (Poodle.)

Premium list: An advance-notice brochure sent to prospective exhibitors and containing details regarding a forthcoming show.

Prick ear: Carried erect and usually pointed at the tip.

Professional handler: A person licensed by the AKC to show dogs for their owners, for a fee.

Put down: To kill a dog, usually old or incurably ill.

Puppy: A dog under twelve months of age.

Pure-bred: A dog whose sire and dam belong to the same breed, and are themselves of unmixed descent since recognition of the breed.

Quality: Refinement, fineness.

Racy: Tall, of comparatively slight build.

Rat tail: The root thick and covered with soft curls; at the tip devoid of hair, or having the appearance of being clipped. (Irish Water Spaniel.)

Register: To record with the AKC a dog's breeding particulars.

Retrieve: A hunting term. The act of bringing back shot game to the handler.

Ringer: A substitute for; a dog closely resembling another dog.

Ring tail: Carried up and around almost in a circle.

Roach back: A convex curvature of the back toward the loin. Carp back.

Roan: A fine mixture of colored hairs with white hairs; blue roan, orange roan, lemon roan, etc. (English Cocker Spaniel.)

Roman nose: A nose whose bridge is so comparatively high as to form a slightly convex line from forehead to nose tip. Ram's nose.

Rose ear: A small drop ear which folds over and back so as to reveal the burr.

Rounding: Cutting or trimming the ends of the ear leather. (English Foxhounds.)

Rudder: The tail.

Ruff: Thick, longer hair growth around the neck.

Sable: A lacing of black hairs over a lighter ground color.

Saddle: A black marking over the back, like a saddle.

Scent: The odor left by an animal on the trail (ground scent), or wafted through the air (air-borne scent).

Scissors bite: A very slight overlapping of the upper teeth over the lower teeth when the mouth is closed.

Screw tail: A naturally short tail twisted in more or less spiral formation.

Second thigh: That part of the hindquarter from the stifle to the hock. Lower thigh.

Sedge: See Deadgrass.

Self color: One color or whole color except for lighter shadings.

Seeing Eye dog: A dog trained by the institution, The Seeing Eye, as guide for the blind.

Semi-prick ears: Ears carried erect with just the tips leaning forward.

Septum: The line extending vertically between the nostrils.

Shelly: A shallow, narrow body lacking an amount of bone commensurate with size and indicative of breed.

Shoulder-height: Height of dog's body as measured from the withers to the ground. *See* Withers.

Sickle tail: Carried out and up in a semicircle.

Sire: The male parent.

Sled dogs: Dogs worked usually in teams to draw sleds.

Sloping shoulder: The shoulder blade set obliquely or "laid back."

Smooth coat: Short hair, close-lying.

Snipy: A pointed, weak muzzle.

Soundness: The state of mental and physical health when all organs and faculties are complete and functioning normally, each in its rightful relation to the other.

Spay: To perform a surgical operation on the bitch's reproductive organs to prevent conception.

Speak: To bark.

Spectacles: Shadings or dark markings over or around the eyes or from eyes to ears.

Splashed: Irregularly patched, color on white or white on color.

Splayfoot: A flat foot with toes spreading. Open foot, open-toed.

Spread: Width between the forelegs when accentuated. (Bulldog.)

Spring: *See* Flush.

Spring of ribs: Degree of rib roundedness.

Squirrel tail: Carried up and curving more or less forward.

Stake: Designation of a class, used in field-trial competition.

Stance: Manner of standing.

Standard: A description of the ideal dog of each recognized breed, to serve as a word pattern by which dogs are judged at shows.

Standoff coat: A long or heavy coat that stands off from the body.

Staring coat: The hair dry, harsh, and sometimes curling at the tips.

Station: Comparative height from the ground, as high-stationed, low-stationed.

Stern: Tail of a sporting dog or hound.

Sternum: Breastbone.

Stifle: The joint of the hind leg between the thigh and the second thigh. The dog's knee.

Stilted: The choppy, up-and-down gait of the straight-hocked dog.

Stop: The step up from nose to skull; indentation between the eyes where the nasal bone and skull meet.

Straight-hocked: Lacking appreciable angulation at the hock joints. Straight behind.

Straight shoulders: The shoulder blades laid rather straight up and down, as opposed to sloping or slanting.

Stud book: A record of the breeding particulars of dogs of recognized breeds.

Stud dog: A dog used for breeding purposes.

Substance: Bone.

Superciliary arches: The ridge, projection, or prominence of the frontal bone of the skull over the eye; the brow.

Swayback: Concave curvature of the back line between the withers and the hipbones.

Team: Usually four dogs.

Terrier: A group of dogs used originally for hunting vermin.

Thigh: The hindquarter from hip to stifle.

Throatiness: An excess of loose skin under the throat.

Thumb marks: Black spots on the region of the pastern.

Ticked: Small, isolated areas of black or colored hairs on a white ground.

Timber: Bone, especially of the legs.

Tongue: The barking or baying of hounds on the trail, as to give tongue, to open or speak.

Topknot: A tuft of longer hair on top of the head.

Toy dog: One of a group of dogs characterized by very small size.

Trace: A dark stripe down the back of the Pug.

Trail: To hunt by following ground scent.

Triangular eye: The eye set in surrounding tissue of triangular shape; three-cornered eye.

Tricolor: Three-color: white, black, and tan.

Trim: To groom the coat by plucking or clipping.

Trumpet: The slight depression or hollow on either side of the skull just behind the orbit or eye socket, the region comparable with the temple in man.

Tucked up: Characterized by markedly shallower body depth at the loin. Small-waisted.

Tulip ear: The ear carried erect with slight forward curvature of the flap along the sides.

Turnup: An uptilted foreface.

Type: The characteristic qualities distinguishing a breed; the embodiment of a standard's essentials.

Undershot: The front teeth (incisors) of the lower jaw overlapping or projecting beyond the front teeth of the upper jaw when the mouth is closed.

Unilateral cryptorchid: See Cryptorchid.

Upper arm: The humerus or bone of the foreleg, between the shoulder blade and the forearm.

Vent: The anal opening. Also, to come to the surface for air, as in otter hunting.

Varminty: A keen, very bright or piercing expression.

Walleye: An eye with a whitish iris; a blue eye, fisheye, pearl eye.

Weaving: When in motion, the crossing of the forefeet or the hind feet. Traveling "in and out."

Weedy: An insufficient amount of bone; light-boned.

Wheaten: Pale yellow or fawn color.

Wheel back: The back line arched markedly over the loin. Roached.

Whelps: Unweaned puppies.

Whip tail: Carried out stiffly straight, and pointed.

Whisker: Longer hairs on muzzle sides and underjaw.

Wind: To catch the scent of game.

Winners: An award given at dog shows to the best dog (winners dogs) and best bitch (winners bitches) competing in regular classes.

Wirehair: A coat of hard, crisp, wiry texture.

Withers: The highest point of the shoulders, immediately behind the neck.

Wrinkle: Loose, folding skin on forehead and foreface.

PART II: BREED HISTORIES

GROUP I: SPORTING DOGS

Griffon, Wirehaired Pointing

THE ORIGIN of the dog known in America as the Wirehaired Pointing Griffon came in the great period of biological awakening—the last quarter of the nineteenth century. Just a few years before, the Austrian abbot, Mendel, had published his experiments on inheritance, and the youth of Western Europe were anxious to try their skill at breeding.

Thus it was that E. K. Korthals, the son of a wealthy banker at Schooten, near Haarlem, in Holland, began to assemble the dogs from which he was to establish a new sporting breed. His first purchase was Mouche, described as a griffon bitch, gray and brown. She was bought in April of 1874, from M. G. Armand of Amsterdam, for sixty florins, or about twenty-five dollars, and was thought to be about seven years old. It is said of her that she was equally excellent in the woods or in the open. There is considerable doubt regarding her ancestry.

Korthals acquired five other dogs during the next three years—Janus, Hector, Satan, Junon, and Banco. Janus had woolly hair, Junon was short-haired, and the others were rough-coated. The first mating was between Mouche and Janus. The result was a puppy named Huzaar, apparently the only one in the litter. The next mating was between Mouche and Hector, and this produced a bitch puppy, Madame Augot. The dog Satan was later bred to Madame Augot, resulting in Zampa.

The first breeding of importance was that of Huzaar, son of the rough-coated Mouche and the woolly-coated Janus, to the short-haired bitch, Junon. From this mating came Trouvee, a bitch with a harder coat than any of the others. Trouvee then was bred to Banco, and she whelped Moustache I, Querida, and Lina—three specimens from which, it is agreed, springs the best line in the breed.

Although the origin of the Wirehaired Pointing Griffon is undoubtedly Dutch, it is regarded principally as a French breed, for it was in France that the major portion of the development took place. This is due, in measure, to the fact that Korthals did not remain in Holland. It seemed that the elder Korthals, who was a successful breeder of cattle, could not understand his son's interest in "insignificant animals," as he termed dogs. They evidently had a number of heated discussions of the matter. Finally, rather than give up his interest in dogs, the son left the parental house.

Young Korthals went to Biebesheim, Germany, and soon resumed his breeding activities again. Yet Korthals was a man of wide acquaintance among the sporting fraternity of Europe, and invariably he was present at any major field activity connected with dogs. Later he followed the bench shows closely, seeking to popularize the type of griffon—for there had been, for several centuries, dogs called griffons—that he had originated.

Perhaps, though, if any single factor can be credited with the spread of interest in the Wirehaired Pointing Griffon, or Korthals griffon as it is known in France, it was the traveling done by the young breeder during the years he spent as the advance agent of the French nobleman, the Duke of Penthievre. Korthals never forgot his hobby, and whenever he found congenial company he extolled the virtues of the new breed. Admitting that it was a deliberate, even slow, worker, his enthusiasm over its keen nose and its ability to point and retrieve game was infectious. Undoubtedly Korthals had sound reasons, even at that early date, for praising this breed, for it has since gained a wide reputation. It is particularly adapted for swampy country, where its harsh coat—unique in a sporting breed—is a great protection. It also is a strong swimmer and serves as an excellent water retriever. But adherents of the breed claim it can be trained and entered to any game.

When Korthals left Holland for Germany, he disposed of the greater portion of his dogs, and as a consequence found it necessary to replenish his stock to some extent. His first new brood matron in Germany was Donna, which he purchased from Heinrich Freytag in February, 1879. She was of the boulet type, which meant that her coat was rather long. Donna was mated twice to Moustache I, and left two daughters, Augot, and Clairette, both of which showed the characteristics desired. Six years later, Korthals effected a lease for the bitch Vesta, and the breeding from her provided another successful line. Vesta had rough hair, and all her descendants were typical species that carried the right sort of coat.

While there remains some doubt as to the various crosses in the background of the dogs known as the "Korthals patriarchs," it has been suggested by a wide number of authorities that they carried setter, spaniel, and Otter Hound blood. It is known that certain specimens, described in *Livre des Origines du Griffon a poil dur,* as true griffons, trace their ancestry back to the ancient breed called the griffon hound; and it also is known that at least one cross with a Pointer—no doubt the German Shorthair—was effected.

The Wirehaired Pointing Griffon was exhibited in England shortly after it was developed, and it attracted considerable attention. Still, classes were not provided until some years later, the first record of these being at the Barn Elms show in the Jubilee year, 1888. The breed came across the Atlantic twelve years later. The first specimen registered by The American Kennel Club was Zolette, 6773, by Guerre, ex Tambour. The registration appears as a "Russian Setter (Griffon)" in Vol. 4, published in 1887. The sire, Guerre, was a grandson of Donna. So started the American fancy.

Pointer

THE Pointer comes by his name honestly. He was the first dog, so far as we know, used to stand game in the sense in which we use the term today, and was developed as a distinct breed much earlier than any of the setters. For years it was believed the first Pointers used in England were importations from Spain and Portugal, but that theory has been pretty thoroughly disproved and it seems far more likely that Pointers came into general use in Spain, Portugal, throughout eastern Europe and in the British Isles at approximately the same time. Whether or not the dogs from which they sprung were native to all these places no one can say, but it can be stated with confidence that the *development* of the English Pointer took place within the confines of Great Britain, most probably in England itself. Later on Spanish Pointers were brought in, but from the first they were considered as a different strain, if not a different breed, from the English dogs.

The first Pointers of which there is any dependable record appeared in England about 1650, some years before the era of wing-shooting with guns, and the use to which they were put is interesting. Coursing with Greyhounds was a favorite sport of those times and the earliest accounts of Pointers reveal that they were taken afield to locate and point hares. When the hare had been found, the Greyhounds were brought up and unleashed, the game was kicked from cover and the fun began. But early in the eighteenth century, at least by 1711, wing-shooting had come into vogue and, from that day on, the "shorthair" has been considered by the majority of sportsmen the equal, if not the superior, of any of the gun dogs.

As to the Pointer's lineage, as usual we find it something of an enigma, but there is no question that the Foxhound, Greyhound and Bloodhound all had a share in his making. Individuals of the three breeds were probably crossed with the inevitable "setting spaniel," which played such a prominent part in the creation of all our modern bird dogs.

Adherents of the Foxhound cross were especially persistent and active. Even as late as 1868 many English breeders were using it, or at least strongly advocating it to improve the Pointer. A well known authority who wrote over the *nom de plume* of "Sixty-one," said that "as far as my experience goes, I consider the Foxhound cross with the Pointer most valuable," and we find Idstone expressing himself as follows: "If the Pointer must be crossed, would it not be advisable to combine Foxhound, Bulldog and Greyhound?" While it is doubtful if any such radical measures were actually used, it was not until the stud-book and dog-show era that the idea was definitely discarded. The importance of our official record of breeding and the value of bench shows in establishing and maintaining the correct standards can hardly be overestimated. Without these two institutions chaos might well have resulted, not only in Pointers, but practically every breed recognized today.

During the first years of the eighteenth century the Spanish Pointer began to appear in England, and he, too, was used for a cross, but as he was exceedingly heavy and very slow in comparison with the English, French, and German Pointers, subsequent breeding operations not only left him out but definitely attempted to correct the faults he had introduced. It appears that his real value was not to improve type but to fix and intensify the pointing instinct, in which, we are told, he was peculiarly strong.

If this was the purpose it seems to have been successful. Remarkable (and incidentally quite unbelievable) stories are to be found in British sporting papers of the early nineteenth century, relating the prodigies performed by certain English Pointers of a former day. Col. Thornton's Pluto and Juno, for example, are said to have held a point on a covey of partridges for an hour and a quarter by the watch. But when we find so solid an authority as Stonehenge telling as gospel truth the now famous yarn of the sportsman who lost his Pointer on the moors, and returning a year later, discovered the skeleton of the dog pointing a skeleton bird, we realize that the statements of these pre-Victorian worthies must be taken with considerably more than a pinch of salt.

During the nineteenth century the English Pointer was repeatedly crossed with the various setters as they came into existence and favor. This, it seems, was partly to improve his disposition, for an old-time writer, commenting on the breed says: "They have a ferocity of temper which will not submit to correction or discipline, unless taken in hand very young." While the Pointer of today is anything but ferocious, it may be that this characteristic, tempered by judicious breeding and in combination with the natural independence that made him object to correction and discipline, has made him the superlative field-trial dog he is today. He certainly possesses the competitive spirit to a greater degree than is usually found in the other bird dogs, a quality that makes him especially suited to public performance.

The modern Pointer is a specialist and looks the part. He is every inch a gun dog. Clean-limbed, lithe, and muscular without being coarse, full of nervous energy and "hunt," put together for speed and endurance, courageous, and with the ability to concentrate on his job, he is an ideal dog for the man or woman who is looking for results when afield. His short hair makes him neat and clean around the house and his disposition makes him adaptable for the kennel. He requires less personal attention than some other gun dogs and he is willing to work satisfactorily for someone other than his own master and handler.

In addition to all this, he has another characteristic—tendency towards early development. As a breed, Pointers seem to acquire the hunting instinct at a tender age, puppies of two months frequently pointing and even backing. For this reason they are especially suited for derby and puppy stakes.

For show purposes, while hardly as attractive in some ways as the Irish Setter, the Pointer is in many respects quite satisfactory. His short coat makes his outline, conformation, and quality easily seen at a glance, and he is a superb poser. His color, usually white with rich liver markings is striking and, like the Irishman, he has an ideal bench temperament. Lemon and white, orange and white, black and white and sometimes solid black are other colorings. Daniel Lambert, an English sportsman, developed a strain of solid blacks as long ago as 1820, and self-colored dogs are still seen in the shows today. But, as already said, the liver and white, lemon and white or black and white specimens are most popular in the ring.

The Pointer is peculiarly fortunate in one all-important respect. He has always been bred for type as well as field ability, hence we have in this case no divergence between the two insofar as appearance goes. From the beginning type has been carefully developed and intelligently preserved. An illustration for Col. Thornton's book *A Tour Through*

Scotland shows Captain Fleming of Barochan out hawking. This picture was drawn or painted about 1786, yet a Pointer, which is among the dogs shown, would pass muster today as an excellent specimen. A reprint of this illustration is to be seen in James Watson's *The Dog Book*.

Pointer, German Shorthaired

THE German Shorthaired Pointer combines in field-dog requirements those qualities which have long popularized the various breeds of hunting dogs. So successfully have keen scenting powers, linked with high intelligence, been fused into the breed through judicious crossing of the old Spanish Pointer, English Foxhound, and Bloodhound, and so varied are this dog's field accomplishments, that his adaptability has earned him the reputation of being an "all-purpose" dog. In fact, the term was given him by the Germans before sportsmen here imported him to any extent in the early twenties.

It would indeed be difficult to find "wrapped up in one package" a staunchly pointing bird dog, a keen-nosed night trailer, a proven duck dog, a natural retriever on land and water, pleasing conformation and markings with great powers of endurance, and an intelligent family watchdog and companion. Indicative of this dog's versatility is his successful work on pheasant, quail, grouse, partridge, jacksnipe, woodcock, duck, rabbits, coon, and possum. He is used, too, to trail and point deer. With a water-resilient coat and webbed feet, he retrieves well from rough terrain or icy waters. However, it is recommended that he be broken first on birds.

In the seventeenth century the Germans imported from Spain some of the old Spanish Pointers which, although mainly hound, they used primarily as pointing bird dogs. Later they found they needed a dog which would point birds and rabbits during the day and trail four-footed animals at night. By crossing the Spanish Pointer with the Bloodhound, they produced a heavy dog that worked satisfactorily at both occupations. This was the German Pointer. Then some time after that German and Austrian sportsmen, looking with envy on the speed and dash of our American Pointers, straightway started to cross their heavy German Pointer with our American or English Pointer. They developed a smaller, faster dog than their old German Pointer, but one which retained the staunchness and keen scenting powers which had made it such a favorite. Selective breeding brought about more pleasing conformation as well as an astonishing degree of endurance. This, then, is the German Short-haired Pointer.

We have only to consider the "shorthair's" pedigree from a quantitative standpoint to account for his exceptional nose. Our American or English Pointer combined the old Spanish Pointer and, among others, the English Foxhound. The old German Pointer was a cross between the old Spanish Pointer and the Bloodhound. Now the German Shorthaired Pointer is a cross between the American Pointer and the old German Pointer. Hence, we have a double cross, or approximately 50 per cent old Spanish Pointer, 25 per cent English Foxhound, and 25 per cent Bloodhound.

Pointer, German Wirehaired

HUNTING has been called our earliest sport, but it is more than that. It was a way of life in ancient times when the ax, the club, and the spear were the sole weapons man had with which to find food for himself and his brood. Throughout the course of time he hunted with traps and pitfalls, hawks and falcons, nets and snares, bows and arrows. Later, the princes, the nobles, and the big landowners hunted not for food but for sport, but to the rank and file such privilege was denied.

However, around 1850 the incidence of political revolt, together with improvements in the shotgun and the cartridge, spurred the business of hunting to such degree that everybody, regardless of class distinction, took to the hunt. The number of sportsmen more than doubled as game-bird shooting grew popular. More dogs were needed, hence more were bred. And slowly but surely the hunting dog became something of a specialist. One kind grew adept at ranging woods and fields where it pointed birds for the huntsman to shoot, others learned to retrieve from land and from water, and as time went on each attained proficiency in its special department.

Continental sportsmen were hard to please; they were not satisfied with a gun dog that would hunt only one kind of game. They envisioned an all-purpose dog, and so it happened that in various European countries retrieving Pointers began to emerge. One of these, native to Germany, was the *Deutsch-Drahthaar* which, literally translated, means German Wirehair. The dog is known today in America, however, as the German Wirehaired Pointer.

In order to understand the heritage of this breed we must bear in mind that there existed abroad a wide variety of retrieving Pointers, all of them more or less interbred. The early Deutsch-Drahthaar Club in fact at first catered to all varieties of wirehaired pointing dogs. Later, however, they thought best to separate their activities into four subdivisions catering to the advancement of the Deutsch-Drahthaar, the Pudelpointer, the Stichelhaar, and the Griffon.

Most of the early wirehaired Pointers represented a combination of Griffon, Stichelhaar, Pudelpointer, and German Shorthair. The Pudel-pointer was a cross between a Poodle dog and an English Pointer bitch, while the Griffon and the Stichelhaar were composed of Pointer, Fox-hound, Pudelpointer, and a Polish water dog. Thus it is easy to appreciate the different hunting skills incorporated in the wirehaired Pointers of a century or more ago.

Admirable breeders and trainers, the Germans demanded a great deal of their sporting dogs. They had no patience with specialists, preferring instead an extra-rugged hunter capable of working on any kind of game and on any terrain. In the German Wirehaired Pointer this is exactly what they got, for they molded into the one breed the distinctive traits of Pointer, Foxhound, and Poodle. Through these avenues of diversified accomplishment they created an all-purpose dog approximating their ideal. He pointed and retrieved equally well on land and in water. He was keen-nosed and constitutionally tough. What is more, he had the courage as well as the coat fit to brave any sort of cover.

Coat has always been emphasized throughout the development of the breed, as indicated by a statement made by members of the Drahthaar Club back in 1902, when they said: "The breeding of a correct wire coat is the most important feature." There was ample reason for this emphasis on coat, considering the work that the German Wirehair was called upon to do. In short, he was designed as an all-weather as well as an all-purpose dog, and he had to negotiate underbrush that would have punished severely any dog not so characteristically armored.

The coat is weather-resisting in every sense of the term, and it is to large extent water-repellent. It is straight, harsh, wiry, and quite flat-lying. One and one half to two inches in length, it is long enough to shield the body from rough cover, yet not so long as to hide the outline. A heavy growth on the brow guards the eyes from injury, and a short beard and whiskers combine to save the foreface from laceration by brush and briar. A very dense undercoat insulates the body against the cold of winter, but it sheds out to such a degree as to be almost invisible in summertime.

As history is reckoned, then, the German Wirehaired Pointer is a comparatively young breed. Developed in Germany from the middle of the previous century on, the dog was recognized as a breed in his native land in 1870, when in just a few short years he supplanted most other breeds of hunting dogs there. Essentially Pointer in type, he is sturdily built, energetic in action, intelligent and determined in expression. He is friendly but not overfriendly; in fact, he may be aloof to all but his own. He was brought to America in 1920 and since then has achieved considerable popularity, especially in the Middle West. The breed was accepted for registration and granted separate show classification in 1959. The first championship points were awarded at the International Kennel Club of Chicago show in April of that year.

Retriever, Chesapeake Bay

WHILE the Chesapeake Bay Retriever originated in this country, he came from stock destined to sail from England. There is no complete and authentic record of his development; at the same time his breed origin as here described is probably correct and at the present time is the one generally accepted. Theories regarding later development are entirely supposition lacking, as yet, definite proof.

In the year 1807 an English brig was wrecked off the coast of Maryland and crew and cargo were rescued by the American ship *Canton*. Also rescued were two Newfoundland puppies, a dingy red dog named "Sailor" and a black bitch called "Canton" after the rescuing boat. Presented to the gentlemen who gave hospitality to the sailors of the wrecked brig, the two dogs were found to possess wonderful qualities as retrievers. Many of the nondescript dogs then used for retrieving were bred to them, although we do not know whether Sailor and Canton themselves were ever mated together. Eventually other outcrosses were used, and of these, the English Otter Hound has been claimed as one of the most influential. However, such a cross would probably have produced different results, since the Chesapeake shows no trace of hound. It is more likely that the Flat-Coated and Curly-Coated Retrievers constituted the most important outcrosses if any were ever purposely made.

By 1885 a definite type of dog was developed. The breed soon became known for its prowess in the rough, icy waters of Chesapeake Bay, where the dogs were often called upon to retrieve 200 or 300 ducks in a day. During World War I continued development was apparent, including the deadgrass color so popular in the Middle West. The Chesapeake of today has improved in appearance, and he is still remarkable in the water.

Retriever, Curly-Coated

THE origin of the Curly Retriever is one of doubt, but he is popularly believed to be descended from the sixteenth-century English Water Spaniel, and from the retrieving setter. Some maintain the Irish Water Spaniel was his ancestor and it is more than probable that a cross was made with this Spaniel from time to time, the liver color being a recognized color for the Curly as well as the black.

Whichever Spaniel was his progenitor, it is certain that added to the mixture of Water Spaniel and retrieving setter was the small, or St. John's Newfoundland, which, according to records, first arrived in England in 1835 as a ship's dog on board the boats that brought salted cod from Newfoundland. The St. John's dog, curiously enough, is sometimes called a Labrador by early writers, a fact which has given rise to some confusion with respect to the modern Labrador.

In the early eighties the Curly is said to have been crossed again with the Poodle (the one-time retriever of France), this cross taken with the object of giving his coat a tight curl. In the absence of very early records, the correct origin of the Curly must, however, always remain a matter of conjecture, but there appears little doubt that he is one of the oldest of all breeds now classified as Retrievers.

The popular gun dog following the old English Water Spaniel, the Curly was first exhibited in 1860 at England's Birmingham show. In 1889 specimens were exported to New Zealand, where they have long been used for retrieving duck and California quail. In Australia, too, where they are used in the swamps and lagoons of the Murray River on duck, they are much admired as steady and tender-mouthed retrievers quite unsurpassed in the water. A dog and a bitch were exported to the United States about 1907; both were trained to the gun and exhibited successfully at shows. Fairly recently, specimens of the breed have taken part in English field trials open to all types of Retrievers, and they have more than held their own.

In the British Isles in 1896 was formed the Curly Retriever Club which, however, ceased to exist some years before the founding in England of the present Curly Retriever Club in 1933. Its object: "To promote the breeding of pure Curly Retrievers and to foster the interests of the breed particularly as a working gun dog, while preserving the correct type for the dual purpose of the field and the show bench." A special committee was selected to consider and possibly revise the standard of the breed as drawn up by the former club. After considerable deliberation at the March, 1933 meeting, our present standard was approved by a general meeting shortly afterward. The club was fortunate to have as president at that time the noted breed enthusiast, Lord Ashburton, who presented a magnificent silver cup to be competed for at field trials organized by the club for Curly Retrievers.

Many assert that the Curly Retriever is temperamentally easy to train. He is affectionate, enduring, hardy, and will practically live in the water. Moreover, his thick coat enables him to face the most punishing covert. He is a charming and faithful companion and an excellent guard.

Retriever, Flat-Coated

THE Flat-Coated Retriever presents something of a paradox as far as the United States is concerned, for the breed traces its ancestry back to two breeds that are indigenous to the North American continent, yet it is one of the least known species of purebred dog in America. Its actual origin and almost its entire development was in England, cradle of so many different varieties of the dog.

The earliest known specimen that approximated the present standard of the Flat-Coated Retriever appeared at the Birmingham show (England) in 1860. This was a dog named Wyndham, owned and exhibited by R. Braisford. The dog excited no little comment, for retrievers of any kind were a rarity in those days. All the sportsmen at the show inspected it closely, and they put all sorts of questions to its owner. The answers were not very satisfactory in regard to its breeding; yet among those who saw this first flat-coated—or wavy-coated, as it was then called—were some experienced authorities who later set their opinions to paper.

Wyndham was very much on the type of the Labrador Retriever, with the exception of coat. Almost wholly black in color, his conformation also followed that of the Labrador; but there the resemblance ended, for Wyndham carried a much heavier coat. Due to his coat, it was reasoned that half of his inheritance came from the St. John's Newfoundland, which then was enjoying great popularity in England. This cross also accounted for Wyndham's size, which was slightly larger than that of the Labrador.

It is impossible to say just how long various sporting dog men had been experimenting with various crosses before the first specimen called the "wavy-coated retriever" was taken to a bench show; but it probably had been at least half a decade. Formal shows were in their infancy, and the greater interest was in work afield. So it is quite probable that a fairly long and varied history lay behind Wyndham. Also, he had many contemporary specimens, some of which carried the same strains and some that were of slightly different type and consequently different ancestors.

The real proof of this breed that since has come to be known as the Flat-Coated Retriever was to be found in the efficiency of its work. It proved a natural water dog, marking, retrieving, and delivering with a style that always elicited favorable comment. Others found the dog equally satisfactory for upland shooting, and it was only a few years before it was used in great numbers on pheasant and other kinds of feather.

The early rapid progress of the breed may be imagined from the fact that it was only four years after its show debut that it had classes at the regular shows. The first exhibition where classes were provided was at the big all-breed event at Ashburnham Hall, Chelsea, in April of 1864. By then there was considerable discussion of type, and the leading breeders were beginning to be rather set in their ideas.

Perhaps the one man who deserves major credit for the pure development of the most desirable type was Dr. Bond Moore of Wolverhampton. He was convinced that the new breed should follow the Labrador in both color and conformation. It is said that he was such a stickler for the solid black that he destroyed all puppies that had any traces of other colors on them.

Dr. Moore's strictness in regard to color and type was inspired by the large number of crosses that had been tried by other breeders, with a consequent confusion in size, type, and color. His aims proved a stabilizing factor at a time when it seemed that no very definite breed would result.

Aside from the Labrador Retriever and the St. John's Newfoundland —the original cross—there is evidence that both the Gordon Setter and the Irish Setter were used to advantage. Some talk of a cross with the Collie is prevalent in the history of the Flat-Coated Retriever, but this is doubtful.

The Flat-Coated Retriever of today is a sturdily made dog of sixty to seventy pounds, with a close-lying, somewhat dense coat that is a splendid protection in the water. The great majority of specimens are wholly black, but occasionally there is found a bit of other color—usually white—on the chest.

While the breed was introduced to the United States many years ago, it never has mustered sufficient supporters to have a specialty club. As a consequence, specimens of the Flat-Coated Retriever are not plentiful, although they may be found scattered through the shooting country.

Retriever, Golden

CRITICAL research within the last few years has revealed information from a variety of sources establishing the logical relationship between the Golden Retriever and other retriever breeds. The revelation stands in striking contrast to the colorful and romantic legend of the Russian circus dogs, long believed by many fanciers to have been the forebears of this beautiful breed.

Retrievers first came into prominence in England during the early part of the nineteenth century when increasing interest in the sport of wild-fowling created a demand for dogs which not only would deliver game to hand but which were rugged enough to withstand the most arduous land and water conditions. To attain the type desired, experimental crosses of setters, water spaniels, and other sporting breeds were made with the small, lighter build of Newfoundland known as the St. John's Newfoundland. These dogs, which had been introduced to the British coast aboard fishing vessels, were noted for their endurance, excellence in swimming, and ability to retrieve. Though their procedures in developing type differed, breeders shared a common purpose in producing strong dogs of moderate size with substance and bone. From their efforts, the four retriever breeds—the Curly Coat, the Wavy or Flat Coat, the Labrador, and the Golden—eventually became standardized. The Wavy-Coated Retriever resulted from the successful crossing of the Gordon Setter with the St. John's dog and is one of the known forebears of the Golden.

Champion of the Golden Retriever was Lord Tweedmouth (formerly Sir Dudley Marjoribanks), whose carefully kept kennel records were made public a few years ago by his grandnephew, the Earl of Ilchester. Written in Tweedmouth's own hand, the records show that a dog called Nous (meaning wisdom), bred by Lord Chichester, was purchased in Brighton in the year 1865. The purchase was made from a cobbler, who explained that he had been given the dog in settlement of a debt and that it had been the odd yellow puppy in a litter of black Wavy Coats. Nous was the first of the yellow retrievers of any renown and he became the foundation stud of the famous Guisachan strain.

The location of Guisachan, Lord Tweedmouth's estate on the Tweed River in southeast Scotland, had a direct bearing upon the program pursued by him to produce the characteristics he desired in his yellow retrievers; for along the shores of this river was a hardy type of spaniel used for retrieving, known as the Tweed Water Spaniel. This dog was descended from the ruggedly built water dogs which for years had been used along the British seacoast by families who depended upon the courage, intelligence, and ability of these animals to retrieve game under all sorts of conditions. According to Dalziel, author of *British Dogs* (1881), Tweed Water Spaniels were light liver in color, so close in curl as to give the idea that they had originally been a cross from a smooth-haired dog; long in tail, ears heavy in flesh and hard like a hound's, but only slightly feathered; forelegs feathered behind, hind legs smooth, head conical, and lips slightly pendulous. The author, "Stonehenge" (John H. Walsh, author of books on dogs and former editor of *The Field* magazine), said they resembled small ordinary English Retrievers. Though this variety of water spaniel has long since sunk into obscurity, its influence on the development of Golden Retrievers cannot be overlooked, for it was to a Tweed Water Spaniel named Belle that Nous was first mated.

This mating resulted in a litter of four yellow puppies in the year 1868, Ada, Crocus, Primrose, and Cowslip. In order to establish uniformity of type, there followed a program of carefully considered line breeding. There were outcrosses to a second Tweed Water Spaniel and also to one of Sir Henry Mieux's Wavy Coats to keep the line strong. Later, experimental crosses were tried with an Irish Setter and another with a Bloodhound, but Tweedmouth's records show these crosses to have been made only once in the Guisachan kennel.

Puppies occasionally were given to members of Lord Tweedmouth's family, who helped to widen public appreciation of the beauty and usefulness of yellow retrievers. It was close to the turn of the century, however, before their color became fashionable in dog shows. By that time there were three other kennels whose names were linked with the yellows and which are known to have had dogs from the Guisachan strain—Ilchester, Ingestre, and Culham. Their methods of selecting breeding stock differed somewhat from those used by Tweedmouth. For instance, the Earl of Ilchester, whose foundation bitch was Ada from the 1868 litter, used black Wavy Coats and Labradors in his breeding program. Unfortunately Tweedmouth and Ilchester did not register their dogs, but to the Ingestre and Culham names a large majority of Goldens may be directly traced today. Yellow Retrievers were classified as Wavy or Flat Coats until 1913, at which time they received recognition from the British Kennel Club as a separate variety and were called "Yellow or Golden Retrievers." In 1920 the name "Yellow" was dropped altogether.

The characteristics which make this breed useful to the sportsman also make it attractive to the pet owner. The Golden is gentle, sensitive, intelligent, and willing. He should be ruggedly built and possess a thick, almost waterproof undercoat to withstand cold temperatures and icy water. His forte is retrieving from water, but he is equally useful on upland birds and can wind game from forty to fifty yards. He has a tender mouth. He is a popular contender in obedience circles and in recent years has gained recognition as a guide dog for the blind.

The Golden Retriever's rise in public esteem and appreciation has been rapid. This popularity can hold merit only so long as breeders are conscientious in their efforts to safeguard, through careful breeding programs, the inherent qualities of type and temperament which Lord Tweedmouth and his followers strove to attain.

Retriever, Labrador

THE Labrador Retriever did not, as his name implies, come from Labrador, but from Newfoundland, although there is no indication of by what means he reached the latter place. However, in 1822 a traveler in that region reported a number of "small water dogs" and said: "The dogs are admirably trained as retrievers in fowling, and are otherwise useful . . . The smooth or short-haired dog is preferred because in frosty weather the long-haired kind become encumbered with ice on coming out of the water."

Early in the nineteenth century the Earl of Malmesbury reputedly saw one of the dogs that had been carried to England by fishermen and immediately arranged to have some imported. In 1830 the noted British sportsman Colonel Hawker referred to the ordinary Newfoundland and what he called the St. John's breed of water dog, mentioning the former as "very large, strong of limb, rough hair, and carrying his tail high." Referring to what is known now as the Labrador, he said they were "by far the best for any kind of shooting. He is generally black and no bigger than a Pointer, very fine in legs, with short, smooth hair and does not carry his tail so much curled as the other; is extremely quick, running, swimming and fighting . . . and their sense of smell is hardly to be credited. . . ."

The dogs were not at first generally known in England as Labradors. In fact, the origin of the name is shown in a letter written in 1887 by an Earl of Malmesbury in which he said: "We always call mine Labrador dogs, and I have kept the breed as pure as I could from the first I had from Poole, at that time carrying on a brisk trade with Newfoundland. The real breed may be known by its close coat which turns the water off like oil and, above all, a tail like an otter." The Labrador gradually died out in Newfoundland on account of a heavy dog tax which, with the English quarantine law, practically stopped the importations into England. Thereafter many Labradors were interbred with other types of retrievers. Fortunately, however, the Labrador characteristics predominated. And finally fanciers, desiring to stop the interbreeding, drew up a standard so as to discourage crossing with other retrievers.

There is a stud book of the Duke of Buccleuch's Labrador Retrievers which made it possible to work out pedigrees of the two dogs that did most to produce the modern Labrador, Mr. A. C. Butter's Peter of Faskally, and Major Portal's Flapper. These pedigrees go back as far as 1878.

The breed was first recognized by the English Kennel Club as a separate breed in 1903 and has since frequently won the Kennel Club's cup for best in show.

Mr. Leslie Sprake's book *The Labrador Retriever* (published in 1933 by H. F. & G. Witherby, London), deals very fully with the breed and its history. He quotes therein from an article written in 1923 by the Hon. A. Holland Hibbert (the late Lord Knutsford) who, in commenting on the two most important points of the Labrador, the eye and the tail, said:

"*Tail.*—The nearer the level carriage and the closer resemblance to an otter tail the better, i.e., short and thick at stump with the hair underneath divided almost as if parted. Otter tails are very rare and straight tails are not common—the more usual carriage being like a Foxhound, except when hunting, and then the tail is almost invariably carried level.

"*Eye.*—The color of the eye, about which much has been written; when Labradors first came into general notice, the dark eye, which was a great point with the flat coat, was supposed to be necessary also for the Labrador. This was nothing but a show ring opinion, and entirely wrong. Although the very light eye has a startled, and I think disagreeable look, yet the dark eye to my mind is lacking in expression, and looks sulky, hence I welcome what is now generally considered the best color, i.e., light brown, the color of burnt sugar."

In England no Labrador can become a bench show champion unless he has received a working certificate. In other words, he must qualify in the field as well as on the bench, so that in looking at an English pedigree if a dog is designated as a champion you know that he must have qualified in the field as well as on the bench.

Setter, English

FROM the best authorities on the subject, it appears that the English Setter was a trained bird dog in England approximately four hundred years ago. A perusal of some of the old writings leads us to believe that the English Setter had its origin in some of the older of the land spaniels that originated in Spain. We are indebted, however, to Hans Bols, who, in *Partridge Shooting and Partridge Hawking*, written in 1582, presents quite definite pictorial evidence that the setter and the spaniel breeds were quite different in appearance and even at that time the tails of the spaniels appeared to have been docked as they are today and the tails of setters left as nature intended them.

There is some evidence in the earlier writings of sportsmen that the old English Setter was originally produced from crosses of the Spanish Pointer, the large Water Spaniel, and the Springer Spaniel, and by careful cultivation attained a high degree of proficiency in finding and pointing game in open country. We can see from examination of the sketches in many of the old writings that this setter-spaniel was an extremely handsome dog, many having a head much longer and with a more classical cut than that of the spaniel, while others had the short spaniel-like head, lacking the well-defined profile of the skull and foreface of the modern dogs. Also most of these older setters had coats which were quite curly, particularly at the thighs. It can be seen from this brief review of the origin of the English Setter that even our oldest authorities were not entirely in accord as to the origin of this breed.

There is little doubt that the major credit for the development of the modern setter should go to Mr. Edward Laverack, who about 1825 obtained from the Rev. A. Harrison, "Ponto" and "Old Moll." The Rev. Harrison had apparently kept this breed pure for thirty-five years or more. From these two Mr. Laverack, through a remarkable process of inbreeding, produced Prince, Countess, Nellie, and Fairy, which were marvelous specimens of English Setters. Along about 1874 Mr. Laverack sold a pair of dogs to Charles H. Raymond of Morris Plains, N.J. During the next ten years the English Setter became more and more popular and it was around this time that many Setters bred by Mr. Llewellin were imported into this country and Canada.

In considering the so-called Llewellin strain it is recorded in the writings of Dr. William A. Bruette that about the time the Laverack strain was at its zenith in England, Mr. R. L. Purcell Llewellin purchased a number of Mr. Laverack's best show dogs of the pure Dash-Moll and Dash-Hill Laverack inheritance. The Laveracks he crossed with some entirely new "blood" which he obtained in the north of England, represented by Mr. Statter's and Sir Vincent Corbet's strain, since referred to as the Duke-Rhoebes, the latter being the two most prominent members of the strain. The result of these crosses was eminently successful, particularly at field trials; they swept everything before them. Their reputation spread to America and many were purchased by sportsmen in different sections of the United States and Canada, so that this line of breeding soon became firmly established in this country.

Probably the name that stands out most conspicuously in the foundation of the field-trial setter in America is Count Noble. This dog was purchased from Mr. Llewellin by Dave Sanborn of Dowling, Michigan, who, after trying him out on the prairies, was upon the point of returning him to England, but was persuaded not to do so by the late B. F. Wilson of Pittsburgh. On the death of Mr. Sanborn, Count passed into the hands of Mr. Wilson, who gave him an opportunity to demonstrate his sterling qualities from coast to coast. The body of this famous dog was mounted at his death and is now in the Carnegie Museum at Pittsburgh, where it is visited annually by many sportsmen.

Dr. Walsh in 1878 stated that Mr. Llewellin's dogs were Dan-Laveracks, because according to him they were all either by Dan out of Laverack bitches or by a Laverack dog out of a sister of Dan. It is quite difficult to give a proper definition of a straight-bred Llewellin, but it is generally accepted that all English Setters may be called Llewellins which trace back in all lines to Duke-Rhoebe-Laverack. This, however, would shut out everything that had Dash II inheritance and this the Llewellin enthusiast does not wish to do, for under such definition it would eliminate a great number of the best known names that appear in the so-called Llewellin pedigrees. R. L. Purcell Llewellin is given credit for making the Duke-Rhoebe-Laverack cross, but in justice to him, according to Mr. A. F. Hochwalt, one of our noted authorities on gun dogs, he is not responsible for the breed being named for him. The name was originated in America by breeders who imported dogs from Mr. Llewellin's kennels and, being great admirers of the man and the dogs he bred, they naturally gave them the name of him from whom they were purchased.

The first show for English Setters was held at Newcastle-on-Tyne on January 28, 1859, and from this time on dog shows flourished throughout England, gradually increasing in popularity. English Setters became increasingly popular, and it is of interest in passing to note that in 1930 for the first time an American was invited abroad to judge English Setters. The expert so honored was none other than the late Benjamin F. Lewis of Lansdowne, Pa., who had been associated with English Setters since his boyhood. His father, B. F. Lewis, born in South Wales, for many years was unquestionably the outstanding handler of all sporting show dogs in America, and it is believed that no one will dissent from the opinion that his son, the late Benny, was without an equal as a handler of sporting dogs.

The English Setter has retained its popularity since its introduction to this country primarily because of its usefulness and beauty. There is little doubt that its usefulness has been a prime factor in this respect, and as a result of intelligent breeding it has been brought to a high state of perfection and there is always to be found a representative entry at all bench shows and field trials.

The mild, sweet disposition characteristic of this breed along with the beauty, intelligence, and aristocratic appearance it makes in the field and in the home has endeared it both to the sportsman as well as all lovers of a beautiful, active, and rugged outdoor dog. A lovable disposition makes it an ideal companion; it is, however, a dog that requires considerable exercise and therefore is better suited to ownership in the suburbs than in the city.

Setter, Gordon

BEAUTY, brains, and bird sense are the outstanding qualities of the handsome black-and-tan Setter from Scotland whose ancient lineage dates back at least to 1620 when Markham, a writer of the time, praised the "black and fallow setting dog" as "hardest to endure labor." Popular among hunters of Scotland for decades, the black-and-tan (or occasionally black-white-and-tan) Setter came into prominence in the kennels of the fourth Duke of Gordon in the late 1700s. Commenting on these kennels, a writer familiar with the Duke's Gordons describes them much as a sportsman would describe a Gordon of today: "The Gordon Castle Setters are as a rule easy to break and naturally back well. They are not fast dogs but they have good staying powers and can keep on steadily from morning until night. Their noses are first class and they seldom make a false point or what is called at field trials a sensational stand. . . . When they stand you may be sure there are birds." A later and illustrious authority, Idstone notes: "I have seen better Setters of the black and tan than of any other breed."

Attracted quite as much by the Gordon's beauty as by his superior hunting ability, George Blunt and Daniel Webster in 1842 imported a brace of the Duke's Gordons to America. In the intervening years other importations from Great Britain and the Scandinavian countries and the perfecting of the American strains helped the Gordon achieve great popularity as a pet and faithful gun dog, particularly in the period when game was marketed commercially and a real "meat" dog assured a full bag at the end of the day's shooting.

With the coming of the field-trial form of competition a few decades back, Gordon popularity waned for a time, as the dog's habit of quartering thoroughly and working close to the gun placed him at a disadvantage where flashing speed was demanded, though as a one-man shooting dog the Gordon knows no peer. However, the recent activities of the fast growing Gordon Setter Club of America in sponsoring regular field trials has turned the tide and the Gordon is being encouraged to develop greater range and speed while maintaining his superiority as a methodical, dependable bird finder, consistently placing well up in the ribbons in all-breed field competition.

The Gordon's characteristic eagerness to work for a loving master has never changed over the centuries, nor have his keen intellect and retentive memory, which enable him to improve with age with no need for retraining each season. This consistency of quality is doubtless due to the fact that, unlike fanciers of some other sporting breeds, Gordon breeders, backed by a strong national club, make no distinction between field or show types. As a rule bench-show champions are used regularly for hunting and give a good account of themselves in the field as do the field trial winners at the bench show.

The oft-quoted comment that the Gordon's coloring makes him difficult to see in the field has doubtless been made by those who have never seen him there. Against the tan fall sedge grass or early snow a black dog is highly conspicuous, and when this black dog is difficult to distinguish against his background, it is then too dark to shoot with safety.

A true Setter, the Gordon is distinctive, resembling the English or Irish Setters only in general type. In field-trial competition the smaller, but not light-boned, Gordon has been more favored while the larger dog is preferred for bench work. The official Standard of the breed allows considerable range in sizes primarily because individual sportsmen from various corners of the nation prefer their Gordons of a size to suit their local hunting terrain. There is general agreement, however, on the aristocratic beauty of the Gordon, with his silky black coat, rich mahogany markings, his well-feathered legs and gaily carried tail. The finely chiseled, somewhat heavy head with long, low-set ears is distinctive for its intelligent expression. His good-sized, sturdy build with plenty of bone and substance and his upstanding, stylish gait give him the necessary stamina to match his ardor for the long days in the field. Few dogs, indeed, can match the Gordon's beauty as he quarters the field, tail wagging constantly while busily in quest of a bird, and few can compare with his quiet dignity as he sleeps at the family fireside.

The quality that endears the Gordon to the pet owner or to the sensitive sportsman is his devoted loyalty to members of the household. Wary of the unwanted intruder, the Gordon is not the chum of every passer-by but lives for the pleasure of being near his owners. This almost fanatical devotion has helped make the Gordon not only a responsive gun dog but a mannerly, eager-to-please dog in the home. His gentleness with children is a byword with those familiar with the breed. His occasional aggressiveness with other dogs occurs as a result of his jealousy guarding his family's affections.

He who acquires a Gordon Setter owns a rare combination: an aristocrat of ancient lineage and rich beauty, a shooting companion of keen intelligence and inbred hunting ability, a loyal family guard, and, as one authority puts it, "a most pettable dog."

Setter, Irish

THE Irish Setter first came into popular notice early in the eighteenth century and less than a hundred years later his reputation was firmly established, not only in his native Ireland but throughout the British Isles. Speculations as to his origin are little more than guesswork, various breeds having been named as his progenitors, but none that can boast a clear title to the honor. Among the conjectures is that he was developed from an Irish Water Spaniel-Irish Terrier cross, but it is far more believable that an English Setter-Spaniel-Pointer combination, with a dash of Gordon thrown in, was the true formula.

The Irish Red Setter is the name officially chosen by the Irish Setter Club of America to designate the breed in this country. His earliest ancestors in the Emerald Isle, on the contrary, were rarely self-colored dogs. By far the larger number were red and white, the white frequently predominating over the red, and even today many individuals across the water are parti-colored. In America, however, solid reds or reds with small and inconspicuous white markings are the only ones accepted as typical, and any large and noticeable white patches are considered blemishes. The Irishman's rich mahogany coat is thoroughly distinctive and has done much to make its wearer the bench show favorite he is today.

The solid red Setter, as distinguished from the red and white, first appeared in Ireland early in the nineteenth century. Mr. Jason Hazzard of Timaskea, County Fermanagh, Sir St. George Gore, and the Earl of Enniskillen all bred self-colored dogs, and it is a matter of record that in 1812 the Earl would have nothing else in his kennels. A few years later Stonehenge wrote: "The blood red, or rich chestnut or mahogany color is the color of an Irish Setter of high mark. This color must be unmixed with black; and studied in a strong light, there must not be black shadows or waves, much less black fringes to the ears, or to the profile of the form." The mention of black in the above is significant as indicating the possibility of the Gordon cross already mentioned. Today this color is absolutely taboo and even a few black hairs are considered enough to disqualify at the shows.

So much for the external appearance of the Irish Setter; now for more important, if less obvious characteristics. The breed is essentially a sporting one, and it is as a gun dog, after all, that this flashy red fellow must stand or fall. The first individuals imported into this country were brought over for use on game and, in spite of the fact that our ruffed grouse, quail, and prairie chicken were new and strange to them, they made good immediately. Elcho, imported in 1875 and one of the first of his breed to make a reputation for himself and his progeny in the United States, was not only a sensational success on the bench but a thoroughly trained and capable shooting dog. To quote Mr. A. F. Hochwalt, in his book *The Modern Setter*, "All through the early field-trial records we find the Irish Setter holding his own with the 'fashionable blue bloods.' Had the Irish Setter fanciers continued on, their favorite breed would no doubt now be occupying a place as high in field trials as the other two breeds"; by which he means, of course, the English Setter and Pointer.

But the Irish Setter men didn't continue on, insofar as field trials were concerned, with the result that the Llewellin Setter and the Pointer have practically cornered the market in public competition in that field. Yet, in spite of this handicap, the red dog from Erin has lost none of the attributes of the good hunting companion, and given a fair chance, can and does demonstrate his quality as a high-class gun dog on all kinds of game. Strange as it may seem, his good looks have been his undoing in a way. His fatal gift of beauty, together with his gaiety, courage, and personality, have made him an ideal show dog. For this reason many fanciers have yielded to the temptation to breed for the bench only and to sacrifice to this most worthwhile object, field ability equally worthwhile and in no way incompatible with proper color, good size, and correct breed type.

Just a word regarding the characteristic personality of the red dog. First and foremost, he is typically Irish, with a devil-may-care something about him that not only makes him tremendously likable but also adds to his value as a bird dog in rough country and briars. He is bold and at the same time gentle and lovable and loyal. He is tough—good and tough. He can stand continued work in the brush, is almost never stiff or sore, has the best of feet and running gear, and almost never gets "sour" when corrected in his work. He is not an early developer and frequently requires more training than some other breeds, but he is not as a rule headstrong in the sense that he is hard to handle in the brush. His outstanding fault as a field-trial performer is that he is not independent enough and pays too much attention to his handler. In reply to the criticism that he develops slowly, it is only fair to say that, once trained on birds, he is trained for the rest of his life and does not require a repetition of the process every fall. When you own a good Irishman, you own him for many years, every day of which you can be proud of his appearance, his personality, and his performance.

Spaniel, American Water

EXACTLY how, when, and where the American Water Spaniel originated is something of a mystery, nevertheless the virtues of the breed have long been appreciated by sportsmen in many parts of the United States. It is principally in the Middle West, however, that the present-day specimen evolved, since the dogs from that section had been known to breed true to type for countless generations. Color, coat, and conformation combine to suggest the Irish Water Spaniel and the Curly-Coated Retriever, together with the latter's forebear the old English Water Spaniel, as progenitors, although this cannot be advanced categorically.

Prior to recognition as a breed by The American Kennel Club in 1940, the American Water Spaniel had been purely a working gun dog. He had never been introduced to the show ring since his admirers evidently feared that bench shows might damage his prowess as a hunter. But they were soon to learn that selective breeding along with bench-show competition actually enhances the value of a dog no matter how well that dog may have been endowed by nature.

As a retriever the American Water Spaniel leaves little to be desired. He will watch the huntsman drop perhaps four or five birds, then work swiftly and merrily until every one is brought in. Rabbits, chickens, grouse, quail, pheasant, ducks—all he handles with unfailing dispatch and tender care. He swims "like a seal," hence few wounded water fowl escape him; his tail serves as a rudder to aid him especially in turbulent water.

He is as well an all-round shooting dog possessed of an excellent nose; he works thicket, rough ground, or covert depending on body scent for location of game. His enthusiasm and thoroughness are an inspiration to the huntsman, while his desire to please makes him easily taught. He learns quickly to drop to shot and wing, although occasionally his eagerness may render him overanxious. He does not point game, but instead he springs it. In addition to all this, he is an efficient watchdog that fits agreeably into the family circle.

Fanciers interested in the breed banded together about 1935 when the American Water Spaniel Club was formed; and from that time on they have been working both individually and as a group to present their favorite in his proper light to the general sporting public.

Spaniel, Brittany

A FRENCH breed known on the Continent for centuries, the Brittany Spaniel might properly be called a setter, judging from his size and manner of working. He is liver and white or, preferably, orange and white; either without a tail or with a tail only a few inches long.

It is generally conceded that the basic stock of all spaniels, pointers and setters came originally from Spain, the migration having taken place so long ago that it cannot be said with certainty exactly when it occurred. Although the greatest development of these breeds took place in the British Isles, they spread through various parts of the Continent so that today some of them—particularly in France—might be traced to the old Spanish strains.

Of ancient lineage, the Brittany Spaniel was bred up from the original spaniel size in much the same manner that the British, using similar stock, produced the setters. In fact, there is reason to believe that the Brittany attained his present size long before his cousins across the channel had taken on a recognizable type. Some maintain that the Brittany was related to the red-and-white Setter which preceded the golden-red Setter in Ireland. Possibly, the Irish chieftains who invaded Gaul—now France —during the first third of the fifth century carried their hunting dogs with them; left in France, these dogs may have contributed something to the development of the Brittany Spaniel. The Irish influence is also seen in the orange-and-white Epagneul Ecossais, or Scotch spaniel, especially in view of the fact that at the time of these invasions the Irish were known as Scoti.

The first tailless ancestor of the modern Brittany Spaniel was bred, about a century ago, at Pontou, a little town situated in the Valley of Douron, the result of a cross between a white-and-mahogany bitch, owned by an old hunter of the region, and a lemon-and-white dog brought to Brittany by an English sportsman for the woodcock shooting. Of two tailless specimens produced in this litter, only one was considered worth keeping. His work in the field has been described as wonderful, and because of it he became a popular stud. All his litters contained puppies either without tails or with short stubs.

The modern history of the Brittany Spaniel dates back only to the beginning of the present century. At that time the breed had degenerated badly, principally because it had been closely inbred, but also because it had not been regarded as a show specimen. Eventually it caught the attention of Arthur Enaud, a French sportsman with a biological turn of mind, who admired the all-around working qualities of the breed so highly that he undertook to improve its appearance.

M. Enaud went about his work thoroughly, and he did not try to accomplish too much in too short a time. He was forced to use certain crosses, but after each cross he returned immediately to the old breed. Unfortunately, like many breeders who have done the same thing with other breeds, he left no clear record of the different dogs that entered into this restoration. In fact, it is only through a study of the other breeds available that it is possible to follow this period in the history of the Brittany Spaniel.

The intensification of the desired orange and white color was one of the chief aims of M. Enaud, and for this he found two breeds that had not only the colors but keen scenting ability. One was the Italian Bracco, or Pointer, the other the Braque de Bourbonnais, also a Pointer. This second breed was the more suitable for his purposes, for besides its other points it was possessed of a very short tail. The only drawback to the use of Pointers was that the coat of the Brittany Spaniel might be affected; but as sparing use was made of crosses and as the rest was a matter of selective breeding, the modern dog was still the counterpart of his ancient Breton ancestors. By 1907 the breed had been restored to all its former glory.

The first Brittany Spaniels were imported to America in 1931, and they have been exhibited at many of our shows since that time. They have proved capable gun dogs and, like most of the Continental-bred sporting dogs, they can be trained easily as retrievers. They are far from being specialists! And they have proved that they can hold their own in field trials—indeed, the first time in competition in America, a Brittany Spaniel carried off a prize against a field of more experienced dogs of other breeds.

Spaniel, Clumber

BECAUSE in type the Clumber Spaniel differs so widely from other members of the great spaniel group, his origin probably will always remain in doubt, as is the case for that matter with many another breed. About all we can do is to ponder the statements of many authorities and then, with the conformation and detail of the breed in mind, resolve the whole into a reasonable supposition, which is that the long, low body resulted from Basset Hound crosses, and the heavy head with noticeable haw from an infusion of the early Alpine Spaniel.

Even within the same litters, the old land spaniels were called by various names—"cockers," "springers," "cock-flushers," and so on, but we do not find the name "Clumber" ascribed at that time. This is not to imply, however, that the Clumber was a later development; indeed, he is believed to be one of the earliest, developed for special uses. The name doubtless arose from Clumber Park, seat of the Duke of Newcastle in Nottingham, to whom the French Duc de Noailles gave several of the dogs which he himself had been breeding carefully for generations.

The year 1859 saw the first class for Clumbers in England and from then on they enjoyed considerable popularity in that country. Due to an abundance of game, there was then no need for a bustling, fast-moving spaniel, consequently the dog was better adapted to foreign shooting conditions than to our own. Nevertheless, he soon made friends in the United States where the breed has been registered since 1883.

He is a dignified, rather slow worker, but a sure finder and a splendid retriever when trained. His most outstanding characteristic, as far as appearances go, is his attractive lemon-and-white coloring.

Spaniel, Cocker

THE spaniel family is a large one, of considerable antiquity. As far back as 1386 we find mention of the *Spanyell*, which came to be divided into two groups, the land spaniel and the water spaniel. A further division separated the land spaniels on a basis of size, when the "cockers" and the very small or toy spaniels were separated from spaniels of larger dimensions. Then, as the cockers and the toys were used for markedly different purposes, these two were once more divided. The toys eventually became the English Toy Spaniels which were maintained principally as pets or comforters, while the Cockers retained their early classification as sporting dogs. That is why the Cocker is called the smallest member of the sporting-dog family.

As a valued helpmeet to the huntsman, this dog was known in his early days by various names, among them "cocker," "cocking spaniel," and finally Cocker Spaniel, the name deriving, according to some authorities, from especial proficiency on woodcock. Not until 1883 were classes provided for him at English bench shows; and not until 1892 was he given breed status in England's Kennel Club stud book. In this country, the Cocker has been exhibited since the early 1880s. Field trials for the breed were started in the United States by the Cocker Spaniel Field Trial Club in 1924. As developed here, the Cocker has evolved somewhat different in type, size, and coloring from the breed now recognized as the English Cocker Spaniel.

The Cocker Spaniel's inherent desire to hunt renders him a capable gun dog when judiciously trained. The usual method of hunting is to let him quarter the ground ahead of the gun, covering all territory within gun range. This he should do at a fast, snappy pace. Upon flushing the game he should stop or preferably drop to a sitting position so as not to interfere with the shot, after which he should retrieve on command only. He should, of course, be so trained that he will be under control at all times. He is likewise valuable for occasional water retrieving and as a rule takes to water readily.

As pet and companion his popularity has been exceptional; he is a great lover of home and family, ordinarily trustworthy and adaptable. Variation in color may have had something to do with the great interest in the breed among which are the solid colors, consisting of black, red, shades of cream or buff and liver, as well as the parti-colors of black and white, black and tan, and combinations of black, tan, and white known as tri-colors. There are, in addition, a few liver-and-whites.

Spaniel, English Cocker

ONE of the oldest types of land spaniel known, the Cocker Spaniel descended from the original spaniels of Spain as one of a family destined to become highly diversified in size, type, coloring, and hunting ability.

Prior to the seventeenth century all members of the group were designated merely as spaniels, whether they were large or small, long-bodied or short, fast or slow on their feet. Gradually the marked difference in size began to impress those who used the dogs for hunting, with the result that the larger dogs were soon springing game and the smaller ones hunting woodcock. The names springer spaniel and cocker, or woodcock, spaniel naturally followed, and in 1892 the Kennel Club (England) finally recognized them as separate breeds. This Cocker Spaniel was the English Cocker Spaniel.

It should be remembered that the Springers and Cockers above described, both before and after the date of their official separation in England, appeared in the same litters. Size alone was the dividing line between them. They enjoyed the same heritage, the same colorings, the same hunting skill and much the same general type. Cocker and Springer developed side by side. In fact, the Springer inheritance, naturally incorporated in the Cocker, was a fortunate directive for the success of the English Cocker, for it enabled him to become one of the finest of the smaller hunting dogs.

Exhaustive research disclosed that during the nineteenth century there were two other lines of "cocker" development. One involved the dogs known as "Field, or Cocker, Spaniels" which eventually branched out into Sussex, Field, and Cocker Spaniels, the latter weighing less than twenty-five pounds and being usually black in color. The other involved the spaniels of the House of Marlborough, of which there were two types—a small, round-headed, short-nosed red-and-white, and a slightly larger dog with shorter ears and longer foreface. The Marlborough "cockers" at long last became the English Toy Spaniels, but before they emerged as a distinct breed, they fused with the smaller cockers of partial Field Spaniel derivation. From these two lines combined came a spaniel approximating the size and type fancied by American importers of that period.

The English Cocker Spaniel Club of America was formed in 1935 to promote the interests of the English Cocker, which had already been recognized as a variety of Cocker Spaniel but not as a breed in its own right. The club's initial specialty show was held the same year on the estate of Mr. E. S. Willing near Bryn Mawr, Pennsylvania, while on May 12, 1936 the standard then operative in England was adopted.

The immediate aim of the club was to discourage the interbreeding of the English and American varieties which English Cocker fanciers considered detrimental to the type they sponsored. Separate classes had been provided at the shows for the English variety; nevertheless, English and American interbred Cockers for some time continued to compete side by side with pure English and pure American specimens. Many an American Cocker, in fact, was entered in the show ring as English on a basis of larger size alone. The resultant confusion militated against the best interests of both varieties, but nothing could be done because no one knew which dogs, genetically, were pure English, which were American, and which a combination of the two.

Under the direction of Mrs. Geraldine R. Dodge, then president of the club, an extensive pedigree search was made of the Cockers of England, Canada, and the United States back to the beginning of official Cocker history abroad in 1892, in order to separate out the pure English lines of descent entirely devoid of American Cocker admixture. When, finally in 1941, this information was obtained, the English Cocker Spaniel Club was in a position to advise authoritatively on the problems of selection and breeding.

Meantime, in 1940 the Canadian Kennel Club recognized the English Cocker Spaniel as a separate breed, as did The American Kennel Club in September, 1946. Not until January, 1947, however, did breed registrations appear in the *Stud Book* under their own heading, for so much had to be done in the interim to comply with the provisions laid down for the official certification of pedigrees.

Spaniel, English Springer

THE name "springing spaniel" included in one classification the ancestral stock from which many of our present-day land spaniels emanated.

In 1902 the Kennel Club of England recognized the English Springer Spaniel as a distinct breed.

Though several individuals in America had these spaniels for their shooting, it was not until 1924, when the English Springer Spaniel Field Trial Association was formed, that they became better known. Field trials were inaugurated, and three years later (1927) the English Springer Spaniel Field Trial Association became the parent club of the breed.

This association has aimed to further the English Springer Spaniel both on the bench and in the field. A Standard was approved when the association was formed and later, in 1932, a committee representing the entire breed drew up a new and better Standard, which was adopted by the English Springer Spaniel Field Trial Association and approved by The American Kennel Club. This Standard was made as nearly as possible to foster the natural ability of the Springer Spaniel, a hunting dog that, with training, could do the work required of him. The association has also conducted field trials every year, and it has endeavored to demonstrate to the public just how good the dogs are as shooting dogs. As competition becomes greater, they must of necessity be able to cover their ground rapidly and, if well trained, to obey signals or orders given them.

Unquestionably the new Standard has helped to make the Springer more uniform as a breed, and as a result the dogs as individuals have become much more uniform at bench shows and in field trials. They are admittedly great sporting dogs, hence should not be allowed to lose any of their standard characteristics; that is, they must not become heavy-boned and stocky in type and thus risk any loss of usefulness in the field. Their one purpose is to hunt and find game.

If more Springer Spaniels were field trained at an early age, and their training continued until the attainment of full physical maturity, they would be far better dogs to put on the bench.

Spaniel, Field

THE Field Spaniel, to probably greater extent than any variety within the great spaniel group, has been taken over the hurdles of man's fancy for exaggerations in type, and as a result the breed suffered greatly. To Mr. Phineas Bullock of England can be given credit for perpetuating a dog of tremendous body length and lowness to the ground, together with phenomenal bone which culminated for a time in a grotesque caricature of a spaniel.

Apparently the type was established by repeated crosses of the "Welsh Cocker" with the Sussex Spaniel. Later, largely through the efforts of Mr. Mortimer Smith, the breed was improved—it took on a type which all who like sporting spaniels can really admire.

Considerable difficulty was encountered in establishing the modern Field Spaniel in the United States due to the necessity for introducing Springer and Cocker crosses in order to eliminate the exaggerations, and this, of course, rendered many individuals ineligible for registration with The American Kennel Club. In fact, in the early 1880's when the Cocker was introduced to America, and for many years thereafter, the sole distinction between the Cockers and the Field Spaniels for show purposes was one of size.

Usually black in color, the Field Spaniel became a useful and handsome breed, sound, straight in the forelegs, and with a height more nearly in balance to length. When built along these lines, he is a dog possessed of endurance, moderate speed and agility. He is level-headed and intelligent, and a dog of great perseverance.

Spaniel, Irish Water

THE Irish Water Spaniel is a dog of very ancient lineage which traces back to the period, centuries ago, when the large and important spaniel group was divided into land spaniels and water spaniels, the latter including both the English and the Irish varieties of water dogs.

As the name implies, the Irish Water Spaniel developed in Ireland, where there were presumably two different strains prior to 1859, namely, the "South Country Water Spaniel" and the "North Country Water Spaniel." Of distinctive color and conformation, the "South Country" variety would appear to have been used more largely for perpetuating the breed as we know it today. The first special class for Irish Water Spaniels was provided in 1859.

The Irish Water Spaniel is often called the clown of the spaniel family, possibly due to the unique appearance of a characteristic topknot together with a peak of curly hair growth between the eyes. He is likewise the tallest of our spaniels. Ordinarily he is loyal to those he knows but forbidding to strangers. He is a grand water dog, not only because he likes water, but because his coat is naturally water-shedding. For this reason, he is used in some parts of the country as a duck retriever, although he is not quite as adaptable for upland work because his coat tends to catch on briars.

Spaniel, Sussex

THE Sussex Spaniel doubtless derives his name from Sussex, England, where the first and most important kennel of these dogs belonged to a Mr. Fuller—he it was who developed the rich golden liver color that has long distinguished the breed. Mr. Phineas Bullock, of Field Spaniel fame, also did notable work in furthering the best interests of the Sussex. Specimens of the breed competed in Britain as far back as the Crystal Palace show of 1862.

During his comparatively early days the Sussex was used for certain types of rough shooting in England, where an abundance of game, together with the custom of hunting on foot, rendered the dog satisfactory as a sporting companion. He has not been imported to any great extent to this country, however, probably due to the fact that he has not sufficient speed for the average sportsman, who faces conditions far different from those abroad.

Although he lacks the speed of the Springer and the Cocker, the Sussex has an extremely good nose, and he is a determined hunter, valuable for all forms of upland shooting. He is inclined to give tongue on scent. In disposition he is an entirely normal dog, not too difficult to train, and when properly taught becomes an excellent retriever.

Spaniel, Welsh Springer

THERE appears to be no authentic information as to the approximate date when the Welsh Springer Spaniel first appeared. However, if we examine old writings, old pictures, old prints, we find that when our ancestors took up shooting over dogs, they undoubtedly used a medium-sized spaniel resembling the Welsh Springer of today more than any other variety. These dogs were always red and white, the one and only color distinguishing the breed.

The Welsh Springer is found principally in Wales and the west of England, where he has been known for several hundred years. More recently he went into Scotland and England, while a large number have been exported from England to America, India, Australia, and Siam. The reason for the breed's distribution into such varied climates is an ability to withstand extremes of heat and cold. The Welshman's coat of course helps him, since it is naturally flat and even, with a soft undercoat which prevents injury from thorns and water.

He is, by the way, an excellent water dog; a keen, hard-working dog —no day is too long, no country too rough—and under all circumstances he is a faithful and willing worker for man. He can be used on any kind of game; in fact, there is no better gun dog than the *well-trained* Welshman. We purposely stress the matter of training because the dog does have a fault: he has an excellent nose, and if not well trained, is inclined to become a lone hunter and subsequently difficult to handle. Even so, he is not hard to train. Taken young—say at six months—and taught first obedience and retrieving, he rarely forgets his early lessons.

As a companion, the Welsh Springer is a true pal of handy size, larger and stronger than the Cocker but smaller than the English Springer. He makes a good guard, too, yet is ordinarily gentle with children and other animals. He is easy to keep, and characteristically vigorous. He can live in town and be happy, but to enjoy life at his best, he should work as a gun dog in the country.

Vizsla

THE origin of the Vizsla, or Hungarian Pointer, has been obscured by the centuries, but it is fair to assume that its ancestors were the hunters and companions of the Magyar hordes which swarmed over Central Europe 1000 years ago and settled in what is now Hungary. Primitive stone etchings of the tenth century show a Magyar huntsman with his falcon and a dog resembling the Vizsla. As far back as the fourteenth century, a manuscript of early Hungarian codes carried a chapter on falconry which was illustrated with a picture of a dog reasonably well identified as a Vizsla. Apparently the breed became a favorite of the early barons and war lords who, either deliberately or by accident, preserved its purity through the years.

The reason for the Vizsla's continued existence even in that far time lay in the fact that its innate hunting ability was fostered and developed by the terrain in which it grew, namely, the plains of Hungary.

Here was a section of that country almost entirely agricultural and pastoral; where grains were raised in great abundance; where the growing season was long, the summers hot, the winters tempered by the proximity of water. Here wheat and corn, rye and barley attracted the partridge and other game birds, while the Hungarian hare flourished and grew large. Amid such plenty, it was inevitable that a hunting dog suited to the climatic conditions, and the available game, would be developed. What the huntsman needed and what he eventually got was a dog swift of foot, and cautious so as not to alert quarry in an almost totally uncovered territory; a close-working dog of superior nose and generally high-class hunting ability; a dog, in short, that would combine the duties of the specialists as both pointer and retriever.

The great wars interfered markedly with what otherwise would have been normal breed progress. The close of World War I found the Vizsla all but extinct, and preserved in only a small way by a few of its firmest friends. The years between the two wars were difficult ones, but those who loved the breed refused to let it die out. Hungarians who fled before the Russian occupation in 1945 took their dogs with them into Austria. One of these, it should be noted, Panni IV, has progeny in the United States. Other refugees fled to Italy and Germany, and with them went their favorite Vizslas. Likewise there are some in Czechoslovakia, Turkey, and southern Russia. And now, here in the United States, where the breed was admitted to AKC registry in 1960, Vizslas are giving a good account of themselves as robust and enduring hunters as well as gentle and friendly companions.

Essentially Pointer in type, the Vizsla is a distinguished looking dog of aristocratic bearing, his short coat an attractive rusty-gold. He is powerfully built, but lithe and well balanced, with a light-footed, smooth, and graceful gait. He is a multiple-purpose dog for work on upland game, on rabbits, and for waterfowl retrieving.

Weimaraner

As HISTORY is reckoned, the Weimaraner is a young dog, dating back only to the early nineteenth century. The Bloodhound is believed to be among its ancestors, if not in direct line of descent, then certainly in a collateral way. In their breed investigations, historians stopped when they got as far back as the Red Schweisshund, but it is difficult to imagine that any of the several varieties of Schweisshund did not trace to the Bloodhound, which was well established in Europe at the time of the Crusades. Indeed, the red-tan Schweisshund found in the vicinity of Hanover is described as having "many of the characteristics of the Bloodhound." It was, however, a breed measuring about twenty-one inches at the shoulder, compared with the Bloodhound's maximum of twenty-seven inches and the Weimaraner's top of twenty-six inches.

The Weimaraner that we know today is the product of selective breeding; of judicious crosses followed by generations of line breeding to fix type and quality. It came from the same general stock which has produced a number of Germany's hunting breeds, one of its cousins being the breed now seen here—the German Shorthaired Pointer. In fact, in its early days, the Weimaraner was known simply as the Weimar Pointer. Since then height and weight have both been increased, but the distinctive coat color, described as silver grizzle or mouse gray, was approximately the same.

Throughout its early career the Weimaraner was sponsored by the sportsmen nobles in the court of Weimar. Long accustomed to many types of hunting, these men determined to meld into one breed all the qualities they had found worth while in their forays against the then abundant game of Germany. In short, the dog had to have good scenting ability, speed, courage, and intelligence.

Formerly the Weimaraner had been a big-game dog used on such quarry as wolves, wild cats, deer, mountain lion, bear, etc. By the time big game in Germany became a rarity, the breed was supported by a club originally started by a few of the men who had drawn up the dog's specifications. They were amateur sportsmen who desired to breed for sport rather than for profit. Accordingly, it was not easy to purchase a Weimaraner in Germany and practically impossible in any foreign country. One had to become a member of the club before purchasing, while gaining admittance to the club meant that the applicant's previous record of sportsmanship must assure proper maintenance of the club's breeding rules. One of these rules demanded that litters resulting from matings deemed unsuitable by a breed survey were not given place in the stud book; another, that specimens, even from approved litters, which did not measure up physically and tempermentally were to be destroyed. Hence there was no chance of a boom in the breed. There have never been more than 1500 specimens in Germany at any time.

America came to know the Weimaraner back in 1929 when an American sportsman and dog breeder, Howard Knight, was made a member of Germany's Weimaraner Club. Permitted to bring back two specimens, he helped found the club in this country and served as its first president. The club has made every effort to carry out the same principles that mapped the career of the breed in its native land.

It should be mentioned in passing that with the demise of big game hunting in Germany, the Weimaraner was trained as a bird dog used on various types of game in upland shooting and as a water retriever noted for its soft mouth. However, both in Germany and in America, the dog has been used more as a personal hunting companion than as a field-trial competitor.

Obedience trials incited the first interest in the breed over here, even before recognition had been granted in 1943 by The American Kennel Club—that was in 1941 when a bitch qualified for her C.D. in three straight shows. Later, another specimen went through all the degrees except the tracking test before reaching his tenth month, while a comparatively young puppy, too, annexed his C.D. Curiously enough, the Weimaraner has seen more actual competition of various kinds in America than it did in all its decades in Germany.

As for temperament, this dog is not happy when relegated to the kennel. He is accustomed to being a member of the family and he accepts the responsibilities which that entails.

GROUP II: HOUNDS

Afghan Hound

It was near Jebel Musa, or the Mountain of Moses, on that small peninsula called Sinai, between the Gulf of Suez and the Gulf of Aqaba, that the breed now known as the Afghan Hound first became a recognizable type of dog. This spot, long held sacred by Hebrew and Christian alike—where Jehovah delivered to Moses the tables of the Ten Commandments—was a part of ancient Egypt at the time when the Afghan's existence was first mentioned on a papyrus.

The document that thus forms the cornerstone of the history of the Afghan Hound has been attributed to the period, 3000 to 4000 B.C., and it mentions the dog so many times that there can be little doubt. According to Major H. Blackstone, an English authority on antiquities who made the translation, the dog is referred to as *cynocephalus*, which may be literally translated as "baboon" or freely translated as "monkey-faced hound." This is the meaning that Major Blackstone ascribes to it, for illustrations of the dog found on the tombs of the time offer convincing proof that even then the Afghan Hound's head was suggestive of the baboon.

The fact that the Afghan Hound was the subject of mention in a valuable document of the times is tantamount to saying that he was accepted among royalty, and that his value as a hunting dog of rare ability had been noted. His development must have progressed systematically under the desert Sheikhs, and although they have left us no stud books, there can be little doubt of the purity of his line for several thousand years. In the beginning it probably was a matter of selective breeding—of breeding that was as successful as its most modern, scientific counterpart.

The tombs on which the Afghan is portrayed are in the Valley of the Nile, so it must be inferred that in the beginning the hound was sent as a regal present to Memphis, or came in the entourage of a Sheikh. His first appearance at the palace must have occasioned some little stir; and there is no doubt that an Egyptian princess claimed him as her pet and applied to him the nickname, "monkey-face."

Considering the turbulent history of Egypt and the nature of the Afghan Hound, it is not unusual that the archaeologists could find no trace of the dog itself when they unearthed the evidence that he had existed in Egypt and that he came from Sinai. He is not a dog that would have prospered in urban surroundings; indeed, only the royal and the wealthy in a land such as Egypt would have been able to maintain him.

Just when the breed became established in the Hill country of the northern part of Afghanistan may remain a mystery for a long time. Likewise the question as to why no traces of the hound were found in Arabia or Persia—across which it would have had to travel—may never be answered.

The modern history of the Afghan Hound dates from World War I. It was taken to England by returning British Army officers after the war, and since then it has become quite the rage across the Atlantic. Also, the British officers were responsible, in great measure, for the spread of the dog into India, Persia, and Arabia, where, today, it is found in increasing numbers. It is the dog most favored for hunting the leopard, and in coursing gazelle and jack rabbits.

While the Egyptian origin of the breed is well founded, there is little doubt that Afghanistan has made the greatest contributions to the development of the Afghan Hound. Bred in mountainous country, and living throughout the ages at high elevations, where the winters are especially severe, the Afghan Hound has defied any change in its distinguishing characteristics. Its coat is of silky thick hair of very fine texture that stands off the body. The quarters, flanks, ribs, and fore-quarters are well covered. The pendulous ears and the four legs are well feathered—the hair on the legs being quite full on the sides and extending right down to the feet. It has a topknot of long, silky hair.

While the tail is set low, the tail carriage is high. This high tail carriage is emphasized in Afghanistan, for the hounds hunt so much in thickets that it is only by watching the tails that the movement of the dogs can be detected. Another most distinguishing point in the Afghan is the assembly of his hipbones. These are considerably higher than in the ordinary dog and set much wider apart. These unique hipbones make it possible for him to negotiate hilly country and uneven ground with ease and give him a motion like that of a monkey. Built in this manner, he turns easily and gets tremendous power into his leaps.

The Afghan hunts by sight, and while he is possessed of great speed, it is doubtful if he is as fast, on the flat, as some of the other hound varieties. However, the Afghan knows no equal as a hurdle racer. Used for countless centuries in a country where leaping over obstacles was even more essential than speed, he has developed this specialty to the ultimate degree. Another heritage he brings to his new abodes in Europe and America is the ability to withstand any temperature—either hot or cold. Summers in Afghanistan are terrifically hot, and winters severely cold.

It was about 1926 that the Afghan Hound first made its appearance in the United States, but for some reason or other the breed did not catch popular fancy at that time. Since then it has enjoyed a rebirth of interest, with a number of kennels that formerly were outstanding in other breeds endeavoring to spread knowledge of it. Gradually it has become known as a splendid all-around dog, quite aside from any ability it may have in the hunting field.

Basenji

THE Basenji, popularly known as the "barkless dog," is one of the oldest breeds. The first specimens were brought from the source of the Nile as presents to the Pharaohs of ancient Egypt. Later, when the civilization of Egypt declined and fell, the Basenji lapsed into obscurity. However, it was still valued and preserved in its native land of Central Africa, where it was highly prized for its intelligence, speed, hunting power, and silence.

Centuries later an English explorer rediscovered the Basenji and a pair was brought to England in 1895. Unfortunately, these little dogs contracted distemper and shortly thereafter died. Aside from that abortive attempt to make the breed known, the "outside" world in general did not hear of the Basenji until 1937, when it was successfully introduced to England. At the same time, a pair was brought to America by Mrs. Byron Rogers of New York City. Unfortunately for America, this pair and a litter of puppies produced from mating these specimens contracted distemper. All died except the older male dog, Bois.

In 1941 a young female Basenji was brought from Africa to Boston; Alexander Phemister of Kingston, Mass., obtained her and shortly afterward also acquired the male dog, Bois, that Mrs. Rogers had brought into the country in 1937. The young female, Congo, and Bois, both African-bred, were mated, resulting in the first litter of Basenji puppies to be raised to maturity in America. Later other Basenjis were imported from the Canadian kennels of Dr. A. R. B. Richmond, and still others were brought over from England.

Dog lovers all over the country became interested in this breed—so old, yet so new to America—and later purchased young specimens as foundation breeding stock. In 1942 the Basenji Club of America was formed with officers from many parts of the country. Mr. Phemister became the president of the club; Miss Ethelwyn Harrison of Euclid, Ohio, and Dr. Eloise Gerry of Madison, Wis., vice-presidents; George Gilkey of Merrill, Wis., treasurer; and George E. Richards of Lynn, Mass., secretary. The Basenji Club of America accepted the Standard of the breed as drawn up by the Basenji Club of England and in 1943, The American Kennel Club accepted the Standard as official and the breed for registration in the Stud Book. Within a few months there were fifty-nine Basenjis registered.

The Basenji is about the size and build of a Fox Terrier. The height for a male is seventeen inches at the shoulder, and sixteen inches for a female. The first impression one gets of a Basenji is that he is a proud little dog, and then one is impressed with his beauty, grace, and intelligence. In fact he has often been compared to a little deer.

The coat of the Basenji is one of his most beautiful features. Coming from a tropical climate, the texture is fine and silky and shines like burnished copper in the sun. In colder countries the coat tends to become more coarse, but it never loses its brilliant luster. The color is preferably red, then come various shades of red and fawn, then chestnut, but always there are white points and invariably there is a white tip to the tightly curled tail, which lies over to one side of the back. Several of the breed's most unusual characteristics are: 1) the lack of bark; 2) the broad forehead deeply furrowed with wrinkles; 3) the prick ears, standing straight up from their heads; 4) the dark, intelligent, far-seeing eyes.

The Basenji's intelligence and courage are proved by his hunting ability in his native habitat. The natives use him for pointing, retrieving, for driving game into nets, and hunting wounded quarry. He is also used for hunting the reed rats—vicious long-toothed creatures weighing from twelve to twenty pounds—and here the silence of the Basenji is a particularly great asset. These dogs have wonderful noses, scenting at eighty yards; so together with their keen scent and gift of silence, it is no wonder the natives value them so highly.

Those in America and England who have had the opportunity to know the little Basenji have found him to be all they could hope for in a dog. He is a fascinating, endearing fellow, full of play, yet gentle as a kitten. His fastidious, dainty habits, such as cleaning himself all over—as does a cat—make him an ideal dog for the immaculate housekeeper.

The Basenji's distinctive sound of happiness fairly thrills one, yet this sound he makes is hard to describe. It is somewhere between a chortle and a yodel. However, he is usually very happy when he makes it and one can't help but share the happiness with him.

The breed is tractable and anxious to please and, by nature, an obedient dog. Already several Basenjis have won obedience degrees in this country and others are being prepared. Their sprightly alert manner in the obedience show rings and their beautiful gait, resembling a thoroughbred horse's, have caused much favorable comment.

The Basenji loves children and is tireless in his play. He has a fascinating manner of teasing one to play. One front paw is brought behind his ear, then down over his nose, and repeated and repeated until he has drawn the desired attention. However, when his owner is ready to call quits, the little Basenji is content to lie right at the feet of his master, just as did his forebears thousands of years ago in the courts of ancient Egypt.

Basset Hound

THE Basset Hound, as the dog is called in the United States and in England, is an old, aristocratic breed. Of ancient lineage, it has flourished for centuries on the continent, chiefly in France and in Belgium, where it was raised by royalty, principally for moderately slow trailing of deer, hares, rabbits, and kindred game. Its traditional origin is in France, where it was called the Basset, and its ancestry was the old French Bloodhound and the St. Hubert hounds.

In the United States, the Basset Hound is used for hunting foxes, rabbits, and pheasants. Also he is trained, for raccoon hunting and for trailing, flushing, and securing wounded pheasants and other game birds. As most sportsmen can follow them easily while on the scent and be ready when the bird rises, Basset Hounds are unexcelled for trailing and flushing pheasants. They are steady, accurate trailers, give plenty of tongue, and with their extremely short legs are particularly valuable in hunting in dense cover. With the exception of the pure Bloodhound, no breed can lay claim to greater scenting ability.

Being bred for centuries as a strictly sporting dog—well disciplined for hunting either in packs or singly—the Basset is both intelligent and docile, with a kindly disposition that makes him a loyal hunting pal. While at work, he will do his best to bring the game around to the waiting hunter. If trained and handled by his master only, the Basset is a one-man dog. He cannot be coaxed away by any stranger, even if the latter has a gun. If kindly raised and trained, a Basset puppy will turn into as loyal, enjoyable, and satisfactory hunting pal as any man would want to own. He is easy to control and as a rule affectionate if treated kindly by his master.

In appearance the Basset Hound is low, from eleven to fifteen inches at the shoulder; of long body and heavy bone; weighing from forty to sixty pounds. In America, the most popular Basset is the crooked or half-crooked front leg type. There is a straight-leg type that is a little rangier and somewhat faster as a rule. The front leg is broad, the foot likewise; the shoulders heavy and well muscled, the chest deep. The hind legs, too, are heavy and well muscled on the hip.

The head is long. The nose is long, also, and well developed clear to the muzzle. The flews are heavy. The dewlap is commonly pendant. In the English type, which has a more recent infusion of the original Bloodhound, the eye is deep-set, with wrinkle above and haw beneath. The ears are long, soft, and pendant—in fact, they are so long that sometimes they may be tied in a knot above the head. The nose usually is black, well developed, and of great scenting power. French Bassets are of the same general lines as the English dog, except that they are of a smaller type, lighter weight, and are more agile.

In recent years, there were two types of smooth Basset Hounds in France, and two strains· the Le Couteulx, and the Lane; named after the two largest breeders in France. Le Cte le Couteulx de Canteleu, and Mons Lane of Francquevilli, near Boos. These hounds differ mostly in the head and eye. The Lane hound has a large eye like a Beagle and a much broader skull. The Le Couteulx hound has that downfaced look, giving it a sad expression; a brown eye, deeply sunken, showing a prominent haw; a domed head of considerable length and narrow in comparison to the Lane hound, which is inclined to cheek bumps.

It is the Le Couteulx type that is most favored in America. Lord Galway was the first to import hounds of this type into England. In 1866, the Comte de Tournow sent Lord Galway a pair of hounds that the latter called Basset and Belle. In 1867, Lord Galway bred a litter of puppies from the pair. In 1872, he sold them to the late Lord Onslow, the 4th Earl. Lord Onslow augmented his pack from the kennels of Le Cte le Couteulx de Canteleu, and about 1882, he sold them—some fourteen or fifteen pairs—to the late George Krehl and the late Sir Everett

Millais, the latter being the son of Sir John Millais. From these hounds, all the best Bassets in England and America are descended.

Until recent years, the French short-legged hound has never been popular in America. The late Sir Everett Millais, who was the first to introduce the dog into England, and also a Bloodhound cross, wrote a description of the breed. So far as it goes, the description is excellent. But Sir Everett made no attempt to go into the history of the breed.

Buffon described it and named two varieties: the crooked and the straight-legged types. However, Millais made the mistake of saying that the latter were the *petit chiens courant*, or small running hound. The probability is that these dogs were descendants from the old breed of greffiers—dogs bred from the white St. Hubert hounds and the hounds of Italy—or else from the St. Hubert hounds direct.

These dogs were used on the liam. And it is easy to understand that a dog which held its nose low to the ground because of its short legs, would be preferred to one which had to make an effort to get his nose equally as low. Undoubtedly, the Basset is the dog most entitled to be considered a direct descendant of the dogs which the Abbots of St. Hubert had to contribute, annually, to the King's kennels, and which were used mainly for tracking on the liam.

It was in 1875, that Sir Everett introduced the Basset to English dog shows. But it was not until 1880, at the Wolverhampton show, that the breed really got its start. At that show, Sir Everett made a large entry, and the breed attracted great attention. The late George R. Krehl then took up the breed, and it became slightly popular on account of its "quaintness." But the difficulty of breeding good dogs caused many in England to give them up; and, except at the larger shows, the Basset was relegated to the variety classes.

Beagle

THE actual origin of the Beagle is lost in the mists of ancient days and no research, it seems, can ever bring its true history to light. Several well-known beaglers have written their opinions on the origin of the breed, and the following remarks are by Captain Otho Paget of Melton Mowbray, England, who was, perhaps, the dean of all Beaglers.

"According to Xenophon there were hounds that hunted by scent in his day and the Romans acquired many of the sports of ancient Greece.

There were, however, in England, packs of hounds before the time of the Romans and it is on record that Pwyll, Prince of Wales, a contemporary of King Arthur, had a special breed of white hounds of great excellence. Wales, to this day is still celebrated for its hounds, generally of a light color. Admirers of shooting dogs, setters, spaniels and other kinds, have asserted that these animals were used in building up the hound. By exercise of a little thought it will seem that this must be wrong and that in fact it is the other way about. The hound was the original progenitor of all sporting dogs, and the two distinct breeds would be the 'Gaze' or 'Greyhound' that hunted by sight alone, and the hound, probably the Bloodhound, that relied entirely on its nose. By the time of good Queen Bess, nearly every country gentleman in England kept a pack of hounds of some sort and hunted the animal of his choice. The fox was not at that time an honored beast of the chase. Hounds in those days seem to have been divided into two classes, the large and the small. The large sort were called 'Buck Hounds' and hunted the deer, and the smaller variety were called 'Beagles' from the French 'Begle' and were hunted on hare."

Coming down to the middle of the eighteenth century, we find fox hunting becoming popular with the younger generations, who wanted something quicker and more exhilarating than watching hounds puzzling out the intricate windings of a hare. The Foxhound was undoubtedly evolved from a mixture of buck hound and Beagle. By this time the vagaries of breeders had produced two distinct types of hare-hunting hounds, one of which was called the Southern hound and the other the North Country Beagle. The former was slow and ponderous, with long ears and deep voice, whilst the other was the exact opposite. According to a writer of that day the "North Country Beagle" was nimble and vigorous and did his business as furiously as Jehu himself could wish him.

In the middle of the nineteenth century Parson Honeywood got together a good pack and showed some excellent sport in Essex. His pack dates as the beginning of the modern Beagle, and nearly every well-known pack of subsequent date owed its origin to that inheritance. The colored engraving "The Merry Beaglers" is as familiar to American sportsmen as it is to anyone in England and will preserve for all time the name of the Reverend Philip Honeywood. We can accept it as true that the Beagle is one of the oldest breeds in history and, with the Bloodhound and perhaps the Otter Hound, closest to the original breed of hounds.

Previous to about 1870 in the United States, the little hunting hounds of the Southern States, then called Beagles, were more of the type of straight-legged Bassets or Dachshunds with weaker heads than the Bassets and were mostly white with a few dark markings. They were said to be snappy, tireless hunters, full of vim and quick at a turn, but not handsome in outline. The importations of the late General Rowett of Carlinsville, Illinois, in the sixties marks the turning point in the history of the American strain or strains of Beagle and brought to this country an acquisition of canine beauty little thought of by those who hitherto had hunted with Beagles. From what packs in England General Rowett obtained his hounds is not known.

About 1880 Mr. Arnold of Providence, R.I., imported a pack from the Royal Rock Beagles in the North of England, and this also has had a good deal of influence on the development of American Beagles. In 1896 Mr. James L. Kernochan imported a pack from England and from then on a great many high-class hounds have been brought over.

Among the first sportsmen of note in the Beagle world, whose importations have helped to create the modern Beagle in America, may be mentioned Mr. Harry Peters of Islip, L.I., Mr. George Post of Bernardsville, N.J., Mr. James W. Appleton of Ipswich, Mass., Mr. Eugene Reynal of Millbrook, N.Y., Mr. H. C. Phipps of Westbury, L.I., and many others.

In 1888 The National Beagle Club was formed and held the first field trial. From that time on field trials carrying championship points have sprung up rapidly all over the United States, and as many more clubs sanctioned to hold informal trials. At all these, packs are run in single classes for hounds thirteen to fifteen inches in height and classes for those under thirteen inches, and at the national trials the pack classes are an important feature. There are single classes for young hounds called "derbies" and all-age classes for large and small dogs and bitches. At the national there are, in addition to these single classes, four pack classes which, of course, cannot be run against each other at the same time, as are the hounds in the single classes. Each pack is hunted separately and scored by the judges.

In addition to the regular all-breed American Kennel Club shows, almost all the field-trial clubs conduct specialty shows in connection with their field trials, and in addition to this again, there are hound shows limited to the various breeds of hounds.

Those who are interested in hunting Beagles as a pack generally enjoy hunting the larger hares, rather than cottontail rabbits. Hares do not go to ground and spoil a hunt, and they give much longer, straighter, and faster runs. Kansas jack rabbits have, therefore, been brought to many parts of the East and have bred extensively in each community in which they have been placed. They are only fairly satisfactory. Several experiments have been made in importing English hares, but they have not been very successful, probably due to the fact that the climate and feed in this part of the world do not suit them. Hares have been imported from Germany, however, with great successs. They show splendid sport and thrive in this country. The white hare, or snowshoe rabbit, is found in northern swamps and provides excellent sport for a pack, but these hares will not do well when imported to other communities and disappear immediately.

There are thousands of men all over the United States who keep a few Beagles and hunt them individually. In addition, there are many packs recorded with the National Beagle Club. They are all hunted in the legitimate manner with a regular hunt staff, in hunt liveries, with their own distinctive colored collar, etc.

In conclusion, a few remarks as to the modern standard for type may be of interest. The height limit of a Beagle in the United States is fifteen inches and in England sixteen inches. Hounds above this height cannot be entered in field trials or shows. The head should be strong and well proportioned, with a fairly long, clean neck. Sloping shoulders are very important for speed and endurance. The body should be close-coupled and well ribbed up. The front legs should be very straight with as much bone as possible and small, round cat-feet. The quarters should be strong and powerful and the hocks set low to the ground. The stern should be set moderately high with a good brush, but a proud or curly stern is most undesirable. Any true hound color is suitable.

Bloodhound

WHEN Claudius Aelianus, or "Aelian," wrote his famous *Historia Animalium* in the third century A.D., he mentioned in especially glowing terms a breed of hound that was unrivaled for its scenting powers and which was possessed of such great determination that it would not leave the trail until the quarry was located. Thus the early Italian scholar gives us a picture of the dog that is known today as the Bloodhound, a breed that has improved considerably in appearance but which still retains its peculiarly intensified ability to follow the faintest scent.

There has been little evidence to prove how far back the origin of the Bloodhound extends, but it is believed by many authorities that it was known throughout the Mediterranean countries long before the Christian Era. It is called the modern representative of the oldest race of hounds that hunt by scent, indicating, of course, that selective breeding over many centuries has made it outwardly changed from the breed the ancients extolled. Yet its characteristics are so distinctive that cynologists have traced it throughout dog history.

The Bloodhound made its appearance in Europe long before the Crusades, the first specimens being brought from Constantinople. There were two strains, black and white. The blacks were the famed St. Huberts of the eighth century, while the whites later became known as the Southern hounds. It was from the black stock that importations were made to England. Both varieties have played big parts in the development of other hounds and hound-type dogs.

In the twelfth century, when even Bishops rode to hounds, dignitaries of the Church were among the foremost in fostering the development of the Bloodhound. A number of high ecclesiastics maintained packs, and the kennel was an important part of every monastery. To them goes a great deal of the credit for keeping the strain clean. In fact, so much care was taken in the breeding of this hound that it came to be called the "blooded hound," meaning aristocratic.

Several centuries later that noted English physician and dog lover, Dr. Johannes Caius, gives a different explanation of the name, but his description of the breed is interesting. It follows:

". . . The larger class remain to be mentioned; these too have drooping lips and ears, and it is well known that they follow their prey not only while alive but also after death when they have caught the scent of blood. For whether the beasts are wounded alive and slip out of the hunter's hands, or are taken dead out of the warren (but with a profusion of blood in either case), these hounds perceive it at once by smell and follow the trail. For that reason they are properly called Sanguinarii.

"Frequently, however, an animal is stolen, and owing to the cleverness of the thieves there is no effusion of blood; but even so they are clever enough to follow dry human footsteps for a huge distance, and can pick a man out of a crowd however large, pressing on through the densest thickets, and they will still go on even though they have to swim across a river. When they arrive at the opposite bank, by a circular movement, they find out which way a man has gone, even if at first they do not hit on the track of the thief. Thus they supplement good luck by artifice and deserve what Aelian says of them in his 'Historia Animalium.' . . ."

Although the Bloodhound reached approximately its modern form in England, the breed has perhaps reached its greatest development in the United States, as far as usefulness is concerned. The breed has been known in America for at least a century. Abolitionists once drew touching pictures of poor fugitive slaves pursued by the Bloodhounds, but it is doubted if many of the breed—then fairly numerous in the South—were so employed. Mongrels were frequently called "bloodhounds" and no doubt some of these did harass the slaves.

The pure-bred Bloodhound is one of the most docile of all breeds. His trailing is more for his own sport than for anything else. Unlike the police-trained dog, he does not attack the man he is trailing. The Bloodhound's task ends once he has followed the trail to its termination. But so accurate is he in following a trail that he is the only dog whose evidence is accepted in a court of law.

Some of the great Bloodhounds of the United States have brought about more convictions for police departments than the best human detectives. One dog was credited with more than 600 actual convictions. The famous dog Nick Carter picked up a trail that was 105 hours old and followed it to a subsequent conviction. The breed's stamina and determination are apparent in the great distances it will travel. Several specimens have followed human quarry for more than fifty miles, and one led the detectives 138 miles—all with success.

Bloodhounds have been exhibited in the United States almost from the beginning of organized dog shows in America.

Borzoi

THE Borzoi, known here prior to 1936 as the Russian Wolfhound, has been used in Russia since the early seventeenth century for hunting wolves and coursing hare and other game, as the *Sloughi*, or Greyhounds of Egypt, were also used many centuries before the time of Christ and depicted on tombs and monuments of that country. As a means of procuring food, and later as a sport, coursing has been known for hundreds of years. There are, in fact, accounts of hunting expeditions of the several Mongol rulers from the time of the conqueror Genghis Khan, in the thirteenth century, in which long hounds, or Greyhounds, were mentioned as the principal coursing dogs. All breeds of coursing hounds resembled each other in general conformation, all having been bred for speed. The Russian Wolfhound, the Borzoi, *Psovoi, Gustopsovoy*, and several other Borzois had many varieties, but all possessed approximately the same characteristics.

Fairly recent research into the much discussed origin of the Borzoi brings to light an interesting discovery, to wit, that in the early seventeenth century a certain Russian duke, who liked very fast dogs for hunting, imported a number of Arabian Greyhounds, probably dogs known as gazelle hounds. These were speedy runners, but it seems that, having thin coats, they were unable to withstand the severe weather and cold winters of Russia and soon died. Undaunted by his first failure, the duke later sent for more of these hounds and carefully crossed them with a native Russian breed somewhat similar to the Collie of today, but slightly more powerful and different in build, having longer legs, longer gracefully curved tail, slightly longer neck, very heavily furred ears, and a carriage more like the Wolfhound of today. This dog's coat was very heavy, wavy or curly, with a tendency to be woolly. In color he was red sable or gray, and in general build powerful and able to withstand great hardship; in fact, he was a real working dog. The result of the crossing was the graceful, elegant and aristocratic dog we know as our own Borzoi.

Of considerable interest is the fact that the ancient type of the Borzoi was difficult to obtain and to breed. This should be explained. It so happened in the early part of the eighteenth century, after many wars, that with subsequent revival of sporting activities in Russia, there arose a great craze to cross Borzois with foreign dogs of the same general type, such as Asiatic Greyhounds, Crimean Greyhounds and gazelle hounds with flapping ears. This crossing was practiced to such an extent that about the middle of the eighteenth century there were few pure-blooded wolfhounds left in the whole of Russia. At this time a large number of the nobility left their estates and repaired to different cities or sojourned in various places in Europe; in many cases their kennels were given up entirely. Thus it will be seen that first from the mixing of other blood with the breed, and later from the decrease in the number of hounds, the ancient type became almost extinct, so that when the first exportations of Borzoi were made from Russia, practically none of the real ancient type hound ever left the country. Of course, in some cases an occasional good specimen may have come out of Russia, but usually any such hounds were duly sent out to individuals as presents.

As far as is known, the first Borzoi which came to America was brought over from England by Mr. William Wade, of Hulton, Pa., in 1889, this hound being purchased from Mr. Freeman Lloyd. This was a bitch named Elsie, described in *The English Stockkeeper* as "Nothing much to look at, being small, light, and weedy, with no bone, straight back, very curly tail and too much bent in stifles." Mr. C. Steadman Hanks in the early or middle nineties imported several Borzois, and the records show that some of them were considered very good ones. Mr. Hanks appears to be the only extensive American importer of these hounds who ever visited Russia until 1903, when Mr. Joseph B. Thomas went there, with the exception of Mr. E. L. Krauss of Pennsylvania, whose importations were of German origin. As somebody wrote, many of them were weedy, although pretty to look at, with good heads and coats, but they had evidently been kennel raised for many generations and seemed to show it in disposition and lack of stamina.

Mr. Joseph B. Thomas's importations were made directly from Russia, from the Perchina Kennels, owned by the Grand Duke Nicholas of Romanoff, and from the Woronzova Kennels of Mr. Arten Balderoff. In these kennels, Mr. Thomas found the good ancient type of hound that everyone interested in the breed was looking for and is still looking for, and about which so much is said. It seems from some of Mr. Thomas's memoirs that the reason these two gentlemen, the Grand Duke and Mr. Balderoff, had the ancient type of the breed well preserved in their kennels was that during the period of the degeneration of the breed, their places and places whence they got their stock were so far out of the way that the craze of crossing did not reach that far.

As you visit different kennels and dog shows and observe Borzois, you will see some well-knit, well-proportioned animals with excellent conformation, that will move elegantly, with great poise, and remind you on the whole of the superiority of a true aristocrat. Then you will also see the hound that apparently does not look just right to the eye, and to the novice this particular dog is a sort of puzzle. He or she will realize that there is something radically wrong, but will be unable to say what it is. This is the type of hound that everyone should try to eliminate. It is either too long for its height, with too small or too large a head for the rest of its body, or fox- or Roman-headed, with improper carriage of tail, which is sometimes too short; these are all out of proportion, not typical or of good conformation, being unable to move properly and lacking the grace and appearance the breed should have. This type is mostly found in the larger-sized hound, which has been raised in confinement and has not had the chance to exercise properly, and as a rule it will be found to be unsound.

Coonhound, Black and Tan

ALTHOUGH a comparatively recent addition to our roster of pure-breds, the Black and Tan Coonhound is actually an old breed as history is reckoned. In all probability he has descended from the Talbot hound which was known in England during the reign of William I, Duke of Normandy, in the eleventh century; thence down through the Bloodhound and the Foxhound via this country's own Virginia Foxhound, frequently referred to as the "black and tan."

Selectively bred on a basis of color (for there were "cooners" of other colors as well) and for proficiency on possum and raccoon, the black-and-tan strain was carefully developed over a period of years and, under the auspices of the Black and Tan Coonhound Club, admitted to registry by The American Kennel Club in 1945.

The Black and Tan Coonhound works his trail with consummate skill and determination, albeit not at a particularly fast pace. In fact, he trails Bloodhound fashion, entirely by scent, with nose to the ground, "barking up" or giving voice the moment his quarry is treed. And despite the fact that the dog has been nurtured as a specialist on coon, he can do equally well in hunting deer, mountain lion, bear, and possibly other big game.

Dachshund

THE name Dachshund (dachs, badger; hund, dog) at once reveals and conceals the origin of the breed. In medieval European books on hunting, dogs similar only in possessing the tracking ability of hounds and the proportions and temperament of terriers, because they were used to follow badger to earth, were called badger-dogs or dachs-hunds. A parallel is suggested by the current use of the name "rabbit dog" in various parts of this country for dogs of various breeding, used to hunt rabbits.

Illustrations dating from the fifteenth, sixteenth, and seventeenth centuries show badgers hunted by dogs with elongated bodies, short legs, and hound-type ears—some with the bent front legs of the Basset, some with the heads of terriers, and some with indications of smooth and long coats. It is well to consider that these illustrations were made before the days of photography, that artists capable of depicting dogs with anatomical fidelity have always been rare, and that woodcuts do not lend themselves to fine reproductions of coat distinctions. At best, the pictures and descriptive words can be interpreted with certainty only as defining the functions of the dogs used on badger.

The preponderance of available evidence indicates that smooth and longhaired coats were separated by selective breeding, long prior to recorded registrations; whereas within such recorded history, the wire-haired coat was produced for protection against briar and thorn by crossing in harsh, wiry terrier coats and then breeding out incompatible characteristics of conformation. Early in the seventeenth century the name Dachshund became the designation of a breed type with smooth and longhaired coat varieties, and since 1890 wirehairs have been registered as the third variety. German breeders early learned that crossing between longhairs and either smooths or wirehairs did more harm than good, and barred such crosses from registration. During the early decades of wirehairs, while breeding stock was comparatively rare, crosses with smooths were permitted. Now, with sufficient breeding stock within each of the three varieties to provide any desired characteristics, there is no advantage in coat crossing, with inevitable production of intermediate coats conforming to neither coat standard, and uncertainty of coat texture for several generations. In the 1956–57 German stud book, including all sizes, there were registered 1348 smooths, 7507 longhairs, and 3099 wirehairs.

The badger was a formidable twenty-five to forty-pound adversary. Strength and stamina as well as keenness and courage above and below ground were required of badger dogs. Weights of thirty to thirty-five pounds were not uncommon. Such Dachshunds in packs also were serviceable against wild boar. With this start the breed was adapted to hunt other game. A smaller sixteen to twenty-two-pound Dachshund proved effective against foxes and to trail wounded deer, and this size has become best known in this country. Still smaller twelve-pound Dachshunds were used on stoat and hare. In the first quarter of the twentieth century, for bolting cottontail rabbits, miniatures with adult weights under five pounds and chest girths under twelve inches, but with plenty of hunting spirit, were produced.

Before the German Dachshund or *Deutscher Teckelklub* was founded in 1888, "racial characteristics," or a standard for the breed had been set up in 1879; and German registration of Dachshunds was included (not always with complete generation data or systematic coat notations) in a general all-breed stud book, the *Deutscher Hunde-Stammbuch*, whose first volume, in 1840, recorded fifty-four Dachshunds and the names of several subsequently prominent breeders, and whose publication continued until officially terminated in 1935. The *Gebrauchsteckel-Klubs,* or hunting Dachshund associations, kept separate stud books, in which were recorded only dogs of demonstrated hunting accomplishment, with scant attention to coat or conformation. From early volumes of the *Deutscher Teckelklub* stud book, first published in 1890, despite meager correlation with older records, pedigrees have been extended back as far as 1860 and 1859. Stud books maintained by clubs devoted to wirehairs, longhairs, and miniatures have waxed and waned. Not until 1915 did the coat-identifying initials K for *Kurzhaar*, or smooth, R for *Rauhhaar*, or wirehair, and L for *Langhaar*, or longhair, become integral components of the *Teckelklub* registration numbers, and later z was added to distinguish *Zwerg* and *Kaninchentechel*, or miniatures, by re-registration after one year on official certification of eligible size. It can be recommended to American Dachshund breeders of longhairs and wirehairs to incorporate the initials L and W, respectively, in names submitted to the AKC for registration of Dachshunds of these coats.

The management of the breed in Germany, as well as the stud books, had been divided. The *Teckelklub* managed the bench shows, while the *Gebrauchsteckel-Klubs* conducted organized hunting activities. In 1935, the nationalized consolidation of all German Dachshund clubs as the *Fachschaft Dachshunde im Reichsverband für das Deutsche Hunde-wesen (FD-RDH)* unified the breed stud books and co-ordinated the conduct of bench shows with natural-hunting field trials.

Since World War II, management of the Dachshund breed in Germany has reverted to the *Deutscher Teckelklub*—whose registrations are accepted by the AKC—and the *Gebrauchsteckelklub*. The balance of breeding for hunting and symmetry, which advanced the breed for twenty-five years before the war, was altered after the war to stress hunting, with a more terrier-like conformation, whereas in this country the prewar objectives have continued to direct the breed.

Importation of Dachshunds into this country antedates the earliest American dog shows or stud books, and eleven were included in *AKC Stud Book, Volume II* in 1885. Our dogs have found little employment in organized hunting, as we lack the badger and wild boar and do not hunt deer with dogs, nor foxes with pick and shovel. The true character and conformation of the breed have been encouraged by frequent importation of German hunting strains; and to encourage hunting capacity and exemplary conformation and temperament, field trials under AKC rules were instituted in 1935.

The advance of the breed in this country has not been without reverses. Fostered since 1895 by The Dachshund Club of America, by 1913 and 1914 it had gained a place among the ten most numerous breeds at the Westminster Kennel Club shows—to fall in the postwar years to a mere dozen and temporarily translate its name to "badger dog."

After World War I, with replenished breeding stock, there were noteworthy gains. From 1930 to 1940, Dachshunds advanced from twenty-eighth to sixth rank among American registrations, and maintained this average rank through World War II by constructive public relations. Since that time, as the all-breed registration totals have continued to increase year by year, the Dachshund has maintained an important place in the proportionate number of dogs registered and exhibited in the ring.

It is unlikely that one American Dachshund in a thousand is used to hunt, but to understand the functional origin and development of the breed helps us appreciate its elegant, streamlined proportions, and gives significance to the application of the breed standard.

Specialized characteristics of the breed for its purposes include a long head and well-developed nose; properly angulated shoulder, pelvis, and leg bones; close elbows, and free, straight gait of forelegs and hind legs; long fore-chest and after-chest with well-sprung ribs for ample lung and heart room without excessive width; supple and elastic skin for free action in restricted quarters underground; a remarkably long, powerful jaw with well-fitted teeth; a long, strong neck, capable as a fencer's wrist; powerful legs and sound feet for digging, a well-muscled back for sustained effort; and above all, that fine, high courage which enables it to measure up to every demand of attack or defense without being quarrelsome or undesirably aggressive.

The medium-sized, smooth-haired Dachshund, which predominates in this country, is small enough to live in house or apartment, yet large enough for street, suburb, or country. Its short legs insure maximum exercise per mile. Its odorless, sleek, dark, short coat leaves no hair on clothes or furniture, requires no plucking, trimming, brushing, combing, oiling, and no bathing except to remove accidental dirt. Outdoors the Dachshund is hardy, vigorous, and tireless; indoors he is affectionate and responsive, companionable in restful mood, hilarious in play, alert in announcing strangers. The breed offers a range of three coat varieties; standard and miniature sizes; red and black-and-tan and a number of other colors.

Deerhound, Scottish

THE origin of the Deerhound breed is of such antiquity and the earliest descriptive names bestowed on it so inextricably mixed that no sound conclusion can be arrived at as to whether the Deerhound was at one time identical with the ancient Irish Wolfdog and, in the course of centuries bred to a type better suited to hunt deer, or whether, as some writers claim, he is the descendant of the hounds of the Picts. Very early descriptive names were used to identify the purpose of the dog rather than to identify species. We find such names as "Irish Wolf Dog," "Scotch Greyhound," "Rough Greyhound," "Highland Deerhound." Dr. Caius, in his book *Englische Dogges* (1576) speaking of Greyhounds, relates: "Some are of a greater sorte, some of a lesser; some are smoothe skynned and some curled, the bigger therefore are appointed to hunt the bigger beastes, the duck, the hart, the doe."

All this is relatively unimportant when we can definitely identify the breed as Deerhounds as early as the sixteenth and seventeenth centuries. From there on the term Deerhound has been applied to the breed, which of all dogs has been found best suited for the pursuit and killing of the deer.

At all times great value has been set on the Deerhound. The history of the breed teems with romance increasing in splendor right down through the Age of Chivalry when no one of rank lower than an earl might possess these dogs. A leash of Deerhounds was held the fine whereby a noble lord condemned to death might purchase his reprieve. Records of the Middle Ages allude repeatedly to the delightful attributes of this charming hound, his tremendous courage in the chase, his gentle dignity in the home.

So highly has the Deerhound been esteemed that the desire for exclusive ownership has at many times endangered the continuance of the breed. As the larger beasts of the chase became extinct, or rare, in England and southern Scotland, the more delicate, smooth Greyhound took the place of the larger Deerhound. The Highlands of Scotland, last territory wherein the stag remained numerous in a wild state, became, as might be expected, the last stronghold of this breed. Here again the Highland Chieftains assumed exclusive proprietorship to such an extent that it was rare to find a good specimen south of the River Forth. So severely was this policy pursued that in 1769 the breed physically and numerically ran very low. This, of course, must be attributed in a great measure to the collapse of the clan system after Culloden 1745. It was not until about 1825, when the restoration of the breed was under-taken very successfully by Archibald and Duncan McNeill (the latter afterwards Lord Colonsay), that the Deerhound regained his place of pre-eminence and former perfection. The Great War, in later times, had considerable effect on the breed when so many of the large estates in Scotland and England were broken up. Although this "Royal Dog of Scotland" is represented at English shows in good numbers and to a considerable extent at shows in the Eastern States of this country, the Deerhound remains a rare dog of such historical interest and character that ownership should give anyone great pride of possession.

The high valuation of the Deerhound is not the result of rarity so much as the fact that as a hunter he is pre-eminent, with a high aggregate of desirable characteristics. He has a keen scent, which may be used in tracking, but it is that combination of strength and speed necessary to cope with the large Scottish deer (often weighing 250 pounds) that is most valued. The hounds are usually hunted singly or in pairs. Centuries of hunting as the companions and guards of Highland Chieftains have given the Deerhound an insatiable desire for human companionship. For this reason the best Deerhounds are seldom raised as kennel dogs. In character the Deerhound is quiet and dignified, keen and alert, and although not aggressive, has great persistence and indomitable courage when necessary. While it might savor of boasting to claim that the Deer-hound of today is identical with the dog of early history, descriptions of which are mostly legendary, it is nevertheless a well-established fact that in type, size, and character he closely conforms to authentic records of the eighteenth and nineteenth centuries.

The hunting of antlered game with dogs is not permitted in the United States, but the Deerhound has been used very successfully on wolves, coyotes, and rabbits, and is keen to match his speed with anything that runs. As a companion the Deerhound is ideal, being tractable and easy to train and possessing the most dependable loyalty and utmost devotion to his master. The most authentic and complete work on the breed is *Scotch Deerhounds and their Masters* written by George Cup-ples. Much has also been written about the Deerhound by Scrope in *Days of Deerstalking* and other works. The best descriptions of the breed are found in nineteenth-century British dog books.

The grace, dignity and beauty of the Deerhound have been faithfully depicted in many of Landseer's paintings and drawings, and Sir Walter Scott, who owned the famous Deerhound Maida, makes many enthusi-astic allusions to the breed, which he describes as "The most perfect creature of Heaven."

Foxhound, American

ACCORDING to well-known authorities on the American Hound, the first mention that we have of hound importations to America appears in a diary of one of De Soto's retainers. It is further mentioned that hounds were utilized to hunt Indians instead of foxes and hare.

From this same good authority we learn that in 1650 Robert Brooke sailed for the Crown Colony in America, taking his pack of hounds with him, which according to this authority were the taproot of several strains of American Hounds and remained in the family for nearly three hundred years. Then Mr. Thomas Walker of Albemarle County, Virginia, imported hounds from England in 1742; in 1770 George Washington subscribed to the importation of hounds from England, and in 1785 received some French Hounds from Lafayette, their voices being "like the bells of Moscow." These importations formed the foundation from which have developed some of the strains of the present day Virginia Hounds.

In 1808 the Gloucester Foxhunting Club imported some of the "best English Hounds," and the Baltimore Hunt Club made many importations from England. Then followed the Rosseau importations from France, and the Irish importations of 1830. The latter are the taproot of the Henry-Birdsong and Trigg strains. Around 1857 General Maupin got from east Tennessee the dog, Tennessee Lead, which, crossed on English importations, produced the "Maupin dog" now known as the Walker hound, another well known strain of American Hound.

The Foxhound in this country is used for four purposes, all of them quite different from each other, and thus calling for hounds of a different characteristic.

1. The field trial hound which is run competitively at field trials where speed and a rather jealous nature are important.

2. A hound for hunting a fox with a gun. Here a slow-trailing hound with a good voice is needed.

3. "Trail" hounds, or drag hounds, which are raced or hunted on a drag, speed alone counting.

4. Hounds to hunt in large numbers (say fifteen to twenty or more) in a pack. This latter class is, of course, the type used by the hunt clubs and hunting farmers.

The types of American hounds have varied widely in different localities, but in the last few years the American Foxhound Club and the hunts which are members of the Masters of Foxhounds Association have made great strides in developing a more standard type.

Foxhound, English

FOXHUNTING in the United States is almost contemporaneous with the sport in Great Britain. The Foxhound with which we are dealing is known in the United States in dog shows and elsewhere as the *English* Foxhound, though why it should be designated by that name any more than a Fox Terrier should be called an *English* Fox Terrier, is hard to understand. The English Foxhound has been bred along careful lines for over one hundred and fifty years, the stud books published by the Masters of Foxhounds Association (of England) dating back before 1800; it is an easy matter for any owner of an English Foxhound to trace its pedigree back. The breeding of Foxhounds in England has always been in the hands of masters of hounds, who kept the most careful records of their breeding operations.

For the benefit of those who may be interested in knowing how long the English Foxhound in his pure state has been in the United States, we find that there are records which established the fact that the first Lord Fairfax imported hounds from England in 1738, and there are unauthenticated records of even earlier importations. The *English Foxhound Stud Book of America*, published by the Masters of Foxhounds Association of America, dates its earliest entries back to 1890, but there are earlier records which would incline one to the belief that there were many earlier importations and certainly the blood of the Genesee Valley pack must date at least twenty years before that time, records having been kept of it with fair accuracy ever since.

In England as in America these hounds have always been used for foxhunting as followed in the English fashion of riding to hounds. There have been over two hundred and fifty packs of hounds in Great Britain, all of which used English Hounds, while in America we have over a hundred packs, of which not over 10 per cent use hounds which would be eligible for the *English Foxhound Stud Book*, although the blood has been freely mixed with the American Foxhound.

In appearance the English Hound is far stouter than his American cousin, and perhaps no better description of his general appearance can be given than to quote a passage from Mr. Cuthbert Bradley's *Reminiscences of Frank Gillard*, in which he describes Belvoir Gambler '85, one of the greatest Foxhounds that was ever bred. He says:

"Although Belvoir Gambler cannot be bred from rule of thumb, the proportions of this remarkable Foxhound are worth preserving as an example of what symmetry should be. Standing twenty-three inches at the shoulder, from the extreme point of his shapely shoulders to the outer curve of his well-turned quarters, he measured twenty-seven and a half inches in length whilst from elbow to ground his height was only twelve inches. Possessing great depth of rib and room round the heart, he girthed thirty-one inches, and his arm below was eight and a quarter inches round. Below the knee he measured eight and a quarter inches of solid bone, while round the thigh he spanned full nine and a quarter inches. The extended neck was ten inches from cranium to shoulder and the head ten inches and a half long. His color was of the richest, displaying all of the beautiful 'Belvoir tan,' and his head had that brainy appearance expressive of the highest intelligence. Gambler might have inspired that earnest poet, Cannon Kingsley, when he described the modern Foxhound, 'The result of nature not limited, but developed by high civilization. Next to an old Greek statue there are few such combinations of grace and strength as in a fine Foxhound.'"

Although the tendency today is to breed hounds a little bigger, the above description cannot be equaled.

Greyhound

Swift as a ray of light, graceful as a swallow, and wise as a Solomon, there is some basis for the prediction that the Greyhound is a breed that will never die. His fame, first written in the hot sands of Egypt, can be traced in the varying terrains of almost every country, on every continent on the globe. His was the type the ancients knew, and from time immemorial he has been a symbol of the aristocracy. Yet the Greyhound is a dog that needs no fanfare to herald his approach, no panoply to keep him in the public eye. His innate qualities give him admittance to any circles, high or low.

The first knowledge of the Greyhound comes from the Tomb of Amten, in the Valley of the Nile, regarded by Egyptologists as belonging to the fourth dynasty, which in modern chronology would be between 2900 and 2751 B.C. The carvings in this old tomb show dogs of unmistakable Greyhound type in three separate scenes. In two they are attacking a deer, while in the other an animal with horns, somewhat similar to the American mountain goat. The dogs have ring tails.

The origin of the name "Greyhound" is somewhat open to dispute, and a number of suppositions have been advanced. One is that it is derived from *Graius*, meaning Grecian, because the dog was in high esteem among the ancient Greeks. Another conjecture is that it derives from the old British *grech* or *greg*, meaning a dog. Also, some say that it came to use because gray was once the prevailing color in the breed.

While the old Egyptian scenes establish the Greyhound as a recognizable type at a very early date, it is from a Grecian source that there has come the first complete description of the breed. This was written by Ovid, who lived from 63 B.C. to 17 A.D. Reading this, one can have little doubt that the dog of ancient times is the same as the one of today. With certain allowances, it fits perfectly.

The Greyhound always has had a cultural and aristocratic background. He was the favorite of royalty in Egypt, and he was bred and raised in such luxurious surroundings that there was every reason for the oppressed races and the common prople of those times to hate this dog. Yet the disposition of the dog was just as lovable and tractable then as it is today. Had the common people been allowed to own specimens of this dog, the story would have been entirely different, but his ownership was restricted to the ruling classes.

The ancient traditions connected with the Greyhound have come down throughout history. He is found in England at a very early date. In fact, a manuscript from the ninth century A.D. is illustrated with a picture of Elfric, Duke of Mercia; and beside this old Saxon chieftain stands his huntsman with a brace of Greyhounds. Just how many centuries before the time of Elfric the Greyhound was known in England is not known, but there is every reason to suppose that the breed had been there a long time.

The famous Canute Laws, written in Danish—for at that time the Danes had conquered much of what is now England—and enacted in a Parliament held at Winchester in 1016, give further evidence as to the status of the Greyhound. No. 31 of these Canute Laws states:

"No meane person may keepe any greihounds, but freemen may keepe greihounds, so that their knees may be cut before the verderons of the forest, and without cutting of their knees also, if he does not abide 10 miles from the bounds of the forest. But if they doe come any nearer to the forest, they shall pay 12 pence for every mile; but if the greihound be found within the forest, the master or owner of the dog shall forfeit the dog and ten shillings to the King."

The Greyhound has been used on practically all kinds of small game from time to time, including deer, stags, foxes, and so forth, but the hare is his natural quarry, and coursing the sport with which he has been associated for centuries. In fact, coursing has been done on an organized basis in England for nearly two centuries.

The famous Waterloo Cup Meet was instituted in England in 1836, and it has been held continuously ever since—with the exception of the war years 1917 and 1918. On the other hand, two meetings were held in 1887, so actually the 1936 event was the one-hundredth. At the beginning this was an eight-dog stake, but in 1837 the number was double, and the next year it was double again to thirty-two dogs. In 1857 it became a sixty-four-dog stake, and it has remained that way ever since.

More than half a century before the Waterloo Cup event, there was organized one of the most colorful clubs in the sporting history of England. This was known as the Swaffham Coursing Society, and it came into being in 1776, organized by the Earl of Orford. It was limited to twenty-five members, using all but one letter of the alphabet, each member being assigned a letter and colors. Still, coursing did not assume uniformity until the Duke of Norfolk drew up a set of rules, some years later, that have been accepted as the standard procedure ever since.

In recent years the Greyhound has added another laurel to his crown. This is his use as a racing dog. This was brought about by the invention of a mechanical "rabbit" that could be used on circular or oval tracks. The first successful tracks were in England, but it is now a growing sport in the United States, where phenomenally fast times are being recorded continually.

Harrier

PROBABLY the oldest work on hare hunting is the famous essay penned by the ancient Greek historian Xenophon about 400 B.C., and with that as a basis, hare hunting has been a favorite subject of the greatest authorities on the dog for the past 2300 years. Regardless of that, there is a striking unanimity of doubt concerning the direct ancestors of this old breed of scent hound.

The Harrier, as he exists today, was unknown in Xenophon's time, although he describes two types of hound that were used with equal success in the early hunting of the hare. One he calls "the Castorean," which was reputed to be the favorite of the demi-god, Castor. The other is designated as "the fox-breed," which is explained as a product of the fox and the dog. On the other hand, Xenophon has listed the qualities of a hound suitable for the purposes, and they bear amazing similarity to the desirable points of modern times.

This early treatise on hunting is no fragmentary remnant of a scholarly mind, but one of the most definite and minute portrayals of a sport that ever has been written. Perhaps the only real difference between the way the Greeks hunted the hare and the manner accepted in England and other countries is that in 400 B.C. the hares were driven into nets. This practice would bring great censure on hunters of today. Still, sportsmanship was given some consideration in ancient times, for Xenophon says: "In tracking the hare, no delay should be made, for it is sportsmanlike, as well as a proof of fondness for exertion, to use every means to capture the animal speedily."

Even the great English authority on all breeds, Stonehenge, was a little mystified by the origin of the Harrier. The theory he advances rather cautiously is that it springs from the old Southern hound, with an infusion of a little Greyhound blood.

Undoubtedly the Southern hound has played a great part in the development of all scent hound breeds in the British Isles, yet there is little or no mention of the origin of this basic breed. The most logical supposition appears to be that it was brought to England by the Normans, for hunting is of great antiquity on the Continent.

The first pack of Harriers in England was the Penistone, which was established by Sir Elias de Midhope in 1260. These Harriers were held together for at least five centuries, and it is recorded that in the fourteenth, the seventeenth, and the eighteenth centuries, the masters were supplied by the Wilsons of Broomhead Hall. Hunting the hare has always had great popularity throughout the British Isles, and in some ways enjoyed greater favor than foxhunting. One great cause of its popularity was that a pack of Harriers could be followed on foot. This enlisted the interest of many, and among the hundred odd packs that hunted regularly in England half a century ago, many were scratch packs. A scratch pack was made up of hounds owned by various individuals —thus bringing the sport down to the level of the poorer man. However, horses are used in most cases today.

In support of the Norman origin of this and other hound breeds, there has been an interesting bit of information supplied by Wynn in regard to the name *harrier*. He shows that this may have come from the Norman word *harier*, denoting Saxon raches, or hounds. Further, *harier* was used down to 1750 for all hounds, not necessarily hare-hounds. And back in 1570, Dr. Caius mentioned stag- and fox-harriers.

Despite all stories of the ancient origin of Harriers, it is the general belief that the dog of today is merely a smaller edition of the Foxhound, and that he has been bred down from the larger hound by selective breeding. Save in size, the Harrier is the external replica of the Foxhound. Some specimens of the Harrier bear a unique, blue mottle color, which is not recognized in English Foxhounds, but in the majority of cases their colors are the same. It also is said that some Harriers are somewhat heavier in the head, in proportion, than is the Foxhound.

Harriers have been known in the United States as long as any of the scent-hound breeds, and they have been used for hunting since Colonial times. In later times, the Harrier proved a great favorite of the drag hunt, in which his slower pace is no detriment.

Irish Wolfhound

THE Irish Wolfhound as we know him today, a large rough-coated hound with piercing eyes, shaggy brows, and built on galloping lines, fits exactly into the picture of the feudal life of the Middle Ages. Yet, beneath this fierce-looking exterior there beats a gentle heart.

An ancient and romantic aura clothes the origin of the great hound from Ireland. Arrian, writing in the second century A.D., mentions the swift hounds brought to Greece during the invasion of the Celts, who sacked Delphi in 273 B.C. Evidence of this is borne out by some of the statues, jewelry, and paintings described, some of which have been recovered.

The breed was well known in Roman days. The first authentic record, however, was in 391 A.D., when the Roman Consul, Quintus Aurelius Symmachus, mentions them in a letter to his brother, Flavianus, in thanking him for the gift of seven Irish Wolfhounds which he had contributed for their circus combats and of which he said, "All Rome viewed them with wonder."

The early literature of Ireland abounds in references to these large dogs, and ancient laws show they were held in great esteem. They were the most valued hunting dogs of early centuries, renowned for their hunting prowess and their wisdom; they were much sought after by foreign monarchs as a fit and pleasing gift to royalty.

In the fourth century, Cormac, a King of Ireland, had a great kennel of hounds, and the master of hounds was the famous Finn. Early Celtic literature is richly endowed with the stories of Finn and his hounds.

In the tenth century, Olaf, a Norwegian, son of an Irish Princess, says to his friend Gunnar, as we find in the Saga of the Burnt Njal: "I will give thee a hound that was given to me in Ireland; he is big, and no worse than a stout man. Besides, it is part of his nature that he has a man's wit, and he will bay at every man whom he knows to be thy foe, but never at thy friends. He can see, too, in any man's face whether he means thee well or ill, and he will lay down his life to be true to thee. This hound's name is 'Sam.' " After that he spoke to the hound: "Now shalt thou follow Gunnar, and do him all the service thou canst." The hound went at once to Gunnar, and laid down at his feet. Later, history relates, when Gunnar's enemies plotted to kill him, they killed the Irish hound first.

A curious old manuscript of the twelfth century mentions a certain Mesrodia, King of Leinsternien, who had a Wolfhound named Aibe. For him six thousand cows and other things were offered by the King of Connacht. At the same time the King of Ulster offered approximately the same sum. Feeling ran so high over the dog that the kings and their retainers betook themselves to their swords and a mighty battle ensued. History does not relate who won the dog.

In 1596 the great Spanish poet, Lope de Vega, wrote a sonnet on the Irish Wolfhound, while in 1790, Bewick said: "The Irish Greyhound is the largest of the dog kind, and its appearance the most beautiful. He is about three feet high, somewhat like a Greyhound, but more robust. His aspect is mild, his disposition peaceable, his strength so great that in combat the Mastiff or Bulldog is far from being equal to him. He mostly seizes his antagonist by the back and shakes him to death, which his great strength enables him to do."

These powerful dogs were used not only in hunting the Irish wolf, but also the gigantic Irish elk, which stood six feet at the shoulder. They are referred to as "Irish dogs," "big dogs of Ireland," "Greyhounds of Ireland," "wolfdogs of Ireland," the "great hounds of Ireland," and the more modern appellative, "the Irish Wolfhounds."

But with the disappearance of wolves and elk, with the steady depletion caused from excessive exportation from now dwindling ranks, the breed was allowed to become almost extinct. It was left to Captain G. A. Graham, of Dursley, Scotchman and officer in the British army, to collect some of the remaining specimens, and by judicious outcrosses to rehabilitate the breed. Captain Graham deserves unlimited credit for his work, which was begun in 1862. He worked for twenty years before his ideal was attained, and a Standard was drafted under his supervision in 1885. Its continued existence until 1950 was justified, inasmuch as it was drawn up after an exhaustive study of old prints and historical references and the findings carefully sifted—and all this by gentlemen who had at some time been on intimate terms with some of the "last remaining specimens" and were fully qualified to do the work. This standard describes the ancient hound, and the present-day effort is to breed it in fullest perfection. The "List of Points in Order of Merit" was added some time after the Standard was written. There is a note at the end which calls attention to the fact that the list in no way alters the Standard, and if in any case it appears at variance, it is the Standard which is correct. So, wisely, the Standard is preserved and affirmed in its true form and by this precedent is protected from modern imaginations.

The sporting afflatus of the Irish Wolfhound cannot be questioned. On the Continent he is used successfully in various hunts: for wild boar, the larger animals, and even in lion hunts in the Kenya Colony, favorable reports have been received. In America he is frequently used in running and killing coyotes, or brush wolves, but he is at his best when tried on the big timber wolf. When in good hard condition, he is capable of overtaking a wolf and dispatching him singly.

But he is rarely used now for this work, since the better specimen quite consistently finds his way into the private home, where he deports himself with credit, being quiet-mannered and dignified. And he must always be a sporting hound if he is bred to meet the requirements of the Standard. Though his usefulness in the field is not so broad as it once was, it is sufficient the world over to make a decent present-day field record.

Norwegian Elkhound

COMRADE to the vikings, guardian of lonely farms and *saeters*, herder of flocks and defender from wolves and bear, a hunter always and a roamer with hardy men, the Norwegian Elkhound comes down to us through more than six millennia with all his Nordic traits untainted, a fearless dog and friendly, devoted to man and the chase. We read of him in sagas, we find his remains by the side of his viking-master along with the viking's weapons—sure proof of the esteem in which he was held; and in the Viste Cave at Jaeren, in western Norway, his skeleton was uncovered among the stone implements in a stratum dating from 4000 to 5000 B.C.

Selected and bred for his ability to accomplish a definite purpose, the Elkhound achieved his distinctive type by natural methods. No form was imposed upon him; he was not squeezed into a preconceived standard; his structure and rare beauty, like those of the thoroughbred horse, were evolved from the tests of performance. Every physical characteristic is the expression of a need. His compactness, his muscled robustness, his squareness, his width and depth are true expressions of nature's requirements for a dog that would hunt day after day and all day long in rugged country, where stamina rather than extreme speed is called for.

For, though the Elkhound in foreign countries has become known and loved chiefly, perhaps, for his engaging and sensitive qualities as a comrade of man, his reliability and quickness to learn and adapt himself to any circumstances and conditions, it should never be forgotten that, from first to last, he has been at all times the peerless hunter of big game.

Many years ago, bear were still common in Norway, but today they are almost extinct, and the native dog's main use is the hunting of elk. (*Elk* is incorrectly used in the United States for the Wapiti, *Cervus Canadensis*, and our *moose* is a true elk.) A century ago, Captain Lloyd, an English sportsman, a mighty hunter, and a fascinating writer, devoted his leisure to the description of bear hunting in Norway; and from that time on, everyone that has seen the Elkhound work in the forests of his native land has added to his praise. Space forbids adequate treatment of the subject here; but those who wish to pursue the matter further and who cannot obtain a copy of Captain Lloyd's books, now long out of print, will find an excellent substitute in Frantz Rosenberg's *Big Game Shooting*, published in England in 1928.

The Elkhound's highly developed senses amount almost to intuition, and it is common to read or, if one is fortunate, experience, such incidents as seeing a seasoned dog take body scent at from two to three miles or to hear him indicating to his master by a slight whimpering that the elk has become alarmed and has begun to run, at a time when no human senses can apprehend any sign by which the hound ascertains this fact. Equally subtle is his method of engaging a bull. Knowing well that an elk can outfoot him, he holds the animal by just enough barking to attract his attention. Even with a skillful dog, however, the elk often moves on before the hunter can get up over the steep countryside; and in that case, the dog, aware that the bull, if not excited by sound or scent, will soon pause, works silently and very carefully up wind until he is once more with his quarry.

After a while, the bull, becoming angry at the small beast annoying him, begins to attack with a wide sweeping movement of the great antlers and by striking with his deadly forefeet; but now, the Elkhound, short-backed so that he can, to use Herr Aarflot's apt expression, bounce like a rubber ball, jumps nimbly in and out, while giving full and furious tongue so that his high-pitched voice will reach his master.

The Elkhound is well adapted to the hunting of any other four-footed game and soon becomes expert on lynx, mountain lion, and raccoon; and Sir Henry Pottinger declares that he is also an excellent tracker of fox. The same authority states: "There is no more deadly way of approaching capercailzie, black game, and other forest birds than with a dog of the breed under discussion held or fastened to the belt by a long leash and allowed to precede the hunter."

The Elkhound, then, is an exceedingly versatile dog developed through constant contact with man in pursuit of game. It was not until 1877 that he began to be considered from an exhibition point of view. In that year the Norwegian Hunters' Association held its first show, and shortly thereafter pedigrees, which had been handed down, were checked and traced as far back as feasible, a stud book (*Norsk Hundestambok*) was published, and a standard drawn up. Before that time, there had been some confusion of type owing to different developments in different parts of the country; but if we study the photograph of such a grand dog as that pillar of the stud book, known to fame as Gamle Bamse Gram (Old Bamse that belonged to Consul Gram), we shall see that all the essential elements of the modern show dog were already there, needing only a little refinement, a little emphasis.

At any rate, by the turn of the century, the breed was making very rapid progress, and, though there were few or no really large kennels, there were many expert breeders devoted to the Elkhound's improvement; and when the Norwegian Kennel Club (Norsk Kennelklub) inaugurated its annual shows at Oslo, the Elkhound came into his own as Norway's great contribution to dogdom. Since then he has been exported in ever-increasing numbers; and his friendly disposition, his intelligence, his staunchness, his absolute dependability and trustworthiness, his eagerness to praise, his sensitivity and his fearless confidence have gained for him everywhere a popularity based even more on his comradely character than on his unsurpassed abilities as a sporting hound.

Otter Hound

WHILE there are allusions to otter hunting and Otter Hounds in the time of King John, who reigned in England from 1199 to 1216, it is not until Edward II (1307–1327) that there is any sort of a description of the kind of dogs that made up a pack of Otter Hounds. This record has been left, fortunately, by William Twici, the huntsman. He makes mention of them as a "rough sort of dog, between a hound and a terrier."

The hunting of the otter never was a so-called major sport in England, but it appears to have existed from very early times. It first was practiced because the otters were preying on the fish in the rivers and streams to an annoying extent. Later it enjoyed a considerable vogue because it was the only kind of hunting possible from April to September.

The undoubted heyday of the Otter Hound in England extended from the middle to the end of the nineteenth century. During many of those years there were eighteen to twenty packs hunting regularly through the season. Most famous, for its record of killing otters, was the Hawkstone pack of the Hon. Geoffrey Hill. From 1870 to 1890 this pack disposed of 704 otters, in 1881, alone, killing sixty-two.

Still, all authorities agree that the best trained pack of Otter Hounds ever hunted in England was that of Squire Lomax of Clitheroe. This was at the peak of its perfection about 1868. The Squire was a stickler for the fine points of the game, and, while results interested him, his major concern was the manner in which his pack worked. It is said that they were trained so well that his signals could be given with the most casual wave of the hand. But then, Squire Lomax had spent the greater part of his life developing this pack; and when the majority of them died in one season, he did not attempt to replace them, believing that enough years did not remain for him to train a new pack as well as the first.

The origin of the Otter Hound is shrouded in mystery, but the earliest writers advance a number of logical opinions as to its origin. According to Stonehenge, its ancestors are the Southern hound and the Welsh Harrier. This is supported by the fact that there were large numbers of Otter Hounds to be found in Devonshire, the chief stronghold of the Southern hound, and in Wales.

A somewhat less acceptable opinion is that of E. Buckley, who ascribes the coat of the Otter Hound to the Water Spaniel—a somewhat different type from the breed known today—and credits the hardiness to the Bulldog. Other writers mention the Bloodhound, supporting this by the domed shape of the skull, and the length of the ears. In fact, writing as early as 1575, Turberville makes no distinction between the Bloodhound and the Otter Hound in describing the hunting of the otter.

The French origin of the Otter Hound appears to be one of the most reasonable. This is the opinion of Marples, who, describing the Otter Hound, says it is the almost exact duplicate of the old Vendee hound of France. The two breeds are alike in both coat and bodily formation.

The Otter Hound is a big dog, standing twenty-four and twenty-six inches, and weighing up to sixty-five pounds. He has a hard, crisp and close coat of an oily nature that can stand any amount of immersion in water. The most desired combination of colors always has been the blue and white, but the breed ranges through many shades to black and tan. It is a peer among swimmers, its progress through the water being aided greatly by its webbed feet.

The working qualities of the Otter Hound always have been emphasized to such an extent that it never has been popularly known as a bench-show specimen in England. Still, it usually was the custom for some of the great packs to send a few couple apiece to the major shows. The Carlisle and Kendal packs were noted for their show dogs.

Otter Hounds first made their appearance in the United States about the year 1900, and they made their bench-show debut in 1907 at shows in Claremont, Okla., and registrations are recorded. These are of Hartland Mosstrooper, 135,335, and Hartland Statesman, 135,334, both owned by H. S. Wardner of New York City. Incidentally, Mr. Wardner was one of the two exhibitors of 1907, and he undoubtedly was America's first breeder.

While the Otter Hound never has grown to wide popularity in the United States, its sagacity and character have retained for it many steadfast friends. What it lacks in smartness of appearance is compensated by its working qualities and its unfailing devotion to its master.

Rhodesian Ridgeback

THE Rhodesian Ridgeback, sometimes referred to as the African Lion Hound, is a native of South Africa having been bred by the Boer farmers to fill their specific need for a serviceable hunting dog in the wilds.

The Dutch, Germans, and Huguenots who emigrated to South Africa in the sixteenth and seventeenth centuries brought with them Danes, Mastiffs, Greyhounds, Bloodhounds, Terriers, and other breeds. For one hundred years from 1707, European immigration was closed, and the native dogs played an important part in the development and ultimate character of the Ridgeback.

The Hottentots, a native race living within range of these early settlers, had a hunting dog that was half wild with a ridge on his back formed by the hair growing forward. There was interbreeding between these dogs and those of the settlers, and this crossbreeding, in due course, established the foundation stock of our present-day Ridgeback.

Good hunting dogs were hard to come by in those days and their value was high. The Boer settler needed a dog that could flush a few partridge, pull down a wounded buck, guard the farm from marauding animals and prowlers at night. He also needed a dog that could withstand the rigors of the African Bush, hold up under the drastic changes in temperature from the heat of the day to nights below freezing, and go a full twenty-four hours or more without water. He required a short-haired dog that would not be eaten by ticks. In addition, he needed a companion that would stay by him while he slept in the Bush and that would be devoted to his wife and children. These were the qualities that the early settlers needed in a dog. Of necessity, then, the Boer farmer developed, by selective breeding, a distinct breed of the African Veldt —the Ridgeback.

In 1877, the Reverend Helm introduced two Ridgebacks into Rhodesia where the big game hunters, Selons, Upcher, Van Rooyen, and others, found them outstanding in the sport of hunting lions on horseback. They raised and bred these dogs with an appreciation of their exceptional hunting qualities, the ridge on their back becoming a unique trademark. In 1922, a group of Rhodesian breeders set up a standard for Ridgebacks which has remained virtually unchanged ever since.

In 1950, the Rhodesian Ridgeback Club of America was founded following the importation of some outstanding specimens.

The Ridgeback, in a comparatively short space of time has won himself many admirers in the United States for his innate qualities. He is clean, an easy keeper and never noisy or quarrelsome. Because of his heritage, obedience training comes readily to him and his desire to please his master, coupled with his general good nature and liking for children, is making him new friends each year.

Saluki

THE Saluki, royal dog of Egypt, is perhaps the oldest known breed of domesticated dog, "a distinct breed and type as long ago as 329 B.C. when Alexander the Great invaded India." He is said to be as old as the earliest known civilization, the claim being based on the fact that the hounds shown on the earliest carvings look more like Salukis than any other breed: they have a Greyhound body with feathered ears, tail, and legs. Exactly the same hound appears on the Egyptian tombs of 2100

B.C. and more recent excavations of the still older Sumerian empire, estimated at 7000–6000 B.C., have produced carvings of striking resemblance to the Saluki.

"Whenever one sees the word 'dog' in the Bible it means the Saluki." As the Mohammedan religion classes the dog as unclean, the Moslem declared the Saluki sacred and called him "the noble one" given them by Allah for their amusement and benefit. This permitted them to eat of the meat brought down in the chase. The Saluki was the only dog of the time allowed to sleep on the carpet of the Sheikh's tent. So great was the esteem in which the dog was held that his body was often mummified like the bodies of the Pharaohs themselves. The remains of numerous specimens have thus been found in the ancient tombs of the Upper Nile region.

As the desert tribes are nomadic, the habitat of the Saluki comprised all the region stretching from the Caspian Sea to the Sahara, including Egypt, Arabia, Palestine, Syria, Mesopotamia, Anatholia, and Persia. Naturally the types varied somewhat in this widely scattered area. However, this difference was mostly in size and coat. Thus we find the Arabian-bred Saluki of a smaller type with less feathering on the legs and ears than the Persian variety.

Salukis were first brought into England in 1840: a bitch owned by Sir Hamilton Smith, a dog in Regents Park Zoological Gardens, and one owned by the Duke of Devonshire at Chatsworth. They were then known as Persian Greyhounds, since these three came from Persia. Evidently there was no real interest, however, in Salukis until the Hon. Florence Amherst imported the first Arabian Salukis in 1895, from the kennels of Prince Abdulla in Transjordania. It is greatly to her credit that the breed has made such headway among European countries.

England later learned more about the Saluki from her army officers stationed in the East during the Great War. Other specimens, either prizes of war or the gifts of friendly tribes, were brought home. Mr. Mervyn Herbert brought back several fine specimens from Egypt while Mr. Vereker-Cowley imported Malik-el-Zobair and Zobeida-el-Zobair. These, with Ch. Sarona Kelb and Sarona-Sarona, imported from Mesopotamia by Brigadier General Lance in 1920, figure prominently in the pedigrees of most of our present-day Salukis.

Having tremendous speed, the Saluki was used by the Arabs principally in bringing down the gazelle, that fastest of antelopes. It is recorded that the Pharaohs rode to the chase with their hawks on their wrists and Salukis on the lead. We also believe the Saluki was used on jackals, foxes, and hares. A cut published in 1852 shows a wild boar hunt in Algeria with Salukis tackling the boar. In England, the dog is used largely on hares, and regular coursing meets are held, with the judging based on ability to turn quickly and overtake the hare in the best possible time. The Saluki hunts largely by sight, although he has a fair nose. The sport of racing Salukis is much enjoyed in England and on the Continent, where a special track with a mechanical rabbit and hurdles at intervals is used.

The Saluki's sight is remarkable, and his hereditary traits often crop out—he loves to lie on the sand and watch an eagle soaring for his prey while paying no attention to the gull. Sarona Dhole, a son of Sarona Kalb, soon after his arrival in America, chased a fox and registered a kill within a few seconds after sighting the quarry.

On his native heath the Saluki gets no pampering. He lives hard, and it is a case of survival of the fittest—one reason for his strong constitution and sturdy frame, enabling him to stand any climate in unheated kennels. His feet are hard and firm, and the hair between the toes is a great protection. In all his running and dodging over the roughest kind of ground and rocky country he never damages pads or toes.

His beauty is that of the thoroughbred horse; grace and symmetry of form; clean-cut and graceful; short silky hair except on the ears, legs, and tail; slender, well-muscled neck, shoulders, and thighs; arched loins; long tail carried naturally in a curve with silky hair hanging from the underside; the arched toes; the rather long head with deep, far-seeing eyes—an expression of dignity mixed with gentleness.

In color, the Saluki can meet the demands of the most fastidious, for while cream and fawn seem to predominate, there is red, grizzle, and tan, white and chestnut, tricolor (black, white, and tan), as well as solid black. In disposition he shows great attachment to his master. He is affectionate without being demonstrative, a good watchdog but not aggressive.

The Saluki was a well-established breed in England for a number of years before he began to come into his own in this country. It was not until November, 1927, that the breed was officially recognized by The American Kennel Club. In July, 1927, the Saluki Club of America was formed, with only seven or eight fanciers among its members, and since that time interest has been steadily growing.

At the Westminster Show of 1927 there were two Salukis entered in the Miscellaneous Class. The following year regular classes were provided, and there were ten. In 1929 there was a further increase in entries, with much more interest shown by the public. Since the breed was officially recognized by The American Kennel Club, there have been regular classes at all the principal shows. So now, instead of being looked upon as something of a curiosity, the Saluki is a familiar sight in the dog world and is becoming more popular year by year.

Whippet

THE Whippet, an English Greyhound in miniature, is a sporting dog of the first flight as well as a very charming, affectionate, and intelligent pet. He is the fastest domesticated animal of his weight, capable of speeds up to thirty-five miles per hour. Though his main forte is as a racedog, he is a rabbit courser of great ability. His rat-killing feats, too, are nearly equal to those of the most hard-bitten terriers. As an animal of beauty, grace of outline, and smoothness of action, he stands near the top in the realm of dogdom.

He is extraordinarily keen when racing or on game, though in the living room he is quiet, dignified, unobtrusive, and above all, highly decorative. His intelligence, when treated as a member of the family, compares favorably with most terriers. He is never snappy or "barky," though as a watchdog he is excellent. Contrary to external appearances, he is by no means delicate and difficult to care for. All in all, he makes an ideal dual-purpose small dog for an owner of discrimination.

As a breed the Whippet is not one of our oldest, having been evolved in England between seventy-five and a hundred years ago, though it was not until 1891 that official recognition was given by the English Kennel Club.

It is said that when such barbaric pastimes as bull- and bearbaiting and dogfighting began to lose favor, the sporting gentry of that period originated the Whippet for the milder (to them) entertainment of coursing rabbits in an enclosure. The early specimens differed a great deal from our best present-day dogs. These were crosses of small English Greyhounds and various terriers, both smooth and rough-coated. It was not until a much later date that fanciers added an infusion of Italian Greyhound blood which aided so materially in improving type.

At first the breed was known as "snap-dog," and the so-called sport was termed "snap-dog coursing." This was because the dog that caught or snapped-up the greatest number of rabbits during a match was declared winner. It will be noted that this ignoble pastime, in which the rabbit had absolutely no chance of escape, differed greatly from legitimate coursing in the open with Greyhounds and was purely a gambling proposition. Later the Whippet was used primarily for straight racing. This sport had its inception, and still flouishes for that matter, in

Lancashire and Yorkshire. Here the colliers nicknamed the Whippet, "the poor man's race horse."

The standard course is 200 yards straightaway, and the method of racing unique. Each dog has two attendants—a slipper and a handler. All dogs are held on their handicap marks by their slippers while their handlers trot up the track and across the finish line, all the while yelling encouragement and frantically waving towels or rags (which the Whippets are trained from puppyhood to run to) to their charges. At the "get-set" command of the starter each slipper picks his dog up by the tail and the skin of the neck and when the pistol cracks the animals are literally thrown into their stride. They then race at top speed up the track and grab the waving rags of their handlers, who are some twenty yards behind the actual finish. Different-colored wool collars are worn to distinguish the entries.

As Whippets vary in weight, from ten to twenty-eight pounds, a rather elaborate system of handicapping was evolved. This is based upon the fact that the heavier the dog, everything else being equal, the faster he should be. Times as fast as eleven and one-half seconds have been recorded, but any dog that can do twelve flat from his handicap mark is considered excellent. Generally speaking, bitches are slightly faster and are usually handicapped accordingly.

Whippets appear first to have been brought to America by English mill operatives of Massachusetts. Lawrence and Lowell, for many years, were the center of Whippet racing in this country. Later, however, the sport moved South when Maryland, particularly in the neighborhood of Baltimore, held the spotlight. Many refinements have been made that have improved racing immensely. Electric starting boxes are used, steeplechases inaugurated, and the entire establishments patterned after the best of horse tracks. The very latest thing in Maryland was a circular track with an electric hare.

From the standpoint of the fancier, Whippets make an ideal exhibition dog. With their small size (around twenty pounds) and smooth coat they are neither difficult to transport nor keep in condition. Their quiet deportment in the ring makes them comparatively easy to show, as is attested by the winnings of numerous novices who handle their own entries.

GROUP III: WORKING DOGS

Alaskan Malamute

THE Alaskan Malamute, one of the oldest Arctic sled dogs, was named after the native Innuit tribe called Mahlemuts, who settled along the shores of Kotzebue Sound in the upper western part of Alaska. Long before Alaska became a possession of the United States, this Arctic region was called by the Russians, who were the discoverers, "Alashak" or "Alyeska," meaning "vast country." Native people were already living in Alyeska land when these Asiatic sailors visited the shores, having been forced by storms when whaling in Bering Strait to land in this North country opposite Siberia. Returned to their homeland, they told stories about seeing "native people using dogs to haul sledges."

The origin of these people and also of the dogs has never been ascertained. We do know that they had been in Alaska for generations; where they came from is as indefinite as it is with any of the other Arctic natives, either of Greenland in the east of North America or the Samoyed tribe of Russia. The same is true about the origin of all Arctic dogs.

The tribe of Mahlemuts, now spelled Malamutes, were called "high-type" Innuits. Many writers of Alaska, in translations from Russian explorers and records left by Englishmen who traveled the Alaskan coast, all give similar accounts about these fine Innuits. *Innuit* means "people" in the Orarian language. Never are the Mahlemuts mentioned without reference to their dogs. One writer, who went to Alaska in the early days of exploration after it had become a possession of the United States, gives interesting references about the Innuits and especially about the Mahlemuts. He uses the original spelling, so that we know the records were taken at an early date.

"Upon arriving at Unalakleet, I found that a party of Mahlemuts had arrived the day before by dog teams. They had carried mail from Point Barrow down along the coast wherever White Men were living. They had also been runners for the Russian Muscovy Whaling Company when they had landed in this Arctic region. These Mahlemuts were wonderful looking natives . . . taller than their Greenland cousins. They were industrious, skilled in hunting and fishing, made perfect sledges, and had dogs of . . . beauty and endurance. These dogs had traveled . . . hundreds of miles and being better cared for by their drivers than is the usual lot of Arctic dogs . . . [they] were affectionate and seemed tireless. . . ."

This description differs from tales told by people who have seen other native dogs in the Arctic, whose dispositions perhaps resulted from the environment in which they lived. The usual treatment of sledge dogs in the North has been harsh, owing to the uncivilized tribes who wandered from place to place until white men invaded their villages.

Another Alaskan traveler, a missionary who journeyed thousands of miles by dog team, writes:

"These Malamutes, now spelled *Malamute*, a corruption of the original word Mahlemut (Mahle meaning name of the Innuit tribe and Mut meaning Village in Orarian vocabulary of the Mahlemut dialect), are a high type people. They are peaceful, happy, hard workers, believe in one wife, are able guides and have wonderful dogs. Even though uncivilized, they have realized that it is important to have fine animals to pull sledges; that without them, means of travel in this sort of country would be impossible at times. The dogs are powerful looking, have thick dense double coats (outer coat of thick coarse fur and inner coat a fuzzy down lying close to skin) called weather coats, erect ears, magnificent bushy tails carried over their backs like waving plumes, tough feet, colors varying but mostly wolf grey or black and white. The dogs have remarkable endurance and fortitude. The Malamute people and their dogs are much respected among other Innuits."

A book entitled *Researches of Alaska* includes several references with these Malamute dogs being called the native dogs of Alaska. "Natives recognized in their crude way the importance of the dogs, as they were considered indispensable for transportation in the North."

Later another reference says: "Dogs were two and two, side by side (gang hitch), leader in front, harnessed to a sledge, colors varying from grey to black and white, and carrying a heavy load. The dogs were powerful looking . . . and did not appear vicious. The natives, called Malamutes, were not Indians but perhaps related to the Asiatic Arctic natives of the Chukchis. [This is a suggestion of their ancestry, but not confirmed.] The Mahlemut dialect is simple to understand and the natives themselves a happy tribe. They are fond of their children and their dogs. The dogs work hard and have wonderful endurance."

A Russian translation gives another reference about the "Mahlemuts found over the sea in the Vast Land" called the "stopping-off" place by the Russian sailors. This writer referred to the workmanship of the Mahlemuts and the sledges, and admitted the "Mahlemut dogs and sledges are better than those of the Russians for interior travel."

It is confirmed that these Alaskan Malamute sledge dogs were used as draught animals and they have never lost their identity. When Alaska became settled by white men, it is true that the Arctic breed was mingled with that of outside dogs, just as they have been in Greenland, Labrador, Siberia, or any of the other Arctic countries. During the Alaskan Sweepstakes, the lure of racing became so popular that many drivers tried all sorts of experiments in mixing the Arctic breed with some outside strain, and this period from 1909 to 1918 was the age of "decay of the Arctic sledge dog." Fortunately, the sport of sled-dog racing became popular in the United States, and interest in developing the pure strain of the native Alaskan Malamute started in 1926 after a careful study of all types of Northern breeds had been made. Malamutes still hold many racing records. During World War I, several Malamutes were among the dogs sent across by A. A. Allen, who assembled 150 dogs for this purpose, 100 coming from Alaska. These Malamutes also made remarkable records for hauling and were distinctive in their appearance. The two recent Byrd Antarctic Expeditions have used Malamutes as well as other Arctic breeds, and again the records have been outstanding.

Some Alaskans today call the Malamute the "personality dog," and several, now owned in the United States, are also called by this term rather than "wolf dogs." The question of the "wolf" ancestry in any of the Arctic breeds is mere supposition; for generations no "wolf blood" has been successfully introduced, even though some of the Alaskan breeders still maintain this is true. One modern dog fancier brings out an important point about the difference of Arctic purebred dogs and wolf dogs. "The Arctic breeds stand erect, have a 'proud appearance' and carry their tails up—while a wolf has a slinking movement and carries his tail down."

The Alaskan Malamute, although quite rare, is becoming more extensively bred in the United States from dogs originally from Alaska. The word *husky*, as sometimes applied to the Malamute, is a misnomer; it was originally a term of disrespect used by the Indians or Aleuts who invaded Alaska and were hostile to the Innuits, calling them "huskies."

This word has gradually been used in the North to describe working dogs of mixed breeds used to pull sledges. No pure breed of Arctic dog is called "husky" except the Siberian Husky. The Alaskan Malamute is the native Alaskan Arctic breed, cousin to the Samoyed of Russia, Siberian Husky (Kolyma River Region), and the Eskimo dogs of Greenland and Labrador.

Well-informed Arctic writers who have made a study of Arctic formations seem to disagree about the origin of the Arctic peoples. Some believe that during the Glacier Age there was land connecting Asia and Alaska, and also Greenland and Labrador. Perhaps our Alaskan natives and Labrador Eskimos came into these countries by dog power. Others claim immigration spread from the Hudson Bay country, east and west; others that Greenland was originated by Norwegians who went "native" and likewise, Alaska by Asiatic people. This happened many generations ago—all we know today is that Arctic breeds were found and that the Alaskan Arctic sledge dog native to that country is the breed now called the Malamute.

In the United States, Alaskan Malamutes are being shown on the bench. As pets they have become popular sled dogs among sportspeople who enjoy this winter recreation. They are very fond of people and especially children, who enjoy driving them to sleds.

Belgian Sheepdog

THE term *Chien de Berger* many years ago was loosely applied to any European dog used for herding sheep. Holland, France, and Belgium all had sheepdogs which varied in coat—there were longhaired, shorthaired, and rough-haired kinds. Anatomically their structure was identical. Some even said that if the dogs were shaved and but casually observed, one could not be distinguished from the other.

However much or little truth there is in this assertion, the fact remains that prior to the year 1891 the Belgian Sheepdog was the genuine shepherd's dog, fairly common throughout the greater part of Europe. It was a potpourri of all sizes, all hairs, all colors, all types. Some of the dogs were cropped. Certain of them had long tails, some naturally short tails, while others were docked. And they reproduced themselves with little if any consistency as regards general appearance and special attributes. Such results were inevitable, since the dogs were bred on a basis of herding aptitude without regard for coat, color, or conformation.

Also inevitable was the fact that gradually a semblance of type did develop, due to the isolation of locality and the way of life; then subsequently the emerging types were named for the districts to which they were native. Such nomenclature of course is not unique in any breed or country, for many of our present-day breed names are geographic.

The modern history of the Belgian Sheepdog begins at the close of the nineteenth century, its most vital development taking place between the years 1891 and 1898, or thereabouts. In 1891 one Professor Reul assembled a group of shepherd dogs for the purpose of studying the different types then existing in Belgium. Sheep raising at that time was in a decline. The dogs had been bred indiscriminately and fed as economically as possible; therefore they tended to be rather slight in frame and quite varied in type, coat, and color. There were, in fact, six varieties—the Belgians called them breeds. The Belgian Kennel Club never wished to recognize them all, but the Royal Society of St. Hubert did deem them deserving of championships.

In his survey Professor Reul noticed three kinds which did exhibit a certain similarity: a longhaired black, a shorthaired fawn and charcoal, and a shaggy-haired, dark ash-gray. He recommended breeding together only those of similar coat. A small group of devotees, who then formed the Belgian Kennel Club, did not immediately go along with Professor Reul's suggestion, and so for a short period fanciers continued to interbreed long-coated and shaggy, or tough-coated, fawns. However in 1897 the Belgian Kennel Club decided to admit only three kinds of coats: the black for long hair, the blackened fawn for short hair, and the ash-gray for tough hair. Since the edict ruled on color as well as coat length and texture, this was a notable step forward in keeping the varieties distinct.

Besides Professor Reul, there was another farsighted pioneer who deserves mention for the part he played in the development of the Belgian Sheepdog, namely, M. Rose of the village of Groenendael. Years before Professor Reul's survey, M. Rose had been breeding longhaired blacks with some success. In 1885 he had found in one of his litters a longhaired black bitch, which he named Petite, presumably a sport, to which he was so attracted that he determined to establish a strain. Blacks were rare in those days, but after a year's search he located Piccard D'Uccle, a black male of similar type which he purchased from its owner, M. Bernaert, for mating with his female. This pair produced a litter whose individual names are engraved on pedigrees of the past as pillars of the breed—Duc, Pitt, Baronne, Margot, and Bergere, all of Groenendael. Duc made his show debut in 1898; he was subsequently mated to several females, and the best of these were used to carry on the strain.

Thus the Groenendael, which took its name from the village of its birth and early development, was started on its way. Its beauty, symmetry and sturdy structure contributed to its growing popularity, which extended before many years to the United States.

The first Belgians came to America in 1907 when five specimens were imported. A few more crossed the sea in 1912 to make their home in Englewood, New Jersey, where they were used in police work. Two years later Mr. Auguste de Conti imported a pair which worked with the Brooklyn police force. Mr. H. Persson, of Staten Island, brought over two from the kennels of M. Madoux, a prominent breeder of Groenendaels.

The Belgian Sheepdog bred in the United States between World War I and World War II was almost exclusively the Groenendael, and this longhaired black dog became generally known as the Belgian Sheepdog in this country.

In 1948 some Malinois, or shorthaired fawn-and-black dogs, were imported from Belgium, but they were not very successful and few of their progeny survive. In 1954 and the years immediately following, a number of Tervuren, or longhaired fawn-and-black dogs, were imported, and these have gained some popularity here. All of these different types were registered and shown as Belgian Sheepdogs up to July 1, 1959, when the AKC established them as three separate breeds, dogs of the Groenendael type alone being registered and shown as Belgian Sheepdogs. The other types are registered as Belgian Malinois and Belgian Tervuren. Separate show classification is provided for the Belgian Tervuren, while the Belgian Malinois is shown in the Miscellaneous Class.

Black has proved to be a dominant characteristic in the breed, and although some few blacks carry the factor for fawn, no case is known in this country where two black parents have reproduced the fawn color. As for imported dogs, Groenendaels are eligible for registration in the United States only if they have at least three generations of pure Groenendael ancestors.

Fanciers are rich in praise of the Belgian Sheepdog's many good qualities, particularly those having to do with devoted companionship. Scientific breeders are equally enthusiastic concerning its intelligence and value as a worker. It has long been used overseas as a police dog; in fact, some authorities credit it as the first breed to be thoroughly trained for such exacting duties. During World War I, thousands were trained as messengers between outflung sectors where human messengers would have met certain death. Many of these dogs gave their lives.

Belgian Tervuren

THE Belgian Tervuren is one of the Belgian types of shepherd dog registered in Belgium and France as the *Chien de Berger Belge*. It is of common origin with the Groenendael and other types, but since 1959 has been registered here as a separate breed. The Tervuren resembles the Groenendael strikingly in conformation, but differs as strikingly in color.

The close relationship between the two breeds grows out of the fact that the earliest of Belgium's sheepdogs incorporated several different kinds or varieties. Some had long hair, some short hair, others tough or shaggy hair, while colors included black, ash-gray, and blackened fawn as well as other shades not so easily identifiable. All were bred together indiscriminately.

A century or more ago, when sheepherding abroad was an important part of rural life, the shepherd's dog was bred solely on a basis of proficiency in herding. The dog's appearance meant nothing to the herdsmen, whose livelihood depended upon the safety and well-being of their sheep. All that mattered was a strong and rugged body, together with superior herding ability. This, without a doubt, the Belgian herdsmen got, but at the same time, by interbreeding, they played havoc with the inheritable factors involved in coat length, color, and texture.

The advent of dog shows in the 1880s coincided with a decline in sheepherding. The wolf menace was on the way out; fences and corrals were coming into greater use, and growing rail facilities helped to obviate the need for quite so much protracted trailing to the markets. Dog shows, however primitive they may have been then as compared with now, tended to direct attention to the dog as an attractive animal in its own right, rather than a mere shepherd's assistant.

From the start of selective breeding, which may be said to have begun with the institution of dog shows, gradually more or less definite types began to emerge from the previous hodgepodge of coat and color.

This volume's history of the Belgian Sheepdog breed explains the evolution of the Groenendael, which began about 1885. The evolution of the Tervuren began in much the same manner, and from identical stock on the sire's side, but exactly when is not clear.

One M. F. Corbeel, of the town of Tervuren, owned Tom and Poes, a pair of sheepdogs with long, black-tipped fawn hair. From this mating

came Miss, a female which fortunately came into the possession of
M. Danhieux, a breeder as astute as M. Rose, which in its way is high
praise. M. Danhieux proceeded to mate Miss with the longhaired black,
Piccard D'Uccle, the very same dog that was progenitor of the Groenendaels. This union produced the justly famed Milsart, a blackened
fawn dog acknowledged to be the best Tervuren whelped in the era before 1900. In 1907 Milsart became the first Tervuren champion.

In the aforementioned discussion of the Groenendael, black was
cited as dominant. In view of Milsart's ancestry, this statement would
cause confusion in the minds of those conversant with Mendelian inheritance unless it were explained further that the longhaired black, Piccard D'Uccle, harbored the fawn factor in his make-up.

Owing to the similarity of the Tervuren with the Groenendael, it is
obvious that the major difference between the two, that of color, should
assume importance. In texture, the hair of the Tervuren is medium harsh,
neither silky nor wiry. In color, it is a rather light fawn at first, but by
the age of eighteen months it takes on a depth and richness approximating warm mahogany overlaid with black. Actually only the tips of the
fawn hairs are black. The blackening extends over the dog like a veil,
much as if it had been stroked with a hand covered with charcoal or
soot. The black is especially pronounced on shoulders and back, face,
ears, and tail tip. The chief consideration is that the coat have sufficient
black, but not too much, since the ground color is a deep, rich fawn.

As regards the breeding potentialities of the Tervuren, the factor for
fawn is a recessive, so despite ancestry two fawns bred together cannot
produce a black. This is the reason the customary three-generation proof
of pure Tervuren ancestry is not required for registration of acceptable
imports.

The first Tervurens apparently came to the United States early in
the 1940s, brought over by Europeans of unknown nationality. One of
the unregistered progeny of the pair was Wolf, a blackened fawn owned
by the William McGees of Toledo. Wolf lived a long and useful life of
fifteen years. Rudy Robinson imported the first registered Tervuren in
1954. Strangely, although the Tervuren orginated in Belgium, almost all
of our imports have come from France.

The breed has not been slow to make its presence felt here; in fact it
has proved especially adept at obedience work. The first American-bred
litter of Tervurens, whelped in 1954, has for its sire and dam two CD
titleholders—Cheri du Clos St. Jacques and Crigga du Clos St. Jacques
—both of which won their degrees before they were a year old. A few
years later, Nightwatch Russet Cavalier earned his tracking degree in
Canada at approximately the same age. D'Jimmy du Clos St. Clair,

owned by Betty C. Hinckley of Chicago, in 1958 became the first champion of the breed in this country.

Previously the Belgian Tervuren was registered and shown as one of the types of Belgian Sheepdog. In 1959, however, it was granted registration as a separate breed with separate classification at the shows.

Bernese Mountain Dog

ARISTOCRATIC in appearance, ancient in lineage, the Bernese Mountain Dog, one of the four varieties of Swiss Mountain dogs, is a worthy addition to The American Kennel Club stud book. Longhaired and distinctive in coloring, these dogs have never been used to herd sheep like the other varieties, but instead were used as draught dogs by the weavers of the Canton of Berne, where it was once a common sight to see them drawing small wagons loaded with baskets to the marketplace.

The dogs were brought into Switzerland over two thousand years ago by the invading Roman soldiers. But until a few years before World War I, they had been almost forgotten by all save the oldest inhabitants of Berne. They were still used by the weavers, but the breed had degenerated to such an extent as to be practically unrecognizable, and when in 1892, a Swiss fancier attempted to find good specimens to be used as breeding stock, his search was a long one. However, he was successful, and several other fanciers became interested as well. A few good examples were unearthed and the rehabilitation was started. In 1907, a specialty club was formed and the breed found favor with many wealthy Swiss, who have developed them as house pets and companions, their old life in harness being a thing of the past.

The popularity of the Bernese Mountain Dog has increased so greatly that they are now to be found all over Switzerland and entries at dog shows are numerous.

A handsome, longhaired dog about the size of a Collie and not unlike him in appearance, the Bernese is jet black in color, with russet brown or rich tan markings on his forelegs, spots over each eye, on either side of the snowy white chest markings, and just above the forelegs. It is highly desirable that the dogs have white feet, white tail-tip, and a pure white blaze, as well as white star-shaped markings on the chest. However, it is not disqualifying if these white marks are missing. The coat is long and silky with a slight wave, but it must not be curly. An impressive looking dog, twenty-three to twenty-seven and one half inches in height for dogs, with bitches slightly smaller, the Bernese is characterized by fiery eyes of dark hazel, V-shaped ears hanging close to the head in repose, but brought slightly forward and raised at the base when alert. His short-backed, compact, and well-ribbed-up body with broad chest, deep brisket, and strong muscular loins show that he is well suited to draught work.

The Bernese is an extremely hardy dog, thriving in an unheated kennel in all weather and needing only a small amount of grooming to look well kept. He is exceptionally faithful, and once having centered his affection on an individual, he does not fawn upon or make friends with strangers.

A few of these Swiss dogs have been imported into the United States and they and their progeny are expected to be a feature of the bench shows of the future.

Bouvier des Flandres

DR. KEUL, of the Veterinary School of Brussels, was the first to call the attention of breeders to the many good qualities of the Bouvier. At that time, the Bouvier was a dog of great size (about twenty-six inches high at the shoulder), with a heavy cylindrical body, rough gray, dark hair, and a rough appearance. It was found in Southwest Flanders and on the French northern hills. As a rule, it was owned by people who occupied themselves with cattle, for the dog's chief aptitude seemed to be cattle-driving.

Most of the early Bouvier breeders were farmers, butchers, or cattle merchants not particularly interested in breeding pure pedigreed dogs. All they wanted was to have help in their work, so one will not be surprised that the first Bouviers were not absolutely uniform in size, weight, and color. Nevertheless, they all had enough characteristics in common to be recognized as Bouviers. They had different names—*Vuilbaard* (dirty beard), *koe hond* (cow dog), *toucheur de boeuf* or *pic* (cattle driver).

The Societe Royale St. Hubert took cognizance of the breed when it appeared on the show benches at the International dog show of May, 1910, in Brussels. The two Bouviers shown there were Nelly and Even, belonging to a Mr. Poiret of Ghent. However, a Standard of the Bouvier type was not adopted until 1912. That was accomplished by a Frenchman, Mr. Fontaine, vice-president of the Club St. Hubert du Nord. At that time a society of Bouvier breeders, founded in Roulers

(West) Flanders, invited many of the most famous Belgian experts to a meeting in August of that year. Among those who attended were M. de Hautvert of Levita, Baron van Zeiglen of Weymons, M. Van Herreweghe, veterinarian of Scharlaken, and others who promulgated a standard of perfection which became the first official standard to be recognized by the Societe Royale St. Hubert.

From then on, the Bouvier des Flandres grew to be more and more appreciated, and several dogs, such as Ch. Nella, Ch. Picard, Ch. Zola of Mr. Re Rycker (Roulers), Pickzwaurt of Mr. Van Herreweghe, Jim and Maerten de lu Wornaffe Domicent, Anna de l'Yperlei and Amic of Mr. Lapierre (Ypres), were enlisted in the L.O.S.H. (the stud book of the Societe Royale St. Hubert).

The breed was making rapid progress when World War I broke out. Those parts of the country where the Bouvier was most largely bred, and where it was becoming popular, were entirely destroyed; the people left the country, and most of the dogs were lost. Many were abandoned and died, others were acquired by the Germans. Nevertheless, a few men succeeded in keeping their dogs all through the war, so Sultan of Mr. Van der Vennet, Picko Carlo of Mr. Perret, Bella and Kit de Ramillies escaped. The dog whose progeny afterwards did much to revive the Bouvier in Belgium lived in the Belgian Army as the property of Veterinarian Captain Darby. This dog, Ch. Nic de Sottegem, was shown in 1920 at the Olympic show in Antwerp, where the judge, M. Charles Hugo said: "Nic is the ideal type of Bouvier. He has a short body, with well developed ribs, short flanks, strong legs, good feet, long and oblique shoulders. His head is of a good shape, with somber eyes and an ideal courageous expression. His hair is dry and dark. The tail should not have been cut so short. I hope that dog will have numerous progeny."

Mr. Hugo's wishes were realized, and when Nic died in 1926, he left many descendants whose names appear in almost every pedigree. Among those worthy of mention are Prince D'or, Ch. Droya, Corshe de Sottegem, Goliath de le Lyt, Lyda Nefte de la Paix, Norah, Siske de Sottegem, Ch. Dragon de la Lys, etc. From these dogs, gathered together one day at Ghent, a group of experts, including Mr. Charles Hugo Vbenret, V. Raymons, Count de Hemptenne, Captain Renon a Gevaert, after examining and measuring each one carefully, established a more comprehensive standard.

Since then Bouviers have attained even greater success abroad, especially in Holland and Belgium. The average number at the shows was thirty, which is relatively large, but so popular did Bouviers become that often this number was exceeded.

Breeders do not forget that the Bouvier is first of all a working dog, and although they try to standardize its type, they do not want it to lose the early qualities which first called attention to its desirability. For that reason, in Belgium a Bouvier cannot win the title of champion unless he has also won a prize in a work-competition as a police, defense, or army dog.

Boxer

ALTHOUGH it has reached its greatest perfection in Germany during the past hundred years, the Boxer springs from a line of dogs known throughout the whole of Europe since the sixteenth century. Prior to that time, ancestors of the breed would hardly be recognized as Boxers could they be placed beside modern specimens. Still, evidence points to the Boxer as one of the many descendants of the old fighting dog of the high valleys of Tibet.

The Boxer is cousin to practically all recognized breeds of the Bulldog type, and these all go back to basic Molossus blood. Few other strains can claim such courage and stamina; and from this line emanates the attractive fawn color that has recurred throughout the centuries.

Flemish tapestries of the sixteenth and seventeenth centuries show scenes of stag and boar hunting; the dogs are the same as the Spanish Alano, found in great numbers in Andalusia and Estramadura, and the Matin de Terceira or Perro do Presa, from the Azores. The Alano and the Matin have been regarded as the same breed—they are either ancestors of the Boxer or they trace back to a common ancestor.

In France, there is a breed known as the Dogue de Bordeaux that is very close, both in appearance and size to the old Tibetan Mastiff, and it is from this massive dog that the Bouldogue du Mida was developed. The Bouldogue du Mida, found principally in the South of France, possesses many of the points of the Boxer.

While all the European breeds mentioned are related to the Boxer, this favorite of Germany has been developed along scientific lines that not only have succeeded in retaining all his old qualitites, but have resulted in a much more attractive appearance. Besides Bulldog blood, the Boxer carries a certain heritage from a terrier strain. There is also some reason to believe that English Bulldogs were at one time imported into Germany. Indeed, Reinagle's noted Bulldog, done in 1803, is not unlike the Boxer, and pictures of some English specimens of 1850 are almost identical with the German dog.

Until dogfighting and bullbaiting were outlawed by most civilized peoples in the middle of the nineteenth century, the Boxer, like all dogs of his type, was used for this purpose. Today he has become an accredited member of society, but he still has the same degree of courage and the ability to defend, as well as aggressiveness when needed. Withal, he is devoted to his master.

The quality of the Boxer is best emphasized, perhaps, when we remember that he was one of the first selected in Germany for police training. This work demands intelligence, fearlessness, agility, and strength.

Considering that the entire modern history of the Boxer is wrapped up with Germany, it seems rather curious that he bears a name obviously English. Yet the name fits him. It arises from his manner of fighting, for invariably he begins a fight with his front paws, somewhat like a man boxing.

The Boxer has been bred and exhibited, sporadically, in the United States since the early days of the present century, but it was not until recent years that the public began to take an interest in the breed. This came about because of the consistent winning of certain outstanding specimens in variety groups.

The first Boxer was registered in 1904; the first championship by a specimen of the breed was finished in 1915. More and more successful breeders are sponsoring the Boxer, and the club is spreading knowledge of his many sterling qualities.

Briard

THE Briard, or Chien Berger de Brie, is descended from a very old race of French dog. Mentioned in records as far back as the twelfth century in France, the breed is accurately described in the fourteenth and sixteenth centuries. In the tapestries and monuments of those times there are dogs closely corresponding in size and appearance to the Briard of today. They were used especially to defend their charges against wolves and robbers, but the dividing up of the land and the increase of the population that followed the French Revolution gradually transformed their work into the more peaceful task of herding, of guiding the flocks, and keeping them from the unfenced fields of the French countryside, and of guarding farm property.

In an article written in 1809 these dogs are definitely referred to as Sheepdogs of Brie (Berger de Brie) and they were entered in dog shows in the latter part of that century. Briards do not come necessarily from the Province of Brie, for they are found all over France and are at present the pre-eminent sheep dog of that country. Everywhere, in the north or the south, they guard the small farms, herd sheep and cattle, and care for property and animals. The society called Les Amis du Briard, formed in France about the year 1900, established a definite standard for size and form, and this, with slight modifications, still prevails and was adopted by the Briard Club of America.

In build the Briard is square, though a little extra length of back may be allowed to bitches. The bushy eyebrows, which are useful in protecting the eyes when the dog is working in rough brushy country, should not be so heavy as to interfere with vision. The tail, which is well feathered and has a small curl at the end called the *crochet*, is carried down under ordinary circumstances and raised to the level of the back only in moments of excitement or very active movement. The coat—hard, wavy, and of moderate length, a real "goat's coat"—sheds water successfully, while caked mud will drop off as it dries. In France the ears are cropped enough to make them stand semierect. This is characteristic of the earliest pictures and standards of the breed, but it lengthens and narrows the look of the head, hence the imported cropped-eared dogs have a different appearance from those bred in this country whose ears are not cropped.

The range of color is wide. In France the dogs are shown in two classes, black and colored, the latter class including tawny and gray with or without black shading on ears and tail. The rules against any white (except a small spot on the chest) and against a lack of dewclaws are strictly enforced, as these defects are considered to signify cross-breeding or degeneracy. The action of the Briard is light and supple—he takes naturally a short trot or the regular amble of a sheep dog circling his flock. He turns readily and quickly and can show great speed if necessary.

Briards learn slowly, but they have a retentive memory. Though they have been used primarily as sheep dogs and guard dogs they have splendid records as police and war dogs. They served as watchers at advance posts, where their acute hearing was invaluable. They accompanied patrols and carried food and supplies and even munitions to the front line. So many died in the service that the race was greatly reduced in numbers and in quality. Briards are used for dragging carts, too, but this is not their natural occupation; their eagerness tempts them to overwork and strain themselves.

Briards are not difficult to raise. The bitches usually have litters of from eight to ten and are careful, sensible mothers. As tawny and gray are racial colors, a litter of pups is likely to be varied even though both parents are black. Characteristically the Briard does not wander, seldom barks unless it is necessary to give warning, and is essentially well mannered.

Bullmastiff

THE known history of Bullmastiff begins about the year 1860 in England. It is probable that the story of the breed is really centuries old, but proof is difficult.

In the latter part of the nineteenth century in England, the problem of keeping large estates and game preserves free from the depredations of poachers was an acute one. Penalties were severe, yet poaching seemed impossible to eradicate by mere laws. Accordingly, the gamekeeper's life was anything but safe. Poachers would often prefer to shoot it out with the keeper on the chance of escape rather than accept the penalties which they would incur upon apprehension.

It is not surprising, therefore, that the gamekeepers decided to enlist the aid of the greatest protector nature has given to man—the dog. These men cared nothing for the looks of a dog as long as he served them well. Numerous breeds were therefore tried. The Mastiff, while courageous and powerful, was not fast enough and not sufficiently aggressive. The Bulldog, big, strong and active in those days, was a trifle too ferocious and not large enough for their needs. These men wanted dogs that would remain silent at the approach of poachers. They needed fearless dogs that would attack on command. They wanted the poachers thrown and held, but not mauled. For these needs, they crossed Mastiff and Bulldog, and the dog they wanted was produced.

From this utilitarian birth, the breed was founded. Inevitably, came the rivalry between keepers as to the quality of their dogs. Inevitably, also, came the breeding to and from outstanding performers of their time—a true survival of the fittest. For many years, then, after the birth of the breed, its history was wholly a utilitarian one. The only contests in which Bullmastiffs engaged were against man, either on the moor or in demonstrations, when they were muzzled and the man was allowed a club, restricted in size to certain weights and measurements. In these contests no man was ever able to hold his feet against a dog of proven worth. In those days the Bullmastiff was known sometimes by his present name, but more usually as the "Gamekeeper's Night-Dog."

During the breed's early years, we find interesting references by contemporary writers. One appears in General William Hutchinson's book *Dog Breaking*, published in London in 1885:

"Bulldogs have good noses. I have known of the cross between them and the Mastiff being taught to follow the scent of a man almost as truly as a Bloodhound."

In 1900, the Westminster *Gazette* reports that Major Crowe of the War Office visited an exhibition of these dogs with a view to reporting on their possible usefulness as an aid to sentries. In *The Field*, August 20, 1901, we find the following:

"Mr. Burton of Thorneywood Kennels brought to the show one Night-Dog (not for competition) and offered any person one pound, who could escape from it while securely muzzled. One of the spectators who had had experience with dogs volunteered and amused a large assembly of sportsmen and keepers who had gathered there. The man was given a long start and the muzzled dog slipped after him. The animal caught him immediately and knocked down his man the first spring. The latter bravely tried to hold his own, but was floored every time he got on his feet, ultimately being kept to the ground until the owner of the dog released him. The man had three rounds with the powerful canine, but was beaten each time and was unable to escape."

For this type of work, dogs of a dark brindle color were preferred owing to their lack of visibility. It was inevitable, however, that as the breed gained in popularity and true Mastiff blood was used, a large number of light fawns should appear. With the gradual disappearance of poaching and the continued demand for Bullmastiffs as guards and watchdogs, this color became popular. The black mask and densely colored ears were often inherited from the Mastiff.

Finally, owing to the increasing popularity of the breed, a number of pioneers started, on a scientific basis, to breed to type in an effort to set a goal which pure-bred dog breeders might seek. This type finally became sufficiently distinct for the English Kennel Club to grant recognition of the Bullmastiff as a pure-bred dog in 1924. At this time the Kennel Club differentiated between the Bullmastiff, crossbred, and the Bullmastiff, pure-bred, the latter being, of necessity, the descendant of three generations of dogs which were neither pure Mastiff nor pure Bulldog. Classes were then provided at a few shows and the dogs were finally awarded Challenge Certificates in 1928. In time the breed became known in many countries, having been exported from England to Siam, India, the Federated Malay States, Africa, and America. The short coat has proved convenient in warm climates, and yet the dog can live in the open in inclement weather.

In October, 1933, The American Kennel Club granted recognition to the Bullmastiff, and since that time the breed has made numerous friends in this country.

Collie

THERE are two varieties of Collie, the rough-coated and the smooth-coated. The Rough Collie of modern times goes back to the rough-coated shepherd's dog which Thomas Bewick depicted in his historic woodcut made prior to 1800, and it is probable that this breed was known in Scotland for more than a century before that time. The dog of olden days lacked today's beauty and majesty, but there has been no serious divergence from the essential type and the outstanding characteristics.

Sheepherding is one of the oldest occupations in the world, and on this basis alone we may assume that the Collie's ancestors go far back in the history of dogs. It may be reasoned, also, that the same conditions which promoted production of the best types of wool also contributed to the rough coat of the shepherd's dog. Except in rare instances, rough-coated dogs have always been associated with sheep. The Smooth Collie, answering to the same standard except in coat, was principally a drover's dog, used for guiding cattle and sheep to market, not for standing watch over them while at pasture.

Inability to give definite dates for the origin of the Collie is due to the fact that until fairly recent times he was solely a working dog, kept pure in strain, but usually without written pedigree; indeed, his untutored masters saw no need of this, even had they been capable of maintaining stud books.

When the Collie first came to the notice of dog fanciers shortly after the start of the nineteenth century, the breed was found principally in northern Scotland. It had a broader, shorter head and measured only fourteen inches at the shoulder. The breed progressed rapidly up to 1859, when the first organized dog show was held in England, and it was one of the first breeds for which classes were provided. This was at the show of the Birmingham Dog Society in 1860.

Early writers on dogs of the British Isles mention a number of crosses, such as the Gordon Setter and the Newfoundland, that went toward the development of the modern Collie, but these may be discounted. They are no more credible than the tale told by old Scotchmen of a century ago that the Collie, the Deerhound, and the Scottish Terrier all descended from a common ancestor. From authentic sources comes the knowledge that the beautiful Rough Collie of modern days has been developed by a careful process of selective breeding. It had reached its present height and weight as long ago as 1886, and breeding since then has been a matter of refinement.

When Queen Victoria paid her first visit to Balmoral in the early sixties she saw specimens of the Rough Collie and took an instant liking to the breed. Of course her opinions became widely known, and the Scotch breeders found an instant market. This stimulus, however, was little beside that of American dog fanciers.

It is probable that working Collies were imported to America as early as Colonial days, but the dogs were scattered and they received little or no attention except from the neighbors of their masters. The start of Collie popularity in the United States dates from about 1880. The first registrations of the breed appear in Vol. 2 of The American Kennel Club *Stud Book*, published in 1885, and, even at that time, a great number were American-breds. In the late eighties, Collies were extremely popular at American bench shows, and there were a number of famous kennels specializing in the breed. The development on both sides of the Atlantic has continued at the same rate, and due to the need for fresh blood, there has been considerable international traffic in them.

There have been occasions when the Rough Collie has been outstripped by other dogs, but its popularity has always been rather consistent. Of the two coats, the smooth was the cattle-driving dog.

The earliest illustration of a Smooth Collie is the woodcut made by Thomas Bewick about 1800; it shows the dog as having a short tail, which may have been docked, for in almost all other respects the dog is similar to specimens of today. Bewick describes the breed as larger, stronger, and fiercer than the shepherd's dog, also illustrated in his *History of Quadrupeds*. Another authority contributes the information that the shepherd's dog, or Rough Collie, was about fourteen inches at the shoulder in 1800, so that the Smooth may not have been very large.

The immediate ancestor of the Smooth Collie probably was the dog that Bewick calls the "ban-dog," which, in turn, was a descendant of the Mastiff, or Canis Molossus, regarded as one of the world's basic breeds.

The earliest known specimens of Smooth Collie carried a great deal of black in the coat; likewise the Roughs were either dark or black. Both varieties were known as the "coally dogs," and from this, undoubtedly, has sprung the modern name of Collie. In 1867, Stonehenge mentions the breed as the "Scotch Colley" or "Highland sheepdog."

There is a striking unanimity of opinion among older authorities that the smooth variety of Collie owes its origin and development to the North of England, although it was known on both sides of the border. The county of Northumberland was a big center of the Smooth, and the black and white mottled strain was distinctly Northumbrian.

Rough and Smooth Collies have been identical in form, aside from coat, for almost three-quarters of a century, but there are reasons for believing that in early days they were two separate breeds. Few types of dog have been more developed and improved in appearance than the Collies, and it is difficult to say just how breeders undertook this task. It is a matter of record, however, that by 1885, when the first specialty show was held for the breed in England, Roughs and Smooths were often found in the same litters.

The first organized dog show took place in England in 1859, and within a year or two the Collie was seen regularly on the benches. The breed as a whole received its first impetus in the early sixties when England's arbiter of fashions and customs, Queen Victoria, expressed her admiration for the dog. At that time, Rough and Smooth competed in the same classes. It was not until the Darlington show of 1870 that separate classes were provided for Smooth Collies, although even then the name "collie" was not commonly applied to the breed.

The Collie was one of the first pure-bred dogs imported to the United States when dog lovers in America began to take an organized interest in the sport of exhibiting. It also is quite probable that specimens had come to this country many years before, purely as working dogs. This is rather difficult to place definitely, since records of such importations have not been kept; but it is certain that the Collies, both Smooth and Rough, were exhibited at some of the earliest bench shows in America.

The development of the Collie in the United States has kept pace with that of England, and the strength of the breed here is evinced by the drop in the number of importations today. However, the Smooth Collie has never received the popular favor enjoyed by the other variety.

Doberman Pinscher

WITH its racial roots somewhat obscure, the Doberman Pinscher became within a comparatively short time a dog of fixed type, whose characteristics of both body and spirit have extended its popularity in many lands. Originating in Apolda, in Thueringen, Germany, around 1890,

the breed was officially recognized in 1900. Since that date the Doberman Pinscher has made fast friends in Europe, in the Orient, and the
Americas. It takes its name from Louis Dobermann of Apolda.

Of medium size and clean-cut appearance, the dog at first glance does
not give evidence of its great muscular power. The adult male in the
pink of condition weighs sixty-five to seventy-five pounds. So compact
is its structure, so dense the laying on of muscle under the short coat,
and so elegant and well chiseled the outline that the novice would probably underestimate the weight by fifteen to twenty pounds. Weight is the
only particular, however, in which the Doberman is deceptive. Its qualities of alertness, agility, muscular and temperamental fire stand patent
for any eye to see. It is an honest dog, uncamouflaged by superfluous
coat or the wiles of the artful conditioner. One gains at once the impression of sinewy nimbleness, of the quick co-ordination of the well-
trained athlete.

There is also an air of nobility about the Doberman Pinscher which
is part of its birthright. More than most other breeds, it gives the impression of a blue-blooded animal, an aristocrat. From the strong muzzle
and wedge-shaped head to the clearly defined stifle, the outline is definite
and sharply etched. The fearless and inquisitive expression of the dark
eye is in harmony with the bodily characteristics. The Doberman looks
upon the stranger boldly and judges him with unerring instinct. He is
ready, if need be, to give prompt alarm and to back his warning with
defense of his master and his master's goods. Yet, he is affectionate,
obedient, and loyal.

Traditionally compounded of the old shorthaired shepherd-dog stock,
with admixtures of Rottweiler, Black and Tan Terrier, and smooth-
haired German Pinscher, the Doberman has been fortunate, with the
aid of selective breeding, to have absorbed the good qualities of the races
which have contributed to its heritage. It has been from the beginning
a working dog devoted to the service of mankind.

At first, the Doberman was used almost exclusively as a guard and
home watchdog. As it developed, its qualities of intelligence and ability
to absorb and retain training brought it into demand as police and war
dog. In this service its agility and courage made it highly prized. An excellent nose adapted the dog to criminal trailing; it has also led to its
use as a hunting dog.

Among the endearing qualities of the Doberman has come to be its
devotion to hearth and home, and its discriminating service as friend
and guardian of the whole family. The properly bred and trained specimen has a sane mind and a sound body; the heart and spirit of a gentleman.

In the United States the breed has been fostered, and its popularity has reached out into every state through The Doberman Pinscher Club of America, which was founded in February, 1921. Through the efforts of this organization, keen interest has been maintained in the breed, further evidenced by the increasing number of breeders and exhibitors.

German Shepherd Dog

DERIVED from the old breeds of herding and farm dogs, and associated for centuries with man as servant and companion, the German Shepherd Dog has been subject to intensive development. Sponsored by the *Verein für Deutsche Schäferhunde*, the parent club of the breed, founded in 1899 in Germany, the cult of the Shepherd spread rapidly from about 1914 onward in many parts of the world. Interest in the breed has been fostered by specialty clubs in many lands as it has been in the United States by the German Shepherd Dog Club of America.

First, last, and all the time a working dog, the German Shepherd has been developed both temperamentally and structurally through selective breeding, through judging which, on the whole, has been of a constructive character, and through specialized training.

Considering first the more important side of the dog—its character— the Shepherd is distinguished for loyalty, courage, and the ability to assimilate and retain training for a number of special services. He should be of equable disposition, poised, unexcitable, and with well-controlled nerves. For his typical work as a herding sheep dog, he must not be gun-shy and must have courage to protect his flock from attacks, either animal or human. For his work as a police dog, a development which followed upon a natural aptitude for training, he must have this courage also, but, in addition, must be able to make use of the excellent nose which he usually possesses. In his work as a leader of the blind, the Shepherd must and does exhibit a high order of intelligence and discrimination involving the qualties of observation, patience, faithful watchfulness, and even, to a certain degree, the exercise of judgment.

These qualities, which have endeared the German Shepherd Dog to a wide public in practically every country of the globe, are those of the companion, protector, and friend. The German Shepherd is not a pugnacious brawler, but a bold and punishing fighter if need be. In his relation to man he does not give affection lightly; he has plenty of dignity and some suspicion of strangers, but his friendship, once given, is given for life.

On the physical side, the German Shepherd has been developed to a point of almost ideal fitness for the work he is called upon to do. He is a dog of middle size with enough weight to be effective as herder or patrolman, but not enough to be cumbersome or unwieldy. The body is relatively long, and the length from the prominent sternum to the back of the well-muscled thigh should always be noticeably more than the height of the dog taken at the withers. A desirable proportion of these measurements runs from ten to nine to ten to eight and a half. Capacious without being barrel-ribbed, the body is marked by great depth of chest and by ribbing carried well back, giving abundant room to the vital organs. The under line of the dog is relatively level. The back is strong and straight, the withers high, the clean-cut neck moderately long and carried rather forward than up. The tail is set on low and carried low when the dog is at rest.

The head is cleanly chiseled, strong without coarseness, but above all, not fine. The muzzle is strong, squarely carried out and level, and the underjaw well developed. The teeth are powerfully developed and the incisors meet in a scissors bite; that is to say, with the inner surfaces of the upper incisors just engaging the upper and outer edge of the lower incisors. The eye is of medium size, set somewhat obliquely, preferably dark with a fearless and alert expression. The ears, of medium size, open to the front and are held erect when the dog is at attention.

By careful selective breeding, the naturally easy trot of the German Shepherd Dog has been brought to a high pitch of nearly effortless motion. Essentially a trotting animal, his structure has been modified so as to increase the power, elasticity and length of his gait. Other things being equal, the best-moving Shepherd is the one which covers the maximum amount of ground with the minimum expenditure of energy. To attain this end three things are essential: an iron-strong back, a hindquarter of deep and clean-cut angulation, and a sloping shoulder with sufficient angulation between the shoulder blade and the upper arm to take up and compensate for the stride of the hindquarter. The hindquarter assembly presents a moderately sloping croup to which is attached a long, wide, and powerfully muscled stifle and, at a sharp angle, a short, strong hock.

At a trot, the hind leg reaches far under the dog, often well past a line perpendicular to the shoulder; the well-arched foot, with thick pad, takes a strong grip on the ground and, with the hock as a fulcrum and the leverage provided by the stifle, propels the dog far forward. At the same time the opposite front foot is stretched far ahead of the animal by means of the opening of the well-angulated shoulder, and a strong, but springy, pastern takes up the shock of the step. So well co-ordinated and harmonious is this gait when properly exemplified that the dog seems to glide forward without visible effort, suspended, one might almost think, from the firm beam of his back.

The German Shepherd Dog has a double coat to protect him in all weathers; a harsh outer coat of medium length, of which the hairs are usually straight, though sometimes somewhat crimped and wavy, and a dense woolly undercoat. In color he may run from jet-black to rather light gray with all sorts of variations in between. Black and tan, brindle, iron gray, gray with sable markings, and other strong colors predominate. Pale or washed-out tones are considered a sign of degeneration and are not wanted.

The impression of the dog as a whole is one of ruggedness combined with nobility, of power combined with agility. There should be a sense of balance, forequarter and hindquarter compensating each other in their development. The outline should be smooth and flowing, and the top line of the dog, from ear to the tip of the full tail, a single sweeping succession of unbroken curves. The German Shepherd is a natural dog, unchanged for any whim of the show ring.

Giant Schnauzer

FEW races have been more prolific in their development of new breeds of dog than the Germanic peoples. Not only have they evinced rare patience in tracing ancestries, but they have proved their ability to fix type. One of the most notable examples of their breeding skill is the Schnauzer, for here is a dog not only brought to splendid physical conformation and keen mental development, but reproduced in three distinct sizes. The one under consideration here is the Riesenschnauzer—the Giant. The others are treated more fully elsewhere.

The remarkable phase of the breeding of the Schnauzers is that all three dogs appear to have been developed toward one standard of perfection from various sources that intermingled, if at all, only in rare instances. Of the three, the dog now known in America as the Standard Schnauzer, which is the medium-sized specimen, is without doubt the oldest. He is the one apparently portrayed in paintings by Dürer, dating from 1492, and he is also the one of the "Nachtwachter-Brunnen," the statue of a night watchman and his dog erected in a square in Stuttgart, Württemberg, in 1620. These instances are important only as they indicate the antiquity of the type of dog perfected at those dates and still retained today.

In unearthing the history of this breed it must be remembered that occupations of men had a great deal to do with all development in dogs. There were no bench shows in those days, and when a new breed was produced it was aimed at a specific work. Also, its characteristics were governed to large extent by weather and living conditions.

All Schnauzers had their origin in the neighboring kingdoms of Württemberg and Bavaria. These are agricultural sections where the raising of sheep, cattle, and other livestock has been a major occupation for years. Since railroads were not known, sheep and cattle had to be driven to market, which meant that dogs were necessary to help the shepherds.

There is little doubt that when Bavarian cattlemen went to Stuttgart they came across the medium-sized Schnauzer. Here was a dog to catch anyone's attention, for even then it was sound, while it showed power throughout its trim lines. The Bavarians liked the dog, but they were not satisfied with its size. The sheepmen could use this size of dog, but the drovers needed a larger specimen for cattle.

The first attempts to produce a drover's dog on terrier lines, with a wiry coat, were no doubt by crossings between the medium-sized Schnauzer and some of the smooth-coated driving and dairymen's dogs then in existence. Later there were crossings with the rough-haired sheep dogs, and much later, with the black Great Dane. There is also reason to believe that the Giant Schnauzer is closely related to the Bouvier des Flandres, which was the driving dog of Flanders.

For many years the Giant Schnauzer was called the Munchener, and it was widely known as a great cattle and driving dog. Von Stephanitz places its origin as Swabia—in the south of Bavaria, and it was found in a state of perfection in the region between Munich and Augsburg.

The Giant Schnauzer was practically unknown outside of Bavaria until nearly the end of the first decade of this century. Cattle-driving was then a thing of the past, but the breed was still found in the hands of butchers, at stockyards, and at breweries. The breweries maintained the dogs as guards, at which duty they are pre-eminently successful.

Not until just before World War I did the Giant Schnauzer begin to come to nationwide attention in Germany as a suitable subject to receive police training at the schools in Berlin and other principal cities. He proved such an intelligent pupil that police work has been his main occupation since that time. His progress in the United States has been very slow. Making his appearance here at the time when the German

Shepherd was reaching its peak, the Bavarian dog had little chance to make headway against such well-established, direct competition. But the soundness and the intelligence of the Giant Schnauzer indicate that someday it is bound to become popular.

Great Dane

IN APPEARANCE and nature the Great Dane is one of the most elegant and distinguished varieties of giant-type dog.

Accurate canine history is limited to but little longer than the last half century. The first dog show was held as recently as 1859 in England, where the "dog game" was born. Before that time, there were occasional records of different sorts of dogs over a period of more than three thousand years; but the items are so few, incomplete, and inaccurate that a student of the dogs of antiquity can "prove" almost anything he cares to imagine.

The name of the breed (in the English language) is a translation of an old French designation, *grand Danois*, meaning "big Danish." This was only one of half a dozen names which had been used for centuries in France. Why the English adopted the name "Great Dane" from the French is a mystery. At the same time the French were also calling it *dogue allemand* or "German Mastiff." "Mastiff" in English, *dogge* in the Germanic, *dogue* or *dogo* in the Latin languages, all meant the same thing: a giant dog with heavy head for fighting or hunting purposes. It was one of the dozen varieties of dog recognized as distinctive enough at that time to have a name of its own.

There is no known reason for connecting Denmark with either the origin or the development of the breed. It was "made in Germany," and it is German fanciers who have led the world in breeding most of the finest specimens.

If the reader is susceptible to the charms of antiquity, he will be interested in Cassel's claim that on Egyptian monuments of about 3000 B.C. there are drawings of dogs much like the Great Dane. Also, the earliest written description of a dog resembling the breed may be found in Chinese literature of 1121 B.C. (an article by Dr. G. Ciaburri, Great Dane Club of Italy publication, 1929).

Eminent zoologists like Keller and Kraemer believe that the Mastiff breeds originated in Asia. They think the modern Tibetan Mastiff, oc-

casionally shown in England, is the most direct descendant of the prototype.

The great naturalist Buffon (1707–1788) claimed the Irish Wolfhound as the principal ancestor of our Great Dane. The comparative
anatomist Cuvier (1769–1832) found more evidence in favor of the
old English Mastiff as the root from which it sprang. Both Irish and
English breeds are known to have been carefully bred for 1300 years
and more. Today most students favor the idea that the Great Dane, or
Deutsche Dogge, resulted from a mixture of both these ancient types.

This is not to say that the German Mastiff or Great Dane is a new
breed. It is, indeed, a very old one which has been cultivated as a distinct type for probably 400 years, if not longer. Like all old varieties of
dog, it was developed for a useful purpose. The Germans used the
Great Dane as a boar hound. Europe's erstwhile boar was one of the
most savage, swift, powerful, and well-armed of all big game on the
Continent. To tackle the wild boar required a superdog, and that is
precisely what the Germans developed. We who fancy him speak of him
as the king of dogs.

In common with all other breeds, the Great Dane's history of and
development to a modern standard type began in the latter nineteenth
century. In 1880 at Berlin, Dr. Bodinus called a meeting of Great Dane
judges who declared that the breed should be known as *Deutsche dogge*
and that all other designations, especially the term "Great Dane,"
should be abolished thereafter. So far as the German people are concerned this declaration has been observed, but English-speaking people
have paid no heed. The Italians, who have a large Great Dane fancy,
have also failed to give Germany credit for the name selected: *alano*. This
word means "a mastiff," consequently the name of their organization
means "Mastiff Club of Italy." This, however, has not prevented close
co-operation between fanciers of the two countries. The leading Italian
breeders have based their operation on nothing but German imported
stock or its descendants.

In 1891 the Great Dane Club of Germany adopted a precise standard,
or official description of the ideal specimen. In 1885 there was a Great
Dane Club in England, and in 1889 at Chicago the German Mastiff
or Great Dane Club of America was founded with the late G. Muss-
Arnoldt as first delegate. Two years later our club reorganized as The
Great Dane Club of America with a membership mostly of Eastern
fanciers, and headquarters since that time has been in New York City.

But the American standard of the Great Dane has always been based
on the German standard as adopted by Deutsche Doggen Club. In fact,
all nations have recognized the authority of the fatherland in this matter.
The English, French, Italian, Indian, and Dutch standards are almost

exact translations from the German. The world over there is a single ideal of excellence in Great Danes. If a Dane rates high in Germany, he will rate high anywhere. This is not true of several breeds which have seen local fads take hold of judges, so that we have a diversity of types in the same breed—English, American, Swiss, or German. This causes confusion in judging and breeding, since a "flyer" in one country will be considered quite undesirable in another. There is nothing like this in Great Danes.

The Great Dane has developed steadily in popularity. He was never the rage outside of Germany in Bismarck's day; nevertheless, year after year all over the world he has slowly increased in numbers. The Germans have kept before them the stern business the boar hound must engage in. A merely "pretty" dog has not been enough. He must have size and weight, nobility and courage, speed and endurance. What more can one ask for in a dog?

Great Pyrenees

PERHAPS no other breed can boast such a colorful history of association with, and service to, mankind through as many centuries as can the Great Pyrenees, Le Grand Chien des Montagnes, Le Chien des Pyrenees, or, as he is known in England and on the Continent, the Pyrenean Mountain Dog, the dog of French royalty and nobility and working associate of the peasant shepherds high on the slopes of the Pyrenees Mountains. His remains are found in the fossil deposits of the Bronze Age, which roughly dates his appearance in Europe between 1800 and 1000 B.C. although it is believed that he came originally from Central Asia or Siberia and followed the Aryan migration into Europe. It is also generally accepted that he is a descendant of the mastiff type whose remains are found in the kitchen-middens of the Baltic and North Sea coasts in the oldest strata containing evidence of the domestic dog, and which appear in Babylonian art about the close of the third millennium B.C. in a size and general appearance resembling the Great Pyrenees.

Once in Europe, the Great Dog of the Mountains developed under climatic conditions similar to those of his habitat and there remained isolated in the high mountainous areas until medieval times, when we find him gracing bas-reliefs at Carcassone, bearing the royal arms of France approximately some five hundred years before his adoption as the court dog in the seventeenth century. As early as 1407 the historian Mons. Bourdet describes the regular guard of Pyrenees dogs owned by the Chateau of Lourdes. These dogs were given a special place in the sentry boxes along with the armed guards; they also accompanied the gaolers on their daily rounds. Their use for these purposes became very general and each large Chateau boasted its band of Great Pyrenees. It was not until the young Dauphin, accompanied by Mme. de Maintenon in 1675 on a visit to Barreges, fell in love with a beautiful *Patou* (a generic name for the breed meaning "shepherd") and insisted on taking it back to the Louvre with him; and not until the Marquis de Louvois also succumbed to their charm that the dog of the shepherd of the Pyrenees became the companion and pet of nobility. Once accepted at court, every noble wanted one, and the breed gained prominence.

It was, however, in the isolation of the lonely mountain pastures that the Pyrenean Mountain Dog developed his inherent traits of devotion, fidelity, sense of guardianship, and intelligent understanding of mankind. Here, in the days when packs of wild animals roamed the mountain slopes freely, he was the official guardian of the flocks. Having a precocious sense of smell and keen sight, he was an invaluable companion of the shepherd, his worth being counted equal to that of two men. Armed by nature with a long, heavy coat which rendered him invulnerable against attack except for the point of the chin and the base of the brain, and armed by his masters with a broad iron collar from which protruded spikes an inch and a half long, the Pyrenees dog was an almost unbeatable foe which won such glory and fame as a vanquisher of wolves and bears that he became known as the Pyrenean wolf dog or hound, and the Pyrenean bearhound.

By disposition and profession, no better dog could have been chosen to assume the role of protector and friend of the early settlements of the Biscay fisherfolk on Newfoundland Island. By 1662, when their first permanent colony at Rougnoust was made, it was the Great Pyrenees dog which had become the companion of the people. Here he was crossed with the black English Retriever, brought over by the English settlers, and from this cross resulted the Newfoundland. The old Landseer type, with its black and white coat, showed the cross far more markedly because of his coloring than the black Newfoundland, although the resemblance in general type is quite noticeable in both.

With the diminution of the wild beasts in the Pyrenees, the breed seemed destined to extinction for a while. Moreover, it was eagerly sought after by breeders in Continental Europe and great numbers were exported from France. However, thanks to the efforts of some gentlemen sportsmen, as well as to the fact that the dogs were of use about the peasants' farms in winter (when their services were not required on the mountain slopes), they were bred in increasing numbers until today the breed is well established in its habitat once again. The dogs are not infrequently referred to as "mat-dogs" because of their habit of lying outside the cottage doors when not busying themselves with menial chores such as pulling carts.

The Great Pyrenees has come into general prominence only since its recognition by The American Kennel Club in February, 1933. It seems hard to realize that the first pair were brought over by General Lafayette for his friend, Mr. J. S. Skinner, in 1824, being "recommended by him from personal experience as of inestimable value to wool-growers in all regions exposed to the depredations of wolves and sheepkilling dogs." Thus writes Mr. Skinner in his book *The Dog and the Sportsman*. Since that date a few scattered specimens have been imported, but not until 1933 was the actual breeding of the dogs launched in America. In the years that have elapsed since their recognition here, champions have been crowned, litters raised and distributed throughout the country, and new dogs imported.

Pre-eminently a watchdog and companion, the Great Pyrenees holds promise also as a dog suited for the sportsman. His love of pulling carts makes him amenable to sled work in winter, and his instinct for feeling out soft places in the snow makes him ideal for pack and guide work on ski trips. He was used during World War I for pack service and for many years for running contraband goods over the Franco-Spanish border by similar methods. Taking dangerous byways impossible for man to travel, he ran the circuit regularly, successfully avoiding the customs officials. His beauty also recommends him for use in the moving picture industry, especially as he has already been used with success for this purpose in France. Certainly no more picturesque animal could be found; he has been aptly called, "an animated snowdrift of the Pyrenees Mountains." The nearer his appearance approaches that of the brown bear, except for the color and the drooping ears, the closer he is to the perfect type.

Komondor

OF THE three breeds of working dog native for ten centuries to the sheep and cattle countries of Hungary, there seems little doubt that the king of them all is the Komondor. This heavily coated dog is an almost direct descendant of the Aftscharka, which the Huns found on the southern steppes when they passed through Russia. Many of today's Komondorok (plural) bear striking resemblance to the massive, long-legged Russian herdsman's dog, but the breed generally has become more compact.

The Komondor, a mighty fellow, with strong bones, stands from twenty-eight to thirty inches at the shoulder. His head is impressive in its generous formation, and his general appearance is commanding. At first sight he is likely to create fear. Strangers of evil intent have reason to be fearful, but he is a devoted companion to his master and readily mingles with friends of the master.

One often sees pictures of the Kormondor that show him with a heavily matted coat and with his head covered all over with long hair. The dog thus seems unkempt, and this is the way he is found in his habitat, where he lives in the open practically all the time. Under such circumstances, it would be impossible for the Komondor to have a well-groomed appearance, but he responds readily to care. When reared in kennels and prepared for shows he is a handsome dog.

The Komondor is the chief of the herdsman's dogs, but he is not often utilized for rounding up the herds. He merely accompanies the flocks and herds in exceptional cases, and then more in the capacity of protector than as herder. His vigilance and courage have earned him a rather enviable position of trust, and much of the routine work is left to the smaller dogs.

The Magyars who have bred the Komondor for more than a thousand years attend principally to their herds and flocks and do not concern themselves with keeping pedigrees of their dogs. However, there is no need of pedigrees for them, as the dogs are not permitted to mate outside their own race.

It is doubtful if any dogs with pedigrees could be found in the so-called "Puszta," for the shepherds and herdsmen do not look upon dog breeding either as a commercial venture or as a hobby. Still, the crossing of a Komondor and a Kuvasz would be unimaginable, and also practically impossible. The Komondor still resides in the Puszta, while the Kuvasz has become, in recent times, more the watchdog of the village.

The history of pure-bred dog breeding in Hungary is not unlike that of any other country in the world. Definite records go back hardly a century, but those in existence are soundly attested by reliable parties. The Hungarian Kennel Club and the Hungarian Komondor Club maintain a strong control over the interests of the Komondor, these organizations having accepted the standard of the breed as drawn up by a committee made up of members of the two clubs. The American Kennel Club's standard of the breed is a translation of the Hungarian.

In reading the Standard, it should be noted that its salient points denote the strength and the protective features that have been bred into the Komondor for centuries, and these should be maintained. Today there is not perhaps as pressing a need for such a self-reliant dog, as there was in the past. In times of old he had to be ready at any moment to fight all manner of beasts of prey, many of which were his superior in size and weight. When the odds were against him, he could depend to some extent on that heavy coat to cover his most vulnerable points, and could call, too, upon an intelligence far superior to that of his wild adversaries.

Kuvasz

FROM Tibet, that strange high-flung domain of the lamas, came the ancestors of the breed that today is known as the Kuvasz (plural, Kuvaszok). Yet this is not a new name for the breed. It is merely a corrupted spelling of Turkish and Arabian words that signified the unexcelled guarding instincts of this big dog.

The Turkish word is *kawasz*, which means "armed guard of the nobility." In the Arabian this appears as *kawwasz*, which signifies "archer," an expression that probably was a mere figure of speech to denote the high esteem in which the dog was held, since many centuries ago an archer was regarded with great respect. Words with nearly the same spelling and meaning are found throughout all the countries whose languages originate in Tibet.

There is little doubt of the part that the Kuvasz played in the history of the kingdoms and empires which flourished throughout Europe five to eight centuries ago. Dogs of this breed were the constant companions of many a ruler of a turbulent country; indeed, none but those within the favor of the royal circles were permitted to own specimens of the Kuvasz.

Known in many countries, it was in Hungary that the Kuvasz developed into the form in which he is seem today. He still is a big dog, but he is not the giant of ancient times. At present he measures approximately twenty-six inches at the shoulder, but there is every reason to believe that the dog which issued from Tibet stood considerably higher.

He was a dog of which the common people stood in awe; his appearance alone was enough to discourage attacks on noblemen by the populace.

The first great period in the Hungarian history of the Kuvasz seemed to reach a climax during the second half of the fifteenth century. His renown reached far and wide. There were numerous big estates that bred the dog and kept their own stud books. Many were trained for hunting, and they proved very successful on the big game of those times.

King Matthias I, who reigned from 1458 to 1490, had at least one Kuvasz with him whenever he traveled, and there were numerous specimens about his palace and the surrounding grounds. Few other rulers have had to strive so hard to hold their domains together. Plots and political intrigue were the rule rather than the exception, while assassinations were not uncommon. It is said that King Matthias was reluctant to place any great trust in even the members of his own household, and his court was filled with ambitious noblemen.

It is no wonder that King Matthias relied more upon his dogs than upon his human guards. He knew that in this big, sturdy fellow he had, perhaps, the only true security that was possible. Often, when the tumultuous day was over—and he waged wars almost continually—the king would retire to his study and spend half the night poring over his books and his maps, preparing his orders for the following day, and while he worked, a big white Kuvasz sprawled just inside the door.

King Matthias became so impressed with the Kuvasz that he developed a large pack to be used for hunting purposes. His kennels on his large estates in Siebenbuergen were among the most impressive in Europe, and the scope of his breeding did a great deal toward perpetuating a splendid strain of the breed. Surplus puppies were presented only to the noblemen and to visiting dignitaries.

Eventually, many specimens got into the hands of the commoners, but this was long after the time of King Matthias I, when herders found them suitable for work with sheep and cattle. It was in this later period that the name of the breed was corrupted to its present spelling. Incidentally, this spelling is rather unfortunate, because it changes the meaning rather ridiculously to that of "mongrel."

According to von Stephanitz, the great German authority on all Central European breeds, the Kuvasz is related to the Komondor, which had been brought from the Russian steppes by the Huns. He ventures the opinion that the *kawasz* or *kawwasz* was crossed with the indigenous country dog of Hungary. While this is something of a conjecture, there is strong evidence that points to truth. At any rate, the original type has proved dominant, and the Kuvasz of today—perhaps a little smaller—is very similar to his earliest progenitors.

Mastiff

THE breed commonly called "Mastiff" in English speaking countries is more properly described as the *Old English* Mastiff. It is a giant short-haired dog, with heavy head and short muzzle, which has been bred in England for over two thousand years as a watchdog.

The term "mastiff" describes a group of giant varieties of dog rather than a single breed. It is supposed to have originated in Asia; and the modern Tibetan Mastiff, seen today at dog shows in England, is thought to be the most direct descendant of the prototype. Next in purity is said to be the Old English Mastiff, which is regarded by some students as the main root whence came many of the others of the Mastiff group.

So little is known about dogs of any sort prior to a century ago that almost all theories of ancestry are of small importance. Every partisan would like to claim the greatest antiquity for his particular sort of Mastiff as well as to say that the other sorts sprang from it. There is very little proof one way or the other.

Cassel finds drawings on Egyptian monuments of typical Mastiffs dating about 3000 B.C. In literature, the earliest reference is in Chinese about 1121 B.C. So much for the undoubted antiquity of the Mastiff group's ancestry.

So far as our breed, the Old English Mastiff, is concerned, it has a longer history than most. Caesar describes them in his account of invading Britain in 55 B.C., when they fought beside their masters against the Roman legions with such courage and power as to make a great impression. Soon afterwards we find several different accounts of the huge British fighting dogs brought back to Rome where they defeated all other varieties in combats at the Circus. They were also matched against human gladiators as well as against bulls, bears, lions, and tigers.

Today we are likely to think of such cruel spectacles as belonging only to the dim ages of the past, but this is not true. Dog fights, bullbaiting, and bearbaiting were respectable and popular forms of amusement in England and America little more than a century ago. Such brutalizing events were patronized by nobility and clergy in England, while public-spirited citizens left legacies so that the common folk might be entertained in this way on holidays.

Dogfighting and animal-baiting were made illegal in England in 1835, due to Queen Victoria's insistence, but for twenty years longer the law was little obeyed. American dog fanciers are interested in the word *fancier*, which was synonymous with *bettor*—meaning especially a bettor on a dog or prize fight—and are interested also in the name of one of the most fashionable sporting establishments in London, over a hundred years ago, called the "Westminster Pit," with 300 seats. *Westminster* meant "dogs" even then—but fighting dogs!

While the Mastiff was always in front rank as a fighting dog, this does not account for his popularity in England for two thousand years. It was as bandogs, or tiedogs (tied by day but loose at night) that they were found everywhere. In fact, long ago, keeping of these Mastiffs was compulsory for the peasants. During Anglo-Saxon times there had to be kept at least one Mastiff for each two villeins. By this means wolves and other savage game were kept under control. They were also used in hunting packs by the nobility. It was as protectors of the home, however, that they were most used, and probably as a result of centuries of such service the Mastiff has acquired unique traits as a family dog.

That the Mastiff has long been numerous is indicated by the development of the English language itself. The ancient word in Anglo-Saxon and in over a score of kindred languages for a member of the canine race is *hound* or something very similar. A rather modern word coming from the Latin languages is like *dog*, but it means one certain *type* of dog in all languages but English. In all but English it means a *Mastiff* sort. So we can believe that when the Normans conquered the Anglo-Saxons in 1066 and made Norman-French the official language of England, *dogues* (or Mastiffs) were so plentiful that people forgot eventually there was any other name for a canine creature. This is the only explanation a dog man can offer for such a peculiar change in a language.

Anecdotes extolling the power and agility of Mastiffs as well as their devotion to their masters would fill a large volume of marvels. Herodotus tells of Cyrus the Great, founder of the Persian Empire about 550 B.C., who received a Mastiff as a gift from the King of Albania. Cyrus matched the dog against another and also sent it against a bull. But the Mastiff acted like a pacificist, so Cyrus in disgust had it killed. News of this reception of his gift came back to the King of Albania. He sent messengers with another Mastiff—a bitch—to Cyrus, telling him that a Mastiff was no ordinary cur and that it scorned to notice such common creatures as a Persian dog or a bull. He urged him to select a worthy opponent such as a lion or even an elephant. The King of Albania concluded by saying Mastiffs were rare and royal gifts and that he would not send Cyrus another. Whereupon, says Herodotus, the Mastiff bitch was set to attack an elephant and did so with such fury and efficiency that she worried the elephant down to the ground and would have killed it.

That is one of the oldest and probably the tallest Mastiff tale on record! However, it gives proof of the reputation of Mastiffs as powerful, agile, and courageous dogs. It is even more interesting to know that Albania was the land of the people known as Alani, an Asiatic race. Also that similar names stand for "mastiffs," *e.g. Alano, Alan,* and *Alaunt.*

The story of Sir Peers Legh, Knight of Lyme Hall, (near Stockport, Cheshire) at the Battle of Agincourt, October 25, 1415, is well-known. He had brought his favorite Mastiff—also a bitch—to France, and when he fell, she stood over and defended him many hours until he was picked up by English soldiers and carried to Paris, where he died of his wounds. The faithful Mastiff was returned to England and from her is descended the famous Lyme Hall strain which the family has bred to this day—a period of over five centuries. In the drawing room of the castle is still to be seen an old stained-glass window portraying the gallant Sir Peers and his devoted Mastiff.

The present-day English Mastiff is based on the strains of Lyme Hall and that of the Duke of Devonshire's Kennels at Chatsworth. Chaucer wrote in Middle English (a mongrel language resulting from a cross between old Anglo-Saxon and Norman-French) 300 years after the Norman Conquest, describing the Old English Mastiff in his "Knight's Tale." He tried to use the Italian-French word for Mastiff, *Alan,*-which is still used in English heraldry to describe the figure of "a Mastiff with cropped ears" on a coat of arms.

Chaucer wrote sometime before his death in 1400:

"Aboute his char ther wenten white *Alaunts*
Twenty and mo, as gret as any stere
To hunten at the leon or the dere."

So here is proof that 600 years ago Mastiffs were hunted in packs in England on such different game as lion or deer. Chaucer says they were as large as a steer! Even though cattle were much smaller in those days, this is hard to credit. The white color is authentic. We have plenty of pictures and descriptions of white and piebald Mastiffs, often with long coats, of about a century ago.

Newfoundland

THERE is much uncertainty about the origin of the Newfoundland. Some say that his ancestors are the white Great Pyrenees, dogs brought to the coast of Newfoundland by the Basque fishermen; others that he descended from a "French hound" (probably the Boarhound); but all agree that he originated in Newfoundland and that his ancestors were undoubtedly brought there by fishermen from the European Continent. Many old prints of Newfoundland show unmistakable evidence of a Husky ancestor, while other traits can be traced to other breeds. At any rate, a dog evolved which was particularly suited to the island of his origin.

He was a large dog, with size and strength to perform the tasks required of him. He had a heavy coat to protect him from the long winters and the icy waters surrounding his native island. His feet were large, strong, and webbed so that he might travel easily over marshes and shores. Admired for his physical powers and attractive disposition, he was taken to England where he was extensively bred until most of the Newfoundlands of pedigree, even in Newfoundland, today are descended from forebears born in England.

At the present time, while not numerous anywhere, the Newfoundland is admired and bred in many different countries including, besides his native land, England, France, Holland, Germany, Switzerland, Italy, Canada, and the United States.

The breed standard was written for a working dog, essentially a dog as much at home in the water as on dry land. Canine literature gives us stories of brave Newfoundlands which have rescued men and women from watery graves; stories of shipwrecks made less terrible by dogs which carried life lines to stricken vessels; of children who have fallen into deep water and have been brought safely ashore by Newfoundlands; and of dogs whose work was less spectacular but equally valuable as they helped their fishermen owners with their heavy nets and performed other tasks necessary to their occupations. Although he is a superior water dog, the Newfoundland has been used and is still used in Newfoundland and Labrador as a true working dog, dragging carts, or more often carrying burdens as a pack horse.

In order to perform these duties the Newfoundland must be a large dog—large enough to bring ashore a drowning man. He must have powerful hindquarters and a lung capacity which enables him to swim for great distances. He must have the heavy coat which protects him from the icy waters. In short, he must be strong, muscular, and sound so that he may do the work for which he has become justly famous. Above all things, the Newfoundland must have the intelligence, the loyalty, and the sweetness which are his best-known traits. He must be able and willing to help his master perform his necessary tasks at command, and also have the intelligence to act on his own responsibility when his rescue work demands it.

In this country, where the Newfoundland is kept, not as an active worker, but as a companion, guard, and friend, we appreciate particularly the sterling traits of the true Newfoundland disposition. Here we have the great size and strength which makes him an effective guard and watchdog combined with the gentleness which makes him a safe companion. For generations he has been the traditional children's protector and playmate. He is not easily hurt by small tugging fingers (as is a smaller dog) and he seems to undertake the duties of nursemaid of his own accord without training. We know of no better description of the character of the Newfoundland dog than the famous epitaph which reads:

"Beneath this spot
Are deposited the remains of a being
Who was possessed of beauty without vanity,
Strength without insolence,
Courage without ferocity,
And all the virtues of man without his vices.

"This praise would be but empty flattery
Were it inscribed upon the ashes of a human being.
And yet it is only what is due to the memory
Of the dog BOATSWAIN:
Born in Newfoundland, May, 1801
Died at Windsor, 18th November, 1815."

Old English Sheepdog

WHILE as compared with some other kinds of dogs the Old English Sheepdog cannot boast the same antiquity, there is nevertheless ample evidence that it can trace its origin to the early nineteenth century or at least 150 years back, thus proving that among recognized breeds it is no mere upstart. As to its real origin, there are conflicting ideas based on premises obscured by the passage of time. A painting by Gainsborough of a Duke of Buccleuch, from which engravings were struck off in 1771, shows the peer with his arms clasped about the neck of what appears to be a fairly good specimen of present-day Old English Sheepdog. This is the earliest picture known that in any manner depicts the breed. What, however, the pictured dog was supposed to be at that period is not certain.

In all probability the breed was first developed in the west of England, in the counties of Devon and Somerset and the Duchy of Cornwall, although from what breeds it was produced is a matter of conjecture. Some maintain that the Scotch bearded Collie had a large part in its making; others claim for one of its progenitors the Russian Owtchar.

At all events, in the beginning of the eighteenth century, we read of a "drover's dog" which was used largely for driving sheep and cattle into the markets of the metropolis. These drover's dogs were exempt from taxes and, to prove their occupation, they were docked. Some believe that the nicknames "bob" and "bobtail" trace to this custom. It is not true, of course, that the practice of removing the tail has produced a breed naturally bobtailed or tailless. In fact, few specimens of the breed are whelped without tails, or with tails long or comparatively short. According to the Standard, the tail should be removed at the first joint, when the puppy is three or four days old, and it should never be longer than one and one-half or two inches in length at maturity. Seldom is an Old English Sheepdog seen in the show ring today with more than a mere thickening of the skin where the tail has been removed. Since this dog has been used more for driving than for herding, the lack of a tail to serve as a rudder, so to speak, has in no wise affected its working ability with heavier kinds of sheep and cattle.

For years after the breed's introduction into this country, fanciers did considerable harm by misinterpreting "profuseness" of coat as "excessiveness." This misled the public into believing that the Old English Sheepdog was difficult to care for, when as a matter of fact a dog with typical coat of the right texture is no harder to keep in shape than is any other longhaired dog. Furthermore, it is homeloving, not given to roaming and fighting, and it is extremely agile; because of its intelligence, affection, and lack of boisterousness, it makes an ideal house dog. It has a tender mouth and can be trained as a retriever; it makes a first-class sledge dog, and is satisfactory as a companion equally at home in apartment, large house, drawing room, and practically anywhere else.

In seeking a good representative of the breed, points to look for include a body practically square; good bone, deep brisket, chest, and spring of rib; strong foreface, dark or walleyes, level teeth, straight forelegs, well-let-down hocks, and a hard coat with good underjacket. Markings are not important. The dogs do well under almost any climatic conditions, their coats serving as insulation against heat, cold, and dampness. A marked characteristic of the breed is its gait, which is quite like the shuffle of a bear.

Puli

THE Puli (plural Pulik), or driver, has been an integral part of the lives of Hungarian shepherds for more than 1000 years. When the Magyars came into Hungary they brought their sheepdogs with them. There were larger kinds similar to the Komondor and the Kuvasz, and a smaller kind which resembled the Puli. Except in color, the Puli was quite similar to the Tibetan Terrier, which may well have been its foundation stock.

Color and size both played a part in the development of Hungary's sheepdogs, each for its particular type of work. The more easily seen, lighter-colored kinds guarded herds and flocks from robbers and wild animals at night, while the smaller, darker-colored Puli was used to drive and herd the sheep during the day. There was ample reason for this, since sheep take direction more certainly from dark dogs than from light-colored ones. Moreover the dark dog was more distinctive to the shepherd's eye, as it worked among the flocks rounding them up and even, so it is claimed, jumping on them or running over their backs to cut off or turn back a runaway.

The dark color has always been recognized as truly characteristic of the Puli. Ordinarily it is called black, but it is a black so unlike that of any other breed as to warrant explanation. It is dull; in some cases bronze-tinged, in others just barely grayed like a weather-worn old coat faded by the sun. An out-of-door life on the hillside, in all weathers but particularly under a constant and glaring sun, robbed the black of its intensity and its sheen. This was the black prized as typical of the breed in its homeland. There are, in addition, Pulik both gray and white. Any shade of gray is allowed so long as it is solid gray. The Puli is first and last a solid-colored dog. There may be some intermixture of hair of different colors usually present in the grays, and this is acceptable if the general appearance of solid color is maintained.

The Puli coat, too, is unique. There is nothing exactly like it in all dogdom. The undercoat is soft, woolly, very dense; the outer coat long and profuse. The puppy coat is tufted, but with growth the undercoat tangles with the top coat in such a manner as to form long cords. This matting and cording is the natural protector of the working Puli, with the over-all effect, as in other Hungarian sheepdogs, best described as unkempt.

Of course in this country more dogs are kept as guards, watchdogs, and companions than as sheepherders, hence we may find the groomed coat preferred to the uniquely corded coat which is the Puli's rightful heritage. But whatever the style of his hair, the Puli's vigor, versatility, and intelligence fit him as well for the home as for the hills.

He is a medium-sized dog averaging seventeen inches height and thirty pounds or so weight, and so striking in appearance that it would be impossible to confuse him with any other kind of dog. His shaggy hair covers his head like an umbrella, and falls all over his body to the very tip of his upcurled tail in such profusion that he seems larger than he actually is. He is keen and quick, and he moves with a gait as springy, almost, as a bouncing ball, this trait a hand-me-down, perhaps, from those dogs of long ago whose dazzling footwork was the admiration of the shepherd boy with his sheep.

Rottweiler

To THE Rottweiler goes considerable credit for helping to change the map and the races of Europe. Of course, the Rottweiler's part in these changes was purely involuntary; nevertheless, if it had not been for him, the Roman armies would not have been able to negotiate the mighty Alps and pour down into Central Europe.

Centuries ago a military expedition was a huge undertaking. The ancient Romans had to assemble vast quantities of food—along with all the other necessary supplies—and its transportation was a matter of major consideration. Perhaps the greatest problem centered around the supply of meat for the soldiers; it had to be carried on the hoof.

The movement of large herds of cattle meant work for many cattle dogs. These were recruited from among the three types then known in Rome: one very heavy and longhaired; the second, shorthaired and wolflike and used even then with sheep; and the third, also shorthaired but of somewhat different build, then used almost solely for herding cattle. This cattle dog was the ancestor of the Rottweiler. Many dogs of the type accompanied the various Roman expeditions as guides and guards of the army's cattle.

In ancient days the principal route of the Romans over the Alps was the historic St. Gotthard Pass. From this point various passages lead downward, and each passage leads to a province that gave a dog breed a home and a name. As the size of the herd grew smaller, fewer dogs were needed, and the Romans found no need of keeping them. Thus we find, today, at least four distinct breeds which have evolved from this one type of cattle dog.

The Rottweiler has developed from Roman cattle dogs that traveled much further afield than their brothers; for their name comes from the township of Rottweil, which lies on a hill on the left bank of the Neckar River, in Württemberg, in the south of Germany. This lies to the west and north of the noted pass, for from St. Gotthard the armies followed over the Furkapass, through Haslital toward the flow of the Aar, to Berne, and from there toward the North into Emmental. Here two other descendants of the original cattle dog are found. But the Romans followed this old military road further north, through Aargu, Schaffhausen, Donaueschingen, and finally came to Rottweil.

Württemberg was conquered by the Romans in the first century, so there is assurance that the breed now called the Rottweiler is some 1900 years old in its present form. The town of Rottweil is in the center of the livestock country, sixty-eight miles south by west of Stuttgart, and favorably close to the borders of France and Hungary. Many things combined to make Rottweil a suitable market place, especially for grain, cattle, and other livestock, and for centuries the buyers and sellers from all over Central Europe flocked there to trade their wares.

The butchers and cattle merchants who settled in Rottweil in increasing numbers adopted a working dog of necessity, and the Roman cattle dog was bred with a view to obtaining a dog capable of hard work. Not only did the butcher-master of Rottweil need a good worker, he needed a trusted companion and a reliable guard. Holdups were the rule rather than the exception, and it was especially dangerous to set forth on a buying expedition. It became the custom for the master to tie his purse around the dog's neck; and few bandits or highwaymen cared to molest one of these sturdy Rottweilers.

Aside from guard work, the principal uses of the Rottweiler always have been driving cattle, oxen, sheep, and pigs, and pulling carts. The smaller dogs were used with cattle, being able to keep up the constant trotting more easily. The larger specimens were considered unsuitable for driving and chasing cattle—some of the heavy dogs being able to knock over a cow by springing against it—and were reserved for draft work.

A few decades ago the Rottweiler was the leader and chaser of the herds on their way to market, but after the driving of cattle by dogs was forbidden by law, gradually more and more were shipped by rail. The larger type Rottweiler also came to be replaced by the donkey for pulling carts; and for a time it seemed that the breed would be lost. In fact, in 1905, the town of Rottweil had only one female representative of the breed.

There came a renaissance for the Rottweiler in 1910 when it was chosen as a desirable type for police training. It joined the Airedale Terrier, the German Shepherd, and its own descendant, the Doberman Pinscher, which were then the only breeds known for their police work. Unfailingly faithful and affectionate, the Rottweiler has developed more character through police work. It has served to emphasize his diligence, understanding, courage, modesty, and self-reliance.

St. Bernard

MANY hypotheses have been advanced to account for the origin of the St. Bernard, but definite proof to substantiate any one of them seems to be lacking. When one has gathered all available information on the subject, however, he is led to the following probability: the breed originated from the heavy Molosser type brought back from Asia by conquering Roman armies, and later, in the dawn of the Christian Era, introduced into Helvetia (Switzerland) during two different invasions.

When St. Bernard de Menthon founded his famous Hospice in the Swiss Alps, in the year 980, it is probable that the *Talhund*, a descendant of the Roman Molosser, was by that time a well-established breed in the Alpine valleys. Just when dogs first were brought to the Hospice is another debatable question, since in the sixteenth century the Hospice was destroyed by fire, and later a large part of the Hospice archives again was lost. In what remains there is nothing to be found as to when or whence the dogs were originally brought to the Great St. Bernard pass. The Prior, Erw. Ch. Lugon, asserts that according to his examination of the archives, the Hospice was still without dogs in the first part of the sixteenth century. Earlier records mention nothing about such animals, and it was not until 1707 that the first notation concerning them was made. This, however, was merely a casual reference to dogs at the Hospice and carried with it the implication that their rescue work at the St. Bernard pass was a fact then well known. An English traveler and painter, writing in 1774, also tells about the life-saving work of the dogs kept at Great St. Bernard, but he, too, mentions it in similar vein as information at that time so widely and commonly known that it needed little comment. From a digest of these early references, it appears probable that dogs were first brought to the Hospice between 1660 and 1670 as watchdogs, that they were recruited from the valleys below and were descendants of the old Roman Molosser.

The lonely monks, who took the dogs along with them on their trips of mercy, soon discovered, not only, that they were excellent pathfinders in the snow, but that their uncanny sense of smell made them invaluable in finding helpless persons overcome during storms. Thus began this working together of monk and dog which made many of the world's most romantic pages of canine history. During the almost three centuries that St. Bernards have been used in rescue work at the Hospice, it is estimated they have been responsible for the saving of approximately 2500 human lives. Building of railroad tunnels through the Alps in recent times has lessened foot and vehicular travel across the St. Bernard pass, and consequently has reduced to a minimum the work of the dogs. Fewer dogs are now kept at the Hospice, but their work is no less important than it was centuries ago. Hardly a season goes by that some rescues from the great white death are not attributed to the heroic dogs of St. Bernard. A new Hospice has been established in Tibet, and in this far outpost of civilization as well as in the frozen Alps the saintly dogs still ply their century-old trade of saving human lives.

St. Bernards required no training for their work, since generations of service in this capacity seem to have stamped the rescuing instinct indelibly upon their characters. The only schooling they received at the Hospice was as young dogs permitted to run with the older dogs on patrol tours. Formerly, the dogs, running in packs of three or four, used to make lone patrols during and following storms in search of possible traveler casualties. When they came upon a victim, two of the animals would lie down on the snow beside him to warm him with their bodies, and one of them would lick the person's face to restore consciousness. In the meantime, one of the other dogs in the pack would be on his way back to the Hospice to give the alarm to the monks and lead them to the scene. As soon as the rescue party of monks arrived, the dogs would retire to a respectful distance and apparently take no further interest in the doings, their part of it being finished.

Today the dogs seldom go on patrols alone. They accompany the monks who go out when warned by telephone that a party of tourists is attempting to go through the pass. Their work on such occasions is invaluable, as the monks themselves could not go more than a few feet from their Hospice door with safety were it not for the unerring sense of direction possessed by the dogs, which can lead them back in the event of a sudden Alpine blizzard that obliterates familiar landmarks.

In addition to their pathfinding capabilities and their sense of smell, which enables them to locate human beings buried under snow, the dogs are reputed to possess an uncanny sixth sense which warns them of approaching avalanches. Instances have been reported wherein a dog would quickly change his position for no apparent reason a few seconds or minutes before an avalanche came hurtling down across the spot where he had stood, burying it under tons of snow and ice.

Although by 1800 it was well known that a special type of dog did rescue work at the Hospice, the breed at that time had been given no name. Between 1800 and 1810, Barry, perhaps the most celebrated dog in history, lived at the Hospice, and for fully half a century after his demise, the Hospice dogs in certain parts of Switzerland were called "Barry hounds" after him. Barry is credited with having saved forty lives. Legend has it that he was killed by the forty-first person he attempted to rescue who mistook his huge bulk for that of a wolf, but this tale appears to be only a pretty story. As a matter of fact, Barry was given a painless death in Berne, in 1814, after he had attained a ripe old age. His likeness in mounted form is now preserved in the Natural History Museum in Berne.

The English, who as early as 1810 imported some of the Hospice dogs to replenish their Mastiff blood, referred to the breed for a number of years as "sacred dog." In Germany, around 1828, the name of "Alpendog" was proposed. In 1823, a writer, Daniel Wilson, first spoke of the so-called St. Bernard dog, but it was not until 1865 that this name definitely appeared, and only since 1880 has it been recognized as the official designation of the breed. The years 1816 to 1818 were seasons of uncommon snows and rigorous weather at the Hospice, and as a result many of the leading Hospice strains perished. It was easy at that time, however, to get good animals of like breed from the underlying valleys, and a few years later the dog situation at the Hospice was again satisfactory.

Confronted by a similar problem in 1830, and also by the fact that their breed was weakened considerably by inbreeding and disease, the monks resorted to an out-cross to give added size and new vigor to their dogs. The Newfoundland, which at that time was larger than the St. Bernard, was the breed decided upon to give the new blood. Results of this crossing showed all of the desired objectives and at the same time did not destroy the St. Bernard type and characteristics. Due to this crossing, however, the first longhaired St. Bernards appeared—previous to 1830 all St. Bernards were shorthaired. There followed years of breeding many St. Bernards in the valleys of Switzerland, in Germany, and in other Continental European countries and England.

In 1887, an International Congress was held in Zurich. Swiss St. Bernard authorities present included Drs. Sigmund, Künzli, and Max Siber. At this Congress an international standard of perfection for the breed was promulgated.

The St. Bernard Club of America was organized in 1888, the year following the Zurich congress, and the international standard was adopted by it. This club still continues to function for the interests of the St. Bernard and is one of the oldest specialty clubs in the United States.

Samoyed

Dog of the ages, with a history and tradition as fascinating as the breed itself! The legend runs that, from the plateau of Iran, man's first earthly habitat, as the sons of man multiplied, the mightier tribes drove the lesser ones, with their families, their herds, and their dogs, farther and farther away in order that the natural food found there might be ample for those remaining. Onward and still farther northward through Mongolia, then the center of the world's culture, on and on, went the lesser tribes, until eventually the Samoyed peoples, primitives of the family of Sayantsi, reliably described as a race in the "transition stages between the Mongol pure and the Finn," found themselves safely entrenched behind bulwarks of snow and ice in the vast stretches of tundra reaching from the White Sea to the Yenisei River. Here for generations they have lived a nomadic life, dependent upon their reindeer herd and upon their dogs as reindeer shepherds, sledge dogs, and household companions.

Here, through the centuries, the Samoyed has bred true. Of all modern breeds, the Samoyed is most nearly akin to the primitive dog—no admixture of wolf or fox runs in the Samoyed strain. The Arctic suns and snows have bleached the harsh stand-off coat and tipped the hairs with an icy sheen. The constant companionship with man through the years has given an almost uncanny "human" understanding, while generations of guarding reindeer, requiring always a protector, never a killer, has developed through the ages in the breed a disposition unique in the canine world. Something of the happy childlike air of these primitive peoples is found as well in every Samoyed.

Nor has the long human association made of the stalwart Samoyed a pampered pet. As work dogs Samoyeds of the great Arctic and Antarctic expeditions have a record of achievement unexcelled in the canine world. The sledge dogs of Nansen, secured from their native masters by a laughable yet pathetic ruse, averaging forty-five pounds each, working day after day under conditions of the utmost hardship, drew one and a half times their own weight of supplies and worked with that joyous abandon and carefree air typical of the breed. Used by Shackleton, Borchgrevinck, Scott, Jackson-Harmsworth, the Duc d'Abruzzi, Fiala, and others, each expedition has added to the unusual history of the breed a new luster. The dogs deserted of necessity by the explorers amid Antarctic wastes had proven their ability to exist by themselves and have multiplied, still true to type, on the ice fields of the Antarctic Circle.

Introduced into England less than a hundred years ago, practically every show sees the Samoyeds in the forefront. The late Queen Alexandra was an ardent fancier, and the descendants of her dogs are found today in many English and American kennels. The dog is found in every region—Samoyeds born in northern Siberia have safely crossed the equator and remained in healthy condition to work in Antarctic snows. Dogs from Antarctic expeditions have survived the suns of Australia to return to England and start great kennels there.

Beautiful, eye-arresting, perhaps the most beautiful breed in existence; gentle and companionable; an excellent watchdog; never a troublemaker, yet able to hold its own when forced into a fight; with an independence born of unusual intelligence, yet marked with a loyalty to a loved owner which wins hearts; the big, white dog with the "smiling" face and dark, intelligent eyes, and the strong, sturdy muscular body, with legs built for speed—that is the Samoyed.

As puppies, "little white teddy bears," the Samoyed characteristics are strongly shown: guardians always, gentle, kindly, sturdy, adaptable, the "big white dog carries in its face and heart the spirit of Christmas the whole year through."

Schnauzer, Standard

OF THE three varieties of Schnauzer: Miniature, Standard, and Giant, all of which are bred and registered as distinct breeds, the medium, or Standard, is the prototype. He is a German breed of great antiquity, which in the fifteenth and sixteenth centuries must have been in high favor as a household companion, for his portrait appears in many paintings of the period. Albrecht Dürer is known to have owned one for at least twelve years, as the portrait of the same dog occurs several times in works of that artist between the years 1492 and 1504. Rembrandt painted several Schnauzers, Lucas Cranach the Elder shows one in a tapestry dated 1501, and in the eighteenth century one appears in a canvas of the English painter Sir Joshua Reynolds. At Mechlinburg, Germany, in the market place there is a statue of a hunter dating from the fourteenth century, with a Schnauzer crouching at his feet which conforms very closely to the present-day show standard.

The general impression of the Schnauzer is that of a compact, sinewy, square-built dog, sturdy and alert, with stiff wiry coat and bristling eyebrows and whiskers. His nature combines high-spirited temperament with unusual intelligence and reliability. He occupies the midway position between the large breeds and the toys.

As far as can be determined, the Schnauzer originated in the crossing of black German Poodle and gray wolf spitz upon wirehaired Pinscher stock. From the Pinscher element derives the tendency to fawn-colored undercoat, and from the wolf spitz is inherited the typical pepper and salt coat color and its harsh wiry character. Solid black specimens of the breed, while fairly common in Germany, are still rather unusual in this country, except in Chicago and the Middle West, where several breeders have taken them up and are endeavoring to correct the tendency shown by the blacks to revert to the soft coat of their Poodle ancestry.

The breed in America was originally classed as a terrier, whereas German breeders have always regarded the Schnauzer principally as a working dog. His principal vocation was that of rat catcher, yard dog, and guard. Before World War I in Germany, fully 90 per cent of the dogs, used to guard the carts of farm produce in the market places while the farmers rested themselves and their teams at the inns, were of strong Schnauzer blood. It was the extraordinary qualities of these dogs that led to further inquiries as to their breed, resulting in the discovery that the land of their origin holds the Schnauzer second to none for sagacity and fearlessness. Owing to these characteristics, the "dogs with the human brain" (as their owners proudly call them) were much used by the army during the war as dispatch carriers and Red Cross aides; they are also employed in Germany in police work.

German breeders are anxious that the Schnauzer shall not deteriorate into a mere show dog. To this end, most of the "Verein von Schnauzern" (Schnauzer Clubs) hold periodical ratting trials. Rats are placed in a large ring surrounded by wire netting, the floor of which is covered with straw or brushwood; two or more dogs are turned in, and the dog which noses out and kills the most rats in the shortest time is declared the winner. Ratting trials have also been held occasionally at some of the larger dog shows in Germany and have proved a great attraction to the public, as well as a telling advertisement for the breed. Schnauzers are also proving themselves apt pupils for obedience tests, which are a feature of so many of the present-day shows.

In this country and in England, they are used mainly as personal guards and companions, for which purpose their devotion and bravery, coupled with an uncanny perception of approaching danger, renders them suitable. They are good water dogs and are easily taught to retrieve; and, on at least one western sheep ranch, Schnauzers have proved themselves the most efficient of various breeds tried as protection for the flocks against marauding coyotes.

Schnauzers were first exhibited in Germany as Wire-Haired Pinschers in 1879 at the Third German International Show at Hanover; they came from the Württemberg Kennels of Burger Leonburg, and a dog named Schnauzer won first prize. Württemberg is the cradle of many of the German breeds, and one of the most important of the early Schnauzer breeders was a Württemberger, Herr Max Hartenstein of the Plavia Kennels.

A standard was published in 1880 and the breed made rapid progress as a show dog. The first specialty show was held at Stuttgart in 1890 with the remarkable entry of ninety-three dogs. The Pinscher Club was founded at Cologne in 1895 and the Bavarian Schnauzer Club at Munich in 1907. In 1918 the Pinscher and Schnauzer Clubs united to become the official representative of the breed in the German Kennel Club—it is known as the Pinscher-Schnauzer Club. There are today clubs devoted to the breed in Holland, Austria, Switzerland, Czechoslovakia, England, and America.

From a breeding point of view, there are two major male lines of descent, tracing back to two unregistered dogs, one the above-mentioned Schnauzer and another called Seppel, while the two most famous basic bitches are Settchen and Jette von Enz. Settchen traces back to

Schnauzer and was bred to a dog of the Seppel line called Prinz Harttmuth; by this mating she became the dam of Sieger Rex von Den Gunthersburg. Rex in turn became the sire of Sieger Rigo Schnauzerlust, and these two dogs, Rex and Rigo, have had a greater influence on the breed than any others in the stud book. Jette von Enz was the dam of Rigo, and her line traces back to Seppel. A litter-brother of Rigo, named Rex von Egelsee, also figures prominently in the early breeding records; both these dogs were used extensively and with excellent results for inbreeding. Demonstrative of the stamina and virility of Schnauzers is the fact that both Rigo and Rex were successfully serving as studs when they were twelve years old.

Schnauzers have become widely known in this country only since World War I, but one is said to have been shown at the Westminster Kennel Club Show in the miscellaneous class in 1899. The first recorded importation was Fingal, brought over by Mr. Leisching of Rochester, N.Y., in 1905. Fingal died in 1914, at the age of ten. The Schnauzer Club of America was formed in 1925. The first Schnauzer to become an American champion was the Swiss bitch, Resy Patricia, imported by Mrs. Maurice Newton, who bred from her the first American-bred champion, Fracas Franconia. The first dog to make the American title was Holm von Egelsee, which was also the first Sieger to come to this country. He was imported by William D. Goff, the president of the Standard Schnauzer Club of America.

All Schnauzers in Germany have their ears cropped, but since cropping in this country is governed by the separate laws of the different states, the American Schnauzer Club Standard permits both the cropped and the natural ear.

Shetland Sheepdog

THE Shetland Sheepdog, as its name implies, is a working Collie in miniature still in process of transformation into a more refined show-type Sheltie with fundamental working traits. There is little doubt that the small working Collie, from which came the modern show Collie evolving on larger lines, was likewise the progenitor of the Shetland Sheepdog evolving on smaller ones. It was assisted in the process by the environment of the Islands, which produces diminutiveness in all its stock, and by crosses with other small breeds residing in, if not indigenous to, the Islands.

The Shetland Islands themselves are not conducive to abundance of fodder or flocks, made up as they are of rugged rocks on which only meager vegetation can survive and surrounded by the sea, which brews frequent and severe storms. Small wonder that only the hardiest of both man and beast, and the smallest, could find subsistence. The actual origin of the breed cannot be traced by reference to records, as none were ever written. Tradition makes the dogs as old as the working Collies of Scotland, which frequently came to Shetland as the breed's forebears, and as old as the Islands themselves.

As the Islands were isolated from the trend of travel, the little dogs were a long time coming to the ken of dog-loving folk. Thus the breed did not take its place on the show bench until well along in the present century. The year 1909 marked the initial recognition of the Sheltie by the English Kennel Club. Not until 1914 did the breed obtain separate classification as Shetland Sheepdogs, and not Shetland Collies, because of pressure brought to bear by the Collie breeders. The first Challenge certificate was awarded to the breed in 1915, after which the war put a stop to all progress for the next few years.

The history of the several clubs catering to the breed has been one of ups and downs centering around the variations in size and type which still linger in a refined form today. The Shetland Sheepdog Club in the Islands, founded in 1908, was, of course, the oldest. They asked for a rough Collie in miniature, height not exceeding 15 inches. The Scottish Shetland Sheepdog Club, a year later, asked for first an "ordinary Collie in miniature" and finally a "modern show Collie in miniature," ideal height 12 inches, and eventually 13½. The English Shetland Sheepdog Club, founded in 1914, was an offshoot of the Scottish requiring "approximately a show Collie in miniature," height (ideal) first 12 inches and finally from 12 to 15, the ideal being 13½. The British Breeders' Association came into being for a time as the offspring of the English Club and asked for a "show Collie in miniature," maintaining the same heights. In 1930 the Scottish and English Clubs revised their standards jointly to read "should resemble a Collie (Rough) in miniature." The American Shetland Sheepdog Association, youngest in years, tried to profit by the experience of its predecessors by combining the best of each in its standard. The current standard specifies height from 13 to 16 inches.

The club controversy was reflected by the struggle of breeders to fix and perpetuate the proper type and size. The smaller breeds intermingling with the working Collies brought in faults quite contradictory to true Collie type. Small spaniels were undoubtedly responsible for contributing undesirable wavy coats, low ears, large round eyes, gay tails, long bodies, and desirable calm, devoted dispositions. Little yellow

Iceland dogs with smutty muzzles and pricked ears made their mark on the breed.

To offset these influences, crosses with modern Collies were resorted to —this introduced a new set of faults along with an undeniable set of virtues derived from long generations of breeding for perfection in Collie points. The chief drawbacks, whose results we are reaping today, were legginess, loss of substance, excess size, and imbalance. At the same time, the breed was given great impetus in the improvement of head properties, especially in type, skull, and expression. While the breed is still suffering somewhat from this inescapable method of its improvement, it is likewise reaping the reward of now having within the breed all the points inseparable from the correct Collie, enabling breeders to produce substantial, beautifully balanced little dogs, with weather-resisting Collie coats, Collie type and expression, and Sheltie size, charm, and character.

The breed characteristics common to all Shelties can be used for two purposes pertaining to their working propensities or their companionship qualities. It is their nature to obey, willingly and naturally, with few or no lessons needed, an instinct coming no doubt from the many generations of obediently trained dogs behind them. The instinct to guard property or places and to give watchdog warning makes them invaluable for work as farm helpers or home protectors, a heritage of the constant vigilance required to protect the crofters' cottages, flocks, and herds from invaders of all kinds. Their ability to run swiftly and gracefully, and jump with agility over obstacles, makes them a delight in fields and woods as well as in farm work. But what most endears them to everybody is their devoted, docile natures and their keen and all but human intelligence and understanding.

Siberian Husky

THE Siberian Husky, often more accurately called the "Siberian Chuchi," is a native of northeastern Siberia particularly the area drained by the Kolyma River, where the strain has been kept pure for untold centuries. The Chuchi natives used their dogs, their most valued possession, as guards for their possessions and as companions for their children, as well as for sled dogs, facts which go far toward explaining the Siberian's gentleness and great versatility.

The first Siberians were imported to Alaska in 1909 for racing purposes; since then a large proportion of sled-dog racing records in Alaska,

Canada, and the United States has been set and held by Siberian leaders and teams.

Contrary to popular opinion, the Siberian Husky, like all true Arctic sled dogs, is naturally gentle and friendly in disposition. He is alert, intelligent, and tractable, and may readily be trained for almost any kind of work. He is by nature almost fastidiously clean, and entirely free from the body odors that many dense-coated breeds have. Remarkable for his adaptability to all kinds of living conditions, a real Siberian Husky makes an ideal pet and companion in either country or city. He is rapidly endearing himself to dog lovers everywhere by his marked intelligence, gentleness, and graceful beauty.

Welsh Corgi, Cardigan

THE Cardigan Welsh Corgi is one of the oldest breeds in the British Isles, yet even in England the breed has come to be a show specimen only in very recent times. The apparent mystery surrounding its origin has been due to the absence of any previously written history, and to the simple fact that the poor hillmen of Wales saw no reason to publicize dogs that had been so useful to them for centuries.

The data upon which this summarized history of the breed is written was collected over a period of twenty years by W. Lloyd-Thomas of Mabws Hall, Llanrhystyd, Cardiganshire, South Wales.

In the beginning, the Corgi came to the high country now known as Cardiganshire with the tall, tawny-headed Celts from Central Europe. The migration of this warrior tribe to Wales is placed, roughly, at about 1200 B.C., which means that the Corgi has been known in the land whence its name comes for more than 3000 years. The dog was a member of the same family that has produced the Dachshund.

The village of Bronant, in Mid-Cardiganshire, became the especial stronghold of those early Celts, for the place is rich in remains of the old fortifications—indeed, Bronant is ringed round with them. The inhabitants, too, give evidence of that early settlement, for considerable numbers of them are tall and auburn-haired. They are said to be the direct descendants of the hard-pressed, fiery race that threw up these mounds.

The vigilance and intelligence of the Corgi must have been a great asset to the Celts from earliest times, and tales handed down from father to son for generations identify him always as a valued member of the family circle. His uses were many and varied, not the least of which were his guardianship of the children and his aid in beating out game, in those times of more than ordinary importance.

Still, the occupation which made the Corgi worth his weight in gold to those Welsh hillmen came at a much later period, but still hundreds of years ago. This was when the Crown owned practically all land, and the tenant farmers, or crofters, were permitted to fence off only a few acres surrounding their dooryards. The rest was open country, known as common land, on which the crofter was permitted to graze his cattle, one of the chief sources of his meager income. It can be imagined that there was great competition among the crofters to secure as much as possible of this pasture land for their own uses, and the task would have been difficult had it not been for the Corgi. The little dog which had been with this Celtic people so long, and which had come to be of almost human intelligence, was trained to perform a service the opposite of that done by the herding dog.

Instead of herding the cattle, the Corgi would nip at their heels and drive them as far afield as desired. Often the crofter called upon his dog to clear "his" ground of the neighbors' cattle. The dog worked the same way in either case. The crofter would stand by his gate and give a soft whistle of two notes, one high, one low. Many times the dog could not see the cattle he was to chase, but he would keep going as long as he could hear that whistle. His speed was remarkable, considering his short legs with their out-turned feet, but the length of his back gave him added spring. When the dog had scattered the cattle by biting their hocks—avoiding death only by ducking close to the ground when they kicked—the crofter would give the recall signal, a shrill, long-drawn-out whistle made by placing the fingers in the mouth. The dog would return at once.

The division of the Crown lands, their subsequent sale to the crofters, and the appearance of fences, removed the usefulness of the Corgi. He was still retained as guard and companion by some of the hillmen, but to most he was a luxury they could not afford. In many instances he was succeeded by the red herder and by the brindle herder. The original type of Corgi known in Bronant since time immemorial became very scarce, and it is due only to the greatest care on the part of modern breeders that the old strains have been preserved.

Needless to say, stud books were unknown to the Celts and to the early Welsh farmer-descendants of the old warrior tribe. But if there were no records, there was a rigid policy of selective breeding unsurpassed in this present day. The original Corgis had to be proficient workers, and no mating was consummated without due consideration.

After the breaking up of the Crown lands, and the introduction of the new breeds, there was a certain amount of experimentation with crosses. The ancient dog of Bronant was crossed with the red herder, but it did not prove very successful and was not attempted many times. The brindle herder, however, made a rather fortuitous cross. The progeny followed the dominant characteristics of the Corgi, and gained a little through the finer coat and the color of the brindle herder. Crossed later with the Collie, there was produced the breed known as the heeler.

The principal strains of the Cardigan Welsh Corgi of today go back to the old Bronant Corgi with a slight infusion of brindle herder blood. This dog approximates as nearly as possible the dog that enjoyed his greatest popularity in Cardiganshire a century and more ago.

Welsh Corgi, Pembroke

ALTHOUGH all evidence seems to point to the fact that the Pembroke Welsh Corgi is a much younger dog than the Cardigan Welsh Corgi, it is still true that the Corgi from Pembrokeshire is a breed of considerable antiquity. No breed that traces its origin back to A.D. 1107 can be regarded as an especially new type of dog.

In modern times there has been an effort to link the two types of Corgi under the heading of a single breed. This is far from the truth, according to W. Lloyd-Thomas, the Welsh authority who has spent so many years digging out the history of these small cattle dogs. He has given some interesting information, that, while it tends to divorce the two Corgis definitely, still gives the Pembroke a colorful past.

The direct ancestors of the Pembroke were brought across the Channel by the Flemish weavers who were induced by Henry I of England and took up their abode in Wales. This occurred in 1107, and it stands as a sturdy cornerstone upon which the development of a breed has been built. While weaving was one of their occupations, these Flemish people were also of an agrarian nature, and they soon had transferred to the southwest corner of Wales, at Haverfordwest, the replicas of the model homes and farms in their native land. The dog fitted into this scheme.

This early progenitor of the Pembroke Welsh Corgi of today has been described as having a noticeable resemblance to the older Schipperkes. It sprang from the same family that includes the Keeshond, the Pomeranian, the Samoyed, the Chow Chow, the Norwegian Elkhound, and the Finnish Spitz. It has little or nothing of the Dachshund characteristics.

In relation to the Cardigan, the Pembroke is higher and shorter in body; the legs are straighter and lighter-boned, while the coat is of finer texture. Two of the most noticeable differences are in the ears and the tail. Cardigan ears are rounded, while the Pembroke's are pointed at the tip and stand erect. The Cardigan has a long tail, and the Pembroke a short one. In disposition, the Pembroke is more restless, more easily excited. If one could see specimens of the early members of both breeds at the same time, the differences would be very marked. In modern times they have become more similar. The whole development of the Pembroke evinces a desire on the part of its breeders to produce a lower, stockier dog. It also may be noted that the head has grown stronger, while, in these times, good sized, round-tipped ears are not unusual.

The manner in which the Pembroke and the Cardigan have approached each other in appearance is not merely a matter of chance or of selective breeding. It is known, rather definitely, that the two were crossed before the middle of the nineteenth century.

The story comes direct from one of the old crofters, a man of nearly ninety years, who spent his whole lifetime in Bronant. It seemed that in his youth, many of the young people in that village found a manner of increasing their pocket money. There were always plenty of the Cardigan puppies; in fact, the majority were a burden on the poor tenant farmers. If these puppies were retained, they would cost money to feed. One day an enterprising young man tucked a couple of Corgi puppies under his arm and set forth into a neighboring shire. When he returned there was the jingle of coins in his pocket. Thereafter, other young men followed the example. The old hillman who relates this incident says that he sold puppies to the farmers in Carmarthenshire and in Pembrokeshire.

It is not known whether any Cardigan Corgis had gone into Pembrokeshire at an earlier date, but it is quite possible, and it is only logical that if the two breeds were in the same section they would be bred together at some time. So far as known, the Pembroke was not taken into Cardiganshire up to the time of World War I, although since then there have been many instances of inter-matings.

The two breeds of Corgi were mated together frequently at the time when these dogs first came to the consciousness of the bench-show fanciers. Little was known about either dog, and crossings were common. This practice has been stopped, or practically so, since more information has become available, and all breeders of today are determined to keep the Pembroke distinct from the Cardigan.

The Pembroke is one of the most agreeable of small house dogs. It has an affectionate nature, but does not force its attentions upon those unwilling to accept them. Its intelligence is undoubted, and it is a remarkably alert, ever-vigilant guard of the fireside.

GROUP IV: TERRIERS

Airedale Terrier

THE origin of the Airedale Terrier is enveloped in the same veil of theory and conjecture which shrouds the origin of all species in man's attempt to retrace the stages in evolution. Antique art records the existence of English dogs having a distinct resemblance to the terriers of later days and from which undoubtedly sprang the Broken-haired or Old English Terrier.

This extinct black and tan tyke is thought by some authorities to have been the common progenitor of the Irish, Fox, Welsh, and Airedale Terrier. At all events, an admixture of his varying types and sizes from seventeen to thirty pounds in weight formed the roots, so to speak, of the genealogical tree of the breed fostered by sporting Yorkshiremen for hunting the fox, badger, weasel, foumart, otter, water rat, and small game in the valleys of the rivers Colne, Calder, Warfe, and Aire. These constant companions and guardians, while excelling in agility, eyesight, hearing, and untiring courage, lacked the keen nose and swimming ability of the rough-coated Otter Hound, with which they competed in the chase, and was the wise reason for crossing the two breeds in the constructive attempt to embody the virtues of both in a better breed of larger and stronger terriers.

From 1864 on, the earlier whelps were called Working, Waterside, and Bingley Terriers. They were shown in increasing numbers at local agricultural shows at the time dog shows were in their early growth.

In 1879 classes were first provided for Airedale Terriers at the Airedale Agricultural Society's show held at Bingley, Yorkshire. Welsh Terriers received classification at shows in 1883, and the Smooth Fox Terrier received separate classifications at Birmingham in 1862. The towns of

Skipton, Bradford, Keighley, and Otley followed Bingley with classifications, and some years later the competition for the Otley gold medal became the premier win in the breed.

Champion Master Briar (1897–1906) is conceded to be the patriarch of the breed. He may be likened to the trunk of the family tree whose branches grew in many directions. His great sons, Ch. Clonmel Monarch and Crompton Marvel, carried on his prepotency. The former was exported to Philadelphia, where ardent fanciers molded the breed in this hemisphere.

Present-day winners in most of the countries which breed, exhibit, and support the breed with Airedale Terrier clubs all now trace to the founders of the modern king of terriers. This honor goes to Ch. Warland Ditto (1919–1927), the Cragsman King family, and the celebrated Warland Kennels, which bred their foundation bitches to Ch. Rhosddu Royalist. His daughter, international Champion, Warland Strategy, produced the key sire, which when bred to her sister, Warland Wingate, produced the great sire Ch. Warland Whatnot. He in turn sired Clonmel Monarque, whose sons Ch. Clee Courtier and Clee Brigand are responsible for the greater number of the 1928–1935 champions when bred to bitches by the record sire of champions, Ch. Flornell Mixer, a Warland Ditto grandson by Moorehead Marquis, whose grandam also owned Ch. Rhosddu Royalist as sire. Warland Ditto, his sire Cragsman Dictator, his dam, Ch. Warland Strategy, and her sire, Ch. Rhosddu Royalist, were all exported to the U.S.A.

Nearly all of the male lines of former families here and in Great Britain have disappeared, leaving few collateral sires for an outcross. We still have a few in descendants of Ch. Ridgewood Rocket, Ch. Geelong Cadet and Ch. Briarcroft Perfection—dogs which held their own in competition with imported champions at the large shows.

The degree of perfection of type attained in the breed by those who have carried on the idea of their standard is attested by the frequency with which Airedales have been judged best of all breeds in the most important all-breed shows of England and America. They shine, however, greatest in the minds of their many fond owners who value the faithful attachment, companionship, and protection of their families as a priceless possession.

Airedale Terriers are used on great game in Africa, India, Canada, and our game lands. They were among the first breeds used for police duty in Germany and Great Britain. They have also been used in several wars as dependable dispatch bearers due to their ability to suffer wounds without faltering at the next order for duty. Their sweet disposition, possibly inherited from the hound blood, has endeared them to many of the best breeders and owners of leading kennels, many of whom are women who take a pride in showing their own stock. The correct temperament in puppyhood is one of discretion, and when mature, a certain dignified aloofness both with strangers and their kind. Their disposition can be molded by the patience of their masters in any environment, but when trained for defense and attack they are usually unbeatable for their weight.

Australian Terrier

As THE history of breeds is reckoned, the Australian Terrier is of comparatively recent origin, dating from the year 1885 when it was first exhibited in Melbourne as the Australian Rough.

Long before that period there was in Australia a dog casually known as the Broken-haired Terrier, that far-flung rootstock of so many terrier breeds. To greater degree than any other so-called breed of bygone times, the Broken-hair or Rough-coated Terrier, as it was sometimes called, resembled the old Scotch or Scottish Terrier. This dog, however, it was discovered later, could not compete successfully with the more modern Scotties being imported from Britain. And so, as has been the case with many another breed during its inception, crosses were resorted to for improvement, and the dog molded to a type in keeping with what Australian fanciers thought it should be. The result was the Australian Terrier.

Several terriers entered into the composition of the Australian Terrier, although few agree as to exactly which ones. The Cairn, the Dandie Dinmont, and the Irish Terrier, the Yorkshire and the prick-eared Skye have all been given credit for participation, by different people at different times. These breeds may have been used as direct crosses but, what is just as likely, their qualities may have been handed down by way of a common or related ancestry. Judging from the standpoint of resemblance, the length of back seems to indicate Skye Terrier heritage; the soft-haired topknot points to the Dandie Dinmont, the weatherproof coat to the Scottie, the erect ears to the Cairn, and the rich blue-and-tan coloration to the Yorkshire.

The Australian Terrier was not long in gathering to itself an enthusiastic coterie of admirers, not alone because of a gratifying individuality of appearance, but because of its adaptability as a useful small hunter in the Australian bushland. It was granted breed status in England in

1933 and, in addition, is currently recognized in Ireland, India, South Africa, Australasia, and Canada. It was introduced into the United States during the first quarter of the century and admitted to registry by the AKC in 1960.

Here is one of the smallest of the working terriers—about ten inches shoulder height and twelve to fourteen pounds weight—but all dog and ready to go. His courage, his spirit, and constant air of assurance are inborn qualities dating back to the days in his native land when he guarded the mines and tended the sheep. Withal, he is affectionate and rather quiet for one of his kind, seeming to accept responsibility for home and household. His harsh coat is good for any weather, while its slight or gradual shedding is only one point of many in his favor as indoor companion.

Bedlington Terrier

THE Bedlington Terrier takes his name from the mining shire of that name, in the County of Northumberland, England. Purely a Northumbrian production, he first came to be known as the Rothbury Terrier, having originated in the Hannys hills, where the sporting squires loved a game terrier.

The origin of the breed remains a mystery. However, going back to 1820, we find that a Joseph Ainsley of Bedlington acquired a bitch, Phoebe, from a friend at Alnwick. This bitch was known as Coates Phoebe, since she found her home at the vicarage where young Coates, the vicar's son, had sporting proclivities. In 1825 Phoebe was mated to a Rothbury dog, Andersons Piper, also acquired by Ainsley of Bedlington, and the fruit of this union was the Bedlington Terrier in question.

About this time there flourished in Bedlington a colony of nailers who took to the breed and became noted for their plucky terriers. Of this dog's gameness there was not the slightest doubt—he never shirked at any kind of vermin and could more than hold his own at drawing a badger or at ratting in or out of Wales.

Although many crosses were introduced, there was always a band of enthusiastic admirers who kept to the original breed, and it was not until 1877 that the National Bedlington Terrier Club (England) was formed by a few influential fanciers who made themselves responsible for bringing him to the notice of the public by exhibiting him on the show bench. Since then the Bedlington has made vast improvement in type.

Many tales have been told by the older generation of matches made by the miners and nailers of that period, where large sums were at stake on the result of a fight between terriers of their respective fancies. The Bedlington was never a mischief seeker, but once he started fighting, it was to the death.

As time went on, he was taken into the homes of the elite, who found him a tractable and first-class companion. He was not long in developing into a pet, his great heart and lovable nature endearing him to all fortunate enough to own him.

There are two distinct colors, liver and blue, and it is only a question of fancy as to which is preferred. In the early days the liver was much in evidence, and some great dogs were of that color; in fact, the liver dog was preferred to the blue which is now so fashionable. Whether the former shade has become rarer from a change of tastes on the part of Bedlington breeders, or whether it is merely a coincidence that so few good liver-colored specimens happen to be shown at the present time, we are unable to say, but the fact remains that of late high-class blue Bedlingtons far outnumber good liver specimens. While there have been many good specimens of both colors, it is noticeable that the mother of the celebrated Piper was a blue-black bitch, possessing a light-colored topknot, a characteristic which has been meticulously preserved.

Both Piper and his mother, Phoebe, were considerably lighter in weight and smaller in stature than the dogs of the present day. But it is on record that Piper was set on a badger at eight months old and was constantly at work, more or less on badgers, foxes, otters and other vermin. He drew a badger after he was fourteen years old, when toothless and nearly blind, after several other terriers had failed.

There are not many today that would face a badger, owing no doubt to the fact that women have adopted the Bedlington and he is becoming more of a pet. However, the old fire is latent within him, for when his jealous nature is aroused, he will fight for his place in one's affection.

One reason there were fewer Bedlingtons at one time than their desirability warranted was the trimming necessary for exhibition in the show ring. Known only to a few so-called experts, this trimming seemed difficult. Gradually, however, the knack was mastered, so that now most owners trim their own dogs and find it quite easy. It is only necessary to see it done by someone who knows how, after which, with a little practice, the novice becomes expert. The dog is hardy and not difficult to raise, and his feeding is the same as that required for other terriers of like weight.

Border Terrier

As THE name suggests, the Border Terrier has its origin on either side of the Cheviot Hills which form the Border country, and may be regarded as one of the oldest kinds of terriers in Great Britain. As a purely "working terrier" Border farmers, shepherds, and sportsmen for generations carefully preserved a particular strain of this dog which could be found in almost every Border homestead.

With the hills at their disposal and miles from habitation, stock was subjected to the ravages of the powerful hill foxes, and to hunt and kill them the Border farmer and shepherd required a game terrier with length of leg sufficient to follow a horse, yet small enough to follow a fox to ground. The dogs had to be active, strong, and tireless; they had to have weather-resisting coats in order to withstand prolonged exposure to drenching rains and mists in the hills.

The Border Terrier is a tireless, hard worker for his size, and he is full of pluck. There is no wall he cannot get over or wire entanglement he cannot scramble through. Should the fox run to earth, he will bolt him every time, or stay the night in the earth until the matter is settled from his point of view. It may therefore be gathered that in order to meet these requirements the Border Terrier, as now known, was evolved by a process of judicious selection from the native hill terriers.

Until the English Kennel Club recognition was given, the Border Terrier was unknown to the great majority, but he was always exhibited in considerable numbers at most of the Agricultural Societies' shows in the Border country. Following recognition by the English Kennel Club and the formation of the Border Terrier Club in 1920, the breed has been catered to at many of the important shows in the British Isles, but few specimens are as yet seen at shows in the United States.

Much has been accomplished toward the improvement of the breed, while keeping in mind its natural vocation together with those breed characteristics which have been the goal of the Border Terrier Club of England in order to further and preserve this ancient sporting terrier.

Bull Terrier

THERE are two varieties of the Bull Terrier breed, the white and the colored. The breed dates back to about 1835. It is almost unanimously admitted that it was established by mating a Bulldog to a white English Terrier, which breed is now extinct. The results were known as the "bull and terrier." Some few years later, to gain size, this dog was crossed with the Spanish Pointer, and even to this day evidence of Pointer inheritance is seen occasionally.

Then about the year 1860 fanciers decided that an entirely white dog would be more attractive, so James Hinks produced an all white one which was taken up enthusiastically by young bloods of the day as the most fashionable dog.

It was a dog for sportsmen in times when life in general was more strenuous and of rougher, coarser fiber—when dog fights were allowed and well attended. As fighting dog, or "gladiator," of the canine world, such a dog had to be of great strength, agility, and courage. Withal, he was bred by gentlemen, for gentlemen, for those who had a great sense of fair play, and who scorned the liar and the deceiver in any game. The dog was taught to defend himself and his master courageously, yet he was not to seek or provoke a fight—and so the white variety became known as "the white cavalier," a title which he bears with distinction to this day.

Contrary to the opinion of those who do not know him, the Bull Terrier is an exceedingly friendly dog; he thrives on affection, yet is always ready for a fight and a frolic. The general preference in this country is for a male dog about fifty pounds, a female about forty-five pounds, well balanced, not freaky in any particular, but a well-put-together, active, agile athlete—a gladiator of perfect form.

There is also the Colored Bull Terrier which, in accordance with its Standard, must be any color other than white, or any color with white just so long as the white does not predominate. The "Colored" was voted a separate variety of Bull Terrier in 1936.

Cairn Terrier

THE history of the Cairn Terrier is enhanced by the fact that the modern Cairn is an attempt to preserve in typical form the old-time working terrier of the Isle of Skye. The fancier, for a proper appreciation of the Cairn, should know what the uses and appearance of these terriers were. Fortunately weights, engravings, measurements, descriptions of their appearance, and accounts of the use of these terriers exist.

From Martin's *History of the Dog* in 1845, Capt. McDonald's description and measurements of the ideal Cairn in 1876, from Ross's *Cairn Terrier*, Darley Matheson's *Terriers*, and many other writers, it is plain that these were working terriers, with courage for the bolting of otter, foxes, and other vermin from among rocks, cliffs, and ledges on the wild shores of their misty isle.

Variation in appearance existed in these early times, as each breeder had his own fancies. But continued selection for a definite purpose soon resulted in the production of a rather definite type. This was a terrier weighing from fourteen to sixteen pounds, with the bitches two pounds or so less; a dog active, game, rather longish in body, short on the leg, with short, pointed muzzle, broad head; ears short, erect, pointed, and set wide apart; large, expressive dark eyes; with hard coat not over an inch and a half long and soft furry undercoat.

The Cairn's sporting instincts and vermin-killing ability made him a useful member of the laird's and crofter's households. Becoming popular with those who desired a sporting terrier capable of hunting in all weather, he was taken up by fanciers and admitted to the English Kennel Club *Stud Book* as a recognized breed.

To retain the best old-working type was the ideal aimed at by the English Cairn Terrier Club on its formation. The Cairn Terrier Club of America has the same object. Both clubs have the same ideal weight for dogs—fourteen pounds or a stone. The two standards with only slight differences in wording describe the same dog—the old-time terrier of the Isle of Skye and the West Highlands of Scotland.

The Cairn has characteristics in common with other breeds of terriers. He should have a level back with tail set on at back level, a straight front, well-sloped shoulders, deep brisket, strong loins and hindquarters, compact feet with thick pads, and he should move easily and freely on a loose lead with terrier smartness and style. But, while these points of contact with other breeds of terriers exist, there are also marked differences which are of great importance to the continuation of the Cairn's distinctive qualities.

In head, the Cairn differs from all other terriers. Short and broad-headed, his foreface should be little, if any, longer than the distance from stop to occiput. The muzzle should be rather pointed and not too heavy or deep. He should have a well-defined stop and a slight indentation between the eyes, flattening out into his broad skull. The ears should be set wide apart, neither too far down on the side nor too high up on the head. They should be small, short, pointed, erect, and free from long hairs. The expression should be keen, alert, varminty. He should have a medium-sized, dark hazel eye, distinct eyelashes, and shaggy protecting brows. He should have plenty of head furnishings, which may be softer than his body coat. Lack of these spoils the characteristic appearance of the head, which is, perhaps, the most important feature of the breed. A Cairn with a good head is half through in the show ring.

The height of the Cairn, which differs from that of other terriers, is important in giving the breed the distinctive conformation which the late Mr. Glynn called "Cairnishness." He should measure at the top of the shoulder about nine and one-half inches, which should be slightly less than two-thirds his body length. He is not so low to ground, and in proportion to his size, is slightly longer in back than the Sealyham and the Scottish Terrier.

The Cairn's typical coat is double with a harsh outer jacket and a soft furry undercoat. Any color except white is permissible, and dark points —muzzle, ears, and tail—are desirable. He is not trimmed, only a certain amount of "tidying up" being allowable. He should always be shown in good coat and with plenty of head furnishings, for a proper coat is one of the breed's distinctive features. There is one, and only one, correct size for the Cairn Terrier—fourteen pounds for dogs, thirteen pounds for bitches, and the dogs should be in proper proportion to those weights.

The modern Cairn should have the hardiness to meet the performance of his old-time prototype. Utility should be the aim of the fancier, since the expressed object of the Cairn Terrier Clubs is to preserve the breed in its best old-working type. If the breed is to resist passing fads and the inroads of modernization, the first consideration in judging should be given to those qualities which are unique in the Cairn.

Dandie Dinmont Terrier

THE Dandie Dinmont Terrier was bred from selected specimens of the rough native terrier of the Border hunters in the Cheviot Hills between England and Scotland and was first recorded as a distinct type of breed about 1700. He was distinguished by his pre-eminence in hunting the otter and the badger. A direct line of these dogs descended to the farmers in the Teviotdale Hills, where Sir Walter Scott in his travels chanced upon them and made them famous in his *Guy Mannering*, published in 1814. His character Dandie Dinmont, a farmer, supposed to have been a Mr. James Davidson of Hindlee, near Hawick, kept the immortal six, Auld Pepper, Auld Mustard, Young Pepper, Young Mustard, Little Pepper, and Little Mustard. Sir Walter gives an excellent description of their pluck: "I have them a' regularly entered, first wi' rottens, then wi' stots or weasles, and then wi' the tods and brocks, and now they fear naething that ever cam' wi' a hairy skin on't." From the time of the popularity of *Guy Mannering* to the present day, the breed has been known as "Dandie Dinmont's Terriers."

There is an excellent picture of a Dandie in the portrait of Henry, third Duke of Buccleuch, painted by Gainsborough in 1770. The present Dandie is identical with the one in this portrait. King Louis Philippe of France owned a pair of the breed in 1845.

Today the hunting qualities of the Dandie are not so often required, but his other qualities make him an excellent house dog. He is intelligent, fond of children, and an excellent guard. He has a will of his own and will sometimes obey a command reluctantly, with a look of "I'll do it, but please don't make me."

The points of a Dandie are quite the opposite of the average terrier—there are no straight lines. Head, large with a full, domed skull; eyes, large, full, of a very deep hazel and luminous, the darker the better; jaw, strong, deep, and punishing; body, long, with slightly arched roach between the center back and the tail, combined with a broad, deep, and powerful chest; front legs, short, with paws slightly outcurved for digging; hind legs, longer and not so heavy; tail, set low, slightly curved and carried at an angle of about forty-five degrees—the shorter and heavier the tail, the better. There are two distinct colors: pepper—blue gray to light silver with light tan or silver points and very light gray or white topknot—and mustard—dark ochre color to cream with white points and topknot. The darker shades in each color are the more desirable. The Dandie has a rough double coat made up of hard and soft hair in the proportion of about double the amount of soft hair to that of hard. This forms a thorough watershed which feels crisp to the touch, but does not have the harsh feel of the wire-coated dog. The topknot and points of the ears are of light silky white hair which when fluffed up forms one of the characteristic features of the "show" Dandie.

In England and increasingly over here, Dandies are shown in their natural state with very little plucking and clipping. A Dandie can be kept in show shape with only a daily brushing and combing which eliminates three or four expensive visits to the dog beauty parlor as is the case with many another breed.

Dandies fit in anywhere, either in a rough-and-tumble out-of-doors life or in the confines of a city apartment. They are an ideal size, between eighteen and twenty-four pounds, small enough to fit a small apartment and yet a dog big in character.

Fox Terrier

THE Fox Terrier is one of the best known and most widely distributed of pure-bred dogs. You may find one wherever the English language is spoken. Clubs have been formed in Belgium, France, Germany, Italy, and other European countries to promote the interests of the breed, which comes in two varieties, the smooth and the wire.

The Fox Terrier is an ancient breed of English origin. In 1790 Colonel Thornton's Pitch, a smooth-coated white terrier with markings, was recorded both in print and on canvas. It is probable that the Smooth and the Wire sprang from widely different sources. A profound student of the related breeds claims that the ancestor of the Wire was the old rough-coated black-and-tan working terrier of Wales, Derbyshire, and Durham, and that the more important ancestors of the Smooth were the smooth-coated black-and-tan, the Bull Terrier, the Greyhound, and the Beagle.

The Smooth antedated the Wire by some fifteen or twenty years in the show ring, and at first was classified among the sporting breeds. This was a tribute to his keen nose, remarkable eyesight, and staying powers in accomplishing his work of driving the fox from his hole or the drain in which he had taken refuge when too closely pursued by the hounds.

Wires were liberally crossed with Smooths in the earlier days of breeding in order to give to the Wire the predominating white pigmentation, the cleaner-cut head, and more classical outline of the Smooth. For this reason no extended pedigree of a Wire Fox Terrier will be found without many Smooth ancestors. On the other hand, the Wire outcross appears only in the pedigrees of such of the modern Smooths as descend in the T-line, so called, from Dusky D'Orsay, bred by Mr. Francis Redmond in England in 1915 in a deliberate attempt, it is alleged, to improve the Smooth. It is believed that the T-line now exists only in Australia.

The practice of interbreeding the Smooth with the Wire and vice versa has been almost universally discontinued for some years.

An English writer has described the ideal Fox Terrier well as follows:

"He should be strong and gay, with a brave, wise way with him in the fields or at home. His head should be long and lean, with much strength in front of his eyes; these should be small and dark and full of the pride of life. His ears should be small, set high on his head, and in shape like a V. His neck be long with a slight arch. The bones from which the forelegs spring should slope well back and be nice and long; these forelegs must be straight and round and thick; his hind legs strong with good reach, and his hocks should be near the ground; his feet should be small and round, and his pads thick. He should have a deep, but not at all a broad, chest; and his ribs should spring well out, so as to make a deep but not a flat side. His back should appear straight, or with but a slight curve; and his loins should be firm and strong. His tail must spring from the top and not from the back of the dog; it should be stout and stand straight up. His coat should be smooth, and straight, and hard, and dense. He should be white, but his marks, black or tan or both, may be of all shapes and on all parts of the dog, but there must be more white than black or tan; he must not have red or blue or liver marks. A dog or bitch should weigh at least a stone (fourteen pounds), and a dog may have up to four more pounds, and a bitch up to two more; much more than this does not help. He should move in a way that shows his limbs are sound and straight and free; but it is hard to make this clear in ink, and if a man can find no guide to help him in this, it will be well to ask a good judge of a horse to show him. In brief, when the dog comes to you or when he goes from you, his legs should seem to be straight and free and not too far each from each, nor yet too near; one's eye must learn to judge this with care."

The original Fox Terrier Standard was so well drawn in 1876 by the Fox Terrier Club (England) that no change has been found necessary except the reducing of the weight of a male dog in show condition from twenty pounds to eighteen pounds.

The American Fox Terrier Club, which is the parent club in this country, adopted this Standard when the club was founded in 1885, and later enlarged upon it only to the extent of giving amplifying measurements to supplement the provisions as to weight.

Irish Terrier

THE Irish Terrier had been established in his native country and elsewhere and truly bred long before entering the show ring in 1879. His origin has been much debated, but there is indisputable evidence that he is one of the oldest of the terrier breeds. In his beautiful red jacket, alert and trim, his piercing eyes reflecting a rare intelligence, he is a gallant picture of authentic terrier type and character.

The outline and conformation of this terrier of Erin are peculiar to the breed and differ markedly from those of any other in the terrier group. The body is longer, proportionately, than the Fox Terrier's, for example, with a much more decided trend to racing lines, but with no lack of substance or sturdiness of bone structure; indeed, the difference in size and shape between the Irish Terrier and the Fox Terrier has been likened to that between hunter and cob. The hunterlike raciness of build and greater freedom of action in the Irish Terrier is alien to the Fox Terrier, in which variety cobbiness is desired. Another comparison may be helpful: the similarity in outline of the Irish Terrier to the grand old Irish Wolfhound is unmistakable; the drawing of one is almost a miniature of the other, and there are equally striking similarities of character.

The Irish Terrier is an incomparable pal, and the loyal, unyielding protector of those he loves. None is hardier or more adaptable. He is equally at home on the country estate, in the city apartment, or in camp; he thrives in the northland or in the tropics. He is the interested playmate and protector of children, eager to join in their fun and frolic. In their service, as in his master's, he challenges whatever may menace. He is a born guardsman.

The Irish Terrier is an accomplished sportsman. In this country he will catch and kill woodchucks and other small game, and rates with any dog in hunting rabbits. He is death on vermin. A natural water dog, and not apt to be gun-shy, he may be trained to retrieve in water as well as on land. Indeed, the Irish Terrier has many of the sporting gifts and talents of the Chesapeake Bay Retriever, the Beagle, and the

Spaniel. He has hunted big game successfully in the far north and in the tropics.

The Irish Terrier scored as a war dog in World War I. He was "over there," and not inconsiderably in evidence. As messenger and sentinel he did his bit with that incomparable spirit and disregard of danger for which he has always been justly famed.

The following is a brief excerpt from an article written by Lt. Col. E. H. Richardson, lately Commandant of the British War-Dog School, reviewing the Irish Terrier's services:

"I can say with decided emphasis that the Irish Terriers of the service more than did their part. Many a soldier is alive today through the effort of one of these very Terriers. Isolated with his unit in some advanced position, entirely cut off from the main body by a wall of shells, and thus prevented communicating his position or circumstance by telephone or runner so that help might follow, this messenger dog was often the only means his officers had of carrying the dispatch which eventually would bring relief. My opinion of this breed is indeed a high one. They are highly sensitive, spirited dogs of fine mettle, and those of us who respect and admire the finer qualities of mind will find them amply reflected in these terriers. They are extraordinarily intelligent, faithful, and honest, and a man who has one of them as a companion will never lack a true friend."

In the show ring the Irish Terrier's style and deportment are peculiarly his own. Alert and grim when challenged, the threatening demeanor of his challenger means nothing at all to him. His fearlessness and disregard of danger have won him the nickname of "dare devil."

In fine, the Irish Terrier is a peerless pal; the playmate and protector of children; a consummate sportsman; and a war dog with the saving of human lives to his credit. In competition he is an impressive picture of intrepid terrier character. He has been styled the D'Artagnan of the show ring.

Kerry Blue Terrier

THE Kerry Blue Terrier originated in Ireland, having been noticed first in the mountainous regions of County Kerry, hence the name. The dogs had been pure-bred in that section for over a hundred years.

Gentle, lovable, and intelligent, the Kerry is an all-round working and utility terrier, used in Ireland and England for hunting small game and birds, and for retrieving from land and water. He is used quite successfully, too, for herding sheep and cattle.

These dogs were always considered as working and sporting terriers, no thought being given to them as a bench-show dog. However, after the formation of the Republic, they began to appear on the bench and met with quick favor. The first few came out at the Dublin show. English fanciers were quick to realize their possibilities if properly groomed, and the Kennel Club there provided regular classification for them. Their rise to popularity was almost instant, and each show brought out increasing numbers of entries.

The Kerry in Ireland is fostered by the Irish Blue Terrier Club of Dublin, organized by H. G. Fotterell. The principal variance in standard is that the Irish will not permit the trimming of coat. Dogs must be shown in the rough.

The Blue Terrier Club of England, organized by Captain Watts Williams, is the supporting organization back of the Blues for England. The English Standard is with a few minor exceptions identical with the American Standard in that coats must be trimmed.

There is more or less conjecture as to who imported the first Kerry and where it was first shown in this country. However, it appears that the first important show at which Kerries appeared was at Westminster in 1922. For two years following their initial exhibition at Madison Square Garden, they were relegated to the miscellaneous class, but in 1924 they were officially recognized by The American Kennel Club as a breed and given championship rating.

During the Westminster show of 1926, a group of fanciers met in the Waldorf-Astoria, New York City, when they organized a specialty club known as the Kerry Blue Terrier Club of America. Among the objects of the club were to encourage the breeding of Kerries and to assist its fanciers; to adopt a standard and to foster both the utilitarian and the sporting qualities of the dog with an aim toward field trials as well as dog shows.

The Kerry is a dog of many-sided accomplishment. He is an instinctive trailer and retrieves well. He is adaptable to all manner of farmwork, for which he is easily trained. He is an indomitable foe and cannot be surpassed as a watchdog and companion. In some instances in England he has even been used for police work. With proper treatment, food, and exercise, the Kerry Blue Terrier is very long-lived and will usually retain his activeness until the end; in fact, Kerries at six and eight years of age might be taken for young dogs.

Lakeland Terrier

THE Lakeland Terrier is one of the oldest working terrier breeds still known today. It was bred, raised, and worked in the lake districts of England long before there was a kennel club or an official stud book. The fact that it has been outstripped by many younger terrier breeds is not so much a reflection on its quality as a tribute to the scope of its working ability. The name "Lakeland," indeed, is a modern acquisition. In olden times the breed was known as the Patterdale Terrier.

It is related that long before the days of the great John Peel, or before any packs of hounds were formed, the Lakeland was kept by the farmers in the mountain districts, who, at that time, would form a hunt with a couple of hounds and these terriers. Their work was to destroy the foxes found raiding the sheepfolds. There was sport, but it was not sport for sport's sake alone. It was a very practical matter.

The color of these dogs did not matter to their owners; they bred principally for gameness at first. The color was quite secondary as long as the dogs were game enough to withstand the punishment meted out by the foxes in their rocky mountain lairs. Later came the packs of hounds, but there was not a single pack in the lake district that did not have one or two game old terriers that had continually shown their courage with fox or otter. These were coveted as breeding material. None of their puppies were ever destroyed. They were given out among various friends and followers of the hunt, later to be tried and the best workers retained to carry on the traditions of the older dogs.

So great was the courage of the native Lakeland Terriers that they would follow underground for tremendous distances. It is told that, in 1871, Lord Lonsdale had one which crawled twenty-three feet under rock after an otter. In order to extricate the dog it was necessary to undertake extensive blasting operations. Finally, after three days' work, they reached the dog, and he was gotten out, none the worse for his experience. Still other dogs have been known to be locked underground for ten or twelve days and have been taken out alive. Others have paid the penalty.

Classes for the likeliest-looking terrier, suitable for fox or otter, were judged in connection with agricultural shows throughout the lake district about 1896, when more interest was evinced in this game old breed. They were judged by masters of hounds or other experienced hunting men. At that time, the color ranged from grizzle to blue and tan, red or wheaten, with a sprinkling of white terriers. Later these classes were divided in color; for white working terriers and for colored working terriers. Always working ability was taken into consideration.

Usually the white terriers were found working with the Otter Hounds, as in many cases a dark terrier got severely mauled in the muddy waters due to the excitement of the younger hounds when the otter had been dislodged from under tree roots and drains.

It is believed by experienced terrier men that the somewhat remote ancestors of the Lakeland Terrier are similar to the progenitor of the Border Terrier. In fact, there is sound evidence that the Lakeland is an offshoot of the breed that became known later as the Bedlington, which was closely related to the Dandie Dinmont.

A hundred-odd years ago—in 1830, or thereabouts—these northern counties of England, Northumberland, Cumberland, and Westmoreland, had many varieties of terrier, each named after the small locality in which it was found in greatest numbers. Many of the old names have been lost since the breeds have gained recognition. This changing of names usually took place when specialist clubs were formed, with breeders unwilling to agree on any of the older names; and, of course, there were cases where the same dog might have been known by half a dozen different names.

Cumberland was the birthplace of the Lakeland Terrier. This is a particularly beautiful country, richly studded with lakes, particularly in the southern part. The Bedlington is attributed to neighboring Northumberland County, but it is not difficult to suppose that there was certain traffic in dogs a century ago.

The first organized effort to promote the interest of this Cumberland County breed came at the Kersurck show in 1912, when a terrier club was formed. The new club made considerable headway for two years, and then came the outbreak of World War I. Naturally, all civilian activities were under a damper, and little or nothing was heard of the Lakeland Terrier again until 1921. That year fanciers met at Whitehaven, in Cumberland. According to Thomas Hosking, who later came to the United States and who was one of the nine fanciers who attended, the name Lakeland Terrier was chosen at that meeting. The Standard was drawn up at that time, and shortly afterward the breed was made eligible for registration in the stud book of the Kennel Club (England).

There is every reason to believe that the Lakeland will find many admirers in the United States. Although a worker for generations, he makes a very good appearance in the ring. He has a dense, weather-resisting, frequently black-and-tan coat, strong jaws of moderate length, powerful hindquarters, and good legs and feet on a short, strong back. And dispite his gameness and courage, he has an attractive, quiet disposition.

Manchester Terrier

GENERATIONS ago, before the days of dog shows, there was in England a Black-and-Tan Terrier, less graceful in outline and coarser in type than those of today. Those early dogs did not have penciled toes and dotted brows, and their tan was smutty; nevertheless they were sound, game, and useful. They were accomplished rat killers, whether in the pits or along the watercourses. In fact their value was reckoned not at all upon any consideration of make and shape but solely upon the number of rats they had killed.

The Black-and-Tan Terrier was one of the breeds mentioned by Dr. Caius in the famous letter concerning the dogs of England that was sent to Gesner for inclusion in his encyclopedic work on the dogs of all nations. Dr. Caius completed his survey in 1570. He described the breed as carrying the essential colors and characteristics, but as being rougher in coat and shorter on the leg.

The Manchester district of England was a noted center for two "poor men's sports," rat killing and rabbit coursing. A fancier by the name of John Hulme, with the idea of producing a dog that could be used at both contests, mated a Whippet bitch with a celebrated rat-killing dog, a crossbred terrier dark brown in color. On this basis the roached back, seldom found in a terrier, is explained. The dogs proved useful, other fanciers took to breeding them, and the Manchester school of terriers was launched.

The name Manchester, however, was regarded as somewhat misleading, for similar dogs were known in many parts of England. Designation of the new breed did not take place until 1860 or thereabouts, at which time the city for which the dog was named had become a breed center. Manchesters soon spread over the British Isles and eventually came to this country in considerable numbers, but years were to pass before the name was stabilized. Actually it was dropped for a time as being too restricted in designation, and the dog was once again known as the Black-and-Tan Terrier. In 1923, however, the newly formed Manchester Terrier Club of America changed the name back to Manchester Terrier, and there it has remained.

Whippet, Greyhound, and Italian Greyhound have all been mentioned (with how much accuracy none can say) as partners of more or less importance in the creation of the Manchester. But supposition regarding heritage does not end there. That extensive investigator, Ash, surmises a bit regarding a Dachshund ancestor. He says it would be interesting to know not whether the Dachshund is related, but how closely it is related to the Manchester Terrier. In substantiation of this conjecture is the description by Whitaker in 1771 of the dog of Manchester as a "short-legged, crooked-legged dog." Such a relationship seems fantastic; even so it is not an impossibility, since the Dachshund's forebears were not so exaggerated as are the dogs of this day.

As a sagacious, intelligent house pet and companion, no breed is superior to the well-bred Manchester. There is a sleek, breedy look about him that no other dog presents. His long, clean head, keen expression, glossy coat, whip tail, and smart, wide-awake appearance always command attention, while his clean habits and short coat admit him to homes which might shut out his rough-haired brothers. Moreover his weight leaves nothing to be desired, for there is a medium-sized type weighing over twelve and not exceeding twenty-two pounds, and a toy weighing twelve pounds or under.

Up until 1959 the Manchester Terrier and the Toy Manchester Terrier were registered as two separate breeds, although interbreeding between the two breeds was permitted. Since that date they have been registered as a single breed, the Manchester Terrier, with two varieties, the toy and the standard, for dog-show purposes.

Development of the toy from the larger dog was first a matter of chance and later a matter of selective breeding. It came about in this manner: Two of the larger specimens would produce a litter in which all but one puppy attained the same size as the parents. As has happened again and again in the breeding of dogs, the tiny prototype attracted attention to such a degree as to create a demand for more. So naturally the breeders tried to produce more puppies of the smaller size. It has been claimed that the toy was so highly prized as to prompt surreptitious matings with Italian Greyhounds in order to keep the dog small. Fortunately these crosses were not perpetuated.

At this point excessive inbreeding took its toll. As can be readily understood, there were few toy-sized dogs to breed from, so inbreeding became the order of the day. In Victorian times size diminished alarmingly to around two and one-half pounds, and the tiny ones were admittedly delicate. Realizing their mistake, breeders endeavored to correct their technique; they aimed for, and got, more normal toy weight together with renewed vigor.

When the anti-cropping edict was passed in England, many of the older fanciers grew discouraged after trying for a time to produce an attractive-looking dog with small button ears, and consequently many ceased breeding. A few staunch devotees, however, kept the breed alive. They loved the game little fellow, whether his ears were up or down, trimmed or untrimmed, and they stayed with him through lean times and good.

No longer are extremes of any sort favored or fostered within the breed, for "the gentleman's terrier," as he was known long ago, has come into his own. He exhibits that true Manchester type, with its flat skull, triangular eyes, accented kiss marks, and sleek ebony coat with clearly delineated markings. The sole difference between the larger dog and the toy is concerned with the ears. Both varieties have moderately small, thin ears, narrow at the base and pointed at the tips. They are set high on the skull and quite close together. In the standard variety, ears may be erect or button; if cropped, they are long and carried straight up. In the toy variety, however, cropping disqualifies. The toy ear is carried naturally erect, without sidewise flare.

Norwich Terrier

THE Norwich Terrier was first introduced into England in 1880, and shortly thereafter became the fad with the undergraduates at Cambridge University. In fact, some people think that the breed should be known as the Cantab Terrier in honor of the collegiate atmosphere in which it made its bow so many years ago.

Following World War I several specimens, then known as Jones Terriers after one of the foremost English breeders of that day, arrived in the United States and were put to work in the hands of various masters of Foxhounds. For some time a small kennel was maintained and kept pure-bred by the Cheshire Hunt in Philadelphia and to lesser extent by other hunt clubs. The dogs have proved their value going to ground and have done excellent work for the hunts that have used them.

Not until 1932 was the breed granted recognition by England's Kennel Club, The American Kennel Club following suit in 1936.

Norwich Terriers enjoy going out with the horses, and notwithstanding their short legs, they have no trouble keeping up. They also make good rabbit dogs. Game to the core, they are real all-weather dogs which in every way answer the requirements of breeders who are looking for a small, wire-coated terrier, eleven to twelve pounds in weight, with good, dark eyes, short legs, stocky build, and true terrier personality. The Standard calls for either an erect ear, a trifle larger than that of the Cairn, or a very neat and small, correctly dropped ear. Although usually red, color may be black and tan or grizzle. White markings are undesirable but not disqualifying.

Here is an ideal house dog, for one reason because his hard, close coat does not collect dirt and needs no trimming. Here is a one-man dog whose loyalty, once given, never swerves. Every effort has been made to perpetuate the interesting Norwich personality and to guard against so-called improvements.

Schnauzer, Miniature

THE Schnauzer is of German origin, and is said to be recognizable in pictures of the fifteenth century. However, the modern breed was probably derived from the crossing of black Poodle and wolf-gray spitz with old German pinscher stock. The last named dogs were probably stocky black and tan, or fawn animals, containing some Württemberg droving blood. The Schnauzer is characterized by his stocky build, wiry coat, and fairly abundant, wiry whiskers. The mixed gray salt-and-pepper color, caused by a mixture of light and dark banded hairs, is peculiar to the breed, although solid black and black-and-tan also occur.

By vocation, the Schnauzer was a yard and stable dog, a guard and a destroyer of vermin, and is consequently a great ratter. However, his size precluded his use in going to ground after small animals, and he is consequently wholly distinct in blood and origin from the British terriers. In general type and temperament he resembles this group and is classed as a terrier in this country, though not in Germany or England.

The Miniature Schnauzer, derived from the Standard, or medium, Schnauzer, was produced by the selection of small specimens and their crossing with Affenpinschers. They were exhibited as a distinct breed at least as early as 1899. They resemble the medium variety in conformation, but vary somewhat more in color and are, as a rule, less aggressive in temperament. Crosses of the two breeds are not eligible for registration.

A typical Miniature is hardy and active, intelligent, fond of children, and a good ratter. His size makes him a suitable dog for town life and small quarters, but he is equally at home in the country and quite up to a dozen miles a day. As a rule, the Miniature is not a fighter, though he can stand up for himself when necessary, and he is seldom addicted to wandering. Size varies considerably, allowing the individual owner to suit his fancy. However, a good medium size is to be preferred, in the neighborhood of twelve inches, or a bit more for males. There is no standard weight, but a grown bitch of reasonable size is likely to weigh around twelve pounds, a dog around fifteen. Weight increases faster than height, so that the larger animals weigh more in proportion, and weight also depends considerably on the amount of bone. Light-boned, leggy animals are decidedly lighter than better-built animals of the same measurement.

The Miniature Schnauzer may be useful as a ratter; he can guard the house and give an alarm as well as a larger dog, but his primary vocation is as a pet. He is admirably fitted to fill this position under almost any circumstances, since good health, good temperament, and an attractive appearance combine to form an attractive personality.

Miniatures have been bred in the United States since 1925, and have gained steadily in popular favor. The American Miniature Schnauzer Club began its independent career in August, 1933.

Scottish Terrier

MOST lovers of the Scottish Terrier have a deep and abiding belief this breed is the most ancient of any of the Highland terriers; that the other breeds are only offshoots from this, the parent stem, and that the Scottie is the original, dyed-in-the-wool, simon-pure Highland terrier. They will tell you that the Skye Terrier mentioned in early histories and chronicles was not the Skye as we know it today, but the forerunner of our favorite and similar in type to it. They will refer you to such early writers as Jacques du Fouilloux, who published *La Venerie* in 1561, Turberville and Dr. Stevens, whose books *The Noble Art of Venerie* and *The Maison Rustique* appeared in 1575 and 1572, respectively. All of these works described an "earth dog used in hunting the fox and the brocke," and these descriptions fit closely to what might have been the forerunner of our present-day Scottie.

In the seventeenth century, when King James VI of Scotland became James I of England, he wrote to Edinburgh to have a half dozen terriers sent to France as a present and addressed the letter to the Laird of Caldwell, naming the Earl of Montieth as having good ones. Later, the great English authority, Rawdon B. Lee, wrote as follows:

"The Scottie is the oldest variety of the canine race indigenous to Britain. . . . For generations he had been a popular dog in the Highlands where, strangely enough, he was always known as the Skye Terrier, although he is different from the long-coated, unsporting-like creature with which that name is now associated."

While all this is very interesting and quite possibly true, the fact remains that it is neither definite nor conclusive.

Leaving the realm of speculation and inference and coming down to history and known facts, we do know that the Scottish Terrier as we find it today has been bred in purity for many years. The first show to have a class for Scottish Terriers was at Birmingham in England, in 1860. Later, a number of other shows carried this classification, but the dogs shown in these classes were not Scottish Terriers, but Skyes, Dandie Dinmonts, and Yorkshires.

All the while, however, Scotchmen who saw these dogs winning as Scottish Terriers were indignant, and about 1877 they broke into print in the *Live Stock Journal* with a series of letters protesting the situation and discussing the points and character of the true Scottish Terrier. The discussion waxed so furious that the editors finally called a halt with the statement, "We see no use in prolonging this discussion unless each correspondent describes the dog which he holds to be the true type." This challenge was taken up by Captain Gordon Murray, who in a letter to the "Stock Keeper" under the *nom de plume* of "Strathbogie," described in detail his conception of a proper Scottish Terrier. This quieted the warring factions and about 1880 J. B. Morrison was persuaded to draw up a standard. This was accepted by all parties.

The essentials of this standard have been retained in all the later standards, only minor changes having been introduced. In 1882 the Scottish Terrier Club was organized, with joint officers for England and Scotland. Later, as interest in the breed grew, the two countries organized separate clubs, although they have always worked harmoniously together. A joint committee revamped the Morrison standard and in 1933 the English club again revised this standard. The present American Standard was adopted in 1925, Messrs. Bixby, Cadwalader, and Megargee being the committee who made the revisions. In most essentials these standards are identical, the chief difference between the American and the foreign standards being in the weight requirements.

John Naylor is credited with being the first to introduce the Scottish Terrier to this country, his initial importation in 1883 consisting of a dog and a bitch, Tam Glen and Bonnie Belle. He showed extensively and continued importing, among his later importations being his famous dogs Glenlyon and Whinstone. The first Scottish Terrier registered in America was Dake (3688), a brindle dog whelped September 15, 1884, bred by O. P. Chandler of Kokomo, Indiana. His sire was Naylor's Glenlyon. This was in the American Kennel *Register*, published by *Forest and Stream*, and about the time The American Kennel Club was being organized. In December, 1887, a bitch Lassie was registered, bred by W. H. Todd of Vermillion, Ohio. Her sire was Glencoe, by Imp. Whinstone *ex.* Imp. Roxie. Here we find Whinstone figuring as a sire. Now Whinstone was by Allister, which together with Dundee formed the two great fountainheads of the breed. Whinstone sired Ch. Bellingham Baliff which was acquired by J. J. Little, founder of the famous Newcastle Kennels. Whinstone therefore was the forerunner and progenitor of the Scottish Terrier in this country today.

Since those days there have been thousands of importations and many notable breeders have carried on the work. Probably very little if any of the early blood is to be found today. Nevertheless, these early dogs must take their place in history; and to that pioneer breeder and missionary of the breed, John Naylor, the great popularity of this staunch little breed today stands as an enduring monument.

Sealyham Terrier

THE Sealyham Terrier derives its name from Sealyham, Haverfordwest, Wales, the estate of the late Captain John Edwardes who, between 1850 and 1891, developed from obscure ancestry a strain of dogs noted for prowess in quarrying badger, otter, and fox. The requisite qualities were extreme gameness and endurance with as much substance as could be encompassed in a dog small and quick enough to dig and battle underground.

As the working ability of Sealyham Terriers drew public interest, they began to take their places with other terrier breeds in prominent homes and on the show bench. Their first recorded appearance at a dog show was at Haverfordwest, Wales, in October, 1903. In January, 1908, a group of Welsh fanciers founded the Sealyham Terrier Club of Haverfordwest and at their first meeting drew up the original standard of points for the breed. The first championship show at which Sealyhams appeared was at the English Kennel Club Show in October, 1910. The breed was recognized on March 8, 1911, by the Kennel Club, which offered the first challenge certificates for Sealyham terriers at the Great Joint Terrier Show, London, June 10, 1911.

There are three clubs that sponsor the breed in Great Britain: the Sealyham Terrier Club of Haverfordwest, which holds an annual show in Wales; the Sealyham Terrier Breeders' Association, which holds an annual championship show near London; and the Midland Sealyham Terrier Club, which holds an annual championship show at Rugby.

The breed was recognized by The American Kennel Club in 1911, shortly after its original importation into the United States. Since its American show debut at San Mateo, California, in September 1911, it has become one of the popular breeds, and it is not uncommon for a Sealyham to be awarded Best in Show at important all-breed fixtures.

The American Sealyham Terrier Club was founded on May 15, 1913, to promote the interests of the breed in the United States and to encourage exhibition and working trials. The club has offered annual trophies for competition among members throughout the country under approved judges; it has held annual specialty shows for American-bred Sealyham Terriers, and futurity stakes, while working certificates have been awarded by a committee or on recommendation of masters of Foxhounds to the club.

Skye Terrier

THE majority of terriers have attained something of their present-day form within the last century; but the Skye Terrier of nearly four centuries ago was so like the specimens of today that his description at the time almost fits the modern standard.

One may find mention of the Skye Terrier in that historic volume called *Englishe Dogges*, which was penned, strangely, by Dr. John Caius, master of Gonville and Caius College, Cambridge University, and court physician to Edward VI, Queen Mary, and Queen Elizabeth. He was a man of broad education aside from the sciences, and also a great traveler and sportsman. Referring to the breed, he says it was "brought out of barbarous borders fro' the uttermost countryes northward," . . . "which, by reason of the length of heare, makes showe neither of face nor of body."

Thus we find the Skye Terrier of today. His flowing coat is the same as the one that proved such a grand protection in the days when his only occupation was to challenge vicious animals that otherwise might have crippled him at a single bite. Perhaps this long coat has been a handicap, for all followers of this game old working terrier have witnessed him surpassed in popularity by one after another of the newer breeds. Still they are reluctant to change him in any manner. Indeed, they stand by the motto of the Skye Club of Scotland—"Wha daur meddle wi' me."

The breed takes its name from the chief of those northwestern islands of Scotland that, as far back as he can be traced, formed his native home, and in which he was found in greatest perfection. He is the only terrier distinctively belonging to the northwestern islands that is not common to the whole of Scotland. Those who have the best practical knowledge of the Skye maintain that he is without rival in his own peculiar domain, and that wherever there are rocks, dens, burrows, cairns, or covers to explore, or waters to take to, his services should be called.

From the nature of Dr. Caius' allusion to him, it is evident that the Skye Terrier had become known in the cities of England, especially in the royal palace. The kings and queens of England have always set the styles in that country, and as soon as the Skye had been accepted in court —evidently in the middle of the sixteenth century when Dr. Caius penned the historic work—he was soon the fashionable pet of all degrees of nobility, and after that of the commoners.

No other definite terrier breed has yet existed long enough to rival the duration of the Skye's popularity, for he still was the most widely known of all the terriers down to the end of the nineteenth century. He was kept in all the English-speaking countries. Since then he has slipped quietly into the background, yet his admirers in England and Scotland— where he has maintained his greatest foothold—are happy to point to the time when "a duchess would almost be ashamed to be seen in the park unaccompanied by her long-coated Skye."

The Skye Terrier was one of the most important breeds at American bench shows before the turn of the century, and the rivalry among the leading kennels was exceptionally keen. Although the frontiers of his activities have been somewhat curtailed, the true value of the Skye Terrier is evinced by the tenacious grasp which he has on those who have come in contact with him. Thus, entries may sometimes be small at bench shows today, but seldom does one find a major show without some specimens of this old terrier breed.

Staffordshire Terrier

To GIVE correctly the origin and history of the Staffordshire Terrier, it is necessary to comment briefly on two other dogs, namely the Bulldog and the terrier.

Until the early part of the nineteenth century, the Bulldog was bred with great care in England for the purpose of baiting the bull. The Bulldog of that day was vastly different from our present-day "sour-mug." Pictures used as late as 1870 represent the Bulldog as agile and as standing straight on his legs—his front legs in particular. In some cases he was even possessed of a muzzle, and long rat tails were not uncommon. In fact, the old Bulldog of years ago, with the exception of head, looks more like our present-day Staffordshire Terrier than like the present-day Bulldog.

Some writers contend it was the white English Terrier, or the Black-and-Tan Terrier that was used as a cross with the Bulldog to perfect the Staffordshire Terrier. It seems easier to believe that any game terriers, such as the Fox Terriers of the early 1800s, were used in this cross, since some of the foremost authorities on dogs of that time state that the Black-and-Tan and the white English Terrier were none too game, but these same authorities go on to stress the gameness of the Fox Terriers. It is reasonable to believe that breeders who were attempting to perfect a dog that would combine the spirit and agility of the terrier with the courage and tenacity of the Bulldog would not use a terrier which was not game. In analyzing the three above-mentioned terriers at that time, we find that there was not a great deal of difference in body conformation, the greatest differences being in color, aggressiveness, and spirit.

In any event, it was this cross between the Bulldog and the terrier that resulted in the Staffordshire Terrier, which was originally called the Bull-and-Terrier Dog, Half and Half, and at times Pit Dog or Pit Bull-terrier, later assuming the name in England of Staffordshire Bull Terrier. As early as 1870 these dogs began to find their way into this country, when they became known as Pit Dog, Pit Bull Terrier, later, American Bull Terrier, and still later, as Yankee Terrier. They were finally recognized by The American Kennel Club under the name Staffordshire Terrier. The name Staffordshire Bull Terrier was originally applied to this dog in England at about the time dogfighting was abolished, the people in and around Staffordshire favoring the continuance of this form of alleged sport.

Breeders in this country have developed a type many of which are a little heavier in weight than the modern Staffordshire of England. These dogs have not been primarily show dogs, but have been bred for gameness, soundness, intelligence, and spirit. The weights in this country for the female are, on the average, from thirty-five to forty-five pounds, and for the male, from about forty to fifty pounds, while in England many specimens weigh approximately ten pounds less. The excess weight that we have acquired in this country is not a result of the infusion of other blood, but was obtained by selecting the larger dogs for breeding purposes, since breeders desired a bit heavier dog. While the weight may vary, it should be in proportion to size; and this dog's chief requisites should be strength unusual for his size, soundness, balance, a strong, powerful head, a well-muscled body, and courage that is proverbial.

To clarify the confusion that may exist even in the minds of dog fanciers concerning the difference between the all-white English Bull Terrier and the Staffordshire Terrier, it is advisable to comment briefly upon Bull Terriers. The all-white English Bull Terrier was introduced by Mr. James Hinks of Birmingham, who had been experimenting for several years with the old bull-and-terrier dog, now known as Staffordshire. It is generally conceded that he used the Staffordshire, crossed with the white English terrier, and some writers contend that a dash of Pointer and Dalmatian blood was also used to help perfect the all-white Bull Terrier.

In mentioning the gameness of the Staffordshire, it is not the intention to tag him as a fighting machine, or to praise this characteristic. These points are discussed because they are necessary in giving the correct origin and history of the breed. The good qualities of the dogs are many, and it would be difficult for anyone to overstress them. In appearance, they are flashy-looking and they attract much attention on the show bench. As to character, they exceed being dead game; nevertheless, they should not be held in ill repute merely because man has been taking advantage of this rare courage to use them in the pit as gambling tools. These dogs are docile, and with a little training are even tractable around other dogs. They are intelligent, excellent guardians, and they protect their masters' property with an air of authority that counts; they easily discriminate between strangers who mean well and those who do not. They have another characteristic that is unusual: when they are sold, or change hands, they accept their new master in a comparatively short time.

Welsh Terrier

JUDGING from the old paintings and prints of the first known terriers, the Welsh Terrier is a very old breed, for these prints show us a rough-haired black-and-tan terrier.

In old times this dog was more commonly known as the Old English Terrier or Black-and-Tan Wire-Haired Terrier, and as late as 1886 the English Kennel Club allotted one class for "Welsh or Old English Wire Haired Black and Tan Terriers." Even to this day the color of the Welsh is as it was a hundred years ago.

In other respects, also, the Welsh Terrier has changed very slightly. He is, as he was then, a sporting dog extensively used in his native home, Wales, for hunting the otter, fox, and badger, and he possesses the characteristic gameness that one naturally looks for in such a dog. Although game, he is not quarrelsome, in fact, he is well mannered and easy to handle.

The first record of Welsh Terriers having a classification of their own in England was in 1884–85 at Carnavon where there were twenty-one entries, but even at this time it was not uncommon for dogs to be shown as Old English Terriers and also as Welsh Terriers. As late as 1893 Dick Turpin, a well-known show dog of those days, continued in this dual role. Welsh Terriers were first brought to this country by the late Mr. Prescott Lawrence in 1888, when he imported a dog and a bitch, T'Other and Which, and showed them at the Old Madison Square Garden in the miscellaneous class. No other Welsh, however, were imported for some time, Ch. Red Palm making his debut over here some years later. But about 1901 classification was offered for Welsh at Westminster, and four or five dogs were shown; from then on their popularity has steadily increased.

Welsh Terriers should stand about fifteen inches and weigh about twenty pounds. Black and a rich tan in color, they should be built like a cleverly made hunter, with plenty of bone and substance. The head should be broader than that of the Fox Terrier, but the skull should be very flat and the eyes set fairly far apart to give that intelligent, unmistakably Welsh expression, so different from other terriers and so characteristic of the breed.

West Highland White Terrier

IT IS probable that the West Highland White Terrier and all the terriers of Scotland came from the same stock; the Scotties, Cairns, Dandie Dinmonts, and West Highland Whites are branches from the same tree and its roots.

The West Highland White Terrier, according to notable authors and the Malcolm family of Poltalloch, Scotland, originated at Poltalloch, where they had been bred and maintained for more than 100 years prior to their appearance at dog shows. In 1916 Colonel Malcolm said that his father and grandfather both kept them. It is probable that the lineage of the Malcolm dogs goes back to the time of King James I, who asked for some "earth-dogges" out of Argyleshire.

Years ago the breed was known as the Roseneath Terrier, also as the Poltalloch Terrier. The name Roseneath was taken from the Duke of Argyll's place in Dumbartonshire, Scotland. The first show held for the breed was at Crufts in London.

Mr. Robert Goelet, among the early fanciers to import the West Highlander to the United States, paid heavy money for the importation of British champions such as Kiltie of Glenmere and Rumpus of Glenmere, both grand dogs in their time. Today the breed is widely known and justly popular.

The West Highland is all terrier—a large amount of Scotch spunk, determination, and devotion crammed into a small body. Outdoors they are truly sporty, good hunters, speedy and cunning, with great intelligence. In the house they are all that can be desired in a pet; faithful, understanding, and devoted, yet gay and light-hearted.

One of the reasons West Highland White Terriers are such delightful little dogs to own is their hardiness. They need no pampering. They love to romp and play in the snow and will follow skaters or walkers for miles across frozen lakes and harbors. They are also easy to show and handle as they require very little trimming and, indeed, look better and more characteristic when in their natural state. Of course, there are always a few hairs which should be pulled out just to smarten the dog up a bit, but there is no prettier sight than a well-kept West Highland White Terrier shown in full coat.

The West Highland's outer coat is hard and stiff and should be kept so by proper grooming and dry-cleaning rather than by washing. There are people who think a white dog hard to keep clean, but this is not so. A little time spent each day with a brush and comb keeps him always in the pink of condition.

GROUP V: TOYS

Affenpinscher

PROGENITOR of the more familiar Brussels Griffon, the Affenpinscher, or Monkey Dog, was well known on the European continent as far back as the seventeenth century. This quaint little dog's popularity has been overshadowed by the Griffon, but more recently he is enjoying a return to favor. The breed has been recognized by The American Kennel Club, admitted to the *Stud Book*, and allowed classification at shows.

A game, alert, intelligent, and sturdy little "terrier type," the Affenpinscher is characterized by his "monkeyish" expression, derived from a prominent chin with hair-tuft and mustache. This expression is further accentuated by his bushy eyebrows, shadowing black-bordered eyelids and large, piercing dark eyes which contrast with his red or gray wiry coat and the black mask which is found on many good specimens. The entire coat is stiff and wiry in texture, and with his cropped ears and docked tail he is every inch a real dog, despite his small size. The ideal Affenpinscher should measure ten and a quarter inches at the shoulder, and weigh no more than seven to eight pounds.

Now that these attractive little dogs are being seen at the shows, their admirers are predicting a rise in popular favor.

Chihuahua

WHILE little or nothing is known of the previous history of the Toltecs, it has been established that they existed in what is now Mexico as early as the ninth century A.D., and that during their several centuries of occupancy they had a breed of dog called the Techichi. This dog was small, although not tiny, and of heavy-boned structure. His coat was long, while his most distinctive feature was muteness.

The Techichi, regarded as indigenous to Central America, is the progenitor of the Chihuahua that now enjoys popularity throughout the United States, where he has been bred to his greatest perfection. No records of the Techichi are, so far, available prior to the ninth century, but it seems probable that his ancestors were in the locality prior to the advent of the Maya tribes about the fifth century.

The evidence firmly establishing the Techichi to the Toltec period is found in pictures carved on stones—they may be found today in the Monastery of Huejotzingo, on the highway from Mexico City to Puebla. This monastery was constructed by the Franciscan Monks around 1530 from materials of the existing Pyramids of Cholula, built by the Toltecs. The carvings give a full-head view and a picture of an entire dog that closely approximates the Chihuahua of modern times. There also are remains of pyramid constructions and some pointers to the early existence of the Techichi at Chichen Itza in distant Yucatan.

Toltec civilization was centered principally around Tula, which is close to the present Mexico City, and there one finds the most abundant relics of this ancient breed. For that reason, there always has been speculation regarding the discovery of the earliest specimens of the modern breed in the State of Chihuahua. The dogs were found, about 1850, in some old ruins close to Casas Grandes, said to be the remains of a palace built by Emperor Montezuma I.

The conclusions of K. de Blinde, a Mexican breeder and authority who has spent years traversing sections of the country on horseback, are that the present form of Chihuahua evolved from crossing the Techichi with the small hairless dog brought from Asia to Alaska over the land bridge where the Bering Strait now runs. This hairless dog, similar to the one found today in China, was responsible for the reduction in size.

The Aztec conquerors of the Toltecs flourished for several centuries, and just prior to the coming of Hernando Cortés civilization was at a high state and the wealth prodigious. Dogs of the rich were highly regarded, and the blue-colored ones were held as sacred. Paradoxical as it seems, the common people found little use for this same breed, and there are even tales that they were eaten.

The stormlike career of Cortés in Mexico during 1519–20 left little of either Aztec wealth or civilization. Practically all Montezuma's possessions were wrung from his dying hands, and it is only natural that his dogs became lost for several centuries.

While the Techichi's principal home was Mexico, there is a historic letter written by Christopher Columbus to the King of Spain that adds a curious note to knowledge of the breed. Reporting on the seizure of the present island of Cuba, Columbus stated that he found: "A small kind of dogs, which were mute and did not bark, as usual, but were domesticated." These dogs could not have been taken to Cuba by the Aztecs, who were not a seafaring people.

Legend and history are rich in tales of the ancestors of the present Chihuahua. He is described as a popular pet, as well as a religious necessity, among the ancient Toltec tribes and later among the Aztecs. Archaeologists have discovered remains of this breed in human graves in Mexico and in parts of the United States.

The phenomenon is believed due to the part the dog played in the religious and mythological life of the Aztecs. He was employed in connection with the worship of deities, with the voyage of the soul in the underworld, and in relation to the human body. With the sacrifice of a dog with a red skin, buring it to ashes with the corpse of the deceased, the sins of the human were supposed to be transferred to the dog, and the indignation of the deity thus averted. The dog also was credited with guiding the human soul through the dark regions of the underworld, fighting off evil spirits and leading the soul of the deceased safely to its ultimate destination.

The modern Chihuahua is quite different from his early ancestors, with his variegated colors ranging from snow white to jet black. Mexico favors the jet black with tan markings, and the black and white spotted. The United States prefers the solid colors.

American breeders have produced a diminutive dog that has few comparisons, even among other breeds, in size, symmetry, and conformation, as well as intelligence and alertness. Curiously, the Chihuahua is clannish, recognizing and preferring his own kind, and, as a rule, not liking dogs of other breeds. The smooth-coated are the most numerous in the United States, and the most clannish, but the long-coated Chihuahua is rapidly increasing. It has all the characteristics of the smooth.

English Toy Spaniel

SINCE the spread of civilization has been from East to West, it is only natural that most of our oldest breeds of dog should trace their origin to the eastern countries. Such is the case of the English Toy Spaniel, an affectionate, intelligent little dog that captivated royalty, aristocrats, and wealthy for at least three centuries.

It has been a widespread fallacy that the Toy Spaniel made its first appearance in England during the reign of King Charles II, in the seventeenth century, for it was in honor of this sovereign that the black-and-tan variety took its name. Yet the Toy Spaniel had been known in England and in Scotland more than a hundred years before.

Just how long the Toy Spaniel had been known in Europe, particularly the south of Europe, before it was carried to England, must remain a matter of doubt. Yet most authorities are agreed that it goes back to Japan, and possibly China, of very ancient times.

According to Leighton, the English Toy Spaniel had its origin in Japan, was taken from there to Spain, and thence to England. Yet the extremely short nose of the breed might constitute evidence that it went from Spain to Japan, where it developed its present characteristics. There is a story, also, that specimens of this toy breed were brought from Japan by Captain Saris, a British naval officer, in 1613. They were presents from the emperor of Japan—every Japanese royal present always included dogs—to King James I.

The tale of Captain Saris seems a logical one, but it cannot be accepted as marking the debut of the Toy Spaniel into England and Scotland. The breed was known in England long before that, for Dr. Johannes Caius, celebrated professor and the physician to Queen Elizabeth, included it in his work *Englishe Dogges*. He refers to it as the "Spaniell Gentle, otherwise called the Comforter." His other references stamp it as almost the identical dog of today.

It is difficult to associate the Toy Spaniel with the austere Elizabeth; evidence that the breed was the favorite of the warmer-hearted Mary, Queen of Scots, in the same century is much more acceptable. The early years of Mary, during the first third of the sixteenth century, were spent in France. When she returned to Scotland as Queen, she brought specimens of the breed with her, and these dogs remained her favorites up to the time of her execution. In fact, her especial pet refused to leave her, even on the scaffold.

All Toy Spaniels up to the time of King Charles II appear to have been of the black-and-tan variety, later called the King Charles. This king's favorites were brought over from France by Henrietta of Orleans, and one is described as a black and white.

The development of the other varieties, the Prince Charles, which is a tricolor of white, black, and tan, the Ruby, which is chestnut red, and the Blenheim, which is white and chestnut red, occurred at later times. All are identical in their characteristics, with the exception of color. For a long time they were bred without any reference to color. Often the same litter would produce dogs of several varieties. It is only in modern times that the science of color breeding set the different varieties apart.

The history of the Blenheim variety seems rather more definite than that of the King Charles, although in some ways incompatible with other data. The development of the Blenheim, or red and white, is credited to John Churchill, the first Duke of Marlborough. Churchill, famous soldier and diplomat, was made an Earl in 1689, and became a Duke in 1702. At that time he acquired Blenheim, which has been the family seat of the Marlboroughs ever since.

It is said by Ash that the first Duke received as a present from China a pair of red-and-white Cocker Spaniels, and that these dogs were the basis of his subsequent breeding. The Chinese origin of the breed is mentioned also by Lady de Gex, who claims that during the fifteenth and sixteenth centuries there were carried from China to Italy numerous specimens of both red-and-white and black-and-white spaniels. These dogs subsequently were crossed with Cockers and Springers, intensifying the sporting instincts which the Toy still retains.

The Dukes of Marlborough bred the Blenheim variety for many generations, and apparently they did so without the infusion of much outside blood—unless it were that of the Cocker and other varieties of spaniel. It was said by Scott in 1800 that the Duke of Marlborough's Blenheims were the smallest and best Cockers in England. They were used very successfully for woodcock shooting. And writers of a still later period describe the dogs found at Blenheim as larger than other specimens of the red and white. Also, the Marlborough strain did not have such exaggerated short noses.

Regardless of the early history of the English Toy Spaniel, it seems certain that many specimens of modern times trace their origin back to various small spaniels of England. Selective breeding has reduced them down to the limits of six to twelve pounds, but it has not altogether erased their natural hunting instincts.

Griffon, Brussels

THE Brussels Griffon is not a dog of beauty as measured by accepted standards, but one teeming with personality, hence it is not surprising that he makes lasting friends wherever he is known. He comes of neither exalted nor ancient lineage, yet is one of the most distinctive and unusual of all dogs. Although classified as a toy, there is nothing of the pampered pet in this bundle of jaunty good nature whose keynote is insouciance from his very turned up nose to the tip of his gaily carried tail. No matter what change of fortune the years may bring, he promises to remain the delightful little Belgian street urchin to the end of time.

The German Affenpinscher and the Belgian street dog, combined, were the true foundation from which our Griffons emanated, and there is only meager data available on both of these seventeenth-century breeds. To all accounts, in Belgium there was a strong conformity to a distinct type in the peasants' dogs of that epoch. These dogs were nearly as large as our Fox Terriers, but heavily built, as are most Belgian animals. Covered with a shaggy, rough, muddy-colored coat and unlovely of feature, but intelligent and interesting in disposition, they were popularly termed Griffons D'Ecurie, Stable Griffons, and they paid for their keep by killing the stable vermin. It is not uncommon to run across mention of these loyal companions as *"chiens barbus"* in the old folk songs and tales of the period, for they were to be found in nearly every household.

On the other hand, the Affenpinscher may be said to resemble the Yorkshire Terrier in many particulars, the likeness being particularly noticeable in head properties as well as in the length of body and leg. Doubtless it was felt that the injection of Affenpinscher into the then Griffons would serve to further increase the ratting ability of the Belgian dogs, although for lack of definite proof, this last must remain a conjecture.

At some later date, the smooth-coated Chinese Pug, already established in neighboring Holland, was used as a cross with the Griffon. This crossbreeding was responsible for the two types of coat which we have even in our present-day litters.

Whether there was any definite reason for adding the Ruby Spaniel to this combination, we cannot say. At any rate this breed was also brought into the picture and is largely responsible for the facial characteristics and expression which are so much a part of our present-day dog, but which have made it impossible for him to do the work to which he was once well suited.

And so we come to the twentieth-century Brussels Griffon, a small, compact dog with a harsh coat similar to that of the Irish Terrier (or else a smooth coat traceable to the Pug and termed Brabancon), with a short upturned face best described as a "speaking countenance" and a gay carriage.

The Griffon's super intelligence causes him to be sensitive, and it is not uncommon for a young dog, when in the presence of strangers, to display the same self-consciousness as a child in its awkward teens. Although obedient and easily managed, Griffons are sometimes difficult to break to the leash, hence this training should always be begun at a very early age. Strange as it may seem, the Brabancons display a marked stubbornness when on leash, although in all other respects they are every bit as tractable as their rough brothers.

As a young puppy, the Griffon must be given the same intelligent care necessary for a puppy of any of the smaller breeds. The average sized Griffon becomes very sturdy as he matures, and he develops into a real comrade, capable of holding his own on hikes and in swimming.

Italian Greyhound

BROUGHT to England during the early years of the seventeenth century, in the reign of Charles I, the Italian Greyhound carried with it a glorious heritage as the favorite of royalty and the privileged classes. Never a dog of great use, it had won high esteem because of its marvelous disposition and small size.

There is evidence that the Italian Greyhound was an effete favorite in the days of ancient Pompeii, and there are relics throughout Italy that point to the breed as the only known pet dog for many centuries. The old Latin motto, "cave canem," or "beware of the dog," is found frequently in old Roman villas. According to Leighton, this did not refer to the huge Mastiff, which invariably was kept chained, but to the tiny Italian Greyhound. The motto meant that guests should take care not to hurt the tiny pet of the matron, for he might easily be crushed by a careless step.

The date, and even the general period, at which the Italian Greyhound appeared as a distinct type is not recorded in any manuscript that has come down to us. It is known only that he has existed in his present form for more than 2000 years. His origin, of course, is not difficult to deduce, for he carries no essential characteristics other than those of the large Greyhound—characteristics that have been weakened and varied, but not radically changed. It is the general belief among accepted authorities that for pet purposes, the breed was dwarfed intentionally from the gazehound of the ancients. Continual inbreeding finally evolved a breed which produced some specimens as small as five pounds.

Possibly the early development of the breed took place in Turkey, according to Dickie, but there remains little supporting evidence for this conclusion. Later it became a favorite in Athens, and by the Middle Ages was very popular throughout all Southern Europe.

The type of the Italian Greyhound has not changed greatly from earliest times down to the present, but like the majority of breeds, it has undergone considerable refinement. The three centuries and more that the breed has been known in England and Scotland have brought it to a high state of perfection. Specimens owned by Mary Beatrice d'Easte of Modena, the Italian consort of James II, and those of Anne of Denmark, consort to James I, would not have done very well if taken into the ring against the delicate little Greyhounds of Queen Victoria.

The Italian Greyhound probably reached its height during the late-Victorian period. There were numerous big breeding kennels throughout England and Scotland at the time the breed was introduced into the United States. It seems curious, indeed, that this breed, designed for warm countries and attuned to an even climate, should have flourished so well under the damp and chilly atmosphere of England and Scotland. Still, the greatest breeder of modern times appears to have been W. Bruce of Falkirk, Scotland. When the breed came to America, it made its greatest early center in Pennsylvania, particularly at the kennels of Dr. F. H. Hoyt, who bred a succession of winners.

There are many interesting stories connected with the Italian Greyhound. Perhaps the most curious is that of King Lobengula, the black monarch of that perpetually warring South African people, the Matabele. One day while in Johannesburg, King Lobengula saw a specimen of Italian Greyhound owned by Luscombe Searelle. The prancing manner of the dog so pleased the king that he made an offer for it. Mr. Searelle was reluctant to part with the dog, but finally succumbed when the monarch promised him 200 head of cattle.

Another story concerns Frederick the Great, King of Prussia. The king had a favorite Italian Greyhound that he carried with him wherever he

went, and once, during the Seven Years' War, the tide of battle turned
so quickly that Frederick found himself in a precarious position. Dog
in arms, he took refuge under the dry arch of a bridge. The dog clung
to his royal master and did not utter a sound. Had the dog barked while
the Austrian dragoons were passing, the fate of the king and of Prussia
would have been decided right there. When this dog died, Frederick
buried him with his own hands in the grounds of the palace in Berlin.

There have been certain yarns that attribute a sporting sense to the
Italian Greyhound, but these are discredited by those who have known
the breed. It is solely a pet, and it has maintained that station throughout
its long history.

Japanese Spaniel

THAT the Japanese Spaniel, or Japanese Chin, is a very old toy breed
is attested to by the fact that dogs closely resembling them have been
noted on the old Chinese temples as well as on ancient pottery and
embroideries. Presumably these dogs originated in China, centuries ago,
since it is reported that one of the Chinese emperors gave a pair to the
emperor of Japan. They were kept in the hands of the nobility and
frequently used as gifts of esteem to diplomats and to foreigners who had
rendered some outstanding service to Japan.

When in 1853 Commodore Perry steamed into the harbor of Wraga
and opened the country's trade to the world, he was presented with some
of these dogs, then he in turn gave a pair to Queen Victoria. In time,
specimens came to America, but there remains no record as to their
final destination here. Others gravitated to this country as a result of
thieving among Japanese kennels, when ships took the dogs all over
the world. Every ship from the Orient carried several to ready buyers.
Unfortunately, the dogs were not long-lived; also, the war cut off the
supply to America to such an extent that we had to use what we had to
maintain and improve the breed. Japan, too, suffered losses among her
prized Chins when earthquakes played havoc among her breeders. Since
then Japanese fanciers have taken up other breeds and the supply of
Chins has diminished. However, Japanese Spaniels are widely distributed,
with breeders in England, France, Switzerland, Austria, and Germany,
where the high quality of the dogs has been maintained.

There are different types of Japanese Spaniels. Essentially, though, the characteristic specimen must look Oriental; must be aristocratic in appearance, stylish in carriage. The larger dog is apt to lack these features, therefore only the small dog is considered of show type. Some specimens carry profuse coats, others shorter and coarser-textured coats; either is correct, but a woolly coat is not favored.

The majority of dogs are black and white, although there are whites with lemon or red markings, including all shades from pale lemon to deep red as well as brindle. In each case the nose color must match the markings, with dark eyes regardless. Colors may be mixed within the litter in cases where the sire or dam is of other than pure black and white inheritance. Frequently a lemon and white produces only black-and-white offspring, and it may require several generations before the colors revert. Years ago, when a black-and-white dog had too much black on the body, a lemon-and-white mate was used in the hope of breaking the color in the next generation. The lemon-and-whites often had more profuse coats, so these were used to improve hair quantity as well as texture. It seems more difficult to produce a good lemon-and-white than a good black-and-white.

A Japanese Spaniel is a good companion, bright and alert. Naturally clean and game, too, he makes an ideal pet that can thrive in almost any climate. He is sensitive, though, with definite likes and dislikes, but rarely, if ever, does he forget friend or foe.

Maltese

THE Maltese is known as "ye ancient dogge of Malta," which for more than twenty-eight centuries has been an aristocrat of the canine world.

Malta has been prominent in history from earliest times. Though settled by the Phoenicians about 1500 B.C., we know that other Mediterranean races lived there as far back as 3500 B.C. Many writers of old have spoken in glowing terms of the fame and opulence of Malta, so justly celebrated for proficiency in the arts and crafts of peace and war as well as for the high state of civilization of its people. Amid these surroundings, among these people, the tiny Maltese lived.

At the time of the Apostle Paul, Publius, the Roman governor of Malta, had a Maltese named Issa of which he was very fond. In this connection the poet Marcus Valerius Martialis, born in A.D. 38 at Bilbilis in Spain, made this attachment famous in one of his famous epigrams:

"Issa is more frolicsome than Catulla's sparrow. Issa is purer than a dove's kiss. Issa is gentler than a maiden. Issa is more precious than Indian gems . . . Lest the last days that she sees light should snatch her from him forever, Publius has had her picture painted."

This last referred to a painting of Issa said to have been so lifelike that it was difficult to tell the picture from the living dog.

Besides Martial, other ancient authors discoursed on the beauty, intelligence, and lovable qualities of Maltese dogs, among them Callimachus the Elder (384–322 B.C.); Strabo (c. 63 B.C.–A.D. 24); Pliny the Elder (23 B.C.–A.D. 79); Saint Clement of Alexandria in the second century; and others equally celebrated.

The Greeks erected tombs to their Maltese, while from the fifth century on Greek ceramic art shows innumerable paintings of these dogs. A fine model of one was dug up in the Fayum, in Egypt—it is not unlikely that this was the kind of dog worshiped by the Egyptians. And it is said that queens of old served the choicest foods out of golden vases to their Maltese.

Dr. Caius (1570), physician to Queen Elizabeth, wrote in Latin: "There is among us another kind of highbred dogs, but outside the common run those which Callimachus called Melitei from the Island of Melita. . . . That kind is very small indeed and chiefly sought after for the pleasure and amusement of women. The smaller the kind, the more pleasing it is; so that they may carry them in their bosoms, in their beds and in their arms while in their carriages."

Aldrovanus, who died in 1607 and who also wrote in Latin, says he saw one of these dogs sold for the equivalent of $2000. Considering the value of the dollar in the time of Queen Elizabeth, the price paid would be equal to a five-figure sum in this day. Since the time of Good Queen Bess the Maltese has often been mentioned, writers invariably drawing attention to its small size. In 1607 E. Topsell said they were "not bigger than common ferrets." Almost 200 years later, in 1792, Linnaeus referred to them as being "about the size of squirrels," while Danberton in his *History Naturelle* writes that "ladies carried them in their sleeves."

The fact that for so many centuries Maltese have been the household pets of people of culture, wealth, and fastidious taste may account for their refinement, fidelity, and cleanliness. It should be remembered that they are spaniels, not terriers, and that, as history has long recorded them, they are healthy and spirited even though tiny.

Papillon

THE Papillon, known in the sixteenth century as the dwarf spaniel, is the modern development of those little dogs often seen pictured in rare old paintings and tapestries. Rubens, Watteau, Fragonard, and Boucher all depicted them, and their popularity was so great that noble ladies of the day did not consider their portraits complete unless one of these elegant little dogs was pictured with them. Madame de Pompadour was the proud possessor of two, Inez and Mimi by name. Marie Antoinette was another ardent admirer, while as early as 1545 there is record of one having been sold to a lady who later ascended the throne of Poland.

It is Spain that we have to thank for the Papillon's primary rise to fame, though Italy, particularly Bologna, probably developed the largest trade. Many were sold to the court of Louis XIV, who had his choice among those brought into France. Prices ran high, and the chief trader, a Bolognese named Filipponi, developed a large business with the court of France and elsewhere. Most of the dogs were transferred from one country to the other upon the backs of mules.

As time went on, a change developed in the dwarf spaniel which gave rise to the present-day name, Papillon. During the days of Louis the Great, the dwarf spaniel possessed large, drooping ears, but gradually there came into being an erect-eared type, the ears being set obliquely on the head and so fringed as to resemble the wings of a butterfly, from which the present breed derives its name. The causes of this change remain largely theoretical, but whatever they may be, we now have a toy dog whose type of body and coat is about the same as that of the original dwarf spaniel of Spain and Italy, but whose ears may be either erect or drooping. Both types may, and often do, appear in the same litter. In continental Europe, as well as Great Britain, the drop-eared variety is called Epagneul Nain, although the breed as a whole carries the nomenclature of Papillon, as it does in this country. Here both types are judged together and with equality. Another change concerns color. Originally, almost all were of solid color, but today white predominates as a ground color, with patches or ticking of other colors.

Papillons are hardy dogs. It is unnecessary to coddle them in winter; and they do not suffer particularly in severe hot weather. They delight in country activities and are equally contented in apartments. As ratters, they are extremely useful. Too small to kill a rat outright, they will worry it until it is exhausted, then dispatch it quickly. As a rule the bitches whelp easily and give little trouble when rearing puppies.

Although they have been exhibited for many years in the United States, it was not until 1935 that Papillons were represented in The American Kennel Club by their own breed club, the Papillon Club of America.

Pekingese

FASCINATING by reason of its Oriental background and distinctive personality, the Pekingese holds honored place in the dog world. In ancient times it was held sacred in China, the land of its origin, and intricately carved Foo Dog idols of varying sizes, ranging in materials from ivory to bronze and jewel-studded wood, have been handed down.

The exact date of origin is debatable, the earliest known record of its existence being traceable to the Tang Dynasty of the eighth century. However, the very oldest strains (held only by the imperial family) were kept pure, and the theft of one of the sacred dogs was punishable by death.

The characteristics we seek to retain and perfect today were in evidence in the earliest Pekingese as shown by three of the names by which they were designated in ancient China. Some were called Lion Dogs, evidently because of their massive fronts, heavy manes and tapering hindquarters. We find a second group termed Sun Dogs because of their strikingly beautiful golden red coats. Since those early days many other darker red shades have become identified with certain strains, but even today we see numerous Sun Dogs at our shows. A third name was Sleeve Dog, this being given only to those diminutive specimens which were carried about in the voluminous sleeves of the members of the imperial household. Although there is not place for even the tiniest Pekingese in the Occidental sleeve, the little ones have found a lasting place in the heart of the fancy, and there are several clubs in existence functioning solely for the improvement of the under-six-pound Pekingese.

Introduction of Pekingese into the western world occurred as a result of the looting of the Imperial Palace at Peking by the British in 1860. It is a matter of history that four were found behind some draperies in the apartments of the aunt of the Chinese emperor. Apparently they were her particular pets—she committed suicide on the approach of the British troops. It is said that throughout the palace the bodies of many of these dogs were found, the Chinese having killed them rather than have them fall into the hands of the Caucasians. The four Pekingese found by the English were of different colors; a fawn and white parti-color was the one presented to Queen Victoria on the return to Great Britain. Lord Hay and the Duke of Richmond kept the remainder and bred them.

Pekingese were not exhibited in England until 1893, when Mrs. Loftus Allen exhibited one at Chester. However, the undeniable beauty and interesting history of the breed placed it in the foreground where it has since remained. The three dogs which were outstanding in the breed's earliest development in the Occident were Ah Cum and Mimosa, termed the "pillars of the stud book" in England, followed by a large black-and-tan specimen named Boxer, so-called because he was obtained by Major Gwynne during the Boxer uprising in 1900. Curiously enough, Boxer had a docked tail and so was never exhibited. He undoubtedly did more for the breed in the early part of the century than any other Pekingese.

That the Oriental dog took quick hold of the American fancy is evidenced by the age of the Pekingese Club of America, which became a member of The American Kennel Club in 1909. So much for the introduction of the Pekingese to the Occident.

The transplanting of the Pekingese into Western soil has in no way changed his personality. He combines marked dignity with an exasperating stubbornness which serves only to endear him the more to his owners. He is independent and regal in every gesture; it would be a great indignity to attempt to make a lap dog out of him. Calm and good-tempered, the Pekingese employs a condescending cordiality toward the world in general, but in the privacy of his family enjoys nothing better than a good romp. Although never aggressive, he fears not the devil himself and has never been known to turn tail and run. He has plenty of stamina, much more in fact than have a number of the larger breeds, and he is very easy to care for.

Since he has been brought down from his pedestal in Chinese temples, the Pekingese has but one purpose in life, to give understanding companionship and loyalty to his owners. It may be truly said that the Pekingese fulfills his mission to perfection.

Pinscher, Miniature

THE Miniature Pinscher has existed for several centuries. Germany, of course, is its native land, but it has been bred as well in the Scandanavian countries for a long time. Real development of the breed abroad began in 1895 when Germany's Pinscher Klub was formed. This club, now called the Pinscher-Schnauzer Klub, gave the breed its initial standard.

From the time of the Pinscher Klub's formation, the breed improved both in type and popularity, but more rapid headway was evident from 1905 up until World War I. That war of course handicapped progress in almost everything. Following it, or in about 1919, fanciers abroad once more started to advance the Miniature Pinscher, and as a result of importations to the United States, breeding was undertaken here to a limited extent.

There were few Miniature Pinschers seen at American dog shows prior to 1928, the impetus to breed advancement dating from 1929 when the Miniature Pinscher Club of America, Inc., was formed. Previously the breed had been shown in the miscellaneous class. The little dog's popularity has increased steadily. Many entries appear at the shows with imported and American-bred specimens winning the toy group on several occasions.

Although the Miniature Pinscher is similar to a Doberman on a smaller scale, it has a nature and a way about it suggestive of a much larger dog. It is especially valuable as a watchdog, sometimes keener even than a dog twice its size. It is a born show dog, too, noted for its lively temperament and intelligence, while it is often used on the stage because of its style, smartness, and pep. The close, slick coat requires scant attention, hence always looks neat and clean. And last but not least, the "Minpin's" fondness for home and master is exceptional.

Pomeranian

A MEMBER of the family of dogs known unofficially as "the spitz group," the Pomeranian has descended from the sled dogs of Iceland and Lapland, if we are to consider type as indicative of heritage. The name, of course, traces to Pomerania, not, however, as a point of origin, but possibly because the breed may have been in process of being bred down to size there. At any rate, in its larger form the dog served as an able herder of sheep. In fact, when it first came into notice in Britain about the middle of the preceding century, some specimens are said to have weighed as much as thirty pounds and to have resembled the German wolf spitz in size, coat, and color.

The Pomeranian was not well known until 1870, when the Kennel Club (England) recognized the so-called spitzdog. Probably the nearest to original type and size of the Poms exhibited in England was the somewhat large sable dog Ruffle, shown by Mrs. Barrett and later brought to this country by Mrs. Smythe. Specimens of the breed were shown in the United States in the miscellaneous class as far back as 1892, but regular classification was not provided until 1900 at New York. In 1911 the American Pomeranian Club held its first specialty show.

The majority of early American winners were heavier in bone, larger in ear, and they usually weighed under six pounds. Generally speaking, they had type and good coat texture, although they lacked the profuseness of coat in evidence today. American-breds show marked improvement over those early winners, as the patient efforts of fanciers have brought them closer to the Standard. Indeed, American-breds have held their own with the best from anywhere; for instance Ch. Pall Mall His Majesty went to Europe and on several occasions defeated all toys for the coveted Best in Show. Over here as well, home-bred Pomeranians have contended successfully for highest honors at all-breed fixtures.

Diminutive size, docile temper, and a vivacious spirit plus sturdiness have made Pomeranians great pets and companions.

Pug

THE Pug dog is sometimes called the Dutch Pug. It is often taken for granted that the breed is indigenous to Holland, since, according to universal but dateless tradition, it came into initial favor in that country. It is easier, however, to attribute the origin of the Pug to China, whence have come practically all of the short-faced dogs with tightly-curled tails.

The Pug was first imported into England by traders from the Dutch East India Company, and that must have been the reason its origin was attributed to the Dutch. Most likely the Pug shares in the claim to antiquity. Upon importation into England it became the favored pet of the ladies of the nobility and its rise to popularity was rapid and deserved. The parent country did little to exploit the breed, and the credit for the acclaim with which the breed was received must go to two well-known British fanciers.

Lady Willoughby de Eresby of Greenthorpe, near Lincoln, was one of the breed's sponsors, and the dogs of her kennels were distinguished by their silver-fawn coloring. Mr. Morrison of Walham Green was also a sponsor; the dogs of his kennels were a brighter golden color. There was nothing to distinguish the two strains other than color, and as they were interbred, the claim that one of the breed is now pure in either strain would be spurious.

The now popular black Pug made his advent many years later, and apparently he traces his origin to an infusion of the Japanese Pug, a breed not dissimilar to our present Toy Spaniels although not so profuse in either coat or feather. The Japanese Pugs were either white or black or a mixture of those two colors, and to this we may also ascribe the tendency of many Pugs to show white on the chest and feet. In addition to the all-black Pug, there have appeared several all-white Pugs which met with little or no favor.

The Willoughby strain was more heavily marked with black tracings than the Morrison Pugs, and the interbreeding of the two strains, with some infusion of black, undoubtedly accounts for the loss of trace in the present-day Pug, since many now have a tendency to smuttiness. Today all colors are bred together indiscriminately and the puppies will be self-colored in either color, with the loss of trace in those other than black as above described.

The Standard, drawn originally in 1883, has been changed considerably since that time.

The breed may well be described as *multum in parvo*. The dogs are compact, alert, cleanly, tractable, and companionable. They breed quite true to size and type. They have merited their popularity of late years, since they require a minimum of care in order to be kept in good condition. They do not require coddling, and many have been known to undertake willingly the tasks of their larger cousins.

Silky Terrier

THE Silky Terrier is a native of Australia, where it has long found favor with the flat or cottage dwellers. Unlike other Australian breeds, it has been a dog not solely of the bush country but, for the most part, a companion in suburban homes. For years it was called the Sydney Silky in honor of its city of origin, but in 1955 it became known abroad as the Australian Silky Terrier. For more than twenty-five years it has been regarded in its homeland as a distinct breed, with stud-book records maintained by both the Royal Agricultural Society Kennel Club and the Kennel Control Council, two separate organizations.

It was first exhibited in Australia in 1907, the period which climaxed years of development. A Standard was drawn up in 1909, after which it went into India and to somewhat smaller extent into Britain. It was admitted to registry in this country as the Silky Terrier in 1959.

The Silky Terrier derives mainly from the Australian Terrier crossed with the Yorkshire. Whether those early breeders of the preceding century planned deliberately to produce a dog different from the then existing Australian Terrier, or whether the Silky was a by-product, a sport perhaps, we do not know. Thus we can but surmise on something less than purely factual basis.

At any rate, by crossbreeding and subsequent development the Australians evolved an appealing toy dog of eight to ten pounds, with a silky-textured coat of blue and tan. Lightly built and rather low-set, the dog is pronounced in terrier character and spirit. The head especially shows strong terrier influence, with its flat skull, level bite, and small, dark eyes.

The erect ear, devoid of sidewise flare, is one of the later-fixed characteristics effected by Australian breeders, since up until just a few years ago both prick and pendant ears were sanctioned. The double ear carriage may have been a holdover from an old Skye Terrier heritage acknowledged to be part and parcel of Australia's terrier family. Likewise the all-soft coat of the Silky Terrier may be accounted for by an influence due not wholly to the Yorkshire cross, for deep within the Skye lay dormant a factor for silkiness. Ash, it will be recalled, mentions "bonnie wee Skyes with long, silky hair." These things, among others, attest to the skill with which early breeders produced and by patient selection developed the Silky Terrier.

The Silky is friendly, and forceful as only a terrier can be. He is agile and light-footed, and he looks out on the world with a curious air which would seem to denote a degree of intelligence seldom encountered in a dog so small. A toy, designed no doubt as a pet, still he has done his share of worth-while work, for it is told that he has helped to control the rats and snakes on many an Australian poultry farm.

Yorkshire Terrier

The Yorkshire Terrier as a breed lays no claim to antiquity, and it became popular within a comparatively few years after it had attained definite form. In fact, its entire history is encompassed within the record of organized dogdom in the English-speaking nations, for it made its first appearance at a bench show in 1861.

The debut of the Yorkshire Terrier took place at the Leeds show, in England, but it was not exhibited under its present name. The name Yorkshire was not applied, in any great extent, until 1886 when the breed was recognized by the Kennel Club in England. According to Marples, the Leeds show of 1861 had a class for Scotch Terriers in which all the specimens were of the breed now known as the Yorkshire. The term Scotch Terrier was applied loosely in those days; indeed, the previous year at Birmingham, all the winners in the classes for Scotch Terriers were Skyes.

The Skye Terrier was definitely Scotch, but the Yorkshire was "invented" and developed in Lancashire and Yorkshire. The fact that the Yorkshire Terrier first was exhibited as a Scotch Terrier gives greater basis for the belief that it is a descendant of the Skye. Considering the recent origin of the breed, it seems rather strange that there should be any doubt as to its ancestors, but breeders long have been noted for their secretiveness when developing new breeds of dogs.

The Yorkshire Terrier in time became the fashionable pet of ladies of the aristocracy and of wealthy families in the late-Victorian era and even before, but in its beginnings it belonged to the working classes. In fact, it was so closely linked to the weavers that many facetious comments were made regarding the fine texture of its extremely long and silky coat, terming it the ultimate product of the looms.

Undoubtedly the Yorkshire is closely related to the Skye and to the Skye's exaggerated progeny, the Clydesdale or Paisley Terrier. When a great number of weavers and their families migrated from Scotland to England in the middle of the nineteenth century, they brought with them numerous specimens of the Skye and the Paisley. Settled in Lancashire and Yorkshire, they found themselves in a region that was quite conversant with practically all existing breeds.

It is doubtful whether many of the early Yorkshire Terriers could trace back to common ancestors, for, in a land that knew so many terriers and toy dogs, it would be unreasonable to suppose that all the breeders used the same crosses. Perhaps the one breed that was found most suitable to complement the qualities of the Skye was the old Black-and-Tan, or Manchester, Terrier, for this coloring long has been dominate in the Yorkshire.

The other breeds credited by old authorities with having a part in the development of the Yorkshire are the Maltese and the Dandie Dinmont Terrier. Of course, the diminutive size cannot be credited alone to crosses. It took many years before the Yorkshire was really small enough to be called a toy. The reduction in size was probably due to selective breeding. Still, it is remarkable that within twenty years of its origin the breed had been dwarfed to such an extent that it was among the smallest of all varieties.

The Yorkshire Terrier was introduced into the United States about 1880, and American writers of that period made rather caustic comments on the fact that its type was not very well fixed. It is not difficult to imagine their perplexity as to just what kind of dog was to be the style, for show records indicate that the weights varied from two and three-fourths pounds to thirteen pounds. In the beginning the weight is said to have been as much as fifteen pounds.

Modern specimens of the Yorkshire breed true to type, and their characteristics are well fixed. Coloring is distinctive, being a dark steel blue from the occiput to the root of the tail, a rich, golden tan on the head, and a bright tan on the chest. It is notable, also, that puppies invariably are born black.

While a toy, and at various times a greatly pampered one, the Yorkshire is a spirited dog. Were it not restrained, it would engage in the roistering activities of the larger terrier breeds—for all agree that the terrier strain in the Yorkshire cannot be denied. However, the extreme length of coat presents such a problem in care that most owners, perforce, must keep their dogs in the house or under strict surveillance. Even the feet must be booted or stockinged so that in scratching he will not ruin his gloriously fine coat.

ANATOMICAL DRAWINGS AND PLATES

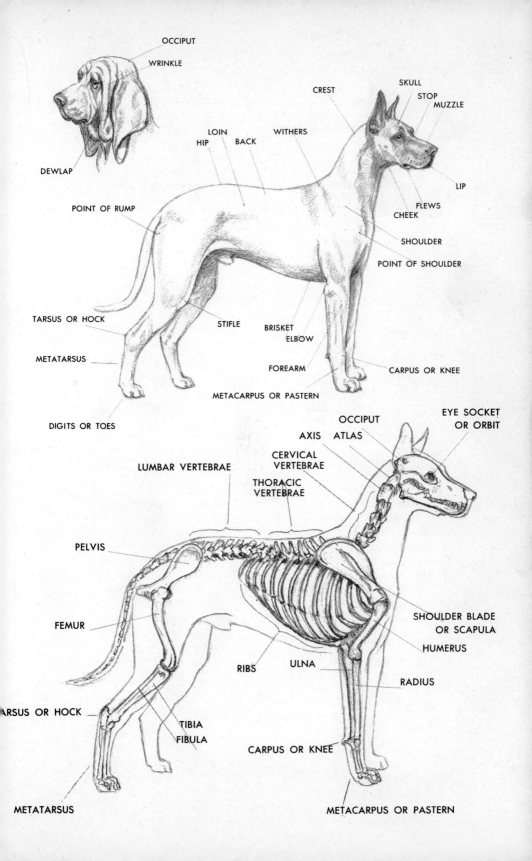

OCCIPUT

WRINKLE

DEWLAP

SKULL

CREST

STOP

MUZZLE

LOIN

BACK

WITHERS

HIP

POINT OF RUMP

LIP

FLEWS

CHEEK

SHOULDER

POINT OF SHOULDER

TARSUS OR HOCK

STIFLE

BRISKET

ELBOW

CARPUS OR KNEE

METATARSUS

FOREARM

METACARPUS OR PASTERN

DIGITS OR TOES

EYE SOCKET
OR ORBIT

OCCIPUT

AXIS   ATLAS

LUMBAR VERTEBRAE

CERVICAL
VERTEBRAE

THORACIC
VERTEBRAE

PELVIS

FEMUR

SHOULDER BLADE
OR SCAPULA

HUMERUS

RIBS   ULNA

RADIUS

ARSUS OR HOCK

TIBIA

FIBULA

CARPUS OR KNEE

METATARSUS

METACARPUS OR PASTERN

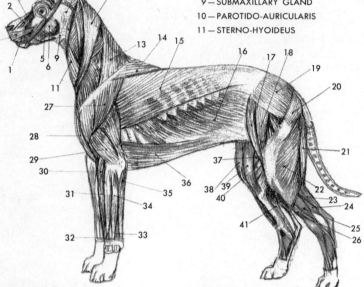

1 — DILATOR NARIS LATERALIS
2 — LEVATOR NASOLABIALIS
3 — LEVATOR LABII SUPERIORIS PROPRIUS

4 — OBICULAR ORIS
5 — ZYGOMATICUS
6 — MASSETER
7 — SCUTULARIS
8 — PAROTID GLAND
9 — SUBMAXILLARY GLAND
10 — PAROTIDO-AURICULARIS
11 — STERNO-HYOIDEUS

12 — BRACHIO-CEPHALICUS
13 — TRAPEZIUS
14 — TRAPEZIUS
15 — LATISSIMUS DORSI
16 — OBLIQUUS ABDOMINIS EXTERNUS
17 — SARTORIUS
18 — TENSOR FASCIAE LATAE
19 — GLUTEUS MEDIUS
20 — GLUTEUS SUPERFICIALIS
21 — SEMITENDINOSUS
22 — BICEPS FEMORIS
23 — GASTROCNEMIUS
24 — SUPERFICIAL DIGITAL FLEXOR
25 — DEEP DIGITAL FLEXOR
26 — ANTERIOR DIGITAL FLEXOR

27 — DELTOID
28 — BRACHIO CEPHALICUS
29 — TRICEPS
30 — EXTENSOR CARPI
31 — ANTERIOR DIGITAL EXTENSOR
32 — TENDON OF EXTENSOR CARPI OBLIQUUS
33 — LATERAL DIGITAL EXTENSOR
34 — EXTENSOR CARPI ULNARIS
35 — FLEXOR CARPI ULNARIS
36 — POSTERIOR DEEP PECTORAL
37 — VASTUS INTERNUS
38 — SARTORIUS
39 — SARTORIUS
40 — ADDUCTOR
41 — DEEP DIGITAL FLEXOR

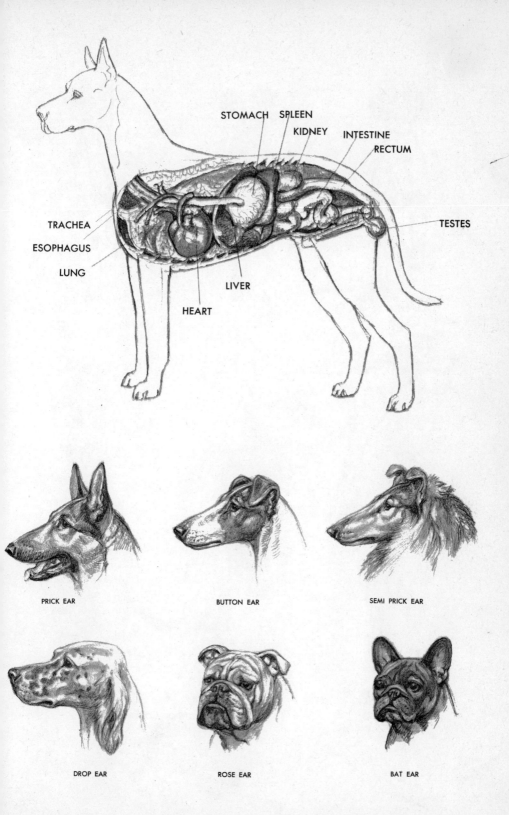

STOMACH   SPLEEN

KIDNEY

INTESTINE

RECTUM

TRACHEA

ESOPHAGUS

LUNG

TESTES

LIVER

HEART

PRICK EAR

BUTTON EAR

SEMI PRICK EAR

DROP EAR

ROSE EAR

BAT EAR

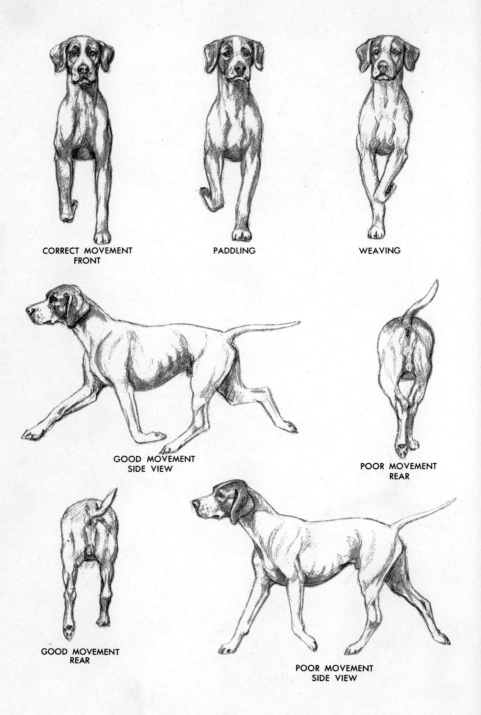

CORRECT MOVEMENT
FRONT

PADDLING

WEAVING

GOOD MOVEMENT
SIDE VIEW

POOR MOVEMENT
REAR

GOOD MOVEMENT
REAR

POOR MOVEMENT
SIDE VIEW

DOWN FACE

DISH FACE

CHEEKY

DOMED HEAD

BUMPY SKULL

FROG FACE

BROKEN UP FACE, LAY BACK

SNIPEY MUZZLE

LEVEL MOUTH

OVERSHOT MOUTH

UNDERSHOT MOUTH

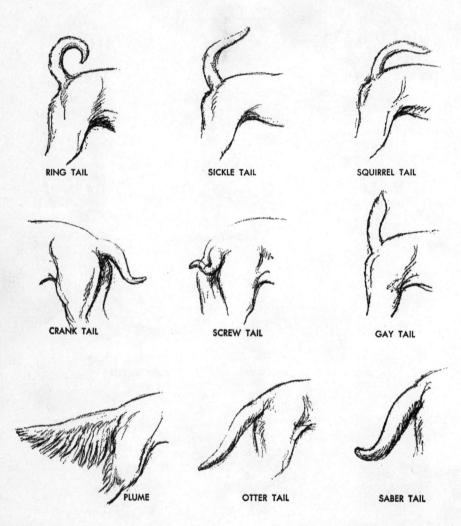

RING TAIL   SICKLE TAIL   SQUIRREL TAIL

CRANK TAIL   SCREW TAIL   GAY TAIL

PLUME   OTTER TAIL   SABER TAIL

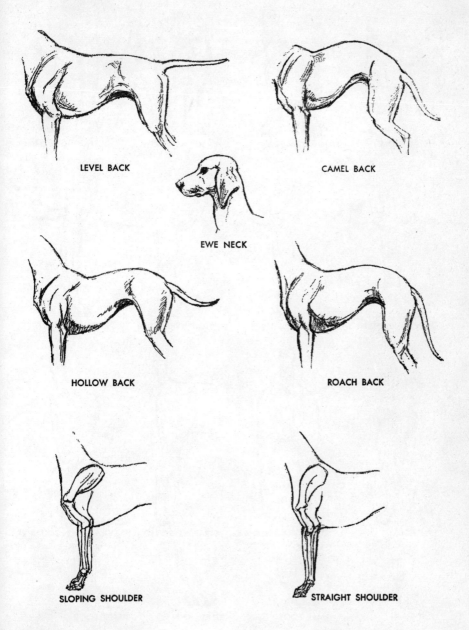

LEVEL BACK

CAMEL BACK

EWE NECK

HOLLOW BACK

ROACH BACK

SLOPING SHOULDER

STRAIGHT SHOULDER

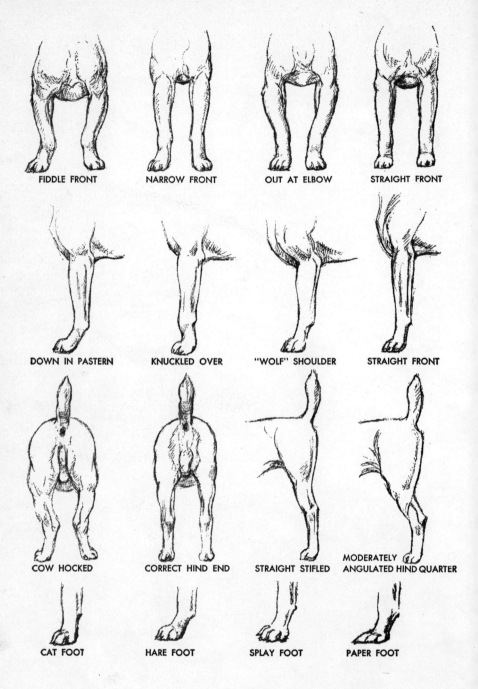

FIDDLE FRONT　　NARROW FRONT　　OUT AT ELBOW　　STRAIGHT FRONT

DOWN IN PASTERN　　KNUCKLED OVER　　"WOLF" SHOULDER　　STRAIGHT FRONT

COW HOCKED　　CORRECT HIND END　　STRAIGHT STIFLED　　MODERATELY ANGULATED HIND QUARTER

CAT FOOT　　HARE FOOT　　SPLAY FOOT　　PAPER FOOT

PLATE 1

Pointer

Wire-haired Pointing Griffon

PLATE 2

German Shorthaired Pointer

German Wirehaired Pointer

PLATE 3

Chesapeake Bay Retriever

Labrador Retriever

PLATE 4

Flat-coated Retriever

Golden Retriever

PLATE 5

Curly-coated Retriever

Gordon Setter

PLATE 6

English Setter

American Water Spaniel

PLATE 7

Irish Setter

Brittany Spaniel

PLATE 8

Clumber Spaniel

Cocker Spaniel

PLATE 9

English Cocker Spaniel

English Springer Spaniel

PLATE 10

Field Spaniel

Sussex Spaniel

PLATE 11

Irish Water Spaniel

Welsh Springer Spaniel

PLATE 12

Vizsla

Weimaraner

PLATE 13

Afghan Hound

Basenji

Beagle

Basset Hound

PLATE 14

Bloodhound

Borzoi

PLATE 15

Black and Tan Coonhound

American Foxhound

English Foxhound

PLATE 16

Smooth-haired Dachshund

Long-haired Dachshund

Wire-haired Dachshund

PLATE 17

Scottish Deerhound

Greyhound

PLATE 18

Harrier

Irish Wolfhound

PLATE 19

Norwegian Elkhound

Otter Hound

Rhodesian Ridgeback

PLATE 20

Saluki

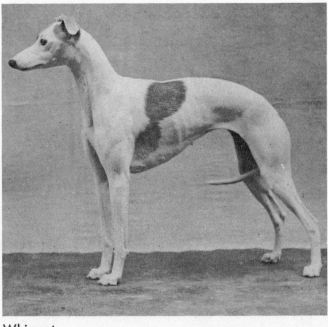

Whippet

PLATE 21

Alaskan Malamute

Briard

PLATE 22

Bernese Mountain Dog

Bouvier des Flandres

Boxer

PLATE 23

Great Pyrenees

Smooth Collie

PLATE 24

Collie

Bullmastiff

PLATE 25

Doberman Pinscher

Belgian Tervuren

Belgian Sheepdog

PLATE 26

German Shepherd Dog

Great Dane

PLATE 27

Komondorok

Giant Schnauzer

PLATE 28

Kuvasz

Mastiff

Old English Sheepdog

PLATE 29

Newfoundland

Puli

Best
17 inches only
nice

PLATE 30

Rottweiler

St. Bernard

PLATE 31

Shetland Sheepdog

Samoyed

Standard Schnauzer

PLATE 32

Siberian Husky

Cardigan Welsh Corgi

Pembroke Welsh Corgi

PLATE 33

Airdale Terrier

Dandie Dinmont Terrier

PLATE 34

Bedlington Terrier

Border Terrier

White Bull Terrier

Colored Bull Terrier

Australian Terrier

Cairn Terrier

PLATE 35

Irish Terrier

Smooth Fox Terrier

PLATE 36

Wire Fox Terrier

Lakeland Terrier

PLATE 37

Kerry Blue Terrier

Manchester Terrier

PLATE 38

Miniature Schnauzer

Norwich Terrier

Scottish Terrier

PLATE 39

Sealyham Terrier

Skye Terrier

Welsh Terrier

PLATE 40

Staffordshire Terrier

West Highland White Terrier

PLATE 41

Affenpinscher

English Toy Spaniel

Italian Greyhound

Brussels Griffon

Smooth-coated Chihuahua

Long-coated Chihuahua

PLATE 42

Maltese

Japanese Spaniel

PLATE 43

Papillon

Silky Terrier

Pomeranian

PLATE 44

Miniature Pinscher

Pekingese

Manchester Terrier (Toy)

Yorkshire Terrier

Pug

PLATE 45

Boston Terrier

Bulldog

PLATE 46

Chow Chow

Dalmatian

PLATE 47

French Bulldog

Keeshond

Lhasa Apso

PLATE 48

Poodle

Schipperke

GROUP VI: NON-SPORTING DOGS

Boston Terrier

ONE of our very few native American breeds, the Boston Terrier was the result of a cross between an English Bulldog and a white English Terrier, later considerably inbred. Incidental peculiarities of the first dogs used as sires are partly responsible for the present type.

About the year 1870 Mr. Robert C. Hooper of Boston came into the possession of an imported dog named Judge, which he purchased from Mr. William O'Brien of the same city. Judge, commonly known as Hooper's Judge and destined to be the ancestor of almost all true modern Bostons, was a cross between a Bulldog and an English Terrier, and in type he resembled the former. He was a well-built, high-stationed dog of about thirty-two pounds, in color dark brindle with white blaze. His head was square and blocky and his mouth nearly even. Judge was mated to "Gyp or Kate," as the name appears on old-time pedigrees. This white bitch, owned by Mr. Edward Burnett of Southboro, Mass., weighed around twenty pounds; she was low-stationed and had a fine, three-quarter tail, while her head was short and square.

From the mating of Judge and Gyp descended Wells' Eph, a dog of strong build and, like his dam, low-stationed. He was dark brindle with even white markings and had a nearly even mouth. Eph was bred to Tobin's Kate, a comparatively small twenty-pound female with fairly short head and straight three-quarter tail. She was golden brindle in color. From these dogs in the main evolved the Boston Terrier breed.

In the year 1889 about thirty fanciers in and around Boston organized what was known as the American Bull Terrier Club, and they exhibited the dogs as Round Heads or Bull Terriers. As time went on, these fanciers met with considerable opposition from Bull Terrier breeders, who did everything possible to discourage them. The Boston Terrier fanciers, however, refused to be discouraged, and in 1891 formed the Boston Terrier Club of America. As their dog was bred in Boston, they changed the name to Boston Terrier. After two years of sustained effort to have the Boston recognized as a pure-bred, they succeeded in persuading The American Kennel Club to admit the breed to the stud book in 1893 and the club to membership.

Up to this time, of course, the Boston Terrier was only in its infancy. There was hard work ahead to standardize the breed and to make the Bostons of that day into a more even lot. Great progress has been made, however, since 1900 in developing different strains by careful, selective breeding which included a certain amount of inbreeding. The result is a clean-cut dog, with short head, snow-white markings, dark, soft eyes, and a body approximating the conformation of the terrier rather than the Bulldog.

The Boston, while not a fighter, is well able to take care of himself. He has a characteristically gentle disposition that has won him the name of the American gentleman among dogs. As a companion and house pet, he is eminently suitable.

Bulldog

To THE best of our knowledge the Bulldog had its origin in the British Isles, the name bull being applied because of the dog's use in connection with bullbaiting.

Exactly when this old English sport first started is hardly possible to say, but in *The Survey of Stamford* the following reference is made to its probable origin:

"William Earl Warren, Lord of this town in the reign of King John (1209), standing upon the walls of his castle at Stamford, saw two bulls fighting for a cow in the castle meadow, till all the butchers' dogs pursued one of the bulls, which was maddened by the noise and multitude, through the town. This so pleased the Earl that he gave the castle meadow where the bulls combat began, for a common to the butchers of the town after the first grass was mowed, on condition that they should find a 'mad bull' on a day six weeks before Christmas for the continuance of that sport for ever."

Anyone who has read about the sport of bullbaiting must have been conscious of its extreme cruelty. From this we can gather that the original Bulldog had to be a very ferocious animal. Beauty and symmetry of form were in no way desirable, the appearance of the dog counting for nothing. The extraordinary courage possessed by these dogs is hardly believable. Bred from a long line of fighting ancestors, they grew to be so savage, so courageous as to be almost insensitive to pain. Such was the Bulldog of British sporting days.

Then came the year 1835, when dogfighting as a sport became illegal in England. To all intents and purposes, therefore, the English Bulldog had outlived his usefulness; his days were numbered. However, there were dog lovers who felt a deep disappointment at the passing of so fine a breed, so forthwith they set themselves the task of preserving it. Though ferocity was no longer necessary or desirable, they wished to retain all the dog's other splendid qualities. With this idea in mind, they proceeded to eliminate the undesirable characteristics and to preserve and accentuate the finer qualities. Scientific breeding brought results, so that within a few generations the English Bulldog became one of the finest physical specimens, minus its original viciousness. Now he was regarded as a dog which anyone could exhibit with pride.

This is the Bulldog we know today; a breed of dog of which we may be justly proud. At the same time we must express our gratitude to our British cousins who realized the value of the English Bull sufficiently to preserve him for posterity.

Chow Chow

DUE in great measure to the ruthlessness with which Chinese emperors destroyed the works of art and the literature of their predecessors, it is difficult to secure evidence of the antiquity of that lordly, aloof dog, the Chow Chow. Still, a bas-relief was discovered not so very long ago, dating back to the Han dynasty, about 150 B.C., that definitely places the Chow as a hunting dog in that period. While this establishes the breed as more than 2000 years old, it is believed by many authorities that the Chow goes back much farther; that it is, indeed, one of the oldest recognizable types of dog.

The theory has been advanced that the Chow originated through a crossing of the old Mastiff of Tibet and the Samoyed, from the northern parts of Siberia. Certainly the Chow evinces some of the characteristics of both breeds. Refutation lies in the fact that the Chow is the only

breed in the world possessing a blue-black tongue. On this score, some
maintain that the Chow is one of the basic breeds, and that he may
have been one of the ancestors of the Samoyed, the Norwegian Elkhound, the Keeshond, and the Pomeranian, all of which are of somewhat
similar type.

In modern times the Chow Chow has become a fashionable pet and
guard dog, but there is plenty of evidence available in China to prove
that for centuries he was the principal sporting dog. Perhaps the most
unusual and lavish kennel in all history was the one maintained by a
T"ang emperor about the seventh century A.D. It was so extensive that
the emperor could not have availed himself of a fraction of the facilities
for sport it afforded. It housed 2500 couples of "hounds" of the Chow
type, and the emperor had a staff of 10,000 huntsmen.

Apparently the Chow has been an unusually gifted breed of dog, since
his uses have run the gamut of work done by nearly all recognized breeds.
Even today, in China, the Chow is used as Occidentals use the setter.
He is credited with great scenting powers, with staunchness on point,
and with cleverness in hunting tactics. He is used frequently on
Mongolian pheasant, and on the francolin of Yunnan, and on both has
received great praise for his speed and stamina.

Undoubtedly the Chow Chow is of far northern origin, but he has
always been found in greatest numbers in the south of China, particularly
in the district centering about Canton. In that region of China where
he is considered indigenous, he is usually called the "black-tongue," or the
"black-mouthed" dog. In the north, as in Peiping, he is called lang kou
(wolf dog), hsiung kou (bear dog) or, the more sophisticated hei she-
t'ou (black-tongued) or Kwantung Kou, i.e. the dog of Canton.

The name Chow Chow has little basis for its origin in China; it
is believed that expression evolved from the pidgin-English term for
articles brought from any part of the Oriental empire during the latter
part of the eighteenth century. It meant knickknacks or bric-a-brac,
including curios such as porcelain and ivory figurines, and finally what is
described today as "mixed pickles," whether of the edible variety or not.
It was far easier for the master of a sailing vessel to write "chow chow"
than it was to describe all the various items of his cargo. So, in time, the
expression came to include the dog.

The first Occidental description of the Chow Chow was penned by
the Reverend Gilbert White, rector of Selborne, England, and this was
published later in the Natural History and Antiquities of Selborne. The
description, which is a most complete one, indicates that the dogs
were not very different from specimens of modern times. It was a
neighbor of the rector who in 1780 brought a brace of Chows from
Canton on a vessel of the East India Company.

The importation of Chows into England did not begin, however, until about 1880, and the breed started toward its present popularity after Queen Victoria took an interest in it. The first specialty club was formed in England in 1895; the dog was exhibited for the first time in the United States in 1890 when a specimen named Takya, owned by Miss A. C. Derby, took a third prize in the miscellaneous class at the Westminster Kennel Club show in New York. Since 1901 the Chow Chow has made steady progress, and today it is one of America's firmly established breeds.

Dalmatian

No BREED has a more interesting background or a more disputed heritage than that dog from long ago, the Dalmatian. His beginning is buried so deep in the past that researchers cannot agree as to his origin. As to the great age of the breed, and the fact that it has come through many centuries unchanged, investigators are in complete agreement.

Models, engravings, paintings, and writings of antiquity have been used with fair excuse but no certainty to claim the spotted dog first appeared in Europe, Asia, and Africa. Perhaps some of the divergencies in opinion as to the original home of the Dalmatian can be accounted for by the fact that the dog has frequently been found in bands of Romanies, and that like his gypsy masters, he has been well known but not located definitely in any one place. Authoritative writers place him first as a positive entity in Dalmatia, a province of Austria on the Eastern shore of the coast of Venice. Though he has been accredited with a dozen nationalities and has as many native names—he is nicknamed by the English, the English Coach Dog, the Carriage Dog, the Plum Pudding Dog, the Fire House Dog, and the Spotted Dick—it is from his first proved home that he takes his correct name, the Dalmatian. We find references to him as Dalmatian in the middle eighteenth century. There is no question whatsoever that his lineage is as ancient and his record as straight as that of other breeds.

His activities have been as varied as his reputed ancestors. He has been a dog of war, a sentinel on the borders of Dalmatia and Croatia. He has been employed as draft dog, as shepherd. He is excellent on rats and vermin. He is well known for his heroic performances as fire-apparatus follower and fire-house mascot. As a sporting dog he has been used as bird dog, as trail hound, as retriever, or in packs for boar or stag hunting. His retentive memory has made him one of the most dependable clowners in circuses and on the stage. Down through the years the intelligence and willingness of the Dalmatian have found him in practically every role to which useful dogs are assigned. Most important among his talents has been his status as the original, one-and-only coaching dog.

The imaginative might say that his coaching days go back to an engraving of a spotted dog following an Egyptian chariot! Even the practical minded will find no end of proof, centuries old, of the Dalmatian, with ears entirely cropped away and padlocked brass collar, plying his natural trade as follower and guardian of the horse-drawn vehicle.

He is physically fitted for road work. In his make-up, speed and endurance are blended to a nicety. His gait has beauty of motion and swiftness, and he has the strength, vitality, and fortitude to keep going gaily till the journey's end. The instinct for coaching is bred in him, born in him, and trained in him through the years. The Dalmatian takes to a horse as a horse takes to him, and that is to say, like a duck to water. He may work in the old way, clearing the path before the Tally Ho with dignity and determination, or following on with his ermine spottings in full view to add distinction to an equipage. He may coach under the rear axle, the front axle, or, most difficult of all, under the pole between the leaders and the wheelers. Wherever he works, it is with the love of the game in his heart and with the skill which has won him the title of the only recognized carriage dog in the world. His penchant for working is his most renowned characteristic, but it in no way approaches his capacity for friendship.

There is no dog more picturesque than this spotted fellow with his slick white coat gaily decorated with clearly defined round spots of jet black, or, in the liver variety, deep brown. He does not look like any other breed, for his markings are peculiarly his own. He is strong-bodied, clean-cut, colorful, and distinctive. His flashy spottings are the culmination of ages of careful breeding.

His aristocratic bearing does not belie him, for the Dalmatian is first of all a gentleman. He is a quiet chap, and the ideal guard dog, distinguishing nicely between barking for fun or with purpose. His courtesy never fails with approved visitors, but his protective instinct is highly developed and he has the courage to defend. As a watch dog he is sensible and dependable. He is not everyone's dog—no casual admirer will break his polite reserve, for he has a fine sense of distinction as to whom he belongs. Fashion has not distorted the Dalmatian. He is born pure white, develops quickly and requires no cropping, docking, stripping, or artifices of any sort. He is all ready for sport or the show ring just as nature made him. He is extremely hardy, an easy keeper, suited to any climate. He requires only the minimum of care, for he is sturdy and neat and clean.

French Bulldog

WHILE there has been a difference of opinion as to the origin of the French Bulldog, it seems pretty well established that one ancestor must have been the English Bulldog—probably one of the toy variety, of which there were a great number in England around 1860. These toy Bulldogs, not finding favor with the English, were sent in large numbers into France. There they were crossed with various other breeds, and finally became popular in fashionable circles, particularly with women. It was then that they were given the name Boule-Dog Français, although later on England scoffed at the idea of applying the word *Français* to a breed so clearly showing a strong strain of English Bulldog. At that time there was little uniformity of type, and one found dogs with rose ears, while others had bat ears which have since come to be recognized as an outstanding feature of the French Bulldog.

There are two distinctive features in French Bulldogs; one, the bat ear, as above mentioned; the other, the skull. The correctly formed skull should be level, or flat, between the ears, while directly above the eyes, extending almost across the forehead, it should be slightly curved, giving a domed appearance. Both of these features add much to the unusual appearance of the French Bulldog.

The preservation of the bat ear as a distinct feature has been due to the persistent efforts of American fanciers, since in the early days of breeding these dogs in Europe the tendency was toward the rose ear. Had this movement not been opposed by America, the breed would eventually have lost the feature that so strongly accentuates its individuality, and the result would have been practically a miniature English Bulldog.

This controversy over type was directly responsible for the formation of the French Bulldog Club of America, the first organization in the world devoted to the breed. Fanciers gave a specialty show in the ballroom of the Waldorf-Astoria in 1898, this being the first of its kind to be held in such de luxe quarters. The affair proved a sensation, and it was due, no doubt, to the resulting publicity that the quaint little chaps became the rage in society. Show entries increased until the peak was reached about 1913, when there were exactly 100 French Bulldogs benched at Westminster, while the following specialty shows had even more.

Unquestionably the dog that did the most toward the establishment of the breed in America was Ch. Nellcote Gamin, imported in 1904 by Mr. and Mrs. Samuel Goldenberg. With the addition of Gamin to the splendid stock already in this country, we were made independent of further importation in order to produce the finest Frenchies in the world. To Gamin goes credit for the greatest influence in molding the breed that can be attributed to any one dog. He was a famous sire, and today it is almost impossible to find a Frenchie that does not have Gamin inheritance.

An ideal French Bulldog should be a well-balanced, compactly built, *sound* dog, having the appearance of an active, intelligent, muscular dog of heavy bone, with a smooth coat, and medium or small stature. The weight may vary (anything up to twenty-eight pounds being permissible under the American Standard), but it is generally conceded that the ideal, or most popular, size is between nineteen and twenty-two pounds. A "Frenchie" may be any color except black (meaning without trace of brindle), black and white, black and tan, liver, or mouse color. Of the allowed colors no one is considered preferable.

In expression, the sour, pugnacious expression of the English Bulldog is not desired; a French Bulldog should have a bright, alert look which gives it the appearance of always being ready for fun and frolic, as it is.

While bred principally as pets and companions, Frenchies are remarkably intelligent and serve as good watchdogs. They are affectionate, sweet-tempered, and dependable. While alert and playful, they are not noisy and, as a rule, bark very little. Their size is another advantage in considering them as indoor pets, while the smooth, short coat is easily kept clean.

Keeshond

It took a national political turnover in Holland to bring the Keeshond (*pl.* Keeshonden) to wide attention in the latter part of the eighteenth century, but the breed had been one of the favorite dogs of the Dutch people for several hundred years before that. Never a hunter, and never used for any of the specialized forms of work that have characterized so many other breeds, the Keeshond had managed by the very force of his personality to win a high place in the affections of a nation.

The events leading up to the recognition of the Keeshond as the national dog of Holland were concerned with the social unrest that seemed to be spreading like a prairie fire throughout the world in the years immediately preceding the French Revolution. Holland was divided into two great camps, the Prinsgezinden, or partisans of the Prince of Orange, and the Patriotten, or Patriots.

The Patriots, consisting principally of the people of the lower and upper middle classes, were led by a man named Kees de Gyselaer, who lived in Dordrecht. Like most of his race, de Gyselaer was a dog lover, and at the time he owned a little dog that he called Kees. This dog gave the breed its name, for it became the symbol of the Patriots. It appeared in countless pictures and cartoons made in those days of civil strife. The men who composed the party were firmly of the opinion that their own spirit was typified in the dog. He was a dog of the people.

Histories are rather vague as to what name the Keeshond bore prior to its adoption as a symbol by the Patriots, but it was known mainly as the barge dog. The breed had served for countless years on the *rijnaken*, or small vessels that were found in great numbers on the Rhine River. These vessels seldom were larger than 200 tons at the time when the Keeshond enjoyed its greatest popularity in Holland, and consequently would not accommodate a very large dog. There probably were more of this breed of dog kept as pets and watchdogs throughout the Netherlands than there were dogs on the barges. It was only natural that the dogs of the barges became better known, for they were continually moving up and down the river, coming in contact with more people.

The origin of the Keeshond undoubtedly is Arctic, or possibly Sub-Arctic, and it is of the same strains that produced the Samoyed, the Chow Chow, the Norwegian Elkhound, the Finnish Spitz, and the Pomeranian. It seems the most closely related to the Pomeranian. Some authorities believe that the Pomeranian was produced by selective breeding of the Keeshond.

The Keeshond has changed little in the past two centuries, for the earliest descriptions represent it as nearly identical with the dog of to-day. There also are a number of old paintings and drawings that prove how well the old Keeshond type has been preserved. A drawing, made in 1794, shows the children and the dog of a burgomaster mourning beside his tomb. The dog is a Keeshond that probably could win at a bench show today. Other evidence is found in the paintings of that famous Dutch artist, Jan Steen.

The close link between the Keeshond and the Patriots in the latter part of the eighteenth century almost proved the dog's undoing. He was so much in the public eye as the symbol of the Patriots that when the Prince of Orange established his party as the dominant one, few people wanted the dog that stood for the opposition. Many who owned Keeshonden disposed of them quietly; and only the most loyal maintained the breed. And then, the type of vessel used on the rivers gradually changed. Each year they seemed to get larger, until, eventually, they were quite pretentious and had plenty of room for large dogs. This affected the popularity of the Keeshond considerably.

The breed was at very low ebb until 1920, at which time the Baroness van Hardencroek became so interested in the old breed that she undertook an investigation to see how much of the old stock still survived. The results of this search were very surprising. Whereas the breed had passed from public attention, it was still kept in its original form by certain captains of riverboats, by farmers, and by truckmen. There were many excellent specimens. Some owners even had maintained their own crude stud books.

The Baroness van Hardencroek began breeding Keeshonden and spreading their story throughout Europe. In ten years she brought the breed to such a solid position that in 1933 De Raad van Beheer op Kynologisch Gebeid in Nederland accepted the standard and the points for judging the breed. Also, there was formed the Dutch Keeshond Club. Prior to this the breed had invaded England, where it made a very good impression as early as 1925.

Alert and intelligent, the Dutch called the Keeshond the ideal companion dog. People in his native land list among his qualities the fact that he has no desire to hunt; that he would much rather remain with his master or mistress.

The whole appearance of the Keeshond gives evidence of his alertness. A wolf-gray in color, he has a stand-off coat that always looks as if it had just been brushed and trimmed, whereas the Keeshond seldom needs attention. The less he is brushed and groomed, the better he appears.

Lhasa Apso

BEYOND the northern boundary of India, where the mighty Mount Everest stands like a guardian sentinel, is the mysterious land of Tibet. It is a country of huge mountains and deep valleys, with a climate of intense cold and great heat, a country where conditions are hard on man and beast. This is the home of the Lhasa Apso, known in that land as Abso Seng Kye, the "Bark Lion Sentinel Dog." Small wonder, then, that these members of dogdom should be of such hardy and vigorous constitution.

There are four breeds native to this country: The Tibetan Terrier, a dog of true terrier type and raised more or less all over the country; the Tibetan Spaniel, a beautiful toy dog; the fierce and powerful Tibetan Mastiff, and the Lhasa Apso, which is raised in the lamaseries and villages around the sacred city of Lhasa. The dogs of Tibet have two characteristics in common, namely, the heavy coat of hair to protect them from the rigors of the climate, and the tail upcurled over the back.

Since danger threatens from without and within in this strange land, a huge Mastiff is chained to a post beside the outer door to prevent intruders from entering, while Lhasa Apsos are kept as special guards inside the dwellings. For this work the little dogs are peculiarly adapted by their intelligence, quick hearing, and finely developed instinct for detecting intimates from strangers.

The crude manner of breeding among the Tibetans is doubtless responsible for the fact that colors are not fixed, that is, if one breeds a black-and-white dog to a honey-colored bitch, he may get a brown or brown-and-white puppy as a result.

The two original dogs brought from Asia to this country were Taikoo, a black-and-white male, and Dinkie, a female the color of raw silk. Both were beautiful specimens of the breed, and from them came offspring colored black and white, grizzle and white, honey, golden, and brown and white. No doubt, under the influence of more scientific western breeding, color inheritance will become more certain.

The little Lhasa Apso has never lost his characteristic of keen watchfulness, nor has he lost his hardy nature. These two features should always be developed, since they are of outstanding merit. We have found that these dogs are easily trained and responsive to kindness. To anyone they trust they are most obedient, and their beautiful dark eyes are certainly appealing as they wait for some mark of appreciation for their efforts.

Poodle

FEW dogs have climbed to such high favor in so many different countries as has the Poodle, but it appeared so early in various parts of the world that there is some doubt as to the land of its origin.

It is supposed to have originated in Germany, where it is known as
the *Pudel* or *Canis Familiaris Aquatius*. However for years it has been
regarded as the national dog of France, where it was commonly used
as a retriever as well as a traveling-circus trick dog. In France it was
and is known as the *Caniche*, which is derived from *chien canard* or
duck dog. Doubtless the English word poodle comes from the German
pudel or *pudelin*, meaning to splash in the water. The expression
"French" Poodle was in all probability a somewhat later cognomen, bestowed as a result of the dog's great popularity in France.

At any rate, the Poodle undoubtedly originated as a water retriever.
In fact the unclipped Poodle of today bears strong resemblance in type
to the old Rough-haired Water Dog of England as painted by Reinagle
at the beginning of the nineteenth century; and except that the Irish
Water Spaniel is born with short hair on its face and tail, there is little
difference between this ancient Irish dog and the Poodle.

Authorities concede that the large, or Standard, Poodle is the oldest of
the three varieties, and that the dog gained special fame as a water
worker. So widely was it used as retriever that it was shorn of portions of
its coat to further facilitate progress in swimming. Thence came the
custom of clipping to pattern which so enhanced the style and general
appearance that its sponsors, particularly in France, were captivated by
it.

All of the Poodle's ancestors were acknowledged to be good swimmers, although one member of the family, the truffle dog (it may have
been of toy or miniature size), it is said, never went near the water.
Truffle hunting was widely practiced in England, and later in Spain
and Germany, where the edible fungus has always been considered a
great delicacy. For scenting and digging up the fungus, the smaller dogs
were favored, since they did less damage to the truffles with their feet
than the larger kinds. So it is rumored that a terrier was crossed with
the Poodle to produce the ideal truffle hunter.

Despite the Standard Poodle's claim to greater age than the other
varieties, there is some evidence to show that the smaller types developed
only a short time after the breed assumed the general type by which it
is recognized today. The smallest, or Toy variety, was known in England in the eighteenth century, when the White Cuban became popular
there. This was a sleeve dog attributed to the West Indian island of
Cuba, whence it traveled to Spain and then to England. Queen Anne,
we are told, admired a troupe of performing dogs that danced to music
in almost human fashion. And this penchant, by the way, Poodles of all
sizes have carried down the years intact.

But the Continent had known the Poodle long before it came to

England. Drawings by the German artist, Albrecht Dürer, establish the breed in the fifteenth and sixteenth centuries. How long the dog had been known in Spain is problematical, but it was the principal pet dog of the latter eighteenth century, as shown by the paintings of the Spanish artist, Goya. And France had Toy Poodles as pampered favorites during the reign of Louis XVI at about the same period.

There is scarcely a pure-bred dog of this day that can claim so many references in art and literature going back into time. Bas-reliefs dating from the first century, found along the shores of the Mediterranean, portray the Poodle very much as it is in this twentieth century. Clipped to resemble the lion, it is not unlike some of the specimens seen at the earliest dog shows. Possibly long ago there was a link between the dog attributed to the Island of Melita—now known as the Maltese—and the Toy Poodle. Similarly there may have been a relationship between the Poodle and the dog of Spain—the spaniel. If they do not come from the same progenitor, at least the paths of their ancestors must have crossed at some remote time.

The universal esteem in which the Poodle has been held since the beginning of modern history is attested by its interesting variations in size and color. In accordance with present-day show classification, we have three sizes—Standard Poodles, Miniature Poodles, Toy Poodles— as well as an array of colors to suit almost anyone's taste. We have white ones, black ones, brown, cream-and-blue ones, gray, apricot, and so on; any solid color is allowed. Some are pink-skinned, some blue- or silver-skinned, others cream-skinned. Hence he who fancies a Poodle is never at a loss: he may choose a big dog to guard and protect, a medium-sized one to fit into restricted quarters, or a tiny tot to serve only as "comforter." And he can pick a color to match whatever his décor may happen to be. Surely such an unusual selection may have played at least some part in the Poodle's continued rise to fame. But beyond that, the dog's innate intelligence and his ability to learn are considered exceptional.

It should be kept in mind that the words *Standard, Miniature,* and *Toy* are used to denote size only. The Standard or large Poodle must be over fifteen inches at the shoulder; the Miniature must be fifteen inches or under, but over ten inches at the shoulder, and the Toy ten inches or less. All are one breed, governed by the same standard of perfection.

In addition to differences in size and color, the Poodle enjoys another characteristic unique among doggy kinds, namely, a coat which lends itself to a choice of hair styling. The top coat is very profuse indeed, wiry in texture and composed of thick, close curls, and the undercoat is woolly and warm. If allowed to grow unhindered, the top coat forms thin, cylindrical mats which form a mass of ropelike cords, thus the curly Poodle becomes what used to be known in the old days as the Corded Poodle. This style, though, went out long ago; it was impractical for everyday living and difficult to keep in condition.

The various clips are of course a matter of taste insofar as the average owner is concerned. If he plans to exhibit in the show ring, however, he must choose between the Continental and the English Saddle clips for a dog that is over a year old. In the Continental clip the hindquarters are shaved bare with rosettes optional on the hips, while in the English Saddle clip a short-clipped blanket of hair covers the hindquarters. Dogs under one year of age may be shown in naturally long coat except for the face, feet, and base of tail, which is shaved.

Schipperke

THE Schipperke originated in the Flemish provinces of Belgium and is sometimes erroneously described as a Dutch dog, due perhaps to a misconception regarding the location of Flanders, a part of which extends into northern France, and to the fact that previous to 1832 Belgium and Holland were at times united. Mr. Charles Huge, the Belgian judge, says: "The Schipperke is not derived from the Spitz or Pomeranian but is really a diminutive of the black sheepdog commonly called the 'Leauvenaar' which used to follow the wagons along our old highways in the provinces. The proof of this is that those specimens that are born with a tail carry it like the Groenendael."

About a hundred years ago some of these forty-pound sheepdogs were still herding sheep in the neighborhood of Louvain, and from these both the Schipperke and the Groenendael have descended. The herd dog was gradually bred larger, and the Schipperke bred down to become that "excellent and faithful" little watchdog that we know. The breed has been known for several hundred years; in fact, it may claim the first known "specialty show," as it might be called, given for any breed. In 1690 a show for the Schipperkes of the Guild workmen was held in the Grand Palace of Brussels; the men were invited to bring their dogs and the hammered brass collars which even at that time custom had ordered for the Schipperke.

The breed was called Spits or Spitske then, the name Schipperke having been given it only after the forming of the specialty club in 1888, when it was chosen as more distinctive, and, as a compliment to Mr.

Renssens, known as "the father of the Schipperke" because of his efforts to gain recognition for the breed. He was the owner of a canalboat line operating between Brussels and Antwerp and had observed that there were many Schipperkes used as guards on these boats. The name is Flemish for "little captain" and is properly pronounced "skeep-er-ker" (the last *r* almost silent). Though called a canalboat dog, the Schipperke was as popular with shoemakers and other workmen as it was on the canals.

The "legend of the Schipperke" relates that the custom of cutting the tails arose in 1609, and it tells the story of a shoemaker who, angered by the repeated thieving of his neighbor's dog, cut off his tail—thereby showing the improved appearance soon copied by others and continued to this day. There is no evidence that the breed was ever born tail-less; in fact, it seems that more dogs are born without tails now than earlier in their history. The Belgian Schipperkes Club has an amusing etching illustrating the legend "The Tail of the Schipperke."

There are few to be found in Holland at present. The canalboat dog of Holland has always been the Keeshond, and Holland does not claim the Schipperke. The few Schips shown at Dutch shows are imported from Belgium. Since the war few are to be seen on the Belgian canalboats. Being a frugal people, the Belgians have bred this small dog to take up little room, to be exceptionally hardy, and to be a keen and alert watchdog. He is often called "the best house dog" (*le meilleur chien de maison*).

The Schipperke has a close undercoat which keeps it warm even in American winters—the latter are far colder than those of its native land; and it sheds water and needs very little attention to keep in order. The dogs have been used to hunt, and at least one American, Mr. Culbertson, a well-known breeder of twenty years ago, wrote that he used them with great success on coons and possums in Minnesota.

The general appearance of the Schipperke is very distinctive, resembling no other breed closely. It has a short and thick-set body with foxy head, intelligent, keen expression, but not at all mean; is rather mischievous, the whole suggesting a dog with plenty of coat and an outstanding ruff and long culotte.

The career of the Schipperke as a fashionable pet began in 1885 when Queen Marie Henriette, wife of Leopold II, saw a Schipperke at a Brussels show and acquired it. Before this time it had been the companion of the lower classes.

The first dog in America was supposed to have been imported in 1888 by Mr. Walter J. Comstock of Providence. A few years later Mr. Frank Dole began showing Schips in the miscellaneous class. There was a specialty club, founded here about 1905, which died out during the war.

After 1918 there was little interest until, after several years of effort by a few fanciers, the present Schipperke Club of America was founded in 1929. The Schipperke Club Standard insists on the distinctive ruff and fairly heavy body coat, to prevent the breed from degenerating into the "black wire-haired terriers" described by Ashe's dog book as undesirable. The dog must not resemble a small black Bull Terrier with the tail cut off. While usually an excellent ratter, the Schip is not a powerful fighter, though he can hold his own with most dogs of his weight and will tackle anything in defense of his household or of his master. He is not aware of the limitations of his size. As Caesar said: "the bravest of these were the Belgians."

Temperament is considered important in judging this breed in France and Belgium and means what we in America would call pep—a Schip without this is not true to type. A judge of the breed for fifty years has said that the most important thing in judging is the correct silhouette: "I first look to see if the dog has the correct silhouette. If not, he is nothing and I look no further. If he has, I look into further details beginning with the bone structure."

This breed is usually long-lived for a small one, many instances of dogs living to be fifteen and sixteen years old being recorded; one dog, bred in Rothesay, Scotland, was reputed to have lived twenty-one years. Schips are very fond of children and in some cases have served as guards; and they have taken the place, to some extent, of human nurses, so devoted are they to their small charges.

PART III: STANDARDS OF THE BREEDS

GROUP I: SPORTING DOGS

Griffon, Wirehaired Pointing

The Wirehaired Griffon is a dog of medium size, fairly short-backed, rather a little low on his legs. He is strongly limbed, everything about him indicating strength and vigor. His coat is harsh like the bristles of a wild boar and his appearance, notwithstanding his short coat, is as unkempt as that of the long-haired Griffon, but on the other hand he has a very intelligent air.

Head—Long, furnished with a harsh coat, forming a mustache and eyebrows, skull long and narrow, muzzle square. *Eyes*—Large, open, full of expression, iris yellow or light brown. *Ears*—Of medium size, flat or sometimes slightly curled, set rather high, very lightly furnished with hair. *Nose*—Always brown.

Neck—Rather long, no dewlap. *Shoulders*—Long, sloping. *Ribs*—Slightly rounded.

Forelegs—Very straight, muscular, furnished with rather short wire hairs.

Hind Legs—Furnished with rather short stiff hair, the thighs long and well developed. *Feet*—Round, firm and well formed. *Tail*—Carried straight or gaily, furnished with a hard coat without plume, generally cut to a third of its length.

Coat—Hard, dry, stiff, never curly, the undercoat downy. *Color*—Steel gray with chestnut splashes, gray white with chestnut splashes, chestnut, dirty white mixed with chestnut, never black.

Height—21½ to 23½ inches for males, and 19½ to 21½ inches for females.

Pointer

General Appearance—The Pointer is bred primarily for sport afield; he should unmistakably look and act the part. The ideal specimen gives the immediate impression of compact power and agile grace; the head noble, proudly carried; the expression intelligent and alert; the muscular body bespeaking both staying power and dash. Here is an animal whose every movement shows him to be a wide-awake, hard-driving hunting dog possessing stamina, courage, and the desire to go. And in his expression are the loyalty and devotion of a true friend of man.

Temperament—The Pointer's even temperament and alert good sense make him a congenial companion both in the field and in the home. He should be dignified, yet showing at all times a responsive attitude.

Head—Skull long and proportionately wide, but indicating length rather than width. Slight furrow between the eyes, cheeks cleanly chiseled. A pronounced stop midway between nostrils and occiput. Muzzle long, in the same plane as the skull. Jaws ending level and square, with scissors or even bite. The flews clean. Nostrils large, spongy, widely open. *Ears*—Set on at eye level. When hanging naturally, they should reach just below the lower jaw, close to the head, with little or no folding. They should be somewhat pointed at the tip—never round—and soft and thin in leather. *Eyes*—Of medium size, rounded, pleasant in expression and the darker the better.

Neck—Long, dry, muscular and slightly arched, springing cleanly from the shoulders. *Shoulders*—Long, thin, and sloping. The top of blades close together.

Front—Elbows well down, directly under the withers and truly parallel, so as to work just clear of the body. Forelegs straight and with oval bone. Knee joint never to knuckle over. Pasterns of moderate length, perceptibly finer in bone than the leg, and slightly slanting. Chest, deep rather than wide, must not hinder free action of forelegs. The breastbone bold, without being unduly prominent. The ribs well sprung, descending as low as the elbow-point. *Back*—Strong and solid, with only a slight rise from croup to top of shoulders. Loin of moderate length, powerful and slightly arched. Croup falling only slightly to base of tail. Tuck-up should be apparent, but not exaggerated.

Tail—Heavier at the root, gradually tapering to a fine point. Length no greater than to reach to the hock joint. Carried straight, ideally on a level with the back.

Hindquarters—Muscular and powerful, with great propelling leverage. Thighs long and well-developed. Stifles well bent. The hocks clean and parallel. Decided angulation is the mark of power and endurance. *Feet*—Oval, with long, closely-set, arched toes, well padded, and deep.

Coat—Short, dense, smooth with a sheen. *Color*—Liver, lemon, black, orange; either in combination with white or solid-colored. A good Pointer cannot be a bad color. In the darker colors, the nose should be black or brown; in the lighter shades it may be lighter or flesh-colored.

Gait—Smooth, frictionless, with a powerful hindquarters' drive. The head should be carried high, the nostrils wide, the tail moving from side to side rhythmically with the pace, giving the impression of a well-balanced, strongly-built hunting dog capable of top speed combined with great stamina.

Balance and Size—Balance, over-all symmetry, is much more important in the Pointer than size. It is just as vital in a dog bred for field work as it is in an athlete or a race horse, and for the same reasons: it indicates muscular co-ordination, endurance, and an equilibrium of power. Whether large or small, a well put-together Pointer, "smooth all over," is to be preferred to an uneven one with contrasting good and bad points. Provided there is balance, considerable variation in size and weight is permissible.

FAULTS

General Appearance—Lack of true Pointer type. Hound or terrier characteristics. *Temperament*—Timidity, unruliness.

Head—Blocky or apple head. Short or snipy muzzle or frog face. Bulging cheeks or pendulous flews. Lack of stop, down-face, Roman nose. Undershot or overshot. Small or dry nostrils. *Ears*—Low set, round, heavy, folded, leathery or hound ears. *Eyes*—Light, hard, almond, or staring eyes.

Neck—Ewe neck. Throatiness. Short, thick neck. *Shoulders*—Loaded or bossy shoulders. Set wide apart at top. Straight shoulders, no slope.

Front—Elbows turned either in or out. Forelegs knuckled over. Straight pasterns, terrier front. Bone of forelegs coarse, fine, or round. Narrow chested, shallow, shelly, pigeon-breasted. Chest too wide, resulting in elbows out. Ribs too flat or too barrelled. *Back*—Roach or sway back. Unbalanced length of body. Cobbiness. Steep rise, or none at all, in topline. Sagging or long, thin loin. Croup falling away too sharply. *Tail*—Rat tail. Set on too high or too low. Carried between the legs, or carried high, flagpole tail.

Hindquarters—Straight stifles. Cow hocks. Lack of angulation or straight in stifle. Any suggestion of weakness in hindquarters. *Feet*—Cat-foot. Thin or soft pads. Splayed feet. Flat toes.

Coat—Long hair or curl. Soft or silky coat. *Color*—Weak or washed-out colors. Light or flesh-colored nose in a dark-colored dog. Butterfly nose. *Gait*—Crossing-over, sprawling or side-tracking. Stepping too high in front— the hackney gait.

SCALE OF POINTS

Head	10	Tail	5
Ears	3	Hindquarters	15
Eyes	4	Feet	9
Neck	5	Coat and color	5
Shoulders	8	Gait	6
Front	6	Balance and true Pointer type	20
Back	4	Total	100

Approved March 10, 1959

Pointer, German Shorthaired

General Appearance—The over-all picture which is created in the observer's eye should be that of an aristocratic, well-balanced, symmetrical animal with conformation indicating power, endurance and agility and a look of intelligence and animation. The dog should be neither unduly small nor conspicuously large. It should rather give the impression of medium size, but be like the proper hunter, "with a short back, but standing over plenty of ground." Tall, leggy individuals seldom possess endurance or sound movement.

Dogs which are ponderous or unbalanced because of excess substance should be definitely rejected. The first impression should be that of a keenness which denotes full enthusiasm for work without indication of nervous or flighty character. Movement should be alertly co-ordinated without waste motion. Grace of outline, clean-cut head, sloping shoulders, deep breast, powerful back, strong quarters, good bone composition, adequate muscle, well-carried tail and taut coat, all of which should combine to produce a look of nobility and an indication of anatomical structure essential to correct gait which must indicate a heritage of purposefully conducted breeding.

Head—Clean-cut, neither too light nor too heavy, in proper proportion to the body. Skull should be reasonably broad, arched on side and slightly round on top. Scissura (median line between the eyes at the forehead) not too deep, occipital bone not as conspicuous as in the case of the Pointer. The foreface should rise gradually from nose to forehead—not resembling the Roman nose. This is more strongly pronounced in the dog than in the bitch, as befitting his sex. The chops should fall away from the somewhat projecting nose. Lips should be full and deep, never flewy. The chops should not fall over too much, but form a proper fold in the angle. The jaw should be powerful and the muscles well developed. The line to the forehead should rise gradually and should never possess a definite stop as in the case of the Pointer, but rather a stop-effect when viewed from the side, due to the position of the eyebrows. The muzzle should be sufficiently long to enable the dog to seize properly and to facilitate his carrying game a long time. A pointed muzzle is not desirable. The entire head should never give the impression of tapering to a point. The depth should be in the right proportion to the length, both in the muzzle and in the skull proper.

Ears—Ears should be broad and set fairly high, lie flat and never hang away from the head. Placement should be above eye level. The ears, when laid in front without being pulled, should about meet the lip angle. In the case of heavier dogs, they should be correspondingly longer. *Eyes*—The eyes should be of medium size, full of intelligence and expressive, good-humored, and yet radiating energy, neither protruding nor sunk. The eyelids should close well. The best color is a dark shade of brown. Light yellow, china or wall (bird of prey) eyes are not desirable. *Nose*—Brown, the larger the better; nostrils well opened and broad. Flesh-colored and spotted noses are not desirable. *Teeth*—The teeth should be strong and healthy. The molars should intermesh properly. Incisors should fit close in a true scissor bite. Jaws should be neither overshot nor undershot.

Neck—Of adequate length to permit the jaws reaching game to be retrieved, sloping downwards on beautifully curving lines. The nape should be rather muscular, becoming gradually larger towards the shoulders. Moderate hound-like throatiness permitted.

Breast and Thorax—The breast in general should give the impression of depth rather than breadth; for all that, it should be in correct proportion to the other parts of the body with fair depth of chest. The ribs forming the thorax should be well-curved and not flat; they should not be absolutely round or barrel-shaped. Ribs that are entirely round prevent the necessary expansion of the chest when taking breath. The back ribs should reach well down. The circumference of the breast immediately behind the elbows should be smaller than that of the breast about a hands-breadth behind elbows, so that the upper arm has room for movement.

Back and Loins—Back should be short, strong and straight with slight rise from root of tail to withers. Excessively long or hog-backed should be penalized. Loin strong, of moderate length and slightly arched. Tuck-up should be apparent.

Assembly of Back Members—The hips should be broad with hip sockets wide apart and fall slightly toward the tail in a graceful curve. Thighs strong and well muscled. Stifles well bent. Hock joints should be well angulated with strong, straight bone structure from hock to pad. Angulation of both stifle and hock joints should be such as to combine maximum combination of both drive and traction. Hocks should turn neither in nor out. *Assembly of Front Members*—The shoulders should be sloping, movable, well covered with muscle. The shoulder blades should lie flat. The upper arm (also called the cross bar, *i.e.* the bones between the shoulder and elbow joints) should be as long as possible, standing away somewhat from the trunk so that the straight and closely muscled legs, when viewed from in front, should appear to be parallel. Elbows which stand away from the body or are pressed right into same indicate toes turning inwards or outwards, which should be regarded as faults. Pasterns should be strong, short and nearly vertical. *Feet*— Should be compact, close-knit and round to spoon-shaped. The toes sufficiently arched and heavily nailed. The pad should be strong and hard.

Coat and Skin—The skin should look close and tight. The hair should be short and thick and feel tough and hard to the hand; it is somewhat longer on the underside of the tail and the back edge of the haunches. It is softer, thinner and shorter on the ears and the head.

Tail—Is set high and firm, and must be docked, leaving approximately two-fifths of length. The tail hangs down when the dog is quiet, is held horizontally when he is walking, never turned over the back or considerably bent but violently wagged when he is on the search.

Bones—Thin and fine bones are by no means desirable in a dog which should be able to work over any and every country and should possess strength. The main importance accordingly is laid not so much on the size as being in proper proportion to the body. Dogs with coarse bones are handicapped in agility of movement and speed.

Desirable Weight and Height—Dogs—55 to 70 pounds. Bitches—45 to 60 pounds. Dogs—23 to 25 inches. Bitches—21 to 23 inches at the shoulders.

Color—Solid liver, liver and white spotted, liver and white spotted and ticked, liver and white ticked, liver roan. Any colors other than liver and white (gray white) are not permitted.

Symmetry and field quality are most essential. A dog well balanced in all points is preferable to one with outstanding good qualities and defects. A smooth, lithe gait is most desirable.

Faults—Bone structure too clumsy or too light, head too large, too many wrinkles in forehead, dish-faced, snipy muzzle, ears too long, pointy or fleshy. flesh-colored nose, eyes too light, too round or too closely set together, excessive throatiness, cowhocks, feet or elbows turned inward or outward, down on pasterns, loose shoulders, sway-back, black coat or tri-colored, any colors except liver or some combination of liver and white.

Approved May 7, 1946

Pointer, German Wirehaired

The German Wirehaired Pointer is a dog that is essentially Pointer in type, of sturdy build, lively manner, and an intelligent, determined expression. In disposition the dog has been described as energetic, rather aloof but not unfriendly.

Head—The head is moderately long, the skull broad, the occipital bone not too prominent. The stop is medium, the muzzle fairly long with nasal bone straight and broad, the lips a trifle pendulous but close and bearded. The nose is dark brown with nostrils wide open, and the teeth are strong with scissors bite. The ears, rounded but not too broad, hang close to the sides of the head. Eyes are brown, medium in size, oval in contour, bright and clear and overhung with bushy eyebrows. Yellow eyes are not desirable. The neck is of medium length, slightly arched and devoid of dewlap, in fact, the skin throughout is notably tight to the body.

Body and Tail—The body is a little longer than it is high, as ten is to nine, with the back short, straight and strong, the entire back line showing a perceptible slope down from withers to croup. The chest is deep and capacious, the ribs well sprung, loins taut and slender, the tuck-up apparent. Hips are broad, with croup nicely rounded and the tail docked, approximately two-fifths of original length.

Legs and Feet—Forelegs are straight, with shoulders obliquely set and elbows close. The thighs are strong and muscular. The hind legs are moderately angulated at stifle and hock and as viewed from behind, parallel to each other. Round in outline, the feet are webbed, high arched with toes close, their pads thick and hard, and their nails strong and quite heavy. Leg bones are flat rather than round, and strong, but not so heavy or coarse as to militate against the dog's natural agility.

Coat—The coat is weather resisting and to some extent water repellent. The undercoat is dense enough in winter to insulate against the cold but so thin in summer as to be almost invisible. The distinctive outer coat is straight, harsh, wiry and rather flat-lying, from one and one-half to two inches in length, it is long enough to protect against the punishment of rough cover but not so long as to hide the outline. On the lower legs it is shorter and between the toes of softer texture. On the skull it is naturally short and close fitting, while over the shoulders and around the tail it is very dense and heavy. The tail is nicely coated particularly on the underside, but devoid of feather. These dogs have bushy eyebrows of strong, straight hair and beards and whiskers of medium length.

A short smooth coat, a soft woolly coat, or an excessively long coat is to be severely penalized.

Color—The coat is liver and white, usually either liver and white spotted, liver roan, liver and white spotted with ticking and roaning or sometimes solid liver. The nose is dark brown. The head is brown, sometimes with a white blaze, the ears brown. Any black in the coat is to be severely penalized. Spotted and flesh-colored noses are undesirable and are to be penalized.

Size—Height of males should be from 24 to 26 inches at the withers, bitches smaller but not under 22 inches.

Approved February 7, 1959

Retriever, Chesapeake Bay

Head—Skull broad and round with medium stop, nose medium short-muzzle, pointed but not sharp. Lips thin, not pendulous. Ears small, set well up on head, hanging loosely and of medium leather. Eyes medium large, very clear, of yellowish color and wide apart. *Neck*—Of medium length with a strong muscular appearance, tapering to shoulders.

Shoulders, Chest and Body—Shoulders, sloping and should have full liberty of action with plenty of power without any restrictions of movement. Chest strong, deep and wide. Barrel round and deep. Body of medium length, neither cobby nor roached, but rather approaching hollowness, flanks well tucked up. *Back Quarters and Stifles*—Back quarters should be as high or a trifle higher than the shoulders. They should show fully as much power as the forequarters. There should be no tendency to weakness in either fore or hindquarters. Hindquarters should be especially powerful to supply the driving power for swimming. Back should be short, well-coupled and powerful. Good hindquarters are essential.

Legs, Elbows, Hocks and Feet—Legs should be medium length and straight, showing good bone and muscle, with well-webbed hare feet of good size. The toes well rounded and close, pasterns slightly bent and both pasterns and hocks medium length—the straighter the legs the better. Dewclaws, if any, must be removed from the hind legs. Dewclaws on the forelegs may be removed. A dog with dewclaws on the hind legs must be disqualified.

Stern—Tail should be medium length—varying from: males, 12 inches to

15 inches, and females from 11 inches to 14 inches; medium heavy at base, moderate feathering on stern and tail permissible.

Coat and Texture—Coat should be thick and short, nowhere over 1½ inches long, with a dense fine woolly under coat. Hair on face and legs should be very short and straight with tendency to wave on the shoulders, neck, back and loins only. The curly coat or coat with a tendency to curl not permissible. *Color*—Any color varying from a dark brown to a faded tan or deadgrass. Deadgrass takes in any shade of deadgrass, varying from a tan to a dull straw color. White spot on breast and toes permissible, but the smaller the spot the better, solid color being preferred.

Weight—Males, 65 to 75 pounds; females 55 to 65 pounds. *Height*—Males, 23 inches to 26 inches; females, 21 inches to 24 inches.

Symmetry and Quality—The Chesapeake dog should show a bright and happy disposition and an intelligent expression, with general outlines impressive and denoting a good worker. The dog should be well proportioned, a dog with a good coat and well balanced in other points being preferable to the dog excelling in some but weak in others.

The texture of the dog's coat is very important, as the dog is used for hunting under all sorts of adverse weather conditions, often working in ice and snow. The oil in the harsh outer coat and woolly undercoat is of extreme value in preventing the cold water from reaching the dog's skin and aids in quick drying. A Chesapeake's coat should resist the water in the same way that a duck's feathers do. When he leaves the water and shakes himself, his coat should not hold the water at all, being merely moist. Color and coat are extremely important, as the dog is used for duck hunting. The color must be as nearly that of his surroundings as possible and with the fact that dogs are exposed to all kinds of adverse weather conditions, often working in ice and snow, the color of coat and its texture must be given every consideration when judging on the bench or in the ring.

Courage, willingness to work, alertness, nose, intelligence, love of water, general quality, and, most of all, disposition should be given primary consideration in the selection and breeding of the Chesapeake Bay dog.

POSITIVE SCALE OF POINTS

Head, inc. lips, ears & eyes ...	16	Color	4
Neck	4	Stern and tail	10
Shoulders and body	12	Coat and texture	18
Back quarters and stifles	12	General conformation	12
Elbows, legs and feet	12	Total	100

Note:—The question of coat and general type of balance takes precedence over any scoring table which could be drawn up.

	Inches		
Length head, nose to occiput...................	9½	to	10
Girth at ears...................................	20	to	21
Muzzle below eyes............................	10	to	10½
Length of ears.................................	4½	to	5
Width between eyes...........................	2½	to	2¾
Girth neck close to shoulder...................	20	to	22
Girth of chest to elbows.......................	35	to	36
Girth at flank.................................	24	to	25
Length from occiput to tail base...............	34	to	35
Girth forearms at shoulders....................	10	to	10½
Girth upper thigh.............................	19	to	20
From root to root of ear, over skull............	5	to	6
Occiput to top shoulder blades.................	9	to	9½
From elbow to elbow over the shoulders..........	25	to	26

DISQUALIFICATIONS

Black or liver colored. Dewclaws on hind legs, white on any part of body, except breast, belly or spots on feet. Feathering on tail or legs over 1¾ inches long. Undershot, overshot or any deformity. Coat curly or tendency to curl all over body. Specimens unworthy or lacking in breed characteristics.

Approved July 9, 1963

Retriever, Curly-Coated

Head—Long and well proportioned, skull not too flat, jaws long and strong but not inclined to snipiness, nose black, in the black coated variety, with wide nostrils. Teeth strong and level. *Eyes*—Black or brown, but not yellow, rather large but not too prominent. *Ears*—Rather small, set on low, lying close to the head, and covered with short curls.

Coat—Should be one mass of crisp curls all over. A slightly more open coat not to be severely penalized, but a saddle back or patch of uncurled hair behind the shoulder should be penalized, and a prominent white patch on breast is undesirable, but a few white hairs allowed in an otherwise good dog. Color, black or liver.

Shoulders, Chest, Body and Loins—Shoulders should be very deep, muscular and obliquely placed. Chest, not too wide, but decidedly deep. Body, rather short, muscular and well ribbed up. Loin, powerful, deep and firm to the grasp.

Legs and Feet—Legs should be of moderate length, forelegs straight and set well under the body. Quarters strong and muscular, hocks low to the ground with moderate bend to stifle and hock. Feet round and compact with well-arched toes.

Tail—Should be moderately short, carried fairly straight and covered with curls, slightly tapering towards the point.

General Appearance—A strong smart upstanding dog, showing activity, endurance and intelligence.

Retriever, Flat-Coated

General Appearance—A bright, active dog of medium size (weighing from 60 pounds to 70 pounds) with an intelligent expression, showing power without lumber and raciness without weediness.

Head—This should be long and nicely molded. The skull flat and moderately broad. There should be a depression or stop between the eyes, slight and in no way accentuated, so as to avoid giving either a down or a dish-faced appearance. The nose of good size with open nostrils. The eyes, of medium size, should be dark brown or hazel, with a very intelligent expression (a round prominent eye is a disfigurement), and they should not be obliquely placed. The jaws should be long and strong, with a capacity of carrying a hare or pheasant. The ears small and well set on close to the side of the head.

Neck, Shoulders and Chest—The head should be well set in the neck, which latter should be long and free from throatiness, symmetrically set and obliquely placed in shoulders running well into the back to allow of easily seeking for the trail. The chest should be deep and fairly broad, with a well-defined brisket, on which the elbows should work cleanly and evenly. The fore ribs should be fairly flat showing a gradual spring and well arched in the center of the body but rather lighter towards the quarters. Open couplings are to be ruthlessly condemned.

Back and Quarters—The back should be short, square and well ribbed up, with muscular quarters. The stern short, straight and well set on, carried gaily but never much above the level of the back. *Legs and Feet*—These are of the greatest importance. The forelegs should be perfectly straight, with bone of good quality carried right down to the feet which should be round and strong. The stifle should not be too straight or too bent and the dog must neither be cowhocked nor move too wide behind, in fact he must stand and move true all round on legs and feet, with toes close and well arched, the soles being thick and strong, and when the dog is in full coat the limbs should be well feathered.

Coat—Should be dense, of fine quality and texture, flat as possible. Color: black or liver.

Retriever, Golden

A symmetrical, powerful, active dog, sound and well put together, not clumsy or long in the leg, displaying a kindly expression and possessing a personality that is eager, alert and self-confident. Primarily a hunting dog, he should be shown in hard working condition. Over-all appearance, balance, gait and purpose to be given more emphasis than any of his component parts. *Size*—Males 23–24 inches in height at withers; females 21½–22½. Length from breastbone to buttocks slightly greater than height at withers in ratio of 12–11. Weight for dogs 65–75 pounds; bitches 60–70 pounds. *Head*—Broad in skull, slightly arched laterally and longitudinally without prominence of frontal or occipital bones. Good stop. Foreface deep and wide, nearly as long as skull. Muzzle, when viewed in profile, slightly deeper at stop than at tip; when viewed from above, slightly wider at stop than at tip. No heaviness in flews. Removal of whiskers for show purposes optional. *Eyes*— Friendly and intelligent, medium large with dark rims, set well apart and reasonably deep in sockets. Color preferably dark brown, never lighter than color of coat. No white or haw visible when looking straight ahead. *Teeth*— Scissors bite with lower incisors touching inside of upper incisors. *Nose*— Black or dark brown, though lighter shade in cold weather not serious. Dudley nose (pink without pigmentation) to be faulted. *Ears*—Rather short, hanging flat against head with rounded tips slightly below jaw. Forward edge attached well behind and just above eye with rear edge slightly below eye. Low, houndlike ear-set to be faulted.

Neck—Medium long, sloping well back into shoulders, giving sturdy muscular appearance with untrimmed natural ruff. No throatiness.

Body—Well balanced, short-coupled, deep through the heart. Chest at least as wide as a man's hand, including thumb. Brisket extends to elbows. Ribs long and well sprung but not barrel shaped, extending well to rear of body. Loin short, muscular, wide and deep, with very little tuck-up. Top line level from withers to croup, whether standing or moving. Croup slopes gently. Slabsidedness, narrow chest, lack of depth in brisket, excessive tuck-up, roach or sway back to be faulted.

Forequarters—Forequarters well co-ordinated with hindquarters and capable of free movement. Shoulder blades wide, long and muscular, showing angulation with upper arm of approximately 90 degrees. Legs straight with good bone. Pastern short and strong, sloping slightly forward with no suggestion of weakness. *Hindquarters*—Well-bent stifles (angulation between femur and pelvis approximately 90 degrees) with hocks well let down. Legs straight when viewed from rear. Cowhocks and sickle hocks to be faulted.

Feet—Medium size, round and compact with thick pads. Excess hair may be trimmed to show natural size and contour. Open or splayed feet to be faulted. *Tail*—Well set on, neither too high nor too low, following natural line of croup. Length extends to hock. Carried with merry action with some upward curve but never curled over back nor between legs.

Coat and Color—Dense and water repellent with good undercoat. Texture not as hard as that of a shorthaired dog nor silky as that of a setter. Lies flat against body and may be straight or wavy. Moderate feathering on back of forelegs and heavier feathering on front of neck, back of thighs and underside of tail. Feathering may be lighter than rest of coat. Color lustrous golden of various shades. A few white hairs on chest permissible but not desirable. Further white markings to be faulted.

Gait—When trotting, gait is free, smooth, powerful and well co-ordinated. Viewed from front or rear, legs turn neither in nor out, nor do feet cross or interfere with each other. Increased speed causes tendency of feet to converge toward center line of gravity.

DISQUALIFICATIONS

Deviation in height of more than one inch from standard either way. Undershot or overshot bite. This condition not to be confused with misalignment of teeth. Trichiasis (abnormal position or direction of the eyelashes).

Approved September 10, 1963

Retriever, Labrador

General Appearance—The general appearance of the Labrador should be that of a strongly built, short-coupled, very active dog. He should be fairly wide over the loins, and strong and muscular in the hindquarters. The coat should be close, short, dense and free from feather.

Head—The skull should be wide, giving brain room; there should be a slight stop, *i.e.* the brow should be slightly pronounced, so that the skull is not absolutely in a straight line with the nose. The head should be clean-cut and free from fleshy cheeks. The jaws should be long and powerful and free from snipiness; the nose should be wide and the nostrils well developed. Teeth should be strong and regular, with a level mouth. The ears should hang moderately close to the head, rather far back, should be set somewhat low and not be large and heavy. The eyes should be of a medium size, expressing great intelligence and good temper, and can be brown, yellow or black, but brown or black is preferred.

Neck and Chest—The neck should be medium length, powerful and not throaty. The shoulders should be long and sloping. The chest must be of good width and depth, the ribs well sprung and the loins wide and strong, stifles well turned, and the hindquarters well developed and of great power.

Legs and Feet—The legs must be straight from the shoulder to ground, and the feet compact with toes well arched, and pads well developed; the hocks should be well bent, and the dog must neither be cowhocked nor be too wide behind; in fact, he must stand and move true all round on legs and feet. Legs should be of medium length, showing good bone and muscle, but not so short as to be out of balance with rest of body. In fact, a dog well balanced in all points is preferable to one with outstanding good qualities and defects.

Tail—The tail is a distinctive feature of the breed; it should be very thick towards the base, gradually tapering towards the tip, of medium length, should be free from any feathering, and should be clothed thickly all round with the Labrador's short, thick, dense coat, thus giving that peculiar "rounded" appearance which has been described as the "otter" tail. The tail may be carried gaily but should not curl over the back.

Coat—The coat is another very distinctive feature; it should be short, very dense and without wave, and should give a fairly hard feeling to the hand.

Color—The colors are black, yellow, or chocolate and are evaluated as follows:

(a) Blacks: All black, with a small white spot on chest permissible. Eyes to be of medium size, expressing intelligence and good temper, preferably brown or hazel, although black or yellow is permissible.

(b) Yellows: Yellows may vary in color from fox-red to light cream with variations in the shading of the coat on ears, the underparts of the dog, or beneath the tail. A small white spot on chest is permissible. Eye coloring and expression should be the same as that of the blacks, with black or dark brown eye rims. The nose should also be black or dark brown, although "fading" to pink in winter weather is not serious. A "Dudley" nose, (pink without pigmentation) should be penalized.

(c) Chocolates: Shades ranging from light sedge to chocolate. A small white spot on chest is permissible. Eyes to be light brown to clear yellow. Nose and eye-rim pigmentation dark brown or liver colored. "Fading" to pink in winter weather not serious. "Dudley" nose should be penalized.

Movement—Movement should be free and effortless. The forelegs should be strong, straight and true, and correctly placed. Watching a dog move towards one, there should be no signs of elbows being out in front, but neatly held to the body with legs not too close together, but moving straight forward without pacing or weaving. Upon viewing the dog from the rear, one should get the impression that the hind legs, which should be well muscled and not cowhocked, move as nearly parallel as possible, with hocks doing their full share of work and flexing well, thus giving the appearance of power and strength.

Approximate weights of dogs and bitches in working condition—Dogs— 60 to 75 pounds; bitches—55 to 70 pounds. *Height at Shoulders*—Dogs— 22½ inches to 24½ inches; bitches—21½ inches to 23½ inches.

Approved April 9, 1957

Setter, English

Head—Long and lean, with a well-defined stop. The skull oval from ear to ear, of medium width, giving brain room but with no suggestion of coarseness, with but little difference between the width at base of skull and at brows and with a moderately defined occipital protuberance. Brows should be at a sharp angle from the muzzle. Muzzle should be long and square, of width in harmony with the skull, without any fullness under the eyes and straight from eyes to tip of the nose. A dish face or Roman nose objectionable. The lips square and fairly pendant. Nose should be black or dark liver in color, except in white, lemon and white, orange and white, or liver and white dogs, when it may be of lighter color. Nostrils should be wide apart and large in the openings. Jaws should be of equal length. Overshot or undershot jaw objectionable. Ears should be carried close to the head, well back and set low, of moderate length, slightly rounded at the ends, and covered with silky hair. Eye should be bright, mild, intelligent and dark brown in color.

Neck—The neck should be long and lean, arched at the crest, and not too throaty. *Shoulders*—Shoulders should be formed to permit perfect freedom of action to the forelegs. Shoulder blades should be long, wide, sloping moderately well back and standing fairly close together at the top.

Chest—Chest between shoulder blades should be of good depth but not of excessive width. *Ribs*—Ribs, back of the shoulders, should spring gradually to the middle of the body and then taper to the back ribs, which should be of good depth.

Back—Back should be strong at its junction with the loin and should be straight or sloping upward very slightly to the top of the shoulder, the whole forming a graceful outline of medium length, without sway or drop. Loins should be strong, moderate in length, slightly arched, but not to the extent of being roached or wheel-backed. Hipbones should be wide apart without too sudden drop to the root of the tail.

Forelegs—The arms should be flat and muscular, with bone fully developed and muscles hard and devoid of flabbiness; of good length from the point of the shoulder to the elbow, and set at such an angle as will bring the legs fairly under the dog. Elbows should have no tendency to turn either in or out. The pastern should be short, strong and nearly round with the slope from the pastern joint to the foot deviating very slightly forward from the perpendicular. *Hind Legs*—The hind legs should have wide, muscular thighs with well developed lower thighs. Stifles should be well bent and strong. Hocks should be wide and flat. The hind pastern or metatarsus should be short, strong and nearly round. *Feet*—Feet should be closely set and strong, pads well developed and tough, toes well arched and protected with short, thick hair.

Tail—Tail should be straight and taper to a fine point, with only sufficient length to reach the hocks, or less. The feather must be straight and silky, falling loosely in a fringe and tapering to the point when the tail is raised. There must be no bushiness. The tail should not curl sideways or above the level of the back.

Coat—Coat should be flat and of good length, without curl; not soft or woolly. The feather on the legs should be moderately thin and regular.

Height—Dogs about 25 inches; bitches about 24 inches.

Colors—Black, white and tan; black and white; blue belton; lemon and white; lemon belton; orange and white; orange belton; liver and white; liver belton; and solid white. *Markings*—Dogs without heavy patches of color on the body, but flecked all over preferred.

Symmetry—The harmony of all parts to be considered. Symmetrical dogs will have level backs or be very slightly higher at the shoulders than at the hips. Balance, harmony of proportion, and an appearance of breeding and quality to be looked for, and coarseness avoided.

Movement and Carriage—An easy, free and graceful movement, suggesting rapidity and endurance. A lively tail and a high carriage of head. Stiltiness, clumsiness or a lumbering gait are objectionable.

SCALE OF POINTS

Head			Feet	6	23
Skull	5		*Coat*		
Ears	5		Length and texture ...	5	
Eyes	5		Color and marking ...	3	8
Muzzle	5	20	*Tail*		
Body			Length and carriage ...	5	5
Neck	5		*General Appearance and Action*		
Chest and shoulders ..	12		Symmetry, style and movement		
Back, loin and ribs ...	10	27	....	12	
Running Gear			Size	5	17
Forelegs	5		Total	100	100
Hips, thighs and hind legs					
....	12				

Approved May 8, 1951

Gordon

ession—The Gordon Setter is a good-sized, sturdily built, black
vell muscled, with plenty of bone and substance, but active,
stylish, appearing capable of doing a full day's work in the
rong, rather short back, with well-sprung ribs and a short
airly heavy and finely chiseled. His bearing is intelligent,
showing no signs of shyness or viciousness. Clear colors
tly waved coat are correct. He suggests strength and
treme speed. Symmetry and quality are most essential.
all points is preferable to one with outstanding good
smooth, free movement, with high head carriage,
is typ

Size—S males, 24 to 27 inches. For females, 23 to 26
inches. W 80 pounds; females, 45 to 70 pounds. Animals
that appe der the prescribed weight limits are to be
judged on rmation and condition. Extremely thin or
fat dogs shou n the basis that under- or overweight ham-
pers the true the Gordon Setter. The weight-to-height
ratio makes hi her setters.

Head—The head n broad, with plenty of brain room; a
nicely rounded, goo est between the ears. The head should
have a clearly indica above the eyes should be lean, and
the cheek as narrow a e head allows. The muzzle is fairly
long and not pointed, e above or from the side. The flews
should not be pendulous. uld be broad, with open nostrils and
black in color. The muzzl same length as the skull from occiput to
stop, and the top of the muzzle is parallel to the line of the skull extended.
The lip line from the nose to the flews shows a sharp, well-defined, square
contour. *Eyes*—Of fair size, neither too deep-set, nor too bulging, dark
brown, bright, and wise. The shape is oval rather than round. The lids
should be tight. *Ears*—Set low on the head approximately on line with the
eye, fairly large and thin, well folded and carried close to the head. *Teeth*—
The teeth should be strong and white, and preferably should meet in front
in a scissors bite, with the upper incisors slightly forward of the lower incisors. A level bite is not to be considered a fault. Pitted teeth from distemper or allied infections should not be penalized.

Neck—Long, lean, arched to the head, and without throatiness. *Shoulders*—
Should be fine at the points, and lying well back, giving a moderately sloping
topline. The tops of the shoulder blades should be close together. When
viewed from behind, the neck appears to fit into the shoulders in smooth,
flat, lines that gradually widen from neck to shoulder. *Chest*—Deep and not

too broad in front; the ribs well sprung, leaving plenty of lung room. The chest should reach to the elbows. A pronounced forechest should be in evidence.

Body—The body should be short from shoulder to hips, and the distance from the forechest to the back of the thigh should approximately equal the height from the ground to the withers. The loins should be short and broad and not arched. The croup is nearly flat, with only a slight slope to the tailhead. *Forequarters*—The legs should be big-boned, straight, and not bowed, with elbows free and not turned in or out. The angle formed by the shoulder blade and upper arm bone should be approximately 90° when the dog is standing so that the foreleg is perpendicular to the ground. The pasterns should be straight. *Hindquarters*—The hind legs from hip to hock should be long, flat, and muscular; from hock to heel, short and strong. The stifle and hock joints are well bent and not turned either in or out. When the dog is standing with the hock perpendicular to the ground the thigh bone should hang downward parallel to an imaginary line drawn upward from the hock. *Feet*—The feet should be formed by close-knit, well-arched toes with plenty of hair between; with full toe pads and deep heel cushions. Feet should not be turned in or out. Feet should be cat-like in shape.

Tail—Short and should not reach below the hocks, carried horizontal or nearly so; thick at the root and finishing in a fine point. The feather which starts near the root of the tail should be slightly waved or straight, having triangular appearance, growing shorter uniformly toward the end. The placement of the tail is important for correct carriage. If the croup is nearly flat, the tail must emerge nearly on the same plane as the croup to allow for horizontal carriage. When the angle of the tail bends too sharply at the first coccygeal bone, the tail will be carried too gaily or will droop. The tail placement should be judged in its relationship to the structure of the croup.

Temperament—The Gordon Setter should be alert, gay, interested, and aggressive. He should be fearless and willing, intelligent and capable. He should be loyal and affectionate, and strong-minded enough to stand the rigors of training.

Gait—The action of the Gordon Setter is a bold, strong, driving, free-swinging gait. The head is carried up and the tail "flags" constantly while the dog is in motion. When viewed from the front the forefeet move up and down in straight lines so that the shoulder, elbow, and pastern joints are approximately in line with each other. When viewed from the rear, the hock, stifle, and hip joints are approximately in line. Thus the dog moves in a straight pattern forward without throwing the feet in or out. When viewed from the side the forefeet are seen to lift up and reach forward to compensate for the driving hindquarters. The hindquarters reach well forward and stretch far back, enabling the stride to be long and the drive powerful. The over-all appearance of the moving dog is one of smooth-flowing, well-balanced rhythm, in which the action is pleasing to the eye, effortless, economical and harmonious.

Coat—Should be soft and shining, straight or slightly waved, but not curly, with long hair on ears, under stomach and on chest, on back of the fore- and hind legs, and on the tail. *Color and Markings*—Black with tan markings, either of rich chestnut or mahogany color. Black penciling is allowed on the toes. The borderline between black and tan colors should be clearly defined. There should not be any tan hairs mixed in the black. The tan markings should be located as follows: (1) Two clear spots over the eyes and not over three quarters of an inch in diameter; (2) On the sides of the muzzle. The tan should not reach to the top of the muzzle, but resembles a stripe around the end of the muzzle from one side to the other; (3) On the throat; (4) Two large clear spots on the chest; (5) On the inside of the hind legs showing down the front of the stifle and broadening out to the outside of the hind legs from the hock to the toes. It must not completely eliminate the black on the back of the hind legs; (6) On the forelegs from the carpus, or a little above, downward to the toes; (7) Around the vent; (8) A white spot on the chest is allowed, but the smaller the better. Predominantly tan, red, or buff dogs which do not have the typical pattern of markings of a Gordon Setter are ineligible for showing and undesirable for breeding.

SCALE OF POINTS

While not a part of the official breed standard, may be helpful in placing proper emphasis upon qualities desired in the physical make-up of the breed.

Head and neck (incl. ears and eyes)	10	Coat	8
Body	15	Color and markings	5
Shoulders, forelegs, forefeet	10	Temperament	10
Hind legs and feet	10	Size, general appearance	15
Tail	5	Gait	12
		Total	100

DISQUALIFICATION

Predominantly tan, red, or buff dogs which do not have the typical pattern of markings of a Gordon Setter.

Approved November 13, 1962

Setter, Irish

General Appearance—The Irish Setter is an active, aristocratic bird-dog, rich red in color, substantial yet elegant in build. Standing over two feet tall at the shoulder, the dog has a straight, fine, glossy coat, longer on ears, chest, tail, and back of legs. Afield he is a swift-moving hunter; at home, a sweet-natured, trainable companion. His is a rollicking personality.

Head—Long and lean, its length at least double the width between the ears. The brow is raised, showing a distinct stop midway between the tip of nose and the well-defined occiput (rear point of skull). Thus the nearly level line from occiput to brow is set a little above, and parallel to, the straight and equal line from eye to nose. The skull is oval when viewed from above or front; very slightly domed when viewed in profile. Beauty of head is emphasized by delicate chiseling along the muzzle, around and below the eyes, and along the cheeks. Muzzle moderately deep, nostrils wide, jaws of nearly equal length. Upper lips fairly square but not pendulous, the underline of the jaws being almost parallel with the top line of the muzzle. The teeth meet in a scissors bite in which the upper incisors fit closely over the lower, or they may meet evenly. *Nose*—Black or chocolate.

Eyes—Somewhat almond-shaped, of medium size, placed rather well apart; neither deep-set nor bulging. Color, dark to medium brown. Expression soft yet alert. *Ears*—Set well back and low, not above level of eye. Leather thin, hanging in a neat fold close to the head, and nearly long enough to reach the nose.

Neck—Moderately long, strong but not thick, and slightly arched; free from throatiness, and fitting smoothly into the shoulders.

Body—Sufficiently long to permit a straight and free stride. Shoulder blades long, wide, sloping well back, fairly close together at the top, and joined in front to long upper arms angled to bring the elbows slightly rearward along the brisket. Chest deep, reaching approximately to the elbows; rather narrow in front. Ribs well sprung. Loins of moderate length, muscular and slightly arched. Top line of body from withers to tail slopes slightly downward without sharp drop at the croup. Hindquarters should be wide and powerful with broad, well-developed thighs. *Legs and Feet*—All legs sturdy, with plenty of bone, and strong, nearly straight pastern. Feet rather small, very firm, toes arched and close. Forelegs straight and sinewy, the elbows moving freely. Hind legs long and muscular from hip to hock, short and nearly perpendicular from hock to ground; well angulated at stifle and hock joints, which, like the elbows, incline neither in nor out. *Tail*—Strong at root, tapering to fine point, about long enough to reach the hock. Carriage straight or curving slightly upward, nearly level with the back.

Coat—Short and fine on head, forelegs, and tips of ears; on all other parts, of moderate length and flat. Feathering long and silky on ears; on back of forelegs and thighs long and fine, with a pleasing fringe of hair on belly and brisket extending onto the chest. Feet well feathered between the toes. Fringe on tail moderately long and tapering. All coat and feathering as straight and free as possible from curl or wave.

Color—Mahogany or rich chestnut red, with no trace of black. A small amount of white on chest, throat, or toes, or a narrow centered streak on skull, is not to be penalized.

Size—There is no disqualification as to size. The make and fit of all parts and their over-all balance in the animal are rated more important. Twenty-seven inches at the withers and a show weight of about 70 pounds is considered ideal for a dog; the bitch 25 inches, 60 pounds. Variance beyond an inch up or down to be discouraged.

Gait—At the trot the gait is big, very lively, graceful, and efficient. The head is held high. The hindquarters drive smoothly and with great power. The forelegs reach well ahead as if to pull in the ground, without giving the appearance of a hackney gait. The dog runs as he stands: straight. Seen from the front or rear, the forelegs, as well as the hind legs below the hock joint, move perpendicularly to the ground, with some tendency toward a single track as speed increases. But a crossing or weaving of the legs, front or back, is objectionable.

Balance—At his best the lines of the Irish Setter so satisfy in over-all balance that artists have termed him the most beautiful of all dogs. The correct specimen always exhibits balance whether standing or in motion. Each part of the dog flows and fits smoothly into its neighboring parts without calling attention to itself.

Approved June 14, 1960

Spaniel, American Water

General Appearance—Medium in size, of sturdy typical spaniel character, curly coat, an active muscular dog, with emphasis placed on proper size and conformation, correct head properties, texture of coat and color. Of amicable disposition; demeanor indicates intelligence, strength and endurance.

Head—Moderate in length, skull rather broad and full, stop moderately defined, but not too pronounced. Forehead covered with short smooth hair and without tuft or topknot. Muzzle of medium length, square and with no inclination to snipiness, jaws strong and of good length, and neither undershot nor overshot, teeth straight and well shaped. Nose sufficiently wide and with well developed nostrils to insure good scenting power. *Faults*—Very flat skull, narrow across the top, long, slender or snipy muzzle. *Eyes*—Hazel, brown or of dark tone to harmonize with coat; set well apart. Expression alert, attractive, intelligent. *Fault*—Yellow eyes to disqualify. *Ears*—Lobular, long and wide, not set too high on head, but slightly above the eyeline. Leather extending to end of nose and well covered with close curls. *Neck*—Round and of medium length, strong and muscular, free of throatiness, set to carry head with dignity, but arch not accentuated.

Body Structure—Well developed, sturdily constructed but not too compactly coupled. General outline is a symmetrical relationship of parts. Shoulders sloping, clean and muscular. Strong loins, lightly arched, and well furnished, deep brisket but not excessively broad. Well-sprung ribs. Legs of medium length and well boned, but not so short as to handicap for field work. *Legs and Feet*—Forelegs powerful and reasonably straight. Hind legs firm with suitably bent stifles and strong hocks well let down. Feet to harmonize with size of dog. Toes closely grouped and well padded. *Fault*—Cowhocks. *Tail*—Moderate in length, curved in a slightly rocker shape, carried slightly below level of back; tapered and covered with hair to tip, action lively. *Faults*—Rat or shaved tail.

Coat—The coat should be closely curled or have marcel effect and should be of sufficient density to be of protection against weather, water or punishing cover, yet not coarse. Legs should have medium short, curly feather. *Faults*—Coat too straight, soft, fine or tightly kinked. *Color*—Solid liver or dark chocolate, a little white on toes or chest permissible.

Height—15 to 18 inches at the shoulder. *Weight*—Males, 28 to 45 pounds; females, 25 to 40 pounds.

DISQUALIFICATION

Yellow eyes.

Spaniel, Brittany

General Description—A compact, closely knit dog of medium size, a leggy spaniel having the appearance as well as the agility of a great ground coverer. Strong, vigorous, energetic and quick of movement. Not too light in bone, yet never heavy-boned and cumbersome. Ruggedness, without clumsiness, is a characteristic of the breed. So leggy is he that his height at the withers is the same as the length of his body. He has no tail, or at most, not more than 4 inches.

Weight—Should weigh between 30 and 40 pounds. *Height*—17½ to 20½ inches—measured from the ground to the highest point of the back—the withers. *Disqualifications*—Any Brittany Spaniel measuring under 17½ inches or over 20½ inches shall be disqualified from bench show competition. Any black in the coat or a nose so dark in color as to appear black shall disqualify. A tail substantially more than 4 inches in length shall disqualify.

Coat—Hair dense, flat or wavy, never curly. Not as fine as in other spaniel breeds, and never silky. Furnishings not profuse. The ears should carry little fringe. Neither the front nor hind legs should carry heavy featherings. Note: Long, curly, or silky hair is a fault. Any tendency toward excessive feathering should be severely penalized, as undesirable in a sporting dog which must face burrs and heavy cover. *Skin*—Fine and fairly loose. (A loose skin rolls with briars and sticks, thus diminishing punctures or tearing. But a skin so loose as to form pouches is undesirable.)

Color—Dark orange and white, or liver and white. Some ticking is desirable, but not so much as to produce belton patterns. Roan patterns or factors of orange or liver shade are permissible. The orange and liver are found in standard parti-color, or piebald patterns. Washed out or faded colors are not desirable. Black is a disqualification.

Skull—Medium length (approximately 4¾ inches). Rounded, very slightly wedge-shaped, but evenly made. Width, not quite as wide as the length (about 4⅜ inches) and never so broad as to appear coarse, or so narrow as to appear racy. Well defined, but gently sloping stop effect. Median line rather indistinct. The occipital crest only apparent to the touch. Lateral walls well rounded. The Brittany should never be "apple-headed" and he should never have an indented stop. (All measurements of skull are for a 19½-inch dog.) *Muzzle*—Medium length, about two thirds the length of the skull, measuring the muzzle from the tip to the stop, and the skull from the occipital crest to the stop between the eyes. Muzzle should taper gradually in both horizontal and vertical dimensions as it approaches the nostrils. Neither a Roman nose nor a concave curve (dish-face) is desirable. Never broad, heavy, or snipy. *Nose*—Nostrils well open to permit deep breathing of air and adequate scenting while at top speed. Tight nostrils should be penalized. Never shiny. Color, fawn, tan, light shades of brown or deep pink. A black nose is a disqualification. A two-tone or butterfly nose should be severely penalized.

Eyes—Well set in head. Well protected from briars by a heavy, expressive eyebrow. A prominent, full or pop eye should be heavily penalized. It is a serious fault in a hunting dog that must face briars. Skull well chiseled under the eyes, so that the lower lid is not pulled back to form a pocket or haw for catching seeds, dirt and weed dust. Judges should check by forcing head down to see if lid falls away from the eye. Preference should be for darker-colored eyes, though lighter shades of amber should not be penalized. Light and mean-looking eyes to be heavily penalized. *Ears*—Set high, above the level of the eyes. Short and leafy, rather than pendulous, reaching about half the length of the muzzle. Should lie flat and close to the head, with the tip rounded very slightly. Ears well covered with dense, but relatively short hair, and with little fringe. *Lips*—Tight to the muzzle, with the upper lip overlapping the lower jaw only sufficiently to cover under lip. Lips dry so that feathers do not stick. Drooling to receive a heavy penalty. Flews to be penalized. *Teeth*—Well joined incisors. Posterior edge of upper incisors in contact with anterior edge of lower incisors, thus giving a true scissors bite. Overshot or undershot jaw to be penalized heavily.

Neck—Medium length. Not quite permitting the dog to place his nose on the ground without bending his legs. Free from throatiness, though not a serious fault unless accompanied by dewlaps. Strong, without giving the impression of being overmuscled. Well set into sloping shoulders. Never concave or ewe-necked.

Body Length—Approximately the same as the height when measured at the withers. Body length is measured from the point of the forechest to the rear of the haunches. A long body should be heavily penalized. *Withers* —Shoulder blades should not protude much. Not too widely set apart with perhaps two thumbs' width or less between the blades. At the withers, the Brittany is slightly higher than at the rump. *Shoulders*—Sloping and muscular. Blade and upper arm should form nearly a 90-degree angle when measured from the posterior point of the blade at the withers to the junction of the blade and upper arm, and thence to the point of the elbow nearest the ribs. Straight shoulders do not permit sufficient reach.

Back—Short and straight. Slight slope from highest point of withers to the root of the tail. Never hollow, saddle, sway or roach-backed. Slight drop from hips to root of tail. Distance from last rib to upper thigh short, about three to four finger widths. *Chest*—Deep, reaching the level of the elbow. Neither so wide nor so rounded as to disturb the placement of the shoulder bones and elbows, which causes a paddling movement, and often causes soreness from elbow striking ribs. Ribs well sprung, but adequate heart room provided by depth as well as width. Narrow or slab-sided chests are a fault.

Flanks—Rounded. Fairly full. Not extremely tucked up, nor yet flabby and falling. Loins short and strong. Narrow and weak loins are a fault. In motion the loin should not sway sideways, giving a zigzag motion to the back, wasting energy. *Hindquarters*—Broad, strong and muscular, with powerful thighs and well-bent stifles, giving a hip set well into the loin and the marked angulation necessary for a powerful drive when in motion. Fat and falling hindquarters are a fault. *Tail*—Naturally tailless, or not over four inches long. Natural or docked. Set on high, actually an extension of the spine at about the same level.

Front Legs—Viewed from the front, perpendicular, but not set too wide as in the case of a dog loaded in shoulder. Elbows and feet turning neither in nor out. Viewed from the side, practically perpendicular to the pastern. Pastern slightly bent to give cushion to stride. Not so straight as in terriers. Falling pasterns, however, are a serious fault. Leg bones clean, graceful, but not too fine. An extremely heavy bone is as much a fault as spindly legs. One must look for substance and suppleness. Height to the elbows should approximately equal distance from elbow to withers. *Hind Legs*—Stifles well bent. The stifle generally is the term used for knee joint. If the angle made by the upper and lower leg bones is too straight, the dog quite generally lacks drive, since his hind legs cannot drive as far forward at each stride as is desirable. However, the stifle should not be bent as to throw the hock joint far out behind the dog. Since factors not easily seen by the eye may give the dog his proper drive, a Brittany should not be condemned for straight stifle until the judge has checked the dog in motion from the side. When at a trot, the Brittany's hind foot should step into or beyond the print left by the front foot. The stifle joint should not turn out making a cowhock. (The cowhock moves the foot out to the side, thus driving out of line, and losing reach at each stride.) Thighs well feathered, but not profusely, halfway to the hock. Hocks, that is, the back pasterns, should be moderately short, pointing neither in nor out; perpendicular when viewed from the side. They should be firm when shaken by the judge. *Feet*—Should be strong, proportionately smaller than other spaniels, with close-fitting, well-arched toes and thick pads. The Brittany is not "up on his toes." Toes not heavily feathered. Flat feet, splayed feet, paper feet, etc., are to be heavily penalized. An ideal foot is half way between the hare- and cat-foot.

A *Guide to the Judge*—The points below indicate only relative values. To be also taken into consideration are type, gait, soundness, spirit, optimum height, body length and general proportions.

SCALE OF POINTS

Head	25	Running gear	40
Body	35	Total	100

DISQUALIFICATIONS

Any Brittany Spaniel measuring under 17½ inches or over 20½ inches. Any black in the coat or a nose so dark in color as to appear black. A tail substantially more than 4 inches in length.

Approved November 18, 1952

Spaniel, Clumber

General Appearance and Size—General appearance, a long, low, heavy-looking dog, of a very thoughtful expression, betokening great intelligence. Should have the appearance of great power. Sedate in all movements, but not clumsy. Weight of dogs averaging between 55 and 65 pounds; bitches from 35 to 50 pounds.

Head—Head large and massive in all its dimensions; round above eyes, flat on top, with a furrow running from between the eyes upon the center. A marked stop and large occipital protuberance. Jaw long, broad and deep. Lips of upper jaw overhung. Muzzle not square, but at the same time powerful-looking. Nostrils large, open and flesh-colored, sometimes cherry-colored. *Eyes*—Eyes large, soft, deep-set and showing haw. Hazel in color, not too pale, with dignified and intelligent expression. *Ears*—Ears long and broad at the top, turned over on the front edge; vine-shaped: close to the head; set on low and feathered only on the front edge, and there but slightly. Hair short and silky, without the slightest approach to wave or curl.

Neck and Shoulders—Neck long, thick and powerful, free from dewlap, with a large ruff. Shoulders immensely strong and muscular, giving a heavy appearance in front.

Body—Long, low and well ribbed up. The chest is wide and deep, the back long, broad, and level, with very slight arch over the loin. *Legs and Feet*—Forelegs short, straight, and very heavy in bone; elbows close. Hind legs only slightly less heavily boned than the forelegs. They are moderately angulated, with hocks well let down. Quarters well developed and muscular. No feather above the hocks, but thick hair on the back of the legs just above the feet. Feet large, compact, and well filled with hair between the toes.

Coat and Feathers—Coat silky and straight, not too long, extremely dense; feather long and abundant. *Color and Markings*—Color, lemon and white, and orange and white. Fewer markings on body the better. Perfection of markings, solid lemon or orange ears, evenly marked head and eyes, muzzle and legs ticked. *Stern*—Stern set on a level and carried low.

SCALE OF POINTS

General appearance and size	10	Body and quarters	20
Head	15	Legs and feet	10
Eyes	5	Coat and feather	10
Ears	10	Color and marking	5
Neck and shoulders	15	Total	100

Approved February 6, 1960

Spaniel, Cocker

Skull—Well developed and rounded with no tendency toward flatness, or pronounced roundness, of the crown (dome). The forehead smooth, the eyebrows and stop clearly defined, the median line distinctly marked and gradually disappearing until lost rather more than halfway up to the crown. The bony structure surrounding the socket of the eye should be well chiseled; there should be no suggestion of fullness under the eyes or prominence in the cheeks which, like the sides of the muzzle, should present a smooth, clean-cut appearance. *Muzzle and Teeth*—To attain a well-proportioned head, which above all should be in balance with the rest of the dog, the distance from the tip of the nose to the stop, at a line drawn across the top of the muzzle between the front corners of the eyes, should approximate one-half the distance from the stop at this point up over the crown to the base of the skull. The muzzle should be broad and deep, with square, even jaws. The upper lip should be of sufficient depth to cover the lower jaw, presenting a square appearance. The teeth should be sound and regular and set at right angles to their respective jaws. The relation of the upper teeth to the lower should be that of scissors, with the inner surface of the upper in contact with the outer surface of the lower when the jaws are closed. The nose of sufficient size to balance the muzzle and foreface, with well-developed nostrils, and black in color in the blacks and black and tans; in the reds, buffs, livers, and parti-colors, and in the roans it may be black or brown, the darker coloring being preferable.

Eyes—The eyeballs should be round and full and set in the surrounding tissue to look directly forward and give the eye a slightly almond-shaped appearance. The eye should be neither weak nor goggled. The expression should be intelligent, alert, soft and appealing. The color of the iris should be dark brown to black in the blacks, black and tans, buffs and creams, and in the darker shades of the parti-colors and roans. In the reds, dark hazel; in the livers, parti-colors, and roans of the lighter shades, not lighter than hazel, the darker the better. *Ears*—Lobular, set on a line no higher than the lower part of the eye, the leather fine and extending to the nostrils, well clothed with long, silky, straight or wavy hair.

Neck and Shoulders—The neck sufficiently long to allow the nose to reach the ground easily, muscular and free from pendulous "throatiness." It should rise strongly from the shoulders and arch slightly as it tapers to join the head. The shoulders deep, clean-cut and sloping without protrusion and so set that the upper points of the withers are at an angle which permits a wide spring of rib.

Body—Its height at the withers should approximate the length from the withers to the set-on of tail. The chest deep, its lowest point no higher than the elbows, its front sufficiently wide for adequate heart and lung space, yet not so wide as to interfere with straightforward movement of the forelegs. Ribs deep and well-sprung throughout. Body short in the couplings and flank, with its depth at the flank somewhat less than at the last rib. Back strong and sloping evenly and slightly downward from the withers to the set-on of tail. Hips wide with quarters well-rounded and muscular. The body should appear short, compact and firmly knit together, giving the impression of strength. *Legs and Feet*—Forelegs, straight, strongly boned and muscular, and set close to the body well under the scapulae. The elbows well let down and turning neither in nor out. The pasterns short and strong. The hind legs strongly boned and muscled with well-turned stifles and powerful, clearly defined thighs. The hocks strong, well let down and paralleled when in motion and at rest. Feet compact, not spreading, round and firm, with deep, strong, horny pads and hair between the toes; they should turn neither in nor out. *Tail*—Set on and carried on a line with the topline of the back and when the dog is at work, its action should be incessant.

Coat—On head, short and fine. On body, flat or slightly wavy (never curly), silky in texture, of medium length, with enough undercoating to give protection. The ears, chest, abdomen, and posterior sides of the legs should be well feathered, but not so excessively as to hide the Cocker Spaniel's true lines and movement or affect his appearance and function as a sporting dog. Excessive coat or feathering shall be penalized. *Color and Markings*—Blacks should be jet black; shadings of brown or liver in the sheen of the coat shall not disqualify; but shall be penalized. A small amount of white on the chest and throat shall not disqualify, but shall be penalized; however, white in any other location shall disqualify.

Solid Colors Other Than Black should be of a sound shade. Lighter coloring of the feathering, while not favored, shall not disqualify. A small amount of white on the chest and throat shall not disqualify, but shall be penalized; however, white in any other location shall disqualify.

In Parti-Colors, at least two definite colors appearing in clearly defined markings, distinctively distributed over the body, are essential. Primary color which is ninety (90%) per cent or more of the specimen, shall disqualify; secondary color or colors which are limited solely to one location shall disqualify. Roans are classified as Parti-Colors and may be of the accepted roaning patterns of mottled appearance or alternating colors of the hairs throughout the whole coat.

Black and Tan, shown under the Variety of Any Solid Color Other Than Black, should have definite tan markings on a jet black body, with clearly defined lines between the two colors. The tan markings should be distinct and plainly visible, and the shade of the tan markings may be from the lightest cream to the darkest red color. The quantity and location of the tan markings are the essence of this description. The amount of tan markings is restricted to ten (10%) per cent or less of the color of the specimen; tan markings in excess of ten (10%) per cent shall disqualify. A mere semblance of tan markings at the specified locations shall not disqualify, but shall be severely penalized; the total absence of tan markings at any of the specified locations, shall disqualify. The marking should be located as follows:

(1) A clear spot over each eye. (2) On the sides of the muzzle, and on the cheeks. (3) On the undersides of the ears. (4) On all feet and legs. (5) Under the tail.

Tan on the muzzle which extends up and over and joins, or tan on the cheeks which is solid, or tan on the feet which does not extend upward towards the knees and hock joints, shall not disqualify, but shall be penalized. Black hairs and penciling on the tan markings shall not be penalized, but tan markings which are "brindled" shall be penalized. A small amount of white on the chest and throat shall not disqualify, but shall be penalized. However, white in any other location shall disqualify.

Height—The ideal height at the withers for an adult dog should be 15 inches. The ideal height at the withers for an adult bitch should be 14 inches. The maximum height at the withers for a dog shall be 15½ inches and the maximum height at the withers for a bitch shall be 14½ inches. A dog or bitch whose height exceeds the maximum heights specified herein shall be disqualified. Note: Height is determined by a line perpendicular to the ground from the top of the shoulder blades, the dog standing naturally with its forelegs and the lower hind legs parallel to the line of measurement.

General Description—Embodying the foregoing we have a serviceable-looking dog with a refinedly chiseled head; standing on straight legs and well up at the shoulders; of compact body and wide, muscular quarters. The Cocker Spaniel's sturdy body, powerful quarters and strong, well-boned legs show him to be a dog capable of considerable speed combined with great endurance. Above all he must be free and merry, sound, well balanced throughout, and in action show a keen inclination to work; equable in temperament with no suggestion of timidity.

SCALE OF POINTS

Skull	8	Legs	9
Muzzle	10	Feet	6
Teeth	4	Stern	3
Eyes	6	Coat	6
Ears	3	Color and Markings	3
Neck and Shoulders	15	Action	12
Body	15	Total	100

DISQUALIFICATIONS

Color and Markings: Blacks—White markings except on chest and throat. Solid Colors Other Than Black—White markings except on chest and throat. Parti-Colors—Ninety (90%) per cent or more of primary color; secondary color or colors limited solely to one location. Black and Tans—Tan markings in excess of ten (10%) per cent; total absence of tan markings at any of the specified locations; white markings except on chest and throat. Height: males over 15½ inches; females over 14½ inches.

Approved December 10, 1957

Spaniel, English Cocker

General Appearance—The English Cocker Spaniel is an attractive, active, merry sporting dog; with short body and strong limbs, standing well up at the withers. His movements are alive with energy; his gait powerful and frictionless. He is alert at all times, and the carriage of head and incessant action of his tail while at work give the impression that here is a dog that is not only bred for hunting but really enjoys it. He is well balanced, strongly built, full of quality and is capable of top speed combined with great stamina. His head imparts an individual stamp peculiar to him alone and has that brainy appearance expressive of the highest intelligence; and is in perfect proportion to his body. His muzzle is a most distinctive feature, being of correct conformation and in proportion to his skull.

Character—The character of the English Cocker is of extreme importance. His love and faithfulness to his master and household, his alertness and courage are characteristic. He is noted for his intelligence and merry disposition; not quarrelsome; and is a responsive and willing worker both in the field and as a companion.

Head—The skull and forehead should be well developed with no suggestion of coarseness, arched and slightly flattened on top when viewed both from the stop to the end of the skull as well as from ear to ear, and cleanly chiseled under the eyes. The proportion of the head desirable is approximately one-half for the muzzle and one-half for the skull. The muzzle should be square with a definite stop where it blends into the skull and in proportion with the width of the skull. As the English Cocker is primarily a sporting dog, the muzzle and jaws must be of sufficient strength and size to carry game; and the length of the muzzle should provide room for the development of the olfactory nerve to insure good scenting qualities, which require that the nose be wide and well developed. Nostrils black in color except in reds, livers, parti-colors and roans of the lighter shades, where brown is permissible, but black preferred. Lips should be square, full and free from flews. Teeth should be even and set squarely. *Faults*—Muzzle too short or snipy. Jaw overshot or undershot. Lips snipy or pendulous. Skull too flat or too rounded, cheeky or coarse. Stop insufficient or exaggerated.

Eyes—The eyes should be of medium size, full and slightly oval shaped; set squarely in skull and wide apart. Eyes must be dark brown except in livers and light parti-colors where hazel is permissible, but the darker the better. The general expression should be intelligent, alert, bright and merry. *Faults* —Light, round or protruding eyes. Conspicuous haw. *Ears*—Lobular; set low and close to the head; leather fine and extending at least to the nose, well covered with long, silky, straight or slightly wavy hair. *Faults*—Set or carried too high; too wide at the top; insufficient feathering; positive curls or ringlets.

Neck—Long, clean and muscular; arched towards the head; set cleanly into sloping shoulders. *Faults*—Short; thick; with dewlap or excessive throatiness.

Body—Close coupled, compact and firmly knit, giving the impression of great strength without heaviness. Depth of brisket should reach to the elbow, sloping gradually upward to the loin. Ribs should spring gradually to middle of body, tapering to back ribs which should be of good depth and extend well back. *Faults*—Too long and lacking depth; insufficient spring of rib; barrel rib. *Shoulders and Chest*—Shoulders sloping and fine; chest deep and well developed but not too wide and round to interfere with the free action of the forelegs. *Faults*—Straight or loaded shoulders.

Back and Loin—Back short and strong. Length of back from withers to tail-set should approximate height from ground to withers. Height of the dog at the withers should be greater than the height at the hip joint, providing a gradual slope between these points. Loin short and powerful, slightly arched. *Faults*—Too low at withers; long, sway-back or roach back; flat or narrow loin; exaggerated tuck-up.

Forelegs—Straight and strong with bone nearly equal in size from elbow to heel; elbows set close to the body with free action from shoulders; pasterns short, straight, and strong. *Faults*—Shoulders loose; elbows turned in or out; legs bowed or set too close or too wide apart; knees knuckled over; light bone.

Feet—Size in proportion to the legs; firm, round and catlike with thick pads and strong toes. *Faults*—Too large, too small; spreading or splayed. *Hindquarters*—The hips should be rounded; thighs broad; well developed and muscular, giving abundance of propelling power. Stifles strong and well bent. Hock to pad moderately short, strong and well let down. *Faults*—Excessive angulation; lightness of bone; stifle too short; hocks too long or turned in or out. *Tail*— Set on to conform with the topline of the back. Merry in action. *Faults*—Set too low; habitually carried too high; too short or too long.

Color—Various. In self colors a white shirt frill is undesirable. In parti-colors, the coloring must be broken on the body and be evenly distributed. No large portion of any one color should exist. White should be shown on the saddle. A dog of any solid color with white feet and chest is not a parti-color. In roans it is desirable that the white hair should be distributed over the body, the more evenly the better. Roans come in various colors: blue, liver, red, orange and lemon. In black and tans the coat should be black; tan spots over the eyes, tan on the sides of the muzzle, on the throat and chest, on forelegs from the knees to the toes and on the hind legs on the inside of the legs, also on the stifle and extending from the hock to the toes. *Faults* —White feet are undesirable in any specimen of self color.

Coat—On head short and fine; on body flat or slightly wavy and silky in texture. Should be of medium length with enough undercoating to give protection. The English Cocker should be well feathered but not so profusely as to hide the true lines or interfere with his field work. *Faults*—Lack of coat; too soft, curly or wiry. Excessive trimming to change the natural appearance and coat should be discouraged.

Height—Ideal heights at withers: Males, 16 to 17 inches; females, 15 to 16 inches. Deviations to be severely penalized but not disqualified. *Weight* —The most desirable weights: Males, 28 pounds to 34 pounds; Females, 26 pounds to 32 pounds. Proper phyical conformation and balance should be considered more important than weight alone.

Approved September 13, 1955

Spaniel, English Springer

General Appearance and Type—The English Springer Spaniel is a medium-size sporting dog with a neat, compact body, and a docked tail. His coat is moderately long, glossy, usually liver and white or black and white, with feathering on his legs, ears, chest and brisket. His pendulous ears, soft gentle expression, sturdy build and friendly wagging tail proclaim him unmistakably a member of the ancient family of spaniels. He is above all a well proportioned dog, free from exaggeration, nicely balanced in every part. His carriage is proud and upstanding, body deep, legs strong and muscular with enough length to carry him with ease. His short level back, well developed thighs, good shoulders, excellent feet, suggest power, endurance, agility. Taken as a whole he looks the part of a dog that can go and keep going under difficult hunting conditions, and moreover he enjoys what he is doing. At his best he is endowed with style, symmetry, balance, enthusiasm and is every inch a sporting dog of distinct spaniel character, combining beauty and utility. To be penalized: Those lacking true English Springer type in conformation, expression, or behavior.

Temperament—The typical Springer is friendly, eager to please, quick to learn, willing to obey. In the show ring he should exhibit poise, attentiveness, tractability, and should permit himself to be examined by the judge without resentment or cringing. To be penalized: Excessive timidity, with due allowance for puppies and novice exhibits. But no dog to receive a ribbon if he behaves in vicious manner toward handler or judge. Aggressiveness toward other dogs in the ring *not* to be construed as viciousness.

Size and Proportion—The Springer is built to cover rough ground with agility and reasonable speed. He should be kept to medium size—neither too small nor too large and heavy to do the work for which he is intended. The ideal shoulder height for dogs is 20 inches; for bitches, 19 inches. Length of topline (the distance from top of the shoulders to the root of the tail) should be approximately equal to the dog's shoulder height—never longer than his height—and not appreciably less. The dog too long in body, especially when long in loin, tires easily and lacks the compact outline characteristic of the breed. Equally undesirable is the dog too short in body for the length of his legs, a condition that destroys his balance and restricts the gait.

Weight is dependent on the dog's other dimensions: a 20-inch dog, well proportioned, in good condition should weigh about 49–55 pounds. The resulting appearance is a well-knit, sturdy dog with good but not too heavy bone, in no way coarse or ponderous. To be penalized: Over-heavy specimens, cloddy in build. Leggy individuals, too tall for their length and substance. Over-size or under-size specimens (those more than one inch under or over the breed ideal).

Color and Coat—Color may be liver or black with white markings; liver and white (or black and white) with tan markings; blue or liver roan; or predominantly white with tan, black or liver markings. On ears, chest, legs and belly the Springer is nicely furnished with a fringe of feathering (of moderate heaviness). On his head, front or forelegs, and below hocks on front of hindlegs the hair is short and fine. The body coat is flat or wavy, of medium length, sufficiently dense to be water-proof, weather-proof and thorn-proof. The texture fine and the hair should have the clean, glossy, live appearance indicative of good health. It is legitimate to trim about head, feet, ears; to remove dead hair; to thin and shorten excess feathering particularly from the hocks to the feet and elsewhere as required to give a smart, clean appearance. To be penalized: Rough, curly coat. Over-trimming especially of the body coat. Any chopped, barbered or artificial effect. Excessive feathering that destroys the clean outline desirable in a sporting dog. Off colors such as lemon, red or orange not to place.

Head—The head is impressive without being heavy. Its beauty lies in a combination of strength and refinement. It is important that the size and proportion be in balance with the rest of the dog. Viewed in profile the head should appear approximately the same length as the neck and should blend with the body in substance. The skull (upper head) to be of medium length, fairly broad, flat on top, slightly rounded at the sides and back. The occiput bone inconspicuous, rounded rather than peaked or angular. The foreface (head in front of the eyes) approximately the same length as the skull, and in harmony as to width and general character. Looking down on the head the muzzle to appear to be about one-half the width of the skull. As the skull rises from the foreface it makes a brow or "stop," divided by a groove or fluting between the eyes. This groove continues upward and gradually disappears as it reaches the middle of the forehead. The amount of "stop" can best be described as moderate. It must not be a pronounced feature as in the Clumber Spaniel. Rather it is a subtle rise where the muzzle blends into the upper head, further emphasized by the groove and by the position and shape of the eyebrows which should be well-developed. The stop, eyebrow and the chiseling of the bony structure around the eye sockets contribute to the Springer's beautiful and characteristic expression.

Viewed in profile the topline of the skull and the muzzle lie in two approximately parallel planes. The nasal bone should be straight, with no inclination downward toward the tip of the nose which gives a down-faced look so undesirable in this breed. Neither should the nasal bone be concave resulting in a "dish-faced" profile; nor convex giving the dog a Roman nose. The jaws to be of sufficient length to allow the dog to carry game easily; fairly square, lean, strong, and even, (neither undershot nor overshot). The upper lip to come down full and rather square to cover the line of the lower jaw, but lips not to be pendulous nor exaggerated. The nostrils, well opened and broad, liver color or black depending on the color of the coat. Flesh-colored ("Dudley noses") or spotted ("butterfly noses") are undesirable. The cheeks to be flat, (not rounded, full or thick) with nice chiseling under the eyes. To be penalized: Oval, pointed or heavy skull. Cheeks prominently rounded, thick and protruding. Too much or too little stop. Over heavy muzzle. Muzzle too short, too thin, too narrow. Pendulous slobbery lips. Under- or over-shot jaws—a very serious fault, to be heavily penalized. *Teeth* —The teeth should be strong, clean, not too small; and when the mouth is closed the teeth should meet in an even bite or a close scissors bite (the lower incisors touching the inside of the upper incisors). To be penalized: Any deviation from above description. One or two teeth slightly out of line not to be considered a serious fault, but irregularities due to faulty jaw formation to be severely penalized.

Eyes—More than any other feature the eyes contribute to the Springer's appeal. Color, placement, size influence expression and attractiveness. The eyes to be of medium size, neither small, round, full and prominent, nor bold and hard in expression. Set rather well apart and fairly deep in their sockets. The color of the iris to harmonize with the color of the coat, preferably a good dark hazel in the liver dogs and black or deep brown in the black and white specimens. The expression to be alert, kindly, trusting. The lids, tight with little or no haw showing. To be penalized: Eyes yellow or brassy in color or noticeably lighter than the coat. Sharp expression indicating unfriendly or suspicious nature. Loose droopy lids. Prominent haw (the third eyelid or membrane in the inside corner of the eye).

Ears—The correct ear set is on a level with the line of the eye; on the side of the skull and not too far back. The flaps to be long and fairly wide, hanging close to the cheeks, with no tendency to stand up or out. The leather, thin, approximately long enough to reach the tip of the nose. To be penalized: Short round ears. Ears set too high or too low or too far back on the head.

Neck—The neck to be moderately long, muscular, slightly arched at the crest gradually blending into sloping shoulders. Not noticeably upright nor coming into the body at an abrupt angle. To be penalized: Short neck, often the sequence to steep shoulders. Concave neck, sometimes called ewe neck or upside down neck (the opposite of arched). Excessive throatiness.

Body—The body to be well coupled, strong, compact; the chest deep but not so wide or round as to interfere with the action of the front legs; the brisket sufficiently developed to reach to the level of the elbows. The ribs fairly long, springing gradually to the middle of the body then tapering as they approach the end of the ribbed section. The back (section between the withers and loin) to be straight and strong, with no tendency to dip or roach. The loins to be strong, short; a slight arch over loins and hip bones. Hips nicely rounded, blending smoothly into hind legs. The resulting topline slopes *very gently* from withers to tail—the line from withers to back descending without a sharp drop; the back practically level; arch over hips somewhat lower than the withers; croup sloping gently to base of tail; tail carried to follow the natural line of the body. The bottom line, starting on a level with the elbows, to continue backward with almost no up-curve until reaching the end of the ribbed section, then a more noticeable up-curve to the flank, but not enough to make the dog appear small waisted or "tucked up." To be penalized: Body too shallow, indicating lack of brisket. Ribs too flat sometimes due to immaturity. Ribs too round (barrel-shaped), hampering the gait. Sway-back (dip in back), indicating weakness or lack of muscular development, particularly to be seen when dog is in action and viewed from the side. Roach back (too much arch over loin and extending forward into middle section). Croup falling away too sharply; or croup too high—unsightly faults, detrimental to outline and good movement. Topline sloping sharply, indicating steep withers (straight shoulder placement) and a too low tail-set.

Tail—The Springer's tail is an index both to his temperament and his conformation. Merry tail action is characteristic. The proper set is somewhat low following the natural line of the croup. The carriage should be nearly horizontal, slightly elevated when dog is excited. Carried straight up is untypical of the breed. The tail should not be docked too short and should be well fringed with wavy feather. It is legitimate to shape and shorten the feathering but enough should be left to blend with the dog's other furnishings. To be penalized: Tail habitually upright. Tail set too high or too low. Clamped down tail (indicating timidity or undependable temperament, even less to be desired than the tail carried too gaily).

Forequarters—Efficient movement in front calls for proper shoulders. The blades sloping back to form an angle with the forearm of approximately 90 degrees which permits the dog to swing his forelegs forward in an easy manner. Shoulders (fairly close together at the tips) to lie flat and mold smoothly into the contour of the body. The forelegs to be straight with the same degree of size to the foot. The bone, strong, slightly flattened, not too heavy or round. The knee, straight, almost flat; the pasterns short, strong; elbows close to the body with free action from the shoulders. To be penalized: Shoulders set at a steep angle limiting the stride. Loaded shoulders (the blades standing out from the body by overdevelopment of the muscles). Loose elbows, crooked legs. Bone too light or too coarse and heavy. Weak pasterns that let down the feet at a pronounced angle. *Hindquarters*—The Springer should be shown in hard muscular condition, well developed in hips and thighs and the whole rear assembly should suggest strength and driving power. The hip joints to be set rather wide apart and the hips nicely rounded. The thighs broad and muscular; the stifle joint strong and moderately bent. The hock joint somewhat rounded, not small and sharp in contour, and moderately angulated. Leg from hock joint to foot pad, short and strong with good bone structure. When viewed from the rear the hocks to be parallel whether the dog is standing or in motion. To be penalized: Too little or too much angulation. Narrow, undeveloped thighs. Hocks too short or too long (a proportion of ⅓ the distance from hip joint to foot is ideal). Flabby muscles. Weakness of joints. *Feet*—The feet to be round, or slightly oval, compact, well arched, medium size with thick pads, well feathered between the toes. Excess hair to be removed to show the natural shape and size of the foot. To be penalized: Thin, open or splayed feet (flat with spreading toes). Hare foot (long, rather narrow foot).

Movement—In judging the Springer there should be emphasis on proper movement which is the final test of a dog's conformation and soundness. Prerequisite to good movement is balance of the front and rear assemblies. The two must match in angulation and muscular development if the gait is to be smooth and effortless. Good shoulders laid back at an angle that permits a long stride are just as essential as the excellent rear quarters that provide the driving power. When viewed from the front the dog's legs should appear to swing forward in a free and easy manner, with no tendency for the feet to cross over or interfere with each other. Viewed from the rear the hocks should drive well under the body following on a line with the forelegs, the rear legs parallel, neither too widely nor too closely spaced. Seen from the side the Springer should exhibit a good, long forward stride, without high-stepping or wasted motion. To be penalized: Short choppy stride, mincing steps with up and down movement, hopping. Moving with forefeet wide, giving roll or swing to body. Weaving or crossing of fore or hind feet. Cow-hocks—hocks turning in toward each other.

In judging the English Springer Spaniel the over-all picture is a primary consideration. It is urged that the judge look for type which includes general appearance, outline and temperament and also for soundness especially as seen when the dog is in motion. Inasmuch as the dog with a smooth easy gait must be reasonably sound and well balanced he is to be highly regarded in the show-ring, however, not to the extent of forgiving him for not looking like an English Springer Spaniel. A quite untypical dog, leggy, foreign in head and expression, may move well. But he should not be placed over a good all-round specimen that has a minor fault in movement. It should be remembered that the English Springer Spaniel is first and foremost a sporting dog of the spaniel family and he must look and behave and move in character.

Approved June 12, 1956

Spaniel, Field

Head—Should be quite characteristic of this grand sporting dog, as that of the Bulldog, or the Bloodhound; its very stamp and countenance should at once convey the conviction of high breeding, character and nobility; skull well developed, with a distinctly elevated occipital tuberosity, which, above all, gives the character alluded to; not too wide across the muzzle, long and lean, never snipy or squarely cut, and in profile curving gradually from nose to throat; lean beneath the eyes—a thickness here gives coarseness to the whole head. The great length of muzzle gives surface for the free development of the olfactory nerve, and thus secures the highest possible scenting powers. *Eyes*—Not too full, but not small, receding or overhung, color dark hazel or brown, or nearly black, according to the color of the dog. Grave in expression and showing no haw. *Ears*—Moderately long and wide, sufficiently clad with nice Setterlike feather and set low. They should fall in graceful folds, the lower parts curling inwards and backwards. *Neck*—Long, strong and muscular, so as to enable the dog to retrieve his game without undue fatigue.

Body—Should be of moderate length, well ribbed up to a good strong loin, straight or slightly arched, never slack. *Nose*—Well developed, with good open nostrils. *Shoulders and Chest*—Former long, sloping and well set back, thus giving great activity and speed; latter deep and well developed, but not too round and wide.

Back and Loin—Very strong and muscular. *Hindquarters*—Strong and muscular. The stifles should be moderately bent, and not twisted either in or out. *Stern*—Well set on and carried low, if possible below the level of the back, in a straight line or with a slight downward inclination, never elevated above the back, and in action always kept low, nicely fringed with wavy feather of silky texture. *Forelegs*—Should be of fairly good length, with straight, clean, flat bone, and nicely feathered. Immense bone is no longer desirable. *Feet*—Not too small; round, with short soft hair between the toes; good, strong pads.

Coat—Flat or slightly waved, and never curled. Sufficiently dense to resist the weather, and not too short. Silky in texture, glossy and refined in nature, with neither duffleness on the one hand, nor curl or wiriness on the other. On the chest, under belly and behind the legs, there should be abundant feather, but never too much, especially below the hocks, and that of the right sort, *viz.* setterlike. The hindquarters should be similarily adorned.

Color—Black, liver, golden liver, mahogany red, or roan; or any one of these colors with tan over the eyes and on the cheeks, feet, and pasterns. Other colors, such as black and white, liver and white, red or orange and white, while not disqualifying, will be considered less desirable since the Field Spaniel should be clearly distinguished from the Springer Spaniel.

Height—About 18 inches to shoulder. *Weight*—From about 35 pounds to 50 pounds.

General Appearance—That of a well-balanced, noble, upstanding sporting dog; built for activity and endurance. A grand combination of beauty and utility, and bespeaking of unusual docility and instinct.

SCALE OF POINTS

Head and jaw	15	Hind legs	10
Eyes	5	Feet	10
Ears	5	Stern	10
Neck	5	Coat and feather	10
Body	10	General appearance	10
Forelegs	10	Total	100

Approved July 14, 1959

Spaniel, Irish Water

Head—Skull rather large and high in dome with prominent occiput; muzzle square and rather long with deep mouth opening and lips fine in texture. Teeth strong and level. The nose should be large with open nostrils, and liver in color. The head should be cleanly chiseled, not cheeky, and should not present a short wedge-shaped appearance. Hair on face should be short and smooth. *Topknot*—Topknot, a characteristic of the true breed, should consist of long loose curls growing down into a well-defined peak between the eyes and should not be in the form of a wig; *i.e.* growing straight across. *Eyes*—Medium in size and set almost flush, without eyebrows. Color of eyes hazel, preferably of dark shade. Expression of the eyes should be keenly alert, intelligent, direct and quizzical. *Ears*—Long, lobular, set low with leathers reaching to about the end of the nose when extended forward. The ears should be abundantly covered with curls becoming longer toward the tips and extending two or more inches below the ends of the leathers.

Neck—The neck should be long, arching, strong and muscular, smoothly set into sloping shoulders. *Shoulders and Chest*—Shoulders should be sloping and clean; chest deep but not too wide between the legs. The entire front should give the impression of strength without heaviness.

Body, Ribs and Loins—Body should be of medium length, with ribs well sprung, pear-shaped at the brisket, and rounder toward the hind quarters. Ribs should be carried well back. Loins should be short, wide and muscular. The body should not present a tucked-up appearance. *Hindquarters*—The hindquarters should be as high as or a trifle higher than the shoulders and should be very powerful and muscular with well-developed upper and second thighs. Hips should be wide; stifles should not be too straight; and hocks low-set and moderately bent. Tail should be set on low enough to give a rather rounded appearance to the hindquarters and should be carried nearly level with the back. Sound hindquarters are of great importance to provide swimming power and drive. *Forelegs and Feet*—Forelegs medium in length, well boned, straight and muscular with elbows close set. Both fore and hind feet should be large, thick and somewhat spreading, well clothed with hair both over and between the toes, but free from superfluous feather.

Tail—The so-called "rat tail" is a striking characteristic of the breed. At the root it is thick and covered for 2 or 3 inches with short curls. It tapers to a fine point at the end, and from the root-curls is covered with short, smooth hair so as to look as if the tail had been clipped. The tail should not be long enough to reach the hock joint.

Coat—Proper coat is of vital importance. The neck, back and sides should be densely covered with tight crisp ringlets entirely free from wooliness. Underneath the ribs the hair should be longer. The hair on lower throat should be short. The forelegs should be covered all around with abundant hair falling in curls or waves, but shorter in front than behind. The hind legs should also be abundantly covered by hair falling in curls or waves, but the hair should be short on the front of the legs below the hocks. *Color*— Solid liver; white on chest objectionable.

Height and Weight—Dogs, 22 to 24 inches; bitches, 21 to 23 inches. Dogs, 55 to 65 pounds; bitches, 45 to 58 pounds.

General Appearance—That of a smart, upstanding, strongly built but not leggy dog, combining great intelligence and the rugged endurance with a bold, dashing eagerness of temperament. *Gait*—Should be square, true, precise and not slurring.

SCALE OF POINTS

Head
Skull and topknot .. 6
Ears 4
Eyes 4
Muzzle and nose... 6   20
Body
Neck 5
Chest, shoulders, back, loin and
ribs 12   17
Driving Gear
Feet, hips, thighs, stifles and
continuity of hindquarter
muscles 14
Feet, legs, elbows and muscles of
forequarters 9   23
Coat
Tightness, denseness of curl and
general texture ... 16
Color 4   20
Tail
General appearance and "set on,"
length and carriage. 5   5
General Conformation and Action
Symmetry, style, gait, weight and
size 15   15
                                 ___
                                 100

Approved June 11, 1940

Spaniel, Sussex

Head—The skull should be moderately long and also wide, with an indention in the middle and a full stop, brows fairly heavy; occiput full, but not pointed, the whole giving an appearance of heaviness without dullness. *Eyes*—Hazel color, fairly large, soft and languishing, not showing the haw overmuch. *Nose*—The muzzle should be about three inches long, square, and the lips somewhat pendulous. The nostrils well developed and liver color. *Ears*—Thick, fairly large and lobe shaped; set moderately low, but relatively not so low as in the black Field Spaniel; carried close to the head and furnished with soft, wavy hair.

Neck—Is rather short, strong and slightly arched, but not carrying the head much above the level of the back. There should not be much throatiness about the skin, but well-marked frill in the coat. *Chest and Shoulders*— The chest is round, especially behind the shoulders, deep and wide giving a good girth. The shoulders should be oblique.

Back and Back Rib—The back and loin is long and should be very muscular, both in width and depth; for this development the back ribs must be deep. The whole body is characterized as low, long and level. *Legs and Feet*— The arms and thighs must be bony as well as muscular, knees and hocks large and strong; pasterns very short and bony, feet large and round, and with short hair between the toes. The legs should be very short and strong, with great bone, and may show a slight bend in the forearm, and be moderately well feathered. The hind legs should not appear to be shorter than the forelegs, nor be too much bent at the hocks. They should be well feathered above the hocks but should not have much hair below that point. The hind legs are short from the hock to the ground, and wide apart. *Tail*—Should be docked from 5 to 7 inches, set low, and not carried above the level of the back, thickly covered with moderately long feather.

Coat—Body coat abundant, flat or slightly waved, with no tendency to curl, moderately well feathered on legs and stern, but clean below the hocks.

Color—Rich golden liver; this is a certain sign of the purity of the breed, dark liver or puce denoting unmistakably a recent cross with the black or other variety of Field Spaniel.

General Appearance—Rather massive and muscular, but with free movements and nice tail action, denoting a cheerful and tractable disposition. Weight from 35 pounds to 45 pounds.

POSITIVE POINTS

Head	10	Legs and feet	10
Eyes	5	Tail	5
Nose	5	Coat	5
Ears	10	Color	15
Neck	5	General appearance	15
Chest and shoulders	5	Total	100
Back and back ribs	10		

Light eyes	5	Color, too light or too	
Narrow head	10	dark	15
Weak muzzle	10	Legginess or light of bone ..	5
Curled ears or set on high ..	5	Shortness of body or flat	
Curled coat	15	sided	5
Carriage of stern	5	General appearance—sour or	
Topknot	10	crouching	10
White on chest	5	Total	100

Approved July 14, 1959

Spaniel, Welsh Springer

The "Welsh Spaniel" or "Springer" is also known and referred to in Wales as a "Starter." He is of very ancient and pure origin, and is a distinct variety which has been bred and preserved purely for working purposes.

Head—Skull—Proportionate, of moderate length, slightly domed, clearly defined stop, well chiseled below the eyes. *Muzzle*—Medium length, straight, fairly square; the nostrils well developed and flesh colored or dark. *Jaw*—Strong, neither undershot nor overshot. *Eyes*—Hazel or dark, medium size, not prominent, nor sunken, nor showing haw. *Ears*—Set moderately low and hanging close to the cheeks, comparatively small and gradually narrowing towards the tip, covered with nice setterlike feathering. A short chubby head is objectionable.

Neck and Shoulders—Neck—Long and muscular, clean in throat, neatly set into long and sloping shoulders. *Forelegs*—Medium length, straight, well boned, moderately feathered.

Body—Not long; strong and muscular with deep brisket, well sprung ribs; length of body should be proportionate to length of leg, and very well balanced; with muscular loin slightly arched and well coupled up. *Quarters*—Strong and muscular, wide and fully developed with deep second thighs. *Hind Legs*—Hocks well let down; stifles moderately bent (neither twisted in nor out), moderately feathered. *Feet*—Round with thick pads. *Stern*—

Well set on and low, never carried above the level of the back; lightly feathered and with lively action.

Coat—Straight or flat and thick, of a nice silky texture, never wiry nor wavy. A curly coat is most objectionable. *Color*—Dark rich red and white.

General Appearance—A symmetrical, compact, strong, merry, very active dog; not stilty, obviously built for endurance and activity.

Vizsla

General Appearance—That of a medium-sized hunting dog of quite distinguished appearance. Robust but rather lightly built, his short coat is an attractive rusty-gold, and his tail is docked. He is a dog of power and drive in the field, and a tractable and affectionate companion in the home.

Head—Lean but muscular. The skull is moderately wide between the ears, with a median line down the forehead. Stop moderate. The muzzle is a trifle longer than the skull and, although tapering, is well squared at its end. Jaws strong, with well-developed white teeth meeting in a scissors bite. The lips cover the jaws completely but they are neither loose nor pendulous. Nostrils slightly open, the nose brown. A black or slate-gray nose is objectionable.

Ears—Thin, silky, and proportionately long, with rounded-leather ends; set fairly low and hanging close to the cheeks. *Eyes*—Medium in size and depth of setting, their surrounding tissue covering the whites, and the iris or color portion harmonizing with the shade of the coat. A yellow eye is objectionable.

Neck—Strong, smooth, and muscular; moderately long, arched, and devoid of dewlap. It broadens nicely into shoulders which are well laid back.

Body—Strong and well proportioned. The back is short, the withers high, and the topline slightly rounded over the loin to the set-on of the tail. Chest moderately broad and deep, and reaching down to the elbows. Ribs well sprung, and underline exhibiting a slight tuck-up beneath the loin.

Legs and Feet—Forelegs straight, strong, and muscular, with elbows close. The hind legs have well-developed thighs, with moderate angulation at stifles and hocks. Too much angulation at the hocks is as faulty as too little. The hocks, which are well let down, are equidistant from each other from the hock joint to the ground. Cowhocks are faulty. Feet are cat-like, round and compact, with toes close. Nails are brown and short; pads thick and tough. Dewclaws, if any, to be removed. Hare feet are objectionable. *Tail*—Set just below the level of the back, thicker at the root, and docked one-third off. *Coat*—Short, smooth, dense, and close-lying, without woolly undercoat. *Color*—Solid. Rusty gold or rather dark sandy yellow in different shades, with darker shades preferred. Dark brown and pale yellow are undesirable. Small white spots on chest or feet are not faulted.

Temperament—That of the natural hunter endowed with a good nose and above-average ability to take training. Lively, gentle-mannered, and demonstratively affectionate. Fearless, and with well-developed protective instinct.

Gait—Far-reaching, light-footed, graceful, smooth.

Size—Males, 22 to 24 inches; females, 21 to 23 inches at the highest point of the shoulders. Any dog measuring over or under these limits shall be considered faulty, the seriousness of the fault depending on the extent of the deviation. Any dog that measures more than 2 inches over or under these limits shall be disqualified.

DISQUALIFICATION

Deviation in height of more than 2 inches from standard either way.
Approved December 10, 1963

Weimaraner

General Appearance—A medium-sized, gray dog with light eyes, he should present a picture of great driving power, stamina, alertness and balance. Above all, the dog *should indicate ability to work hard in the field. Height*— Height at withers: dogs, 25 to 27 inches; bitches, 23 to 25 inches.

Head—Moderately long and aristocratic, with moderate stop and slight median line extending back over the forehead. Rather prominent occipital bone and trumpets set well back, beginning at the back of the eyesockets. Measurement from tip of nose to stop to equal that from stop to occipital bone. The flews should be moderately deep, enclosing a powerful jaw. Foreface perfectly straight, delicate at the nostrils. Skin tightly drawn. Neck clean-cut and moderately long. Expression kind, keen, intelligent. *Ears*—Long and lobular, slightly folded and set high. The ear when drawn snugly alongside the jaw should end approximately 2 inches from the point of the nose. *Eyes* —In shades of light amber, gray or blue-gray, set well enough apart to indicate good disposition and intelligence. When dilated under excitement the eyes may appear almost black. *Teeth*—Well-set, strong and even; well-developed and proportionate to jaw with correct scissors bite, the upper teeth protruding slightly over the lower teeth but not more than 1/16 of an inch. Complete dentition is greatly to be desired. *Nose*—Gray. *Lips and Gums*—Pinkish flesh shades.

Body—The back should be moderate in length, set in straight line, strong, and should slope slightly from the withers. The chest should be well developed and deep, shoulder well laid on and snug. Ribs well sprung and long. Abdomen firmly held; moderately tucked-up flank. The brisket should drop to the elbow.

Coat—Short, smooth and sleek in shades of mouse-gray to silver-gray, usually blending to a lighter shade on the head and ears. Small white mark allowable on the chest, but not on any other part of the body. White spots that have resulted from injuries shall not be penalized.

Legs—*Forelegs*—Straight and strong, with the measurement from the elbow to the ground approximately equaling the distance from the elbow to the top of the withers. *Hindquarters*—Well-angulated stifles and straight hocks. Musculation well developed. *Feet*—Firm and compact, webbed, toes well arched, pads closed and thick, nails short and gray or amber in color. *Dewclaws*—Allowable only on forelegs, there optional.

Tail—Docked. At maturity it should measure approximately 6 inches with a tendency to be light rather than heavy and should be carried in a manner expressing confidence and sound temperament.

Gait—The walk is rather awkward. The trot should be effortless, ground covering and should indicate smooth co-ordination. When seen from the rear, the hind feet should parallel the front feet. When viewed from the side, the topline should remain strong and level. *Temperament*—The dog should display a temperament that is keen, fearless, friendly, protective and obedient.

VERY SERIOUS FAULTS

Any longhaired coat or coat darker than mouse-gray to silver-gray is considered a most undesirable recessive trait. White, other than a spot on chest. Eyes any other color than gray, blue-gray or light amber. Black, mottled mouth. Non-docked tail. Dogs exhibiting strong fear. Viciousness.

SERIOUS FAULTS

Poor gait. Very poor feet. Cowhocks. Faulty backs, either roached or sway. Badly overshot or undershot jaw. Snipy muzzle. Short ears. Yellow in white marking. Undersize.

FAULTS

Doggy bitches. Bitchy dogs. Improper muscular condition. Badly affected teeth. More than four missing teeth. Back too long or too short. Faulty coat. Neck too short, thick or throaty. Low tail set. Elbows in or out; feet east and west.

MINOR FAULTS

Tail too short or too long. Pink nose. Oversize should not be considered a serious fault, providing correct structure and working ability are in evidence.

Approved April 14, 1959

GROUP II: HOUNDS

Afghan Hound

General Appearance—The Afghan Hound is an aristocrat, his whole appearance one of dignity and aloofness with no trace of plainness or coarseness. He has a straight front, proudly carried head, eyes gazing into the distance as if in memory of ages past. The striking characteristics of the breed—exotic, or "eastern," expression, long silky topknot, peculiar coat pattern, very prominent hip bones, large feet, and the impression of a somewhat exaggerated bend in the stifle due to profuse trouserings—stand out clearly, giving the Afghan Hound the appearance of what he is, a king of dogs, that has held true to tradition throughout the ages.

Head—The head is of good length, showing much refinement, the skull evenly balanced with the foreface. There is a slight prominence of the nasal bone structure causing a slightly Roman appearance, the center line running up over the foreface with little or no stop, falling away in front of the eyes so there is an absolutely clear outlook with no interference; the underjaw showing great strength, the jaws long and punishing; the mouth level, meaning that the teeth from the upper jaw and lower jaw match evenly, neither overshot nor undershot. This is a difficult mouth to breed. A scissors bite is even more punishing and can be more easily bred into a dog than a level mouth, and a dog having a scissors bite, where the lower teeth slip inside and rest against the teeth of the upper jaw, should not be penalized. The occipital bone is very prominent. The head is surmounted by a topknot of long silky hair. *Ears*—The ears are long, set approximately on level with outer corners of the eyes, the leather of the ear reaching nearly to the end of the dog's nose, and covered with long silky hair. *Eyes*—The eyes are almond-shaped (almost triangular), never full or bulgy, and are dark in color. *Nose*—Nose is of good size, black in color. *Faults*—Coarseness; snipiness; overshot or undershot; eyes round or bulgy or light in color; exaggerated Roman nose; head not surmounted with topknot.

Neck—The neck is of good length, strong and arched, running in a curve to the shoulders which are long and sloping and well laid back. *Faults*—Neck too short or too thick; a ewe neck; a goose neck; a neck lacking in substance.

Body—The black line appearing practically level from the shoulders to the loin. Strong and powerful loin and slightly arched, falling away toward the stern, with the hipbones very pronounced; well ribbed and tucked up in flanks. The height at the shoulders equals the distance from the chest to the buttocks; the brisket well let down, and of medium width. *Faults*—Roach back, sway-back, goose rump, slack loin; lack of prominence of hipbones; too much width of brisket causing interference with elbows. *Tail*—Tail set not too high on the body, having a ring, or a curve on the end; should never be curled over, or rest on the back, or be carried sideways; and should never be bushy.

Legs—Forelegs are straight and strong with great length between elbow and pastern; elbows well held in; forefeet large in both length and width; toes well arched; feet covered with long thick hair; fine in texture; pasterns long and straight; pads of feet unusually large and well down on the ground. Shoulders have plenty of angulation so that the legs are well set underneath the dog. Too much straightness of shoulder causes the dog to break down in the pasterns, and this is a serious fault. All four feet of the Afghan Hound are in line with the body, turning neither in nor out. The hind feet are broad and of good length; the toes arched, and covered with long thick hair; hindquarters powerful and well muscled with great length between hip and hock; hocks are well let down; good angulation of both stifle and hock; slightly bowed from hock to crotch. *Faults*—Front or back feet thrown outward or inward; pads of feet not thick enough; or feet too small; or any other evidence of weakness in feet; weak or broken down pasterns; too straight in stifle; too long in hock.

Coat—Hindquarters, flanks, ribs, forequarters, and legs well covered with thick, silky hair, very fine in texture; ears and all four feet well feathered; from in front of the shoulders, and also backwards from the shoulders along the saddle from the flanks and the ribs upwards, the hair is short and close, forming a smooth back in mature dogs—this is a traditional characteristic of the Afghan Hound. The Afghan Hound should be shown in its natural state; the coat is not clipped or trimmed; the head is surmounted (in the full sense of the word) with a topknot of long, silky hair—that is also an outstanding characteristic of the Afghan Hound. Showing of short hair on cuffs on either front or back legs is permissible.

Faults—Lack of shorthaired saddle in mature dogs.

Height—Dogs, 27 inches, plus or minus one inch; bitches, 25 inches, plus or minus one inch. *Weight*—Dogs, about 60 pounds; bitches, about 50 pounds. *Color*—All colors are permissible, but color or color combinations are pleasing; white markings, especially on the head, are undesirable.

Gait—When running free, the Afghan Hound moves at a gallop, showing great elasticity and spring in his smooth, powerful stride. When on a loose lead, the Afghan can trot at a fast pace; stepping along, he has the appearance of placing the hind feet directly in the foot prints of the front feet, both thrown straight ahead. Moving with head and tail high, the whole appearance of the Afghan Hound is one of great style and beauty.

Temperament—Aloof and dignified, yet gay. *Faults*—Sharpness or shyness.

Approved September 14, 1948

Basenji

Characteristics—The Basenji should not bark, but is not mute. The wrinkled forehead and the swift, tireless running gait (resembling a racehorse trotting full out) are typical of the breed.

General Appearance—The Basenji is a small, lightly built, short backed dog, giving the impression of being high on the leg compared to its length. The wrinkled head must be proudly carried, and the whole demeanor should be one of poise and alertness.

Head and Skull—The skull is flat, well chiseled and of medium width, tapering towards the eyes. The foreface should taper from eye to muzzle and should be shorter than the skull. Muzzle, neither coarse, nor snipy but with rounded cushions. Wrinkles should appear upon the forehead, and be fine and profuse. Side wrinkles are desirable, but should never be exaggerated into dewlap. *Nose*—Black greatly desired. A pinkish tinge should not penalize an otherwise first class specimen, but it should be discouraged in breeding. *Eyes*—Dark hazel, almond shaped, obliquely set and far seeing.

Ears—Small, pointed and erect, of fine texture, set well forward on top of head. *Mouth*—Teeth must be level with scissors bite.

Neck—Of good length, well crested and slightly full at base of throat. It should be well set into flat, laid back shoulders. *Forequarters*—The chest should be deep and of medium width. The legs straight with clean fine bone, long forearm and well defined sinews. Pasterns should be of good length, straight and flexible.

Body—The body should be short and the back level. The ribs well sprung, with plenty of heart room, deep brisket, short coupled, and ending in a definite waist. *Hindquarters*—Should be strong and muscular, with hocks well let down, turned neither in nor out, with long second thighs. *Feet*—Small, narrow and compact, with well arched toes. *Tail*—Should be set on top and curled tightly over to either side.

Coat—Short and silky. Skin very pliant. *Color*—Chestnut red (the deeper the better) or pure black, or black and tan, all with white feet, chest and tail tip. White legs, white blaze and white collar optional.

Weight—Bitches 22 pounds approximately. Dogs 24 pounds approximately. *Size*—Bitches 16 inches and dogs 17 inches from the ground to the top of the shoulder. Bitches 16 inches and dogs 17 inches from the front of the chest to the farthest point of the hindquarters. *Faults*—Coarse skull or muzzle. Domed or peaked skull. Dewlap. Round eyes. Low set ears. Overshot or undershot mouths. Wide chest. Wide behind. Heavy bone. Creams, shaded or off colors, other than those defined above, should be heavily penalized.

Approved June 8, 1954

Basset Hound

General Appearance—The Basset Hound possesses in marked degree those characteristics which equip it admirably to follow a trail over and through difficult terrain. It is a short-legged dog, heavier in bone, size considered, than any other breed of dog, and while its movement is deliberate, it is in no sense clumsy. In temperament it is mild, never sharp or timid. It is capable of great endurance in the field and is extreme in its devotion.

Head—The head is large and well proportioned. Its length from occiput to muzzle is greater than the width at the brow. In over-all appearance the head is of medium width. *The skull* is well domed, showing a pronounced occipital protuberance. A broad flat skull is a fault. The length from nose to stop is approximately the length from stop to occiput. The sides are flat and free from cheek bumps. Viewed in profile the top lines of the muzzle and skull are straight and lie in parallel planes, with a moderately defined stop. The skin over the whole of the head is loose, falling in distinct wrinkles over the brow when the head is lowered. A dry head and tight skin are faults. *The muzzle* is deep, heavy, and free from snipiness. *The nose* is darkly pigmented, preferably black, with large wide-open nostrils. A deep liver-colored nose conforming to the coloring of the head is permissible but not desirable. *The teeth* are large, sound, and regular, meeting in either a scissors or an even bite. A bite either overshot or undershot is a serious fault. *The lips* are darkly pigmented and are pendulous, falling squarely in front and, toward the back, in loose hanging flews. *The dewlap* is very pronounced. *The neck* is powerful, of good length, and well arched. *The eyes* are soft, sad, and slightly sunken, showing a prominent haw, and in color are brown, dark brown preferred. A somewhat lighter-colored eye conforming to the general coloring of the dog is acceptable but not desirable. Very light or protruding eyes are faults. *The ears* are extremely long, low set, and when drawn forward, fold well over the end of the nose. They are velvety in texture, hanging in loose folds with the ends curling slightly inward. They are set far back on the head at the base of the skull and, in repose, appear to be set on the neck. A high set or flat ear is a serious fault.

Forequarters—*The chest* is deep and full with prominent sternum showing clearly in front of the legs. *The shoulders* and elbows are set close against the sides of the chest. The distance from the deepest point of the chest to the ground, while it must be adequate to allow free movement when working in the field, is not to be more than one-third the total height at the withers of an adult Basset. The shoulders are well laid back and powerful. Steepness in shoulder, fiddle fronts, and elbows that are out, are serious faults. *The forelegs* are short, powerful, heavy in bone, with wrinkled skin. Knuckling over of the front legs is a disqualification. *The paw* is massive, very heavy with tough heavy pads, well rounded and with both feet inclined equally a trifle outward, balancing the width of the shoulders. Feet down at the pastern are a serious fault. *The toes* are neither pinched together nor splayed, with the weight of the forepart of the body borne evenly on each. The dewclaws may be removed.

Body—The rib structure is long, smooth, and extends well back. The ribs are well sprung, allowing adequate room for heart and lungs. Flat-sidedness and flanged ribs are faults. The topline is straight, level, and free from any tendency to sag or roach, which are faults.

Hindquarters—The hindquarters are very full and well rounded, and are approximately equal to the shoulders in width. They must not appear slack or light in relation to the over-all depth of the body. The dog stands firmly on its hind legs showing a well-let-down stifle with no tendency toward a crouching stance. Viewed from behind, the hind legs are parallel, with the hocks turning neither in nor out. Cowhocks or bowed legs are serious faults. The hind feet point straight ahead. Steep, poorly angulated hindquarters are a serious fault. The dewclaws, if any, may be removed.

Tail—The tail is not to be docked, and is set in continuation of the spine with but slight curvature, and carried gaily in hound fashion. The hair on the underside of the tail is coarse.

Size—The height should not exceed 14 inches. Height over 15 inches at the highest point of the shoulder blades is a disqualification.

Gait—The Basset Hound moves in a smooth, powerful, and effortless manner. Being a scenting dog with short legs, it holds its nose low to the ground. Its gait is absolutely true with perfect co-ordination between the front and hind legs, and it moves in a straight line with hind feet following in line with the front feet, the hocks well bent with no stiffness of action. The front legs do not paddle, weave, or overlap, and the elbows must lie close to the body. Going away, the hind legs are parallel.

Coat—The coat is hard, smooth, and short, with sufficient density to be of use in all weather. The skin is loose and elastic. A distinctly long coat is a disqualification.

Color—Any recognized hound color is acceptable and the distribution of color and markings is of no importance.

Height of more than 15 inches at the highest point of the shoulder blades. Knuckled over front legs. Distinctly long coat.

Approved January 14, 1964

Beagle

Head—The skull should be fairly long, slightly domed at occiput, with cranium broad and full. *Ears*—Ears set on moderately low, long, reaching when drawn out nearly, if not quite, to the end of the nose; fine in texture, fairly broad—with almost entire absence of erectile power—setting close to the head, with the forward edge slightly inturning to the cheek—rounded at tip. *Eyes*—Eyes large, set well apart—soft and houndlike—expression gentle and pleading; of a brown or hazel color. *Muzzle*—Muzzle of medium length—straight and square-cut—the stop moderately defined. *Jaws*—Level. Lips free from flews; nostrils large and open. *Defects*—A very flat skull, narrow across the top; excess of dome, eyes small, sharp and terrierlike, or prominent and protruding; muzzle long, snipy or cut away decidedly below the eyes, or very short. Roman-nosed, or upturned, giving a dish-face expression. Ears short, set on high or with a tendency to rise above the point of origin.

Body—Neck and Throat—Neck rising free and light from the shoulders strong in substance yet not loaded, of medium length. The throat clean and free from folds of skin; a slight wrinkle below the angle of the jaw, however, may be allowable. *Defects*—A thick, short, cloddy neck carried on a line with the top of the shoulders. Throat showing dewlap and folds of skin to a degree termed "throatiness." *Shoulders and Chest*—Shoulders sloping—clean, muscular, not heavy or loaded—conveying the idea of freedom of action with activity and strength. Chest deep and broad, but not broad enough to interfere with the free play of the shoulders. *Defects*—Straight, upright shoulders. Chest disproportionately wide or with lack of depth. *Back, Loin and Ribs*—Back short, muscular and strong. Loin broad and slightly arched, and the ribs well sprung, giving abundance of lung room. *Defects*—Very long or swayed or roached back. Flat, narrow loin. Flat ribs.

Forelegs and Feet—Forelegs—Straight, with plenty of bone in proportion to size of the hound. Pasterns short and straight. *Feet*—Close, round and firm. Pad full and hard. *Defects*—Out at elbows. Knees knuckled over forward, or bent backward. Forelegs crooked or Dachshundlike. Feet long, open or spreading.

Hips, Thighs, Hind Legs and Feet—Hips and thighs strong and well muscled, giving abundance of propelling power. Stifles strong and well let down. Hocks firm, symmetrical and moderately bent. Feet close and firm. *Defects* —Cowhocks, or straight hocks. Lack of muscle and propelling power. Open feet.

Tail—Set moderately high; carried gaily, but not turned forward over the back; with slight curve; short as compared with size of the hound; with brush. *Defects*—A long tail. Teapot curve or inclined forward from the root. Rat tail with absence of brush.

Coat—A close, hard, hound coat of medium length. *Defects*—A short, thin coat, or of a soft quality. *Color*—Any true hound color.

General Appearance—A miniature Foxhound, solid and big for his inches, with the wear-and-tear look of the hound that can last in the chase and follow his quarry to the death.

SCALE OF POINTS

Head			Running Gear		
Skull	5		Forelegs	10	
Ears	10		Hips, thighs and hind		
Eyes	5		legs	10	
Muzzle	5	25	Feet	10	30
Body					
Neck	5		Coat	5	
Chest and shoulders	15		Stern	5	10
Back, loin and ribs	15	35	Total		100

Varieties—There shall be two varieties. Thirteen Inch—which shall be for hounds not exceeding 13 inches in height. Fifteen Inch—which shall be for hounds over 13 but not exceeding 15 inches in height.

DISQUALIFICATION

Any hound measuring more than 15 inches shall be disqualified.

PACKS OF BEAGLES
SCORE OF POINTS FOR JUDGING

Hounds—General levelness of pack	40%	
Individual merit of hounds	30%	
		70%
Manners		20%
Appointments		10%
Total		..100%

Levelness of Pack—The first thing in a pack to be considered is that they present a unified appearance. The hounds must be as near of the same height, weight, conformation and color as possible.

Individual Merit of the Hounds—Is the individual bench-show quality of the hounds. A very level and sporty pack can be gotten together and not a single hound be a good Beagle. This is to be avoided.

Manners—The hounds must all work gaily and cheerfully, with flags up —obeying all commands cheerfully. They should be broken to heel up, kennel up, follow promptly and stand. Cringing, sulking, lying down to be avoided. Also, a pack must not work as though in terror of master and whips. In Beagle packs it is recommended that the whip be used as little as possible.

Appointments—Master and whips should be dressed alike, the master or huntsman to carry horn—the whips and master to carry light thong whips. One whip should carry extra couplings on shoulder strap.

RECOMMENDATIONS FOR SHOW LIVERY

Black velvet cap, white stock, green coat, white breeches or knickerbockers, green or black stockings, white spats, black or dark brown shoes. Vest and gloves optional. Ladies should turn out exactly the same except for a white skirt instead of white breeches.

Approved September 10, 1957

Bloodhound

General Character—The Bloodhound possesses, in a most marked degree, every point and characteristic of those dogs which hunt together by scent (Sagaces). He is very powerful, and stands over more ground than is usual with hounds of other breeds. The skin is thin to the touch and extremely loose, this being more especially noticeable about the head and neck, where it hangs in deep folds.

Height—The mean average height of adult dogs is 26 inches, and of adult bitches 24 inches. Dogs usually vary from 25 inches to 27 inches, and bitches from 23 inches to 25 inches; but, in either case, the greater height is to be preferred, provided that character and quality are also combined. *Weight*— The mean average weight of adult dogs, in fair condition, is 90 pounds, and of adult bitches 80 pounds. Dogs attain the weight of 110 pounds, bitches 100 pounds. The greater weights are to be preferred, provided (as in the case of height) that quality and proportion are also combined.

Expression—The expression is noble and dignified, and characterized by solemnity, wisdom, and power. *Temperament*—In temperament he is extremely affectionate, neither quarrelsome with companions nor with other dogs. His nature is somewhat shy, and equally sensitive to kindness or correction by his master.

Head—The head is narrow in proportion to its length, and long in proportion to the body, tapering but slightly from the temples to the end of the muzzle, thus (when viewed from above and in front) having the appearance of being flattened at the sides and of being nearly equal in width throughout its entire length. In profile the upper outline of the skull is nearly in the same plane as that of the foreface. The length from end of nose to stop (midway between the eyes) should be not less than that from stop to back of occipital protuberance (peak). The entire length of head from the posterior part of the occipital protuberance to the end of the muzzle should be 12 inches, or more, in dogs, and 11 inches, or more, in bitches. *Skull*— The skull is long and narrow, with the occipital peak very pronounced. The brows are not prominent, although, owing to the deep-set eyes, they may have that appearance. *Foreface*—The foreface is long, deep, and of even width throughout, with square outline when seen in profile. *Eyes*—The eyes are deeply sunk in the orbits, the lids assuming a lozenge or diamond shape, in consequence of the lower lids being dragged down and everted by the heavy flews. The eyes correspond with the general tone of color of the animal, varying from deep hazel to yellow. The hazel color is, however, to be preferred, although very seldom seen in red-and-tan hounds. *Ears*—The ears are thin and soft to the touch, extremely long, set very low, and fall in graceful folds, the lower parts curling inwards and backwards.

Wrinkle—The head is furnished with an amount of loose skin, which in nearly every position appears superabundant, but more particularly so when the head is carried low; the skin then falls into loose, pendulous ridges and folds, especially over the forehead and sides of the face. *Nostrils*—The nostrils are large and open. *Lips, Flews, and Dewlap*—In front the lips fall squarely, making a right angle with the upper line of the foreface; whilst behind they form deep, hanging flews, and, being continued into the pendant folds of loose skin about the neck, constitute the dewlap, which is very pronounced. These characters are found, though in a less degree, in the bitch.

Neck, Shoulders, and Chest—The neck is long, the shoulders muscular and well sloped backwards; the ribs are well sprung; and the chest well let down between the forelegs, forming a deep keel. *Legs and Feet*—The forelegs are straight and large in bone, with elbows squarely set; the feet strong and well knuckled up; the thighs and second thighs (gaskins) are very muscular; the hocks well bent and let down and squarely set.

Back and Loin—The back and loins are strong, the latter deep and slightly arched. *Stern*—The stern is long and tapering, and set on rather high, with a moderate amount of hair underneath.

Gait—The gait is elastic, swinging and free, the stern being carried high, but not too much curled over the back.

Color—The colors are black and tan, red and tan, and tawny; the darker colors being sometimes interspersed with lighter or badger-colored hair, and sometimes flecked with white. A small amount of white is permissible on chest, feet, and tip of stern.

Borzoi

Head—Skull slightly domed, long and narrow, with scarcely any perceptible stop, rather inclined to be Roman-nosed; jaws long, powerful and deep; teeth strong, clean and even, neither pig-jawed nor undershot; nose large and black. *Ears*—Small and fine in quality, lying back on the neck when in repose with the tips when thrown back almost touching behind occiput; raised when at attention. *Eyes*—Set somewhat obliquely, dark in color, intelligent, but rather soft in expression, never full nor staring, nor light in color, eyelids dark.

Neck—Clean, free from throatiness, somewhat shorter than in the Greyhound, slightly arched, very powerful and well set on. *Shoulders*—Sloping, should be fine at the withers and free from coarseness or lumber. *Chest*—Rather narrow, with great depth of brisket. *Ribs*—Only slightly sprung, but very deep, giving room for heart and lung play. *Back*—Rising a little at the loins in a graceful curve. *Loins*—Extremely muscular, but rather tucked up, owing to the great depth of chest and comparative shortness of back and ribs.

Forelegs—Bone flat, straight, giving free play for the elbows, which should be neither turned in nor out; pasterns strong. *Feet*—Hare-shaped, with well-arched knuckles, toes close and well padded. *Hindquarters*—Long, very muscular and powerful, with well bent stifles and strong second thighs, hocks broad, clean and well let down. *Tail*—Long, set on and carried low in a graceful curve.

Coat—Long, silky (not woolly), either flat, wavy or rather curly. On the head, ears and front of legs it should be short and smooth; on the neck the frill should be profuse and rather curly. Feather on hindquarters and tail, long and profuse, less so on the chest and back of forelegs. *Color*—Any color, white usually predominating, more or less marked with lemon, tan, brindle, gray or black. Whole-colored specimens of these tints occasionally appear.

General Appearance—Should be that of an elegant, graceful aristocrat among dogs, possessing courage and combining muscular power with extreme speed.

Size—Dogs, average height at shoulder from 28 to 31 inches; average weight from 75 to 105 pounds. Larger dogs are often seen, extra size being no disadvantage when it is not acquired at the expense of symmetry, speed and staying quality. Bitches are invariably smaller than dogs, and two inches less in height, and from 15 to 20 pounds less in weight is a fair average.

SCALE OF POINTS

Head	12	Legs and feet	10
Eyes	5	Coat and feather	10
Ears	3	Tail	3
Neck	5	Conformation and gait	15
Shoulders and brisket	10	Total	100
Ribs, back and loins	15		
Hindquarters, stifles and hocks	12		

Coonhound, Black and Tan

The Black and Tan Coonhound is first and fundamentally a working dog, capable of withstanding the rigors of winter, the heat of summer, and the difficult terrain over which he is called upon to work. Judges are asked by the club sponsoring the breed to place great emphasis upon these facts when evaluating the merits of the dog. The general impression should be that of power, agility, and alertness. His expression should be alert, friendly, eager, and aggressive. He should immediately impress one with his ability to cover the ground with powerful rhythmic strides.

Head—The head should be cleanly modeled, with medium stop occurring midway between occiput bone and nose. The head should measure from 9 to 10 inches in males and from 8 to 9 inches in females. Viewed from the profile the line of the skull is on a practically parallel plane to the foreface or muzzle. The skin should be devoid of folds or excess dewlap. The flews should be well developed with typical hound appearance. Nostrils well open and always black. Skull should tend toward oval outline. Eyes should be from hazel to dark brown in color, almost round and not deeply set. The ears should be low set and well back. They should hang in graceful folds giving the dog a majestic appearance. In length they should extend well beyond the tip of the nose. Teeth should fit evenly with slightly scissors bite.

Body—Neck, Shoulders, and Chest—The neck should be muscular, sloping, medium length, extending into powerfully constructed shoulders and deep chest. The dog should possess full, round, well-sprung ribs, avoiding flatsidedness. *Back and Tail*—The back should be level, powerful and strong, with a visible slope from withers to rump. Tail should be strong, with base slightly below level of back line, carried free, and when in action at approximately right angle to back.

Legs and Feet—The forelegs should be straight, with elbows well let down, turning neither in nor out; pasterns strong and erect. Feet should be catlike with compact, well-arched toes and thick strong pads. *Hindquarters*— Quarters should be well boned and muscled. From hip to hock long and sinewy, hock to pad short and strong. Stifles and hock well bent and not inclining either in or out. When standing on a level surface the hind feet should set back from under the body, and leg from pad to hock be at right angles to the ground when viewed both from profile and the rear. The stride of the Black and Tan Coonhound should be easy and graceful with plenty of reach in front and drive behind.

Coat and Color—The coat should be short but dense to withstand rough going. As the name implies, the color should be coal black, with rich tan markings above eyes, on sides of muzzle, chest, legs and breeching with black pencil markings on toes.

Size—Measured at the shoulder: males, 25 to 27 inches; females, 23 to 25 inches. Height should be in proportion to general conformation so that dog appears neither leggy nor close to the ground. Dogs oversized should not be penalized when general soundness and proportion are in favor.

Judges should penalize the following defects: Undersize, elbows out at shoulder, lack of angulation in hindquarters, splay feet, sway- or roach back, flatsidedness, lack of depth in chest, yellow or light eyes, shyness and nervousness. *Fault*—Dewclaws; white on chest or other parts of body is highly undesirable and if it exceeds 1½ inches in diameter should be disqualified.

DISQUALIFICATION

White on chest or other parts of the body if it exceeds 1½ inches in diameter.

Approved July 10, 1945

Dachshund

SUMMARY

General Appearance—Short-legged, long-bodied, low-to-ground; sturdy, well muscled, neither clumsy nor slim, with audacious carriage and intelligent expression; conformation pre-eminently fitted for following game into burrows.

Head—Long, uniformly tapered, clean-cut; teeth well fitted, with scissors bite; eyes medium oval; ears broad, long, rounded, set on high and well back; neck long, muscular. *Forequarters*—Muscular, compact. Chest deep, long, full and oval; breastbone prominent. Broad, long shoulder, and oblique humerus forming right angle; heavy, set close; forearm short, inclined slightly in. Foreleg straight and vertical in profile, covering deepest point of chest. Feet broad, firm, compact, turned slightly out. *Hindquarters*—Well-muscled and rounded. Pelvis, femur and tibia oblique, forming right angles; tarsus inclined forward. Hip should be level with shoulder, back strong, neither sagged nor more than very slightly arched. Tail strong, tapered, well-covered with hair, not carried gaily.

Varieties—Three coat types: *Smooth* or Shorthaired, short and dense, shining, glossy. *Wirehaired*, like German Wirehaired Pointer, hard, with good undercoat. *Longhaired*, like Irish Setter.

Note—In each coat variety there are divisions of open classes restricted to Miniatures, under 9 pounds, minimum age 12 months.

Color—Solid red (tan) of various shades, and black with tan points, should have black noses and nails, and narrow black line edging lips and eyelids; chocolate with tan points permits brown nose. Eyes of all, lustrous, the darker the better.

Faults—Overshot or undershot, knuckling over, loose shoulders; high on legs, clumsy gait, long, splayed or twisted feet, sagged or roached back, high croup, small, narrow or short chest, faulty angulation of fore or hindquarters, weak loins, narrow hindquarters, bowed legs, cowhocks; weak or dish-faced muzzle, dewlaps, uneven or scanty coat.

GENERAL FEATURES

General Appearance—Low to ground, short-legged, long-bodied, but with compact figure and robust muscular development; with bold and confident carriage of the head and intelligent facial expression. In spite of his shortness of leg, in comparison with his length of trunk, he should appear neither crippled, awkward, cramped in his capacity for movement, nor slim and weasel-like. *Qualities*—He should be clever, lively, and courageous to the point of rashness, persevering in his work both above and below ground; with all the senses well developed. His build and disposition qualify him especially for hunting game below ground. Added to this, his hunting spirit, good nose, loud tongue, and small size, render him especially suited for beating the bush. His figure and his fine nose give him an especial advantage over most other breeds of sporting dogs for trailing.

CONFORMATION OF BODY

Head—Viewed from above or from the side, it should taper uniformly to the tip of the nose, and should be clean-cut. The skull is only slightly arched, and should slope gradually without stop (the less stop the more typical) into the finely-formed slightly-arched muzzle (ram's nose). The bridge bones over the eyes should be strongly prominent. The nasal cartilage and tip of the nose are long and narrow; lips tightly stretched, well covering the lower jaw, but neither deep nor pointed; corner of the mouth not very marked. Nostrils well open. Jaws opening wide and hinged well back of the eyes, with strongly developed bones and teeth.

(*a*) Teeth: Powerful canine teeth should fit closely together, and the outer side of the lower incisors should tightly touch the inner side of the upper. (Scissors bite.) (*b*) Eyes: Medium size, oval, situated at the sides, with a clean, energetic, though pleasant expression; not piercing. Color, lustrous dark reddish-brown to brownish-black for all coats and colors. Wall (fish or pearl) eyes in the case of gray or dapple-colored dogs are not a very bad fault, but are also not desirable. (*c*) Ears: Should be set near the top of the head, and not too far forward, long but not too long, beautifully rounded, not narrow, pointed, or folded. Their carriage should be animated, and the forward edge should just touch the cheek. (*d*) Neck: Fairly long, muscular, clean-cut, not showing any dewlap on the throat, slightly arched in the nape, extending in a graceful line into the shoulders, carried proudly but not stiffly.

Front—To endure the arduous exertion underground, the front must be correspondingly muscular, compact, deep, long and broad. Forequarters in detail: (*a*) Shoulder Blade: Long, broad, obliquely and firmly placed upon the fully developed thorax, furnished with hard and plastic muscles. (*b*) Upper Arm: Of the same length as the shoulder blade, and at right angles to the latter, strong of bone and hard of muscle, lying close to the ribs, capable of free movement. (*c*) Forearm: This is short in comparison to other breeds, slightly turned inwards; supplied with hard but plastic muscles on the front and outside, with tightly stretched tendons on the inside and at the back. (d) Joint between forearm and foot (wrists): These are closer together than the shoulder joints, so that the front does not appear absolutely straight. (e) Paws: Full, broad in front, and a trifle inclined outwards; compact, with well-arched toes and tough pads. (f) Toes: There are five of these, though only four are in use. They should be close together, with a pronounced arch; provided on top with strong nails, and underneath with tough toe-pads.

Trunk—The whole trunk should in general be long and fully muscled. The back, with sloping shoulders, and short, rigid pelvis, should lie in the straightest possible line between the withers and the very slightly arched loins, these latter being short, rigid, and broad. (a) Chest: The breastbone should be strong, and so prominent in front that on either side a depression (dimple) appears. When viewed from the front, the thorax should appear oval, and should extend downward to the mid-point of the forearm. The enclosing structure of ribs should appear full and oval, and when viewed from above or from the side, full-volumed, so as to allow by its ample capacity, complete development of heart and lungs. Well ribbed up, and gradually merging into the line of the abdomen. If the length is correct, and also the anatomy of the shoulder and upper arm, the front leg when viewed in profile should cover the lowest point of the breast line. (b) Abdomen: Slightly drawn up.

Hindquarters—The hindquarters viewed from behind should be of completely equal width. (a) Croup: Long, round, full, robustly muscled, but plastic, only slightly sinking toward the tail. (b) Pelvic Bones: Not too short, rather strongly developed, and moderately sloping. (c) Thigh Bone: Robust and of good length, set at right angles to the pelvic bones. (d) Hind Legs: Robust and well-muscled, with well-rounded buttocks. (e) Knee Joint: Broad and strong. (f) Calf Bone: In comparison with other breeds, short; it should be perpendicular to the thigh bone, and firmly muscled. (g) The bones at the base of the foot (*tarsus*) should present a flat appearance, with a strongly prominent hock and a broad tendon of Achilles. (h) The central foot bones (*metatarsus*) should be long, movable towards the calf bone, slightly bent toward the front, but perpendicular (as viewed from behind). (i) Hind Paws: Four compactly closed and beautifully arched toes, as in the case of the front paws. The whole foot should be posed equally on the ball and not merely on the toes; nails short.

Tail—Set in continuation of the spine, extending without very pronounced curvature, and should not be carried too gaily.

Note—*Inasmuch as the Dachshund is a hunting dog, scars from honorable wounds shall not be considered a fault.*

SPECIAL CHARACTERISTICS OF THE THREE COAT-VARIETIES

The Dachshund is bred with three varieties of coat: (1) Shorthaired (or Smooth); (2) Wirehaired; (3) Longhaired. All three varieties should conform to the characteristics already specified. The longhaired and shorthaired are old, well-fixed varieties, but into the wirehaired Dachshund, the blood of other breeds has been purposely introduced; nevertheless, in breeding him, the greatest stress must be placed upon conformity to the general Dachshund type. The following specifications are applicable separately to the three coat-varieties, respectively:

SHORTHAIRED (OR SMOOTH) DACHSHUND

(1) Hair: Short, thick, smooth and shining; no bald patches. Special faults are: Too fine or thin hair, leathery ears, bald patches, too coarse or too thick hair in general. Tail: Gradually tapered to a point, well but not too richly haired; long, sleek bristles on the underside are considered a patch of strong-growing hair, not a fault. A brush tail is a fault, as is also a partly or wholly hairless tail.

Color of hair, nose and nails: (a) One-colored Dachshund—This group includes red (often called tan), red-yellow, and yellow, with or without a shading of interspersed black hairs. Nevertheless a clean color is preferable, and red is to be considered more desirable than red-yellow or yellow. Dogs strongly shaded with interspersed black hairs belong to this class, and not to the other color groups. No white is desirable, but a solitary small spot is not exactly disqualifying. Nose and Nails—Black; red is admissible, but not desirable.

(b) Two-Colored Dachshund—These comprise deep black, chocolate, gray, and white; each with rust-brown or yellow marks over the eyes, on the sides of the jaw and underlip, on the inner edge of the ear, front, breast, inside and behind the front leg, on the paws and around the anus, and from there to about one-third to one-half of the length of the tail on the under side. (The most common two-colored Dachshund is usually called black-and-tan.) Except on white dogs, no white is desirable, but a solitary small spot is not exactly disqualifying. Absence, or undue prominence of tan markings is undesirable. Nose and Nails—In the case of black dogs, black; for chocolate, brown or black; for gray, gray or even flesh color, but the last named color is not desirable; in the case of white dogs, black nose and nails are to be preferred.

(c) Dappled and Striped Dachshund—The color of the dappled (or tiger) Dachshund is a clear brownish or grayish color, or even a white ground, with dark irregular patches of dark-gray, brown, red-yellow or black (large areas of one color not desirable). It is desirable that neither the light nor the dark color should predominate. The color of the striped (brindle) Dachshund is red or yellow with a darker streaking. Nose and Nails—As for One- and Two-Colored Dachshund.

WIREHAIRED DACHSHUND

(2) The general appearance is the same as that of the shorthaired, but without being long in the legs, it is permissible for the body to be somewhat higher off the ground.

Hair: With the exception of jaw, eyebrows, and ears, the whole body is covered with a perfectly uniform tight, short, thick, rough, hard coat, but with finer, shorter hairs (undercoat) everywhere distributed between the coarser hairs, resembling the coat of the German Wirehaired Pointer. There should be a beard on the chin. The eyebrows are bushy. On the ears the hair is shorter than on the body; almost smooth, but in any case conforming to the rest of the coat. The general arrangement of the hair should be such that the wirehaired Dachshund, when seen from a distance should resemble the smooth-haired. Any sort of soft hair in the coat is faulty, whether short or long, or wherever found on the body; the same is true of long, curly, or wavy hair, or hair that sticks out irregularly in all directions; a flag tail is also objectionable. Tail: Robust, as thickly haired as possible, gradually coming to a point, and without a tuft. Color of Hair, Nose and Nails: All colors are admissible. White patches on the chest, though allowable, are not desirable.

LONGHAIRED DACHSHUND

(3) The distinctive characteristic differentiating this coat from the shorthaired, or smooth-haired Dachshund is alone the rather long silky hair. Hair: The soft, sleek, glistening, often slightly wavy hair should be longer under the neck, on the underside of the body, and especially on the ears and behind the legs, becoming there a pronounced feather; the hair should attain its greatest length on the underside of the tail. The hair should fall beyond the lower edge of the ear. Short hair on the ear, so-called "leather" ears, is not desirable. Too luxurious a coat causes the longhaired Dachshund to seem coarse, and masks the type. The coat should remind one of the Irish Setter, and should give the dog an elegant appearance. Too thick hair on the paws, so-called "mops," is inelegant, and renders the animal unfit for use. It is faulty for the dog to have equally long hair over all the body, if the coat is too curly, or too scrubby, or if a flag tail or overhanging hair on the ears are lacking; or if there is a very pronounced parting on the back, or a vigorous growth between the toes. Tail: Carried gracefully in prolongation of the spine; the hair attains here its greatest length and forms a veritable flag. Color of Hair, Nose and Nails: Exactly as for the smooth-haired Dachshund.

Note—Miniature Dachshunds are bred in all three coats. They are not undersized or undeveloped specimens of full-size Dachshunds, but have been purposely produced to work in burrows smaller than standard Dachshunds can enter. The limits set upon their size have inevitably resulted in a more slender body structure. Depth of chest and shortness of leg proportionate to the regular conformation would, in these diminutive animals, prove impractical for their active hunting purposes.

The German specifications limit Zwergteckel *(dwarf Dachshund) to a chest circumference of 13.8 inches and limit* Kaninchenteckel *(rabbit Dachshunds) to a chest circumference of 11.8 inches, certified at a minimum age of 12 months. Rather than the ideal, these sizes represent instead the upper limit for miniature re-registration; and thus in pedigrees provide an index to purity of miniature breeding.*

In the United States Miniature Dachshunds have not been given separate classification. At American shows, a division of the open class for "under 9 pounds and 12 months old or over" permits class competition as miniatures, and opportunity in winners classes to compete for championship points in each coat variety. Within the limits imposed, symmetrical adherence to the general Dachshund conformation, combined with smallness, and mental and physical vitality should be outstanding characteristics of the Miniature Dachshund.

GENERAL FAULTS

Serious Faults (which may prevent a dog from receiving any show rating): Overshot or undershot jaws, knuckling over, very loose shoulders.

Secondary Faults (which may prevent a dog from receiving a high show rating): A weak, long-legged, or dragging figure; body hanging between the shoulders; sluggish, clumsy, or waddling gait; toes turned inwards or too obliquely outwards; splayed paws; sunken back, roach (or carp) back; croup higher than withers; short-ribbed or too weak chest; excessively drawn-up flanks like those of a Greyhound; narrow, poorly muscled hindquarters; weak loins; bad angulation in front or hindquarters; cowhocks; bowed legs; "glass" eyes, except for gray or dappled dogs; a bad coat.

Minor Faults (which may prevent a dog from receiving the highest rating in championship competition): Ears wrongly set, sticking out, narrow or folded; too marked a stop; too pointed or weak a jaw; pincer teeth, distemper teeth; too wide or too short a head; goggle eyes, "glass" eyes in the case of gray and dappled dogs, insufficiently dark eyes in the case of all other coat-colors; dewlaps; short neck; swan neck; too fine or too thin hair.

Approved July 9, 1935

Deerhound, Scottish

Head—Should be broadest at the ears, narrowing slightly to the eyes, with the muzzle tapering more decidedly to the nose. The muzzle should be pointed, but the teeth and lips level. The head should be long, the skull flat rather than round with a very slight rise over the eyes but nothing approaching a stop. The hair on the skull should be moderately long and softer than the rest of the coat. The nose should be black (in some blue fawns—blue) and slightly aquiline. In lighter colored dogs the black muzzle is preferable. There should be a good mustache of rather silky hair and a fair beard. *Ears*—Should be set on high; in repose, folded back like a Greyhound's, though raised above the head in excitement without losing the fold, and even in some cases semierect. A prick ear is bad. Big thick ears hanging flat to the head or heavily coated with long hair are bad faults. The ears should be soft, glossy, like a mouse's coat to the touch and the smaller the better. There should be no long coat or long fringe, but there is sometimes a silky, silvery coat on the body of the ear and the tip. On all Deerhounds, irrespective of color of coat, the ears should be black or dark colored.

Neck and Shoulders—The neck should be long—of a length befitting the Greyhound character of the dog. Extreme length is neither necessary nor desirable. Deerhounds do not stoop to their work like the Greyhounds. The mane, which every good specimen should have, sometimes detracts from the apparent length of the neck. The neck, however, must be strong as is necessary to hold a stag. The nape of the neck should be very prominent where the head is set on, and the throat clean cut at the angle and prominent. Shoulders should be well sloped; blades well back and not too much width between them. Loaded and straight shoulders are very bad faults.

Tail—Should be tolerably long, tapering and reaching to within 1½ inches off the ground and about 1½ inches below the hocks. Dropped perfectly down or curved when the Deerhound is still, when in motion or excited, curved, but in no instance lifted out of line of the back. It should be well covered with hair, on the inside, thick and wiry, underside longer and towards the end a slight fringe is not objectionable. A curl or ring tail is undesirable.

Eyes—Should be dark—generally dark brown, brown or hazel. A very light eye is not liked. The eye should be moderately full, with a soft look in repose, but a keen, far-away look when the Deerhound is roused. Rims of eyelids should be black.

Body—General formation is that of a Greyhound of larger size and bone. Chest deep rather than broad but not too narrow or slab-sided. Good girth of chest is indicative of great lung power. The loin well arched and drooping to the tail. A straight back is not desirable, this formation being unsuited for uphill work, and very unsightly. *Legs and Feet*—Legs should be broad and flat, and good broad forearms and elbows are desirable. Forelegs must, of course, be as straight as possible. Feet close and compact, with well-arranged toe. The hindquarters drooping, and as broad and powerful as possible, the hips being set wide apart. A narrow rear denotes lack of power. The stifles should be well bent, with great length from hip to hock, which should be broad and flat. Cowhocks, weak pasterns, straight stifles and splay feet are very bad faults.

Coat—The hair on the body, neck and quarters should be harsh and wiry, about 3 or 4 inches long; that on the head, breast and belly much softer. There should be a slight fringe on the inside of the forelegs and hind legs but nothing approaching the "feather" of a Collie. A woolly coat is bad. Some good strains have a mixture of silky coat with the hard which is preferable to a woolly coat. The climate of the United States tends to produce the mixed coat. The ideal coat is a thick, close-lying ragged coat, harsh or crisp to the touch. *Color* is a matter of fancy, but the dark blue-gray is most preferred. Next come the darker and lighter grays or brindles, the darkest being generally preferred. Yellow and sandy red or red fawn, especially with black ears and muzzles, are equally high in estimation. This was the color of the oldest known strains—the McNeil and Chesthill Menzies. White is condemned by all authorities, but a white chest and white toes, occurring as they do in many of the darkest-colored dogs, are not objected to, although the less the better, for the Deerhound is a self-colored dog. A white blaze on the head, or a white collar, should entirely disqualify. The less white the better but a slight white tip to the stern occurs in some of the best strains.

Height of Dogs—From 30 to 32 inches, or even more if there be symmetry without coarseness, which is rare. *Height of Bitches*—From 28 inches upwards. There is no objection to a bitch being large, unless too coarse, as even at her greatest height she does not approach that of the dog, and therefore could not be too big for work as overbig dogs are. *Weight*—From 85 to 110 pounds in dogs, and from 75 to 95 pounds in bitches.

POINTS OF THE DEERHOUND
ARRANGED IN ORDER OF IMPORTANCE

1. *Typical*—A Deerhound should resemble a rough-coated Greyhound of larger size and bone. 2. *Movements*—Easy, active and true. 3. As tall as possible consistent with quality. 4. *Head*—Long, level, well balanced, carried high. 5. *Body*—Long, very deep in brisket, well-sprung ribs and great breadth across hips. 6. *Forelegs*—Strong and quite straight, with elbows neither in nor out. 7. *Thighs*—Long and muscular, second thighs well muscled, stifles well bent. 8. *Loins*—Well arched, and belly well drawn up. 9. *Coat*—Rough

and hard, with softer beard and brows. 10. *Feet*—Close, compact, with well-knuckled toes. 11. *Ears*—Small (dark) with Greyhoundlike carriage. 12. *Eyes*—Dark, moderately full. 13. *Neck*—Long, well arched, very strong with prominent nape. 14. *Shoulders*—Clean, set sloping. 15. *Chest*—Very deep but not too narrow. 16. *Tail*—Long and curved slightly, carried low. 17. *Teeth*—Strong and level. 18. *Nails*—Strong and curved.

DISQUALIFICATION

White blaze on the head, or a white collar.

Approved March, 1935

Foxhound, American

HEAD. *Skull*—Should be fairly long, slightly domed at occiput, with cranium broad and full. *Ears*—Ears set on moderately low, long, reaching when drawn out nearly, if not quite, to the tip of the nose; fine in texture, fairly broad, with almost entire absence of erectile power—setting close to the head with the forward edge slightly inturning to the cheek—round at tip. *Eyes*—Eyes large, set well apart—soft and houndlike—expression gentle and pleading; of a brown or hazel color. *Muzzle*—Muzzle of fair length—straight and square-cut—the top moderately defined. *Defects*—A very flat skull, narrow across the top; excess of dome; eyes small, sharp and terrier-like, or prominent and protruding; muzzle long and snipy, cut away decidedly below the eyes, or very short. Roman-nosed, or upturned, giving a dish-face expression. Ears short, set on high, or with a tendency to rise above the point of origin.

BODY. *Neck and Throat*—Neck rising free and light from the shoulders, strong in substance yet not loaded, of medium length. The throat clean and free from folds of skin, a slight wrinkle below the angle of the jaw, however, is allowable. *Defects*—A thick, short, cloddy neck carried on a line with the top of the shoulders. Throat showing dewlap and folds of skin to a degree termed "throatiness." *Shoulders, Chest and Ribs*—Shoulders sloping—clean, muscular, not heavy or loaded—conveying the idea of freedom of action with activity and strength. Chest should be deep for lung space, narrower in proportion to depth than the English hound—28 inches (*girth*) in a 23-inch hound being good. Well-sprung ribs—back ribs should extend well back—a three-inch flank allowing springiness. *Back and Loins*—Back moderately long, muscular and strong. Loins broad and slightly arched. *Defects*—Very long or swayed or roached back. Flat, narrow loins.

FORELEGS AND FEET. *Forelegs*—Straight, with fair amount of bone. Pasterns short and straight. *Feet*—Foxlike. Pad full and hard. Well-arched toes. Strong nails. *Defects*—Straight, upright shoulders, chest disproportionately wide or with lack of depth. Flat ribs. Out at elbow. Knees knuckled over forward, or bent backward. Forelegs crooked. Feet long, open or spreading.

Hips, Thighs, Hind Legs and Feet—Hips and thighs, strong and muscled, giving abundance of propelling power. Stifles strong and well let down. Hocks firm, symmetrical and moderately bent. Feet close and firm. *Defects*—Cowhocks, or straight hocks. Lack of muscle and propelling power. Open feet.

Tail—Set moderately high; carried gaily, but not turned forward over the back; with slight curve; with very slight brush. *Defects*—A long tail. Teapot curve or inclined forward from the root. Rat tail, entire absence of brush.

Coat—A close, hard, hound coat of medium length. *Defects*—A short thin coat, or of a soft quality.

Height—Dogs should not be under 22 or over 25 inches. Bitches should not be under 21 or over 24 inches measured across the back at the point of the withers, the hound standing in a natural position with his feet well under him. *Color*—Any color.

SCALE OF POINTS

Head				*Running Gear*		
Skull	5			Forelegs	10	
Ears	5			Hips, thighs and hind		
Eyes	5			legs	10	
Muzzle	5	20		Feet	15	35
Body				*Coat and Tail*		
Neck	5			Coat	5	
Chest and shoulders	15			Tail	5	10
Back, loins and ribs	15	35		Total		100

Foxhound, English

Head—Should be of full size, but by no means heavy. Brow pronounced, but not high or sharp. There should be a good length and breadth, sufficient to give in a dog hound a girth in front of the ears of fully 16 inches. The nose should be long (4½ inches) and wide, with open nostrils. Ears set on low and lying close to the cheeks. Most English hounds are "rounded" which means that about 1½ inches is taken off the end of the ear. The teeth must meet squarely, either a *pig-mouth* (overshot) or undershot being a disqualification.

Neck—Must be long and clean, without the slightest throatiness, not less than 10 inches from cranium to shoulder. It should taper nicely from shoulders to head, and the upper outline should be slightly convex. The *Shoulders* should be long and well clothed with muscle, without being heavy, especially at the points. They must be well sloped, and the true arm between the front and the elbow must be long and muscular, but free from fat or lumber. *Chest and Back Ribs*—The chest should girth over 31 inches in a 24-inch hound, and the back ribs must be very deep.

Back and Loin—Must both be very muscular, running into each other without any contraction between them. The couples must be wide, even to raggedness, and the topline of the back should be absolutely level, the *Stern* well set on and carried gaily but not in any case curved *over* the back like a squirrel's tail. The end should taper to a point and there should be a fringe of hair below. The *Hindquarters* or propellers are required to be very strong, and as endurance is of even greater consequence than speed, straight stifles are preferred to those much bent as in a Greyhound. *Elbows* set quite straight, and neither turned in nor out are a *sine qua non*. They must be well let down by means of the long true arm above mentioned.

Legs and Feet—Every Master of Foxhounds insists on legs as straight as a post, and as strong; size of bone at the ankle being especially regarded as all important. The desire for straightness had a tendency to produce knuckling-over, which at one time was countenanced, but in recent years this defect has been eradicated by careful breeding and intelligent adjudication, and one sees very little of this trouble in the best modern Foxhounds. The bone cannot be too large, and the feet in all cases should be round and catlike, with well-developed knuckles and strong horn, which last is of the greatest importance.

Color and Coat—Not regarded as very important, so long as the former is a good "hound color," and the latter is short, dense, hard, and glossy. Hound colors are black, tan, and white, or any combination of these three, also the various "pies" compounded of white and the color of the hare and badger, or yellow, or tan. The *Symmetry* of the Foxhound is of the greatest importance, and what is known as "quality" is highly regarded by all good judges.

SCALE OF POINTS

Head	5	Elbows	5
Neck	10	Legs and feet	20
Shoulders	10	Color and coat	5
Chest and back ribs	10	Stern	5
Back and loin	15	Symmetry	5
Hindquarters	10	Total	100

DISQUALIFICATION

Pig-mouth (overshot) or undershot.

Greyhound

Head—Long and narrow, fairly wide between the ears, scarcely perceptible stop, little or no development of nasal sinuses, good length of muzzle, which should be powerful without coarseness. Teeth very strong and even in front.

Ears—Small and fine in texture, thrown back and folded, except when excited, when they are semipricked. *Eyes*—Dark, bright, intelligent, indicating spirit.

Neck—Long, muscular, without throatiness, slightly arched, and widening gradually into the shoulder. *Shoulders*—Placed as obliquely as possible, muscular without being loaded. *Forelegs*—Perfectly straight, set well into the shoulder, neither turned in nor out, pasterns strong. *Chest*—Deep, and as wide as consistent with speed, fairly well-sprung ribs.

Back—Muscular and broad. *Loins*—Good depth of muscle, well arched, well cut up in the flanks. *Hindquarters*—Long, very muscular and powerful, wide and well let down, well-bent stifles. Hocks well bent and rather close to ground, wide but straight fore and aft. *Feet*—Hard and close, rather more hare than cat-feet, well knuckled up with good strong claws. *Tail*—Long, fine and tapering with a slight upward curve.

Coat—Short, smooth and firm in texture. *Color*—Immaterial. *Weight*—Dogs, 65 to 70 pounds; bitches, 60 to 65 pounds.

SCALE OF POINTS

General symmetry and quality	10	Back	10
		Quarters	20
Head and neck	20	Legs and feet	20
Chest and shoulders	20	Total	100

Harrier

The points of the modern Harrier are very similar to those of the English Foxhound. The Harrier, however, is smaller than the English Foxhound and the most popular size is 19 to 21 inches. They should be active, well balanced and full of strength and quality, with shoulders sloping into the muscles of the back, clean and not loaded on the withers or point.

The back level and muscular, and not dipping behind the withers or arching over the loin. The elbow's point set well away from the ribs, running parallel with the body and not turning outwards. Deep, well-sprung ribs, running well back, with plenty of heart room, and a deep chest.

Good straight legs with plenty of bone running well down to the toes, but not overburdened, inclined to knuckle over very slightly but not exaggerated in the slightest degree. Round catlike feet, and close toes turning inwards. Hind legs and hocks stand square, with a good sweep and muscular thigh to take the weight off the body.

The head should be of a medium size with good bold forehead, and plenty of expression; head must be well set up on a neck of ample length, and not heavy; stern should be set well up, long and well controlled.

Irish Wolfhound

General Appearance—Of great size and commanding appearance, the Irish Wolfhound is remarkable in combining power and swiftness with keen sight. The largest and tallest of the galloping hounds, in general type he is a rough-coated, Greyhoundlike breed; very muscular, strong though gracefully built; movements easy and active; head and neck carried high, the tail carried with an upward sweep with a slight curve towards the extremity. The minimum height and weight of dogs should be 32 inches and 120 pounds; of bitches, 30 inches and 105 pounds; these to apply only to hounds over 18 months of age. Anything below this should be debarred from competition. Great size, including height at shoulder and proportionate length of body, is the desideratum to be aimed at, and it is desired to firmly establish a race that shall average from 32 to 34 inches in dogs, showing the requisite power, activity, courage and symmetry.

Head—Long, the frontal bones of the forehead very slightly raised and very little indentation between the eyes. Skull, not too broad. Muzzle, long and moderately pointed. Ears, small and Greyhoundlike in carriage. *Neck* —Rather long, very strong and muscular, well arched, without dewlap or loose skin about the throat.

Chest—Very deep. Breast, wide. *Back*—Rather long than short. Loins arched. *Tail*—Long and slightly curved, of moderate thickness, and well covered with hair. *Belly*—Well drawn up.

Forequarters—Shoulders, muscular, giving breadth of chest, set sloping. Elbows well under, neither turned inwards nor outwards. *Leg*—Forearm muscular, and the whole leg strong and quite straight. *Hindquarters*— Muscular thighs and second thigh long and strong as in the Greyhound, and hocks well let down and turning neither in nor out. *Feet*—Moderately large and round, neither turned inwards nor outwards. Toes, well arched and closed. Nails, very strong and curved.

Hair—Rough and hard on body, legs and head; especially wiry and long over eyes and underjaw.

Color and Markings—The recognized colors are gray, brindle, red, black, pure white, fawn, or any other color that appears in the Deerhound.

Faults—Too light or heavy a head, too highly arched frontal bone; large ears and hanging flat to the face; short neck; full dewlap; too narrow or too broad a chest; sunken or hollow or quite straight back; bent forelegs; overbent fetlocks; twisted feet; spreading toes, too curly a tail; weak hindquarters and a general want of muscle too short in body. Lips or nose liver-colored or lacking pigmentation.

LIST OF POINTS IN ORDER OF MERIT

1. *Typical.* The Irish Wolfhound is a rough-coated Greyhoundlike breed, the tallest of the coursing hounds and remarkable in combining power and swiftness. 2. *Great* size and commanding appearance. 3. Movements easy and active. 4. Head, long and level, carried high. 5. Forelegs, heavily boned, quite straight; elbows well set under. 6. Thighs long and muscular; second thighs, well muscled, stifles nicely bent. 7. Coat, rough and hard, specially wiry and long over eyes and under jaw. 8. Body, long, well ribbed up, with ribs well sprung, and great breadth across hips. 9. Loins arched, belly well drawn up. 10. Ears, small, with Greyhoundlike carriage. 11. Feet, moderately large and round; toes, close, well arched. 12. Neck, long, well arched and very strong. 13. Chest, very deep, moderately broad. 14. Shoulders, muscular, set sloping. 15. Tail, long and slightly curved. 16. Eyes, dark.

Note—The above in no way alters the "Standard of Excellence," which must in all cases be rigidly adhered to; they simply give the various points in order of merit. If in any case they appear at variance with Standard of Excellence, it is the latter which is correct.

Approved September 12, 1950

Norwegian Elkhound

General Description—The Norwegian Elkhound is a typical northern dog, of medium size, with a compact, proportionately short body, with a thick and rich, but not bristling, gray coat, with prick ears, and with a tail that is curled and carried over the back. His temperament is bold and energetic.

Head—"Dry" (without any loose skin), broad at the ears; the forehead and back of the head only slightly arched; the stop not large, yet clearly defined. The muzzle is of medium length, thickest at the base and, seen from above or from the side, tapers evenly without being pointed. The bridge of the nose is straight; the lips are tightly closed. *Ears*—Set high, firm and erect, are higher than they are wide at the base, pointed (not rounded) and very mobile. When the dog is listening, the orifices are turned forward. *Eyes*

—Not protruding, brown in color, preferably dark, lively, with a fearless energetic expression. *Neck*—Of medium length, "dry" (without any loose skin), strong, and well set up.

Body—Powerful, *compact*, and short, with broad deep chest, well-sprung ribs, straight back, well-developed loins, and stomach very little drawn up.

Legs—Firm, straight and strong; elbows closely set on; hind legs with little angulation at knees and hocks. Seen from behind, they are straight. *Feet*— Comparatively small, somewhat oblong, with tightly closed toes, not turned out. There should be no dewclaws on hind legs. *Tail*—Set high, short, thickly and closely haired, but without brush; tightly curled, not carried too much to one side.

Coat—Thick, rich and hard, but rather smooth-lying. On head and front of legs, short and even; longest on neck and chest, on buttocks, on hindside of forelegs and on underside of tail. It is made up of longer and harder covering hairs, dark at the tips, and of a light, soft, woolly undercoat. *Color*—Gray, with black tips to the long covering hairs; somewhat lighter on chest, stomach, legs, underside of tail, and around anus. The color may be lighter or darker, with a slight shading towards yellow; but a pronounced variation from the gray color disqualifies. Too dark or too light individuals should be avoided; also, yellow markings or uneven coloring. There should be no pronounced white markings.

Height at Shoulder—Dogs, about 20.5 inches; bitches, about 18 inches.

DISQUALIFICATION

Pronounced variation from gray color.

Approved November 12, 1935

Otter Hound

In general appearance—always excepting the coat—the Otter Hound much resembles the Bloodhound; he should be perfect in symmetry, strongly built, hard and enduring, with unfailing powers of scent, and a natural antipathy to the game he is bred to pursue. The head should be large, broader in proportion than the Bloodhound's, the forehead high, the muzzle a fair length and the nostrils wide. The ears are long, thin and pendulous, fringed with hair. The neck is not naturally long, and looks shorter than it really is from the abundance of hair on it; the shoulders should slope well, the legs be straight and the feet a good size, but compact; the back strong and wide, the ribs, and particularly the back ribs, well let down; the thighs should be big and firm, and the hocks well let down; the stern well and thickly covered with hair and carried well up, but not curled; the colors are generally grizzle or sandy, with black and tan more or less clearly defined.

SCALE OF POINTS

Skull	10	Legs and feet	10
Jaws	10	Coat	10
Eyes	5	Stern	5
Ears	10	Symmetry and strength	10
Chest and shoulders	15	Total	100
Body and loin	15		

Rhodesian Ridgeback

The peculiarity of this breed is the *ridge* on the back, which is formed by the hair growing in the opposite direction to the rest of the coat. The ridge must be regarded as the characteristic feature of the breed. The ridge should be clearly defined, tapering and symmetrical. It should start immediately behind the shoulders and continue to a point between the prominence of the hips, and should contain two identical crowns opposite each other. The lower edges of the crown should not extend further down the ridge than one third of the ridge.

General Appearance—The Ridgeback should represent a strong muscular and active dog, symmetrical in outline, and capable of great endurance with a fair amount of speed.

Head—Should be of a fair length, the skull flat and rather broad between the ears and should be free from wrinkles when in repose. The stop should be reasonably well defined. *Muzzle*—Should be long, deep and powerful, jaws level and strong with well-developed teeth, especially the canines or holders. The lips clean, closely fitting the jaws. *Eyes*—Should be moderately well apart, and should be round, bright and sparkling, with intelligent expression, their color harmonizing with the color of the dog. *Ears*—Should be set rather high, of medium size, rather wide at base, and tapering to a rounded point. They should be carried close to the head. *Nose*—Should be black, or brown, in keeping with the color of the dog. No other colored nose is permissible. A black nose should be accompanied by dark eyes, a brown nose by amber eyes.

Neck and Shoulders—The neck should be fairly strong and free from throatiness. The shoulders should be sloping, clean and muscular, denoting speed.

Body, Back, Chest and Loins—The chest should not be too wide, but very deep and capacious; ribs moderately well sprung, never rounded like barrel hoops (which would indicate want of speed), the back powerful, the loins strong, muscular and slightly arched. *Legs and Feet*—The forelegs should be perfectly straight, strong and heavy in bone; elbows close to the body. The feet should be compact, with well-arched toes, round, tough, elastic pads, protected by hair between the toes and pads. In the hind legs the muscles should be clean, well defined, and hocks well down. *Tail*—Should be strong at the insertion, and generally tapering towards the end, free from coarseness. It should not be inserted too high or too low, and should be carried with a slight curve upwards, never curled.

Coat—Should be short and dense, sleek and glossy in appearance, but neither woolly nor silky. *Color*—Light wheaten to red wheaten. A little white on the chest and toes permissible but excessive white there and any white on the belly or above the toes is undesirable.

Size—A mature Ridgeback should be a handsome, upstanding dog; dogs should be of a height of 25 to 27 inches, and bitches 24 to 26 inches. *Weight*—(Desirable) dogs 75 pounds, bitches 65 pounds.

SCALE OF POINTS

Ridge	20	Coat	5
Head	15	Tail	5
Neck and shoulders	10	Size, symmetry, general	
Body, back, chest, loins	10	appearance	20
Legs and feet	15	Total	100

Approved November, 1955

Saluki

Head—Long and narrow, skull moderately wide between the ears, not domed, stop not pronounced, the whole showing great quality. Nose black or liver. *Ears*—Long and covered with long silky hair hanging close to the skull and mobile. *Eyes*—Dark to hazel and bright; large and oval, but not prominent. *Teeth*—Strong and level. *Neck*—Long, supple and well muscled.

Chest—Deep and moderately narrow. *Forequarters*—Shoulders sloping and set well back, well muscled without being coarse. *Forelegs*—Straight and long from the elbow to the knee. *Hindquarters*—Strong, hipbones set well apart and stifle moderately bent, hocks low to the ground, showing galloping and jumping power. *Loin and Back*—Back fairly broad, muscles slightly arched over loin. *Feet*—Of moderate length, toes long and well arched, not splayed out, but at the same time not cat-footed; the whole being strong and supple and well feathered between the toes. *Tail*—Long, set on low and carried naturally in a curve, well feathered on the underside with long silky hair, not bushy.

Coat—Smooth and of a soft silky texture, slight feather on the legs, feather at the back of the thighs and sometimes with slight woolly feather on the thigh and shoulder. *Colors*—White, cream, fawn, golden, red, grizzle and tan tricolor (white, black and tan) and black and tan.

General Appearance—The whole appearance of this breed should give an impression of grace and symmetry and of great speed and endurance coupled with strength and activity to enable it to kill gazelle or other quarry over deep sand or rocky mountains. The expression should be dignified and gentle with deep, faithful, far-seeing eyes. Dogs should average in height from 23 to 28 inches and bitches may be considerably smaller, this being very typical of the breed.

The Smooth Variety—In this variety the points should be the same with the exception of the coat, which has no feathering.

Whippet

General Appearance—The Whippet should be a dog of moderate size, very alert, that can cover a maximum of distance with a minimum of lost motion, a true sporting hound. Should be put down in hard condition but with no suggestion of being muscle-bound.

Head—Long and lean, fairly wide between the ears, scarcely perceptible stop, good length of muzzle which should be powerful without being coarse. Nose entirely black. *Ears*—Small, fine in texture, thrown back and folded. Semipricked when at attention. Gay ears are incorrect and should be severely penalized. *Eyes*—Large, intelligent, round in shape and dark hazel in color, must be at least as dark as the coat color. Expression should be keen and alert. Light yellow or oblique eyes should be strictly penalized. A sulky expression and lack of alertness to be considered most undesirable. *Teeth*—White, strong and even. Teeth of upper jaw should fit closely over the lower. *An undershot mouth shall disqualify.*

Neck—Long and muscular, well-arched and with no suggestion of throatiness, widening gradually into the shoulders. Must not have any tendency to a "ewe" neck. *Shoulders*—Long, well-laid back with long, flat muscles. Loaded shoulders are a *very* serious fault. *Brisket*—Very deep and strong, reaching as nearly as possible to the point of the elbow. Ribs well sprung but with no suggestion of barrel shape. Should fill in the space between the forelegs so that there is no appearance of a hollow between them.

Forelegs—Straight and rather long, held in line with the shoulders and *not* set under the body so as to make a forechest. Elbows should turn neither in nor out and move freely with the point of the shoulder. Fair amount of bone, which should carry right down to the feet. Pasterns strong. *Feet*—Must be well formed with strong, thick pads and well-knuckled-up paws. A thin, flat, open foot is a serious fault. *Hindquarters*—Long and powerful, stifles well bent, hocks well let down and close to the ground. Thighs broad and muscular, the muscles should be long and flat. A steep croup is most undesirable.

Back—Strong and powerful, rather long with a good, natural arch over the loin creating a definite tuck-up of the underline but covering a lot of ground. *Tail*—Long and tapering, should reach to a hipbone when drawn through between the hind legs. Must not be carried higher than the top of the back when moving.

Coat—Close, smooth and firm in texture. *Color*—Immaterial. *Size*—Ideal height for dogs, 19 to 22 inches; for bitches, 18 to 21 inches. These are not intended to be definite limits, only approximate.

Gait—Low, free moving and smooth, as long as is commensurate with the size of the dog. A short, mincing gait with high knee action should be severely penalized.

DISQUALIFICATION

Undershot mouth.

Approved November 9, 1955

GROUP III: WORKING DOGS

Alaskan Malamute

General Appearance and Characteristics—The Alaskan Malamute is a powerful and substantially built dog with deep chest and strong, compact body, not too short coupled, with a thick, coarse guard coat of sufficient length to protect a dense, woolly undercoat, from 1 to 2 inches in depth when dog is in full coat. Stands well over pads, and this stance gives the appearance of much activity, showing interest and curiosity. The head is broad, ears wedge-shaped and erect when alerted. The muzzle is bulky with only slight diminishing in width and depth from root to nose, not pointed or long, but not stubby. The Malamute moves with a proud carriage, head erect and eyes alert. Face markings are a distinguishing feature. These consist of either cap over head and rest of face solid color, usually grayish white, or face marked with the appearance of a mask. Combinations of cap and mask are not unusual. The tail is plumed and carried over the back, not like a fox brush, or tightly curled, more like a plume waving.

Malamutes are of various colors, but are usually wolfish gray or black and white. Their feet are of the "snowshoe" type, tight and deep, with well-cushioned pads, giving a firm and compact appearance. Front legs are straight with big bone. Hind legs are broad and powerful, moderately bent at stifles, and without cowhocks. The back is straight, gently sloping from shoulders to hips. The loin should not be so short or tight as to interfere with easy, tireless movement. Endurance and intelligence are shown in body and expression. They have a "wolf-like" appearance by their position, but the expression is soft and indicates an affectionate disposition.

Temperament—The Alaskan Malamute is an affectionate, friendly dog, not a "one-man" dog. He is a loyal, devoted companion, playful on invitation, but generally impressive by his dignity after maturity.

Head—The head should indicate a high degree of intelligence, and is broad and powerful as compared with other "natural" breeds, but should be in proportion to the size of the dog so as not to make the dog appear clumsy or coarse. *Skull*—The skull should be broad between the ears, gradually narrowing to eyes, moderately rounded between ears, flattening on top as it approaches the eyes, rounding off to cheeks, which should be moderately flat. There should be a slight furrow between the eyes, the topline of skull and topline of the muzzle showing but little break downward from a straight line as they join. *Muzzle*—The muzzle should be large and bulky in proportion to size of skull, diminishing but little in width and depth from junction with skull to nose; lips close fitting; nose black; upper and lower jaws broad with large teeth, front teeth meeting with a scissors grip but never overshot or undershot.

Eyes—Brown, almond shaped, moderately large for this shape of eye, set obliquely in skull. Dark eyes preferred. *Ears*—The ears should be of medium size, but small in proportion to head. The upper halves of the ears are triangular in shape, slightly rounded at tips, set wide apart on outside back edges of the skull with the lower part of the ear joining the skull on a line with the upper corner of the eye, giving the tips of the ears the appearance, when erect, of standing off from the skull. When erect, the ears point slightly forward, but when the dog is at work the ears are sometimes folded against the skull. High-set ears are a fault.

Neck—The neck should be strong and moderately arched.

Body—The chest should be strong and deep; body should be strong and compactly built but not short coupled. The back should be straight and gently sloping to the hips. The loins should be well muscled and not so short as to interfere with easy, rhythmic movement with powerful drive from the hindquarters. A long loin which weakens the back is also a fault. No excess weight. *Shoulders, Legs and Feet*—Shoulders should be moderately sloping; forelegs heavily boned and muscled, straight to pasterns, which should be short and strong and almost vertical as viewed from the side. The feet should be large and compact, toes tight-fitting and well arched, pads thick and tough, toenails short and strong. There should be a protective growth of hair between toes. Hind legs must be broad and powerfully muscled through thighs; stifles moderately bent, hock joints broad and strong, moderately bent and well let down. As viewed from behind, the hind legs should not appear bowed in bone, but stand and move true in line with movement of the front legs, and not too close or too wide. The legs of the Malamute must indicate unusual strength and tremendous propelling power. Any indication of unsoundness in legs or feet, standing or moving, is to be considered a serious fault. Dewclaws on the hind legs are undesirable and should be removed shortly after pups are whelped.

Tail—Moderately set and following the line of the spine at the start, well furred and carried over the back when not working—not tightly curled to rest on back—or short furred and carried like a fox brush, a waving plume appearance instead.

Coat—The Malamute should have a thick, coarse guard coat, not long and soft. The undercoat is dense, from 1 to 2 inches in depth, oily and woolly. The coarse guard coat stands out, and there is thick fur around the neck. The guard coat varies in length, as does the undercoat; however, in general, the coat is moderately short to medium along the sides of the body with the length of the coat increasing somewhat around the shoulders and neck, down the back and over the rump, as well as in the breeching and plume. Malamutes usually have shorter and less dense coats when shed out during the summer months.

Color and Markings—The usual colors range from light gray through the intermediate shadings to black, always with white on underbodies, parts of legs, feet, and part of mask markings. Markings should be either cap-like and/or mask-like on face. A white blaze on forehead and/or collar or spot on nape is attractive and acceptable, but broken color extending over the body in spots or uneven splashings is undesirable. One should distinguish between mantled dogs and splash-coated dogs. The only solid color allowable is the all-white.

Size—There is a natural range in size in the breed. The desirable freighting sizes are: *Males:* 25 inches at the shoulders—85 pounds. *Females:* 23 inches at the shoulders—75 pounds. However, size consideration should not outweigh that of type, proportion, and functional attributes, such as shoulders, chest, legs, feet, and movement. When dogs are judged equal in type, proportion, and functional attributes, the dog nearest the desirable freighting size is to be preferred.

IMPORTANT.—*In judging Alaskan Malamutes their function as a sledge dog for heavy freighting must be given consideration above all else.* The judge must bear in mind that this breed is designed primarily as the working sledge dog of the North for hauling heavy freight, and therefore he should be a heavy-boned, powerfully built, compact dog with sound legs, good feet, deep chest, powerful shoulders, steady, balanced, tireless gait, and the other physical equipment necessary for the efficient performance of his job. He isn't intended as a racing sled dog designed to compete in speed trials with the smaller Northern breeds. The Malamute as a sledge dog for heavy freighting is designed for strength and endurance and any characteristic of the individual specimen, including temperament, which interferes with the accomplishment of this purpose is to be considered the most serious of faults. Faults under this provision would be splayfootedness, any indication of unsoundness or weakness in legs, cowhocks, bad pasterns, straight shoulders, lack of angulation, stilted gait or any gait which isn't balanced, strong, and steady, ranginess, shallowness, ponderousness, lightness of bone, poor over-all proportion, and similar characteristics.

SCALE OF POINTS

General Appearance 20

Head 15

Body 20

Legs and Movement 20

Feet 10

Coat and Color 10

Tail 5

Total 100

Approved April 12, 1960

Belgian Sheepdog

Personality—The Belgian Sheepdog should reflect the qualities of intelligence, courage, alertness, and devotion to master. To his inherent aptitude as guardian of flocks should be added protectiveness of the person and property of his master. He should be watchful, attentive, and always in motion when not under command. In his relationship with humans he should be observant and vigilant with strangers but not apprehensive. He should not show fear or shyness. He should not show viciousness by unwarranted or unprovoked attack. With those he knows well, he is most affectionate and friendly, zealous of their attention, and very possessive.

General Appearance—The first impression of the Belgian Sheepdog is that of a well-balanced, square dog, elegant in appearance, with an exceedingly proud carriage of the head and neck. He is a strong, agile, well-muscled animal, alert and full of life. His whole conformation gives the impression of depth and solidity without bulkiness. The male dog is usually somewhat more impressive and grand than his female counterpart. The bitch should have a distinctly feminine look.

Size and Substance—Males should be 24–26 inches in height and females 22–24 inches, measured at the withers. The length, measured from point of breast bone to point of rump, should equal the height. Bitches may be slightly longer. Bone structure should be moderately heavy in proportion to his height so that he is well balanced throughout and neither spindly or leggy nor cumbersome and bulky. *Stance*—The Belgian Sheepdog should stand squarely on all fours. Side view: the topline, front legs, and back legs should closely approximate a square. *Expression*—Indicates alertness, attention, readiness for activity. Gaze should be intelligent and questioning.

Coat—The guard hairs of the coat must be long, well-fitting, straight, and abundant. They should not be silky or wiry. The texture should be a medium harshness. The undercoat should be extremely dense, commensurate, however, with climatic conditions. The Belgian Sheepdog is particularly adaptable to extremes of temperature or climate. The hair is shorter on the head, outside of the ears, and lower part of the legs. The opening of the ear is protected by tufts of hair. Ornamentation: especially long and abundant hair, like a collarette, around the neck; fringe of long hair down the back of the forearm; especially long and abundant hair trimming the hindquarters, the breeches; long, heavy, and abundant hair on the tail.

Color—Black. May be completely black or may be black with white, limited as follows: Small to moderate patch or strip on forechest. Between pads of feet. On *tips* of hind toes. On chin and muzzle (frost—may be white or gray). On *tips* of front toes—allowable but a fault.

Head—Cleancut and strong, overall size should be in proportion to the body. *Skull*—Top flattened rather than rounded. The width approximately the same, but not wider, than the length. *Stop*—Moderate. *Muzzle, Jaws, Lips*—Muzzle moderately pointed, avoiding any tendency to snipiness, and approximately equal in length to that of the topskull. The jaws should be strong and powerful. The lips should be tight and black, with no pink showing on the outside. *Ears*—Triangular in shape, stiff, erect, and in proportion to the head in size. Base of the ear should not come below the center of the eye. *Eyes*—Brown, preferably dark brown. Medium size, slightly almond shaped, not protruding. *Nose*—Black, without spots or discolored areas. *Teeth*—A full complement of strong, white teeth, evenly set. Should not be overshot or undershot. Should have either an even bite or a scissors bite.

Torso—Neck—Round and rather outstretched, tapered from head to body, well muscled, with tight skin. *Topline*—The withers are slightly higher and slope into the back which must be level, straight, and firm from withers to hip joints. The loin section, viewed from above, is relatively short, broad and strong, but blending smoothly into the back. The croup is medium long, sloping gradually. *Tail*—Strong at the base, bone to reach hock. At rest the dog holds it low, the tip bent back level with the hock. When in action he raises it and gives it a curl, which is strongest toward the tip, without forming a hook. *Chest*—Not broad, but deep. The lowest point should reach the elbow, forming a smooth ascendant curve to the abdomen. *Abdomen*—Moderate development. Neither tucked-up nor paunchy.

Forequarters—Shoulder—Long and oblique, laid flat against the body, forming a sharp angle (approximately 90°) with the upper arm. *Legs*—Straight, strong, and parallel to each other. Bone oval rather than round. Development (length and substance) should be well proportioned to the size of the dog. Pastern: medium length, strong, and very slightly sloped. *Feet*—Round (cat footed), toes curved close together, well padded. Nails strong and black except that they may be white to match white toe tips.

Hindquarters—Thighs—Broad and heavily muscled. The upper and lower thigh bones approximately parallel the shoulder blade and upper arm respectively, forming a relatively sharp angle at stifle joint. *Legs*—Length and substance well proportioned to the size of the dog. Bone oval rather than round. Legs are parallel to each other. The angle at the hock is relatively sharp, although the Belgian Sheepdog does not have extreme angulation. Metatarsus medium length, strong, and slightly sloped. Dewclaws, if any, should be removed. *Feet*—Slightly elongated. Toes curved close together, well padded. Nails strong and black except that they may be white to match white toe tips.

Gait—Motion should be smooth, free and easy, seemingly never tiring, exhibiting facility of movement rather than a hard driving action. He tends to single-track on a fast gait; the legs, both front and rear, converging toward the center line of gravity of the dog. The backline should remain firm and level, parallel to the line of motion with no crabbing. He shows a marked tendency to move in a circle rather than a straight line.

Faults—Any deviation from these specifications is a fault. In determining whether a fault is minor, serious, or major, these two factors should be used as a guide: 1. The extent to which it deviates from the Standard. 2. The extent to which such deviation would actually affect the working ability of the dog.

DISQUALIFICATIONS

Viciousness. Color—any color other than black, except for white in specified areas. Ears—hanging (as on a hound). Tail—cropped or stump. Males under 22½ or over 27½ inches in height. Females under 20½ or over 25½ inches in height.

Approved June 9, 1959

Belgian Tervuren

Personality—The Belgian Tervuren should reflect the qualities of intelligence, courage, alertness and devotion to master. To his inherent aptitude as guardian of flocks should be added protectiveness of the person and property of his master. He should be watchful, attentive and usually in motion when not under command. In his relationship with humans he should be observant and vigilant with strangers but not apprehensive. He should not show fear or shyness. He should not show viciousness by unwarranted or unprovoked attack. With those he knows well, he is most affectionate and friendly, zealous for their attention and very possessive.

General Appearance—The first impression of Belgian Tervuren is that of a well-balanced square dog, elegant in appearance, with proud carriage of the head and neck. He is a strong, agile, well-muscled animal, alert and full of life. His whole conformation gives the impression of depth and solidity without bulkiness. The male is usually somewhat more impressive and grand than the female. The female should have a distinctly feminine look. Because of frequent comparisons between the Belgian Tervuren and the German Shepherd Dog, it is to be noted that these two breeds differ considerably in size, substance and structure, the difference being especially noticeable in the formation of the topline and the hindquarters.

Size and Substance—Males 24–26 inches in height, and females 22–24 inches, measured at the withers. The length, measured from point of breastbone to point of rump, should equal the height. Bone structure medium in proportion to height so that he is well balanced throughout and neither spindly or leggy nor cumbersome and bulky. *Stance*—The Belgian Tervuren should stand squarely on all fours. Viewed from the side, the topline, ground level, front legs, and back legs should closely approximate a perfect square.

Expression—Intelligent and questioning, indicating alertness, attention and readiness for action.

Coat—The guard hairs of the coat must be long, well-fitting, straight and abundant. They should not be silky or wiry. The texture should be a medium harshness. The undercoat should be very dense commensurate, however, with climatic conditions. The Belgian Tervuren is particularly adaptable to extremes of temperature or climate. The hair is shorter on the head, outside the ears and on the lower part of the legs. The opening of the ear is protected by tufts of hair. Ornamentation: especially long and abundant hair, like a collarette, around the neck; fringe of long hair down the back of the forearm; especially long and abundant hair trimming the hindquarters—the breeches; long, heavy and abundant hair on the tail.

Color—Rich fawn to russet mahogany with black overlay. The coat is characteristically double pigmented, wherein the tip of each fawn hair is blackened. On mature males, this blackening is especially pronounced on the shoulders, back and rib section. The chest color is a mixture of black and gray. The face has a black mask, and the ears are mostly black. The tail typically has a darker or black tip. The underparts of the body, tail and breeches are light beige. A small white patch is permitted on the chest, not to extend to the neck or breast. The tips of the toes may be white. White or gray hair (frost) on chin or muzzle is normal. Although some allowance is to be made for dogs under 18 months of age, when true color is attained, washed-out color or color too black resembling the Belgian Sheepdog is undesirable.

Head—Well chiseled, dry, long without exaggeration. Skull and muzzle, measuring from the stop, should be of equal length. Over-all size should be in proportion to the body. Top of skull flattened rather than rounded, the width approximately the same but not wider than the length. Stop moderate. Muzzle moderately pointed, avoiding any tendency to snipiness. The jaws should be strong and powerful. The lips should be tight and black, with no pink showing on the outside. Ears are equilateral triangles in shape, well cupped, stiff, erect, not too large. Set high, the base of the ear should not come below the center of the eye. Eyes brown, preferably dark brown, medium size, slightly almond shaped, not protruding. Light or yellow eyes are a fault. Nose black, without spots or discolored areas. Nostrils well defined. There should be a full complement of strong white teeth evenly set. Either a scissors or even bite is acceptable. Should not be overshot or undershot. Teeth broken by accident should not be severely penalized, but worn teeth, especially incisors, are often indicative of the lack of proper bite, although some allowance should be made for age. Discolored (distemper) teeth are not to be penalized.

Torso—Neck round, muscular, rather outstretched, slightly arched and tapered from head to body. Skin well fitting with no loose folds. Topline horizontal, straight and firm from withers to hip joints. The loin section, viewed from above, is relatively short, broad and strong, but blending smoothly into the back. The croup is medium long, sloping gradually. Tail strong at the base, the last vertebra to reach the hock. At rest the dog holds it low, the tip bent back level with the hock. When in action he raises it and gives it a curl, which is strongest toward the tip, without forming a hook. Tail should not be carried too high nor turned to one side. Chest not broad but deep, the lowest point should reach the elbow, forming a smooth ascendant curve to the abdomen. Abdomen moderately developed, neither tucked-up nor paunchy.

Forequarters—Legs straight, parallel, perpendicular to the ground. Shoulders long and oblique, laid flat against the body, forming a sharp angle (approximately 90°) with the upper arm. Top of the shoulder blades should be roughly a thumb's width apart. Arms should move in a direction exactly parallel to the axis of the body. Forearms long and well muscled. Bone flat rather than round. Pasterns short and strong, slightly sloped. Feet round (cat-footed), toes curved close together, well padded, strong nails. Nail color can vary from black to transparent. *Hindquarters*—Legs powerful without heaviness, moving in the same pattern as the limbs of the forequarters. Thighs broad and heavily muscled. Stifles clearly defined, with upper shank at right angles to the hip bones. Bone flat rather than round. Hocks moderately bent. Metatarsi short, perpendicular to the ground, parallel to each other when viewed from the rear. Dewclaws, if any, should be removed. Feet slightly elongated, toes curved close together, heavily padded, strong nails. Nail color may vary from black to transparent.

Gait—The gait is lively and graceful, covering the maximum of ground. Always in motion, seemingly never tiring, he shows facility of movement rather than a hard driving action. He tends to single-track at a fast gait, the legs both front and rear converging toward the center line of gravity of the dog. The back line should remain firm and level, parallel to the line of motion with no crabbing. His natural tendency is to move in a circle rather than a straight line.

DISQUALIFICATIONS

Ears—hanging, as on a hound. Tail—cropped or stump. Color—white markings anywhere except as specified. Teeth—pronounced undershot. Size—males under 22½ or over 27½ inches in height; females under 20½ or over 25½ inches in height.

Approved May 12, 1959

Bernese Mountain Dog

General Appearance—A well-balanced dog, active and alert; a combination of sagacity, fidelity and utility. *Height*—Dogs, 23 inches to 27½ inches; bitches, 21 inches to 26 inches at shoulder.

Head—Skull flat, defined stop and strong muzzle. Dewlaps very slightly developed, flews not too pendulous, jaw strong with good, strong teeth. Eyes dark, hazel-brown, full of fire. Ears V-shaped, set on high, not too pointed at tips and rather short. When in repose, hanging close to head; when alert, brought slightly forward and raised at base.

Body—Rather short than too long in back, compact and well ribbed up. Chest broad with good depth of brisket. Loins strong and muscular. *Legs and Feet*—Forelegs perfectly straight and muscular, thighs well developed and stifles well bent. Feet round and compact. Dewclaws should be removed.

Tail—Of fair thickness and well covered with long hair, but not to form a flag; moderate length. When in repose, should be carried low, upward swirl permissible; when alert, may be carried gaily, but may never curl or be carried over back.

Coat—Soft and silky with bright, natural sheen; long and slightly wavy but may never curl. *Color and Markings*—Jet-black with russet-brown or deep tan markings on all four legs, a spot just above forelegs, each side of white chest markings and spots over eyes, which may never be missing. The brown on the forelegs must always be between the black and white. *Preferable, but not a condition, are*—White feet, tip of tail, pure white blaze up foreface, a few white hairs on back of neck, and white star-shaped markings on chest. When the latter markings are missing, it is not a disqualification.

Faults—Too massive in head, light or staring eyes, too heavy or long ears, too narrow or snipy muzzle, undershot or overshot mouth, pendulous dewlaps, too long or Setterlike body, splay or hare feet, tail curled or carried over back, cowhocks and white legs.

SCALE OF POINTS

General appearance	15	Tail	10
Size and height	5	Coat	10
Head	15	Color and markings	15
Body	15	Total	100
Legs and feet	15		

Approved April 13, 1937

Bouvier des Flandres

The Bouvier des Flandres is a rough-coated dog of notably rugged appearance as befitting an erstwhile cattle driver and farmers' helper of Flandres, and later an ambulance dog and messenger in World War I. He is a compact-bodied, powerfully built dog of upstanding carriage and alert, intelligent expression.

Head—The head is medium long, with the skull slightly longer than the muzzle. *Skull*—Almost flat on top, moderately wide between the ears, and sloping slightly toward the muzzle. The brow is noticeably arched over the eyes. The stop is shallow, and the under-eye fill-in good. *Ears*—Rough-coated, set high on the head and cropped to a triangular contour. They stand erect and are carried straight up. *Eyes*—Neither protruding nor sunken, the eyes are set a trifle obliquely in the skull and not too far apart. They are of medium size and very nearly oval. Preferred color, a dark nut-brown. Black eyes, although not considered faulty, are less desirable as contributing to a somber expression. Light-colored eyes, and staring or wild expression are faulty. *Muzzle*—Wide, deep and well filled out, the width narrowing gradually toward the tip of the nose. Cheeks are clean or flat-sided, the jaws powerful, and the lips dry and tight-fitting. A narrow muzzle, suggestive of weakness, is faulty. *Teeth*—Strong and white, with the canines set well apart, the teeth meet in a scissors bite. *Nose*—Black and well developed, the nostrils wide open. Across the top the contour is a trifle rounded as opposed to flat. Brown, pink and spotted noses are faulty.

Neck and Shoulders—The neck is well rounded, slightly arched, and carried almost upright, its thickness gradually increasing as it fits gracefully into the shoulders. Clean and dry at the throat. The shoulders are long and sloping.

Body—The brisket is deep, extending down at least to the point of the elbows, and of moderate width. *Back*—Short, strong and straight. *Loins*— Short, taut, and slightly arched in topline, while the rump is broad and square rather than sloping. Ribs are deep and well sprung. As advantageous for breeding purposes, slightly greater length of loin is permissible in bitches.

Tail—Set high, carried up, and docked to about 4 inches.

Legs and Feet—The leg bones, although only moderate in girth, are made to appear heavy because of their covering with thick, rough hair. *Forelegs*— Straight as viewed from the front or side, with elbows turned neither in nor out. *Hind Legs*—Hindquarters are firm and well muscled, with large, powerful hams. Legs are strong and sturdy, with hocks well let down and wide apart. They are slightly angulated at stifle and hock joints. Viewed from the back, they are absolutely parallel. *Feet*—Round, compact, with toes arched and close. The nails are black, the pads thick and tough.

Coat—Rough, touseled and unkempt in appearance, the coat is capable of withstanding the hardest work in the most inclement weather. *Topcoat*— Harsh, rough and wiry, and so thick that when separated by the hand the skin is hardly visible. *Undercoat*—Fine and soft in texture, and thicker in winter. On the skull the hair is shorter and almost smooth. On the brows it is longer, thus forming eyebrows. Longer growth on muzzle and underjaw from mustache and beard. On the legs it is thick and rough, on the feet rather short. Soft, silky or woolly topcoats are faulty. *Color*—From fawn to black; pepper and salt, gray and brindle. A white star on the chest is allowed. Chocolate brown with white spots is faulty.

Height—Dogs from 23½ to 27½ inches; bitches, a minimum of 22¾ inches.

SCALE OF POINTS

Coat	20	Back, loin, brisket, belly ...	15
Head (eyes, ears, skull, foreface)		Feet and legs	10
....	20	Symmetry, size and character	
Shoulders and style	10	....	15
Hindquarters (hams and		Total	100
legs)	10		

Approved April 14, 1959

Boxer

The Boxer is a medium-sized, sturdy dog, of square build, with short back, strong limbs, and short tight-fitting coat. His musculation, well developed, should be clean, hard and appear smooth (not bulgy) under taut skin. His movements should denote energy. The gait although firm is elastic (springy), the stride free and ground-covering, the carriage proud and noble. Developed to serve the multiple purposes of guard, working, and escort-dog, he must combine elegance with substance and ample power, not alone for beauty but to insure the speed, dexterity, and jumping ability essential to arduous hike, riding expedition, police or military duty. Only a body whose individual parts are built to withstand the most strenuous efforts, assembled as a complete and harmonious whole, can respond to these combined demands. Therefore, to be at his highest efficiency he must never be plump or heavy and, while equipped for great speed, he must never be racy.

The head imparts to the Boxer a unique individual stamp peculiar to him alone. It must be in perfect proportion to his body, never small in comparison to the over-all picture. His muzzle is his most distinctive feature, and the greatest value is to be placed on its being of correct form and in absolute proper proportion to the skull.

In judging the Boxer, the first thing to be considered is general appearance, then balance; the relation of substance to elegance and of the desired proportions of the individual parts of the body to each other. Consideration is to be given to an attractive color, after which the individual parts are to be examined for their correct constructions and their functions. Special attention is to be devoted to the head. *Faults*—Head not typical, plump bull-doggy appearance, light bone, lack of balance, bad condition, deficiency in nobility.

Head—The beauty of the head depends upon the harmonious proportion between the muzzle and the skull. The muzzle should always appear powerful, never small in its relationship to the skull. The head should be clean, not showing deep wrinkles. Folds will normally appear upon the forehead when the ears are erect, and they are always indicated from the lower edge of the stop running downward on both sides of the muzzle. The dark mask is confined to the muzzle and is in distinct contrast to the color of the head. Any extension of the mask to the skull, other than dark shading around the eyes, creates a somber undesirable expression. The muzzle is powerfully developed in length, width and depth. It is not pointed, narrow, short, or shallow. Its shape is influenced first through the formation of both jawbones, second through the placement of the teeth, and third through the texture of the lips.

The two jawbones do not terminate in the usual scissor-bite; instead the lower jaw protrudes moderately beyond the upper and bends *slightly* upward. The Boxer is normally undershot. The upper jaw is broad where attached to the skull and maintains this breadth except for a very slight tapering to the front. The lower jaw incisor teeth are in a straight line. In the upper jaw they are slightly rounded. The middle incisors should not project. This formation creates frontal width in both jaws and results in the canine teeth being widely separated from each other. The upper corner incisors should fit snugly back of the lower canine teeth, the pre-molars, anterior palliative foramen (a technical term pertaining to the placing of teeth), and molars fitting in the most normal possible manner, creating a sound, powerful bite.

The lips complete the formation of the muzzle. The upper lip is thick and padded, filling out the frontal space formed by the projection of the lower jaw and it is supported by the jaw's fangs. Therefore, these fangs must stand far apart and be of good length so that the front surface of the muzzle shall become broad and squarish and, when viewed from the side, form a rounded angle with the topline of the muzzle. The lower edge of the upper lip rests on the edge of the lower lip. The repandous (bent upward) part of the under-jaw with the lower lip (sometimes called the chin) must not rise above the front of the upper lip, but much less may it disappear under it. It must be perceptible when viewed from the front as well as the side, without protruding and bending upward in the manner of the English Bulldog. The Boxer must not show his teeth or his tongue when his mouth is closed. Excessive flews are not desirable.

The top of the skull is slightly arched, not rotund, or flat, or noticeably broad, and the occiput must not be too pronounced. The forehead forms a distinct stop with the topline of the muzzle, which must not be forced back into the forehead like that of a Bulldog. It should not slant up, or down (down-faced), or be dished. The tip of the nose lies somewhat higher than the root of the muzzle. The forehead shows a suggestion of furrow which, however, must never be too deep, especially between the eyes. Corresponding with the powerful set of teeth, the cheeks are accordingly well developed, without protruding from the head with too bulgy an appearance, preferably they should taper into the muzzle in a slight, graceful curve. The ears are cut rather long, well trimmed, and carried erect. The dark brown eyes, not too small, not protruding or deep-set, disclose an alert and intelligent expression and must never appear gloomy, threatening, or piercing; they should be encircled by dark hair. The nose is broad and black, very slightly turned up; the nostrils are broad with the nasolabial line running between them.

Faults—Lack of nobility and expression, somber face, unserviceable bite. Pinscher or Bulldog head, badly trimmed ears, visible conjunctiva (haw), driveling, showing teeth or tongue, light so-called "Bird of Prey" eyes. Sloping top line of muzzle, too pointed or too light a bite (snipy).

Neck—Round, of ample length, not too short; strong and muscular and clean throughout, without dewlap, with a distinctly marked nape and an elegant arch running down to the back. *Faults*—Dewlap.

Body—Body is square. Measured in profile, a horizontal line from the front of the forechest to the rear projection of the upper thigh should equal a vertical line dropped from the top of the withers to the ground.

Chest and Front Leg Measurements—The brisket is deep, reaching down to the elbows; the depth of the body at the lowest point of the brisket amounts to half the height of the dog at the withers. The ribs, extending far to the rear, are well arched but not barrel-shaped. The loins are short and muscular; the lower stomach line, lightly tucked up, blending into a graceful curve to the rear. The shoulders are long and sloping, close lying, and not excessively covered with muscle. The upper arm is long, closely approaching a right angle to the shoulder blade. The forelegs, when seen from the front, must be straight, stand parallel to each other, and have strong, firmly joined bones. Chest of fair width, and forechest well defined. The elbows must not press too closely to the chest wall or stand off visibly from it. The forearm is straight, long, and firmly muscled. The pastern (knee) joint of the foreleg is clearly defined but not distended. The pastern is short, slightly slanting, but standing almost perpendicular to the ground. Feet compact, turning neither in nor out, with tightly arched toes and hard soles (cat's paws).

Faults—Too broad and low in front, loose shoulders, chest hanging between the shoulders, hare's feet, hollow flanks, hanging stomach, turned feet, tied-in elbows.

Back—The withers should be clearly defined, the whole back short, straight, and very muscular. *Faults*—Roach back, sway back, thin lean back, long narrow loins, weak union with croup.

Hindquarters—In balance with forequarters; strongly muscled. The thighs broad and curved, the breech musculation strongly developed. The croup very slightly sloped, broad. Tail attachment high, rather than low. Tail clipped, carried upward. The pelvis should be long and especially broad in females. Upper and lower thigh long, leg well angulated. In standing position, the leg below the hock joint should be practically perpendicular to the ground (a slight slope is permissible). Viewed from behind the hind legs are straight. The hocks (metatarsus) clean, strong, and short, supported by powerful rear pads with hock joint clean-cut and clearly defined. The rear toes just a little longer than the front toes, but similar in all other respects.

Faults—Falling off or too rounded or narrow croup, low-set tail, higher in back than in front; steep, stiff, or too slightly angulated hindquarters, light thighs, cowhocks, bowlegs and crooked legs, rear dewclaws, soft hocks, narrow heel, tottering, waddling gait, hare feet, hindquarters too far under or too far behind.

Height—Males—22 inches to 24 inches at the withers. Females—21 inches to 23 inches at the withers. Males should not go under 22 inches and females should not go over 23 inches.

Coat—Short, shiny, lying smooth and tight to the body.

Color—The colors are fawn and brindle. Fawn in various shades from light yellow to dark deer red. The brindle variety should have clearly defined black stripes on fawn background. White markings in fawn and brindle dogs are not to be rejected; in fact, they are often very attractive in appearance. The black mask is absolutely required. When white occurs on the muzzle it should be edged by remnants of the black mask. Black toenails are preferred but not essential. Even distribution of head markings is desirable.

Character—The character of the Boxer is of the greatest importance and demands the most solicitous attention. He should be alert and fearless; willing to make friends, but not necessarily effusive. *Faults*—Shyness—A dog should be considered shy if he shrinks away from a friendly approach or displays timidity when approached from the rear, or displays cowardice over sudden and unusual noises. *Viciousness*—A dog should be considered vicious that attempts to attack either his handler or the judge. Belligerency toward other dogs should not be considered viciousness.

DISQUALIFICATIONS

Boxers with white or black ground color, or entirely white or black or any color other than fawn or brindle. (White markings are allowed but must not exceed one-third (⅓) of the ground color.)

Approved May 10, 1960

Briard

General Appearance—A strong and substantially built dog, fitted for field work, lithe, muscular, and well proportioned, alert and active. *Size*—Height at shoulders: Dogs, 23 to 27 inches; bitches, 22 to 25½ inches. Young dogs may be below the minimum.

Head—Large and rather long. Stop well marked and placed at equal distance from top of head and tip of nose. Forehead very slightly rounded. Line from stop to tip of nose straight. Teeth strong, white, and meeting exactly even. Muzzle neither narrow nor pointed. Nose rather square than rounded, always black. Hair heavy and long on top of head, the ears, and around the muzzle forming eyebrows standing out and not veiling the eyes too much. Eyes horizontal, well opened, dark in color and rather large; intelligent and gentle in expression. *Ears*—Placed high, alert, may be cropped or left natural. If cropped the ears are carried erect; if uncut they should not be too large or carried too flat. There shall be no preference shown to either cropped or uncropped ears.

Conformation—Neck muscular and distinct from the shoulders. Chest broad and deep. Back straight. Rump slightly sloped. Legs muscular with heavy bones. Hock not too near the ground, making a well-marked angle, the leg below the hock being not quite vertical. *Tail*—Uncut, well feathered, forming a crook at the end, carried low and twisted neither to right nor left. The length of the tail should equal the distance from the root of the tail to the point of the hock. *Feet*—Strong, round, with toes close together and hard pads; nails black.

Coat—Long, slightly wavy, stiff and strong. *Color*—All solid colors are allowed except white. Dark colors are preferable. Usual colors: black, and black with some white hairs, dark and light gray, tawny, and combinations of two of these colors, provided there are no marked spots and the transition from one to the other takes place gradually and symmetrically.

Dewclaws—Two dewclaws on each hind leg are required. A dog with only one cannot be given a prize.

Faults—Muzzle pointed. Eyes small, almond-shaped or light in color. Rump straight or too sloped. White spot on the breast (a large white spot is very bad). Tail too short or carried over the back. White nails.

DISQUALIFICATIONS

Size below the limit. Absence of dewclaws. Short hair on the head, face or feet. Tail lacking or cut. Nose light in color or spotted. Eyes spotted. Hair curled. White hair on feet. Spotted colors of the coat.

Approved March 12, 1963

Bullmastiff

General Appearance—That of a symmetrical animal, showing great strength; powerfully built but active. The dog is fearless yet docile, has endurance and alertness. The foundation breeding was 60% Mastiff and 40% Bulldog.

Head—Skull large, with a fair amount of wrinkle when alert; broad, with cheeks well developed. Forehead flat. Muzzle broad and deep; its length, in comparison with that of the entire head, approximately as 1 is to 3. Lack of foreface with nostrils set on top of muzzle is a reversion to the Bulldog and is very undesirable. Nose black with nostrils large and broad. Flews not too pendulous, stop moderate, and the mouth (bite) preferably level or slightly undershot. Canine teeth large and set wide apart. A dark muzzle is preferable. *Eyes*—Dark and of medium size. *Ears*—V-shaped and carried close to the cheeks, set on wide and high, level with occiput and cheeks, giving a square appearance to the skull; darker in color than the body and medium in size. *Neck*—Slightly arched, of moderate length, very muscular, and almost equal in circumference to the skull.

Body—Compact. Chest wide and deep, with ribs well sprung and well set down between the forelegs. *Forequarters*—Shoulders muscular but not loaded, and slightly sloping. Forelegs straight, well boned and set well apart; elbows square. Pasterns straight, feet of medium size, with round toes well arched. Pads thick and tough, nails black. *Back*—Short, giving the impression of a well balanced dog. *Loins*—Wide, muscular and slightly arched, with fair depth of flank. *Hindquarters*—Broad and muscular with well developed second thigh denoting power, but not cumbersome. Moderate angulation at hocks. Cowhocks and splay feet are bad faults. *Tail*—Set on high, strong at the root and tapering to the hocks. It may be straight or curved, but never carried hound fashion.

Coat—Short and dense, giving good weather protection. *Color*—Red, fawn or brindle. Except for a very small white spot on the chest, white marking is considered a fault.

Size—Dogs, 25 to 27 inches at the shoulder, and 110 to 130 pounds weight. Bitches, 24 to 26 inches at the shoulder, and 100 to 120 pounds weight. Other things being equal, the heavier dog is favored.

Approved February 6, 1960

Collie

ROUGH

General Character—The Collie is a lithe, strong, responsive, active dog, carrying no useless timber, standing naturally straight and firm. The deep, moderately wide chest shows strength, the sloping shoulders and well-bent hocks indicate speed and grace, and the face shows high intelligence. The Collie presents an impressive, proud picture of true balance, each part being in harmonious proportion to every other part and to the whole. Except for the technical description that is essential to this Standard and without which no Standard for the guidance of breeders and judges is adequate, it could be stated simply that no part of the Collie ever seems to be out of proportion to any other part. Timidity, frailness, sullenness, viciousness, lack of animation, cumbersome appearance and lack of over-all balance impair the general character.

Head—The head properties are of great importance. When considered in proportion to the size of the dog the head is inclined to lightness and never appears massive. A heavy-headed dog lacks the necessary bright, alert, full-of-sense look that contributes so greatly to expression. Both in front and profile view the head bears a general resemblance to a well-blunted lean wedge, being smooth and clean in outline and nicely balanced in proportion. On the sides it tapers gradually and smoothly from the ears to the end of the black nose, without being flared out in backskull ("cheeky") or pinched in muzzle ("snipy"). In profile view the top of the backskull and the top of the muzzle lie in two approximately parallel, straight planes of equal length, divided by a very slight but perceptible stop or break. A mid-point between the inside corners of the eyes (which is the center of a correctly placed stop) is the center of balance in length of head.

The end of the smooth, well-rounded muzzle is blunt but not square. The underjaw is strong, clean-cut and the depth of skull from the brow to the under part of the jaw is not excessive. The teeth are of good size, meeting in a scissors bite. *Overshot or undershot jaws are undesirable, the latter being more severely penalized.* There is a very slight prominence of the eyebrows. The backskull is flat, without receding either laterally or backward and the occipital bone is not highly peaked. The proper width of backskull necessarily depends upon the combined length of skull and muzzle and the width of the backskull is less than its length. Thus the correct width varies with the individual and is dependent upon the extent to which it is supported by length of muzzle. Because of the importance of the head characteristics, *prominent head faults are very severely penalized.*

Eyes—Because of the combination of the flat skull, the arched eyebrows, the slight stop and the rounded muzzle, the foreface must be chiseled to form a receptacle for the eyes and they are necessarily placed obliquely to give them the required forward outlook. Except for the blue merles, they are required to be matched in color. They are almond-shaped, of medium size and never properly appear to be large or prominent. The color is dark and the eye does not show a yellow ring or a sufficiently prominent haw to affect the dog's expression. The eyes have a clear, bright appearance, expressing intelligent inquisitiveness, particularly when the ears are drawn up and the dog is on the alert. In blue merles, dark brown eyes are preferable, but either or both eyes may be merle or china in color without specific penalty. A large, round, full eye seriously detracts from the desired "sweet" expression. *Eye faults are heavily penalized. Ears*—The ears are in proportion to the size of the head and, if they are carried properly and unquestionably "break" naturally, are seldom too small. Large ears usually cannot be lifted correctly off the head, and even if lifted, they will be out of proportion to the size of the head. When in repose the ears are folded lengthwise and thrown back into the frill. On the alert they are drawn well up on the backskull and are carried about three-quarters erect, with about one-fourth of the ear tipping or "breaking" forward. *A dog with prick ears or low ears cannot show true expression and is penalized accordingly.*

Neck—The neck is firm, clean, muscular, sinewy and heavily frilled. It is fairly long, carried upright with a slight arch at the nape and imparts a proud, upstanding appearance showing off the frill.

Body—The body is firm, hard and muscular, a trifle long in proportion to the height. The ribs are well-rounded behind the well-sloped shoulders and the chest is deep, extending to the elbows. The back is strong and level, supported by powerful hips and thighs and the croup is sloped to give a well-rounded finish. The loin is powerful and slightly arched. *Noticeably fat dogs, or dogs in poor flesh, or with skin disease, or with no undercoat are out of condition and are moderately penalized accordingly.*

Legs—The forelegs are straight and muscular, with a fair amount of bone considering the size of the dog. A cumbersome appearance is undesirable. *Both narrow and wide placement are penalized.* The forearm is moderately fleshy and the pasterns are flexible but without weakness. The hind legs are less fleshy, muscular at the thighs, very sinewy and the hocks and stifles are well bent. *A cowhocked dog or a dog with straight stifles is penalized.* The comparatively small feet are approximately oval in shape. The soles are well padded and tough, and the toes are well arched and close together. When the Collie is not in motion the legs and feet are judged by allowing the dog to come to a natural stop in a standing position so that both the forelegs and the hind legs are placed well apart, with the feet extending straight forward. Excessive "posing" is undesirable.

Gait—The gait or movement is distinctly characteristic of the breed. A sound Collie is not out at the elbows but it does, nevertheless, move toward an observer with its front feet tracking comparatively close together at the ground. The front legs do not "cross over," nor does the Collie move with a pacing or rolling gait. Viewed from the front, one gains the impression that the dog is capable of changing its direction of travel almost instantaneously, as indeed it is. When viewed from the rear, the hind legs, from the hock joint to the ground, move in comparatively close-together, parallel, vertical planes. The hind legs are powerful and propelling. Viewed from the side, the gait is smooth not choppy. The reasonably long, "reaching" stride is even, easy, light and seemingly effortless.

Tail—The tail is moderately long, the bone reaching to the hock joint or below. It is carried low when the dog is quiet, the end having an upward twist or "swirl." When gaited or when the dog is excited it is carried gaily but not over the back.

Coat—The well-fitting, proper-textured coat is the crowning glory of the rough variety of Collie. It is abundant except on the head and legs. The outer coat is straight and harsh to the touch. *A soft, open outer coat or a curly outer coat, regardless of quantity, is penalized.* The undercoat, however, is soft, furry and so close together that it is difficult to see the skin when the hair is parted. The coat is very abundant on the mane and frill. The face or mask is smooth. The forelegs are smooth and well feathered to the back of the pasterns. The hind legs are smooth below the hock joints. Any feathering below the hocks is removed for the show ring. The hair on the tail is very profuse and on the hips it is long and bushy. The texture, quantity and the extent to which the coat "fits the dog" are important points.

Color—The four recognized colors are sable and white, tri-color, blue merle and white. There is no preference among them. The sable and white is predominantly sable (a fawn sable color of varying shades from light gold to dark mahogany) with white markings usually on the chest, neck, legs, feet and the tip of the tail. A blaze may appear on the foreface or backskull or both. The tri-color is predominantly black, carrying white markings as in a sable and white and has tan shadings on and about the head and legs. The blue merle is a mottled or "marbled" color, predominantly blue-gray and black with white markings as in the sable and white and usually has tan shadings as in the tri-color. The white is predominantly white, preferably with sable or tri-color markings. Blue merle coloring is undesirable in whites.

Size—Dogs are from 24 to 26 inches at the shoulder and weigh from 60 to 75 pounds. Bitches are from 22 to 24 inches at the shoulder, weighing from 50 to 65 pounds. *An undersize or an oversize Collie is penalized according to the extent to which the dog appears to be undersize or oversize.*

Expression—Expression is one of the most important points in considering the relative value of Collies. *Expression*, like the term "character" is difficult to define in words. It is not a fixed point as in color, weight or height and it is something the uninitiated can properly understand only by optical illustration. In general, however, it may be said to be the combined product of the shape and balance of the skull and muzzle, the placement, size, shape and color of the eye and the position, size and carriage of the ears. An expression that shows sullenness or which is suggestive of any other breed is entirely foreign. The Collie cannot be judged properly until its expression has been carefully evaluated.

SMOOTH

The Smooth Variety of Collie is judged by the same Standard as the Rough Variety, except that the references to the quantity and the distribution of the coat are not applicable to the Smooth Variety, which has a hard, dense, smooth coat.

Approved March 10, 1959

Doberman Pinscher

General Conformation and Appearance—The *Appearance* is that of a dog of good middle size, with a body that is square, the height, measured vertically from the ground to the highest point of the withers, equaling the length, measured horizontally, from the forechest to the rear projection of the upper thigh. Height, at the withers, males 26 to 28 inches, ideal being about 27 inches; bitches, 24 to 26 inches, ideal being about 25½ inches. Compactly built, muscular and powerful, for great endurance and speed. Elegant in appearance, of proud carriage, reflecting great nobility and temperament. Energetic, watchful, determined, alert, fearless, loyal, and obedient. *Faults* —Coarseness. Fine Greyhound build. Undersized or oversized. *Disqualifying Faults*—Shyness, viciousness. *Shyness*—A dog shall be judged fundamentally shy if, refusing to stand for examination, it shrinks away from the judge; if it fears an approach from the rear; if it shies at sudden and unusual noises to a marked degree. *Viciousness*—A dog that attacks, or attempts to attack, either the judge or its handler is definitely vicious. An aggressive or belligerent attitude towards other dogs shall not be deemed viciousness.

HEAD (shape, eyes, teeth, ears). *Shape*—Long and dry, resembling a blunt wedge, both frontal and profile views. When seen from the front, the head widens gradually toward the base of the ears in a practically unbroken line.

Top of skull flat, turning with slight stop to bridge of muzzle, with muzzle line extending parallel to the top line of the skull. Cheeks flat and muscular. Lips lying close to jaws, and not drooping. Jaws full and powerful, well filled under the eyes. Nose, solid black in black dogs, dark brown in brown ones, and dark gray in blue ones. *Faults*—Head out of balance in proportion to body. Ram's, dishfaced, cheeky, or snipy heads. *Eyes*—Almond-shaped, *not* round, moderately deep set, *not* prominent, with vigorous, energetic expression. Iris of uniform color, ranging from medium to darkest brown in black dogs, the darker shade being the more desirable. In reds or blues, the color of the iris should blend with that of the markings, but not be of a lighter hue than that of the markings. *Faults*—Slit eyes. Glassy eyes. *Teeth*—Strongly developed and white. Lower incisors upright and touching inside of upper incisors—a true scissors bite. Forty-two teeth (22 in lower jaw, 20 in upper jaw). Distemper teeth should not be penalized. *Disqualifying Faults*—Overshot more than 3/16 of an inch. Undershot more than 1/8 of an inch. *Ears*—Well trimmed and carried erect. (In all states where ear trimming is prohibited, or where dogs with cropped ears cannot be shown, the foregoing requirements are waived.) The upper attachment of the ear, when held erect, should be on a level with the top of the skull.

Neck—Carried upright, well muscled and dry. Well arched, and with nape of neck widening gradually toward body. Length of neck proportioned to body and head.

BODY. *Back* short, firm, of sufficient width, and muscular at the loin extending in a straight line from withers to the slightly rounded croup. *Withers* pronounced and forming the highest point of body. *Brisket* full and broad, reaching deep to the elbow. *Chest* broad, and *forechest* well defined. *Spring of ribs* pronounced. *Belly* well tucked up, extending in a curved line from chest. *Loins* wide and muscled. *Hips* broad in proportion to body, breadth of hips being approximately breadth of body at rib spring. *Tail*, docked at approximately second joint, should appear to be the continuation of the spine, without material drop.

FOREQUARTERS. *Shoulder blade and upper arm* should meet at an angle of 90 degrees. Relative length of shoulder and upper arm should be as one to one, excess length of upper arm being much less undesirable than excess length of shoulder blade. *Legs*, seen from the front and side, perfectly straight and parallel to each other from elbow to pastern; muscled and sinewy, with round, heavy bone. In a normal position, and when gaiting, the elbow should lie close to the brisket. *Pasterns* firm, with an almost perpendicular position to the ground. *Feet* well arched, compact, and catlike, turning neither in nor out. HINDQUARTERS. In balance with forequarters. *Upper shanks* long, wide and well muscled on both sides of thigh, with clearly defined stifle. *Hocks* while the dog is at rest: hock to heel should be perpendicular to the ground. *Upper shanks, lower shanks, and hocks* parallel to each other, and wide enough apart to fit in with a properly built body. The *hipbone* should fall away from the spinal column at an angle of about 30 degrees. The *upper shank* should be at right angles to the hip bone. Croup well filled out. *Cat-feet*, as on front legs, turning neither in nor out.

Gait—The *gait* should be free, balanced, and vigorous, with good reach in the forequarters and good driving power in the hindquarters. When trotting, there should be a strong rear action drive, with rotary motion of hindquarters. Each rear leg should move in line with the foreleg on the same side. Rear and front legs should be thrown neither in nor out. Back should remain strong, firm and level.

COAT, COLOR, MARKINGS. *Coat*, smooth-haired, short, hard, thick, and close-lying. Invisible gray undercoat on neck permissible. Allowed *colors*, black, brown, or blue. *Markings*, rust red, sharply defined, and appearing above each eye, and on muzzle, throat, and forechest, and on all legs and feet, and below tail. White on chest, not exceeding one-half square inch, permissible.

The foregoing description is that of the ideal Doberman Pinscher. Any deviation from the above-described dog must be penalized in proportion to the extent of the deviation, and in accordance with the appended scale of points.

SCALE OF POINTS

General Conformation and Appearance

Proportions	8	
Bone—Substance	8	
Temperament—Expression—Nobility	8	
Condition	5	29

Head

Shape	6	
Teeth	5	
Eyes	3	
Ears	1	15

Neck | 3 | 3

Body

Backline—Withers—Loins—Tail Placement	8
Chest—Brisket—Rib Spring—Tuck-up	8

Shape and proportions

	4	20

Forequarters

Shoulders—Upper arms—Legs—Pasterns	5	
Angulation	4	
Paws	2	11

Hindquarters

Upper thigh—Stifle—Hocks	5	
Angulation	4	
Paws	2	11

Gait | 6 | 6

Coat—Color—Markings

	5	5
Total	100	100

DISQUALIFICATIONS

Shyness, viciousness. Overshot more than 3/16 of an inch; undershot more than ⅛ of an inch.

Approved February 9, 1948

German Shepherd Dog

General Appearance—The first impression of a good German Shepherd Dog is that of a strong, agile, well-muscled animal, alert and full of life. It should both be and appear to be well balanced, with harmonious development of the forequarter and hindquarter. The dog should appeal to the eye, and actually be, longer than tall; deep-bodied, and presenting an outline of smooth curves rather than corners. It should look substantial and not spindly, giving the impression, both at rest and in motion, of muscular fitness and nimbleness without any look of clumsiness or soft living.

The ideal height for dogs is 25 inches, and for bitches, 23 inches at the shoulder. This height is established by taking a perpendicular line from the top of the shoulder blade to the ground with the coat parted or so pushed down that this measurement will show only the actual height of the frame or structure of the dog. The working value of dogs above or below the indicated heights is proportionately lessened, although variations of an inch above or below the ideal height are acceptable, while greater variations must be considered as faults. Weights of dogs of desirable size in proper flesh and condition average between 75 and 85 pounds, and of bitches, between 60 and 70 pounds.

The Shepherd should be stamped with a look of quality and nobility—difficult to define but unmistakable when present. The good Shepherd Dog never looks common. The breed has a distinct personality marked by a direct and fearless, but not hostile, expression; self-confidence and a certain aloofness which does not lend itself to immediate and indiscriminate friendships. Secondary sex characteristics should be strongly marked, and every animal should give a definite impression of masculinity or femininity, according to its sex. Dogs should be definitely masculine in appearance and deportment; bitches, unmistakably feminine, without weakness of structure or apparent softness of temperament. The condition of the dog should be that of an athlete in good condition, the muscles and flesh firm and the coat lustrous.

The Shepherd is normally a dog with a double coat, the amount of undercoat varying with the season of the year and the proportion of the time the dog spends out of doors. It should, however, always be present to a sufficient degree to keep out water, to insulate against temperature extremes, and as a protection against insects. The outer coat should be as dense as possible, hair straight, harsh and lying close to the body. A slightly wavy outer coat, often of wiry texture, is equally permissible. The head, including the inner ear, foreface and legs and paws are covered with short hair, and the neck with longer and thicker hair. The rear of forelegs and hind legs has somewhat longer hair extending to the pastern and hock respectively. Faults in coat include complete lack of any undercoat, soft, silky or too long outer coat and curly or open coat.

Structure—A German Shepherd is a trotting dog and his structure has been developed to best meet the requirements of his work in herding. That is to say, a long, effortless trot which shall cover the maximum amount of ground with the minimum number of steps, consistent with the size of the animal. The proper body proportion, firmness of back and muscles and the proper angulation of the forequarters and hindquarters serve this end. They enable the dog to propel itself forward by a long step of the hindquarter and to compensate for this stride by a long step of the forequarter. The high withers, the firm back, the strong loin, the properly formed croup, even the tail as balance and rudder, all contribute to this same end.

Proportion—The German Shepherd Dog is properly longer than tall with the most desirable proportion as 10 is to 8½. We have seen how the height is ascertained; the length is established by a dog standing naturally and four-square, measured on a horizontal line from the point of the prosternum, or breastbone, to the rear edge of the pelvis, the ischium tuberosity, commonly called the sitting bone.

Angulation—(*a*) Forequarter: The shoulder blade should be long, laid on flat against the body with its rounded upper end in a vertical line above the elbow, and sloping well forward to the point where it joins the upper arm. The withers should be high, with shoulder blades meeting closely at the top, and the upper arm set on at an angle approaching as nearly as possible a right angle. Such an angulation permits the maximum forward extension of the foreleg without binding or effort. Shoulder faults include too steep or straight a position of either blade or upper arm, too short a blade or upper arm, lack of sufficient angle between these two members, looseness through lack of firm ligamentation, and loaded shoulders with prominent pads of flesh or muscles on the outer side. Construction in which the whole shoulder assembly is pushed too far forward also restricts the stride and is faulty.

(*b*) Hindquarters: The angulation of the hindquarter also consists ideally of a series of sharp angles as far as the relation of the bones to each other is concerned, and the thigh bone should parallel the shoulder blade while the stifle bone parallels the upper arm. The whole assembly of the thigh, viewed from the side, should be broad, with both thigh and stifle well muscled and of proportionate length, forming as nearly as possible a right angle. The metatarsus (the unit between the hock joint and the foot commonly and erroneously called the hock) is strong, clean and short, the hock joint clean-cut and sharply defined.

Head—Clean-cut and strong, the head of the Shepherd is characterized by nobility. It should seem in proportion to the body and should not be clumsy, although a degree of coarseness of head, especially in dogs, is less of a fault than overrefinement. A round or domey skull is a fault. The muzzle is long and strong with the lips firmly fitted, and its top line is usually parallel with an imaginary elongation of the line of the forehead. Seen from the front, the forehead is only moderately arched and the skull slopes into the long wedge-shaped muzzle without abrupt stop. Jaws are strongly developed. Weak and too narrow underjaws, snipy muzzles and no stop are faults.

(*a*) Ears: The ears should be moderately pointed, open toward the front, and are carried erect when at attention, the ideal carriage being one in which the center lines of the ears, viewed from the front, are parallel to each other and perpendicular to the ground. Puppies usually do not permanently raise their ears until the fourth or sixth month, and sometimes not until later. Cropped and hanging ears are to be discarded. The well-placed and well-carried ear of a size in proportion to the skull materially adds to the general appearance of the Shepherd. Neither too large nor too small ears are desirable. Too much stress, however, should not be laid on perfection of carriage if the ears are fully erect.

(*b*) Eyes: Of medium size, almond-shaped, set a little obliquely and not protruding. The color as dark as possible. Eyes of lighter color are sometimes found and are not a serious fault if they harmonize with the general coloration, but a dark brown eye is always to be preferred. The expression should be keen, intelligent and composed.

(*c*) Teeth: The strong teeth, 42 in number—20 upper and 22 lower— are strongly developed and meet in a scissor grip in which part of the inner surface of the upper teeth meets and engages part of the outer surface of the lower teeth. This type of bite gives a more powerful grip than one in which the edges of the teeth meet directly, and is subject to less wear. The dog is overshot when the lower teeth fail to engage the inner surfaces of the upper teeth. This is a serious fault. The reverse condition—an undershot jaw—is a very serious fault. While missing premolars are frequently observed, complete dentition is decidedly to be preferred. So-called distemper teeth and discolored teeth are faults whose seriousness varies with the degree of departure from the desired white, sound coloring. Teeth broken by accident should not be severely penalized but worn teeth, especially the incisors, are often indicative of the lack of a proper scissor bite, although some allowance should be made for age.

Neck—The neck is strong and muscular, clean-cut and relatively long, proportionate in size to the head and without loose folds of skin. When the dog is at attention or excited, the head is raised and the neck carried high, otherwise typical carriage of the head is forward rather than up and but little higher than the top of the shoulder, particularly in motion.

Topline—(*a*) Withers: The withers should be higher than, and sloping into, the level back to enable a proper attachment of the shoulder blades.

(b) Back: The back should be straight and very strongly developed without sag or roach, the section from the wither to the croup being relatively short. (The desirable long proportion of the Shepherd Dog is not derived from a long back but from over-all length with relation to height, which is achieved by breadth of forequarter and hindquarter viewed from the side.)

(c) Loin: Viewed from the top, broad and strong, blending smoothly into the back without undue length between the last rib and the thigh, when viewed from the side.

(d) Croup: Should be long and gradually sloping. Too level or flat a croup prevents proper functioning of the hindquarter, which must be able to reach well under the body. A steep croup also limits the action of the hindquarter.

(e) Tail: Bushy, with the last vertebra extended at least to the hock joint, and usually below. Set smoothly into the croup and low rather than high, at rest the tail hangs in a slight curve like a sabre. A slight hook— sometimes carried to one side—is faulty only to the extent that it mars general appearance. When the dog is excited or in motion, the curve is accentuated and the tail raised, but it should never be lifted beyond a line at right angles with the line of the back. Docked tails, or those which have been operated upon to prevent curling, disqualify. Tails too short, or with clumpy ends due to the ankylosis or growing together of the vertebrae, are serious faults.

Body—The whole structure of the body gives an impression of depth and solidity without bulkiness.

(a) Forechest: Commencing at the prosternum, should be well-filled and carried well down between the legs with no sense of hollowness.

(b) Chest: Deep and capacious with ample room for lungs and heart. Well carried forward, with the prosternum, or process of the breastbone, showing ahead of the shoulder when the dog is viewed from the side.

(c) Ribs: Should be well sprung and long, neither barrel-shaped nor too flat, and carried down to a breastbone which reaches to the elbow. Correct ribbing allows the elbow to move back freely when the dog is at a trot, while too round a rib causes interference and throws the elbow out. Ribbing should be carried well back so that loin and flank are relatively short.

(d) Abdomen: Firmly held and not paunchy. The bottom line of the Shepherd is only moderately tucked up in flank, never like that of a Greyhound.

Legs—(a) The bone of the legs should be straight, oval rather than round or flat and free from sponginess. Its development should be in proportion to the size of the dog and contribute to the over-all impression of substance without grossness. Crooked leg bones and any malformation such as, for example, that caused by rickets, should be penalized.

(b) Pastern: Should be of medium length, strong and springy. Much more spring of pastern is desirable in the Shepherd Dog than in many other breeds, as it contributes to the ease and elasticity of the trotting gait. The upright terrier pastern is definitely undesirable.

(c) Metatarsus (the so-called "hock"): Short, clean, sharply defined and of great strength. This is the fulcrum upon which much of the forward movement of the dog depends. Cowhocks are a decided fault, but before penalizing for cowhocks, it should be definitely determined, with the animal in motion, that the dog has this fault, since many dogs with exceptionally good hindquarter angulation occasionally stand so as to give the appearance of cowhockedness which is not actually present.

(d) Feet: Rather short, compact, with toes well-arched, pads thick and hard, nails short and strong. The feet are important to the working qualities of the dog. The ideal foot is extremely strong with good gripping power and plenty of depth of pad. The so-called cat-foot, or terrier foot, is not desirable. The thin, spread or hare-foot is, however, still more undesirable.

Pigment—The German Shepherd Dog differs widely in color and all colors are permissible. Generally speaking, strong, rich colors are to be preferred, with definite pigmentation and without the appearance of a washed-out color. White dogs are not desirable and are to be disqualified if showing albino characteristics.

Gait—(a) General impression: The gait of the German Shepherd Dog is outreaching, elastic, seemingly without effort, smooth and rhythmic. At a walk it covers a great deal of ground, with long step of both hind leg and foreleg. At a trot, the dog covers still more ground and moves powerfully but easily with a beautiful co-ordination of back and limbs so that, in the best examples, the gait appears to be the steady motion of a well-lubricated machine. The feet travel close to the ground, and neither fore nor hind feet should lift high on either forward reach or backward push.

(b) The hindquarter delivers, through the back, a powerful forward thrust which slightly lifts the whole animal and drives the body forward. Reaching far under, and passing the imprint left by the front foot, the strong arched hind foot takes hold of the ground; then hock, stifle and upper thigh come into play and sweep back, the stroke of the hind leg finishing with the foot still close to the ground in a smooth follow-through. The over-reach of the hindquarter usually necessitates one hind foot passing outside and the other hind foot passing inside the track of the forefeet and such action is not faulty unless the locomotion is crabwise with the dog's body sideways out of the normal straight line.

(c) In order to achieve ideal movement of this kind, there must be full muscular co-ordination throughout the structure with the action of muscles and ligaments positive, regular and accurate.

(d) Back transmission: The typical smooth, flowing gait of the Shepherd Dog cannot be maintained without great strength and firmness (which does not mean stiffness) of back. The whole effort of the hindquarter is transmitted to the forequarter through the muscular and bony structure of the loin, back and withers. At full trot, the back must remain firm and level without sway, roll, whip or roach.

(e) To compensate for the forward motion imparted by the hindquarter, the shoulder should open to its full extent—the desirability of good shoulder angulation now becomes apparent—and the forelegs should reach out in a stride balancing that of the hindquarter. A steep shoulder will cause the dog either to stumble or to raise the forelegs very high in an effort to co-ordinate with the hindquarter, which is impossible when shoulder structure is faulty. A serious gait fault results when a dog moves too low in front, presenting an unlevel top line with the wither lower than the hips.

(f) The Shepherd Dog does not track on widely separated parallel lines as does the terrier, but brings the feet inward toward the middle line of the body when at trot in order to maintain balance. For this reason a dog viewed from the front or rear when in motion will often seem to travel close. This is not a fault if the feet do not strike or cross, or if the knees or shoulders are not thrown out, but the feet and hocks should be parallel even if close together.

(g) The excellence of gait must also be evaluated by viewing from the side the effortless, properly co-ordinated covering of ground.

Character—As has been noted before, the Shepherd Dog is not one that fawns upon every new acquaintance. At the same time, it should be approachable, quietly standing its ground and showing confidence and a willingness to meet overtures without itself making them. It should be poised, but when the occasion demands, eager and alert; both fit and willing to serve in any capacity as companion, watch dog, blind leader, herding dog or guardian, whichever the circumstances may demand. The Shepherd Dog must not be timid, shrinking behind its master or handler; nervous, looking about or upward with anxious expression or showing nervous reactions to strange sounds or sights, nor lackadaisical, sluggish or manifestly disinterested in what goes on about him. Lack of confidence under any surroundings is not typical of good character; cases of extreme timidity and nervous unbalance sometimes give the dog an apparent, but totally unreal, courage and it becomes a "fear biter," snapping not for any justifiable reason but because it is apprehensive of the approach of a stranger. This is a serious fault subject to heavy penalty.

In summary: It should never be forgotten that the ideal Shepherd is a working animal, which must have an incorruptible character combined with body and gait suitable for the arduous work which constitutes its primary purpose. All its qualities should be weighed in respect to their contribution to such work, and while no compromise should be permitted with regard to its working potentiality, the dog must nevertheless possess a high degree of beauty and nobility.

Evaluation of Faults—Note: Faults are important in the order of their group, as per group headings, irrespective of their position in each group. *Disqualifying Faults*—Albino characteristics; cropped ears; hanging ears (as in a hound); docked tails. *Very Serious Faults*—Major faults of temperament; undershot lower jaw. *Serious Faults*—Faults of balance and proportion; poor gait, viewed either from front, rear or side; marked deficiency of substance (bone or body); bitchy male dogs; faulty backs; too level or too short croup; long and weak loin; very bad feet; ring tails; tails much too short; rickety condition; more than four missing premolars or any other missing teeth, unless due to accident; lack of nobility; badly washed-out color; badly overshot bite. *Faults*—Doggy bitches; poorly carried ears; too fine heads; weak muzzles; improper muscular condition; faulty coat, other than temporary condition; badly affected teeth. *Minor Faults*—Too coarse heads; hooked tails; too light, round or protruding eyes; discolored teeth; condition of coat, due to season or keeping.

DISQUALIFICATIONS

White if indicative of albino characteristics. Cropped ears, hanging ears. Docked tail.

Approved December 9, 1958

Giant Schnauzer

General Impression—The Giant Schnauzer is a robust, sinewy, more heavy-set than slender dog, of somewhat rectangular build. His nature combines high-spirited temperament with extreme reliability.

Head—Strong and elongated, gradually narrowing from the ears to the eyes and thence toward the tip of the nose, in proportion to the size of the body. Its total length (tip of nose to occiput) should compare approximately to one-third the length of the back (withers—first dorsal vertebra—to the beginning of the tail). Upper part of the head (occiput to the base of the forehead) broad between the ears—its width should not be more than two-thirds of the length—with flat, creaseless forehead and well-muscled but not too strongly developed cheeks. Ears, small and V-shaped, of moderate thickness, set well on the head and dropping forward closely to the cheek, or cropped, with ears evenly cut, placed high and carried erect in excitement. Eyes medium-sized, dark, oval, turned forward, brows arched and wiry. The powerful, ferreting snout formed by the upper and lower jaw (base of forehead to the tip of nose) should be in proportion to the upper head and should end in a moderately blunt manner, with heavy stubby whiskers. Ridge of the nose straight and running almost parallel to the extension of the forehead. The tip of the nose is black and full. Lips tight and not overlapping, with strongly developed fangs, healthy and pure white.

Neck—Not too short, with skin close-fitting at the throat. Nape strong and slightly arched.

Forequarters—Shoulders slanting and flat, but strongly muscled. Forelegs (upper and under arm) seen from all sides are vertical without any curve.

Chest—Moderately broad with visible, strong breastbone and reaching at least to the height of the elbow and slowly extending backwards. Back strong and straight with well-developed short thighs. The length of back equal to shoulder height (from withers vertical to floor) built squarely, belly well drawn up towards the back. *Tail*—Carried high and cut down to three joints.

Hindquarters—Thighs slanting and flat, but strongly muscled. Hind legs (upper and lower thighs) at first vertical to the knee, from knee to hock in line with the extension of the upper neckline, from hock vertical to ground.

Paws—Short, round, extremely compact paws, with close, arched toes (cat's paws) dark nails and hard soles.

Hair—Close, strong, hard and wiry, on the back seen against the grain— unruly—that is, neither short nor smooth; shorter on ears, forehead, legs and paws.

Height—From 21½ to 25½ inches shoulder height. *Color*—All pepper-and-salt colored or similar equal mixtures, pure black or black with tan.

Faults—Too plump or too light; low or high-legged build; too heavy around head; creased forehead; sticking-out or badly carried ears; light eye (with yellow or light-gray rings); strongly protruding cheekbones; flabby throat skin; undershot or overshot jaw. Teeth too pointed, too small or too long; sunken or roached back; chest with barrel ribs (tubby); slanting crupper; elbows turned out; heels turned in; hind part overbuilt; too steep; spread-open toes; long and flat (hare) paws; too short, sleek, too long, soft, silky, curled, rolled, shaggy hair; all white, spotty, tigered, red and reddish colors. Small white breast spot or marking on the breast is not a fault.

Great Dane

STANDARD OF POINTS

1. General Conformation
   - (*a*) General appearance 10
   - (*b*) Color and markings 8
   - (*c*) Size 5
   - (*d*) Condition of coat 4
   - (*e*) Substance 3   30
2. Movement
   - (*a*) Gait 10
   - (*b*) Rear end (croup, legs, paws) 10
   - (*c*) Front end (shoulders, legs, paws) 8   28
3. Head
   - (*a*) Head conformation 12
   - (*b*) Teeth 4
   - (*c*) Eyes (nose and ears) 4   20
4. Torso
   - (*a*) Neck 6
   - (*b*) Loin and back 6
   - (*c*) Chest 4
   - (*d*) Ribs and brisket 4   20
5. Tail   2

   Total 100

1. General Conformation .... 30 points

(*a*) *General Appearance* (10 points)—The Great Dane combines in its distinguished appearance dignity, strength and elegance with great size and a powerful, well-formed, smoothly muscled body. He is one of the giant breeds, but is unique in that his general conformation must be so well-balanced that he never appears clumsy and is always a unit—the Apollo of dogs. He must be spirited and courageous—never timid. He is friendly and dependable. This physical and mental combination is the characteristic which gives the Great Dane the majesty possessed by no other breed. It is particularly true of this breed that there is an impression of great masculinity in dogs as compared to an impression of femininity in bitches. The male should appear more massive throughout than the bitch, with larger frame and heavier bone. In the ratio between length and height, the Great Dane should appear as square as possible. In bitches, a somewhat longer body is permissible. Faults: Lack of unity; timidity; bitchy dogs; poor musculature; poor bone development; out of condition; rickets; doggy bitches.

(b) *Color and Markings* (8 points)—(i) Color: Brindle Danes. Base color ranging from light golden yellow to deep golden yellow always brindled with strong black cross stripes. The more intensive the base color and the more intensive the brindling, the more attractive will be the color. Small white marks at the chest and toes are not desirable. Faults: Brindle with too dark a base color; silver-blue and grayish-blue base color; dull (faded) brindling; white tail tip.

(ii) Fawn Danes. Golden yellow up to deep golden yellow color with a deep black mask. The golden deep-yellow color must always be given the preference. Small white spots at the chest and toes are not desirable. Faults: Yellowish-gray, bluish-yellow, grayish-blue, dirty yellow color (drab color), lack of black mask.

(iii) Blue Danes. The color must be a pure steel blue as far as possible without any tinge of yellow, black or mouse gray. Faults: Any deviation from a pure steel-blue coloration.

(iv) Black Danes. Glossy black. Faults: Yellow-black, brown-black or blue-black. White markings, such as stripes on the chest, speckled chest and markings on the paws are permitted but not desirable.

(v) Harlequin Danes. Base color: pure white with black torn patches irregularly and well-distributed over the entire body; pure white neck preferred. The black patches should never be large enough to give the appearance of a blanket nor so small as to give a stippled or dappled effect. (Eligible but less desirable are a few small gray spots, also pointings where instead of a pure white base with black spots there is a white base with single black hairs showing through which tend to give a salt and pepper or dirty effect.) Faults: White base color with a few large spots; bluish-gray pointed background.

(c) *Size* (5 points)—The male should not be less than 30 inches at the shoulders, but it is preferable that he be 32 inches or more, providing he is well proportioned to his height. The female should not be less than 28 inches at the shoulders, but it is preferable that she be 30 inches or more, providing she is well proportioned to her height.

(d) *Condition of Coat* (4 points)—The coat should be very short and thick, smooth and glossy. Faults: Excessively long hair (stand-off coat); dull hair (indicating malnutrition, worms and negligent care).

(e) *Substance* (3 points)—Substance is that sufficiency of bone and muscle which rounds out a balance with the frame. Faults: Lightweight whippety Danes; coarse, ungainly proportioned Danes; always there should be balance.

2. Movement .... 28 points

(a) *Gait* (10 points)—Long, easy, springy stride with no tossing or rolling of body. The back line should move smoothly, parallel to the ground. The gait of the Great Dane should denote strength and power. The rear legs should have drive. The forelegs should track smoothly and straight. The Dane should track in two parallel straight lines. Faults: Short steps. The rear quarters should not pitch. The forelegs should not have a hackney gait (forced or choppy stride). When moving rapidly the Great Dane should not pace for the reason that it causes excessive side-to-side rolling of the body and thus reduces endurance.

(b) *Rear End (Croup, Legs, Paws)* (10 points)—The croup must be full, slightly drooping and must continue imperceptibly to the tail root. Hind legs, the first thighs (from hip joint to knee) are broad and muscular. The second thighs (from knee to hock joint) are strong and long. Seen from the side, the angulation of the first thigh with the body, of the second thigh with the first thigh, and the pastern root with the second thigh should be very moderate, neither too straight nor too exaggerated. Seen from the rear, the hock joints appear to be perfectly straight, turned neither towards the inside nor towards the outside. Faults: A croup which is too straight; a croup which slopes downward too steeply; and too narrow a croup. Hind legs: Soft, flabby, poorly muscled thighs; cowhocks which are the result of the hock joint turning inward and the hock and rear paws turning outward; barrel legs, the result of the hock joints being too far apart; steep rear. As seen from the side, a steep rear is the result of the angles of the rear legs forming almost a straight line; overangulation is the result of exaggerated angles between the first and second thighs and the hocks and is very conducive to weakness. The rear legs should never be too long in proportion to the front legs.

Paws, round and turned neither towards the inside nor towards the outside. Toes short, highly arched and well closed. Nails short, strong and as dark a possible. Faults: Spreading toes (splay foot); bent, long toes (rabbit paws); toes turned towards the outside or towards the inside. Furthermore, the fifth toe on the hind legs appearing at a higher position and with wolf's claw or spur; excessively long nails; light-colored nails.

(c) *Front End (Shoulders, Legs, Paws)* (8 points)—*Shoulders:* The shoulder blades must be strong and sloping and seen from the side, must form as nearly as possible a right angle in its articulation with the humerus (upper arm) to give a long stride. A line from the upper tip of the shoulder to the back of the elbow joint should be as nearly perpendicular as possible. Since all dogs lack a clavicle (collar bone) the ligaments and muscles holding the shoulder blade to the rib cage must be well developed, firm and secure to prevent loose shoulders. Faults: Steep shoulders, which occur if the shoulder blade does not slope sufficiently; overangulation; loose shoulder which occur if the Dane is flabbily muscled, or if the elbow is turned toward the outside; loaded shoulders.

Forelegs: The upper arm should be strong and muscular. Seen from the side or front the strong lower arms run absolutely straight to the pastern joints. Seen from the front, the forelegs and the pastern roots should form perpendicular lines to the ground. Seen from the side, the pastern root should slope only very slightly forward. *Faults:* Elbows turned toward the inside or toward the outside, the former position caused mostly by too narrow or too shallow a chest, bringing the front legs too closely together and at the same time turning the entire lower part of the leg outward; the latter position causes the front legs to spread too far apart, with the pastern roots and paws usually turned inwards. Seen from the side, a considerable bend in the pastern toward the front indicates weakness and is in most cases connected with stretched and spread toes (splay foot); seen from the side a forward bow in the forearm (chair leg); an excessively knotty bulge in the front of the pastern joint. *Paws:* Round and turned neither toward the inside nor toward the outside. Toes short, highly arched and well closed. Nails short, strong and as dark as possible. *Faults:* Spreading toes (splay foot), bent, long toes (rabbit paws); toes turned toward the outside or toward the inside; light-colored nails.

3. Head . . . . 20 points

(*a*) *Head Conformation* (12 points)—Long, narrow, distinguished, expressive, finely chiseled, especially the part below the eyes (which means that the skull plane under and to the inner point of the eye must slope without any bony protuberance in a pleasing line to the full square jaw), with strongly pronounced stop. The masculinity of the male is very pronounced in the expression and structure of head (this subtle difference should be evident in the dog's head through massive skull and depth of muzzle); the bitch's head may be more delicately formed. Seen from the side, the forehead must be sharply set off from the bridge of the nose. The forehead and the bridge of the nose must be straight and parallel to one another. Seen from the front, the head should appear narrow, the bridge of the nose should be as broad as possible. The cheek muscles must show slightly but under no circumstances should they be too pronounced (cheeky). The muzzle part must have full flews and must be as blunt vertically as possible in front; the angles of the lip must be quite pronounced. The front part of the head, from the tip of the nose up to the center of the stop should be as long as the rear part of the head from the center of the stop to the only slightly developed occiput. The head should be angular from all sides and should have definite flat planes and its dimensions should be absolutely in proportion to the general appearance of the Dane. *Faults:* Any deviation from the parallel planes of skull and foreface; too small a stop; a poorly defined stop or none at all; too narrow a nose bridge; the rear of the head spreading laterally in a wedgelike manner (wedge head); an excessively round upper head (apple head); excessively pronounced cheek musculature; pointed muzzle; loose lips hanging over the lower jaw (fluttering lips) which create an illusion of a full deep muzzle. The head should be rather shorter and distinguished than long and expressionless.

(*b*) *Teeth* (4 points)—Strong, well developed and clean. The incisors of the lower jaw must touch very lightly the bottoms of the inner surface of the upper incisors (scissors bite). If the front teeth of both jaws bite on top of each other, they wear down too rapidly. Faults: Even bite; undershot and overshot; incisors out of line; black or brown teeth; missing teeth.

(*c*) *Eyes* (4 points)—Medium size, as dark as possible, with lively intelligent expression; almond-shaped eyelids, well-developed eyebrows. Faults: Light-colored, piercing, amber-colored, light blue to a watery blue, red or bleary eyes; eyes of different colors; eyes too far apart; Mongolian eyes; eyes with pronounced haws; eyes with excessively drooping lower eyelids. In blue and black Danes, lighter eyes are permitted but are not desirable. In harlequins, the eyes should be dark. Light colored eyes, two eyes of different color and walleyes are permitted but not desirable.

Nose (0 points)—The nose must be large and in the case of brindled and "single-colored" Danes, it must always be black. In harlequins, the nose should be black; a black spotted nose is permitted; a pink-colored nose is not desirable.

Ears (0 points)—Ears should be high, set not too far apart, medium in size, of moderate thickness, drooping forward close to the cheek. Top line of folded ear should be about level with the skull. Faults: hanging on the side, as on a Foxhound. Cropped ears; high set: not set too far apart, well pointed but always in proportion to the shape of the head and carried uniformly erect.

4. Torso .... 20 points

(*a*) *Neck* (6 points)—The neck should be firm and clean, high-set, well arched, long, muscular and sinewy. From the chest to the head, it should be slightly tapering, beautifully formed, with well-developed nape. Faults: Short, heavy neck, pendulous throat folds (dewlaps).

(*b*) *Loin and Back* (6 points)—The withers forms the highest part of the back which slopes downward slightly toward the loins which are imperceptibly arched and strong. The back should be short and tensely set. The belly should be well shaped and tightly muscled, and, with the rear part of the thorax, should swing in a pleasing curve (tuck-up). Faults: Receding back; sway back; camel or roach back; a back line which is too high at the rear; an excessively long back; poor tuck-up.

(*c*) *Chest* (4 points)—Chest deals with that part of the thorax (rib cage) in front of the shoulders and front legs. The chest should be quite broad, deep and well muscled. Faults: A narrow and poorly muscled chest; strong protruding sternum (pigeon breast).

(*d*) *Ribs and Brisket* (4 points)—Deals with that part of the thorax back of the shoulders and front legs. Should be broad, with the ribs sprung well out from the spine and flattened at the side to allow proper movement of the shoulders extending down to the elbow joint. Faults: narrow (slab-sided) rib cage; round (barrel) rib cage; shallow rib cage not reaching the elbow joint.

5. Tail .... 2 points

Should start high and fairly broad, terminating slender and thin at the hock joint. At rest, the tail should fall straight. When excited or running, slightly curved (saberlike). Faults: A too high, or too low set tail (the tail set is governed by the slope of the croup); too long or too short a tail; tail bent too far over the back (ring tail); a tail which is curled; a twisted tail (sideways); a tail carried too high over the back (gay tail); a brush tail (hair too long on lower side). Cropping tails to desired length is forbidden.

FAULTS

Disqualification Faults: Deaf Danes. Danes under minimum height. White Danes without any black marks (albinos). Merles, a solid mouse-gray color or a mouse-gray base with black or white or both color spots or white base with mouse-gray spots. Harlequins and solid-colored Danes in which a large spot extends coatlike over the entire body so that only the legs, neck and the point of the tail are white. Brindle, fawn, blue and black Danes with white forehead line, white collars, high white stockings and white bellies. Danes with predominantly blue, gray, yellow or also brindled spots. Docked tails. Split noses.

The faults below are important according to their grouping (very serious, serious, minor) and not according to their sequence as placed in each grouping:

Very serious: Lack of unity. Poor bone development. Poor musculature. Lightweight whippety Danes. Rickets. Timidity. Bitchy dog. Sway-back. Roach back. Cowhocks. Pitching gait. Short steps. Undershot teeth.

Serious: Out of condition. Coarseness. Any deviation from the standard on all coloration. Deviation from parallel planes of skull and foreface. Wedgehead. Poorly defined stop. Narrow nose bridge. Snipy muzzle. Any color but dark eyes in fawns and brindles. Mongolian eyes. Missing teeth. Overshot teeth. Heavy neck. Short neck. Dewlaps. Narrow chest. Narrow rib cage. Round rib cage. Shallow rib cage. Loose shoulders. Steep shoulders. Elbows turned inward. Chair legs (front). Knotty bulge in pastern joint (adult dog). Weak pastern roots. Receding back. Too long a back. Back high in rear. In harlequins, a pink nose. Poor tuck-up (except in bitches that have been bred). Too straight croup. Too sloping croup. Too narrow croup. Overangulation. Steep rear. Too long rear legs. Poorly muscled thighs. Barrel legs. Paws turned outward. Rabbit paws. Wolf's claw. Hackney gait.

Minor: Doggy bitches. Small white marks on chest and toes—blues, blacks, brindles and fawns. Few gray spots and pointings on Harlequins. In Harlequins, black-spotted nose. White-tipped tail except on Harlequins. Excessively long hair. Excessively dull hair. Apple head. Small stop. Fluttering lips. Eyes too far apart. Drooping lower eyelids. Haws. Any color but dark eyes in blacks, blues and harlequins. Discolored teeth. Even bite. Pigeon breast. Loaded shoulders. Elbows turned outward. Paws turned inward. Splay foot. Excessively long toenails. Light nails (except in harlequins). Low-set tail. Too long a tail. Too short a tail. Gay tail. Curled tail. Twisted tail. Brush tail.

DISQUALIFICATIONS

Danes under minimum height. White Danes without any black marks (albinos). Merles, a solid mouse-gray color or a mouse-gray base with black or white or both color spots or white base with mouse-gray spots. Harlequins and solid-colored Danes in which a large spot extends coatlike over the entire body so that only the legs, neck and the point of the tail are white. Brindle, fawn, blue and black Danes with white forehead line, white collars, high white stockings and white bellies. Danes with predominantly blue, gray, yellow or also brindled spots. Docked tails. Split noses.

Approved November 14, 1944

Great Pyrenees

General Appearance—A dog of immense size, great majesty, keen intelligence, and kindly expression; of unsurpassed beauty and a certain elegance, all white or principally white with markings of badger, gray, or varying shades of tan. In the rolling, ambling gait it shows unmistakably the purpose for which it has been bred, the strenuous work of guarding the flocks in all kinds of weather on the steep mountain slopes of the Pyrenees. Hence soundness is of the greatest importance and absolutely necessary for the proper fulfillment of his centuries' old task.

Size—The average height at the shoulder is 27 inches to 32 inches for dogs, and 25 inches to 29 inches for bitches. The average length from shoulder blades to root of tail should be the same as the height in any given specimen. The average girth is 36 inches to 42 inches for dogs and 32 inches to 36 inches for bitches. The weight for dogs runs 100 to 125 pounds and 90 to 115 pounds for bitches. A dog heavily boned; with close cupped feet; double dewclaws behind and single dewclaws in front.

Head—Large and wedge-shaped, measuring 10 inches to 11 inches from dome to point of nose, with rounding crown, furrow only slightly developed and with no apparent stop. *Cheeks*—Flat. *Ears*—V-shaped, but rounded at the tips, of medium size, set parallel with the eyes, carried low and close to the head except when raised at attention. *Eyes*—Of medium size set slightly obliquely, dark rich brown in color with close eyelids, well pigmented. *Lips*—Close-fitting, edged with black. *Dewlaps*—Developed but little. The head is in brief that of a brown bear, but with the ears falling down. *Neck*—Short, stout and strongly muscular.

Body—Well-placed shoulders set obliquely, close to the body. *Back and Loin* —Well coupled, straight and broad. *Haunches*—Fairly prominent. *Rump*—Sloping slightly. *Ribs*—Flat-sided. *Chest*—Deep. *Tail*—Of sufficient length to hang below the hocks, well plumed, carried low in repose, and curled high over the back, "making the wheel" when alert.

Coat—Created to withstand severe weather, with heavy fine white undercoat and long flat thick outer coat of coarser hair, straight or slightly undulating.

Qualities—In addition to his original age-old position in the scheme of pastoral life as protector of the shepherd and his flock, the Great Pyrenees has been used for centuries as a guard and watchdog on the large estates of his native France, and for this he has proven ideal. He is as serious in play as he is in work, adapting and molding himself to the moods, desires and even the very life of his human companions, through fair weather and foul, through leisure hours and hours fraught with danger, responsibility and extreme exertion; he is the exemplification of gentleness and docility with those he knows, of faithfulness and devotion for his master even to the point of self-sacrifice; and of courage in the protection of the flock placed in his care and of the ones he loves.

SCALE OF POINTS

Head

Shape of skull	5	Back 5	
Ears	5	Loins 5	
Eyes	5	Feet 5	25
Muzzle	5	Coat	10
Teeth	5 25	Size and Soundness	25
General Conformation		Expression and General	
Neck	5	Appearance	15
Chest	5	Total	100

Approved February 13, 1935

Komondor

General Appearance—The Komondor is characterized by imposing strength, courageous demeanor and pleasing conformation. In general he is a big muscular dog with plenty of bone and substance.

Nature and Characteristics—As a houseguard as well as a guardian of herds he is, when grown up, an earnest, courageous, and very faithful dog. The young dog, however, is just as playful as any other puppy. He is much devoted to his master and will defend him against attack by any stranger. On account of this trait he is not used for driving the herds, but only for guarding them. His special task is to protect the animals, and he lives during the greater part of the year in the open air without protection against strange dogs and all kinds of beasts of prey.

Head—The head of the Komondor is covered all over with long hair, and thus the head looks somewhat short, in comparison to the seemingly wide forehead. When the hair is smoothed, it will be seen that the skull is somewhat arched if viewed from the side; the forehead is not wide, but appears, however, wider through the rich growth of hair. The stop is moderate, it is the starting point of the muzzle which is somewhat shorter than the length of the skull. The top line of the muzzle is straight and about parallel with the line of the top of the skull. The muzzle should be fairly square. The lips cover the teeth closely and are black. The muzzle is mostly covered by long hair. The edges of the muzzle are black or steel blue-gray. The jaws are powerful, and the teeth are level and close together evenly. *Ears*—The ears are rather low set and hang along the side of the head. They are medium-sized, and their surface is covered with long hair. *Eyes*—The eyes express fidelity. They are medium-sized and almond-shaped, not too deeply set and surrounded by rough, unkempt hair. The iris of the eyes is of coffee or darker brown color, light color is not desirable. Blue-white eyes are disqualifying. The edges of the eyelids are slate-gray. *Muzzle*—In comparison to the length given in the head description, the muzzle is wide, coarse and not pointed. The nostrils are wide. The color of the nose is black. Komondors with flesh-colored noses must absolutely be excluded from breeding. A slate-colored or dark brown nose is undesirable but may, however, be accepted for breeding purposes.

Neck—The neck is covered with long hair, is muscular, of medium length, moderately arched. The head erect. No dewlap is allowed.

Body—The body is characterized chiefly by the powerful, deep chest which is muscular and proportionately wide. The height at the top of shoulders is 23½ inches to 31½ inches, the higher, the better. The shoulders slope into the neck without apparent protrusion. The body is moderately long and level. Back and loins are wide. The rump is wide, muscular, moderately sloping towards the root of the tail. The body should be somewhat drawn up at the rear, but not Greyhoundlike. *Tail*—The tail is as a straight continuation of the rump-line, and reaches down to the hocks slightly curved upwards at its end. It is covered in its full length with long hair, which when the dog is at ease almost touches the ground. When the dog is excited the tail is raised up to the level of the back. The tail should not be docked. Komondors born with short tails must be excluded even for breeding purposes.

Forelegs—The forelegs should be straight, well boned and muscular. Viewed from any side, the legs are like vertical columns. The upper arm joins the body closely, without loose elbows. The legs are covered all around by long, evenly hanging hair. *Hindquarters and Legs*—The steely, strong bone structure is covered with highly developed muscles, and the legs are evenly covered with long hair, hanging down in matted clods. The legs should be straight as viewed from the rear. Stifles well bent. Dewclaws must be removed. The body and the legs should about form a rectangle. *Feet*—The feet should be strong, rather large and with close, well-arched toes. The hind feet are stronger, and all are covered with long hair. The nails are black or slate-gray. The pads are hard, elastic and black.

Coat—The entire body of the Komondor is covered with a long, soft woolly, dense hair of different length on the different parts of the body, with inclination to entanglement and shagginess. If the dog is not taken care of, the hair becomes shaggy on the forelegs, chest, belly, rump and on the sides of the thigh and the tail. The longer and the more ragged, the better, though, as above stated, the length of the hair varies on the different parts of the body. The longer hair begins on the head and ears and lengthens gradually on the body, being longest on the thighs and the tail. A somewhat shorter, but still long hair is found on the legs, the muzzle and the cheeks. Too curly hair is undesirable. *Color*—The color of the hair is white. Any other color is disqualifying.

Size—The bigger the Komondor, the better, a minimum height of 25½ inches at top of shoulders for males and 23½ inches for females is required.

Faults—Light or flesh-colored nose, albino or blue eyes, highly set and small ears. Short, smooth hair, on the head and legs, strongly curled tail, color other than white.

DISQUALIFICATIONS

Blue-white eyes; color other than white.

Approved November 9, 1937

Kuvasz

General Appearance—Being a working dog of the larger size, the Kuvasz should be sturdily built and impress the eye with its strength and activity combined with light footedness. He should move freely on strong legs and any tendency to a weak or hollow back is a decided fault.

Head—Should be in proportion to the body, skull broad and flat with not too decided a stop. *Muzzle*—Should be clean cut, rather square in shape and covered with short, fine hair. *Ears*—Rather small, set well back, folded over level with the top of skull and lying close to the head. They should be covered with fine, short hair but no fringe. *Eyes*—Should be of medium size, set slightly obliquely and rather wide apart. They should be as dark as possible. *Nose*—Nostrils well developed. The nose together with the flews should be black.

Color—Pure white. Occasionally specimens appear with a yellow saddle, but this is a decided fault and such dogs are not to be recommended for breeding purposes. *Coat*—Rather long on neck and croup becoming a little shorter and slightly wavy on sides.

Body—Should be well ribbed up with a fairly broad back, neck is fairly short, strong, well set on sloping shoulders with strong muscular loins. *Forelegs*—Should have strong bone, be perfectly straight and well muscled, elbows should be in but well let down. Hair short on front and sides of legs. Slightly feathered on back of legs. *Hindquarters*—Should be strong, legs should have great freedom of action, lightness of loins and cowhocks are a great defect. *Chest*—Should be deep and fairly broad. *Feet*—Should be strong and well shaped; splay or turned out feet are objectionable. *Tail*—Should be of moderate length reaching a little below the hocks and covered with thick, fairly long hair.

Height—Dogs about 26 inches at shoulder, bitches somewhat less.

Approved August 13, 1935

Mastiff

General Character and Symmetry—Large, massive, symmetrical and well-knit frame. A combination of grandeur and good nature, courage and docility.

General Description of Head—In general outline giving a massive appearance when viewed from any angle. Breadth greatly to be desired. *Skull*—Broad and somewhat rounded between the ears, forehead slightly curved, showing marked wrinkles which are particularly distinctive when at attention. Brows (superciliary ridges) moderately raised. Muscles of the temples well developed, those of the cheeks extremely powerful. Arch across the skull a flattened curve with a furrow up the center of the forehead. This extends from between the eyes to halfway up the skull. *Ears*—Small, V-shaped, rounded at the tips. Leather moderately thin, set widely apart at the highest points on the sides of the skull continuing the outline across the summit. They should lie close to the cheeks when in repose. Ears dark in color, the blacker the better, conforming to the color of the muzzle. *Eyes*—Set wide apart, medium in size, never too prominent. Expression alert but kindly. The stop between the eyes well marked but not too abrupt. Color of eyes brown, the darker the better and showing no haw.

Face and Muzzle—Short, broad under the eyes and running nearly equal in width to the end of the nose. Truncated, *i.e.* blunt and cut off square, thus forming a right angle with the upper line of the face. Of great depth from the point of the nose to underjaw. Underjaw broad to the end and slightly rounded. Canine teeth healthy, powerful and wide apart. Scissors bite preferred but a moderately undershot jaw permissible providing the teeth are not visible when the mouth is closed. Lips diverging at obtuse angles with the septum and sufficiently pendulous so as to show a modified square profile. Nose broad and always dark in color, the blacker the better, with spread flat nostrils (not pointed or turned up) in profile. Muzzle dark in color, the blacker the better. Muzzle should be half the length of the skull, thus dividing the head into three parts—one for the foreface and two for the skull. In other words, the distance from tip of nose to stop is equal to one-half the distance between the stop and the occiput. Circumference of muzzle (measured midway between the eyes and nose) to that of the head (measured before the ears) as 3 is to 5.

Neck—Powerful and very muscular, slightly arched, and of medium length. The neck gradually increases in circumference as it approaches the shoulder. Neck moderately "dry" (not showing an excess of loose skin).

Chest and Flanks—Wide, deep, rounded and well let down between the forelegs, extending at least to the elbow. Forechest should be deep and well defined. Ribs extremely well rounded. False ribs deep and well set back. There should be a reasonable, but not exaggerated, cut-up. *Shoulder and Arm*—Slightly sloping, heavy and muscular. No tendency to looseness of shoulders.

Forelegs and Feet—Legs straight, strong and set wide apart, heavy-boned. Elbows parallel to body. Feet heavy, round and compact with well-arched toes. Pasterns strong and bent only slightly. Black nails preferred. *Hind Legs*—Hindquarters broad, wide and muscular. Second thighs well developed, hocks set back, wide apart and parallel when viewed from the rear. *Back and Loins*—Back muscular, powerful and straight. Loins wide and muscular, slightly rounded over the rump. *Tail*—Set on moderately high and reaching to the hocks or a little below. Wide at the root, tapering to the end, hanging straight in repose, forming a slight curve but never over the back when dog is in action.

Coat—Outer coat moderately coarse. Undercoat, dense, short and close lying.

Color—Apricot, silver fawn or dark fawn-brindle. Fawn-brindle should have fawn as a background color which should be completely covered with very dark stripes. In any case muzzle, ears and nose must be dark in color, the blacker the better, with similar color tone around the orbits, extending upwards between them.

Size—Dogs, minimum, 30 inches at the shoulder; bitches, minimum, 27½ inches at the shoulder.

SCALE OF POINTS

General character and symmetry	10	Chest and ribs	10
Height and substance	10	Forelegs and feet	10
Skull	10	Back, loins and flanks	10
Face and muzzle	12	Hind legs and feet	10
Ears	5	Tail	3
Eyes	5	Coat and color	5
		Total	100

Approved July 8, 1941

Newfoundland

Symmetry and General Appearance—The dog should impress the eye with strength and great activity. He should move freely on his legs with the body swung loosely between them, so that a slight roll in gait should not be objectionable; but at the same time a weak or hollow back, slackness of the loins or cowhocks should be a decided fault.

Head—Should be broad and massive, the occipital bone well developed, there should be no decided stop, the muzzle should be short, clean cut, and rather square in shape, and covered with short fine hair.

Coat—Should be flat and dense, of a coarsish texture and oily nature, and capable of resisting the water. If brushed the wrong way it should fall back into its place naturally.

Body—Should be well ribbed up with a broad back. A neck, strong, well set on to the shoulders and back, with strong muscular loins. *Forelegs*— Should be perfectly straight, well covered with muscle, elbows in but well let down and feathered all down. *Hindquarters and Legs*—Should be very strong; the legs should have great freedom of action, and a little feather. Slackness of loins and cowhocks are a great defect; dewclaws are objectionable and should be removed. *Chest*—Should be deep and fairly broad and well covered with hair, but not to such an extent as to form a frill. *Bone*— Massive throughout, but not to give a heavy inactive appearance. *Feet*— Should be large and well shaped. Splayed or turned out feet are objectionable.

Tail—Should be of moderate length, reaching down a little below the hocks, it should be of fair thickness, and well covered with long hair, but not to form a flag. When the dog is standing still, and not excited, it should hang downwards with a slight curve at the end; but when the dog is in motion it should be carried a trifle up, and when he is excited straight out with a slight curve at the end. Tails with a kink in them, or curled over the back, are very objectionable.

Ears—Should be small, set well back, square with the skull, lie close to the head, and be covered with short hair and no fringe. *Eyes*—Should be small, of a dark brown color, rather deeply set but not showing any haw, and they should be rather widely apart.

Color—Dull jet black. A slight tinge of bronze, or a splash of white on chest and toes is not objectionable.

Height and Weight—Size and weight are very desirable so long as symmetry is maintained. A fair average height at the shoulders is 28 inches for a dog, and 26 inches for a bitch, and a fair average weight is, respectively: dogs, 140 to 150 pounds; bitches, 110 to 120 pounds.

Other Than Black (Landseers)—Should in all respects follow the black except in color, which may be almost any, so long as it disqualifies for the black class, but the colors most to be encouraged are white and black or bronze. Beauty in markings to be taken greatly into consideration. Black dogs that have only white toes and white breasts and white tip to tail, should be exhibited in the classes provided for "black."

SCALE OF POINTS

Head			
Shape of skull	8	Loin and back	12
Ears	10	Hindquarters and tail	10
Eyes	8	Legs and feet	10
Muzzle	8 34	Coat	12
Body		Size, height and general	
Neck	4	appearance	8 66
Chest	6	Total points	100
Shoulders	4		

MARKINGS OF WHITE AND BLACK DOGS

Head	3	Rump	2
Saddle	5	Total	10

DEFINITION FOR PREFERENCE

Black head marked with narrow blaze. Even-marked saddle. Black rump, extending on to tail. The ten points above are to be considered in differentiating between "Landseers" not added to Standard.

Old English Sheepdog

Skull—Capacious and rather squarely formed, giving plenty of room for brain power. The parts over the eyes should be well arched and the whole well covered with hair. *Jaw*—Fairly long, strong, square and truncated. The top should be well defined to avoid a Deerhound face. (The attention of judges is particularly called to the above properties, as a long, narrow head is a deformity.) *Eyes*—Vary according to the color of the dog. Very dark preferred, but in the glaucous or blue dogs a pearl, walleye or china eye is considered typical. (A light eye is most objectionable.) *Nose*—Always black, large and capacious. *Teeth*—Strong and large, evenly placed and level in opposition. *Ears*—Medium-sized, and carried flat to side of head, coated moderately.

Legs—The forelegs should be dead straight, with plenty of bone, removing the body a medium height from the ground, without approaching legginess, and well coated all around. *Feet*—Small, round; toes well arched, and pads thick and hard. *Tail*—It is preferable that there should be none. Should never, however, exceed 1½ or 2 inches in grown dogs. When not natural-born bobtails however, puppies should be docked at the first joint from the body and the operation performed when they are from three to four days old.

Neck and Shoulders—The neck should be fairly long, arched gracefully and well coated with hair. The shoulders sloping and narrow at the points, the dog standing lower at the shoulder than at the loin.

Body—Rather short and very compact, ribs well sprung and brisket deep and capacious. *Slabsidedness highly undesirable.* The loin should be very stout and gently arched, while the hindquarters should be round and muscular and with well-let-down hocks, and the hams densely coated with a thick, long jacket in excess of any other part.

Coat—Profuse, but not so excessive as to give the impression of the dog being overfat, and of a good hard texture; not straight, but shaggy and free from curl. *Quality and texture of coat to be considered above mere profuseness.* Softness or flatness of coat to be considered a fault. The undercoat should be a waterproof pile, when not removed by grooming or season.

Color—Any shade of gray, grizzle, blue or blue-merled with or without white markings or in reverse. *Any shade of brown or fawn to be considered distinctly objectionable and not to be encouraged.*

Size—Twenty-two inches and upwards for dogs and slightly less for bitches. Type, character and symmetry are of the greatest importance and are on no account to be sacrificed to size alone.

General Appearance and Characteristics—A strong, compact-looking dog of great symmetry, practically the same in measurement from shoulder to stern as in height, absolutely free from legginess or weaselness, very elastic in his gallop, but in walking or trotting he has a characteristic ambling or pacing movement, and his bark should be loud, with a peculiar "pot-casse" ring in it. Taking him all round, he is a profusely, but not *excessively* coated, thickset, muscular, able-bodied dog with a most intelligent expression, free from all Poodle or Deerhound character. *Soundness should be considered of greatest importance.*

Skull	5	Body and loins	10
Eyes	5	Hindquarters	10
Ears	5	Legs	10
Teeth	5	Coat (texture, quality and	
Nose	5	condition)	15
Jaw	5	General appearance and movement	
Foreface	5		15
Neck and shoulders	5	Total	100

Approved October 13, 1953

Puli

General Appearance—A dog of medium size, vigorous, alert, and extremely active. By nature affectionate, he is a devoted and home-loving companion, sensibly suspicious of strangers and therefore an excellent guard. Striking and highly characteristic is the shaggy coat which centuries ago fitted him for the strenuous work of herding the flocks on the plains of Hungary.

Head—Of medium size, in proportion to the body. The skull is slightly domed and not too broad. Stop clearly defined but not abrupt, neither dished nor downfaced, with a strong muzzle of medium length ending in a nose of good size. Teeth are strong and comparatively large, and the bite may be either level or scissors. Flews tight. *Ears*—Hanging and set fairly high, medium size, and V-shaped. *Eyes*—Deep-set and rather large, should be dark brown, but lighter color is not a serious fault.

Neck and Shoulders—Neck strong and muscular, of medium length, and free of throatiness. Shoulders clean-cut and sloping, with elbows close.

Body—The chest is deep and fairly broad with ribs well sprung. Back of medium length, straight and level, the rump sloping moderately. Fairly broad across the loins and well tucked up. *Tail*—Occasionally born bobtail, which is acceptable, but never cut. The tail is carried curled over the back when alert, carried low with the end curled up when at rest. *Legs and Feet* —Forelegs straight, strong, and well boned. Feet round and compact with thick-cushioned pads and strong nails. Hindquarters well developed, moderately broad through the stifle which is well bent and muscular. Dewclaws, if any, may be removed from both forelegs and hind legs.

Coat—Characteristic of the breed is the dense, weather-resisting double coat. The outer coat, long and of medium texture, is never silky. It may be straight, wavy, or slightly curly, the more curly coat appearing to be somewhat shorter. The undercoat is soft, woolly, and dense. The coat mats easily, the hair tending to cling together in bunches, giving a somewhat corded appearance even when groomed. The hair is profuse on the head, ears, face, stifles, and tail, and the feet are well haired between the toes. Usually shown combed, but may also be shown uncombed with the coat hanging in tight, even cords.

Color—Solid colors, black, rusty-black, various shades of gray, and white. The black usually appears weathered and rusty or slightly gray. The intermixture of hair of different colors is acceptable and is usually present in the grays, but must be uniform throughout the coat so that the over-all appearance of a solid color is maintained. Nose, flews, and eyelids are black.

Height—Males about 17 inches, and should not exceed 19 inches. Females about 16 inches, and should not exceed 18 inches.

Serious Faults—Overshot or undershot. Lack of undercoat, short or sparse coat. White markings such as white paws or spot on chest. Flesh color on nose, flews, or eyelids. Coat with areas of two or more colors at the skin.

Approved April 12, 1960

Rottweiler

General Appearance and Character—The Rottweiler is a good-sized, strongly built, active dog. He is affectionate, intelligent, easily trained to work, naturally obedient and extremely faithful. While not quarrelsome, he possesses great courage and makes a splendid guard. His demeanor is dignified and he is not excitable.

Head—Is of medium length, the skull broad between the ears. Stop well pronounced as is also the occiput. Muzzle is not very long. It should not be longer than the distance from the stop to the occiput. Nose is well developed, with relatively large nostrils and is always black. Flews which should not be too pronounced are also black. Jaws should be strong and muscular;

teeth strong—incisors of lower jaw must touch the inner surface of the upper incisors. Eyes are of medium size, dark brown in color and should express faithfulness, good humor and confidence. The ears are comparatively small, set high and wide and hang over about on a level with top of head. The skin on head should not be loose. The neck should be of fair length, strong, round and very muscular, slightly arched and free from throatiness.

Forequarters—Shoulders should be well placed, long and sloping, elbows well let down, but not loose. Legs muscular and with plenty of bone and substance, pasterns straight and strong. Feet strong, round and close, with toes well arched. Soles very hard, toe nails dark, short and strong. *Body*— The chest is roomy, broad and deep. Ribs well sprung. Back straight, strong and rather short. Loins strong and deep, and flanks should not be tucked up. Croup short, broad, but not sloping. *Hindquarters*—Upper thigh is short, broad and very muscular. Lower thigh very muscular at top and strong and sinewy at the bottom. Stifles fairly well bent, hocks strong. The hind feet are somewhat longer than the front ones, but should be close and strong with toes well arched. There should be no dewclaws. Tail should be short, placed high (on level with back) and carried horizontally. Dogs are frequently born with a short stump tail and when tail is too long it must be docked close to body.

Coat—Hair should be short, coarse and flat. The undercoat which is absolutely required on neck and thighs should not show through outer coat. The hair should be a little longer on the back of front and hind legs and on tail. *Color*—Black, with clearly defined markings on cheeks, muzzle, chest and legs, as well as over both eyes. Color of markings: tan to mahogany brown. A small spot of white on chest and belly is permissible but not desirable.

Height—Shoulder height for males is 23¾ to 27 inches, for females, 21¾ to 25¾ inches, but height should always be considered in relation to the general appearance and conformation of the dog.

Faults—Too lightly built or too heavily built, sway-back, roach back, too long body, lack of spring of ribs. Head too long and narrow or too short and plump. Lack of occiput, snipy muzzle, cheekiness, top line of muzzle not straight, light or flesh colored nose, hanging flews, overshot or undershot, loose skin on head, ears set too low, or ears too heavy, long or narrow or rose ear, or ears uneven in size. Light, small or slanting eyes, or lack of expression, neck too long, thin or weak, or very noticeable throatiness. Lack of bone and muscle, short or straight shoulders, front legs too close together or not straight, weak pasterns, splay feet, light nails, weak toes. Flat ribs, sloping croup. Too heavy or plump body. Flanks drawn up. Flat thighs, cowhocks or weak hocks, dewclaws. Tail set too high or too low or that is too long or too thin. Soft, too short, too long or too open coat, wavy coat or lack of undercoat. White markings on toes, legs, or other parts of body, markings not well defined or smudgy. The one-color tan Rottweiler with either black or light mask or with black streak on back as well as other colors such as brown or blue are not recognized and are believed to be cross bred, as is also a longhaired Rottweiler. Timid or stupid-appearing animals are to be positively rejected.

Approved April 9, 1935

St. Bernard

SHORTHAIRED

General—Powerful, proportionately tall figure, strong and muscular in every part, with powerful head and most intelligent expression. In dogs with a dark mask the expression appears more stern, but never ill-natured.

Head—Like the whole body, very powerful and imposing. The massive skull is wide, slightly arched and the sides slope in a gentle curve into the very strongly developed, high cheek bones. Occiput only moderately developed. The supra-orbital ridge is very strongly developed and forms nearly a right angle with the horizontal axis of the head. Deeply imbedded between the eyes and starting at the root of the muzzle, a furrow runs over the whole skull. It is strongly marked in the first half, gradually disappearing toward the base of the occiput. The lines at the sides of the head diverge considerably from the outer corner of the eyes toward the back of the head. The skin of the forehead, above the eyes, forms rather noticeable wrinkles, more or less pronounced, which converge toward the furrow. Especially when the dog is in action, the wrinkles are more visible without in the least giving the impression of morosity. Too strongly developed wrinkles are not desired. The slope from the skull to the muzzle is sudden and rather steep.

The muzzle is short, does not taper, and the vertical depth at the root of the muzzle must be greater than the length of the muzzle. The bridge of the muzzle is not arched, but straight; in some dogs, occasionally, slightly broken. A rather wide, well-marked, shallow furrow runs from the root of the muzzle over the entire bridge of the muzzle to the nose. The flews of the upper jaw are strongly developed, not sharply cut, but turning in a beautiful curve into the lower edge, and slightly overhanging. The flews of the lower jaw must not be deeply pendant. The teeth should be sound and strong and should meet in either a scissors or an even bite; the scissors bite being preferable. The undershot bite, although sometimes found with good specimens, is not desirable. The overshot bite is a fault. A black roof to the mouth is desirable. *Nose* (Schwamm)—Very substantial, broad, with wide open nostrils, and, like the lips, always black.

Ears—Of medium size, rather high set, with very strongly developed burr (Muschel) at the base. They stand slightly away from the head at the base, then drop with a sharp bend to the side and cling to the head without a turn. The flap is tender and forms a rounded triangle, slightly elongated toward the point, the front edge lying firmly to the head, whereas the back edge may stand somewhat away from the head, especially when the dog is at attention. Lightly set ears, which at the base immediately cling to the head, give it an oval and too little marked exterior, whereas a strongly developed base gives the skull a squarer, broader and much more expressive appearance. *Eyes*—Set more to the front than the sides, are of medium size, dark brown, with intelligent, friendly expression, set moderately deep. The lower eyelids, as a rule, do not close completely and, if that is the case, form an angular wrinkle toward the inner corner of the eye. Eyelids which are too deeply pendant and show conspicuously the lachrymal glands, or a very red, thick haw, and eyes that are too light, are objectionable.

Neck—Set high, very strong and in action is carried erect. Otherwise horizontally or slightly downward. The junction of head and neck is distinctly marked by an indentation. The nape of the neck is very muscular and rounded at the sides which makes the neck appear rather short. The dewlap of throat and neck is well-pronounced: too strong development, however, is not desirable.

Shoulders—Sloping and broad, very muscular and powerful. The withers are strongly pronounced. *Chest*—Very well arched, moderately deep, not reaching below the elbows. *Back*—Very broad, perfectly straight as far as the haunches, from there gently sloping to the rump, and merging imperceptibly into the root of the tail. *Hindquarters*—Well-developed. Legs very muscular. *Belly*—Distinctly set off from the very powerful loin section, only little drawn up.

Tail—Starting broad and powerful directly from the rump is long, very heavy, ending in a powerful tip. In repose it hangs straight down, turning gently upward in the lower third only, which is not considered a fault. In a great many specimens the tail is carried with the edge slightly bent and therefore hangs down in the shape of an f. In action all dogs carry the tail more or less turned upward. However it may not be carried too erect or by any means rolled over the back. A slight curling of the tip is sooner admissible.

Forearms—Very powerful and extraordinarily muscular. *Forelegs*—Straight, strong. *Hind Legs*—Hocks of moderate angulation. Dewclaws are not desired; if present, they must not obstruct gait. *Feet*—Broad, with strong toes, moderately closed, and with rather high knuckles. The so-called dewclaws which sometimes occur on the inside of the hind legs are imperfectly developed toes. They are of no use to the dog and are not taken into consideration in judging. They may be removed by surgery.

Coat—Very dense, short-haired (stockhaarig), lying smooth, tough, without however feeling rough to the touch. The thighs are slightly bushy. The tail at the root has longer and denser hair which gradually becomes shorter toward the tip. The tail appears bushy, not forming a flag. *Color*—White with red or red with white, the red in its various shades; brindle patches with white markings. The colors red and brown-yellow are of entirely equal value. Necessary markings are: white chest, feet and tip of tail, nose band, collar or spot on the nape; the latter and blaze are very desirable. Never of one color or without white. Faulty are all other colors, except the favorite dark shadings on the head (mask) and ears. One distinguishes between mantle dogs and splash-coated dogs.

Height at Shoulder—Of the dog should be 27½ inches minimum, of the bitch 25½ inches. Female animals are of finer and more delicate build.

Considered as faults are all deviations from the standard, as for instance a sway-back and a disproportionately long back, hocks too much bent, straight hindquarters, upward growing hair in spaces between the toes, out at elbows, cowhocks and weak pasterns.

LONGHAIRED

The longhaired type completely resembles the shorthaired type except for the coat which is not shorthaired (stockhaarig) but of medium length plain to slightly wavy, never rolled or curly and not shaggy either. Usually, on the back, especially from the region of the haunches to the rump, the hair is more wavy, a condition, by the way, that is slightly indicated in the shorthaired dogs. The tail is bushy with dense hair of moderate length. Rolled or curly hair on the tail is not desirable. A tail with parted hair, or a flag tail, is faulty. Face and ears are covered with short and soft hair; longer hair at the base of the ear is permissible. Forelegs only slightly feathered; thighs very bushy.

Approved May 12, 1959

Samoyed

General Conformation—(a) *General Appearance*—The Samoyed, being essentially a working dog, should present a picture of beauty, alertness and strength, with agility, dignity and grace. As his work lies in cold climates, his coat should be heavy and weather resistant, well groomed, and of good quality rather than quantity. The male carries more of a "ruff" than the female. He should not be long in the back as a weak back would make him practically useless for his legitimate work, but at the same time, a close-coupled body would also place him at a great disadvantage as a draft dog. Breeders should aim for the happy medium, a body not long but muscular, allowing liberty, with a deep chest and well-sprung ribs, strong neck, straight front and especially strong loins. Males should be masculine in appearance and deportment without unwarranted aggressiveness; bitches feminine without weakness of structure or apparent softness of temperament. Bitches may be slightly longer in back than males. They should both give the appearance of being capable of great endurance but be free from coarseness. Because of the depth of chest required, the legs should be moderately long. A very short-legged dog is to be deprecated. Hindquarters should be particularly well developed, stifles well bent and any suggestion of unsound stifles or cowhocks severely penalized. General appearance should include movement and general conformation, indicating balance and good substance.

(b) *Substance*—Substance is that sufficiency of bone and muscle which rounds out a balance with the frame. The bone is heavier than would be expected in a dog of this size but not so massive as to prevent the speed and agility most desirable in a Samoyed. In all builds, bone should be in proportion to body size. The Samoyed should never be so heavy as to appear clumsy nor so light as to appear racy. The weight should be in proportion to the height.

(c) *Height*—Males—21 to 23½ inches; females—19 to 21 inches at the withers. An oversized or undersized Samoyed is to be penalized according to the extent of the deviation.

(d) *Coat* (Texture & Condition)—The Samoyed is a double-coated dog. The body should be well-covered with an undercoat of soft, short, thick, close wool with longer and harsh hair growing through it to form the outer coat, which stands straight out from the body and should be free from curl. The coat should form a ruff around the neck and shoulders, framing the head (more on males than on females). Quality of coat should be weather resistant and considered more than quantity. A droopy coat is undesirable. The coat should glisten with a silver sheen. The female does not usually carry as long a coat as most males and it is softer in texture.

(e) *Color*—Samoyeds should be pure white, white and biscuit, cream, or all biscuit. Any other colors disqualify.

Movement—(a) *Gait*—The Samoyed should trot, not pace. He should move with a quick agile stride that is well timed. The gait should be free, balanced and vigorous, with good reach in the forequarters and good driving power in the hindquarters. When trotting, there should be a strong rear action drive. Moving at a slow walk or trot, they will not single track, but as speed increases the legs gradually angle inward until the pads are finally falling on a line directly under the longitudinal center of the body. As the pad marks converge the forelegs and hind legs are carried straight forward in traveling, the stifles not turned in nor out. The back should remain strong, firm and level. A choppy or stilted gait should be penalized.

(b) *Rear End*—Upper thighs should be well developed. Stifles well bent—approximately 45 degrees to the ground. Hocks should be well developed, sharply defined and set at approximately 30 per cent of hip height. The hind legs should be parallel when viewed from the rear in a natural stance, strong, well developed, turning neither in nor out. Straight stifles are objectionable. Double jointedness or cowhocks are a fault. Cowhocks should only be determined if the dog has had an opportunity to move properly. (c) *Front End*—Legs should be parallel and straight to the pasterns. The pasterns should be strong, sturdy and straight, but flexible with some spring for proper let-down of feet. Because of depth of chest, legs should be moderately long. Length of leg from the ground to the elbow should be approximately 55 per cent of the total height at the withers—a very short-legged dog is to be deprecated. Shoulders should be long and sloping, with a layback of 45 degrees and be firmly set. Out at the shoulders or out at the elbow should be penalized. The withers separation should be approximately 1–1½ inches.

(d) *Feet*—Large, long, flattish—a hare-foot, slightly spread but not splayed; toes arched; pads thick and tough, with protective growth of hair between the toes. Feet should turn neither in nor out in a natural stance but may turn in slightly in the act of pulling. Turning out, pigeon-toed, round or cat-footed or splayed are faults. Feathers on feet are not too essential but are more profuse on females than on males.

Head—(a) *Conformation*—Skull is wedge-shaped, broad, slightly crowned, not round or apple-headed, and should form an equilateral triangle on lines between the inner base of the ears and the center point of the stop. *Muzzle*— Muzzle of medium length and medium width, neither coarse nor snipy; should taper toward the nose and be in proportion to the size of the dog and the width of skull. The muzzle must have depth. *Stop*—Not too abrupt, nevertheless well defined. *Lips*—Should be black for preference and slightly curved up at the corners of the mouth, giving the "Samoyed smile." Lip lines should not have the appearance of being coarse nor should the flews drop predominately at corners of the mouth.

Ears—Strong and thick, erect, triangular and slightly rounded at the tips; should not be large or pointed, nor should they be small and "bear-eared." Ears should conform to head size and the size of the dog; they should be set well apart but be within the border of the outer edge of the head; they should be mobile and well covered inside with hair; hair full and stand-off before the ears. Length of ear should be the same measurement as the distance from inner base of ear to outer corner of eye.

Eyes—Should be dark for preference; should be placed well apart and deep-set; almond shaped with lower lid slanting toward an imaginary point approximating the base of ears. Dark eye rims for preference. Round or protruding eyes penalized. Blue eyes disqualifying.

Nose—Black for preference but brown, liver, or Dudley nose not penalized. Color of nose sometimes changes with age and weather.

Jaws and Teeth—Strong, well set teeth, snugly overlapping with scissors bite. Undershot or overshot should be penalized.

(b) *Expression*—The expression, referred to as "Samoyed expression," is very important and is indicated by sparkle of the eyes, animation and lighting up of the face when alert or intent on anything. Expression is made up of a combination of eyes, ears and mouth. The ears should be erect when alert; the mouth should be slightly curved up at the corners to form the "Samoyed smile."

Torso—(a) *Neck*—Strong, well muscled, carried proudly erect, set on sloping shoulders to carry head with dignity when at attention. Neck should blend into shoulders with a graceful arch.

(b) *Chest*—Should be deep, with ribs well sprung out from the spine and flattened at the sides to allow proper movement of the shoulders and freedom for the front legs. Should not be barrel-chested. Perfect depth of chest approximates the point of elbows, and the deepest part of the chest should be back of the forelegs—near the ninth rib. Heart and lung room are secured more by body depth than width.

(c) *Loin and Back*—The withers forms the highest part of the back. Loins strong and slightly arched. The back should be straight to the loin, medium in length, very muscular and neither long nor short-coupled. The dog should be "just off square"—the length being approximately 5 per cent more than the height. Females allowed to be slightly longer than males. The belly should be well shaped and tightly muscled and, with the rear of the thorax, should swing up in a pleasing curve (tuck-up). Croup must be full, slightly sloping, and must continue imperceptibly to the tail root.

Tail—The tail should be moderately long with the tail bone terminating approximately at the hock when down. It should be profusely covered with long hair and carried forward over the back or side when alert, but sometimes dropped when at rest. It should not be high or low set and should be mobile and loose—not tight over the back. A double hook is a fault. A judge should see the tail over the back once when judging.

Disposition—Intelligent, gentle, loyal, adaptable, alert, full of action, eager to serve, friendly but conservative, not distrustful or shy, not overly aggressive. Unprovoked aggressiveness to be severely penalized.

DISQUALIFICATIONS

Any color other than pure white, cream, biscuit, or white and biscuit. Blue eyes.

Approved April 9, 1963

Schnauzer, Standard

The Standard Schnauzer is a robust, sinewy, heavy-set dog of terrier type, sturdily built, square in the proportion of body length to height, with good muscle and plenty of bone. His nature combines high-spirited temperament with extreme reliability. His rugged build and dense, harsh coat are accentuated by arched eyebrows, bristly mustache and luxurious whiskers. *Height*—At withers, from 18 to 20 inches for males, and from 17 to 19 inches for females. *Disqualification*—Animals under or over these measurements.

Head—Strong and rectangular, diminishing slightly from the ear to the eyes, and again to the tip of the nose. Total length about one-third the length of the back, measuring from the withers to the beginning of the tail. *Skull*—Moderately broad between the ears, width not exceeding two-thirds of the length. *Faults*—Too narrow or pronounced. *Forehead*—Flat and unwrinkled. *Cheeks*—Well muscled, but not too strongly developed. *Faults* —Protruding cheek bones. *Muzzle*—Strong and in proportion to the skull, ending in moderately blunt manner, with wiry whiskers accenting the rectangular shape of the head. *Faults*—Too long or too short, pointed or lacking whiskers; dish-faced or down-faced. *Nose*—Powerful, black and full, with ridge running almost parallel to the extension of the forehead. Lips tight and not overlapping. *Ears*—Evenly shaped, set high and carried erect when cropped. If uncropped, they should be small and V-shaped, of moderate thickness and carried rather high and close to the head. *Faults*—Low-set, houndy ears and badly cut ears. *Eyes*—Medium size, dark brown, oval and turned forward. Vision should not be obstructed from the front or profile by too long an eyebrow. The brow should be arched and wiry. *Faults*—Too large, round, or protruding, light or yellow-ringed eyes. *Jaw*—Level, powerful and square. *Faults*—Overshot or undershot. *Teeth*—Sound, strong and white, with canines meeting in scissors bite. *Faults*—Pointed or irregular.

Neck—Nape should be strong, slightly arched and set cleanly on the shoulders. Skin should be tight, fitting closely to the throat. *Faults*—Too short, thick, long and throaty. *Shoulders*—Somewhat sloping, strongly muscled. *Faults*—Loose, straight or low shoulders, or steep-set front. *Chest*— Moderately broad, with the breastbone plainly discernible and reaching at least to the height of the elbows, extending slowly backwards. Belly well drawn up toward the back, but no tuck-up. *Faults*—Too broad or too narrow, shallow or false chest.

Back—Strong, stiff, straight and short, with a well-developed short loin section, the ribs well sprung. Length of the back from the withers to the set-on of tail should approximate the height at withers.

Forelegs—Straight and vertical when seen from all sides, with bone carried well down to the feet; elbows set close to body and pointing directly backward. *Faults*—Legs too high, low, thin, or weak; elbows turned out or in. Pasterns sunken or any weakness of joint, bone or muscular development. *Feet*—Small and compact; round with thick pads, strong nails. Toes well arched and pointing straight ahead. *Faults*—Toed-in or toed-out and long or spreading feet. *Hindquarters*—Strongly muscled, with thighs slanting and flat, never appearing overbuilt or higher than the shoulders. *Faults*—Hocks let down, cowhocks or any weakness of joint.

Body—Compact, strong, short coupled and substantial so as to permit great flexibility. *Tail*—Set moderately high and carried erect. Cut down to two joints and should not be longer than two inches. *Faults*—Too steep, level or too long a croup.

Coat—Hard and wiry, standing up on the back and, when seen against the course of the hair, neither short nor lying flat. The outer coat should be harsh, the undercoat soft. It should be trimmed only to accent the body outline and should not be more than an inch long except on the ears and skull. *Faults*—Soft, smooth, curly; too long or short; too closely trimmed, dyed or excessively powdered. *Color*—Pepper and salt or similar equal mixtures, light or dark including pure black. *Faults*—Solid colors other than black, also very light or whitish, spotted or tiger colors. A small white spot on the breast is not a fault.

Action—The gait should be sound, strong, quick, free, true and level.

DISQUALIFICATIONS

Shy, savage or highly nervous dogs and dogs which are in excess of or less than the standard in height.

Approved April 11, 1939

Shetland Sheepdog

Preamble—The Shetland Sheepdog, like the Collie, traces to the Border Collie of Scotland, which, transported to the Shetland Islands and crossed with small, intelligent, longhaired breeds, was reduced to miniature proportions. Subsequently crosses were made from time to time with Collies. This breed now bears the same relationship in size and general appearance to the Rough Collie as the Shetland Pony does to some of the larger breeds of horses. Although the resemblance between the Shetland Sheepdog and the Rough Collie is marked, there are differences which may be noted.

General Description—The Shetland Sheepdog is a small, alert, rough-coated, longhaired working dog. He must be sound, agile and sturdy. The outline should be so symmetrical that no part appears out of proportion to the whole. Dogs should appear masculine; bitches feminine.

Size—The Shetland Sheepdog should stand between 13 and 16 inches at the shoulder. Note: Height is determined by a line perpendicular to the ground from the top of the shoulder blades, the dog standing naturally, with forelegs parallel to line of measurement. *Disqualification*—Heights below or above the desired size range are to be disqualified from the show ring.

Coat—The coat should be double, the outer coat consisting of long, straight, harsh hair; the undercoat short, furry, and so dense as to give the entire coat its "stand-off" quality. The hair on face, tips of ears and feet should be smooth. Mane and frill should be abundant, and particularly impressive in males. The forelegs well feathered, the hind legs heavily so, but smooth below the hock joint. Hair on tail profuse. Note: Excess hair on ears, feet, and on hocks may be trimmed for the show ring. *Faults*—Coat short or flat, in whole or in part; wavy, curly, soft or silky. Lack of undercoat. Smooth-coated specimens. *Color*—Black, blue merle, and sable (ranging from golden through mahogany); marked with varying amounts of white and/or tan. *Faults*—Rustiness in a black or a blue coat. Washed out or degenerate colors, such as pale sable and faded blue. Self-color in the case of blue merle, that is, without any merling or mottling and generally appearing as a faded or dilute tricolor. Conspicuous white body spots. Specimens with more than 50 per cent white shall be so severely penalized as to effectively eliminate them from competition. *Disqualification*—Brindle.

Temperament—The Shetland Sheepdog is intensely loyal, affectionate, and responsive to his owner. However, he may be reserved toward strangers but not to the point of showing fear or cringing in the ring. *Faults*—Shyness, timidity, or nervousness. Stubbornness, snappiness, or ill temper.

Head—The head should be refined and its shape, when viewed from top or side, be a long, blunt wedge tapering slightly from ears to nose, which must be black. *Skull and Muzzle*—Top of skull should be flat, showing no prominence at nuchal crest (the top of the occiput). Cheeks should be flat and should merge smoothly into a well-rounded muzzle. Skull and muzzle should be of equal length, balance point being inner corner of eye. In profile the top line of skull should parallel the top line of muzzle, but on a higher plane due to the presence of a slight but definite stop. Jaws clean and powerful. The deep, well-developed underjaw, rounded at chin, should extend to base of nostril. Lips tight. Upper and lower lips must meet and fit smoothly together all the way around. Teeth level and evenly spaced. Scissors bite. *Faults*—Two-angled head. Too prominent stop, or no stop. Overfill below, between, or above eyes. Prominent nuchal crest. Domed skull. Prominent cheekbones. Snipy muzzle. Short, receding, or shallow under-jaw, lacking breadth and depth. Overshot or undershot, missing or crooked teeth. Teeth visible when mouth is closed. *Eyes*—Medium size with dark, almond-shaped rims, set somewhat obliquely in skull. Color must be dark, with blue or merle eyes permissible in blue merles only. *Faults*—Light, round, large or too small. Prominent haws. *Ears*—Small and flexible, placed high, carried three-fourths erect, with tips breaking forward. When in repose the ears fold lengthwise and are thrown back into the frill. *Faults*—Set too low. Hound, prick, bat, twisted ears. Leather too thick or too thin.

Expression—Contours and chiseling of the head, the shape, set and use of ears, the placement, shape and color of the eyes, combine to produce expression. Normally the expression should be alert, gentle, intelligent and questioning. Toward strangers the eyes should show watchfulness and reserve, but no fear. *Neck*—Neck should be muscular, arched, and of sufficient length to carry the head proudly. *Faults*—Too short and thick.

Body—In over-all appearance the body should appear moderately long as measured from shoulder joint to ischium (rearmost extremity of the pelvic bone), but much of this length is actually due to the proper angulation and breadth of the shoulder and hindquarter, as the back itself should be comparatively short. Back should be level and strongly muscled. Chest should be deep, the brisket reaching to point of elbow. The ribs should be well sprung, but flattened at their lower half to allow free play of the foreleg and shoulder. Abdomen moderately tucked up. *Faults*—Back too long, too short, swayed or roached. Barrel ribs. Slab side. Chest narrow and/or too shallow.

Forequarters—From the withers the shoulder blades should slope at a 45-degree angle forward and downward to the shoulder joints. At the withers they are separated only by the vertebra, but they must slope outward sufficiently to accommodate the desired spring of rib. The upper arm should join the shoulder blade at as nearly as possible a right angle. Elbow joint should be equidistant from the ground or from the withers. Forelegs straight viewed from all angles, muscular and clean, and of strong bone. Pasterns very strong, sinewy and flexible. Dewclaws may be removed. *Faults*—Insufficient angulation between shoulder and upper arm. Upper arm too short. Lack of outward slope of shoulders. Loose shoulders. Turning in or out of elbows. Crooked legs. Light bone. *Feet (front and hind)*—Feet should be oval and compact with the toes well arched and fitting tightly together. Pads deep and tough, nails hard and strong. *Faults*—Feet turning in or out. Splay-feet. Hare-feet. Cat-feet.

Hindquarters—There should be a slight arch at the loins, and the croup should slope gradually to the rear. The hipbone (pelvis) should be set at a 30-degree angle to the spine. The thigh should be broad and muscular. The thighbone should be set into the pelvis at a right angle corresponding to the angle of the shoulder blade and upper arm. Stifle bones join the thighbone and should be distinctly angled at the stifle joint. The over-all length of the stifle should at least equal the length of the thighbone, and preferably should slightly exceed it. Hock joint should be clean-cut, angular, sinewy, with good bone and strong ligamentation. The hock (metatarsus) should be short and straight viewed from all angles. Dewclaws should be removed. Feet (*see* Forequarters). *Faults*—Croup higher than withers. Croup too straight or too steep. Narrow thighs. Cowhocks. Hocks turning out. Poorly defined hock joint. Feet (*see* Forequarters). *Tail*—The tail should be sufficiently long so that when it is laid along the back edge of the hind legs the last vertebra will reach the hock joint. Carriage of tail at rest is straight down or in a slight upward curve. When the dog is alert the tail is normally lifted, but it should not be curved forward over the back. *Faults*—Too short. Twisted at end.

Gait—The trotting gait of the Shetland Sheepdog should denote effortless speed and smoothness. There should be no jerkiness, nor stiff, stilted, up-and-down movement. The drive should be from the rear, true and straight, dependent upon correct angulation, musculation, and ligamentation of the entire hindquarter, thus allowing the dog to reach well under his body with his hind foot and propel himself forward. Reach of stride of the foreleg is dependent upon correct angulation, musculation and ligamentation of the forequarters, together with correct width of chest and construction of rib cage. The foot should be lifted only enough to clear the ground as the leg swings forward. Viewed from the front, both forelegs and hind legs should move forward almost perpendicular to ground at the walk, slanting a little inward at a slow trot, until at a swift trot the feet are brought so far inward toward center line of body that the tracks left show two parallel lines of footprints actually touching a center line at their inner edges. *There should be no crossing of the feet nor throwing of the weight from side to side.* *Faults*—Stiff, short steps, with a choppy, jerky movement. Mincing steps, with a hopping up and down, or a balancing of weight from side to side (often erroneously admired as a "dancing gait" but permissible in young puppies). Lifting of front feet in hackneylike action, resulting in loss of speed and energy. Pacing gait.

SCALE OF POINTS

General Appearance			Forequarters		
Symmetry	10		Shoulder	10	
Temperament	10		Forelegs and feet	5	15
Coat	5	25	Hindquarters		
Head			Hip, thigh and stifle		
Skull and stop	5			10	
Muzzle	5		Hocks and feet	5	15
Eyes, ears and expression			Gait		
	10	20	Gait—smoothness and		
Body			lack of waste motion		
Neck and back	5		when trotting		
Chest, ribs and brisket					5
	10		Total		100
Loin, croup, and tail					
	5	20			

DISQUALIFICATIONS

Heights below or above the desired range, i.e. 13–16 inches. Brindle color.
Approved May 12, 1959

Siberian Husky

General Appearance—The Siberian Husky is a medium-sized working dog of powerful but graceful build. His moderately compact and well-furred body, erect ears, and brush tail curved over the back suggest the Northern heritage of the capable sled dog. His characteristic gait is free and effortless but unbelievably strong when called upon to pull. And the keen and friendly expression in his slightly oblique eyes indicates the amenable disposition of the good companion.

Head. Skull—Of medium size, in proportion to the body; a trifle rounded on top and tapering gradually to the eyes, the width between the ears medium to narrow. Muzzle medium long, that is, the distance from nose to stop is about equal to the distance from stop to occiput. Skull and muzzle are finely chiseled. Lips dark and close-fitting, the jaws strong, and the teeth meeting in a scissors bite. *Faults*—Head too heavy; skull too wide;

the muzzle either bulky, snipy, or coarse. *Ears*—Medium in size, set high, and carried erect. When at attention, they are practically parallel to each other. They are moderately rounded at the tips and well furred on the inner side. *Faults:* Too large, too low-set, and not strongly erect. *Eyes*—Set a trifle obliquely, their expression keen but friendly, interested, and even mischievous. Color may be either brown or blue, one brown eye and one blue eye being permissible but not desirable. *Faults:* Eyes set too obliquely.

Nose—Preferably black, with brown allowed in specimens of reddish-colored coats; and flesh-colored nose and eye rims allowed in white dogs. The nose that is temporarily pink-streaked in winter is permissible but not desirable.

Neck—Strong, arched, and fairly short.

Body—Moderately compact but never cobby. Chest deep and strong but not too broad, the ribs well sprung and deep. Shoulders powerful and well laid back. Back of medium length and strong, the back line level. Loins taut, lean, and very slightly arched. *Faults:* Weak or slack back; roach back.

Legs and Feet. Legs—The legs are straight and well muscled, with bone substantial but not heavy. Hindquarters powerful with good angulation. Well bent at stifles. Dewclaws on the rear legs, if any, are to be removed. *Feet*—Oval in shape, medium in size; compact and well furred between the toes. Pads tough and deeply cushioned. In short, a typical snowshoe foot, somewhat webbed between the toes. *Faults:* Bone too light or too heavy; insufficient bend at stifles; weak pasterns; feet soft and/or splayed.

Tail—A well-furred brush carried over the back in a sickle curve when the dog runs or stands at attention, and trailing out behind when working or in repose. When carried up, the typical tail does not curl to either side of the body, nor does it snap flat to the back. The tail hair is usually of medium length, although length varies somewhat with over-all coat length.

Coat—Double. The undercoat is dense, soft and downy, and should be of sufficient length and density to support the outer coat. The outer coat is very thick, smooth-textured and soft, giving a smooth, full-furred appearance and a clean-cut outline. It is usually medium in length; a longer coat is allowed so long as the texture is soft and remains the same in any length. *Faults:* Harsh texture, or a rough look which obscures the clean-cut outline of the dog; absence of undercoat, except while actually shedding.

Color—All colors and white, and all markings are allowed. The various shades of wolf and the silver grays, tan and black with white points are most usual. A variety of markings, especially on the head, are common to the breed, these including many striking and unusual patterns not found in other breeds. The cap-like mask and spectacles are typical.

Size. Both height and weight are very important. *Height*—Dogs, from 21 to 23½ inches at the shoulder; bitches, from 20 to 22 inches. *Weight*—Dogs, from 45 to 60 pounds; bitches, from 35 to 50 pounds. Dogs over 23½ inches and bitches over 22 inches are to be disqualified.

Summary—Most important of the Siberian Husky's characteristics are medium size and moderate bone, soft coat, high-set ears, ease and freedom of action, and good disposition. A gait, or a general appearance in any way clumsy, heavy, or unwieldy is to be penalized. In addition to the faults already noted, obvious structural faults common to all breeds, such as cow-hocks, for instance, are as undesirable in the Siberian Husky as in any other breed, even though they are not specifically mentioned therein.

DISQUALIFICATION

Height over 23½ inches in dogs; over 22 inches in bitches.

Approved March 12, 1963

Welsh Corgi, Cardigan

Head—To be foxy in shape and appearance. Skull to be fairly wide between the ears and flat, tapering toward the eyes. Muzzle to measure about three inches in length (or in proportion to skull as 3 to 5) and to taper toward the snout. Nose to be rather pointed. Teeth—strong, level and sound. *Eyes* —To be of medium size, but giving a sharp and watchful expression, preferably dark in color but clear. Silver eyes permissible in blue merles. *Ears*—Proportionate to size of dog and prominent; preferably pointed at the tips; moderately wide at the base; carried erect and set about 3½ inches apart and well back so that they can be laid flat along neck, sloping forward slightly when erect.

Neck—To be fairly long and without throatiness, fitting into well sloped and strong muscular shoulders. *Front*—To be slightly bowed, with strong bone. Chest to be moderately broad with prominent breastbone.

Body—To be fairly long and strong, with deep brisket, well sprung ribs and clearly defined waist. Hindquarters to be strong with muscular thighs. *Feet*—To be round and well-padded. Legs, short and strong (front forelegs slightly bowed or straight). Dewclaws removed. *Tail*—To be moderately long and set in line with body (not curled over back) and resembling that of a fox.

Coat—Short or medium, of hard texture. Any color except pure white. Other points being equal, preference to be given in following order: Red (sable, fawn or golden); brindle; black and tan; black and white; blue merles. (White markings are considered to enhance the general appearance.)

Height—To be as near as possible to 12 inches at shoulder. *Weight*— Dogs, 18 to 25 pounds; bitches, 15 to 22 pounds.

General Appearance and Expression—To be as foxy as possible; alertness essential, the body to measure about 34 to 36 inches from point of nose to tip of tail. *Faults*—(Examples.) Overshot or undershot mouth; high, peaked occiput; prominent cheeks, low, flat forehead; expressionless eyes, crooked forearms; splayed feet; tail curled over back; silky coat, etc.

Head	15	Tail	5
Eyes	5	Coat	10
Ears	10	Height	10
Neck	5	General appearance and	
Front	10	expression	10
Body	10	Total	100
Feet	10		

Welsh Corgi, Pembroke

General Appearance—Low-set, strong, sturdily built, alert and active, giving an impression of substance and stamina in a small space; outlook bold, expression intelligent and workmanlike. The movement should be free and active, elbows fitting closely to the sides, neither loose nor tied. Forelegs should move well forward, without too much lift, in unison with thrusting action of hind legs.

Head and Skull—Head to be foxy in shape and appearance, with alert and intelligent expression, skull to be fairly wide and flat between the ears; moderate amount of stop. Length of foreface to be in proportion to the skull as three is to five. Muzzle slightly tapering. Nose black. *Eyes*—Well set, medium size, hazel in color and blending with color of coat. *Ears*—Pricked, medium-sized, slightly pointed. A line drawn from the tip of the nose through the eye should, if extended, pass through, or close to, the tip of the ear.

Mouth—Teeth level, or with the inner side of the upper front teeth resting closely on the front of the under ones.

Neck—Fairly long.

Forequarters—Legs short and as straight as possible. "Straight as possible" means straight as soundness and deep broad chest will permit. It does not mean terrier-straight. Ample bone carried right down to the feet. Elbows should fit closely to the sides, neither loose nor tied. Forearm should curve slightly round the chest. *Body*—Of medium length, with well-sprung ribs. Not short-coupled or terrierlike. Level top line. Chest broad and deep, well let down between the forelegs. *Hindquarters*—Strong and flexible, slightly tapering. Legs short. Ample bone carried right down to the feet. Hocks straight when viewed from behind. *Feet*—Oval, the two center toes slightly in advance of two outer toes, pads strong and well arched. Nails short. *Tail*—Short, preferably natural.

Coat—Of medium length and dense; not wiry. *Color*—Self colors in red, sable, fawn, black and tan, or with white markings on legs, chest and neck. Some white on head and foreface is permissible.

Weight and size—Dogs, 20 to 24 pounds; bitches, 18 to 22 pounds. Height, from 10 to 12 inches at shoulder.

Approved February 10, 1952

GROUP IV: TERRIERS

Airedale Terrier

Head—Should be well balanced with little apparent difference between the length of skull and foreface. *Skull* should be long and flat, not too broad between the ears and narrowing very slightly to the eyes. Scalp should be free from wrinkles, stop hardly visible and cheeks level and free from fullness. *Ears* should be V-shaped with carriage rather to the side of the head, not pointing to the eyes, small but not out of proportion to the size of the dog. The topline of the folded ear should be above the level of the skull. *Foreface* should be deep, powerful, strong and muscular. Should be well filled up before the eyes. *Eyes* should be dark, small, not prominent, full of terrier expression, keenness and intelligence. *Lips* should be tight. *Nose* should be black and not too small. *Teeth* should be strong and white, free from discoloration or defect. Bite either level or vise-like. A slightly overlapping or scissors bite is permissible without preference.

Neck—Should be of moderate length and thickness gradually widening towards the shoulders. Skin tight, not loose. *Shoulders and Chest*—Shoulders long and sloping well into the back. Shoulder blades flat. From the front, chest deep but not broad. The depth of the chest should be approximately on a level with the elbows.

Body—Back should be short, strong and level. Ribs well sprung. Loins muscular and of good width. There should be but little space between the last rib and the hip joint. *Hindquarters*—Should be strong and muscular with no droop. *Tail*—The root of the tail should be set well up on the back. It should be carried gaily but not curled over the back. It should be of good strength and substance and of fair length. *Legs*—*Forelegs* should be perfectly straight, with plenty of muscle and bone. *Elbows* should be perpendicular to the body, working free of sides. *Thighs* should be long and powerful with muscular second thigh, stifles well bent, not turned either in or out, hocks well let down parallel with each other when viewed from behind. *Feet* should be small, round and compact with a good depth of pad, well cushioned; the toes moderately arched, not turned either in or out.

Coat—Should be hard, dense and wiry, lying straight and close, covering the dog well over the body and legs. Some of the hardest are crinkling or just slightly waved. At the base of the hard very stiff hair should be a shorter growth of softer hair termed the undercoat. *Color*—The head and ears should be tan, the ears being of a darker shade than the rest. Dark markings on either side of the skull are permissible. The legs up to the thighs and elbows and the under-part of the body and chest are also tan and the tan frequently runs into the shoulder. The sides and upper parts of the body should be black or dark grizzle. A red mixture is often found in the black and is not to be considered objectionable. A small white blaze on the chest is a characteristic of certain strains of the breed.

Size—Dogs should measure approximately 23 inches in height at the shoulder; bitches, slightly less. Both sexes should be sturdy, well muscled and boned.

Movement—Movement or action is the crucial test of conformation. Movement should be free. As seen from the front the forelegs should swing perpendicular from the body free from the sides, the feet the same distance apart as the elbows. As seen from the rear the hind legs should be parallel with each other, neither too close nor too far apart, but so placed as to give a strong well-balanced stance and movement. The toes should not be turned either in or out. Yellow eyes, hound ears, white feet, soft coat, being much over or under the size limit, being undershot or overshot, having poor movement, are faults which should be severely penalized.

SCALE OF POINTS

Head	10	Color	5
Neck, shoulders and chest	10	Size	10
Body	10	Movement	10
Hindquarters and tail	10	General characteristics and	
Legs and feet	10	expression	15
Coat	10	Total	100

Approved July 14, 1959

Australian Terrier

General Appearance—A small, sturdy, rough-coated terrier of spirited action and self-assured manner.

Head—Long, flat-skulled, and full between the eyes, with the stop moderate. The muzzle is no longer than the distance from the eyes to the occiput. Jaws long and powerful, teeth of good size meeting in a scissors bite, although a level bite is acceptable. Nose black. *Ears* set high on the skull and well apart. They are small and pricked, the leather either pointed or slightly rounded and free from long hairs. *Eyes* small, dark, and keen in expression; not prominent. Light-colored and protruding eyes are faulty.

Neck—Inclined to be long, and tapering into sloping shoulders; well furnished with hair which forms a protective ruff.

Body—Low-set and slightly longer from the withers to the root of the tail than from the withers to the ground. *Chest* medium wide, and deep, with ribs well sprung but not round. Topline level. *Tail* set on high and carried erect but not too gay; docked leaving two fifths. *Legs and Feet*—Forelegs straight and slightly feathered to the carpus or so-called knee; they are set well under the body with elbows close and pasterns strong. Hindquarters strong and well muscled but not heavy; legs moderately angulated at stifles and hocks, with hocks well let down. Bone medium in size. Feet are small, clean, and catlike, the toes arched and compact, nicely padded and free from long hair. Nails strong and black.

Coat—Outer coat harsh and straight, and about two and one half inches all over the body. Under coat short and soft. The topknot, which covers only the top of the skull, is of finer texture and lighter color than the body coat.

Color—May be blue-black or silver-black, with rich tan markings on head and legs. The blue-black is bluish at the roots and dark at the tips. In the silver-blacks each hair carries black and silver alternating with black at the tips. The tan is rich and deep, the richer the better. Also, sandy color and clear red are permissible but not as desirable, other things being equal, as the blue and tan. In the sandies, any suggestion of shading or smuttiness is undesirable.

Gait—Straight and true; sprightly, indicating spirit and assurance.

Temperament—That of a hard-bitten terrier, with the aggressiveness of the natural ratter and hedge hunter, but as a companion friendly, affectionate, and biddable.

Size—Shoulder height, about 10 inches. Average weight 12 to 14 pounds.

Approved September 13, 1960

Bedlington Terrier

Skull—Narrow, but deep and rounded, high at the occiput, wedge-shaped, covered with profuse topknot, which should be nearly white, and, when trimmed, should give a Roman nose appearance. *Jaws*—Long and tapering. There must be no "stop" and the line from occiput to nose end straight and unbroken. Well filled up beneath the eye. Close fitting lips, no flews. *Teeth* —Level or pincer-jawed. The teeth should be large and strong. *Nose*—The nostrils must be large and well defined. Blues and blue and tans have black noses; livers, sandies, etc., have brown noses. *Eyes*—Small, bright and well sunk. The ideal eyes have the appearance of being triangular. Blue should have a dark eye; blue and tans have light eyes with amber lights; liver and sandies have a light hazel eye. *Ears*—Moderate sized, filbert shaped; set on low and hanging flat to the cheek. They should be covered with short, fine hair, with a fringe of silky hair at the tip.

Legs and Feet—Muscular and moderate length. The hind legs, by reason of the roach back and arched loin, have the appearance of being longer than the forelegs. The forelegs should be straight, with a moderately wide chest and hare-feet.

Body—Muscular, yet markedly flexible. Flat-ribbed and deep through the brisket, well ribbed up. The chest should be deep and fairly broad. The back should be roached and the loin markedly arched. Light, muscular, galloping quarters, which are also fine and graceful. *Neck*—Long, tapering arched neck, deep at the base. The neck should spring well from the shoulders, which should be flat, and head should be carried high.

Coat—The coat is very distinctive and unlike that of any other terrier in that it should be thick and linty (not wiry), and when in show condition should not exceed one inch in length. It should be brushed on the body and back from the root of the tail toward the head, and should not lie flat against the body. There should be an absence of hair on the ears except at the tip, where the *fringe* should be from one-half to one inch long. The hair on the legs should be slightly longer and straighter than that of the body. The topknot should be highest at the occiput and taper gradually to just in back of the nose. It (the topknot) should be rounded from side to side from an imaginary line drawn from the outer corner of the eye to the top of the ear on one side to a like line on the opposite side.

Tail—Of moderate length, thick at the root, tapering to a point and gracefully curved, slightly feathered, 9 to 11 inches long, scimitar shaped, carried elevated but not over the back.

Color—Blue, blue and tan, liver, liver and tan, sandy, sandy and tan.

Height—About 15 or 16 inches. *Weight*—Dogs, about 24 pounds; bitches, about 22 pounds.

Action—Very distinctive. Rather mincing, light and springy, must gallop like a Greyhound, with the whole body.

General—A graceful, lithe but not shelly, muscular dog, with no sign of coarseness or weakness. The whole head should be pear-shaped or wedge-shaped. The expression in repose is mild and gentle. When roused, the eyes should sparkle and the dog look full of temper and courage.

VALUE OF POINTS

Head	20	Eyes	5
Size	10	Nose	5
Teeth	10	Body	15
Color	5	Coat	10
Legs and feet	10	Tail	5
Ears	5	Total	100

Approved February 17, 1937

Border Terrier

Since the Border Terrier is a working terrier of a size to go to ground and able, within reason, to follow a horse, his conformation should be such that he be ideally built to do his job. No deviations from this ideal conformation should be permitted, which would impair his usefulness in running his quarry to earth and in bolting it therefrom. For this work he must be alert, active and agile, and capable of squeezing through narrow apertures and rapidly traversing any kind of terrain. His head, "like that of an otter," is distinctive, and his temperament ideally exemplifies that of a Terrier. By nature he is good-tempered, affectionate, obedient, and easily trained. In the field he is hard as nails, "game as they come" and driving in attack. It should be the aim of Border Terrier breeders to avoid such over-emphasis of any point in the Standard as might lead to unbalanced exaggeration.

General Appearance—He is an active terrier of medium bone, strongly put together, suggesting endurance and agility, but rather narrow in shoulder, body and quarter. The body is covered with a somewhat broken though close-fitting and intensely wiry jacket. The characteristic "otter" head with its keen eye, combined with a body poise which is "at the alert," gives a look of fearless and implacable determination characteristic of the breed. The proportions should be that the height at the withers is slightly greater than the distance from the withers to the tail, *i.e.* by possibly 1–1½ inches in a 14-pound dog.

Weight—Dogs, 13–15½ pounds, bitches, 11½–14 pounds, are appropriate weights for Border Terriers in hard-working condition.

Head—Similar to that of an otter. Moderately broad and flat in skull with plenty of width between the eyes and between the ears. A slight, moderately broad curve at the stop rather than a pronounced indentation. Cheeks slightly full. *Ears*—Small, V-shaped and of moderate thickness, dark preferred. Not set high on the head but somewhat on the side, and dropping forward close to the cheeks. They should not break above the level of the skull. *Eyes*—Dark hazel and full of fire and intelligence. Moderate in size, neither prominent nor small and beady. *Muzzle*—Short and "well filled." A dark muzzle is characteristic and desirable. A few short whiskers are natural to the breed. *Teeth*—Strong, with a scissors bite, large in proportion to size of dog. *Nose*—Black, and of a good size.

Neck—Clean, muscular and only long enough to give a well-balanced appearance. It should gradually widen into the shoulder. *Shoulders*—Well laid back and of good length, the blades converging to the withers gradually from a brisket not excessively deep or narrow. *Forelegs*—Straight and not too heavy in bone and placed slightly wider than in a Fox Terrier. *Feet*—Small and compact. Toes should point forward and be moderately arched with thick pads.

Body—Deep, fairly narrow and of sufficient length to avoid any suggestion of lack of range and agility. Deep ribs carried well back and not oversprung in view of the desired depth and narrowness of the body. The body should be capable of being spanned by a man's hands behind the shoulders. Back strong but laterally supple, with no suspicion of a dip behind the shoulder. Loin strong and the under line fairly straight. *Tail*—Moderately short, thick at the base, then tapering. Not set on too high. Carried gaily when at the alert, but not over the back. When at ease, a Border may drop his stern.

Hindquarters—Muscular and racy, with thighs long and nicely molded. Stifles well bent and hocks well let down.

Coat—A short and dense undercoat covered with a very wiry and somewhat broken top coat which should lie closely, but it must not show any tendency to curl or wave. With such a coat a Border should be able to be exhibited almost in his natural state, nothing more in the way of trimming being needed than a tidying-up of the head, neck and feet. *Hide*—Very thick and loose fitting.

Movement—Straight and rhythmical before and behind, with good length of stride and flexing of stifle and hock. The dog should respond to his handler with a gait which is free, agile and quick.

Color—Red, grizzle and tan, blue and tan, or wheaten. A small amount of white may be allowed on the chest but white on the feet should be penalized.

SCALE OF POINTS

Head, ears, neck and teeth ..	20	Back and loin	10
Legs and feet	15	Hindquarters	10
Coat and skin	10	Tail	5
Shoulders and chest	10	General appearance	10
Eyes and expression	10	Total	100

Approved March 14, 1950

Bull Terrier

WHITE

The Bull Terrier must be strongly built, muscular, symmetrical and active, with a keen determined and intelligent expression, full of fire but of sweet disposition and amenable to discipline.

The Head should be long, strong and deep right to the end of the muzzle, but not coarse. Full face it should be oval in outline and be filled completely up giving the impression of fullness with a surface devoid of hollows or indentations, *i.e.*, egg shaped. In profile it should curve gently downwards from the top of the skull to the tip of the nose. The forehead should be flat across from ear to ear. The distance from the tip of the nose to the eyes should be perceptibly greater than that from the eyes to the top of the skull. The underjaw should be deep and well defined. *The Lips* should be clean and tight. *The Teeth* should meet in either a level or in a scissors bite. In the scissors bite the upper teeth should fit in front of and closely against the lower teeth, and they should be sound, strong and perfectly regular.

The Ears should be small, thin and placed close together. They should be capable of being held stiffly erect, when they should point upwards. *The Eyes* should be well sunken and as dark as possible, with a piercing glint and they should be small, triangular and obliquely placed; set near together and high up on the dog's head. *The Nose* should be black, with well developed nostrils bent downwards at the tip.

The Neck should be very muscular, long, arched and clean, tapering from the shoulders to the head and it should be free from loose skin. *The Chest* should be broad when viewed from in front, and there should be great depth from withers to brisket, so that the latter is nearer the ground than the belly.

The Body should be well rounded with marked spring of rib, the back should be short and strong. The back ribs deep. Slightly arched over the loin. The shoulders should be strong and muscular but without heaviness. The shoulder blades should be wide and flat and there should be a very pronounced backward slope from the bottom edge of the blade to the top edge. Behind the shoulders there should be no slackness or dip at the withers. The underline from the brisket to the belly should form a graceful upward curve.

The Legs should be big boned but not to the point of coarseness; the forelegs should be of moderate length, perfectly straight, and the dog must stand firmly upon them. The elbows must turn neither in nor out, and the pasterns should be strong and upright. The hind legs should be parallel viewed from behind. The thighs very muscular with hocks well let down. Hind pasterns short and upright. The stifle joint should be well bent with a well developed second thigh. *The Feet* round and compact with well arched toes like a cat.

The Tail should be short, set on low, fine, and ideally should be carried horizontally. It should be thick where it joins the body, and should taper to a fine point.

The Coat should be short, flat, harsh to the touch and with a fine gloss. The dog's skin should fit tightly. *The Color* should be pure white, though markings on the head are permissible. Any markings elsewhere on the coat shall disqualify.

Movement. The dog shall move smoothly, covering the ground with free, easy strides, fore and hind legs should move parallel each to each when viewed from in front or behind. The forelegs reaching out well and the hind legs moving smoothly at the hip and flexing well at the stifle and hock. The dog should move compactly and in one piece but with a typical jaunty air that suggests agility and power.

Faults. Any departure from the foregoing points shall be considered a fault, and the seriousness of the fault shall be in exact proportion to its degree, *i.e.* a very crooked front is a very bad fault; a rather crooked front is a rather bad fault; and a slightly crooked front is a slight fault.

Color—Any markings other than on the head shall disqualify.

COLORED

The Standard for the Colored Variety is the same as for the White except for the sub-head "Color" which reads: *Color.* Any color other than white, or any color with white markings. Preferred color, brindle. A dog which is predominately white shall be disqualified.

Color—Any dog which is predominantly white shall be disqualified.
Approved December 11, 1956

Cairn Terrier

General Appearance—That of an active, game, hardy, small working terrier of the short-legged class; very free in its movements, strongly but not heavily built, standing well forward on its forelegs, deep in the ribs, well coupled with strong hindquarters and presenting a well proportioned build with a medium length of back, having a hard, weather-resisting coat; head shorter and wider than any other terrier and well furnished with hair giving a general foxy expression.

Skull—Broad in proportion to length with a decided stop and well furnished with hair on the top of the head, which may be somewhat softer than the body coat. *Muzzle*—Strong but not too long or heavy. Teeth large —mouth neither overshot or undershot. Nose black. *Eyes*—Set wide apart, rather sunken, with shaggy eyebrows, medium in size, hazel or dark hazel in color, depending on body color, with a keen terrier expression. *Ears*—Small, pointed, well carried erectly, set wide apart on the side of the head. Free from long hairs.

Tail—In proportion to head, well furnished with hair but not feathery. Carried gaily but must not curl over back. Set on at back level.

Body—Well muscled, strong, active body with well-sprung, deep ribs, coupled to strong hindquarters, with a level back of medium length, giving an impression of strength and activity without heaviness. *Shoulders, Legs and Feet*—A sloping shoulder, medium length of leg, good but not too heavy bone; forelegs should not be out at elbows, and be perfectly straight, but forefeet may be slightly turned out. Forefeet larger than hind feet. Legs must be covered with hard hair. Pads should be thick and strong and dog should stand well up on its feet.

Coat—Hard and weather resistant. Must be double-coated with profuse harsh outer coat and short, soft, close furry undercoat. *Color*—May be of any color except white. Dark ears, muzzle and tail tip are desirable.

Ideal Size—Involves the weight, the height at the withers and the length of body. Weight for bitches, 13 pounds, for dogs, 14 pounds. Height at the withers—bitches, 9½ inches, dogs, 10 inches. Length of body from 14¼ to 15 inches from the front of the chest to back of hindquarters. The dog must be of balanced proportions and appear neither leggy or too low to ground; and neither too short or too long in body. Weight and measurements are for matured dogs at two years of age. Older dogs may weigh slightly in excess and growing dogs may be under these weights and measurements.

Condition—Dogs should be shown in good hard flesh, well muscled and neither too fat or thin. Should be in full good coat with plenty of head furnishings, be clean, combed, brushed and tidied up on ears, tail, feet and general outline. Should move freely and easily on a loose lead, should not cringe on being handled, should stand up on their toes and show with marked terrier characteristics.

FAULTS

1. *Skull*—Too narrow in skull. 2. *Muzzle*—Too long and heavy a foreface; mouth overshot or undershot. 3. *Eyes*—Too large, prominent, yellow, and ringed are all objectionable. 4. *Ears*—Too large, round at points, set too close together, set too high on the head; heavily covered with hair. 5. *Legs and Feet*—Too light or too heavy bone. Crooked forelegs or out at elbow. Thin, ferrety feet; feet let down on the heel or too open and spread. Too high or too low on the leg. 6. *Body*—Too short back and compact a body, hampering quickness of movement and turning ability. Too long, weedy and snaky a body, giving an impression of weakness. Tail set on too low. Back not level. 7. *Coat*—Open coats, blousy coats, too short or dead coats, lack of sufficient undercoat, lack of head furnishings, lack of hard hair on the legs. Silkiness or curliness. A slight wave permissible. 8. *Nose*—Flesh or light-colored nose. 9. *Color*—White on chest, feet or other parts of body.

Approved May 10, 1938

Dandie Dinmont Terrier

Head—Strongly made and large, not out of proportion to the dog's size, the muscles showing extraordinary development, more especially the maxillary. *Skull* broad between the ears, getting gradually less towards the eyes, and measuring about the same from the inner corner of the eye to back of skull as it does from ear to ear. The forehead well domed. The head is *covered* with very soft silky hair, which should not be confined to a mere topknot, and the lighter in color and silkier it is the better. The *Cheeks*, starting from the ears proportionately with the skull have a gradual taper towards the muzzle, which is deep and strongly made, and measures about three inches in length, or in proportion to skull as 3 is to 5. The *Muzzle* is covered with hair of a little darker shade than the topknot, and of the same texture as the feather of the forelegs. The top of the muzzle is generally bare for about an inch from the back part of the nose, the bareness coming to a point towards the eye, and being about 1 inch broad at the nose. The nose and inside of *Mouth* black or dark-colored. The *Teeth* very strong, especially the canines, which are of extraordinary size for such a small dog. The canines fit well into each other, so as to give the greatest available holding and punishing power, and the teeth are level in front, the upper ones very slightly overlapping the under ones. (Many of the finest specimens have a "swine mouth," which is very objectionable, but it is not so great an objection as the protrusion of the underjaw.)

Eyes—Set wide apart, large, full, round, bright, expressive of great determination, intelligence and dignity; set low and prominent in front of the head; color, a rich dark hazel. *Ears*—Pendulous, set well back, wide apart, and low on the skull, hanging close to the cheek, with a very slight projection at the base, broad at the junction of the head and tapering almost to a point, the forepart of the ear tapering very little—the tapering being mostly on the back part, the forepart of the ear coming almost straight down from its junction with the head to the tip. They should harmonize in color with the body color. In the case of a Pepper dog they are covered with a soft straight brownish hair (in some cases almost black). In the case of a Mustard dog the hair should be mustard in color, a shade darker than the body, but not black. All should have a thin feather of light hair starting about 2 inches from the tip, and of nearly the same color and texture as the topknot, which gives the ear the appearance of a *distinct point*. The animal is often 1 or 2 years old before the feather is shown. The cartilage and skin of the ear should not be thick, but rather thin. Length of ear from 3 to 4 inches.

Neck—Very muscular, well-developed and strong, showing great power of resistance, being well set into the shoulders.

Body—Long, strong and flexible; ribs well sprung and round, chest well developed and let well down between the forelegs; the back rather low at the shoulder, having a slight downward curve and a corresponding arch over the loins, with a very slight gradual drop from top of loins to root of tail; both sides of backbone well supplied with muscle. *Tail*—Rather short, say from 8 inches to 10 inches, and covered on the upper side with wiry hair of darker color than that of the body, the hair on the under side being lighter in color and not so wiry, with nice feather about 2 inches long, getting shorter as it nears the tip; rather thick at the root, getting thicker for about four inches, then tapering off to a point. It should not be twisted or curled in any way, but should come up with a curve like a scimitar, the tip, when excited, being in a perpendicular line with the root of the tail. It should neither be set on too high nor too low. When not excited it is carried gaily, and a little above the level of the body.

Legs—The forelegs short, with immense muscular development and bone, set wide apart, the chest coming well down between them. The feet well formed *and not flat*, with very strong brown or dark-colored claws. Bandy legs and flat feet are objectionable. The hair on the forelegs and feet of a Pepper dog should be tan, varying according to the body color from a rich tan to a pale fawn; of a Mustard dog they are of a darker shade than its head, which is a creamy white. In both colors there is a nice feather, about two inches long, rather lighter in color than the hair on the forepart of the leg. The hind legs are a little longer than the forelegs, and are set rather wide apart but not spread out in an unnatural manner, while the feet are much smaller; the thighs are well developed, and the hair of the same color and texture as the forelegs, but having no feather or dewclaws; the whole claws should be dark; but the claws of all vary in shade according to the color of the dog's body.

Coat—This is a very important point; the hair should be about 2 inches long; that from skull to root of tail, a mixture of hardish and soft hair, which gives a sort of crisp feel to the hand. The hard should not be wiry; the coat is what is termed piley or penciled. The hair on the under part of the body is lighter in color and softer than on the top. The skin on the belly accords with the color of dog. *Color*—The color is pepper or mustard. The pepper ranges from a dark bluish black to a light silvery gray, the intermediate shades being preferred, the body color coming well down the shoulder and hips, gradually merging into the leg color. The mustards vary from a reddish brown to a pale fawn, the head being a creamy white, the legs and feet of a shade darker than the head. The claws are dark as in other colors. (Nearly all Dandie Dinmont Terriers have some white on the chest, and some have also white claws.)

Size—The height should be from 8 to 11 inches at the top of shoulder.

Length from top of shoulder to root of tail should not be more than twice the dog's height, but preferably 1 or 2 inches less. *Weight*—The preferred weight from 18 to 24 pounds. These weights are for dogs in good working condition.

The relative value of the several points in the standard are apportioned as follows:

SCALE OF POINTS

Head	10	Legs and feet	10
Eyes	10	Coat	15
Ears	10	Color	5
Neck	5	Size and weight	5
Body	20	General appearance	5
Tail	5	Total	100

Approved May 10, 1960

Fox Terrier

SMOOTH

The following shall be the standard of the Fox Terrier amplified in part in order that a more complete description of the Fox Terrier may be presented. The standard itself is set forth in ordinary type, the amplification in italics.

Head—The skull should be flat and moderately narrow, gradually decreasing in width to the eyes. Not much stop should be apparent, but there should be more dip in the profile between the forehead and the top jaw than is seen in the case of a Greyhound. The cheeks must not be full. The ears should be V-shaped and small, of moderate thickness, and drooping forward close to the cheek, not hanging by the side of the head like a Foxhound. *The topline of the folded ear should be well above the level of the skull.* The jaws, upper and lower, should be strong and muscular and of fair punishing strength, but not so as in any way to resemble the Greyhound or modern English Terrier. There should not be much falling away below the eyes. This part of the head should, however, be moderately chiseled out, so as not to go down in a straight slope like a wedge. The nose, toward which the muzzle must gradually taper, should be black. *It should be noticed that although the foreface should gradually taper from eye to muzzle and should tip slightly at its juncture with the forehead, it should not "dish" or fall away quickly below the eyes, where it should be full and well made up, but relieved from "wedginess" by a little delicate chiseling.* The eyes and the rims should be dark in color, *moderately* small and rather deep-set, full of fire, life and intelligence and as nearly as possible circular in shape. *Anything approaching a yellow eye is most objectionable.* The teeth should be as nearly as possible together, *i.e. the points* of the upper (*incisors*) teeth on the outside of or *slightly overlapping* the lower teeth. *There should be apparent little difference in length between the skull and foreface of a well-balanced head.*

Neck—Should be clean and muscular, without throatiness, of fair length, and gradually widening to the shoulders. *Shoulders*—Should be long and sloping, well laid back, fine at the points, and clearly cut at the withers. *Chest* —Deep and not broad. *Back*—Should be short, straight (*i.e.* level), and strong, with no appearance of slackness. *Brisket should be deep, yet not exaggerated. Loin*—Should be very powerful, *muscular* and very slightly arched. The foreribs should be moderately arched, the back ribs deep *and well sprung,* and the dog should be well ribbed up.

Hindquarters—Should be strong and muscular, quite free from droop or crouch; the thighs long and powerful; *stifles well curved and turned neither in nor out;* hocks *well bent* and near the ground *should be perfectly upright and parallel each with the other when viewed from behind,* the dog standing well up on them like a Foxhound, and not straight in the stifle. *The worst possible form of hindquarters consists of a short second thigh and a straight stifle. Stern*—Should be set on rather high and carried gaily, but not over the back or curled. It should be of good strength, anything approaching a "pipe-stopper" tail being especially objectionable. *Legs*—The forelegs viewed from any direction must be straight with bone strong right down to the feet, showing little or no appearance of ankle in front, and being short and straight in pasterns. Both forelegs and hind legs should be carried straight forward in traveling, the stifles not turning outward. The elbows should hang perpendicularly to the body, working free of the sides. *Feet*—Should be round, compact and not large; the soles hard and tough; the toes moderately arched and turned neither in nor out.

Coat—Should be smooth, flat, but hard, dense and abundant. The belly and under side of the thighs should not be bare. *Color*—White should predominate; brindle, red, or liver markings are objectionable. Otherwise this point is of little or no importance.

Symmetry, Size and Character—The dog must present a generally gay, lively and active appearance; bone and strength in a small compass are essentials, but this must not be taken to mean that a Fox Terrier should be cloddy, or in any way coarse—speed and endurance must be looked to as well as power, and the symmetry of the Foxhound taken as a model. The terrier, like the hound, must on no account be leggy, nor must he be too short in the leg. He should stand like a cleverly made hunter, covering a lot of ground, yet with a short back, as before stated. He will then attain the highest degree of propelling power, together with the greatest length of stride that is compatible with the length of his body. Weight is not a certain criterion of a terrier's fitness for his work—general shape, size and contour are the main points; and if a dog can gallop and stay, and follow his fox up a drain, it matters little what his weight is to a pound or so. *According to present-day requirements, a full-sized, well-balanced dog should not exceed 15½ inches at the withers, the bitch being proportionately lower—nor should the length of back from withers to root of tail exceed 12 inches, while, to maintain the relative proportions, the head should not exceed 7¼ inches or be less than 7 inches. A dog with these measurements should scale 18 pounds in show condition—a bitch weighing some 2 pounds less—with a margin of 1 pound either way.*

Balance—This may be defined as the correct proportions of a certain point, or points, when considered in relation to a certain other point or points. It is the keystone of the terrier's anatomy. The chief points for consideration are the relative proportions of skull and foreface; head and back; height at withers and length of body from shoulder-point to buttock —the ideal of proportion being reached when the last two measurements are the same. It should be added that, although the head measurements can be taken with absolute accuracy, the height at withers and length of back and coat are approximate, and are inserted for the information of breeders and exhibitors rather than as a hard and fast rule.

Movement—Movement, or action, is the crucial test of conformation. The terrier's legs should be carried straight forward while traveling, the forelegs hanging perpendicular and swinging parallel with the sides, like the pendulum of a clock. The principal propulsive power is furnished by the hind legs, perfection of action being found in the terrier possessing long thighs and muscular second thighs well bent at the stifles, which admit of a strong forward thrust or "snatch" of the hocks. When approaching, the forelegs should form a continuation of the straight line of the front, the feet being the same distance apart at the elbows. When stationary, it is often difficult to determine whether a dog is slightly out at shoulder, but, directly he moves, the defect—if it exists—becomes more apparent, the forefeet having a tendency to cross, "weave," or "dish." When, on the contrary, the dog is tied at the shoulder, the tendency of the feet is to move wider apart, with a sort of paddling action. When the hocks are turned in—cowhock— the stifles and feet are turned outwards, resulting in a serious loss of propulsive power. When the hocks are turned outwards the tendency of the hind feet is to cross, resulting in an ungainly waddle.

N.B.—Old scars or injuries, the result of work or accident, should not be allowed to prejudice a terrier's chance in the show ring, unless they interfere with its movement or with its utility for work or stud.

WIRE

This variety of the breed should resemble the smooth sort in every respect except the coat, which should be broken. The harder and more wiry the texture of the coat is, the better. On no account should the dog look or feel woolly; and there should be no silky hair about the poll or elsewhere. The coat should not be too long, so as to give the dog a shaggy appearance, but, at the same time, it should show a marked and distinct difference all over from the smooth species.

SCALE OF POINTS

Head and ears	15	Legs and feet	15
Neck	5	Coat	15
Shoulders and chest	10	Symmetry, size and	
Back and loin	10	character	10
Hindquarters	15	Total	100
Stern	5		

DISQUALIFICATIONS

Nose—White, cherry or spotted to a considerable extent with either of these colors. Ears—Prick, tulip or rose. Mouth—Much undershot, or much overshot.

Irish Terrier

Head—Long, but in nice proportion to the rest of the body; the skull flat, rather narrow between the ears, and narrowing slightly towards the eyes; free from wrinkle, with the stop hardly noticeable except in profile. The jaws must be strong and muscular, but not too full in the cheek, and of good punishing length. The foreface must not fall away appreciably between or below the eyes; instead, the modeling should be delicate and in contradistinction, for example, to the fullness of foreface of the Greyhound. An exaggerated foreface, which is out of proportion to the length of the skull from the occiput to the stop, disturbs the proper balance of the head, and is not desirable. Also, the head of exaggerated length usually accompanies oversize or disproportionate length of body, or both, and such conformation is not typical. On the other hand, the foreface should not be noticeably shorter than is the skull from occiput to stop. Excessive muscular development of the cheeks, or bony development of the temples, conditions which are described by the fancier as "cheeky," or "strong in head," or "thick in skull," are objectionable. The "bumpy" or "alligator" head, sometimes described as the "taneous" head, in which the skull presents two lumps of bony structure with or without indentations above the eyes, is unsightly and to be faulted. The hair on the upper and lower jaw should be similar in quality and texture to that on the body, and only of sufficient length to present an appearance of additional strength and finish to the foreface. The profuse, goatlike beard is unsightly and undesirable, and almost invariably it betokens the objectionable linty and silken hair in the coat.

Teeth—Should be strong and even, white and sound; and neither overshot nor undershot. *Lips*—Should be close and well-fitting, almost black in color.

Nose—Must be black. *Eyes*—Dark hazel in color; small, not prominent; full of life, fire and intelligence. The light or yellow eye is most objectionable.

Ears—Small and V-shaped; of moderate thickness; set well on the head, and dropping forward closely to the cheek. The ear must be free of fringe, and the hair much shorter and somewhat darker in color than on the body. A "dead" ear, houndlike in appearance, must be severely penalized. It is not characteristic of the Irish Terrier. An ear which is too slightly erect is undesirable.

Neck—Should be of fair length and gradually widening towards the shoulders; well and proudly carried, and free from throatiness. Generally there is a slight frill in the hair at each side of the neck, extending almost to the corner of the ear. *Shoulders and Chest*—Shoulders must be fine, long, and sloping well into the back. The chest should be deep and muscular, but neither full nor wide.

Back and Loin—The body should be moderately long—neither too long nor too short. The short back, so coveted and so appealing in the Fox Terrier, is *not* characteristic of the Irish Terrier. It is objectionable. The back must be symmetrical, strong and straight, and free from an appearance of slackness or "dip" behind the shoulders. The loin strong and muscular, and slightly arched. The ribs fairly sprung, deep rather than round, with a well-ribbed back. The bitch may be slightly longer in appearance than the dog. *Hindquarters*—Should be strong and muscular; powerful thighs; hocks near the ground; stifles moderately bent. *Stern*—Should be docked, and set on rather high, but not curled. It should be of good strength and substance; of fair length and well covered with harsh, rough hair, and free from fringe or feather. The three-quarters dock is about right.

Feet and Legs—The feet should be strong, tolerably round, and moderately small; toes arched and turned neither out nor in, with black toenails. The pads should be deep, not hard, but with a pleasing velvety quality, and perfectly sound; they must be entirely free from cracks or horny excrescences. Corny feet, so-called, are to be regarded as an abominable blemish; as a taint which must be shunned. Cracked pads frequently accompany corny growths, and these conditions are more pronounced in hot and dry weather. In damp weather and in winter such pads may improve temporarily, but these imperfections inevitably reappear and the result is unsound feet, a deplorable fault which must be heavily penalized. There seems to be no permanent cure for this condition, and even if a temporary cure were possible, the disease is seldom, if ever, eradicated, and undoubtedly it is transmitted in breeding. The one sure way to avoid corny and otherwise unsound feet is to avoid breeding from dogs or bitches which are not entirely free from this taint. Legs, moderately long, well set from the shoulders, perfectly straight, with plenty of bone and muscle; the elbows working clear of the sides; pastern short, straight, and hardly noticeable. Both forelegs and hind legs should move straight forward when traveling; the stifles should not turn outward. Cowhocks—that is, where the hocks are turned in, and the stifles and feet turned out, are intolerable. The legs should be free from feather, and covered, like the head, with hair of similar texture to that on the body, but not so long.

Coat—Should be dense and wiry in texture, rich in quality, having a broken appearance, but still lying fairly close to the body, the hairs growing so closely and strongly together that when parted with the fingers the skin is hardly visible; free of softness or silkiness, and not so long as to alter the outline of the body, particularly in the hindquarters. At the base of the stiff outer coat there should be a growth of finer and softer hair, differing in color, termed the undercoat. Single coats, which are without any undercoat, and wavy coats, are undesirable; the curly coat is most objectionable. On the sides of the body the coat is never as harsh as on the back and the quarters, but it should be plentiful and of good texture. *Color*—Should be whole-colored; the bright red, red wheaten, or golden red colors are preferable. A small patch of white on the chest, frequently encountered in all whole-colored breeds, is permissible but not desirable. White on any other part of the body is most objectionable.

Size and Symmetry—The most desirable weight in show condition is 27 pounds for the dog and 25 pounds for the bitch. The height at the shoulder should be approximately 18 inches. This terrier must be active, lithe and wiry in movement, with great animation; sturdy and strong in substance and bone structure, but at the same time free from clumsiness, for speed, power and endurance are most essential. The Irish Terrier must be neither "cobby" nor "cloddy," but should be built on lines of speed, with a graceful, racing outline.

The weights herein mentioned are ideal and serve as a guide to both breeder and judge. In the show ring, however, the informed judge readily identifies the oversized or undersized Irish Terrier by its conformation and general appearance. The weights named should be regarded as limit weights, as a rule, but it must be considered that a comparatively small, heavily built and "cloddy" dog—which is most undesirable, and not at all typical—may easily be of standard weight, or over it; whereas another Terrier which is long in leg, lacking in substance and built somewhat upon the lines of a Whippet—also undesirable and not at all typical—may be of the exact weight, or under it; therefore, although the standard weights must be borne well in mind, weight is not the last word in judgment. It is of the greatest importance to select, in so far as possible, terriers of moderate and generally accepted size, possessing the other various necessary characteristics.

Temperament—The Irish Terrier is game and asks no quarter. He is of good temper, most affectionate, and absolutely loyal to mankind. Tender and forbearing with those he loves, this rugged, stout-hearted terrier will guard his master, his mistress, children in his charge, or their possessions, with unflinching courage and with utter contempt of danger or hurt. His life is one continuous and eager offering of loyal and faithful companionship, and devoted, loving service. He is ever on guard, and stands between his house and all that threatens.

POSITIVE POINTS

Head, ears and expression ...	20	Hindquarters and stern	10
Legs and feet	15	Coat	15
Neck	5	Color	10
Shoulders and chest	10	Size and symmetry	10
Back and loin	5	Total	100

NEGATIVE POINTS

White nails, toes and feet,		Coat shaggy, curly or soft	10
minus	10	Uneven in color	5
Much white on chest	10	Total	50
Dark shadings on face	5		
Mouth undershot or			
cankered	10		

DISQUALIFICATIONS

Nose—Any other color than black. Mouth—Much undershot or overshot. Ears—Cropped ears. Color—Any other color than red, golden red, or red wheaten. A small patch of white on the chest is permissible; otherwise parti-colored coats disqualify.

Approved July, 1929

Kerry Blue Terrier

Head—Long, but not exaggerated and in good proportion to the rest of the body. Well balanced, with little apparent difference between the length of the skull and foreface. (20 points) *Skull*—Flat, with very slight stop, of but moderate breadth between the ears, and narrowing very slightly to the eyes. *Cheeks*—Clean and level, free from bumpiness. *Ears*—V-shaped, small but not out of proportion to the size of the dog, of moderate thickness, carried forward close to the cheeks with the top of the folded ear slightly above the level of the skull. A "dead" ear houndlike in appearance is very undesirable. *Foreface*—Jaws deep, strong and muscular. Foreface full and well made up, not falling away appreciably below the eyes but moderately chiseled out to relieve the foreface from wedginess. *Nose*—Black, nostrils large and wide. *Teeth*—Strong, white and either level or with the upper (incisors) teeth slightly overlapping the lower teeth. An undershot mouth should be strictly penalized. *Eyes*—Dark, small, not prominent, well placed and with a keen terrier expression. Anything approaching a yellow eye is very undesirable.

Neck—Clean and moderately long, gradually widening to the shoulders upon which it should be well set and carried proudly. (5 points) *Shoulders and Chest*—Shoulders fine, long and sloping, well laid back and well knit. Chest deep and of but moderate breadth. (10 points) *Legs and Feet*—Legs moderately long with plenty of bone and muscle. The forelegs should be straight from both front and side view, with the elbows hanging perpendicularly to the body and working clear of the sides in movement, the pasterns short, straight and hardly noticeable. Both forelegs and hind legs should move straight forward when traveling, the stifles turning neither in nor out. (10 points) Feet should be strong, compact, fairly round and moderately small, with good depth of pad free from cracks, the toes arched, turned neither in nor out, with black toenails.

Body—Back short, strong and straight (*i.e.* level), with no appearance of slackness. Loin short and powerful with a slight tuck-up, the ribs fairly well sprung, deep rather than round. (10 points) *Hindquarters and Stern*—Hindquarters strong and muscular with full freedom of action, free from droop or crouch, the thighs long and powerful, stifles well bent and turned neither in nor out, hocks near the ground and, when viewed from behind, upright and parallel with each other, the dog standing well up on them. Tail should be set on high, of moderate length and carried gaily erect, the straighter the tail the better. (10 points)

Color—The correct mature color is any shade of blue gray or gray blue from deep slate to light blue gray, of a fairly uniform color throughout except that distinctly darker to black parts may appear on the muzzle, head, ears, tail and feet. (10 points) Kerry color, in its process of "clearing" from an apparent black at birth to the mature gray blue or blue gray, passes through one or more transitions—involving a very dark blue (darker than deep slate), shades or tinges of brown, and mixtures of these, together with a progressive infiltration of the correct mature color. Up to 18 months such deviations from the correct mature color are permissible without preference and without regard for uniformity. Thereafter, deviation from it to any significant extent must be severely penalized. Solid black is never permissible in the show ring. Up to 18 months any doubt as to whether a dog is black or a very dark blue should be resolved in favor of the dog, particularly in the case of a puppy. Black on the muzzle, head, ears, tail and feet is permissible at any age. *Coat*—Soft, dense and wavy. A harsh, wire or bristle coat should be severely penalized. In show trim the body should be well covered but tidy, with the head (except for the whiskers) and the ears and cheeks clear. (15 points)

General Conformation and Character—The typical Kerry Blue Terrier should be upstanding, well knit and in good balance, showing a well developed and muscular body with definite Terrier style and character throughout. A low-slung Kerry is not typical. (10 points)

Height—The ideal Kerry should be 18½ inches at the withers for a dog, slightly less for a bitch. In judging Kerries, a height of 18–19½ inches for a dog, and 17½–19 inches for a bitch should be given primary preference. Only where the comparative superiority of a specimen outside of the ranges noted clearly justifies it, should greater latitude be taken. In no case should it extend to a dog over 20 inches or under 17½ inches, or to a bitch over 19½ inches or under 17 inches. The minimum limits do not apply to puppies. *Weight*—The most desirable weight for a fully developed dog is from 33–40 pounds, bitches weighing proportionately less.

DISQUALIFICATIONS

Solid black. Dewclaws on hind legs.

Approved September 15, 1959

Lakeland Terrier

General Appearance—The Lakeland Terrier is a small, workman-like dog of square, sturdy build and gay, friendly, self-confident demeanor. He stands on his toes as if ready to go, and he moves, lithe and graceful, with a straight-ahead, free stride of good length. His head is rectangular in contour, ears V-shaped, and wiry coat finished off with fairly long furnishings on muzzle and legs.

Head—Well balanced, rectangular, the length of skull equaling the length of the muzzle when measured from occiput to stop, and from stop to nose-tip. *The skull* is flat on top and moderately broad, the cheeks almost straight-sided, and the stop barely perceptible. *The muzzle* is broad with straight nose bridge and good fill-in beneath the eyes. *The nose* is black, except that liver-colored noses shall be permissible on liver-coated dogs. *Jaws* are powerful. *The teeth*, which are comparatively large, may meet in either a level, edge-to-edge bite, or a slightly overlapping scissors bite. Specimens with teeth overshot or undershot are to be disqualified. *The ears* are small, V-shaped, their fold just above the top of the skull, the inner edge close to the cheeks, and the flap pointed down. *The eyes,* moderately small and somewhat oval in outline, are set squarely in the skull, fairly wide apart. Their normally dark color may be a warm brown or black. *The expression* depends upon the dog's mood of the moment; although typically alert, it may be intense and determined, or gay and even impish.

Neck—Reachy and of good length; refined but strong; clean at the throat, slightly arched, and widening gradually into the shoulders. The withers, that point at the back of the neck where neck and body meet, are noticeably higher than the level of the back.

Body—In over-all length-to-height proportion, the dog is approximately square. The moderately narrow *chest* is deep; it extends to elbows which are held close to the body. Shoulder blades are sloping, that is, well laid back, their musculature lean and almost flat in outline. *The ribs* are well sprung and moderately rounded. *The back* is short and level in topline. *Loins* are taut and short, although they may be a trifle longer in bitches than in dogs. *Quarters* are strong, broad, and muscular.

Legs and Feet—Forelegs are strongly boned, clean, and absolutely straight as viewed from the front or side, and devoid of appreciable bend at the pasterns. *Hind legs* too are strong and sturdy, the second thighs long and nicely angulated at the stifles and the hocks. *Hocks* are well let down, with the bone from hock to toes straight and parallel to each other. The small *feet* are round, the toes compact and well padded, the nails strong. Dewclaws, if any, are to be removed.

Tail—Set high on the body, the tail is customarily docked so that when the dog is set up in show position, the tip of the docked tail is on an approximate level with the skull. In carriage it is gay or upright, although a slight curve in the direction of the head is considered desirable. The tail curled over the back is faulty.

Coat and Color—Two-ply or double, the outer coat is hard and wiry in texture, the undercoat soft. Furnishings on muzzle and legs are plentiful as opposed to profuse. *The color* may be blue, black, liver, black and tan, blue and tan, red, red grizzle, grizzle and tan, or wheaten. Tan, as desirable in the Lakeland Terrier, is a light wheaten or straw color, with rich red or mahogany tan to be penalized. Otherwise, colors, as specified, are equally acceptable. Dark-saddled specimens (whether black grizzle or blue) are nearly solid black at birth, with tan points on muzzle and feet. The black recedes and usually turns grayish or grizzle at maturity, while the tan also lightens.

Size—The ideal *height* of the mature dog is 14½ inches from the withers to the ground, with up to a ½-inch deviation either way permissible. Bitches may measure as much as one inch less than dogs. The *weight* of the well-balanced, mature specimen in hard, show condition, averages approximately 17 pounds, those of other heights proportionately more or less.

Size is to be considered of lesser importance than other qualities, that is, when judging dogs of equal merit, the one nearest the ideal size is to be preferred. Symmetry and proportion, however, are paramount in the appraisal, since all qualities together must be considered in visualizing the ideal.

Movement—Straight and free, with good length of stride. Paddling, moving close, and toeing-in are faulty.

Temperament—The typical Lakeland Terrier is bold, gay, and friendly, with a self-confident, cock-of-the-walk attitude. Shyness, especially shy-sharpness, in the mature specimen is to be heavily penalized.

SCALE OF POINTS

Head	15	Legs and feet	10
Eyes, ears, expression	15	Size and symmetry	10
Neck	5	Movement	10
Body	10	Temperament	10
Coat	15	Total	100

DISQUALIFICATION

The front teeth overshot or undershot.

Approved May 14, 1963

Manchester Terrier

Head—Long, narrow, tight-skinned, almost flat, with a slight indentation up the forehead; slightly wedge-shaped, tapering to the nose, with no visible cheek muscles, and well filled up under the eyes; tight-lipped jaws, level in mouth, and functionally level teeth, or the incisors of the upper jaw may make a close, slightly overlapping contact with the incisors of the lower jaw. *Eyes*—Small, bright, sparkling and as near black as possible; set moderately close together; oblong in shape, slanting upwards on the outside; they should neither protrude nor sink in the skull. *Nose*—Black.

Ears (Toy Variety)—Of moderate size; set well up on the skull and rather close together; thin, moderately narrow at base; with pointed tips; naturally erect carriage. Wide, flaring, blunt-tipped or "bell" ears are a serious fault; cropped or cut ears shall disqualify.

Ears (Standard Variety)—Erect, or button, small and thin; smaller at the root and set as close together as possible at the top of the head. If cropped, to a point, long and carried erect.

Neck and Shoulders—The neck should be a moderate length, slim and graceful; gradually becoming larger as it approaches, and blend smoothly with the sloping shoulders; free from throatiness; slightly arched from the occiput.

Chest—Narrow between the legs; deep in the brisket.

Body—Moderately short, with robust loins; ribs well sprung out behind the shoulders; back slightly arched at the loin, and falling again to the tail to the same height as the shoulder. *Legs*—Forelegs straight, of proportionate length, and well under body. Hind legs should not turn in or out as viewed from the rear; carried back; hocks well let down. *Feet*—Compact, well arched, with jet black nails; the two middle toes in the front feet rather longer than the others; the hind feet shaped like those of a cat. *Tail*— Moderately short, and set on where the arch of the back ends; thick where it joins the body, tapering to a point, not carried higher than the back.

Coat—Smooth, short, thick, dense, close and glossy; not soft.

Color—Jet black and rich mahogany tan, which should not run or blend into each other but abruptly forming clear, well-defined lines of color division. A small tan spot over each eye; a very small tan spot on each cheek; the lips of the upper and lower jaws should be tanned, extending under the throat, ending in the shape of the letter V; the inside of the ears partly tanned. Tan spots, called rosettes, on each side of the chest above the front legs, more pronounced in puppies than in adults. There should be a black "thumb mark" patch on the front of each foreleg between the pastern and the knee. There should be a distinct black "pencil mark" line running lengthwise on the top of each toe on all four feet. The remainder of the forelegs to be tan to the knee. Tan on the hind legs should continue from the penciling on the feet up the inside of the legs to a little below the stifle joint; the outside of the hind legs to be black. There should be tan under the tail, and on the vent, but only of such size as to be covered by the tail. White in any part of the coat is a serious fault, and shall disqualify whenever the white shall form a patch or stripe measuring as much as one-half inch in its longest dimension.

Weight (Toy Variety)—Not exceeding 12 pounds. It is suggested that clubs consider dividing the American-bred and open classes by weight as follows: 7 pounds and under, over 7 pounds and not exceeding 12 pounds.

Weight (Standard Variety)—Over 12 pounds and not exceeding 22 pounds. Dogs weighing over 22 pounds shall be disqualified. It is suggested that clubs consider dividing the American-bred and open classes by weight as follows: over 12 pounds and not exceeding 16 pounds, over 16 pounds and not exceeding 22 pounds.

DISQUALIFICATIONS

Color—*White in any part of the coat, forming a patch or stripe measuring as much as ½ inch in its longest dimension.*
   Weight (Standard Variety)—*Over 22 pounds.*
   Ears (Toy Variety)—*Cropped or cut ears.*

Approved June 12, 1962

Norwich Terrier

Head—Skull wide, slightly rounded with good width between the ears. Muzzle strong but not long or heavy, with slightly "foxy" appearance. Length about one-third less than the measurement from the occiput to the bottom of the stop, which should be well defined. *Faults*—A long narrow head; over square muzzle; highly rounded dome. *Ears*—Prick or drop. If pricked, small, pointed, erect and set well apart. If dropped, neat, small, with break just above the skull line, front edge close to cheek, and not falling lower than the outer corner of the eye. *Faults*—Oversize; poor carriage. *Eyes*—Very bright, dark and keen. Full of expression. *Faults*—Light or protruding eyes. *Jaw*—Clean, strong, tight lipped, with strong, large, closely-fitting teeth; scissors bite. *Faults*—A mouth badly over- or undershot. *Neck*—Short and strong, well set on clean shoulders.

Body—Moderately short, compact and deep with level topline, ribs well sprung. *Faults*—Long weak back, loaded shoulders. *Legs*—Short and powerful and as straight as is consistent with the short legs for which we aim. Sound bone, round feet, thick pads. *Faults*—Out at elbow, badly bowed, knuckled over. Too light in bone. *Quarters*—Strong, rounded, with great powers of propulsion. *Faults*—Cowhocks. *Tail*—Medium docked, carriage not excessively gay.

Color—Red (including red-wheaten), black and tan or grizzle. White markings on the chest, though allowable, are not desirable. *Faults*—White markings elsewhere or to any great extent on the chest. *Coat*—As hard and wiry as possible, lying close to the body, with a definite undercoat. Top coat absolutely straight; in full coat longer and rougher forming almost a mane on shoulders and neck. Hair on head, ears and muzzle, except for slight eyebrows and slight whiskers, is absolutely short and smooth. These dogs should be shown with as nearly a natural coat as possible. A minimum amount of tidying is permissible but excessive trimming, shaping and clipping shall be heavily penalized by the judge. *Faults*—Silky or curly coat.

Weight—Ideal, 11 to 12 pounds.

Height—Ideal, 10 inches at the withers.

General Appearance—A small, low rugged terrier, tremendously active. A perfect demon yet not quarrelsome and of a lovable disposition, and a very hardy constitution. Honorable scars from fair wear and tear shall not count against.

DISQUALIFICATION

Cropped ears shall disqualify.

Approved May 9, 1961

Schnauzer, Miniature

General Appearance—The Miniature Schnauzer is a robust, active dog of terrier type, resembling his larger cousin, the Standard Schnauzer, in general appearance, and of an alert, active disposition. He is sturdily built, nearly square in proportion of body length to height, with plenty of bone, and without any suggestion of toyishness.

Head—Strong and rectangular, its width diminishing slightly from ears to eyes, and again to the tip of the nose. The forehead is unwrinkled. The topskull is flat and fairly long. The foreface is parallel to the topskull, with a slight stop, and is at least as long as the topskull. The muzzle is strong in proportion to the skull; it ends in a moderately blunt manner, with thick whiskers which accentuate the rectangular shape of the head. *Teeth*—The teeth meet in a scissors bite. That is, the upper front teeth overlap the lower front teeth in such a manner that the inner surface of the upper incisors barely touches the outer surface of the lower incisors when the mouth is closed. *Eyes*—Small, dark brown and deep-set. They are oval in appearance and keen in expression. *Ears*—When cropped the ears are identical in shape and length, with pointed tips. They are in balance with the head and not exaggerated in length. They are set high on the skull and carried perpendicularly at the inner edges, with as little bell as possible along the outer edges. When uncropped, the ears are small and V-shaped, folding close to the skull.

Neck—Strong and well arched, blending into the shoulders, and with the skin fitting tightly at the throat.

Body—Short and deep, with the brisket extending at least to the elbows. Ribs are well sprung and deep, extending well back to a short loin. The underbody does not present a tucked-up appearance at the flank. The topline is straight; it declines slightly from the withers to the base of the tail. The over-all length from chest to stern bone equals the height at the withers.

Forequarters—The forequarters have flat, somewhat sloping shoulders and high withers. Forelegs are straight and parallel when viewed from all sides. They have strong pasterns and good bone. They are separated by a fairly deep brisket which precludes a pinched front. The elbows are close, and the ribs spread gradually from the first rib so as to allow space for the elbows to move close to the body. *Hindquarters*—The hindquarters have strong-muscled, slanting thighs: they are well bent at the stifles and straight from hock to so-called heel. There is sufficient angulation so that, in stance, the hocks extend beyond the tail. The hindquarters never appear overbuilt or higher than the shoulders. *Feet*—Short and round (cat-feet) with thick, black pads. The toes are arched and compact.

Action—The trot is the gait at which movement is judged. The dog must gait in a straight line. Coming on, the forelegs are parallel, with the elbows close to the body. The feet turn neither inward nor outward. Going away, the hind legs are parallel from the hocks down, and travel wide. Viewed from the side, the forelegs have a good reach, while the hind legs have a strong drive with good pick-up of hocks.

Tail—Set high and carried erect. It is docked only long enough to be clearly visible over the topline of the body when the dog is in proper length of coat.

Coat—Double, with a hard, wiry outer coat and a close undercoat. The body coat should be plucked. When in show condition, the proper length is not less than three-quarters of an inch except on neck, ears and skull. Furnishings are fairly thick but not silky.

Size—From 12 to 14 inches. Ideal size 13½ inches. (*See disqualifications.*)

Color—The recognized colors are salt and pepper, black and silver, and solid black. The typical color is salt and pepper in shades of gray; tan shading is permissible. The salt and pepper mixture fades out to light gray or silver white in the eyebrows, whiskers, cheeks, under throat, across chest, under tail, leg furnishings under body, and inside legs. The light under-body hair is not to rise higher on the sides of the body than the front elbows.

The black and silvers follow the same pattern as the salt and peppers. The entire salt-and-pepper section must be black.

Black is the only solid color allowed. It must be a true black with no gray hairs and no brown tinge except where the whiskers may have become discolored. A small white spot on the chest is permitted.

FAULTS

Type—Toyishness, raciness, or coarseness. *Structure*—Head coarse and cheeky. Chest too broad or shallow in brisket. Tail set low. Sway or roach back. Bowed or cowhocked hindquarters. Loose elbows. *Action*—Sidegaiting. Paddling in front, or high hackney knee action. Weak hind action. *Coat*—Too soft or too smooth and slick in appearance. *Temperament*—Shyness or viciousness. *Bite*—Undershot or overshot jaw. Level bite. *Eyes*—Light and/or large and prominent in appearance.

DISQUALIFICATIONS

Dogs or bitches under 12 inches or over 14 inches. Color solid white or white patches on the body.

Approved May 13, 1958

Scottish Terrier

Skull (5 points)—Long, of medium width, slightly domed and covered with short, hard hair. It should not be quite flat, as there should be a slight stop or drop between the eyes. *Muzzle* (5 points)—In proportion to the length of skull, with not too much taper toward the nose. Nose should be black and of good size. The jaws should be level and square. The nose projects somewhat over the mouth, giving the impression that the upper jaw is longer than the lower. The teeth should be evenly placed, having a scissors or level bite, with the former being preferable. *Eyes* (5 points)—Set wide apart, small and of almond shape, not round. Color to be dark brown or nearly black. To be bright, piercing and set well under the brow. *Ears* (10 points)—Small, prick, set well up on the skull, rather pointed but not cut. The hair on them should be short and velvety.

Neck (5 points)—Moderately short, thick and muscular, strongly set on sloping shoulders, but not so short as to appear clumsy. *Chest* (5 points)— Broad and very deep, well let down between the forelegs.

Body (15 points)—Moderately short and well ribbed up with strong loin, deep flanks and very muscular hindquarters. *Legs and Feet* (10 points)— Both forelegs and hind legs should be short and very heavy in bone in proportion to the size of the dog. Forelegs straight or slightly bent with elbows close to the body. Scottish Terriers should not be out at the elbows. Stifles should be well bent and legs straight from hock to heel. Thighs very muscular. Feet round and thick with strong nails, forefeet larger than the hind feet. *Note:* The gait of the Scottish Terrier is peculiarly its own and is very characteristic of the breed. It is not the square trot or walk that is desirable in the long-legged breeds. The forelegs do not move in exact parallel planes —rather in reaching out incline slightly inward. This is due to the shortness of leg and width of chest. The action of the rear legs should be square and true and at the trot both the hocks and stifles should be flexed with a vigorous motion. *Tail* (2½ points)—Never cut and about 7 inches long, carried with a slight curve but not over the back.

Coat (15 points)—Rather short, about 2 inches, dense undercoat with outer coat intensely hard and wiry.

Size and Weight (10 points)—Equal consideration must be given to height, length of back and weight. Height at shoulder for either sex should be about 10 inches. Generally, a well-balanced Scottish Terrier dog of correct size should weigh from 19 to 22 pounds and a bitch, from 18 to 21 pounds. The principal objective must be symmetry and balance.

Color (2½ points)—Steel or iron gray, brindled or grizzled, black, sandy or wheaten. White markings are objectionable and can be allowed only on the chest and that to a slight extent only.

General Appearance (10 points)—The face should wear a keen, sharp and active expression. Both head and tail should be carried well up. The dog should look very compact, well muscled and powerful, giving the impression of immense power in a small size.

Penalties: Soft coat, round or very light eye, overshot or undershot jaw, obviously oversize or undersize, shyness, timidity or failure to show with head and tail up are faults to be penalized. No judge should put to Winners or Best of Breed any Scottish Terrier not showing real terrier character in the ring.

SCALE OF POINTS

Skull	5	Legs and feet	10
Muzzle	5	Tail	2½
Eyes	5	Coat	15
Ears	10	Size	10
Neck	5	Color	2½
Chest	5	General appearance	10
Body	15	Total	100

Approved June 10, 1947

Sealyham Terrier

The Sealyham should be the embodiment of power and determination, ever keen and alert, of extraordinary substance, yet free from clumsiness.

Height—At withers about 10½ inches. *Weight:* 21 pounds for dogs, and 20 pounds for bitches. It should be borne in mind that size is more important than weight.

Head—Long, broad and powerful, without coarseness. It should, however, be in perfect balance with the body, joining neck smoothly. Length of head roughly, three-quarters height at withers, or about an inch longer than neck. Breadth between ears a little less than one-half length of head. *Skull*—Very slightly domed, with a shallow indentation running down between the brows, and joining the muzzle with a moderate stop. *Cheeks*—Smoothly formed and flat, without heavy jowls. *Jaws*—Level, powerful and square. Overshot or undershot bad faults. *Teeth*—Sound, strong and white, with canines fitting closely together. *Nose*—Black, with large nostrils. White, cherry or butterfly bad faults. *Eyes*—Very dark, deeply set and fairly wide apart, of medium size, oval in shape with keen terrier expression. Light, large or protruding eye bad faults. *Ears*—Folded level with top of head, with forward edge close to cheek. Well rounded at tip, and of length to reach outer corner of eye. Thin, not leathery, and of sufficient thickness to avoid creases. Prick, tulip, rose or hound ears bad faults.

Neck—Length slightly less than two-thirds of height of dog at withers. Muscular without coarseness, with good reach, refinement at throat, and set firmly on shoulders. *Shoulders*—Well laid back and powerful, but not over-muscled. Sufficiently wide to permit freedom of action. Upright or straight shoulder placement highly undesirable.

Legs—Forelegs strong, with good bone; and as straight as is consistent with chest being well let down between them. Down on pasterns, knuckled over, bound, and out at elbow, bad faults. Hind legs longer than forelegs and not so heavily boned. *Feet*—Large but compact, round with thick pads, strong nails. Toes well arched and pointing straight ahead. Forefeet larger, though not quite so long as hind feet. Thin, spread or flat feet bad faults.

Body—Strong, short-coupled and substantial, so as to permit great flexibility. Brisket deep and well let down between forelegs. Ribs well sprung.

Back—Length from withers to set on of tail should approximate height at withers, or 10½ inches. Topline level, neither roached nor swayed. Any deviations from these measurements undesirable. *Hindquarters*—Very powerful, and protruding well behind the set on of tail. Strong second thighs, stifles well bent, and hocks well let down. Capped or cowhocks bad faults.

Tail—Docked and carried upright. Set on far enough forward so that spine does not slope down to it.

Coat—Weather-resisting, comprised of soft, dense undercoat and hard, wiry top coat. Silky or curly coat bad fault. *Color*—All white, or with lemon, tan or badger markings on head and ears. Heavy body markings and excessive ticking should be discouraged. *Action*—Sound, strong, quick, free, true and level.

Note—The measurements were taken with calipers.

SCALE OF POINTS

General character, balance and size	15	Hindquarters 10	
		Legs and feet 10	
Head 5		Coat 10	50
Eyes 5		Tail 5	
Mouth 5		Color	
Ears 5		(body marking & ticking) 5	10
Neck 5	25	Total 100	
Shoulders and brisket . 10			
Body, ribs, & loin 10			

Approved March 12, 1935

Skye Terrier

General Appearance—The Skye Terrier is a dog of style, elegance, and dignity; agile and strong with sturdy bone and hard muscle. Long, low, and lank—he is twice as long as he is high—he is covered with a profuse coat that falls straight down either side of the body over oval-shaped ribs. The hair well feathered on the head veils forehead and eyes to serve as protection from brush and briar as well as amid serious encounters with other animals. He stands with head high and long tail hanging, and moves with a seemingly effortless gait. Of suitable size for his hunting work, strong in body, quarters, and jaw.

Temperament—That of the typical working terrier capable of overtaking game and going to ground, displaying stamina, courage, strength, and agility. Fearless, good-tempered, loyal, and canny, he is friendly and gay with those he knows and reserved and cautious with strangers.

Head—Long and powerful, strength being deemed more important than extreme length. Moderate width at the back of the skull tapers gradually to a strong muzzle. The stop is slight. The dark muzzle is just moderately full as opposed to snipy, and the nose is always black. Powerful and absolutely true jaws and mouth with the incisor teeth closing level, or with the upper teeth slightly overlapping the lower. *Eyes*—Brown, preferably dark brown, medium in size, close-set, and alight with life and intelligence. *Ears*—Symmetrical and gracefully feathered. They may be carried prick or drop. When prick, they are medium in size, placed high on the skull, erect at their outer edges, and slightly wider at the peak than at the skull. Drop ears, somewhat larger in size and set lower, hang flat against the skull.

Neck—Long and gracefully arched, carried high and proudly.

Body—Pre-eminently long and low. The backline is level, the chest deep, with oval-shaped ribs. The sides appear flattish due to the straight falling and profuse coat.

Legs and Feet. Forequarters—Legs short, muscular, and straight as possible. "Straight as possible" means straight as soundness and chest will permit; it does not mean "terrier straight." Shoulders well laid back, with tight placement of shoulder blades at the withers, and elbows should fit closely to the sides and be neither loose nor tied. Forearm should curve slightly around the chest. *Hindquarters*—Strong, full, well developed, and well angulated. Legs short, muscular, and straight when viewed from behind. *Feet*—Large hare-feet preferably pointing forward, the pads thick and nails strong and preferably black.

Movement—The legs proceed straight forward when traveling. When approaching, the forelegs form a continuation of the straight line of the front, the feet being the same distance apart as the elbows. The principal propelling power is furnished by the hind legs, which travel straight forward. Forelegs should move well forward, without too much lift. The whole movement may be termed free, active, and effortless and give a more or less fluid picture.

Tail—Long and well feathered. When hanging, its upper section is pendulous, following the line of the rump, its lower section thrown back in a moderate arc without twist or curl. When raised, its height makes it appear a prolongation of the backline. Though not to be preferred, the tail is sometimes carried high when the dog is excited or angry. When such carriage arises from emotion only, it is permissible. But the tail should not be constantly carried above the level of the back nor hang limp.

Coat—Double. Undercoat short, close, soft, and woolly. Outer coat hard, straight, and flat, 5½ inches long without extra credit granted for greater length. The body coat hangs straight down each side, parting from head to tail. The head hair, which may be shorter and softer, veils forehead and eyes and forms a moderate beard and apron. The long feathering on the ears falls straight down from the tips and outer edges, surrounding the ears like a fringe and outlining their shape. The ends of the hair should mingle with the coat at the sides of the neck.

Color—The coat must be of one over-all color at the skin but may be of varying shades of the same color in the full coat, which may be black, blue, dark or light gray, silver, platinum, fawn, or cream. The dog must have no distinctive markings except for the desirable black points of ears, muzzle, and tip of tail, all of which points are preferably dark even to black. The shade of head and legs should approximate that of the body. There must be no trace of pattern, design, or clear-cut color variations, with the exception of the breed's only permissible white which occasionally exists on the chest not exceeding 2 inches in diameter.

The puppy coat may be very different in color from the adult coat. As it is growing and clearing, wide variations of color may occur; consequently this is permissible in dogs under 18 months of age. However, even in puppies there must be no trace of pattern, design, or clear-cut variations with the exception of the black band of varying width frequently seen encircling the body coat of the cream-colored dog, and the only permissible white which, as in the adult dog, occasionally exists on the chest not exceeding 2 inches in diameter.

Size—Dogs: Shoulder height, 10 inches. Length, chest bone over tail at rump, 20 inches. Head, 8½ inches. Tail, 9 inches. Bitches: Shoulder height, 9½ inches. Length, chest bone over tail at rump, 19 inches. Head, 8 inches. Tail, 8½ inches. A slightly higher or lower dog of either sex is acceptable, providing body, head, and tail dimensions are proportionately longer or shorter. The ideal ratio of body length to shoulder height is 2 to 1, which is considered the correct proportion.

Measurements are taken with the Skye standing in natural position with feet well under. A box caliper is used vertically and horizontally. For the height, the top bar should rest on the withers. The head is measured from the tip of the nose to the back of the occipital bone, and the tail from the root to tip. Dogs 8 inches or less at the withers and bitches 7½ inches or less at the withers are to be penalized.

Approved February 8, 1964

Staffordshire Terrier

General Impression—The Staffordshire Terrier should give the impression of great strength for his size, a well put-together dog, muscular, but agile and graceful, keenly alive to his surroundings. He should be stocky, not long-legged or racy in outline. His courage is proverbial.

Head—Medium length, deep through, broad skull, very pronounced cheek muscles, distinct stop; and ears are set high. *Ears*—Cropped or uncropped, the latter preferred. Uncropped ears should be short and held half rose or prick. Full drop to be penalized. *Eyes*—Dark and round, low down in skull and set far apart. No pink eyelids. *Muzzle*—Medium length, rounded on upper side to fall away abruptly below eyes. Jaws well defined. Underjaw to be strong and have biting power. Lips close and even, no looseness. Upper teeth to meet tightly outside lower teeth in front. Nose definitely black.

Neck—Heavy, slightly arched, tapering from shoulders to back of skull. No looseness of skin. Medium length. *Shoulders*—Strong and muscular with blades wide and sloping. *Back*—Fairly short. Slight sloping from withers to rump with gentle short slope at rump to base of tail. Loins slightly tucked.

Body—Well-sprung ribs, deep in rear. All ribs close together. Forelegs set rather wide apart to permit of chest development. Chest deep and broad.

Tail—Short in comparison to size, low set, tapering to a fine point; not curled or held over back. Not docked. *Legs*—The front legs should be straight, large or round bones, pastern upright. No resemblance of bend in front. Hindquarters well-muscled, let down at hocks, turning neither in nor out. Feet of moderate size, well-arched and compact. Gait must be springy but without roll or pace.

Coat—Short, close, stiff to the touch, and glossy. *Color*—Any color, solid, parti, or patched is permissible, but all white, more than 80 per cent white, black and tan, and liver not to be encouraged.

Size—Height and weight should be in proportion. A height of about 18 to 19 inches at shoulders for the male and 17 to 18 inches for the female is to be considered preferable.

Faults—Faults to be penalized are Dudley nose, light or pink eyes, tail too long or badly carried, undershot or overshot mouths.

Approved June 10, 1936

Welsh Terrier

Head—The skull should be flat, and rather wider between the ears than the Wirehaired Fox Terrier. The jaw should be powerful, clean-cut, rather deeper, and more punishing—giving the head a more masculine appearance than that usually seen on a Fox Terrier. Stop not too defined, fair length from stop to end of nose, the latter being of a black color. *Ears*—The ear should be V-shaped, small, not too thin, set on fairly high, carried forward and close to the cheek. *Eyes*—The eye should be small, not being too deeply set in or protruding out of skull, of a dark hazel color, expressive and indicating abundant pluck. *Neck*—The neck should be of moderate length and thickness, slightly arched and sloping gracefully into the shoulders.

Body—The back should be short, and well-ribbed up, the loin strong, good depth, and moderate width of chest. The shoulders should be long, sloping, and well set back. The hindquarters should be strong, thighs muscular and of good length, with the hocks moderately straight, well let down, and fair amount of bone. The stern should be set on moderately high, but not too gaily carried. *Legs and Feet*—The legs should be straight and muscular, possessing fair amount of bone, with upright and powerful pasterns. The feet should be small, round and catlike.

Coat—The coat should be wiry, hard, very close and abundant. *Color*—The color should be black and tan, or black grizzle and tan, free from black penciling on toes.

Size—The height at shoulder should be 15 inches for dogs, bitches proportionately less. Twenty pounds shall be considered a fair average weight in working condition, but this may vary a pound or so either way.

SCALE OF POINTS

Head and jaws	10	Legs and feet	10
Ears	5	Coat	15
Eyes	5	Color	5
Neck and shoulders	10	Stern	5
Body	10	General appearance	15
Loins and hindquarters	10	Total	100

DISQUALIFICATIONS

(1) *Nose: white, cherry or spotted to a considerable extent with either of these colors.* (2) *Ears: prick, tulip or rose.* (3) *Undershot jaw or pig-jawed mouth.* (4) *Black below hocks or white to an appreciable extent.*

West Highland White Terrier.

General Appearance of the West Highland White Terrier is that of a small, game, hardy-looking terrier exhibiting good showmanship, possessed with no small amount of self-esteem, with varminty appearance strongly built, deep in chest and back ribs, straight back and powerful hindquarters on muscular legs, and exhibiting in a marked degree a great combination of strength and activity. The coat should be about 2 inches long, white in color, hard, with plenty of soft undercoat, and no tendency to wave or curl. The tail should be as straight as possible and carried not too gaily, and covered with hard hair, but not bushy. The skull should be not too broad, being in proportion to the terribly powerful jaws. The ears shall be as small and sharp-pointed as possible and carried tightly up, and must be absolutely erect. The eyes of moderate size, as dark as possible, widely placed with a sharp, bright, intelligent expression. The muzzle should not be too long, powerful and gradually tapering toward the nose; the roof of mouth and pads of feet are usually black in color. The dog should be tidied up. Considerable hair should be left around the head to act as a frame for the face to yield a typical Westie expression.

Color—Pure white; any other color objectionable.

Coat—Very important, and seldom seen to perfection; must be double-coated. The outer coat consists of hard hair, about 2 inches long, and free from any curl. The undercoat, which resembles fur, is short, soft and close. Open coats are objectionable.

Size—Dogs should measure about 11 inches at the withers, bitches, about one inch less.

Skull—Should not be too narrow, being in proportion to his powerful jaw, not too long, slightly domed, and gradually tapering to the eyes, between which there should be a slight indentation or stop, eyebrows heavy. There should be little apparent difference in length between the muzzle and the skull. *Eyes*—Widely set apart, medium in size, as dark as possible in color, slightly sunk in the head, sharp and intelligent, which, looking from under the heavy eyebrows give a piercing look. Full eyes and also light-colored eyes are very objectionable. *Muzzle*—Should be nearly equal in length to the rest of the skull, powerful and gradually tapering toward the nose, which should be fairly wide. The nose itself should be black in color. The jaws level and powerful, the teeth square or evenly met, well set and large for the size of the dog. Teeth much overshot or much undershot should be heavily penalized. Muzzles longer than the skull and not in proportion thereto are objectionable. *Ears*—Small, carried tightly erect and never dropped, set wide apart and terminating in a sharp point. The hair on them should be short, smooth and velvety and they should never be cut. The ears should be free from fringe at the top. Round-pointed, broad and large ears are very objectionable as are ears set too closely together or heavily covered with hair.

Neck—Muscular and nicely set on sloping shoulders. *Chest*—Very deep, with breadth in proportion to the size of the dog. *Body*—Compact, straight back, ribs deep and well arched in the upper half of rib, presenting a flattish side appearance, loins broad and strong, hindquarters strong, muscular and wide across the top.

Legs and Feet—Both fore- and hind legs should be short and muscular. The shoulder blades should be comparatively broad, and well sloped backwards. The points of the shoulder blades should be closely knitted into the backbone, so that very little movement of them should be noticeable when the dog is walking. The elbow should be close into the body both when moving or standing, thus causing the foreleg to be well placed in under the shoulder. The forelegs should be straight and thickly covered with short hard hair. The hind legs should be short and sinewy. The thighs very muscular and not too wide apart. The hocks bent and well set in under the body, so as to be fairly close to each other either when standing, walking, or trotting. The forefeet are larger than the hind feet; are round, proportionate in size, strong, thickly padded, and covered with short hard hair. The hind feet are smaller and thickly padded. Cowhocks detract from the general appearance. Straight or weak hocks, both kinds, are undesirable, and should be guarded against.

Tail—Five or 6 inches long, covered with hard hairs, no feather, as straight as possible, carried gaily but not curled over back. Tails longer than 6 inches are objectionable.

Movement—Should be free, straight and easy all round. In front the leg should be freely extended forward by the shoulder. The hind movement should be free, strong and close. The hocks should be freely flexed and drawn close in under the body, so that when moving off on the foot the body is thrown or pushed forward with some force. Stiff, stilty movement behind is very objectionable.

ATTENTION OF JUDGES

Under no consideration should a West Highland White Terrier be judged or trimmed as a Scottish Terrier. They are a distinct breed differing in head, body, hindquarters, movement and general over-all type. They are *not* white Scottish Terriers.

SCALE OF POINTS

Value

General appearance	15	Neck	5
Color	7½	Chest	5
Coat	10	Body	10
Size	7½	Legs and feet	7½
Skull	5	Tail	5
Eyes	5	Movement	7½
Muzzle	5	Total value	100
Ears	5		

FAULTS

Coat—Any silkiness, wave or tendency to curl is a serious blemish as is an open coat, single coat or one having black, gray or wheaten hairs therein.

Size—Any specimens under the minimum or over the maximum height limits are objectionable. *Eyes*—Full or light-colored. *Ears*—Round-pointed, poorly placed, drop, semierect or overly large. *Muzzle*—Overly long forefaces, teeth too much overshot or too much undershot or defective teeth.

Approved September 15, 1959

GROUP V: TOYS

Affenpinscher

As in most toys, general appearance is one of, if not the most important single point in the Affenpinscher. Details are of secondary importance and anatomical variations are of small concern.

General Appearance—Small, but rather sturdy in build and not delicate in any way. He carries himself with comical seriousness and he is generally quiet and a very devoted pal. He can get vehemently excited, however, when attacked and is fearless toward any aggressor.

Coat—A very important factor. It is short and dense in certain parts and shaggy and longer in others, but should be hard and wiry. It is longer and more loose and shaggy on the legs and around the eyes, nose and chin, giving the typical monkeylike appearance from whence comes his name. The best color is black, matching his eyes and fiery temperament. However, black with tan markings, red, gray and other mixtures are permissible. Very light colors and white markings are a fault.

Head—Should be round and not too heavy, with well-domed forehead. *Eyes*—Should be round, of good size, black and very brilliant. *Ears*—Rather small, set high, pointed and erect, usually clipped to a point. *Muzzle*—Must be short and rather pointed with a black nose. The upper jaw is a trifle shorter than the lower jaw, while the teeth should close together; a slight undershot condition is not material. The teeth, however, should not show.

Neck—Short and straight.

Body—The back should be straight with its length about equal to the height at the shoulder. Chest should be reasonably deep and the body should show only a slight tuck-up at the loin. *Legs*—Front legs should be straight as possible. Hind legs without much bend at the hocks and set well under the body. *Feet*—Should be round, small and compact. Turned neither in nor out, with preferably black pads and nails. *Tail*—Cut short, set and carried high.

Size—The smaller dog, if of characteristic type, is more valuable, and the shoulder height should not exceed 10¼ inches in any case.

Approved September 15, 1936

Chihuahua

SMOOTH COAT

Head—A well-rounded-apple, dome skull, with or without molera. Cheeks and jaws lean. Nose moderately short, slightly pointed (self-colored, in blond types, or black). In moles, blues, and chocolate, they are self-colored. In blond types, pink nose permissible. *Ears*—Large, held erect when alert, but flaring at the sides at about an angle of 45 degrees when in repose. This gives breadth between the ears. *Eyes*—Full, but not protruding, balanced, set well apart—dark, ruby, or luminous. (Light eyes in blond types, permissible.) *Teeth*—Level.

Neck and Shoulders—Slightly arched, gracefully sloping into lean shoulders, may be smooth in the very short types, or with ruff about neck preferred. Shoulders lean, sloping into a slightly broadening support above straight forelegs that are set well under, giving a free play at the elbows. Shoulders should be well up, giving balance and soundness, sloping into a level back. (Never down or low.) This gives a chestiness, and strength of forequarters, yet not of the "Bulldog" chest; plenty of brisket.

Back and Body—Level back, slightly longer than height. Shorter backs desired in males. Ribs rounded (but not too much "barrel-shaped"). *Hindquarters*—Muscular, with hocks well apart, neither out or in, well let down, with firm sturdy action. *Tail*—Moderately long, carried cycle either up or out, or in a loop over the back, with tip just touching the back. (Never tucked under.) Hair on tail in harmony with the coat of the body, preferred furry. A natural bobtail or tailless permissible, if so born, and not against a good dog. *Feet*—Small, with toes well split up, but not spread, pads cushioned, with fine pasterns. (Neither the hare nor the cat-foot.) A dainty, small foot with nails moderately long.

Coat—In the smooth, the coat should be soft texture, close and glossy. (Heavier coats with undercoats permissible.) Coat placed well over body with ruff on neck, and more scanty on head and ears. *Color*—Any color—solid, marked or splashed.

Weight—One to 6 pounds, with 2 to 4 pounds preferable, if 2 dogs are equally good in type, the more diminutive is preferred.

General Appearance—A graceful, alert, swift-moving little dog with saucy expression. Compact, and with terrierlike qualities.

SCALE OF POINTS

Head, including ears	20	Legs	15
Body	20	Weight	10
Coat	10	General appearance and action	
Tail	5		15
Color	5	Total	100

DISQUALIFICATIONS

Cropped tail, broken down or cropped ears.

LONG COAT

The long-coated variety of the Chihuahua is judged by the same standard as the smooth-coated variety, except for the following: *Coat*—In the Long Coats, the coat should be of a soft texture, either flat or slightly curly, with undercoat preferred. Ears fringed (heavily fringed ears may be tipped slightly, never down), feathering on feet and legs, and pants on hind legs. Large ruff on neck desired and preferred. Tail full and long (as a plume).

Disqualifications—Too thin coat, that resembles bareness.

SCALE OF POINTS

Head, including ears	20	Legs	10
Body	20	Weight	5
Coat	20	General appearance	
Tail	5	and action	15
Color	5	Total	100

DISQUALIFICATIONS

Cropped tail, broken down or cropped ears, too thin coat that resembles bareness.

Approved January 12, 1954

English Toy Spaniel

KING CHARLES, PRINCE CHARLES, RUBY AND BLENHEIM

Head—Should be well domed, and in good specimens is absolutely semi-globular, sometimes even extending beyond the half-circle, and absolutely projecting over the eyes, so as nearly to meet the upturned nose. *Eyes*—The eyes are set wide apart, with the eyelids square to the line of the face—not oblique or foxlike. The eyes themselves are large and dark as possible, so as to be generally considered black, their enormous pupils, which are absolutely of that color, increasing the description. *Stop*—The stop, or hollow between the eyes, is well marked, as in the Bulldog, or even more so; some good specimens exhibit a hollow deep enough to bury a small marble in it. *Nose*—The nose must be short and well turned up between the eyes, and without any indication of artificial displacement afforded by a deviation to either side. The color of the end should be black, and it should be both deep and wide with open nostrils. A light-colored nose is objectionable, but shall not disqualify. *Jaw*—The muzzle must be square and deep, and the lower jaw wide between the branches, leaving plenty of space for the tongue, and for the attachment of the lower lips, which should completely conceal the teeth. It should also be turned up or "finished," so as to allow of its meeting the end of the upper jaw, turned up in a similar way as above described. A protruding tongue is objectionable, but does not disqualify. *Ears*—The ears must be long, so as to approach the ground. In an average-sized dog they measure 20 inches from tip to tip, and some reach 22 inches or even a trifle more. They should be set low down on the head and hang flat to the sides of the cheeks, and be heavy-feathered.

Size—The most desirable size is from 9 pounds to 12 pounds. *Shape*—In compactness of shape these Spaniels almost rival the Pug, but the length of coat adds greatly to the apparent bulk, as the body, when the coat is wetted, looks small in comparison with that dog. Still, it ought to be decidedly "cobby," with strong, stout legs, short broad back and wide chest.

Coat—The coat should be long, silky, soft and wavy, but not curly. There should be a profuse mane, extending well down in the front of the chest. The feather should be well displayed on the ears and feet, and in the latter case so thickly as to give the appearance of being webbed. It is also carried well up the backs of the legs. In the Black and Tan the feather on the ears is very long and profuse, exceeding that of the Blenheim by an inch or more. The feather on the tail (which is cut to the length of about 1½ inches) should be silky, and from 3 to 4 inches in length, constituting a marked "flag" of a square shape, and not carried above the level of the back.

COLORS OF THE TWO VARIETIES

King Charles and Ruby—The King Charles and Ruby types which comprise one show variety are solid-colored dogs. The King Charles are black and tan (considered a solid color), the black rich and glossy with deep mahogany tan markings over the eyes and on the muzzle, chest and legs. The presence of a few white hairs intermixed with the black on the chest is to be faulted, but a white patch on the chest or white appearing elsewhere disqualifies. The Ruby is a rich chestnut red and is whole-colored. The presence of a few white hairs intermixed with the red on the chest is to be faulted, but a white patch on the chest or white appearing elsewhere disqualifies.

Blenheim and Prince Charles—The Blenheim and Prince Charles types which comprise the other show variety are broken-colored dogs. The Blenheim is red and white. The ground color is a pearly white which has bright red chestnut or ruby red markings evenly distributed in large patches. The ears and cheeks should be red, with a blaze of white extending from the nose up the forehead and ending between the ears in a crescentic curve. In the center of the blaze at the top of the forehead, there should be a clear "spot" of red, the size of a dime. The Prince Charles, a tri-colored dog, is white, black and tan. The ground color is a pearly white. The black consists of markings which should be evenly distributed in large patches. The tan appears as spots over the eyes, on the muzzle, chest and legs; the ears and vent should also be lined with tan. The Prince Charles has no "spot," that being a particular feature of the Blenheim.

SCALE OF POINTS

King Charles, or Black and Tan. Prince Charles, White, with Black and Tan Markings. Ruby, or Red.

Symmetry, condition, size and soundness of limb	20	Eyes	10
		Ears	15
Head	15	Coat and feathering	15
Stop	5	Color	10
Muzzle	10	Total	100

Blenheim, or White with Red Markings

Symmetry, condition, size and soundness of limb	15	Ears	10
Head	15	Coat and feathering	15
Stop	5	Color and markings	15
Muzzle	10	Spot	5
Eyes	10	Total	100

King Charles and Ruby: A white patch on the chest, or white on any other part.

Approved July 14, 1959

Griffon, Brussels

General Appearance—A toy dog, intelligent, alert, sturdy, with a thick-set short body, a smart carriage and set-up, attracting attention by an almost human expression.

Head—Skull—Large and round, with a domed forehead. *Ears*—Small and set rather high on the head. May be shown cropped or natural. If natural they are carried semi-erect. *Eyes*—Should be set well apart, very large, black, prominent, and well open. The eyelashes long and black. Eyelids edged with black. *Nose*—Very black, extremely short, its tip being set back deeply between the eyes so as to form a lay-back. The nostrils large, the stop deep. *Lips*—Edged with black, not pendulous but well brought together, giving a clean finish to the mouth. *Jaws*—Chin must be undershot, prominent, and large with an upward sweep. The incisors of the lower jaw should protrude over the upper incisors, and the lower jaw should be rather broad. Neither teeth nor tongue should show when the mouth is closed. A wry mouth is serious fault.

Body and Legs—Brisket should be broad and deep, ribs well sprung, back level and short. *Neck*—Medium length, gracefully arched. *Tail*—Set and held high, docked to about one third. *Forelegs*—Of medium length, straight in bone, well muscled, set moderately wide apart and straight from the point of the shoulders as viewed from the front. Pasterns short and strong. *Hind legs*—Set true, thighs strong and well muscled, stifles bent, hocks well let down, turning neither in nor out. *Feet*—Round, small, and compact, turned neither in nor out. Toes well arched. Black pads and toenails preferred.

Coat—There are two distinct types of coat—rough and smooth. The rough coat should be wiry and dense, the harder and more wiry the better. On no account should the dog look or feel woolly, and there should be no silky hair anywhere. The coat should not be so long as to give a shaggy appearance, but should still be distinctly different all over from the smooth coat. The head should be covered with wiry hair slightly longer around the eyes, nose, cheeks, and chin, thus forming a fringe. The Smooth coat is similar to that of the Boston Terrier or English Bulldog, with no trace of wire hair.

Color—In the rough-coated type, coat is either 1. reddish brown, with a little black at the whiskers and chin allowable, or 2. black and reddish brown mixed, usually, with black mask and whiskers, or 3. black with uniform reddish brown markings, usually appearing under the chin, on the legs, over the eyebrows, around the edges of the ears and around the vent, or 4. solid black. The colors of the smooth-coated type are the same as those of the rough-coated type except that solid black is not allowable. Any white hairs in either the rough or smooth coat are a serious fault, except for "frost" on the black muzzle of a mature dog, which is natural.

Weight—Usually 8 to 10 pounds, and should not exceed 12 pounds. Type and quality are of greater importance than weight, and a smaller dog that is sturdy and well proportioned should not be penalized.

SCALE OF POINTS

Head

Skull	5
Nose and stop	10
Eyes	5
Chin and jaws	10
Ears	5 35

Coat

Color	12
Texture	13 25

Body and General Conformation

Body (brisket and rib)		
....		15
Legs		10
Feet		5
General Appearance (neck, topline, and tail carriage)		
....		10 40
Total		100

DISQUALIFICATIONS

Dudley or butterfly nose, white spot or blaze anywhere on coat, hanging tongue, jaw overshot, solid black coat in the smooth type.

Approved February 6, 1960

Italian Greyhound

General Appearance—A miniature English Greyhound, more slender in all proportions, and of ideal elegance and grace in shape, symmetry and action.

Head—Skull, long, flat and narrow. Muzzle, very fine, nose dark, teeth level. Ears, rose shaped, placed well back, soft and delicate. Eyes, rather large, bright and full of expression.

Body—Neck, long and gracefully arched. Shoulders, long and sloping. Chest, deep and narrow. Back, curved and drooping at the hindquarters. *Legs and Feet*—Forelegs, straight, set well under the shoulders, fine pasterns, small delicate bones. Hind legs—hocks well let down, thighs muscular. Feet, the long hare foot. *Tail*—Rather long, fine and with low carriage.

Coat—Skin fine and supple, hair thin and glossy like satin. *Color*—All shades of fawn, red, mouse, blue, cream and white are recognized. Black and Tan Terrier markings not allowed.

Action—High-stepping and free. *Size*—Two classes, one of 8 pounds and under, and one over 8 pounds. A good small dog is preferable to an equally good large one but a good larger dog is preferable to a poor smaller one.

SCALE OF POINTS

Skull	6	Forelegs	8
Muzzle	8	Hind legs	8
Ears	8	Feet	8
Eyes	5	Tail	8
Neck	8	Coat	4
Shoulders	5	Color	3
Chest	5	Action	8
Back	8	Total	100

Japanese Spaniel

General Appearance—That of a lively, high-bred little dog with dainty appearance, smart, compact carriage and profuse coat. These dogs should be essentially stylish in movement, lifting the feet high when in action, carrying the tail (which is heavily feathered, proudly curved or plumed) over the back. In size they vary considerably, but the smaller they are the better, provided type and quality are not sacrificed. When divided by weight, classes should be under and over 7 pounds.

Head—Should be large for the size of the dog, with broad skull, rounded in front. *Eyes*—Large, dark, lustrous, rather prominent and set wide apart. *Ears*—Small and V-shaped, nicely feathered, set wide apart and high on the head and carried slightly forward. *Nose*—Very short in the muzzle part. The end or nose proper should be wide, with open nostrils, and must be the color of the dog's markings, *i.e.* black in black-marked dogs, and red or deep flesh color in red or lemon-marked dogs. It shall be a disqualification for a black and white Japanese Spaniel to have a nose any other color than black. *Neck*—Should be short and moderately thick.

Body—Should be squarely and compactly built, wide in chest, "cobby" in shape. The length of the dog's body should be about its height. *Tail*—Must be well twisted to either right or left from root and carried up over back and flow on opposite side; it should be profusely covered with long hair (ring tails not desirable). *Legs*—The bones of the legs should be small, giving them a slender appearance, and they should be well feathered. *Feet*—Small and shaped somewhat long; the dog stands up on its toes somewhat. If feathered, the tufts should never increase in width of the foot, but only its length a trifle.

Coat—Profuse, long, straight, rather silky. It should be absolutely free from wave or curl, and not lie too flat, but have a tendency to stand out, especially at the neck, so as to give a thick mane or ruff, which with profuse feathering on thighs and tail gives a very showy appearance. *Color*—The dogs should be either black and white or red and white, *i.e.* parti-colored. The term red includes all shades of sable, brindle, lemon and orange, but the brighter and clearer the red the better. The white should be clear white, and the color, whether black or red, should be evenly distributed, patches over the body, cheek and ears.

SCALE OF POINTS

Head and neck	10	Tail		10
Eyes	10	Feet and legs		5
Ears	5	Coat and markings		15
Muzzle	10	Action		5
Nose	5	Size		10
Body	15	Total		100

DISQUALIFICATION

In black and whites, a nose any other color than black.

Maltese

General Appearance—The Maltese is a toy dog covered from head to foot with a mantle of long, silky, white hair. He is gentle-mannered and affectionate, eager and sprightly in action, and, despite his size, possessed of the vigor needed for the satisfactory companion.

Head—Of medium length and in proportion to the size of the dog. *The skull* is slightly rounded on top, the stop moderate. *The drop ears* are rather low set and heavily feathered with long hair that hangs close to the head. *Eyes* are set not too far apart; they are very dark and round, their black rims enhancing the gentle yet alert expression. *The muzzle* is of medium length, fine and tapered but not snipy. *The nose* is black. *The teeth* meet in an even, edge-to-edge bite, or in a scissors bite.

Neck—Sufficient length of neck is desirable as promoting a high carriage of the head.

Body—Compact, the height from the withers to the ground equaling the length from the withers to the root of the tail. Shoulder blades are sloping, the elbows well knit and held close to the body. The back is level in topline, the ribs well sprung. The chest is fairly deep, the loins taut, strong, and just slightly tucked up underneath.

Tail—A long-haired plume carried gracefully over the back, its tip lying to the side over the quarter.

Legs and Feet—Legs are fine-boned and nicely feathered. Forelegs are straight, their pastern joints well knit and devoid of appreciable bend. Hind legs are strong and moderately angulated at stifles and hocks. The feet are small and round, with toe pads black. Scraggly hairs on the feet may be trimmed to give a neater appearance.

Coat and Color—The coat is single, that is, without undercoat. It hangs long, flat, and silky over the sides of the body almost, if not quite, to the ground. The long head-hair may be tied up in a topknot or it may be left hanging. Any suggestion of kinkiness, curliness, or woolly texture is objectionable. Color, pure white. Light tan or lemon on the ears is permissible, but not desirable.

Size—Weight under 7 pounds, with from 4 to 6 pounds preferred. Over-all quality is to be favored over size.

Gait—The Maltese moves with a jaunty, smooth, flowing gait. Viewed from the side, he gives an impression of rapid movement, size considered. In the stride, the forelegs reach straight and free from the shoulders, with elbows close. Hind legs to move in a straight line. Cowhocks or any suggestion of hind leg toeing in or out are faults.

Temperament—For all his diminutive size, the Maltese seems to be without fear. His trust and affectionate responsiveness are very appealing. He is among the gentlest mannered of all little dogs, yet he is lively and playful as well as vigorous.

Approved November 12, 1963

Manchester Terrier (Toy)

The Standard for the Manchester Terrier (Toy Variety) is the same as for the Manchester Terrier except as regards weight and ears. (*See page* 459)

Papillon

General Appearance—The Papillon is a toy dog of fine-boned structure. It is gentle, intelligent, dainty, and of lively action. It is not a diminutive form of a breed. There is only one classification—the toy.

Head—The head of the Papillon is well proportioned to the body. It may appear small because it is covered with short hair while the rest of the body is heavily coated. The skull should be of medium width and slightly rounded between the ears. A well-defined stop is formed where the muzzle joins the skull. The muzzle is shorter than the skull and is fine; it is abruptly thinner than the head, becoming more slender down to the nose. *Nose*— The nose of the Papillon is small and rounded, and is slightly flat on top. It should be black. *Disqualification*—Pink nose, or one with pink spots. *Eyes*—The eyes of the Papillon are dark and expressive. The center of the eyes is on a line with the stop. The shape of the eye is round. Rim around the eyes should be black. Eyes must not bulge. *Mouth*—The jaws of the Papillon are well adjusted; the lips are tight and thin, and should be black. Teeth should meet in a scissors bite. *Fault*—The jaw should not be overshot or undershot. *Ears*—The ears of Papillons of either the erect or the drop type should be large and set on the sides of the head. The ears should be fringed. (1) The erect type of ears is carried obliquely and moves like the spread wings of a butterfly. At rest or when relaxed, their position forms an angle of approximately 45 degrees to the head. The concha is largely open, and the inside is entirely visible and covered with silken hair. The ears should be of fine leather and of sufficient strength to maintain the opened-up position. (2) The drop type of ears (known on the Continent as Phalene), is similar to the erect type, but the ears are carried drooping, and must be completely down. *Major fault*—Ears partly down.

Neck—The neck is slender, and is lost in the collarette.

Body—The body must be slightly longer than high. The Papillon is not a cobby dog. The back is level. The chest is of medium depth and width. The ribs are arched. The loins are tucked up. *Shoulders*—The shoulders should be flexible and well-angulated, and are hidden by hair. *Forelegs*—The forelegs are fine and straight. It stands with front feet rather close together. The back of the forelegs is covered with abundant fringes, diminishing to the pastern; the front of the forelegs is covered with short hair. *Hind Legs*—The thighs are fairly muscular and well-angulated. The hind legs are slender and parallel when viewed from behind. They are covered to the hocks with abundant breeches (culottes); the hind pastern is covered with short, smooth hair. The stifles are well angulated. The hocks are placed fairly high. *Fault*— Cowhocks. *Feet*—The feet are thin and elongated (hare-like). The toes are close and arched. The hair on the feet is short, but fine tufts may appear between the toes and grow beyond them, forming a point. *Tail*—The tail is set high and carried well arched over the body. The plume on the tail usually hangs to the side of the body.

Coat—The coat is short and smooth on the head, muzzle, front of legs, and back of legs from the hocks downward. The hair around the neck forms a collarette. The hair on the neck, shoulders, and breast is abundant in comparison with that on the rest of the body. The back of the forelegs should be well fringed, the length of the fringes shortening down to the pastern. The tail is covered with a long abundant plume. *Quality of Coat*— The coat is profuse and shiny, and may be slightly wavy, but not curly. There is no undercoat. The hair on the back is flat. The coat is soft and comparatively fine, but has a resilient quality.

Size—The height at the withers should be 11 inches or under. The weight and height should be in good proportion. *Disqualification*—12 inches and over.

Gait—The gait is free, quick, easy, and graceful.

Color and Markings—Papillons are two-colored or tri-colored. The usual two colors are white and black, white and sable or white and some shade of red, varying from light tan to deep red. The color is usually in spots or patches thrown in relief against white, which predominates. The size, shape, and placement, of the patches are without importance. A tri-colored Papillon is black and white with tan spots. The tan spots may appear over the eyes, on the cheeks, in the ears, and under the tail. The exact placement or omission of the tan spots is of no importance. The black appears in patches on white in the same manner as in the dog of two colors. A saddle is permissible. A blaze is desirable but not essential. Among the allowable colors and markings, there is no preference.

Fault—A coat of solid color.

DISQUALIFICATIONS

Nose—*Pink nose, or one with pink spots.* *Size*—*12 inches and over.*
Approved May 13, 1958

Pekingese

Expression—Must suggest the Chinese origin of the Pekingese in its quaintness and individuality, resemblance to the lion in directions and independence and should imply courage, boldness, self-esteem and combativeness rather than prettiness, daintiness or delicacy.

Skull—Massive, broad, wide and flat between the ears (not dome-shaped), wide between the eyes. *Nose*—Black, broad, very short and flat. *Eyes*—Large, dark, prominent, round, lustrous. *Stop*—Deep. *Ears*—Heart-shaped, not set too high, leather never long enough to come below the muzzle, nor carried erect, but rather drooping, long feather. *Muzzle*—Wrinkled, very short and broad, not overshot nor pointed. Strong, broad underjaw, teeth not to show.

Shape of Body—Heavy in front, well-sprung ribs, broad chest, falling away lighter behind, lionlike. Back level. Not too long in body; allowance made for longer body in bitch. *Legs*—Short forelegs, bones of forearm bowed, firm at shoulder; hind legs lighter but firm and well shaped. *Feet*—Flat, toes turned out, not round, should stand well up on feet, not on ankles.

Action—Fearless, free and strong, with slight roll.

Coat, Feather and Condition—Long, with thick undercoat, straight and flat, not curly nor wavy, rather coarse, but soft; feather on thighs, legs, tail and toes long and profuse. *Mane*—Profuse, extending beyond the shoulder blades, forming ruff or frill round the neck.

Color—All colors are allowable. Red, fawn, black, black and tan, sable, brindle, white and parti-color well defined: black masks and spectacles around the eyes, with lines to ears are desirable. *Definition of a Parti-Color Pekingese*—The coloring of a parti-colored dog must be broken on the body. No large portion of any one color should exist. White should be shown on the saddle. A dog of any solid color with white feet and chest is *not* a parti-color.

Tail—Set high; lying well over back to either side; long, profuse, straight feather.

Size—Being a toy dog, medium size preferred, providing type and points are not sacrificed; extreme limit 14 pounds.

SCALE OF POINTS

Expression	5	Shape of body	15
Skull	10	Legs and feet	15
Nose	5	Coat, feather and condition	
Eyes	5		15
Stop	5	Tail	5
Ears	5	Action	10
Muzzle	5	Total	100

Penalizations—Protruding tongue, badly blemished eye, overshot, wry mouth.

DISQUALIFICATIONS

Weight—over 14 pounds; Dudley nose.

Approved April 10, 1956

Pinscher, Miniature

General Appearance—The Miniature Pinscher was originated in Germany and named the "Reh Pinscher" due to his resemblance in structure and animation to a very small specie of deer found in the forests. This breed is structurally a well-balanced, sturdy, compact, short-coupled, smooth-coated toy dog. He is naturally well groomed, proud, vigorous and alert. The natural characteristic traits which identify him from other toy dogs are his precise Hackney gait, his fearless animation, complete self-possession, and his spirited presence. *Faults*—Structurally lacking in balance, too long- or short-coupled, too coarse or too refined (lacking in bone development causing poor feet and legs), too large or too small, lethargic, timid or dull, shy or vicious, low in tail placement and poor in action (action not typical of the breed requirements). Knotty overdeveloped muscles.

Head—In correct proportion with the body. *From Top:* Tapering, narrow with well-fitted but not too prominent foreface which should balance with the skull. No indication of coarseness. *From Front:* Skull appears flat, tapering forward toward the muzzle. Muzzle itself strong rather than fine and delicate, and in proportion to the head as a whole; cheeks and lips small, taut and closely adherent to each other. Teeth in perfect alignment and apposition. *From Side*: Well-balanced with only a slight drop to the muzzle, which should be parallel to the top of the skull. *Eyes*: Full, slightly oval, almost round, clear, bright and dark even to a true black; set wide apart and fitted well into the sockets. *Ears*: Well-set and firmly placed, upstanding (when cropped, pointed and carried erect in balance with the head). *Nose*: Black only (with the exception of chocolates, which may have a self-colored nose).

Faults—Too large or too small for the body, too coarse or too refined, pinched and weak in foreface, domed in skull, too flat and lacking in chiseling, giving a vapid expression. *Jaws and teeth* overshot or undershot. *Eyes* too round and full, too large, bulging, too deep-set or set too far apart; or too small, set too close (pig eyes). Light-colored eyes not desirable. *Ears* poorly placed, low-set hanging ears (lacking in cartilage) which detract from head conformation. (Poorly cropped ears if set on the head properly and having sufficient cartilage should not detract from head points, as this would be a man-made fault and automatically would detract from general appearance.) *Nose* any color other than black (with the exception of chocolates which may have a self-colored nose).

Neck—Proportioned to head and body. Slightly arched, gracefully curved, clean and firm, blending into shoulders, length well-balanced, muscular and free from a suggestion of dewlap or throatiness. *Faults*—Too straight or too curved; too thick or too thin; too long or short; knotty muscles; loose, flabby or wrinkled skin.

Body—From Top: Compact, slightly wedge-shaped, muscular with well-sprung ribs. *From Side*: Depth of brisket, the base line of which is level with the points of the elbows; short and strong in loin with belly moderately tucked up to denote grace in structural form. Back level or slightly sloping toward the rear. Length of males equals height at withers. Females may be slightly longer. *From Rear*: High tail-set; strong, sturdy upper shanks, with croup slope at about 30 degrees; vent opening not barreled. *Forequarters*: Forechest well-developed and full, moderately broad, shoulders clean, sloping with moderate angulation, co-ordinated to permit the true action of the Hackney pony. *Hindquarters*: Well-knit muscular quarters set wide enough apart to fit into a properly balanced body.

Faults—From top—too long, too short, too barreled, lacking in body development. *From side*—too long, too short, too thin or too fat, hips higher or considerably lower than the withers, lacking depth of chest, too full in loin, sway back, roach back or wry back. *From rear*—quarters too wide or too close to each other, overdeveloped, barreled vent, underdeveloped vent, too sloping croup, tail set low. *Forequarters*—forechest and spring of rib too narrow (or too shallow and underdeveloped), shoulders too straight, too loose, or too short and overloaded with muscles. *Hindquarters*—too narrow, undermuscled or overmuscled, too steep in croup.

Legs and Feet—Strong bone development and small clean joints; feet catlike, toes strong, well-arched and closely knit with deep pads and thick, blunt nails. *Forelegs and Feet*: As viewed from the front straight and upstanding, elbows close to body, well-knit, flexible yet strong with perpendicular pasterns. *Hind Legs*: All adjacent bones should appear well-angulated with well-muscled thighs or upper shanks, with clearly well-defined stifles, hocks short, set well apart turning neither in nor out, while at rest should stand perpendicular to the ground and upper shanks, lower shanks and hocks parallel to each other. *Faults*—Too thick or thin bone development, large joints, spreading flat feet. *Forelegs and Feet*—bowed or crooked, weak pasterns, feet turning in or out, loose elbows. *Hind legs*—thin undeveloped stifles, large or crooked hocks, loose stifle joints.

Tail—Set high, held erect, docked to ½ to 1 inch. *Faults*—Set too low, too thin, drooping, hanging or poorly docked.

Coat—Smooth, hard and short, straight and lustrous, closely adhering to and uniformly covering the body. *Faults*—Thin, too long, dull; upstanding; curly; dry; area of various thickness or bald spots.

Color—1. Solid red or stag red. 2. Lustrous black with sharply defined tan, rust-red markings on cheeks, lips, lower jaw, throat, twin spots above eyes and chest, lower half of forelegs, inside of hind legs and vent region, lower portion of hocks and feet. Black pencil stripes on toes. 3. Solid brown or chocolate with rust or yellow markings. *Faults*—Any color other than listed; very dark or sooty spots. *Disqualifications*—thumb marks or any area of white on feet or forechest exceeding one-half (½) inch in its longest dimension.

Size—Desired height 11 inches to 11½ inches at the withers. A dog of either sex measuring under 10 inches or over 12½ inches shall be disqualified. *Faults*—Oversize; undersize; too fat; too lean.

SCALE OF POINTS

General appearance and movement		Body	15
—(*very important*)	30	Feet	5
Skull	5	Legs	5
Muzzle	5	Color	5
Mouth	5	Coat	5
Eyes	5	Tail	5
Ears	5	Total	100
Neck	5		

DISQUALIFICATIONS

Color—*Thumb marks or any area of white on feet or forechest exceeding one-half (½) inch in its longest dimension. Size*—*A dog of either sex measuring under 10 or over 12½ inches.*

Approved May 13, 1958

Pomeranian

Appearance—The Pomeranian in build and appearance should be a compáct, short-coupled dog, well-knit in frame. He should exhibit great intelligence in his expression, docility in his disposition, and activity and buoyancy in his deportment, and be sound in action.

Head—The head should be wedge-shaped, somewhat foxy in outline, the skull being slightly flat, large in proportion to the muzzle. In its profile it has a little stop which must not be too pronounced, and the hair on the head and face must be smooth or short-coated. The muzzle should finish rather fine. The teeth should meet in a scissors grip, in which part of the inner surface of the upper teeth meets and engages part of the outer surface of the lower teeth. This type of bite gives a firmer grip than one in which the edges of the teeth meet directly, and is subject to less wear. The mouth is considered *overshot* when the lower teeth fail to engage the inner surfaces of the upper teeth. The mouth is *undershot* when the lower teeth protrude beyond the upper teeth. One tooth out of line does not mean an undershot or overshot mouth. *Eyes*—The eyes should be medium in size, rather oblique in shape, not set too wide apart, or too close together, bright and dark in color. The eye rims of the blues and browns are self-colored. In all other colors the eye rims must be black. *Ears*—The ears should be small, not set too far apart or too low down, and carried perfectly erect, and should be covered with soft, short hair. Trimming unruly hairs on edges of ears permissible. *Nose*—Should be self-colored in blues and browns. In all other colors should be black.

Neck and Shoulders—The neck rather short, well set in, and lionlike, covered with a profuse mane and frill of long, straight hair sweeping from the underjaw and covering the whole of the front part of the shoulders and chest as well as the top part of the shoulders. The shoulders must be clean and laid well back.

Body—The back must be short and level, and the body compact, being well ribbed up and rounded. The chest must be fairly deep. *Legs*—The forelegs must be well feathered and perfectly straight, of medium length and strength in due proportion to a well-balanced frame. The feet small, compact in shape, standing well up on toes. The hind legs and thighs must be well feathered down to the hocks, and must be fine in bone and free in action.

Trimming around the edges of the toes and up the back of the legs to the first joint is permissible. *Tail*—The tail is characteristic of the breed, and should be turned over the back and carried flat, set high. It is profusely covered with long, spreading hair.

Coat—There should be two coats, an under- and an over coat; the first a soft, fluffy undercoat, and the other a long, perfectly straight and glistening coat covering the whole body, being very abundant around the neck and forepart of the shoulders and chest where it should form a frill of profuse, standing-off, straight hair extending over the shoulders. The hindquarters should be clad with long hair or feathering from top of rump to the hocks. The texture of the guard hairs must be harsh to the touch.

Color—Twelve colors, or color combinations, are permissible and recognized, namely, black, brown, chocolate, beaver, red, orange, cream, orange-sable, wolf-sable, blue, white, and parti-color. The beaver color is a dark beige. A parti-color dog is white with orange or black color distributed in even patches on the body, with white blaze on head desirable. Where whole-colored and parti-colored Pomeranians compete together, the preference should, other points being equal, be given to the whole-colored specimen. Sable-colored dogs must be shaded throughout as uniformly as possible, with no self-colored patches. In orange-sable, the undercoat must be a light tan with deeper orange guard hairs ending in black tippings. In wolf-sable, the undercoat is light gray with a deeper shade of steel-gray guard hairs ending in black tippings. A shaded muzzle on the sables is permissible, but a black mask on sables is a minor fault. Orange Pomeranians must be self-colored throughout, with light shadings of the same tone (not white) on breechings permitted. A black mask on an orange Pomeranian is a major fault. White chest, white foot, or white leg on whole-colored dogs are major faults. White hairs on black, brown, blue or sable Pomeranians are objectionable. Tinges of lemon or any other color on white dogs are objectionable. The above colors, as described, are the only allowable colors or combination of colors for Pomeranians.

Size—The weight of a Pomeranian for exhibition is 3 pounds to 7 pounds. The ideal size for show specimens is from 4 to 5 pounds.

Classification—The classes for Pomeranians may be divided by color in open classes as follows: Black and brown; red, orange or cream; sable. Any other allowable color.

FAULTS

Major—Round, domey skull. Too large ears. Undershot. Pink eye rims. Light or Dudley nose. Out at elbows or shoulders. Flat-sided dogs. Down in pasterns. Cowhock. Soft, flat, open coat. Whole-colored dogs with white chest, or white foot or leg. Black mask on an orange. *Objectionable*—Overshot. Large, round or light eyes. High or low on legs. Long toes. Too wide in hind legs. Trimming too close to show date. Tail set too low on rump. Black, brown, blue, and sable should be free from white hairs. Whites should be free from lemon or any other color. Black and tan. Underweight or overweight. *Minor*—Must be free from lippiness, wide chest. Tail should not curl back. Black mask on sable. White shadings on orange.

Approved April 12, 1960

Poodle (Toy)

The Standard for the Poodle (Toy variety) is the same as for the Standard and the Miniature varieties except as regards height. (*See page 517*)

Pug

Symmetry—Symmetry and general appearance, decidedly square and cobby. A lean, leggy Pug and a dog with short legs and a long body are equally objectionable. *Size and Condition*—The Pug should be *multum in parvo*, but this condensation (if the word may be used) should be shown by compactness of form, well-knit proportions, and hardness of developed muscle. Weight from 14 to 18 pounds (dog or bitch) desirable.

Body—Short and cobby, wide in chest and well ribbed up. *Legs*—Very strong, straight, of moderate length and well under. *Feet*—Neither so long as the foot of the hare, nor so round as that of the cat; well-split-up toes, and the nails black.

Muzzle—Short, blunt, square, but not up-faced. *Head*—Large, massive, round—not appleheaded, with no indentation of the skull. *Eyes*—Dark in color, very large, bold and prominent, globular in shape, soft and solicitous in expression, very lustrous, and, when excited, full of fire. *Ears*—Thin, small, soft, like black velvet. There are two kinds—the "rose" and "button." Preference is given to the latter.

Markings—Clearly defined. The muzzle or mask, ears, moles on cheeks, thumb mark or diamond on forehead, back-trace should be as black as possible. *Mask*—The mask should be black. The more intense and well defined it is the better. *Wrinkles*—Large and deep. *Trace*—A black line extending from the occiput to the tail.

Tail—Curled tightly as possible over the hip. The double curl is perfection.

Coat—Fine, smooth, soft, short and glossy, neither hard nor woolly.

Color—Silver or apricot-fawn. Each should be decided, to make the contrast complete between the color and the trace and the mask. Black.

SCALE OF POINTS

	Fawn	Black		Fawn	Black
Symmetry	10	10	Eyes	10	10
Size	5	10	Mask	5	....
Condition	5	5	Wrinkles	5	5
Body	10	10	Tail	10	10
Legs and feet	5	5	Trace	5	....
Head	5	5	Coat	5	5
Muzzle	10	10	Color	5	10
Ears	5	5	Total	100	100

Silky Terrier

The Silky Terrier is a lightly built, moderately low-set toy dog of pronounced terrier character and spirited action.

Head—The head is strong, wedge-shaped, and moderately long. The skull is a trifle longer than the muzzle, in proportion about three-fifths for the skull, two-fifths for the muzzle. *Skull*—Flat, and not too wide between the ears. *Stop*—Shallow. *Ears*—Small, V-shaped and pricked. They are set high and carried erect without any tendency to flare obliquely off the skull.

Eyes—Small, dark in color, and piercingly keen in expression. Light eyes are a fault. *Teeth*—Strong and well aligned, scissors bite. A bite markedly undershot or overshot is a serious fault. *Nose*—The nose is black.

Neck and Shoulders—The neck fits gracefully into sloping shoulders. It is medium long, fine and to some degree crested along its top line.

Body—Low-set, about one fifth longer than the dog's height at the withers.

A too short body is a fault. The back line is straight, with a just perceptible rounding over the loins. Brisket medium wide, and deep enough to extend down to the elbows. *Tail*—The tail is set high and carried erect or semierect but not over-gay. It is docked and well coated but devoid of plume.

Forequarters—Well laid back shoulders, together with good angulation at the upper arm, set the forelegs nicely under the body. Forelegs are strong, straight and rather fine-boned. *Hindquarters*—Thighs well muscled and strong, but not so developed as to appear heavy. Legs moderately angulated at stifles and hocks, with the hocks low and equidistant from the hock joints to the ground. *Feet*—Small, cat-like, round, compact. Pads are thick and springy while the nails are strong and dark colored. White or flesh colored nails are a fault. The feet point straight ahead, with no turning in or out. Dewclaws, if any, are removed.

Coat—Flat, in texture fine, glossy, silky; on matured specimens the desired length of coat from behind the ears to the set-on of the tail is from five to six inches. On the top of the head the hair is so profuse as to form a topknot, but long hair on face and ears is objectionable. Legs from knee and hock joints to feet should be free from long hair. The hair is parted on the head and down over the back to the root of the tail. *Color*—Blue and tan. The blue may be silver blue, pigeon blue or slate blue, the tan deep and rich. The blue extends from the base of the skull to the tip of the tail, down the forelegs to the pasterns, and down the thighs to the hocks. On the tail the blue should be very dark. Tan appears on muzzle and cheeks, around the base of the ears, below the pasterns and hocks, and around the vent. There is a tan spot over each eye. The topknot should be silver or fawn.

Temperament—The keenly alert air of the terrier is characteristic, with shyness or excessive nervousness to be faulted. The manner is quick, friendly, responsive.

Movement—Should be free, light footed, lively, and straightforward. Hindquarters should have strong propelling power. Toeing in or out is to be faulted.

Size—Weight ranges from eight to ten pounds. Shoulder height from nine to ten inches. Pronounced diminutiveness (such as a height of less than 8 inches) is not desired; it accentuates the quality of toyishness as opposed to the breed's definite terrier character.

Approved April 14, 1959

Yorkshire Terrier

General Appearance—Should be that of a long-coated toy terrier, the coat hanging quite straight and evenly down each side, a parting extending from the nose to the end of the tail. The animal should be very compact and neat, the carriage being very upright, and having an important air. The general outline should convey the existence of a vigorous and well-proportioned body.

Head—Should be rather small and flat, not too prominent or round in the skull, nor too long in the muzzle, with a perfect black nose. The fall on the head to be long, of a rich golden tan, deeper in color at the sides of the head about the ear roots, and on the muzzle where it should be very long. The hair on the chest a rich bright tan. On no account must the tan on the head extend on to the neck, nor must there be any sooty or dark hair intermingled with any of the tan. *Eyes*—Medium, dark and sparkling, having a sharp, intelligent expression, and placed so as to look directly forward. They should not be prominent, and the edge of the eyelids should be of a dark color. *Ears*—Small, V-shaped, and carried semierect, or erect, and not far apart, covered with short hair, color to be of a very deep rich tan. *Mouth*—Perfectly even, with teeth as sound as possible. An animal having lost any teeth through accident not a fault, providing the jaws are even.

Body—Very compact, and a good loin. Level on the top of the back.

Coat—The hair on body moderately long and perfectly straight (not wavy), glossy like silk, and of a fine silky texture. Color, a dark steel blue (not silver blue) extending from the occiput (or back of skull) to the root of tail, and on no account mingled with fawn, bronze or dark hairs.

Legs—Quite straight, well covered with hair of a rich golden tan a few shades lighter at the ends than at the roots, not extending higher on the forelegs than the elbow, nor on the hind legs than the stifle. *Feet*—As round as possible, and the toenails black.

Tail—Cut to medium length; with plenty of hair, darker blue in color than the rest of the body, especially at the end of the tail, and carried a little higher than the level of the back.

Tan—All tan hair should be darker at the roots than in the middle, shading to a still lighter tan at the tips.

SCALE OF POINTS

Formation and terrier appearance.............	15	Head....................	10
Color of hair on body......	15	Mouth..................	5
Richness of tan on head and legs...............	15	Legs and feet............	5
		Ears...................	5
Quality and texture of coat..	10	Eyes...................	5
Quantity and length of coat	10	Tail (carriage of).........	5
		Total................	100

GROUP VI: NON-SPORTING DOGS

Boston Terrier

General Appearance—The general appearance of the Boston Terrier should be that of a lively, highly intelligent, smooth-coated, short-headed, compactly built, short-tailed, well-balanced dog of medium station, of brindle color and evenly marked with white. The head should indicate a high degree of intelligence, and should be in proportion to the size of the dog; the body rather short and well knit, the limbs strong and neatly turned; tail short; and no feature be so prominent that the dog appears badly proportioned. The dog should convey an impression of determination, strength and activity, with style of a high order; carriage easy and graceful. A proportionate combination of "color" and "ideal markings" is a particularly distinctive feature of a representative specimen, and a dog with a preponderance of white on body, or without the proper proportion of brindle and white on head, should possess sufficient merit otherwise to counteract its deficiencies in these respects. The ideal "Boston Terrier expression" as indicating "a high degree of intelligence," is also an important characteristic of the breed. "Color and markings" and "expression" should be given particular consideration in determining the relative value of "general appearance" to other points.

Skull—Square, flat on top, free from wrinkles; cheeks flat; brow abrupt, stop well defined. *Eyes*—Wide apart, large and round, dark in color, expression alert, but kind and intelligent. The eyes should set square in the skull, and the outside corners should be on a line with the cheeks as viewed from the front. *Muzzle*—Short, square, wide and deep, and in proportion to skull; free from wrinkles; shorter in length than in width and depth, not exceeding in length approximately one-third of length of skull; width and depth carried out well to end; the muzzle from stop to end of nose on a line parallel to the top of the skull; nose black and wide, with well defined line between nostrils. The jaws broad and square, with short regular teeth. Bite even or sufficiently undershot to square muzzle. The chops of good depth but not pendulous, completely covering the teeth when mouth is closed. *Ears*—Carried erect, either cropped to conform to the shape of head, or natural bat, situated as near the corners of skull as possible.

Head Faults—Skull "domed" or inclined; furrowed by a medial line; skull too long for breadth, or *vice versa*; stop too shallow; brow and skull too slanting. Eyes small or sunken; too prominent; light color or walleye; showing too much white or haw. Muzzle wedge-shaped or lacking depth; downfaced; too much cut out below the eyes; pinched or wide nostrils; butterfly nose; protruding teeth; weak lower jaw; showing turn-up, layback, or wrinkled. Ears poorly carried or in size out of proportion to head.

Neck—Of fair length, slightly arched and carrying the head gracefully; setting neatly into shoulders. *Neck Faults*—Ewe-necked; throatiness; short and thick.

Body—Deep with good width of chest; shoulders sloping; back short; ribs deep and well sprung, carried well back to loins; loins short and muscular; rump curving slightly to set-on of tail; flank very slightly cut up. The body should appear short but not chunky. *Body Faults*—Flat sides; narrow chest; long or slack loins; roach back; sway-back; too much cut up in flank. *Elbows* —Standing neither in nor out. *Forelegs*—Set moderately wide apart and on a line with the point of the shoulders; straight in bone and well muscled; pasterns short and strong. *Hind Legs*—Set true; bent at stifles; short from hocks to feet; hocks turning neither in nor out; thighs strong and well muscled. *Feet*—Round, small and compact and turned neither in nor out; toes well arched. *Leg and Feet Faults*—Loose shoulders or elbows; hind legs too straight at stifles; hocks too prominent; long or weak pastern; splay feet.

Gait—The gait of the Boston Terrier is that of a sure-footed, straight-gaited dog, forelegs and hind legs moving straight ahead in line with perfect rhythm, each step indicating grace with power. *Gait Faults*—There shall be no rolling, paddling or weaving when gaited and any crossing movement, either front or rear, is a serious fault.

Tail—Set-on low; short, fine and tapering; straight; or screw; devoid of fringe or coarse hair, and not carried above horizontal. *Tail Faults*—A long or gaily carried tail; extremely gnarled or curled against body. (Note—The preferred tail should not exceed in length approximately half the distance from set-on to hock.)

Ideal Color—Brindle with white markings. The brindle to be evenly distributed and distinct. Black with white markings permissible but brindle with white markings preferred. *Ideal Markings*—White muzzle, even white blaze over head, collar, breast, part or whole of forelegs, and hind legs below hocks. *Color and Markings Faults*—All white; absence of white marking; preponderance of white on body; without the proper proportion of brindle and white on head; or any variations detracting from the general appearance.

Coat—Short, smooth, bright and fine in texture. *Coat Faults*—Long or coarse; lacking luster.

Weight—Not exceeding 25 pounds, divided by classes as follows: lightweight, under 15 pounds; middleweight, 15 and under 20 pounds; heavyweight, 20 and not exceeding 25 pounds.

SCALE OF POINTS

General appearance	10	Forelegs	5
Skull	10	Hind legs	5
Eyes	5	Gait	10
Muzzle	10	Feet	5
Ears	2	Tail	5
Neck	3	Color	4
Body	15	Ideal markings	5
Elbows	4	Coat	2
		Total	100

DISQUALIFICATIONS

Solid black; black and tan; liver or mouse colors. Dudley nose. Docked tail or any artificial means used to deceive the judge.

Approved April 9, 1957

Bulldog

General Appearance, Attitude, Expression, etc.—The perfect Bulldog must be of medium size and smooth coat; with heavy, thick-set, low-swung body, massive, short-faced head, wide shoulders and sturdy limbs. The general appearance and attitude should suggest great stability, vigor and strength. The disposition should be equable and kind, resolute and courageous (not vicious or aggressive), and demeanor should be pacific and dignified. These attributes should be countenanced by the expression and behavior.

Gait—The style and carriage are peculiar, his gait being a loose-jointed, shuffling, sidewise motion, giving the characteristic "roll." The action must, however, be unrestrained, free and vigorous.

Proportion and Symmetry—The "points" should be well distributed and bear good relation one to the other, no feature being in such prominence from either excess or lack of quality that the animal appears deformed or ill-proportioned. *Influence of Sex*—In comparison of specimens of different sex, due allowance should be made in favor of the bitches, which do not bear the characteristics of the breed to the same degree of perfection and grandeur as do the dogs.

Size—The size for mature dogs is about 50 pounds; for mature bitches about 40 pounds.

Coat—The coat should be straight, short, flat, close, of fine texture, smooth and glossy. (No fringe, feather or curl.) *Color of Coat*—The color of coat should be uniform, pure of its kind and brilliant. The various colors found in the breed are to be preferred in the following order: (1) Red Brindle, (2) all other brindles, (3) solid white, (4) solid red, fawn or fallow, (5) piebald, (6) inferior qualities of all the foregoing. *Note:* A perfect piebald is preferable to a muddy brindle or defective solid color. Solid black is very undesirable, but not so objectionable if occurring to a moderate degree in piebald patches. The brindles to be perfect should have a fine, even and equal distribution of the composite colors. In brindles and solid colors a small white patch on the chest is not considered detrimental. In piebalds the color patches should be well defined, of pure color and symmetrically distributed.

Skin—The skin should be soft and loose, especially at the head, neck and shoulders. *Wrinkles and Dewlap*—The head and face should be covered with heavy wrinkles, and at the throat, from jaw to chest, there should be two loose pendulous folds, forming the dewlap.

Skull—The skull should be very large, and in circumference, in front of the ears, should measure at least the height of the dog at the shoulders. Viewed from the front, it should appear very high from the corner of the lower jaw to the apex of the skull, and also very broad and square. Viewed at the side, the head should appear very high, and very short from the point of the nose to occiput. The forehead should be flat (not rounded or domed), neither too prominent nor overhanging the face. *Cheeks*—The cheeks should be well rounded, protruding sideways and outward beyond the eyes. *Stop*— The temples or frontal bones should be very well defined, broad, square and high, causing a hollow or groove between the eyes. This indentation, or stop, should be both broad and deep and extend up the middle of the forehead, dividing the head vertically, being traceable to the top of the skull. *Eyes and Eyelids*—The eyes, seen from the front, should be situated low down in the skull, as far from the ears as possible, and their corners should be in a straight line at right angles with the stop. They should be quite in front of the head, as wide apart as possible, provided their outer corners are within the outline of the cheeks when viewed from the front. They should be quite round in form, of moderate size, neither sunken nor bulging, and in color should be very dark. The lids should cover the white of the eyeball, when the dog is looking directly forward, and the lid should show no "haw." *Ears* —The ears should be set high in the head, the front inner edge of each ear joining the outline of the skull at the top back corner of skull, so as to place them as wide apart, and as high, and as far from the eyes as possible. In size they should be small and thin. The shape termed "rose ear" is the most desirable. The rose ear folds inward at its back lower edge, the upper front edge curving over, outwards and backwards, showing part of the inside of the burr. (The ears should not be carried erect or prick-eared or buttoned and should never be cropped.)

Face—The face, measured from the front of the cheekbone to the tip of the nose, should be extremely short, the muzzle being very short, broad, turned upwards and very deep from the corner of the eye to the corner of the mouth. *Nose*—The nose should be large, broad and black, its tip being set back deeply between the eyes. The distance from bottom of stop, between the eyes, to the tip of nose should be as short as possible and not exceed the length from the tip of nose to the edge of under lip. The nostrils should be wide, large and black, with a well-defined line between them. Any nose other than black is objectionable and "Dudley" or flesh-colored nose absolutely disqualified from competition. *Chops*—The chops or "flews" should be thick, broad, pendant and very deep, completely overhanging the lower jaw at each side. They join the under lip in front and almost or quite cover the teeth, which should be scarcely noticeable when the mouth is closed. *Jaws*—The jaws should be massive, very broad, square and "undershot," the lower jaw projecting considerably in front of the upper jaw and turning up. *Teeth*—The teeth should be large and strong, with the canine teeth or tusks wide apart, and the 6 small teeth in front, between the canines, in an even, level row.

Neck—The neck should be short, very thick, deep and strong and well arched at the back. *Shoulders*—The shoulders should be muscular, very heavy, wide-spread and slanting outward, giving stability and great power. *Chest*—The chest should be very broad, deep and full.

Brisket and Body—The brisket and body should be very capacious, with full sides, well-rounded ribs and very deep from the shoulders down to its lowest part, where it joins the chest. It should be well let down between the shoulders and forelegs, giving the dog a broad, low, short-legged appearance. The body should be well ribbed up behind with the belly tucked up and not rotund. *Back*—The back should be short and strong, very broad at the shoulders and comparatively narrow at the loins. There should be a slight fall in the back, close behind the shoulders (its lowest part), whence the spine should rise to the loins (the top of which should be higher than the top of the shoulders), thence curving again more suddenly to the tail, forming an arch (a very distinctive feature of the breed), termed "roach back" or, more correctly, "wheel-back."

Forelegs—The forelegs should be short, very stout, straight and muscular, set wide apart, with well developed calves, presenting a bowed outline, but the bones of the legs should not be curved or bandy, nor the feet brought too close together. *Elbows*—The elbows should be low and stand well out and loose from the body. *Hind Legs*—The hind legs should be strong and muscular and longer than the forelegs, so as to elevate the loins above the shoulders. Hocks should be slightly bent and well let down, so as to give length and strength from loins to hock. The lower leg should be short, straight and strong, with the stifles turned slightly outward and away from the body. The hocks are thereby made to approach each other, and the hind feet to turn outward. *Feet*—The feet should be moderate in size, compact and firmly set. Toes compact, well split up, with high knuckles and with short stubby nails. The front feet may be straight or slightly out-turned, but the hind feet should be pointed well outward.

Tail—The tail may be either straight or "screwed" (but never curved or curly), and in any case must be short, hung low, with decided downward carriage, thick root and fine tip. If straight, the tail should be cylindrical and of uniform taper. If "screwed" the bends or kinks should be well defined, and they may be abrupt and even knotty, but no portion of the member should be elevated above the base or root.

SCALE OF POINTS

General Properties				
Proportion and symmetry	5		Chops	2
			Jaws	5
Attitude	3		Teeth	2	39
Expression	2		*Body, Legs, etc.*	
Gait	3		Neck	3
Size	3		Dewlap	2
Coat	2		Shoulders	5
Color of coat	4	22	Chest	3
Head			Ribs	3
Skull	5		Brisket	2
Cheeks	2		Belly	2
Stop	4		Back	5
Eyes and eyelids	3		Forelegs and elbows	4
Ears	5		Hind legs	3
Wrinkle	5		Feet	3
Nose	6		Tail	4	39
			Total	100

DISQUALIFICATION

Dudley or flesh-colored nose.

Chow Chow

General Appearance—A massive, cobby, powerful dog, active and alert, with strong, muscular development, and perfect balance. Body squares with height of leg at shoulder; head, broad and flat, with short, broad, and deep muzzle, accentuated by a ruff; the whole supported by straight, strong legs. Clothed in a shining, offstanding coat, the Chow is a masterpiece of beauty, dignity, and untouched naturalness.

Head—Large and massive in proportion to size of dog, with broad, flat skull; well filled under the eyes; moderate stop; and proudly carried. Expression— Essentially dignified, lordly, scowling, discerning, sober, and snobbish—one of independence. *Muzzle*—Short in comparison to length of skull; broad from eyes to end of nose, and of equal depth. The lips somewhat full and overhanging. *Teeth*—Strong and level, with a scissors bite; should neither be overshot, nor undershot. *Nose*—Large, broad, and black in color. Disqualification—nose spotted or distinctly other color than black, except in blue Chows, which may have solid blue or slate noses. *Tongue*—A blue-black. The tissues of the mouth should approximate black. Disqualification—tongue red, pink, or obviously spotted with red or pink. *Eyes*—Dark, deep-set, of moderate size, and almond-shaped. *Ears*—Small, slightly rounded at tip, stiffly carried. They should be placed wide apart, on top of the skull, and set with a slight, forward tilt. Disqualification—drop ear or ears. A drop ear is one which is stiffly carried or stiffly erect, but which breaks over at any point from its base to its tip.

Body—Short, compact, with well-sprung ribs, and let down in the flank. *Neck*—Strong, full, set well on the shoulders. *Shoulders*—Muscular, slightly sloping. *Chest*—Broad, deep, and muscular. A narrow chest is a serious fault. *Back*—Short, straight, and strong. *Loins*—Broad, deep, and powerful. *Tail* —Set well up and carried closely to the back, following line of spine at start. *Forelegs*—Perfectly straight, with heavy bone and upright pasterns. *Hind Legs* —Straight-hocked, muscular, and heavy boned. *Feet*—Compact, round, cat-like, with thick pads.

Gait—Completely individual. Short and stilted because of straight hocks.

Coat—Abundant, dense, straight, and off-standing; rather coarse in texture with a soft, woolly undercoat. It may be any clear color, solid throughout, with lighter shadings on ruff, tail, and breechings.

Nose spotted or distinctly other color than black, except in blue Chows, which may have solid blue or slate noses. Tongue red, pink or obviously spotted with red or pink. Drop ear or ears.

Approved March 11, 1941

Dalmatian

The Dalmation should represent a strong, muscular, and active dog; poised and alert; free of shyness; intelligent in expression; symmetrical in outline; and free from coarseness and lumber. He should be capable of great endurance, combined with a fair amount of speed.

Head—Should be of a fair length, the skull flat, proportionately broad between the ears, and moderately well defined at the temples, and not in one straight line from the nose to the occiput bone as required in a Bull Terrier. It should be entirely free from wrinkle. *Muzzle*—Should be long and powerful—the lips clean. The mouth should have a scissors bite. Never undershot or overshot. It is permissible to trim whiskers. *Eyes*—Should be set moderately well apart, and of medium size, round, bright, and sparkling, with an intelligent expression; their color greatly depending on the markings of the dog. In the black-spotted variety the eyes should be dark (black or brown or blue). In the liver-spotted variety they should be lighter than in the black-spotted variety (golden or light brown or blue). The rim around the eyes in the black-spotted variety should be black; in the liver-spotted variety, brown. Never flesh-colored in either. Lack of pigment a major fault.

Ears—Should be set rather high, of moderate size, rather wide at the base, and gradually tapering to a rounded point. They should be carried close to the head, be thin and fine in texture, and preferably spotted. *Nose*—In the black-spotted variety should always be black; in the liver-spotted variety, always brown. A butterfly or flesh-colored nose is a major fault.

Neck and Shoulders—The neck should be fairly long, nicely arched, light and tapering, and entirely free from throatiness. The shoulders should be oblique, clean, and muscular, denoting speed.

Body, Back, Chest, and Loins—The chest should not be too wide, but very deep and capacious, ribs well sprung but never rounded like barrel hoops (which would indicate want of speed). Back powerful; loin strong, muscular and slightly arched. *Legs and Feet*—Of great importance. The forelegs should be straight, strong, and heavy in bone; elbows close to the body; feet compact, well-arched toes, and tough, elastic pads. In the hind legs the muscles should be clean, though well defined; the hocks well let down. Dewclaws may be removed from legs. *Nails*—In the black-spotted variety, black or white; or a nail may be both black and white. In the liver-spotted variety, brown or white; or a nail may be both brown and white.

Gait—Length of stride should be in proportion to the size of the dog, steady in rhythm of 1, 2, 3, 4 as in the cadence count in military drill. Front legs should not paddle, nor should there be a straddling appearance. Hind legs should neither cross nor weave; judges should be able to see each leg move with no interference of another leg. Drive and reach are most desirable. Cowhocks are a major fault.

Tail—Should ideally reach the hock joint, strong at the insertion, and tapering toward the end, free from coarseness. It should not be inserted too low down, but carried with a slight curve upwards, and never curled.

Coat—Should be short, hard, dense, and fine, sleek and glossy in appearance, but neither woolly nor silky. *Color and Markings*—Are most important points. The ground color in both varieties should be pure white, very decided, and not intermixed. The color of the spots in the black-spotted variety should be dense black; in the liver-spotted variety they should be liver brown. The spots should not intermingle, but be as round and well defined as possible, the more distinct the better. In size they should be from that of a dime to a half-dollar. The spots on the face, head, ears, legs, and tail to be smaller than those on the body. Patches, tri-colors, and any color markings other than black or liver constitute a disqualification. A true patch is a solid, sharply defined mass of black or liver that is appreciably larger than any of the markings on the dog. Several spots that are so adjacent that they actually touch one another at their edges do not constitute a patch.

Size—The desirable height of dogs and bitches is between 19 and 23 inches at the withers, and any dog or bitch over 24 inches at the withers is to be disqualified.

MAJOR FAULTS

Butterfly or flesh-colored nose. Cowhocks. Flat feet. Lack of pigment in eye rims. Shyness. Trichiasis (abnormal position or direction of the eyelashes).

FAULTS

Ring or low-set tail. Undersize or oversize.

SCALE OF POINTS

Body, back, chest and loins .	10	Legs and feet	10
Coat	5	Neck and shoulders	10
Color and markings	25	Size, symmetry, etc.	10
Ears	5	Tail	5
Gait	10	Total	100
Head and eyes	10		

Any color markings other than black or liver. Any size over 24 inches at the withers. Patches. Tri-colors. Undershot or overshot bite.

Approved December 11, 1962

French Bulldog

General Appearance—The French Bulldog should have the appearance of an active, intelligent, muscular dog, of heavy bone, smooth coat, compactly built, and of medium or small structure. *Proportion and Symmetry*—The points should be well distributed and bear good relation one to the other, no feature being in such prominence from either excess or lack of quality that the animal appears deformed or poorly proportioned. *Influence of Sex*—In comparison of specimens of different sex, due allowance should be made in favor of the bitches, which do not bear the characteristics of the breed to the same marked degree as do the dogs.

Weight—A lightweight class under 22 pounds; heavyweight class, 22 pounds, and not over 28 pounds.

Head—The head should be large and square. The top of the skull should be flat between the ears; the forehead should not be flat but slightly rounded. The stop should be well defined, causing a hollow or groove between the eyes. The muzzle should be broad, deep and well laid back; the muscles of the cheeks well developed. The nose should be extremely short; nostrils broad with well defined line between them. The nose and flews should be black, except in the case of the lighter-colored dogs, where a lighter color nose is acceptable. The flews should be thick and broad, hanging over the lower jaw at the sides, meeting the underlip in front and covering the teeth which should not be seen when the mouth is closed. The underjaw should be deep, square, broad, undershot and well turned up. *Eyes*—The eyes should be wide apart, set low down in the skull, as far from the ears as possible, round in form, of moderate size, neither sunken nor bulging, and in color dark. No haw and no white of the eye showing when looking forward.

Neck—The neck should be thick and well arched, with loose skin at throat.

Ears—The ears shall hereafter be known as the bat ear, broad at the base, elongated, with round top, set high on the head, but not too close together, and carried erect with the orifice to the front. The leather of the ear, fine and soft.

Body—The body should be short and well rounded. The chest, broad, deep and full, well ribbed with the belly tucked up. The back should be a roach back, with a slight fall close behind the shoulders. It should be strong and short, broad at the shoulders and narrowing at the loins. *Legs*—The forelegs should be short, stout, straight and muscular, set wide apart. The hind leg should be strong and muscular, longer than the forelegs, so as to elevate the loins above the shoulders. Hocks well let down. *Feet*—The feet should be moderate in size, compact and firmly set. Toes compact, well split up, with high knuckles and short, stubby nails; hind feet slightly longer than forefeet. *Tail*—The tail should be either straight or screwed (but not curly), short, hung low, thick root and fine tip; carried low in repose.

Color, Skin and Coat—Acceptable colors are: All brindle, fawn, white, brindle and white, and any color except those which constitute disqualification. The skin should be soft and loose, especially at head and shoulders, forming wrinkles. Coat moderately fine, brilliant, short and smooth.

SCALE OF POINTS

General Properties				Jaws	6	
Proportion and symmetry		5		Teeth	2	40
Expression		5		Body, Legs, etc.		
Gait		4		Shoulders	5	
Color		4		Back	5	
Coat		2	20	Neck	4	
Head				Chest	3	
Skull		6		Ribs	4	
Cheeks and chops		2		Brisket	3	
Stop		5		Belly	2	
Ears		8		Forelegs	4	
Eyes		4		Hind legs	3	
Wrinkles		4		Feet	3	
Nose		3		Tail	4	40
				Total		100

DISQUALIFICATIONS

Other than bat ears; black and white, black and tan, liver, mouse or solid black (black means black without any trace of brindle) eyes of different color; nose other than black except in the case of the lighter-colored dogs, where a lighter color nose is acceptable; hare lip; any mutilation; over 28 pounds in weight.

Approved February 11, 1947

Keeshond

General Appearance and Conformation—The Keeshond is a handsome dog, of well-balanced, short-coupled body, attracting attention not only by his alert carriage and intelligent expression, but also by his luxurious coat, his richly plumed tail, well curled over his back, and by his foxlike face and head with small pointed ears. His coat is very thick round the neck, fore part of the shoulders and chest, forming a lionlike mane. His rump and hind legs, down to the hocks, are also thickly coated forming the characteristic "trousers." His head, ears and lower legs are covered with thick short hair. The ideal height of fully matured dogs (over 2 years old), measured from top of withers to the ground, is: for males, 18 inches; bitches, 17 inches. However, size consideration should not outweigh that of type. When dogs are judged equal in type, the dog nearest the ideal height is to be preferred. Length of back from withers to rump should equal height as measured above.

HEAD. *Expression*—Expression is largely dependent on the distinctive characteristic called "spectacles"—a delicately penciled line slanting slightly upward from the outer corner of each eye to the lower corner of the ear, coupled with distinct markings and shadings forming short but expressive eyebrows. Markings (or shadings) on face and head must present a pleasing appearance, imparting to the dog an alert and intelligent expression. *Fault* —Absence of "spectacles." *Skull*—The head should be well proportioned to the body, wedge-shaped when viewed from above. Not only in muzzle, but the whole head should give this impression when the ears are drawn back by covering the nape of the neck and the ears with one hand. Head in profile should exhibit a definite stop. *Fault*—Apple head, or absence of stop. *Muzzle*—The muzzle should be dark in color and of medium length, neither coarse nor snipy, and well proportioned to the skull. *Mouth*—The mouth should be neither overshot nor undershot. Lips should be black and closely meeting, not thick, coarse or sagging; and with no wrinkle at the corner of the mouth. *Fault*—Overshot or undershot. *Teeth*—The teeth should be white, sound and strong (but discoloration from distemper not to penalize severely); upper teeth should just overlap the lower teeth. *Eyes*—Eyes should be dark brown in color, of medium size, rather oblique in shape and not set too wide apart. *Fault*—Protruding round eyes or eyes light of color. *Ears*—Ears should be small, triangular in shape, mounted high on head and carried erect; dark in color and covered with thick, velvety, short hair. Size should be proportionate to the head—length approximating the distance from outer corner of the eye to the nearest edge of the ear. *Fault*—Ears not carried erect when at attention.

BODY. *Neck and Shoulders*—The neck should be moderately long, well shaped and well set on shoulders; covered with a profuse mane, sweeping from under the jaw and covering the whole of the front part of the shoulders and chest, as well as the top part of the shoulders. *Chest, Back and Loin*—The body should be compact with a short straight back sloping slightly downward toward the hindquarters; well ribbed, barrel well rounded, belly moderately tucked up, deep and strong of chest. *Legs*—Forelegs should be straight seen from any angle, and well feathered. Hind legs should be profusely feathered down to the hocks—not below, with hocks only slightly bent. Legs must be of good bone and cream in color. *Fault*—Black markings below the knee, penciling excepted. *Feet*—The feet should be compact, well rounded, catlike, and cream in color. Toes are nicely arched, with black nails. *Fault*—White foot or feet.

Tail—The tail should be set on high, moderately long, and well feathered, tightly curled over back. It should lie flat and close to the body with a very light gray plume on top where curled, but the tip of the tail should be black. The tail should form a part of the "silhouette" of the dog's body, rather than give the appearance of an appendage. *Fault*—Tail not lying close to the back. *Action*—Dogs should show boldly and keep tails curled over the back. They should move cleanly and briskly; and the movement should be straight and sharp (not lope like a German Shepherd). *Fault*—Tail not carried over back when moving.

Coat—The body should be abundantly covered with long, straight, harsh hair; standing well out from a thick, downy undercoat. The hair on the legs should be smooth and short, except for a feathering on the front legs and "trousers," as previously described, on the hind legs. The hair on the tail should be profuse, forming a rich plume. Head, including muzzle, skull and ears, should be covered with smooth, soft, short hair—velvety in texture on the ears. Coat must not part down the back. *Fault*—Silky, wavy or curly coats. Part in coat down the back.

Color and Markings—A mixture of gray and black. The undercoat should be very pale gray or cream (not tawny). The hair of the outer coat is black tipped, the length of the black tips producing the characteristic shading of color. The color may vary from light to dark, but any pronounced deviation from the gray color is not permissible. The plume of the tail should be very light gray when curled on back, and the tip of the tail should be black. Legs and feet should be cream. Ears should be very dark—almost black. Shoulder line markings (light gray) should be well defined. The color of the ruff and "trousers" is generally lighter than that of the body. "Spectacles" and shadings, as previously described, are characteristic of the breed and must be present to some degree. There should be no pronounced white markings.

Very Serious Fault—Entirely black or white or any other solid color; any pronounced deviation from the gray color.

SCALE OF POINTS

General conformation and appearance	20	Tail 10	
Head:		Neck and shoulders 8	
Shape	6	Legs 4	
Eyes	5	Feet 3	35
Ears	5	*Coat*	15
Teeth	4 20	*Color and markings* ...	10
Body:		Total	100
Chest, back and loin	10		

Approved July 12, 1949

Lhasa Apso

Character—Gay and assertive, but chary of strangers. *Size*—Variable, but about 10 inches or 11 inches at shoulder for dogs, bitches slightly smaller. *Color*—Golden, sandy, honey, dark grizzle, slate, smoke, parti-color, black, white or brown. This being the true Tibetan Lion-dog, golden or lionlike colors are preferred. Other colors in order as above. Dark tips to ears and beard are an asset.

Body Shape—The length from point of shoulders to point of buttocks longer than height at withers, well ribbed up, strong loin, well-developed quarters and thighs. *Coat*—Heavy, straight, hard, not woolly nor silky, of good length, and very dense.

Mouth and Muzzle—Mouth level, otherwise slightly undershot preferable. Muzzle of medium length; a square muzzle is objectionable.

Head—Heavy head furnishings with good fall over eyes, good whiskers and beard; skull narrow, falling away behind the eyes in a marked degree, not quite flat, but not domed or apple-shaped; straight foreface of fair length. Nose black, about 1½ inches long, or the length from tip of nose to eye to be roughly about one-third of the total length from nose to back of skull.

Eyes—Dark brown, neither very large and full, nor very small and sunk.

Ears—Pendant, heavily feathered.

Legs—Forelegs straight; both forelegs and hind legs heavily furnished with hair. *Feet*—Well feathered, should be round and catlike, with good pads.

Tail and Carriage—Well feathered, should be carried well over back in a screw; there may be a kink at the end. A low carriage of stern is a serious fault.

Approved April 9, 1935

Poodle

General Appearance, Carriage and Condition—That of a very active, intelligent and elegant-looking dog, squarely built, well-proportioned, moving soundly and carrying himself proudly. Properly clipped in the traditional fashion and carefully groomed, the Poodle has about him an air of distinction and dignity peculiar to himself.

Head and Expression—(a) *Skull:* moderately rounded, with a slight but definite stop. Cheek-bones and muscles flat. *Muzzle:* long, straight and fine, with slight chiseling under the eyes. Strong without lippiness. The chin definite enough to preclude snipiness. Teeth white, strong and with a scissors bite. Nose sharp with well-defined nostrils. (b) *Eyes:* set far apart, very dark, full of fire and intelligence, oval in appearance. (c) *Ears:* set low and hanging close to the head. The leather should be long, wide and heavily feathered.

Neck and Shoulders—Neck well proportioned, strong and long to admit of the head being carried high and with dignity. Skin snug at throat. The neck should rise from strong muscular shoulders which slope back from their point of angulation at the upper foreleg to the withers.

Body—The chest deep and moderately wide. The ribs well sprung and braced up. The back short, strong and slightly hollowed, the loins short, broad and muscular. (Bitches may be slightly longer in back than dogs.)

Tail—Straight, set on rather high, docked, but of sufficient length to insure a balanced outline. It should be carried up and in a gay manner.

Legs—The forelegs straight from the shoulder, parallel and with bone and muscle in proportion to size of dog. The pasterns should be strong. The hind legs very muscular, stifles well bent and hocks well let down. The thigh should be well developed, muscular and showing width in the region of the stifle to insure strong and graceful action. The four feet should turn neither in nor out. *Feet*—Rather small and oval in shape. Toes arched, close and cushioned on thick, hard pads.

Coat—Quality: very profuse, of harsh texture and dense throughout. *Clip*: A Poodle may be shown in the "Puppy" Clip or in the traditional "Continental" Clip or the "English Saddle" Clip. A Poodle under a year old may be shown in the "Puppy" Clip with the coat long except the face, feet and base of tail, which should be shaved. Dogs one year old or older must be shown in either the "Continental" Clip or "English Saddle" Clip.

In the "Continental" Clip the hindquarters are shaved with pompons on hips (optional). The face, feet, legs and tail are shaved leaving bracelets on the hind legs, puffs on the forelegs and a pompon at the end of the tail. The rest of the body must be left in full coat.

In the "English Saddle" Clip the hindquarters are covered with a short blanket of hair except for a curved shaved area on the flank and two shaved bands on each hind leg. The face, feet, forelegs and tail are shaved leaving puffs on the forelegs and a pompon at the end of the tail. The rest of the body must be left in full coat.

Color—The coat must be an even and solid color at the skin. In blues, grays, silvers, browns, cafe-au-laits, apricots and creams the coats may show varying shades of the same color. This is frequently present in the somewhat darker feathering of the ears and in the tipping of the ruff. While clear colors are definitely preferred such natural variation in the shading of the coat is not to be considered a fault. Brown and cafe-au-lait Poodles have liver-colored noses, eye-rims and lips, dark toenails and dark amber eyes. Black, blue, gray, silver, apricot, cream and white Poodles have black noses, eye-rims and lips, black or self-colored toenails and very dark eyes. In the apricots while black is preferred, liver-colored noses, eye-rims and lips, self-colored toenails and amber eyes are permitted but are not desirable.

Gait—A straightforward trot with light springy action. Head and tail carried high. Forelegs and hind legs should move parallel turning neither in nor out. Sound movement is essential.

SIZE

Standard—The Standard Poodle is over 15 inches at the withers. Any Poodle which is 15 inches or less in height shall be disqualified from competition as a Standard Poodle.

Miniature—The Miniature Poodle is 15 inches or under at the withers, with a minimum height in excess of 10 inches. Any Poodle which is over 15 inches, or 10 inches or less at the withers shall be disqualified from competition as a Miniature Poodle.

Toy—The Toy Poodle is 10 inches or under at the withers. Any Poodle which is more than 10 inches at the withers shall be disqualified from competition as a Toy Poodle.

VALUE OF POINTS

General appearance, carriage and condition	20	Body and tail	15
Head, ears, eyes and expression	20	Legs and feet	15
		Coat—color and texture	10
		Gait	10
Neck and shoulders	10	Total	100

MAJOR FAULTS

Eyes: round in appearance, protruding, large or very light. Jaws: undershot, overshot or wry mouth. Cowhocks. Feet: flat or spread. Tail: set low, curled or carried over the back. Shyness.

DISQUALIFICATIONS

Parti-colors: The coat of a parti-colored dog is not an even solid color at the skin but is variegated in patches of two or more colors. Any type of clip other than those listed in section on coat.

Any size over or under the limits specified in section on size.

Approved July 14, 1959

Schipperke

Appearance and General Characteristics—Excellent and faithful little watchdog, suspicious of strangers. Active, agile, indefatigable, continually occupied with what is going on around him, careful of things that are given him to guard, very kind with children, knows the ways of the household; always curious to know what is going on behind closed doors or about any object that has been moved, betraying his impressions by his sharp bark and upstanding ruff, seeking the company of horses, a hunter of moles and other vermin; can be used to hunt, a good rabbit dog. *Color*—Solid black.

Head—Foxlike, fairly wide, narrowing at the eyes, seen in profile slightly rounded, tapering muzzle not too elongated nor too blunt, not too much stop.

Nose—Small and black. *Eyes*—Dark brown, small, oval rather than round, neither sunken nor prominent. *Expression*—Should have a questioning expression: sharp and lively, not mean or wild. *Ears*—Very erect, small, triangular, placed high, strong enough not to be capable of being lowered except in line with the body. *Teeth*—Meeting evenly. A tight scissors bite is acceptable.

Neck—Strong and full, slightly arched, rather short. *Shoulders*—Muscular and sloping. *Chest*—Broad and deep in brisket.

Body—Short, thick-set and cobby. Broad behind the shoulders, seeming higher in front because of ruff. Back strong, short, straight and level or slightly sloping down toward rump. Ribs well sprung. *Loins*—Muscular and well drawn up from the brisket but not to such an extent as to cause a weak and leggy appearance of the hindquarters. *Forelegs*—Straight under body, with bone in proportion, but not coarse. *Hindquarters*—Somewhat lighter than the foreparts, but muscular, powerful, with rump well rounded, tail docked to no more than 1 inch in length. *Feet*—Small, round and tight (not splayed), nails straight, strong and short.

Coat—Abundant and slightly harsh to the touch, short on the ears and on the front of legs and on the hocks, fairly short on the body, but longer around neck beginning back of the ears, and forming a ruff and a cape; a jabot extending down between the front legs, also longer on rear where it forms a culotte, the points turning inward. Undercoat dense and short on body, very dense around neck making ruff stand out. Culotte should be as long as the ruff.

Weight—Up to 18 pounds.

Faults—Light eyes, large round prominent eyes, ears too long or too rounded, narrow head and elongated muzzle, too blunt muzzle, domed skull, smooth short coat with short ruff and culotte, lack of undercoat, curly or silky coat, body coat more than three (3) inches long, slightly overshot or undershot, sway-back, Bull Terrier shaped head, straight hocks. Straight stifles and shoulders, cowhocks, feet turning in or out, legs not straight when viewed from front. Lack of distinction between length of coat, ruff and culotte.

DISQUALIFICATIONS

Any color other than solid black. Drop or semi-erect ears. Badly overshot or undershot.

Approved May 12, 1959

INDEX